by John Updike

PICKED-UP PIECES

John Updike

PICKED-UP PIECES

New York · Alfred · A · Knopf

1975

THIS IS A BORZOI BOOK
PUBLISHED BY ALFRED A. KNOPF, INC.

Library of Congress Cataloging in Publication Data
Updike, John.   Picked-up pieces.
Includes index.   I. Title.
PS3571.P4P48   813'.5'4   75–8252
ISBN 0–394–49849–6

Manufactured in the United States of America

First Edition

Acknowledgments

Grateful acknowledgment is made to the following magazines and publishers, who first printed the pieces specified, sometimes under other titles:

THE NEW YORKER: "Amor Vincit Omnia Ad Nauseam," "The First Lunar Invitational," "Letter from Anguilla," "Voznesensky Met," and fifty of the book reviews, including seven published as "Briefly Noted."

THE NEW YORK TIMES: "On Meeting Writers," "Bech Meets Me," "Tips on a Trip," "His Own Horn," and "Coffee-Table Books for High Coffee Tables."

THE NEW REPUBLIC: "The Mastery of Miss Warner" and the poem in "P. S."

THE NEW STATESMAN: "Papa's Sad Testament" and "Notes to a Poem."

THE LISTENER: "Notes of a Temporary Resident."

THE SUNDAY TIMES (London): "And Yet Again Wonderful."

TRANSATLANTIC REVIEW: "Cemeteries."

THE ATLANTIC MONTHLY: "Black Suicide" and "Talk of a Sad Town."

HORIZON: "Remembrance of Things Past Remembered."

MOTIVE: "Auden Fecit."

LIFE: "Mnemosyne Chastened" and "A Raw Something."

PLAYBOY: Comment on creativity.

MADEMOISELLE: Comment on female sexuality.

BOOKS AND BOOKMEN: "The Future of the Novel."

THE AMERICAN PEN (Vol. 2, No. 3): "Humor in Fiction."

SOUTHERN REVIEW (South Australia): "Why Write?"

GAMBIT, INC.: Introduction to Pens and Needles, drawings by David Levine.

HOUGHTON MIFFLIN CO.: Introduction to *The Harvard Lampoon Centennial Celebration 1876—1973.*

SHEED AND WARD, INC.: Introduction to *Soundings in Satanism.*

DELACORTE PRESS AND PENGUIN BOOKS, LTD., LONDON: Three translations of Borges poems from *Jorge Luis Borges: Selected Poems 1924—1967,* edited by Norman Thomas di Giovanni, Copyright © 1972 by Delacorte Press.

SUNTORY LTD. (Tokyo, Japan): "Farewell to the Middle Class" reprinted from *Suntory Fiction and Essays.*

TRIQUARTERLY BOOKS (Northwestern University Press): "A Tribute" from *Nabokov,* edited by Alfred Appel, Jr., and Charles Newman (1970).

UNITED STATES INFORMATION SERVICE: Excerpts from "Reality and the Novel in Africa and America," a symposium (Lagos, 1972).

TO ROGERS WHITAKER

Contents

Reviews

JOYCE AND PROUST

BORGES

NABOKOV

ENGLISH LIVES

FRENCH DEATHS

EUROPE

AFRICA

THE AVANT GARDE

YOUNG AMERICANS

OLDER AMERICANS

FOREWORD

Since the publication, ten years ago, of *Assorted Prose*, most of my pieces of non-fictional prose have been book reviews. And these were written mostly for *The New Yorker*. It has not been easy, I dare say, for the editors of "the kindest magazine in the world" (as Nabokov describes its pseudonym *The Beau and the Butterfly*) to locate books that might fall within my nebulous competence. When, *circa* 1960, I gratuitously volunteered to be a critic, humorous verse and theology were the only areas where a data-density map of my brain would have shown even a faint darkening. In this latter area my information appeared out-of-the-ordinary primarily because the ordinary, in those bad old materialist days, before the Beatles spiritualized us all, was nil. Out of deference to my curious hobby, Christianity, I was permitted to treat, at suitably anxious length, of Karl Barth (in the earlier collection) and (in this) of Kierkegaard. For a time, indeed, there was some danger of my becoming a kind of *ad hominem* Religious Department; those slim, worthy-looking volumes by Tillich and Heidegger that keep cluttering a book editor's desk—what better disposal than to send them off to Updike for a "note"? The section "Religious Notes" remembers this epoch, a time of faith on all sides.

An aspiring American writer myself, I clearly could not be trusted to clip the tender new shoots of my competitors. The esoteric fiction of Europe, however, was an ocean removed from envy's blight, and my practitioner's technical side was glad to investigate imported gadgetry. Borges, Queneau, Pinget, van Ostaijen, Cortázar—I am happy thus to have made their acquaintance, and made note of their lessons. Sure enough, when an American (Kosinski, Piercy) or an Englishman (Ayrton, Collier) got mixed into my periodic dose of the avant garde, a brusquer assurance and a chummy impatience did creep into my tone, which when dealing with translated works assumed the even omnivorous rumble of a grist mill.

More lately, the Fates that spin *The New Yorker*'s "Books" Department have taken to testing my iron digestion with books about Brazilian Indians and body cells. Evidently I can read anything in English and muster up an opinion about it. I am not sure, however, the stunt is good for me. Among these reviews I am proudest of—though what I feel for my utmost favorites is still a step-emotion to the parent's pride taken in the feeblest tyke of a story or poem—those most voluntary: essays of celebration and promulgation moved by a prior enthusiasm (Kierkegaard, Borges, Proust, Fuchs) or assignments that provoked me to read more, or think deeper, than was strictly called for (the pieces on Camus, Hamsun, Hemingway, Joyce, and Africans seem such). Apologies, if any, would be tendered to those authors, like Grass and Gombrowicz, who came to me coated with a muffling murk of missed nuances—dusty plaster replicas of statues whose pure marble glowed in an inaccessible museum. But even when the visibility was poorest I tried to give each book the benefit of a code of reviewing drawn up inwardly when I embarked on this craft, or ("a man should have a trade," my father used to insist) trade.

My rules, shaped intaglio-fashion by youthful traumas at the receiving end of critical opinion, were and are:

1. Try to understand what the author wished to do, and do not blame him for not achieving what he did not attempt.

2. Give enough direct quotation—at least one extended passage—of the book's prose so the review's reader can form his own impression, can get his own taste.

3. Confirm your description of the book with quotation from the book, if only phrase-long, rather than proceeding by fuzzy *précis*.

4. Go easy on plot summary, and do not give away the ending. (How astounded and indignant was I, when innocent, to find reviewers blabbing, and with the sublime inaccuracy of drunken lords reporting on a peasants' revolt, all the turns of my suspenseful and surpriseful narrative! Most ironically, the only readers who approach a book as the author intends, unpolluted by pre-knowledge of the plot, are the detested reviewers themselves. And then, years later, the blessed fool who picks the volume at random from a library shelf.)

5. If the book is judged deficient, cite a successful example along the same lines, from the author's *oeuvre* or elsewhere. Try to understand the failure. Sure it's his and not yours?

To these concrete five might be added a vaguer sixth, having to do with maintaining a chemical purity in the reaction between product and appraiser. Do not accept for review a book you are predisposed to dislike, or committed by friendship to like. Do not imagine yourself a caretaker of any tradition, an enforcer of any party standards, a warrior in any ideological battle, a corrections officer of any kind. Never, never (John Aldridge, Norman Podhoretz) try to put the author "in his place," making of him a pawn in a contest with other reviewers. Review the book, not the reputation. Submit to whatever spell, weak or strong, is being cast. Better to praise and share than blame and ban. The communion between reviewer and his public is based upon the presumption of certain possible joys of reading, and all our discriminations should curve toward that end.

Easier said than done, of course. Here and there filial affection for an older writer has pulled my punch. Fear of reprisal may have forced a grin or two. In a few reprehensible cases I may have dreamed of sleeping with the authoress. In other cases irritations of the moment added their personal pepper. A reviewer, unlike an ideal reader, is committed to finish the book; I read slower than I write, and sheer exasperation over time expended may have shortened my patience with the Cozzens novel and, even, *Ada*. The little Dostoevsky review was done for *Life* during a mysterious attack of tendonitis; I could not sleep, and sat up all one night, watching dawn infiltrate Menemsha Bight, my throbbing left wrist held above my head while my right hand confidently advised Dostoevsky to keep trying. "The Crunch of Happiness" was composed shortly after my leg had been broken, making me perhaps unduly sensitive to the hugs and crunches in Nabokov's *Glory.* One of the oldest pieces here, on Sylvia Townsend Warner (who deserves, ten years later, an extended tribute to her vigorously continuing production), was hilariously fractured and mis-assembled when printed in *The New Republic;* this collection holds for me no greater satisfaction than that of getting its hexed text at last correct.

The fabled care *The New Yorker* takes with the texts it prints presides like Providence over most of these reviews. Many the untruth quietly curbed, the misspelling invisibly mended. My habit of ample quotation compels the "checkers" virtually to read the book through, a scrupulousness that amounts to sanctity. My editor for the "Books" pieces has been Mr. Rogers Whitaker (telephone operators, take note of the *s*). Gruff wise bear of a man, he has given most of these contents a lick and a spank, and in gratitude for his collaboration I dedicate this book to him. May he edit *ad infinitum.*

The "Views" section (which ends with a review) salvages some of the debris of a writer's life. One is invited to do this and that, and one doesn't always refuse. My year in London (1968–1969) was especially prolific of accepted invitations. Also while there I composed my decade's one precious parody, and a necrotic meditation ("Cemeteries") that didn't quite make it into fiction. My four speeches, delivered on as many continents, serve as index of the itinerary that even a reluctantly public man can find himself undergoing. I have restrained myself from including a talk in Venezuela comparing *Doña Barbara* with movie Westerns, and a weighty speech on the American writer's cultural situation that I kept giving as I moved across central Africa, shedding large chunks of it as I went. If there's one thing the Third World does *not* want to hear about, it's parallelisms with the United States. Henry Bech should write a story.

And I, no doubt, should write, in the decades left to me, in the highest forms I can reach, matter of my own devising. There was an educational value, for a man with lazy eyes, in accepting some review assignments; but my laziness is now such that I can scarcely read a book without a pencil in my hand, and without the expectation of being paid for a verdict. Innocence deserts one's tryst with a printed page when a review has been promised and begins writing itself in the margin. Meanwhile, the classics languish, and even blank pages begin to look suspect. Let us hope, for the sakes of artistic purity and paper conservation, that ten years from now the pieces to be picked up will make a smaller heap.

There could have been a third section, "Interviews." They are a form to be loathed, a half-form like maggots, but in some cases (notably my *Paris Review* travail with Charles Samuels) have benefitted from written revisions; and one is forced to say things sometimes true and not always said elsewhere. The only topic upon which my offhand opinions carry authority is, of course, my own works; so I have excerpted a few self-centered quotations from the six or so interviews I have saved, and closeted them in an appendix, where none but the morbidly curious, or academically compelled, need peek.

And, speaking of half-forms: hard-pressed magazine editors perpetually bombard a writer's tenuous vicinity with questions, questionnaires, and quizzes. Most of these meteors from outer space burn up in the ionosphere of unanswered mail, but a few get through, coinciding with a moment of euphoria or efficiency in the inscrutable authorial rhythms, and receive an answer. Here are two Answers to Hard Questions that turned up in my files, which are hereby, as of October 25, 1974, exhausted.

MADEMOISELLE: *What is female sexuality?*

You ask me about this most wordless of subjects. I know nothing; but the "nothing" stirs, breathes, takes on a vague and vaguely inviting form. To begin, I would understand "sexuality" to be the subject and "male" and "female" to be adjectives, not polar opposites. In infancy both sexes enjoy an identical introduction to erotic sensation, so that fondling, sucking, teasing, cradling, crooning, tickling, rocking, stroking, and murmuring form a common base of amorous vocabulary. Somewhere before adolescence the male, that little hunter, tips his sexual curiosity with an optical point, whereas the female remains a blind snuggler, impervious to photo-

pornography, dependent to some extent upon brute *duration* of contact. When the sexual functions ripen, the male assignment becomes
penetration and distribution, the female duty acceptance and re-
tention. Yet our insatiable minds, with their unique gift for empathy,
seek to broaden sexual experience into the domain of the opposite
(*en face* rather than inimical) number; the rapacious female and
passive male are delightful variations. Harmlessly, insofar as any
human transaction is harmless, they seek to appropriate sensations
biology has only diffidently made possible for them. Again, our aspiring spirits drive erotic sensitivity outward from the monstrous
and gummy organs of sex, which look like wounds, to the ethereal
fringes of the body; the hands, the skull, the soles of the feet, the
backs of the knees are where perhaps you, *mademoiselle*, begin to
quicken. There is a poetry in sexual convolution that would bring
the scattered centers of our being—the brain, the heart, the genitals—into a unity of juxtaposition. The sexual unpredictability of
females must be, in part, an attempt to subordinate to the angelic
prerogatives of choice and will the sexual function still bewilder-
ingly mired in the ancient ooze of the involuntary. Perversion, like
continence, would reclaim from our animal ore the gold of the
purely human. In females, if anatomy is an adequate metaphor,
sexuality is more central and more buried than in males. Love, then,
becomes an exploration toward a muffled center, a quest whose
terrain is the woman and the grail her deep self. The man who
advances this exploration bestows a totality meagerly paid for with
anything less than enslavement. The man who does not fails disastrously. Hence the extremes of fastidiousness and wantonness that
perennially astound men, and the strange sharp note of bitter disappointment we hear whenever women offer to throw light into
these warm shadows.

PLAYBOY: *What is creativity?*

For one thing, creativity is merely a plus name for regular activity; the ditchdigger, dentist, and artist go about their tasks in
much the same way, and any activity becomes creative when the
doer cares about doing it right, or better. Out of my own slim experience, I would venture the opinion that the artistic impulse is a
mix, in varying proportions, of childhood habits of fantasizing
brought on by not necessarily unhappy periods of solitude; a certain
hard wish to perpetuate and propagate the self; a craftsmanly affection for the materials and process; a perhaps superstitious receptivity
to moods of wonder; and a not-often-enough-mentioned ability,
within the microcosm of the art, to organize, predict, and persevere.

PICKED-UP PIECES

Views

THE LITERARY LIFE

On Meeting Writers

THE LUST to meet authors ranks low, I think, on the roll of holy appetites; but it is an authentic pang. The county where I and my literary ambitions were conceived held only one writer, whose pen name, Mildred Jordan, masked her true identity as an unmeetably rich industrialist's wife. At Harvard I stood with crowds of other students to hear, and to glimpse in the mysterious flesh, anthology presences like Eliot, Sandburg, Frost, and Wilder. After his lecture in Sanders Theater, Eliot, a gem of composure within a crater of applause, inserted his feet into his rubbers, first the right, then the left, as we poured down upon him a grateful tumult that had less to do with his rather sleepy-making discourse on poetic drama than with the fabulous descent of his vast name into an actual, visible, and mortal body. Whereas Sandburg, playing ballads in New Lecture Hall, rambled on into our dinner hour; as the audience noisily diminished he told us, his white bangs glowing in the gloom, that it was all right, that often in his life he had sat in hotel rooms with only his guitar for company.

The first author I met socially was Joyce Cary. It was in England's Oxford. Someone kindly had us to tea, and into the stiff little party bounced a well-knit sandy man with light quick eyes and an intensely handsome chin; unhesitatingly he assumed his right to dominate the conversation. He was full of a tender excitement, the excitement of those certain they are loved, and anxious to share, before it spills over and is wasted, the bubbling treasure of themselves. He described to us his sitting in Paris writing at an outdoor table while around him in the Tuileries little boys were going pee-

pee; he read us, with an excessive Irish accent, the opening and then the closing words of *Finnegans Wake*, to show that they interlocked.

Now I had never read Cary, but had myself recently tasted the emboldening black blood of print. When he stated that Joyce's influence was enormous, I churlishly grunted disagreement; he cited e. e. cummings, and I absurdly shook my head No. His eyebrows lifted, and for a second I lived within the curiosity of those very quick eyes. They flicked away, and somewhat later I began to read him, and found him to be—above all in his two African novels—a splendid writer, peculiarly alive to nuances of power and competition such as my jealous rudeness that afternoon. For years the incident embarrassed me in memory, and in 1957 Cary heroically suffered his prolonged death, and I lost forever my chance to apologize.

Quite different was my preparation for meeting James Thurber, in London later that year. As a boy I had hoarded pennies to buy Thurber's books, and owned them all; he was for me the brightest star in that galaxy of New York wits I yearned to emulate, however dimly. A college acquaintance who knew of my adoration arranged the meeting: into her flat Thurber was led by his wife Helen. He was taller than I had expected, not Walter Mitty but a big-boned blind giant, and his upstanding hair was snowier than photographs had led me to expect, and there could have been no anticipating the alarming way his eyes caromed around under the refracting magnification of his glasses.

He sat, talking and drinking tea until I wondered why his bladder didn't burst. We listened, I raptly at first and finally becoming, to my own amazement, bored. Though Thurber cocked his head alertly at my poor fawning attempts to make conversation, these attempts did not appreciably distract him from the anecdotes of Columbus, Ohio, he had told a thousand times before, and that I had read ten years before, in their definitive, printed versions. Pages of *The Thurber Album* and *My Life and Hard Times* issued from his lips virtually intact.

His performance, though remarkable, was, alas, a performance; I had been privileged to join an auditory audience slightly less anonymous than readership, and there was no question of living for even a second in his curiosity. Fifteen years later, with another adored writer, Jorge Luis Borges, I was to reëxperience the disappointing revelation that blindness and fame and years do island a man, do isolate him within a monologue that, if he is a literary man, he had delivered to you already, in finer and grander form— "grander" because literary obsessions appear to have been selected from an infinite field, whereas personal obsessions seem to betray a mere narrowness. Sad to say, my love of Thurber's works was slightly stunted ever after his generous teatime monologue.

All the writers I have met—and they have not been many; I must be one of the few Americans with a bachelor-of-arts degree who has never met either Robert Lowell or Norman Mailer *— carry around with them a field force that compels objects in the vicinity to conform to their literary style. Standing next to E. B. White, one is imbued with something of the man's fierce modesty, and one's sentences haltingly seek to approximate the wonderful way his own never say more than he means. Whereas Thurber's humor bore a trace of the tyrannical, a wish to impose confusion from above, White's seems to stem from an extreme of attentiveness that would grant to things the graceful completion they lack in reality. Once I barged through a door in *The New Yorker* offices, and powerfully struck an obstacle on the other side; White had been hurrying down the hall, and stood there dazed. Reading in my face my horror, my fear that I had injured this sacred and fragile person, this living embodiment of the magazine's legend, he obligingly fell down as if dead.

A room containing Philip Roth, I have noticed, begins hilariously to whirl and pulse with a mix of rebelliousness and constriction that I take to be Oedipal. And I have seen John Cheever, for ten days we shared in Russia, turn the dour world of Soviet literary officials

---

* True in 1968 but no longer. Lowell, who seemed to be leaning above me like a raked mast, later described me to a mutual friend as "elusive and shy." I think I was afraid he would fall on me from his height of eminence. Mailer, as much shorter than I had expected as Lowell was taller, danced about me on a darkened street corner (44th and Second Avenue, if memory serves), taunting me with my supposed handsomeness, with being the handsomest guy he had ever seen. I took it to be Maileresque hyperbole, absurd yet nevertheless with something profound in it—perhaps my secret wish to *be* handsome, which only he, and that by dim streetlight, at a drunken hour, has ever perceived.

into a bright scuttle of somehow suburban characters, invented with marvellous speed and arranged in sudden tableaux expressive, amid wistful neo-Czarist trappings, of the lyric desperation associated with affluence. As if transported to the moon, people in Cheever's neighborhood lose half their bodily weight. My most traumatic experience of gravitational attraction came with John O'Hara. I had consented to read at a White House entertainment for the National Honor Students; crossing the lobby of the Hay-Adams, I spied brooding on a chair a broad-shouldered presence strongly reminiscent of the back of a book jacket. Deferentially I moved closer. "Mr. O'Hara?" said I.

O'Hara held out his hand. "Pull," he said. I hesitated. "My back," O'Hara explained. I pulled. He grunted in pain and did not budge. "Again," said O'Hara.

This time he made it, wincing, to his feet. Our laconic but characteristic dialogue continued. He, too, was attending the White House function. I offered him a ride in the limousine that had been sent for me, since I was one of the entertainers. I explained to the suspicious driver that this gentleman was John O'Hara, a very great writer and a guest of the President. The driver with maximum grudgingness made space for him in the front seat, while my wife and I settled regally in the back.

Within the few seconds of this encounter I had been plunged into a cruel complex of stoic pain and social irony—a Negro chauffeur and a stammering light-verse writer had transformed a millionaire author into a front-seat hitchhiker. Mortified by the situation, feeling all its edges grating on O'Hara's acute nerves, I fled conversationally to the state of Pennsylvania, which we had in common. O'Hara moved us to a plane both higher and more concrete—the number of Updikes in Princeton, New Jersey. At the White House he showed a distinct preference for the company of Marianne Moore, bending his big ear to her tiny precise voice like a schoolboy listening to a transistor radio he has smuggled into class.

These not entirely fanciful reminiscences (which have omitted how I met Bernard Malamud in a museum lavatory, or how James Dickey entertained me one hungover 6 a.m. with a concert of country guitar music that fetched tears to my hillbilly eyes) mean to suggest that writers, like everyone else, see a world their personalities to some extent create. Denis de Rougemont claims that Chateaubriand could never have written Stendhal's essays on seduction because seduction was simply no problem for Chateaubriand. The cosmos of delay and obfuscation rendered in *The Castle* surely in part reflects the special environment Kafka's neurotic mannerisms spun around him. And we all recall how Hemingway scouted the world for those marginal places where violence might feed his style.

Also, as one who in a small way is himself now and then "met," I suggest that forces within the writer-reader personal encounter foment unreality. The reader comes equipped with a vivid, fresh, outside impression of works the writer remembers wearily from the inside, as a blur of intention, a stretch of doubting drudgery, a tangle of memories and fabrications, a batch of nonsensical reviews, and a disappointed sigh from the publisher. The reader knows the writer better than he knows himself; but the writer's physical presence is light from a star that has moved on.

Evasive temperaments are drawn to the practice of fiction. Their work is done far behind the heat-shield of face and voice that advances against a room of strangers. The performance can be a shambling and ingratiating one as much as a cocksure and intimidating one, but performance it is: a pity, for these anonymous devoted readers who press affectionately toward a blind man are his lovers, who have accepted into themselves his most intimate and earnest thrusts. I would like to meet, I suppose, Vladimir Nabokov and Henry Green, but recognize the urge as superstitious, a seeking of a physical ritual to formalize the fact that we already are (I write as a reader) so well met.

Voznesensky Met

(*A* New Yorker *Notes and Comment: August 1967*)

SEVERAL TIMES, a few years ago, we dined with Andrei Voznesensky in the dining hall of the Writers' Union in Moscow. The Union's building, on Vorovsky Street, was Tolstoy's Moscow mansion, and the model for the home of the Rostovs in *War and Peace*. One drives in through the gates through which the Rostovs and a wagonload of possessions fled Napoleon's approaching armies; straight ahead, past a bust of Tolstoy, are the yellow doors to the long, parqueted ballroom. The dining hall—to the right, in a wing of the building—is still pleasantly redolent of Czarist days. Walnut panelling reaches to the ceiling; a carved staircase leads up to a balcony. Here, in the same smoky atmosphere of clashing silver and prolonged table talk that one finds in any New York club for the privileged, come and go the local members of the immense Soviet literary Establishment. We met a few of them: the perky young *Yunost* editor, full of chaffing and "routines"; the cheerful translatoress, spouting the latest names in beatnik poetry; the tough yet comradely gray-haired lady who sat on the editorial board that had declined to publish *Doctor Zhivago;* the war novelist who after three vodkas began to look through us toward something desolating he had once seen; the round-faced art critic whose subtlest thoughts had to be couched, protectively, in French; the Union official, all a-twinkle—gold teeth, gold spectacles—a volley in his laugh and an executioner's chop in his hands. In this company, Voznesensky was a pet, a shy, shrugging pet, with a cold sore on his lower lip, politely sipping water at each toast offered in vodka, but nevertheless, amid so many literary foremen and mechanics, the real thing, a poet—a poet whose voice had already broken through to Russian youth and was on the verge of being heard in the West. Now his breakthrough has been made, and has led him to a perhaps disastrous defiance of the Writers' Union, which tried, as far as its fundamentally anti-artistic function permitted, to cherish him.

We worry that our side might do him in. Introducing him at a poetry reading in this country last May, Robert Lowell confided to the audience that he thought both he and Voznesensky had "really terrible governments." Such a remark could not hurt Lowell but would certainly arrest the attention of the Russian Embassy watchdog who invariably attends displays of Russo-American cultural exchange. Now the *Times* has zealously and, we suppose, rightly, published the outraged letter from Voznesensky denouncing the Writers' Union's clumsy and mendacious cancellation of his scheduled reading at Lincoln Center in June—a letter that *Pravda* declined to print. Perhaps the time is ripe for open opposition to the "atmosphere of blackmail, confusion, and provocation"—as Voznesensky put it—in which the heirs of Tolstoy and Chekhov and Pushkin do their work. The Writers' Union's control over publication is absolute. Yet a poet of Voznesensky's fame and genius is not defenseless; the Soviet system, unlike ours, admits that it needs artists, as blazoners of the ideals of the state. Hence, along with the censorship, there are the summer dachas and assured incomes and pleasant dining halls and erratic indulgences. Stalin sheltered the maverick Mayakovsky; Khrushchev let Yevtushenko keep writing. The Sinyavsky-Daniel trial was carried to its foregone conclusion, but a petition of dissent was signed by Russia's best writers. Thaw cannot be imported from the West. If Voznesensky carries his point, it will not be thanks to indignant editorials in this country or petitions signed by writers smug in their pre-bought freedom. If he cannot carry his point, let him at least survive. His mere survival, like Pasternak's, would be a victory.

Studying his photograph in the *Times* (our own delicate experts in propaganda have selected one that looks especially worried), we remember him across the table trying, in his then fragmentary English, to communicate. His pale face appeared faintly bloated, like a nun's squeezed in her wimple. His manner was both boyish and elderly, his thinning hair studiously licked down, his nose an innocent ski jump. Only a certain steadiness in his heavy blue eyes betrayed awareness that to be Pasternak's spiritual son, the hope of poetry in a nation hungry for poetry, was a mighty thing. One does not advance in post-Stalin Russia without some steel. Voznesensky, the gentlest of men until he stands to recite, becomes then a prophet, clangorous and stern; the reunion of Russian and modern poetry demands an ambitious campaign. To speak and write honestly in the Soviet Union is still a more difficult enterprise than an American can imagine.

Bech Meets Me

(The New York Times Book Review *Persuades Henry Bech,*
Literary Man for All Thin Seasons,
to Conduct an Interview: November 1971)

UPDIKE'S OFFICE is concealed in a kind of false-bottomed drawer in the heart of downtown Ipswich (Mass.), but the drowsy locals, for a mere 30 pieces of silver, can be conned into betraying its location. A stuck-looking door is pulled open; an endless flight of stairs, lit by a team of dusty fireflies, is climbed. Within the sanctum, squalor reigns unchallenged. A lugubrious army-green metal desk rests in the center of a threadbare Oriental rug reticulate with mouse-paths; the walls are camouflaged in the kind of cardboard walnut panelling used in newly graduated lawyers' offices or in those Los Angeles motels favored by the hand-held cameramen and quick-tongued *directeurs* of blue movies. On these sad walls hang pictures, mostly souvenirs of his childhood, artistic or otherwise. On the bookshelves, evidently stained by a leopard in the process of shedding his spots, rest repellent books—garish schoolboy anthologies secreting some decaying Updikean morsel, seven feet of James Buchanan's bound works adumbrating the next opus, some daffodil-yellow building-trade manuals penumbrating *Couples;* and, most repellent of all, a jacketless row of the total *oeuvre,* spines naked as the chorus of *Hair,* revealing what only the more morbid have hitherto suspected, that since 1959 (*The Poorhouse Fair,* surely his masterpiece) Updike with Alfred A. Knopf's connivance has been perpetrating a uniform edition of himself. Beclouding all, the stink of nickel cigarillos, which the shifty, tremulous, asthmatic author puffs to sting the muse's eyes into watering ever since, at the Surgeon General's behest, he excised cigarettes from his armory of crutches.

Updike, at first sight, seems bigger than he is, perhaps because the dainty stitchwork of his prose style readies one for an apparition of elfin dimensions. An instant layer of cordial humorousness veneers a tough thickness of total opacity, which may in turn coat a center of heartfelt semi-liquid. Shamefacedly I confessed my errand—to fabricate an "interview" for one of those desperate publications that seek to make weekly "news" of remorselessly accumulating Gutenbergian silt. Shamefacedly, Updike submitted. Yet, throughout the interview that limped in the van of this consent, as the pumpkin-orange New England sun lowered above the chimney pots of a dry-cleaning establishment seen darkly through an unwashed window, Updike gave the impression of (and who wouldn't?) wanting to be elsewhere. He kept interjecting his desire to go "home" and "shingle" his "barn"; it occurred to this interviewer (the Interviewer, as Mailer would say), that the uniform books, varied in tint and size as subtly as cedar shakes, were themselves shingles, with the which this shivering poor fellow hopes to keep his own skin dry in the soaking downpour of mortality.

I observed, feinting for an opening, that he has stopped writing about Jews. He replied that the book about me had not so much been about a Jew as about a writer, who was a Jew with the same inevitability that a fictional rug-salesman would be an American. I riposted that *he* was a writer, though a Wasp. With the languid shrug of the chronically pained, he bitterly inveighed against the term Wasp, which implies, he said, wealth where he had been poor, Calvinism where he had been Lutheran, and ethnic consciousness where he had had none. That his entire professional life had been spent among Jews and women, that his paternal grandmother had been partly Irish, that he had disliked James Gould Cozzens' last novel, that false loyalties were the plague of a divided Republic, that racism as an aesthetic category was one thing but as an incitement to massacre another, etc.

With the chinks in his armor gaping before me like marigolds at the height of noon, I lunged deftly as a hummingbird. Didn't I detect, I asked, in his later work, an almost blunt determination to, as it were, sing America? Would he describe himself, I asked, switching the tape recorder up to fortissimo, as (a) pro-American, (b) a conservative? His turtleish green eyes blinked, recognizing that his shell was being tickled, and that there was no way out but forward. He said he was pro-American in the sense that he was married to America and did not wish a divorce. That the American style and landscape and impetus were, by predetermination, his meat; though he had also keenly felt love of fatherland in England, in Russia, in Egypt. That nations were like people, lovable and wonderful in their simple existence. That, in answer to the second prong of my probe, there were some things he thought worth conserving, such as the electoral college and the Great Lakes; but that by registration he was a Democrat and by disposition an apologist for the spirit of anarchy—our animal or divine margin of resistance to the social contract. That, given the need for a contract, he preferred the American Constitution, with its 18th-century bow to the pursuit of individual happiness, to any of the totalisms presently running around rabid. That the decisions of any establishment, though properly suspect and frightfully hedged by self-interest and the myopia power brings, must be understood as choices among imperfect alternatives; power participates in the weight and guilt of the world and shrill impotence never has to cash in its chips.

I inkled that this diatribe was meant to lead up to some discussion of his new novel, with its jacket of red, gray, and blue stripes, but, having neglected to read more than the first pages, which concern a middle-aged ex-athlete enjoying a beer with his elderly father, I was compelled to cast my interrogation in rather general terms. Viz.:

Q: Are you happy?

A: Yes, this is a happy limbo for me, this time. I haven't got the first finished copies yet, and haven't spotted the first typo. I haven't had to read any reviews.

Q: How do you find reviews?

A: Humiliating. It isn't merely that the reviewers are so much cleverer than I, and could write such superior fictions if they deigned to; it's that even the on-cheering ones have read a different book than the one you wrote. All the little congruences and arabesques you prepared with such delicate anticipatory pleasure are gobbled up as if by pigs at a pastry cart. Still, the ideal reader must —by the ontological argument—exist, and his invisibility therefore be a demonic illusion sustained to tempt us to despair.

Q: Do you envision novels as pills, broadcasts, tapestries, explosions of self, cantilevered constructs, or what?

A: For me, they are crystallizations of visceral hopefulness extruded as a slow paste which in the glitter of print regains something of the original, absolute gaiety. I try to do my best and then walk away rapidly, so as not to be incriminated. Right now, I am going over old short stories, arranging them in little wreaths, trimming away a strikingly infelicitous sentence here, adding a paper ribbon there. Describing it like this makes me sound more Nabokovian than I feel. Chiefly, I feel fatigued by my previous vitality.

Q: I'd like to talk about the new book, but the truth is I can't hold bound galley pages, my thumbs keep going to sleep, so I didn't get too far into this, what? *Rabbit Rerun?*

A (*eagerly, pluggingly*): *Redux*. Latin for led back. You know Latin: *Apologia Pro Vita Sua*. The next installment, ten years from now, I expect to call *Rural Rabbit*—you'll notice at the end of this book Janice talks about them getting a farm. The fourth and last, to come out in 1991 if we all live, is tentatively titled *Rabbit Is Rich*. Nice, huh?

Q (*turning tape recorder down to pianissimo*): Not bad. *Pas mal*. Not bad.

A (*gratefully, his shingling hand itching*): Thanks. Thanks a lot.

Farewell to the Middle Class

*(Hitherto Published Only, Strange to Say, in Japanese,
as One of a Series of Ads for Suntory Whisky,
on the Strength of its having been Written
under the Influence of Alcohol)*

TODAY I WAS TOLD I had made half a million dollars. My wife calls me a half-ass millionaire. The man on the other end of the phone seemed a little disappointed that I couldn't react. He had swung the deal and felt closer to it than I did. I expressed a doubt, just to make conversation, and that produced a series of phone calls on his part that produced another hundred thousand dollars. The second time he called, my wife kept shouting "Give it away!"

from the other room, and I could hardly hear him, and explained that he had given my wife a headache, and he laughed, thinking I was making a joke. I wasn't.

Sad, yes. I couldn't think of how to keep the government from taking the major share. The contract wasn't even signed, and I was a tax dodger. I couldn't think where to put the money. Our savings accounts were full to the insurable maximum. My wife had a new electric dishwasher, and I had a new pair of Fiberglas skis. We lived in an old house in the middle of an old neighborhood, making a little more than our neighbors but too lazy to spend it and taking a (if you examine it closely) snobbish pride in our worn-out sneakers, our dented cars, our threadbare backyard full of broken toys and unharvested dog dung.

Tonight I am a rich man. Tomorrow my wife is thirty-eight. I went out in a blizzard and bought her, rapidly, at the five and ten and then the local electric shop, a Joan Baez record, an electric waffle iron, and a four-slice toaster. In the old days, I would have bought her either the toaster or the waffle iron, but not both. I also bought some four-ninety wine. I said to the liquor-store proprietor, with whom I have grown intimate over the years, that people who paid five bucks for a bottle of wine must be nuts. Then I bought some. It was all a routine, half-planned on my part. He laughed, though. And the strange thing is, the wine was terrific, really distinctly better than three-dollar Bordeaux, or two-dollar Almadén. Fuller, smokier, with more grape, more landscape, more sorrow in it. We drank it all and, drunk, horsed around with the kids, who were feeling sorry for the old toaster and old waffle iron. The smaller girl took these appliances up to her bed and tucked them in. The snow kept coming. I had to cancel a church meeting that was going to be held at my house—too many old people on the committee to make it up the slippery curb.

Now I stand here, frugging to the Joan Baez record, looking out my window at my neighbor's television screen through the snow-storm. He is a train conductor and watches television every night from six to midnight. His endurance is fabulous. It is beautiful. His bluish set, more familiar to my wife and myself than the moon, is beautiful. We have watched it from our bedroom window often, before making love, after making love, before fights, after them.

Its electric shadows twitch. Its blue is smeared, glorified, made abstract by the snow, the falling flurrying flying snow, falling in clumps, bunched; only God could make so much snow. Five hundred thousand flakes. My neighbor's wife's head, silhouetted by the set, turns, and I guess I am visible, and she is watching. I turn off the light and keep frugging. Go, Joan. Good-bye, good-bye. She is doing "Where Have All the Flowers Gone?" in German. *Sagt mir wo die Blumen sind.* Good-bye, dear neighborhood of smoking chimneys and speckled roofs. My children yearn to be put to bed. One of the boys had a bath and is running around the house naked, flipping his penis; somehow he knows already we are rich and anything goes. The smaller girl comes to me and cries; she wants me to protect her in our storm of good fortune. My wife is out getting gas for the car. It didn't need gas but she loves snowstorms, whirlwinds, births, menstrual periods, and other such inexpensive excitements. Maybe she is saying good-bye to thirty-seven, hello to middle age. She sees money as a curse, that is why I love her. Who else would have lived here so long, on this noisy nondescript corner, amid widows and semi-shaven men who mutter off to mysterious jobs before the sun is up? Lord, I have loved them. I love you too, Joan. And you, old house, and you, Old Toaster. And you, you blue-smeared snow. Let's fuck once more. Good-bye, good-bye.

FOUR SPEECHES

Accuracy

I THANK the donors of the prize and the judges of the award for this honor. Its receipt makes me both glad and uneasy—uneasy perhaps because the writing of fiction is so rewarding in itself, so intimately necessary, that public bonuses seem bestowed under some misapprehension, to somebody else, to that fantastical and totally remote person whose picture very occasionally appears in the Sunday book supplements and whose opinions of art, life, and technology are so hopefully solicited by the editors of undergraduate magazines. On his behalf, as it were, I gratefully accept; and since he has been asked to say a few words, I will mention, in the manner of writing fiction, a virtue seldom extolled these days, that of *accuracy*, or *lifelikeness*.

It may seem too daring of me to touch on this when my book appeared, to many, a bewildering, arbitrary, and forced mixture of uncongenial elements, of mythology and remembrance, of the drably natural and the bookishly supernatural. I can only plead that the shape of the book formally approximates, for me, the mixed and somewhat antic experience it was trying to convey. The book as well as the hero is a centaur. Anyone dignified with the name of "writer" should strive, surely, to discover or invent the verbal texture that most closely corresponds to the tone of life as it arrives on his nerves. This tone, whose imitation induces style, will vary from soul to soul. Glancing upward, one is struck by the dispersion of recent constellations, by how far apart the prose masters of the century—say, Proust and Joyce, Kafka and Hem-

Given in New York City, in March 1964, in acceptance of the 1963 National Book Awards fiction prize, awarded to *The Centaur*.

ingway—are from one another. It may be partly an optical illusion, but modern fiction does seem, more than its antecedents, the work of eccentrics. The writer now makes his marks on paper blanker than it has ever been. Our common store of assumptions has dwindled, and with it the stock of viable artistic conventions. Each generation—and readers and writers are brothers in this—inherits a vast attic of machinery that once worked and decorative dodads whose silhouettes no longer sing. We must each of us clear enough space in this attic so that we in turn can unpack. Does plot, for example, as commonly understood and expected, mirror Providential notions of retribution and ultimate balance that our hearts doubt? Is the syntactical sentence plastic enough to render the flux, the blurring, the endless innuendo of experience as we feel it? No aesthetic theory will cover the case; what is needed is a habit of honesty on the part of the writer. He must, rather athletically, instill his wrists with the refusal to write whatever is lazily assumed, or hastily perceived, or piously hoped. Fiction is a tissue of literal lies that refreshes and informs our sense of actuality. Reality is—chemically, atomically, biologically—a fabric of microscopic accuracies. Language approximates phenomena through a series of hesitations and qualifications; I miss, in much contemporary writing, this sense of self-qualification, the kind of timid reverence toward what exists that Cézanne shows when he grapples for the shape and shade of a fruit through a mist of delicate stabs. The intensity of the grapple is the surest pleasure a writer receives. Though our first and final impression of Creation is not that it was achieved by taking pains, perhaps we should proceed in the humble faith that, by taking pains, word by word, to be accurate, we put ourselves on the way toward making something useful and beautiful and, in a word, good.

The Future of the Novel

First, let us ask, to what extent is The Future of the Novel a non-question, a non-issue repeatedly raised by literary journalists about a non-thing, the Novel? Do we worry ourselves with the future of

Given in Bristol, England, in February 1969, after a dinner arranged by the Bristol Literary Society.

the Poem? Surprisingly, not. Yet verse, compared to narrative prose, would seem to be the more fragile device, far more vulnerable to the clamorous counterclaims of television, the cinema, and traffic noise, far less likely to survive into an age of McLuhanism, Computerization, and whatever other polysyllables would dull our sensibilities and eclipse our humanistic heritage. In fact, poetry has survived. Great poets appear, do their work, and die. Waves of excitement and revolution occur, and are followed by lulls of consolidation and repose. An Ezra Pound or an Allen Ginsberg issues proclamations and generates apostles; relatively isolated and softspoken figures such as our Wallace Stevens and your Philip Larkin also meditate, and create. No doubt some decades are more fruitful of enduring verse than others; but each generation seems to supply its quota of poets and, odder still, of poetry readers. A certain slender ardent audience for poetry persists, and indeed in the United States seems to be widening; and if we include as "poets" (and why not?) the ubiquitous pop lyricists in the style of Bob Dylan and the Beatles, the audience is very wide indeed. The appetite for song—for things singingly said—would seem to be so fundamental to human nature that no foreseeable turn of technology or history could soon root it out.

Now, might we not assume the same of prose narrative? Perhaps; but the impression does linger that the Novel is not quite a category of human expression as eternal as Poetry, or the Dance, or the Joke, but is instead, like the Verse Epic, like the dramatic form called Tragedy, a genre with a life cycle and a death—a death, indeed, that may have already occurred.

Dr. Johnson, in his Dictionary, defined the word "novel" as "a small tale, generally of love." What he had in mind, of course, were the Italian *novelle*, written in great quantity from the 14th century to the 17th, of which Boccaccio's were the most famous, and from which Shakespeare derived the plots of, among other plays, *Romeo and Juliet* and *Othello*. The novel form in England was greatly enriched and broadened: Richardson brought to it the imitation of the epistle and Defoe the imitation of the journal; with Fielding and Jane Austen it becomes an inhabitable microcosm of society; and with Dickens the many-chambered Novel is expanded to include a courtroom for the indictment of social abuse. In the 19th century, length—physical bulk, the rendering of the sonorous music of passing time—becomes so intrinsic to the idea of the once-modest *novella* that Tennyson speaks of the ideal novel as one that will just "go on and on and never end." Throughout, however, and right down to the classics of modernism, love is a pervasive, perhaps obsessive, thread. The French say, "Without adultery, there is no novel," and while this may be more true of *their* novels than yours, it is indeed difficult to imagine a novel, even one by Lord Snow, without its—as the phrase goes—"romantic interest."

I would suggest that this is a *genre* trait of the Novel rather than an undistorted reflection of our lives. There *are* areas of concern in our lives apart from love; yet as a literary practitioner, and as a sometimes compulsory reader of unsuccessful novels, I have observed that it is difficult to make them interesting in a novel. Disease and pain, for instance, are of consuming concern to the person suffering from them, but while we will follow for eight hundred pages the course of a romance, and suffer with each love pang, the course of a physical disease, and the description of pain and discomfort, however sympathetic the character afflicted, weary us within a few paragraphs. Similarly, the amassment of sums of money, fascinating in reality, acquires interest in a novel only if the acquisition of wealth advances the hero or heroine toward that eventual copulation that seems to be every reader's insatiable and exclusive desire. Indeed, it is part of the peculiar democracy of fiction, and one way in which the air of its world is fresher than our own, that although in real life we *do* find wealthy and famous men more interesting than poor and obscure ones, in novels we do not. Even intelligence does not recommend a fictional character to us. No, in the strange egalitarian world of the Novel a man must earn our interest by virtue of his—how shall I say?—his *authentic sentiments.*

So we arrive at the not very spectacular inkling that the Novel is by nature sentimental. I use the word without pejorative intent, but merely as descriptive of the kind of coinage with which we transact our business in one literary realm. This coinage is not legal tender, I think, in the New Testament, or in *Beowulf*, or in *Prometheus Bound*, or to any predominant degree in the *Odyssey* or *Para-*

dise Lost. It is current, though not the only currency, in *The Divine Comedy*, and it would seem to have been introduced in Italy, with the breakup of the Middle Ages, and to be concurrent with the rise of capitalism. That is, when human worth began to be measured in terms of capital, and men became counters upon a board of productivity, the uneconomic emotions went underground, into literature. We can scarcely imagine it: but with the massive cosmic drama of Fall and Redemption always before him, and the momentous potentialities of sin and repentance always alive within him, medieval man may well have needed less reassurance than we that his emotions were substantial and significant, that his inner life and outward status were integrated. Even today, religious fundamentalists are not notable novel-readers.

This scale of generalization is uncomfortable for a novelist, concerned as he properly is with the strict small circumstance, the quizzical but verifiable fact. I wish to describe, merely, the Novel as a product of private enterprise, for which a market is created when the state, or tribe, or church, withdraws itself from the emotional sector of the individual's life. Erotic love then becomes a symbol, a kind of code for all the nebulous, perishable sensations which we persist in thinking of as *living*. Living and loving: the titles of two novels by the splendid Henry Green, and an equation, but for one transposed vowel, to which all novel readers consent— the housewife reading away the dull afternoon, the schoolboy concentrating amid the stupid family din, the banker sitting prim in the homeward commuting train. All are members of a conspiracy to preserve the secret that people *feel*. Please do not suppose that I am describing only penny fiction, trash. The most elegant and respectable of modern novels, from *Remembrance of Things Past* to *Lolita*, enlist in this conspiracy with all the boldness of their virtuosity. Even as all-including and unyielding a masterwork as *Ulysses* is finally about lovers; Leopold and Molly Bloom are great lovers, great in compassion and fidelity, fidelity to each other and to their inner sensations, their authentic sentiments. Perhaps the reason Stephen Dedalus is slightly tedious in this novel is that he is not in love. Not to be in love, the capital N Novel whispers to capital W Western Man, is to be dying.

*

So much for the past; what of the future? The Novel's Victorian heyday has passed. If my impression is correct, that capitalism put sex in a treasure chest, the chest, after so many raids upon it, is battered to the point of collapse. The set of tensions and surprises we call *plot* to a great extent depends upon the assumption that bourgeois society discourages and obstructs free-ranging sex. In the 19th-century novels and the 20th-century movies, the punishment for adultery is death. Yet even in *Madame Bovary*, one feels, reading it, that the heroine in swallowing arsenic is being hysterical, that there is nothing in her situation a sudden inheritance of money wouldn't solve. In the novels, say, of Evelyn Waugh, adultery has become a dangerous pleasantry, and by now I think even the aura of danger is fading. As Denis de Rougemont has pointed out, the conventional obstructions to love no longer impress us; a somewhat extravagant situation, such as in *Lolita*, alone can bestow dignity upon a romantic passion. Freud, misunderstood or not, has given sex the right to be free, and the new methods of contraception have minimized the bail. Remove the genuine prohibitions and difficulty, and the three-dimensional interweave of the Novel collapses, becomes slack and linear. The novels of Henry Miller are not novels, they are acts of intercourse strung alternately with segments of personal harangue. They are closer to the *Arabian Nights* than to Tolstoy; they are not novels but *tales*.

Dr. Johnson defined "novel" as a type of tale; and, though the classic Novel, the sentimental underground of bourgeois Europe, may belong to a moment of history that is passing, the appetite for tales is probably not less fundamental to the human species than the appetite for songs. Books of prose about imaginary events will continue to appear, and they will be called, out of semantic inertia, novels.

What will be the shape of these books? Some will continue the direction of Miller, and be more or less angry personal accounts of coitus and conversation among bohemians. The tradition is not dishonorable—Dostoevsky's *Notes from the Underground* is such a book—and will veer very close to pornography, which itself has a tradition that is, at the least, venerable. The subversive burden will shift, I fear, from sex to violence, and the threat of society, and the problem for censorship, lies not, in my opinion, with the description of sexual acts but with fantasies of violence and torture. Books like *Last Exit to Brooklyn* and *The Painted Bird*, with their unrelieved brutality, and the relish that seethes beneath their creditable surface pretensions, augur an unhappy direction. Cruel events do occur in reality, of course; but the obligation of the artist, when dealing with them, as with sex, is to be, not inexplicit, but accurately alive to their complicated human context. Today's bohemia, or hippiedom, seems to aspire toward a political effectiveness that precludes much compass of sympathy or subtlety of craft. Rather, a fanatic and dazed narrowing of comprehension seems to be in progress. The sour riots of the Sixties are not likely to call forth the ebullient rapture of a Kerouac, let alone the refined anguish of a Huysmans.

Other books of fiction will, I think, try to employ the inherited machinery of the romantic novel for drier purposes than the dramatization of erotic vicissitudes. The novels of Vladimir Nabokov already ingeniously toy with romantic triangles to produce more intricate patterns. His novels approach the condition of puzzles—*Pale Fire* was rigged on the scheme of an annotated poem and the introduction playfully invited us to buy two copies to read it properly. Novels by other men play hopscotch with us, or invite us to shuffle the pages and make our own plots. Robbe-Grillet gives us an overlapping sequence of repetitions of actions; all such inventions have a somewhat capricious air, but I think the two directions, of novel as philosophy, of novel as object, will be fruitfully pursued. Heightened intellectual demands should compress the conventional size of the novel; hundreds of thousands of words in Dickens' time, it may settle at around two hundred pages, the length of a mystery story, of *Candide*, or of a novel by Samuel Beckett.

The surface of the page, now a generally dead rectangle of gray, a transparent window into the action, could be a lively plane of typographic invention, as it was for Apollinaire—a surface that says "This is printing" much as Impressionism forsook the licked illusionistic surface and announced, "This is painting." The comic strip offers a blend of picture and word that, though it has not attained the status of high art, has, in strips like the old "Krazy Kat" and the contemporary "Peanuts," climbed rather high. I see no intrinsic reason why a doubly talented artist might not arise and create a comic-strip novel masterpiece. Artistically, this century has belonged to the eye; concrete poetry, medieval manuscripts, and Egyptian hieroglyphs all hint at paths of accommodation in an ecumenical movement among eye-oriented media.

If these suggestions sound frivolous, let me say that tale-telling *is* a kind of toying, and that something of primitive magic does linger about the manipulation of verbal dolls. When the speaker was an undergraduate student of "creative writing," a guest writer, John Hawkes, told our class—amazingly, I thought— "When I want a character to fly, I just say, 'He flew.'" We are, all of us novelists, like neoclassic playwrights captive to the three unities, prisoners of conventions we cannot imagine our way around; a wonderful freedom awaits us, and extraordinary opportunities. Let me admit to the hopeful fancy that some book such as I have imagined—a short novel, approaching the compact, riddling condition of an object—may serve as the vehicle of a philosophic revolution. That a new Rousseau or a new Marx or a new Kierkegaard may choose to speak to us through the Novel. That the Novel, relieved of some of its old duties as an emotional masseur, may prove to be a light and nimble messenger. That, though at the moment the Novel roosts a little heavily in the bookshops, to fly it only needs him to come along who will say, "It flies."

From *Humor in Fiction*

THE TITLE of this talk has been assigned to me; and, though I confess I find it congenial, I confess also that I can hardly imagine a language *less* international than that of written humor. For humor, written or otherwise, operates in the nuancé margins of experience and communication; not only is a pun lost in translation from one language to another, but also lost are rhythm, slang, and the many fine halftones of verbal allusion. The Argentine writer Jorge Luis Borges, in parenthetically discussing the failure of Shake-

---

Given in Seoul, South Korea, in June 1970, at a conference of the International P.E.N.; the general conference theme was "Humor."

speare's humor to amuse him, ventures the surprising thought that "humor . . . is an oral genre, a sudden spark in conversation, not a written thing." And, if we reflect upon those occasions when we laugh, we perceive how delicate and complex are the forces giving rise to our reaction, how close to pathos or banality these forces verge, and how difficult it is to describe, later, what, in the heat of conversation or, it may be, in the forward surge of reading, seemed so funny.

The phenomenon of humor, or laughter, has not failed to attract theorists. Henri Bergson locates the comic essence in an "encrustation of the mechanical upon the organic." Twins, for example, are humorous because duplication of individuals hints at a mechanical intervention in the species; a man slipping upon a banana peel is comic in that he behaves like a machine, rigidly perpetuating his motion without the foresight and allowances proper to vitality. By Bergson's theory, the comic incident is a misapplication of momentum and the comic character is a monomaniac, which well enough describes the heroes of French farce but does not encompass such a nimble and many-faced comic hero as Shakespeare's Falstaff.

Confusingly, just as weeping can express joy as well as sorrow, laughter arises from states of mind that appear not merely various but even opposite: laughter can announce scorn and contempt, but may also be applause. Our laughter at Falstaff, for instance, has much applause and admiration in it, as well as feelings of superiority, and in literary humor especially, we find an ingredient of the genial. Within a comic work we are relaxed in a world of essential safety, where the dangers of death and destruction have been exchanged for mock penalties, for semblances of defeat and punishment that are erased by the next comic scene. The comic character, whether a cat in an animated cartoon or the hero of a classic like Don Quixote, is rubbery; he bounces back, and suffers no scars. Contrast the brittle, stony characters of Greek tragedy, who, under the unforgiving pressure of fate's engines, irrevocably shatter.

Sigmund Freud attempted to extend the methods of his dream analysis into the analysis of jokes. His book *Wit and Its Relation to the Unconscious* explains jokes and examples of verbal wit and, by extension, all instances of the comic in terms of a difference in psychical expenditures; the characteristic joke sets up an instant of bewilderment, and laughter follows in the recognition that a kind of sense has been made, but different from what we expected. As Kant said, the comic is "an expectation that has turned to nothing." Certainly jokes, like dreams, do function in a realm liberated from the laws of logic and logical consequence; and there is melancholy profundity in Freud's tentative suggestion that humor, the art of the comic, is an intellectual adult attempt to recover "the lost laughter of childhood."

And what might be this original laughter, the laughter of childhood? A recent, popular, but not uninformative book called, a little provocatively, *The Naked Ape*, discusses, from a zoologist's point of view, the origin of laughter. Desmond Morris first notes that crying is present from birth but laughter does not appear until the third or fourth month of life. It arises in circumstances like these: the mother, holding the child in her lap, pretends to let him drop, or does something else startling. The infant's instinctive crying reaction is cancelled by his recognition that he is safe, that the mother is with him, and his cry merges with the parental-recognition gurgle that by this time is part of his vocabulary. In this manner, laughter is born. How many of the games parents instinctively play with infants, for instance, the tossing and clutching, the chasing and tickling, are in fact a systematic daring and scaring, a systematic widening of the circle of safety in which the children may feel privileged to laugh? A hundred and fifty years ago, William Hazlitt wrote this on the theory of laughter:

> If we hold a mask before our face, and approach a child with this disguise on, it will at first, from the oddity and incongruity of the appearance, be inclined to laugh; if we go nearer to it, steadily, and without saying a word, it will begin to be alarmed, and be half inclined to cry; if we suddenly take off the mask, it will recover from its fears, and burst out a-laughing; but if, instead of presenting the old well-known countenance, we have concealed a satyr's head or some frightful caricature behind the first mask, the suddenness of the change will not in this case be a source of merriment to it, but will convert its surprise into an agony of consternation, and will make it scream out for help, even though it may be convinced that the whole thing is a trick at bottom.

The alternation of tears and laughter, in this little episode in common life, depends almost entirely on the greater or less degree of interest attached to the different changes of appearance. The mere suddenness of the transition, the mere baulking our expectations, and turning them abruptly into another channel, seems to give additional liveliness and gaiety to the animal spirits; but the instant the change is not only sudden, but threatens serious consequences, or calls up the shape of danger, terror supersedes our disposition to mirth, and laughter gives place to tears.

Laughter, then, can be construed as a signal of danger past or dismissed. It occurs within an arena, whether the arms of a mother or the covers of a novel, where the customary threats of life have been suspended. Dreams, jokes, play, and aesthetic pleasure alike mark a truce with the destructive forces of life. The oldest laugh may be the crow of triumph a warrior emits when his enemy is at his feet. We giggle when we are nervous; we scream hilariously when, in the old silent pictures, the comedian totters on the parapet of the skyscraper. The margin of glee in our scream is the knowledge that, being a comedian, he will not fall. The clown, the fool, is traditionally exempt from laws and taboos. Yet his activities, and our laughter, take their point from the backdrop of gravity, of necessary prohibition and actual danger. In literature, comic adventure is woven from the same threads as tragedy and pathos; we laugh within the remittance from seriousness that the artist has momentarily won for us. . . .

The episode, in *Don Quixote*, of the windmills contains many of the elements that our theorists of the comic would have us look for. Don Quixote's monomania, his determination to see romantic adventures in mundane happenstance, is comic in its rigidity, and admirable in its ingenuity. At first he seems to see the windmills through a cloud, so that sails of wood and canvas take on the appearance of giant human arms; he charges forward despite the shouted warnings of his clear-sighted squire. Then, rebuffed by a whack one sail gives him, and perhaps his vision clarified by his physical closeness to these supposed giants, he reconstructs his delusion upon a new, and invulnerable, ground: his enemy the magician Freston has turned real giants into apparent windmills. All of Sancho's realism is overthrown by sublime assertions: "Thou art but little acquainted with adventures" and "There is nothing so subject to the Inconstancy of Fortune as War." Like some modern statesmen, Don Quixote has constructed from much real information and one wildly false premise an impregnable castle of self-justification; awkward realities are made to argue against themselves, and to reconfirm the malice of the enemy and the nobility of the unreal quest.

His dream does not shatter under reality because the author and Sancho Panza protect him; the author by conferring upon this lean old man a magical rubbery toughness, and Sancho Panza—with a loving and wondering fidelity that is one of the book's masterstrokes—by always rushing forward and picking up the pieces. Don Quixote suffers no ill effects from this adventure; it is Rozinante, his horse, who limps, his shoulder half dislocated by their fall. It is the horse, who cannot reason or go mad but who can suffer, who absorbs and mutely carries off this adventure's residue of pain.

Even this early in the novel, Cervantes seems indifferent to his stated objective—of burlesquing the pseudo-medieval adventures of Tasso and Ariosto. A cruder author would have hurt his hero severely, or had him spin delusions less plausibly, or accompanied him with a mocking and sardonic squire. Our laughter would have been quicker and sharper, but thin, and quickly automatic. Satire, as an attack upon an idea or set of ideas, quickly bores us, since the author, manipulating his puppets, makes the same statement over and over. Here, with Cervantes—himself as often battered and disappointed as his hero—our laughter is deepened by a certain ambiguous poetry in the narrative; the windmills are not merely mistaken for giants but somehow loom *as* giants. The wind, springing up opportunely to turn their giant arms, seems to join the fun; and the knight's unshakable dignity in some sense argues for his delusions, and gives him that air of triumph which is, we noted above, an ancient tributary of laughter. . . .

Dr. Pangloss, like Don Quixote, irrepressibly applies the mechanism of his *idée fixe* to the incongruous material of life. But here there is no mistaking the satiric edge, and the author performs his comedy on the edge of pain. We are anesthetized, and allowed therefore to laugh, by the flitting quickness and neatness of the narrative style. When the Lisbon earthquake occurs in *Candide*, we are told, as if the statistic had been gathered in an instant, that "Thirty thousand men, women and children were crushed to death." The characters with mechanical promptness react in character: the pious and innocent Candide exclaims that the Day of Judgment is near, Dr. Pangloss poses himself a philosophical riddle amid the toppling ruins, and the sailor, cheerfully heartless, seizes the opportunity for theft and lechery. Such stylization preserves the earthquake as an item in an abstract argument and heightens our sense of play. In a sentence, we are told Candide is injured and half-buried, but are not asked to dwell upon his condition—Rozinante's limp is more sensuously present. The central figure remains Dr. Pangloss, whose musing in such circumstances approaches heroic detachment and whose lack of pity for Candide is partially redeemed by his equal lack of self-pity. Pangloss' preposterous conclusion of a vein of sulphur running halfway around the world, defended with the stoutness of a Quixote, makes us laugh; and if we look into our laughter we detect there:

1. a sense of superiority to the scientific speculation of the 18th century;

2. a certain pleasure in the image, gaudy and simple as a child's crayon stroke;

3. applause at the good doctor's unfailing intellectual curiosity;

4. a kind of hysteria at the frightful facts of calamity and heavenly indifference that Voltaire sets before us;

5. a confession of pleasurable warmth, which the farcical tempo of the narrative has created in us, and which disposes us to laugh reflexively.

Laughter, as we know from its social instances, is infectious and carries a curious momentum; an image, mixed of such incongruities as a man's call for the oil and wine of the last rites mixed with another man's meditations upon sulphur, trips the trigger of laughter and, recurring (as it does when Pangloss insists, "I maintain it's proved!"), trips it again, harder. Here we touch upon the mystery, in presentation of the comic, of *timing;* in personal presentation, of timing and facial expression. A wrong twist of the face, betraying over-eagerness, like an excessive adjective in a sentence, will with mysterious thoroughness defuse a joke and frustrate a laugh. The moment of blank bewilderment that Freud describes has been sullied. There must be a headlong, clean, economical some-thing, a swift and careless music perhaps descended from the rhythm of ticklings in infancy. No purer example of this comic music exists than *Candide*. Indeed, its example leads us to wonder if any efficient display of energy—an elegant mathematical proof, a well-made young woman briskly walking by—doesn't dispose us to jubilation, to a smile or laugh that is a salute, a shout of greeting to the angels of health and life. . . .

Why Write?

MY TITLE offers me an opportunity to set a record of brevity at this Festival of Arts; for an adequate treatment would be made were I to ask, in turn, "Why not?" and sit down.

But instead I hope to explore, for not too many minutes, the question from the inside of a man who, rather mysteriously to him-self, has earned a livelihood for close to twenty years by engaging in the rather selfish and gratuitous activity called "writing." I do *not* propose to examine the rather different question of what use is writing to the society that surrounds and, if he is fortunate, sup-ports the writer. The ancients said the purpose of poetry, of writ-ing, was to entertain and to instruct; Aristotle put forward the still fascinating notion that a dramatic action, however terrible and piteous, carries off at the end, in catharsis, the morbid, personal, subjective impurities of our emotions. The enlargement of sym-pathy, through identification with the lives of fictional others, is frequently presented as an aim of narrative; D. H. Lawrence, with characteristic fervor, wrote, "And here lies the vast importance of the novel, properly handled. It can inform and lead into new places the flow of our sympathetic consciousness, and can lead our sym-pathy away in recoil from things that are dead." Kafka wrote that a book is an ax to break the frozen sea within us. The frozen sea within himself, he must have meant; though the ax of Kafka's own art (which, but for Max Brod's posthumous disobedience, Kafka

---

Given in Adelaide, South Australia, in March 1974.

would have taken with him into the grave), has served an analogous purpose for others. This note of pain, of saintly suffering, is a modern one, far removed from the serene and harmonious bards and poets of the courts of olden time. Listen to Flaubert, in one of his letters to Louise Colet:

> I love my work with a love that is frenzied and perverted, as an ascetic loves the hair shirt that scratches his belly. Sometimes, when I am empty, when words don't come, when I find I haven't written a single sentence after scribbling whole pages, I collapse on my couch and lie there dazed, bogged in a swamp of despair, hating myself and blaming myself for this demented pride which makes me pant after a chimera. A quarter of an hour later everything changes; my heart is pounding with joy. Last Wednesday I had to get up and fetch my handkerchief; tears were streaming down my face. I had been moved by my own writing; the emotion I had conceived, the phrase that rendered it, and satisfaction of having found the phrase—all were causing me to experience the most exquisite pleasure.

Well, if such is the writer at work, one wonders why he doesn't find a pleasanter job; and one also wonders why he appears himself to be the chief market for his own product.

Most people sensibly assume that writing is propaganda. Of course, they admit, there is bad propaganda, like the boy-meets-tractor novels of socialist realism, and old-fashioned propaganda, like Christian melodrama and the capitalist success stories of Horatio Alger or Samuel Smiles. But that some message is intended, wrapped in the story like a piece of crystal carefully mailed in cardboard and excelsior, is not doubted. Scarcely a day passes in my native land that I don't receive some letter from a student or teacher asking me *what I meant to say* in such a book, asking me to elaborate more fully on some sentence I deliberately whittled into minimal shape, or inviting me to speak on some topic, usually theological or sexual, on which it is pleasantly assumed I am an expert. The writer as hero, as Hemingway or Saint-Exupéry or D'Annunzio, a tradition of which Camus was perhaps the last example, has been replaced in America by the writer as educationist. Most writers teach, a great many teach writing; writing is furiously taught in the colleges even as the death knell of the book and the written word is monotonously tolled; any writer, it is assumed, can give a lecture, and the purer products of his academic mind, the "writings" themselves, are sifted and, if found of sufficient quality, installed in their places on the assembly belt of study, as objects of educational contemplation.

How dare one confess, to the politely but firmly inquiring letter-writer who takes for granted that as a remote but functioning element of his education you are duty-bound to provide the information and elucidating essay that will enable him to complete his term paper, or his Ph.D. thesis, or his critical *opus*—how dare one confess that the absence of a swiftly expressible message is, often, *the* message; that reticence is as important a tool to the writer as expression; that the hasty filling out of a questionnaire is not merely irrelevant but *inimical* to the writer's proper activity; that this activity is rather curiously private and finicking, a matter of exorcism and manufacture rather than of toplofty proclamation; that what he makes is ideally as ambiguous and opaque as life itself; that, to be blunt, the social usefulness of writing matters to him primarily in that it somehow creates a few job opportunities—in Australia, a few government grants—a few opportunities to live as a writer.

Not counting journalists and suppliers of scripts to the media, hardly a hundred American men and women earn their living by writing, in a wealthy nation of two hundred million. Does not then, you ask, such a tiny band of privileged spokesmen owe its country, if not the trophy of a Nobel Prize,* at least the benign services of a spiritual aristocracy? Is not the writer's role, indeed, to speak for humanity, as conscience and prophet and servant of the billions not able to speak for themselves? The conception is attractive, and there are some authors, mostly Russian, who have aspired to such grandeur without entirely compromising their gifts. But in general, when a writer such as Sartre or Faulkner becomes a great man, a well-intentioned garrulity replaces the specific witness that has been theirs to give.

The last time I dared appear on a platform in a foreign land, it was in Kenya, where I had to confess, under some vigorous questioning from a large white man in the audience, that the general

---

* That year awarded to Australia's Patrick White.

betterment of mankind, and even the improvement of social conditions within my own violently imperfect nation, were *not* my basic motivation as a writer. To be sure, *as a citizen* one votes, attends meetings, subscribes to liberal pieties, pays or withholds taxes, and contributes to charities even more generously than—it turns out—one's own President. But as a writer, for me to attempt to extend my artistic scope into all the areas of my human concern, to substitute nobility of purpose for accuracy of execution, would certainly be to forfeit whatever social usefulness I *do* have. It has befallen a Solzhenitsyn to have experienced the Soviet labor camps; it has befallen Miss Gordimer and Mr. Mtshali * to suffer the tensions and paradoxes and outrages of a racist police state; social protest, and a hope of reform, is in the very fiber of their witness. But a writer's witness, surely, is of value in its circumstantiality. Solzhenitsyn's visible and brave defiance of the Soviet state is magnificent; but a novel like *The First Circle* affords us more than a blind flash of conditioned and—let's face it—chauvinistic indignation; it affords us entry into an unknown world, it offers a complex and only implicitly indignant portrait of how human beings live under a certain sort of political system. When I think of the claustrophobic and seething gray world of *The First Circle*, I am reminded in texture of Henry Miller's infamous Paris novels. Here, too, we have truth, and an undeniable passion to proclaim the truth—a seedy and repellent yet vital truth—though the human conditions Miller describes are far removed from any hope of political cure. And Miller, in his way, was also a martyr: as with Solzhenitsyn, his works could not be published in his native land.

We must write where we stand; wherever we do stand, there is life; and an imitation of the life we know, however narrow, is our only ground. As I sat on that stage in Kenya, a symbolic American in a corner of that immense range of peoples symbolically called The Third World, I felt guilty and bewildered that I could not hear in my formidable accuser's orotund phrases anything that had to do with my practice of the writer's profession; I was discomfited that my concerns—to survive, to improve, to make my microcosms amusing to me and then to others, to fail, if fail I must, through

---

* Oswald Mtshali, Zulu poet. Both he and Nadine Gordimer were present at the Adelaide Festival.

neither artistic cowardice nor laziness, to catch all the typographical errors in my proofs, to see that my books appear in jackets
both striking and fairly representative of the contents, to arrange
words and spaces and imagined realities in patterns never exactly
achieved before, to be able to defend any sentence I publish—I was
embarrassed that my concerns were so ignoble, compared to his.
But, once off the stage (where a writer should rarely be), I tend to
be less apologetic, and even to believe that my well-intentioned
questioner, and the silent faces in the same audience looking to me
to atone for America's sins real and supposed, and the touching
schoolchildren begging me by letter to get them through the seventh grade—that none of these people have any felt comprehension
of my vocation.

Why write? As soon ask, why rivet? Because a number of personal accidents drift us toward the occupation of riveter, which
pre-exists, and, most importantly, the riveting-gun exists, and we
love it.

Think of a pencil. What a quiet, nimble, slender and then stubby
wonder-worker he is! At his touch, worlds leap into being; a tiger
with no danger, a steam-roller with no weight, a palace at no cost.
All children are alive to the spell of pencil and crayons, of making something, as it were, from nothing; a few children never
move out from under this spell, and try to become artists. I
was once a rapturous child drawing at the dining-room table,
under a stained-glass chandelier that sat like a hat on the swollen
orb of my excitement. What is exciting that child, so distant from
us in time and space? He appears, from the vantage of this lectern
unimaginable to him, to be in the grip of two philosophical perceptions.

One, mimesis demands no displacement; the cat I drew did not
have to fight for food or love with the real cat that came to the
back porch. I was in drawing *adding* to the world rather than rearranging the finite amount of goods within it. We were a family
struggling on the poverty edge of the middle class during the Depression; I was keen to avoid my father's noisy plight within the
plague of competition; pencil and paper were cheap, unlike most
other toys.

And, Two, the world called into being on the pencilled paper admitted of connections. An early exercise, whose pleasure returns to me whenever I assemble a collection of prose or poetry or whenever, indeed, I work several disparate incidents or impressions into the shape of a single story, was this: I would draw on one sheet of paper an assortment of objects—flowers, animals, stars, toaster, chairs, comic-strip creatures, ghosts, noses—and connect them with lines, a path of two lines, so that they all became the fruit of a single impossible tree. The exact age when this creative act so powerfully pleased me I cannot recall; the wish to make collections, to assemble sets, is surely a deep urge of the human mind in its playful, artistic aspect. As deep, it may be, as the urge to hear a story from beginning to end, or the little ecstacy of extracting resemblances from different things. Proust, of course, made simile the cornerstone of his theory of aesthetic bliss, and Plato, if I understand him right, felt that that which a set of like objects have in common *must* have a separate existence in itself, as the *idea* which delivers us, in our perception of the world, from the nightmare of nominalism. At any rate, to make a man of pencil and paper is as much a magical act as painting a bison with blood on the wall of a cave; a child, frail and overshadowed, and groping for his fate, herein *captures* something and, further, brings down praise from on high.

I have described the artistic transaction as being between the awakening ego and the world of matter to which it awakes; but no doubt the wish to please one's parents enters early, and remains with the artist all his life, as a desire to please the world, however displeasing his behavior may seem, and however self-satisfying the work pretends to be. We are surprised to discover, for instance, that Henry James hoped to make lots of money, and that James Joyce read all of his reviews. The artist's personality has an awkward ambivalence: he is a cave dweller who yet hopes to be pursued into his cave. The need for privacy, the need for recognition: a child's vulnerability speaks in both needs, and in my own reaction to, say, the beseeching mail just described, I detect the live ambiguity—one is avid to receive the letters, and loath to answer them. Or (to make some reference to the literary scene I know best) consider the striking contrast between the eager, even breathless warmth of Saul Bellow's fiction, inviting our love and closeness with every phrase, and Bellow's own faintly haughty, distinctly edgy personal surface. Again, J. D. Salinger wrote a masterpiece, *The Catcher in the Rye*, recommending that readers who enjoy a book call up the author; then he spent his next twenty years avoiding the telephone. A writer, I would say, out of no doubt deficiencies of character, has constructed a cave-shaped organ, hollow more like a mouth than like an ear, through which he communicates with the world at one remove. Somewhat, perhaps, as his own subconscious communicates with him through dreams. Because the opportunities for feedback have been reduced to letters that need not be answered and telephones that can be unlisted, to an annual gauntlet of reviews and non-bestowal of prizes, the communication can be more honest than is any but the most trusting personal exchange; yet also great opportunities for distortion exist unchecked. For one more of these rather sub-terranean and reprehensible satisfactions of writing that I am here confessing is that the world, so balky and resistant and humiliating, can in the act of mimesis be rectified, adjusted, chastened, purified. Fantasies defeated in reality can be fully indulged; tendencies de-flected by the cramp of circumstance can be followed to an end. In my own case I have noticed, so often it has ceased to surprise me, a prophetic quality of my fictions, even to the subsequent appearance in my life of originally fictional characters. We write, that is, out of latency as much as memory; and years later our laggard lives in reality act out, often with eerie fidelity, the pat-terns projected in our imaginings.

But we have come too far, too fast, from that ambitious child making his pencil move beneath the stained-glass chandelier. In my adolescence I discovered one could write with a pencil as well as draw, without the annoying need to consult reality so frequently. Also, the cave beneath the written page holds many more kinds of space than the one beneath the drawing pad. My writing tends, I think, to be pictorial, not only in its groping for visual precision but in the way the books are conceived, as objects in space, with events and persons composed within them like shapes on a canvas. I do not recommend this approach; it is perhaps a perversion of the primal narrative urge. Storytelling, for all its powers of depiction, shares with music the medium of time, and perhaps its genius, its most central transformation, has to do with time, with rhythm and echo and the sense of time not frozen as in a painting but channelled and harnessed as in a symphony.

But one can give no more than what one has received, and we try to create for others, in our writings, aesthetic sensations we have experienced. In my case, some of these would be: the graphic precision of a Dürer or a Vermeer, the offhand-and-backwards-feeling verbal and psychological accuracy of a Henry Green, the wonderful embowering metaphors of Proust, the enigmatic concreteness of Kafka and Joyce, the collapse into components of a solved mathematical problem, the unriddling of a scrupulous mystery story, the earth-scorning scope of science fiction, the tear-producing results of a truly humorous piece of writing. Writing, really, can make us do rather few substantial things: it can make us laugh, it can make us weep, and if it is pornography and we are rather young, it can make us come. It can also, of course, make us sleep; and though in the frequent discussion of the writer's social purpose this soporific effect is unfailingly ignored, I suspect it is the most widespread practical effect of writing—a book is less often a flaming sword or a beam of light than a bedtime toddy. Whatever the use, we hope that some members of society will find our product useful enough to purchase; but I think it would be a hypocrisy to pretend that these other people's welfare, or communication with them, or desire to ennoble or radicalize or terrify or lull them, is the primary reason why one writes.

No, what a writer wants, as every aspiring writer can tell you, is to *get into print*. To transform the changing shadows of one's dimly and fitfully lived life into print—into metal or, with the advent of offset printing, into rather mysteriously electrified rubber —to lift through the doubled magic of language and mechanical reproduction our own impressions and dreams and playful constructions into another realm of existence, a multiplied and far-flung existence, into a space far wider than that which we occupy, into a time theoretically eternal: *that* is the siren song that holds us to our desks, our dismal revisions, our insomnia panics, our dictionaries and encyclopedias, our lonely and, the odds long are, superfluous labor. "Of making many books there is no end; and much study is a weariness of the flesh." A weariness one can certainly feel entering even a modestly well-stocked bookstore. Yet it is just this involvement in the world of commerce and industry, this imposition of one's otherwise evanescent fancies upon the machinery of manufacture and distribution, that excites the writer's ego, and gives an illusion of triumph over his finitude.

Although, as a child, I lived what was to become my material and message, my wish to write did not begin with that material and message; rather, it was a wish to escape from it, into an altogether better world. When I was thirteen, a magazine came into the house, *The New Yorker* by name, and I loved that magazine so much I concentrated all my wishing into an effort to make myself small and inky and intense enough to be received into its pages. Once there, I imagined, some transfigured mode of being, called a "writer's life," would begin for me. My fantasy was not entirely fantastic, as my domineering position on this platform and the first-class airplane tickets that brought me halfway around the world testify. But what I would not altogether insincerely ask you to accept is something shabby, precarious, and even craven about a writer's life.

Among artists, a writer's equipment is least out-of-reach—the language we all more or less use, a little patience at grammar and spelling, the common adventures of blundering mortals. A painter must learn to paint; his studio is redolent of alchemic substances and physical force. The musician's arcanum of specialized knowledge and personal dexterity is even more intimidating, less accessible to the untrained, and therefore somehow less corruptible than the writer's craft. Though some painters and musicians go bad in the prime of their lives, far fewer do, and few so drastically, as writers. Our trick is treacherously thin; our art is so incorrigibly amateur that novices constantly set the world of letters on its ear, and the very phrase "professional writer" has a grimy sound. Hilaire Belloc said that the trouble with writing was that it was never meant to be a profession, it was meant to be a hobby. An act of willful play, as I have described it.

So I have not spoken up to now of language, of the joys of using it well, of the role of the writer as a keeper of the keys of language, a guardian of usage and enforcer of precision. This does not seem to me a very real notion, however often it is put forward.* Language goes on evolving in the street and in the spoken media, and well-written books are the last places it looks for direction. The writer follows after the spoken language, usually timidly. I see myself described in reviews as a doter upon words. It is true, I am grateful to have been born into English, with its polyglot flexibility and the happy accident, in the wake of two empires, of its worldwide currency. But what I am conscious of doting on is not English *per se*, its pliable grammar and abundant synonyms, but its potential, for the space of some phrases or paragraphs, of becoming reality, of engendering out of imitation another reality, infinitely lesser but thoroughly possessed, thoroughly human.

Pascal says, "When a natural discourse paints a passion or an effect, one feels within oneself the truth of what one reads, which was there before, although one did not know it. Hence one is inclined to love him who makes us feel it, for he has not shown us his own riches, but ours." The writer's strength is not his own; he is a conduit who so positions himself that the world at his back flows through to the readers on the other side of the page. To keep this conduit scoured is his laborious task; to be, in the act of writing, anonymous, the end of his quest for fame.

Beginning, then, with cunning private ambitions and a childish fascination with the implements of graphic representation, I find myself arrived, in this audible search for self-justification, at an embarrassed altruism. Beginning with the wish to make an impression, one ends wishing to erase the impression, to make of it a perfect transparency, to make of oneself a point of focus purely, as selfless as a lens. One begins by seeking celebrity and ends by feeling a terrible impatience with everything—every flattering attention, every invitation to speak and to impersonate a wise man, every hunger of the ego and of the body—an impatience with everything that clouds and clots our rapt witness to the world that surrounds and transcends us. A writer begins with his personal truth, with that obscure but vulnerable and, once lost, precious life that he lived before becoming a writer; but, those first impressions dis-

---

* As, say, by Iris Murdoch, in the 1972 Blashfield Address.

charged—a process of years—he finds himself, though empty, still posed in the role of a writer, with it may be an expectant audience of sorts and certainly a habit of communion. It is then that he dies as a writer, and becomes an inert cultural object merely, or is born again, by re-submitting his ego, as it were, to fresh drafts of experience and refined operations of his mind. *To remain interested* —of American novelists, only Henry James continued in old age to advance his art; most, indeed, wrote their best novels first, or virtually first. Energy ebbs as we live; success breeds disillusion as surely as failure; the power of hope to generate action and vision lessens. Almost alone the writer can reap profit from this loss. An opportunity to sing louder from within the slackening ego is his. For his song has never been all his own: he has been its excuse as much as its source. The little tyrant's delight in wielding a pencil always carried with it an empathy into the condition of *being* a pencil; more and more the writer thinks of himself as an instrument, a means whereby a time and a place make their mark. To become less and transmit more, to replenish energy with wisdom— some such hope, at this more than mid-point of my life, is the reason why I write.

LONDON LIFE

Notes of a Temporary Resident
(for *The Listener*)

January 1969

AN AMERICAN IN LONDON, whether he has come here to work for
Esso or to escape the draft, cannot but be impressed and charmed
by the city. The monumentality of Washington, the thriving busy-
ness of New York, the antique intimacy of Boston, plus a certain
spacious and open feeling reminiscent of Denver and San Francisco
—all these he finds combined for his pleasure. If he is on foot, con-
siderately designed buses and taxis offer to lift him along a maze of
streets; if he has a car, the roadways, however intimidating to a
pedestrian instinctively looking in the wrong direction, reveal
themselves as paragons of clear marking and disciplined flow. This,
surely, is a city, a *civitas* in the root sense, a collection of citizens
whose collective life and conscience is bespoken by the wealth of
parks and museums, the gracious abundance of public services.
Food, for example, which in France must be won by slightly daring
forays into restaurants and *épiceries* that have the shuttered air of
brothel-fronts, is here everywhere—fresh fruit heaped for sale in
the most densely trafficked streets, candy machines on trees, counters of meat in clothing stores. If the telephone booths are scarcer
than an American is used to, at least the ones he finds have not been
vandalized. He moves through London with no fear, as in Rome, of
being cheated and with no fear, as in Paris, of being willfully misunderstood. It is not merely the English language that makes this
ease, it is a language of social expectation and response that in his
own country is a rather harsh dialect. He finds, in London, tickets
to concerts and plays easy to come by; yet when he arrives the

hall is full, or nearly. The balance between supply and demand is maintained with a reasonableness as mysterious as the opaque imbalances of Moscow. Its central institution is, I suppose, the docile, ubiquitous queue.

In the house that I rent hangs a large map of London and environs in 1741. City blocks stop at Marylebone: the eye travels north across stippled fields to Hampstead. Paddington, St. Pancras, and Kentish Towns are villages; St. John's Wood a matter of two or three houses. Elsewhere on the map, Brompton and Chelsea, Camberwell, Peckham, and Stepney are all distinct and full of delicately etched orchards. Why should this seem special to me? All cities grow by swallowing their satellite towns. But these have kept their names and, somehow beneath the asphalt, a sense of locality, of neighborhood. If, as everyone (or at least every American) says, London is a city one can live in, credit the variety of demi-cities within it, few of them hopelessly unfashionable or ugly, all of them with some possibilities and style. London's genius is conglomerate; how restricted, relatively, is New York, four of its five boroughs more or less unheard-of and the Manhattanites with pretensions to respectability penned into a few dozen blocks east of lower Central Park, or clinging to several side-streets in the increasingly decadent Village, or to the once solidly middle-class West Side. And these are sizable enclaves, compared to the "good" neighborhoods of inner-core Philadelphia or Cleveland. No doubt the contrast can be overdrawn. The square miles of chimney pots and sullen slate one sees from a southbound train window match for dreariness any American ghetto. Yet some of the factors blighting American cities (their ruthless grid-plan expansion, our centuries of racial discrimination and the bitter harvest of impoverishment, the rural nostalgia that foments the flight to the suburbs) do seem to have been absent or mitigated here, and London's long primacy has made possible a kind of civic self-confidence absent or ambiguously ironical in America, except in small towns. I have moved here from a small American town, and find familiar virtues: some things are free, some are cheap, one walks among strangers without feeling menaced, the institutions of communal existence feel accessible.

A city, then, of sections rather than layers, where latitude mitigates pressure. The latitude of costume, for instance: it is impossible to dress too oddly for the streets. The clothes along Piccadilly are a spree for the eyes, as shameless as the underwear ads that flow past the startled standee on the Underground escalator, as hard to believe, at first sight, as the Post Office Tower. On a sunny day along Regent Street it is as if England has costumed itself for one more Gilbert and Sullivan operetta, bobbies in their helmets and bankers in their bowlers and a chorus of clowns in bell-bottomed pants and slouch hats, with powdered faces and painted doll's eyes. The miniskirts, too (unlike the ones on Fifth Avenue, perhaps because they are shorter) have a dolly look of unassailable innocence. The spirit of comedy lurks beneath the jubilantly erotic surfaces —and after all isn't English literature, from the Wife of Bath and Rosalind to Moll Flanders and Sara Monday, peculiarly rich in comic heroines? Women parade in everything from yak hides to cellophane—everything except the stern little uniform of black cocktail dress and single pearl strand in which the sleek matron of Park Avenue or Paris sallies forth, sweet soldier, to do battle with her lover, broker, or furrier.

The hip young men seem sad. The uncut hair, which in America does hark back to a native wildness, to Davy Crockett and the redmen, here evokes some sickly Prince Valiant—a squad of pallid, faithless Christs. The faces of the American young reflect excitement: their struggle is for the center of the world stage, and there is an impressive largeness in their dreams of revolutionizing Western morality. I do not feel that excitement here; *Private Eye* is an updated *Tidbits*, the young socialists on television have the rabid punctilio of Dracula turned commissar, and the music is all sung in an American accent. What does Dusty Springfield know about a "preacher man"? Insofar as the popular music here is not derivative, it is Elizabethan balladeering beamed back after centuries of fermentation in the Appalachians, by way of Elvis Presley. It is white man's music, grown in the package. Beyond the luxuriance of London (all those Rolls-Royces!) and the bustling bravura of its shopping streets, there is an England a foreigner glimpses mostly on television—a soggy little island huffing and puffing to keep up with Western Europe, John Bull counting his change as he runs for the bus. An American has difficulty understanding the technical headlines promulgated by your government of glum economists.* But even your Queen looks somehow thrifty. The television news can seem desperately local —for a fortnight this fall, one besieged man in Shropshire eclipsed Asia, Africa, and our elections. Asia, indeed, appears as remote as the moon—let the Yanks and the Reds fight over it. As to Africa, and ex-colonies elsewhere—"our commonwealth friends," as Mr. Wilson a shade wryly terms them—they are like people with whom one was very intimate once, on a long lovely cruise, but who now are, well, *embarrassing.* Embarrassing, too, are all these darkish immigrants that make Mr. Powell's eyebrows lift so high, and those marching Catholics in Londonderry (what *do* they want?), and the crazy Welsh (not Tom Jones and Burton, but the ones that blew up the reservoir), and those impossible French (we'd let them into *our* club, if we had one) and rude Herr Hochhuth . . . really, if we'd known the world was going to be such a nagging bore, we wouldn't have bothered to beat the Spanish Armada.

Marcus Cunliffe, in his biography of Washington, says of the American outlook: "In comparison with the dense, shrewd, worldly British texture from which it is derived, it is surprisingly thin, diffuse, and romantic." True; yet, like an Andean Indian, one born to this thin air learns to breathe it and feels a slight heaviness on the chest elsewhere. There come moments when the "dense, shrewd" texture seems stifling. Two enjoyable American experiences are mailing letters and going to the movies; post offices and movie houses are central in most towns, yet rarely crowded and briskly managed. In England I have learned to dread the moment in the cinema, so stuffy with smoke, when after the short subjects the lights shockingly leap on and weary-looking girls in white insist that we purchase from them yet more sweets before being allowed, freighted with pap, to plunge back into dreamland. And in the post office, after floundering to the stamp counter past the long queues waiting to purchase licenses, receive pensions, and whatever else their life-long wrangle with the Welfare State involves, it is maddening to watch the clerk (whose clerkliness is of Gogolian intensity, the product of generations of breeding carried

---

* No sentence in this set of aging impressions seems farther away than this one now, when all Western governments are of glum economists.

on with dip pens and inkwells) as he tries to balance your letter against a number of brass weights, fiddling to find the right combination, having the letter slip from its tray, replacing it, and at last like blind Justice locating a state approximating balance and then mincing out your postage to you in a series of oddly denominated stamps whose sum he frequently botches, thanks to the intrinsic awkwardness of non-decimal addition. And the way one can get a bank statement only by writing for it to the manager! And those ponderous three-prong electric plugs! Clumsiness, I suspect, is cherished as a British resource, like muddle and heroism. It forms a code, a lock, to which one needs a key. In the end, there are recesses of England that exist only for initiates. The alien moves through pleasant green hallways and anterooms, always conscious of spike fences and polished locks. Some Duchess, if memory serves, said at the funeral of our greatest Anglophile, Henry James: "Poor Mr. James. He never quite met the right people."

June 1969

THE AMERICAN (ME) who last winter thrust upon the readers of *The Listener* his impressions of London left so much still to say that, with his homeward flight number announced for the second time and all suitcases excitedly popping their catches, he feels compelled to add a ragged postscript.

The English National Character. Such a thing must exist, yet residing in England has not brought me closer to it. Quintessential Englishmen here, with their combed tweeds and calibrated drawls, turn out to come from Hungary or Buffalo. In conjuring up for myself the essence of Britishness, I remember men encountered far from Albion. For example, I remember A.B., with his leather-patched elbows and hideously sensible shoes, who walked miles of Manhattan, unmarried, alone, unafraid, cheerful. The bookcases of his West Side room, amid the siren-loud night and the scuttle of Puerto Rican heroin pushers, breathed of Oxford—dear little blue classics, Waugh and Powell in their pastel British jackets, and poetry volumes as thin as shingles. Over a decade has rolled by; he lives in Connecticut, has four daughters, sails boats, wears the same shoes, and takes a tolerant anthropological interest in local rites like P.-T.A. meetings and three-hour cocktail hours. America amuses him. Or I think of C.D., met in Cairo, with the same bony pink forehead and strategic, disarming stammer. He had been a professor of moral philosophy; abruptly, on some road to Damascus, he had switched to Islamic architecture and mastered Turkish, Arabic, and Russian. That morning when he took me on a tour of mosques, he brushed away begging children as one would brush away the summer midges that come between you and the page of a book. Dazed by his torrent of precise information about a succession of indistinguishably murky and friable buildings, I asked him, with an American's naïve faith that the universe is a collection of Freudian symbols, the significance of the dome. I shall not soon forget the quality of his blue gaze as his tongue shifted gears. I had become a begging child. "The dome?" he at last said. "It has no significance. It is a *dome*."

Only in England would Donne's assertion that no man is an island have seemed a paradox and not a commonplace. Son of an island, each man is himself an island, secure in the certainty of his own boundaries. Things foreign break upon him like waves. He is the world's toughest traveller. What an incredible diaspora of amateur explorers, footloose second sons, dissatisfied colonels, and inquisitive ladies in hoop skirts creates and fills an Empire between Drake's accidental circumnavigation of the globe and Scott's doomed saunter toward the South Pole! The Africans called Mungo Park "the one who travels alone," and the same term would apply to Livingstone, Lawrence, Doughty, Burton. The attraction between the British and the Arabs must rest in part on a common austerity, an ability to travel light.

When did this character differentiate itself from the German character, from the Germans who cannot go anywhere except as a gang? Geographical insularity, relatively early consolidation as a nation, an underlying Celtic pawkishness, a dash of French bitters via the Normans—whatever its cause, its enforcer is the public school system that tears a lad from his mother's still-foaming breast and plunges him into ice water. To those prophets distressed by the possibility of test-tube conception and mechanized rearing, the

British national character should be a great reassurance. After the shock of his education, nothing can shake an Englishman. True, he might emerge a little woozy, and mistake a sports car for a woman, or a birch rod for a mother's kiss. But in this kingdom of bachelors, hobbyists, and pet-lovers, a little amiable confusion is wisely allowed. Recently I took my innocent children to a British movie about a man who fell in love with an otter. Our hero is first seen morosely strolling London's streets with one of those Nero haircuts that signify a queer as surely as a dangling handbag used to signify a prostitute. He spies an otter in a pet-shop window, buys it, and more or less marries it. For their honeymoon they go to remotest, most picturesque Scotland, where the otter (chummily dubbed "Mitch") eats eels in the cove. To make the abnormality of these arrangements unignorable, the plot provides a Scots lass who, though pretty as a picture and loyal to a fault, is not only denied physical satisfaction by the hero but is degradingly compelled to feign fondness for his hirsute, quadruped, amphibian little consort. Providence is not entirely a-doze, however; a burly Scots ditch-digger dispatches "Mitch" with a shovel. The man with the Nero hairdo never stops mooning, and the fade-out shows him penning the first lines of a kind of *In Memoriam* for Mitch, just like Tennyson for Hallam. Now, I suppose such a bestial film might be made in other countries, but only in England would it be given a U rating.

English Women. They are wonderful. They remind me of, in America, those tall, precocious boys of education-oriented households who are given rooms of their own and plenty of time for model airplanes. Only ample neglect brings such dreamy, disdainful poise. They are masterful flirts and have the miraculously steady hands of rhinoceros hunters and of women who apply eye make-up first thing in the morning. Shaw doubted that England deserved its great men; I wonder if it deserves its women. But what land does? "You Americans," said Lady Pynchme, "you are so romantic. You all think your little dolly is Helen of Troy." "You mean," said I, startled, "she's not? What, then, is she?" "Simply a jolly good lay," was the answer. Two things shocked me here: the dog-food ads on television and the language of the upper classes.

*

Great Men. The British seem to prefer, in leaders, rogues or men with a streak of the rogue. Henry VIII, Charles II, Nelson, Disraeli, Lloyd George, Churchill. If a rogue is unattainable, the next best thing is a nonentity. An earnest, clever man like Harold Wilson is universally distrusted.

Class Warfare. The only phenomenon in the United States comparable to the catting, at an English party, between an *arriviste* working-class intellectual and a swinging duchess is the banter, at a Manhattan conclave, between a liberated Negro and a liberalized lady of Southern birth. The hostile tension of sexual attraction. Maxim of human behavior: we want to fuck what we fear. The primordial drive toward cross-fertilization.

All those "pleases" and "thank you's," which the fresh visitor mistakes for elaborate courtesy, in fact prove, like the chirps of birds, to be warnings establishing territoriality. Those fierce fences and high brick walls, sometimes enclosing scarcely a square yard of cement. The passion for separation and class distinction leads to absurdities: a fourpenny post it costs money to delay, an A classification at the cinema that compels parents to accompany their children to puerile films.

The Englishman is under no constitutional obligation to believe that all men are created equal. The American agony is therefore scarcely intelligible, like a saint's self-flagellation viewed by an atheist.

The beheading of Charles I, the repeal of the Corn Laws: the only times an *idea* has entered English politics. A king easier to restore than foreign markets.

America is a land whose center is nowhere; England one whose center is everywhere. In America every town has its Chamber of Commerce; here every shire has been the site of a poem.

Christianity has been disposed of by giving the clergy a social status, a part in the pageant. After Trollope's novels, there can be no apocalypse. An odd number of steeples with their tips cut off, like daggers made safe for children to play with.

Americans love England. For every tulip that comes up in Hyde Park, a tourist lands at Heathrow. I have not spoken to one American resident in London, not counting my eight-year-old daughter, who wouldn't like to stay. And there are thousands, thousands of those mysterious men "in oil," with their haircuts transparently cleaving to their skulls, with their expensively dressed wives, whose very good legs and taut figures are disappointingly capped by tan, hard, rather cross faces. (What do we *do* to our women, I ask myself, that is so brutalizing? What happens to our magnificent teen-age girls, with their clothes allowances, their fuzzy sweaters, their convertibles and batons and "steadies," to give them as adults such a bitter, pushy narrowness and voices from which all melody has been squeezed?) America is uncomfortable now. On the continent fascism or anarchy reigns. Here things are civilized, cheap, pretty, educational, clean, green. Here the police and the poor are polite. The bully of the seven seas is in danger of becoming a nation of gigolos and tour guides. In the newspapers, imbalance of trade and impending bankruptcy; in the restaurants, girls dressed like houris and men with nugget cuff-links.

Living in Regent's Park. During a candle-lit dinner there comes a moment when one does not know whether a lion in the zoo, or the stomach of one's table partner, has just growled.

Notes to a Poem
(for *The New Statesman*)

MINORITY REPORT

My beloved land,   1
here I sit in London   2
   overlooking Regent's Park ⎫   3
   overlooking my new Citroën ⎭ both green,   4
exiled by success of sorts.   5
I listen to Mozart   6
   in my English suit and weep,   7
      remembering a Swedish film.   8
But it is you,   9
   really you I think of: 10
      your nothing streetcorners   11
      your ugly eateries   12
      your dear barbarities   13
      and vacant lots   14
(Br'er Rabbit demonstrated: 15
      freedom is made of brambles).   16
They say over here you are choking   17
  to death on your cities and slaves,   18
     but they have never smelled dry grass, 19
     smoked Kools in a drugstore,   20
     or pronounced a flat "a," an honest "r." 21
Don't read your reviews,   22
    A☆M☆E☆R☆I☆C☆A: 23
you are the only land.   24

Line 2. At 59, Cumberland Terrace, N.W.1, where I can no longer be found. In a sense I never was found there. For nine months in England I felt like a balloon on too long a tether.

*

Lines 6–8. The Mozart would be Piano Concerto No. 21, in C Major, and the Swedish film, of course, *Elvira Madigan.* The English suit is by Cyril A. Castle, 42 Conduit Street.

Line 12. Is this fair? Many are ugly from the outside (see Nabokov, V., *Lolita,* on roadside restaurants) but inside have a certain appropriateness and comfort. Though America's "better" restaurants are stuffy and pappy compared to those you can find on almost any side-street on the Continent, our casual food—the hurried hamburger, the presto pastrami—is unsurpassed. At a formative stage of my life, at the age when young Frenchmen are being seduced by their governesses and young Englishmen by their headmasters, I was compelled to spend hours of every day in a homely luncheonette next to a small post office. There was nothing ugly about it except the griddle and the politics, possibly, of the proprietor. But then being economically dependent upon a crowd of teen-agers would bring out the reactionary in anyone. I have never been happier than in those idle hours mixed of cigarette smoke, pinball clatter, schoolgirl odors, hot dogs, and the recorded voices of Doris Day and Frankie Laine. Come to think of it, there was one period, many months long, when Petrillo had called all the musicians out on strike and the jukebox was supplied with strange recordings of humming voices and scab oddball instruments like the banjo and the sweet potato. But I ramble.

Line 14. Common in the land of my childhood. There was one beside our house, and others dotted all over the town. They were not parks, of course; they lacked daffodil beds and small mumbling men with turf edgers, but they made their own gift of space and freedom. Nobody owned them. Not even the Queen. Those vacant lots where the thistles waxed tall and we played fungo and kick-the-can were scraps of surviving Indian land, nowhereland. Compare parks: Hyde Park is a piece of royal domain graciously released to the commonweal, Central Park a wilderness of rape, torture, drug-induced trance, and savage whoops.

Lines 15–16. Br'er Rabbit is a native folk hero like Till Eulenspiegel in Scandinavia and Ra in Egypt. The reference is to his escape from Br'er Fox and other enemies; he said, Do anything you want to me, but don't, please *don't,* throw me into the briar patch. So they did. It was where he wanted to be. He had immigrated.

Line 17. "over here"—in fact the English press seemed to me to be sufficiently fair and wise in scrutinizing its alarming trans-Atlantic offspring. The poet, perhaps, is expressing an irritation with the new style of American self-criticism, a kind of Calvinism that assumes all those who hold power are damned, that nothing is relative, that rhetoric is truth, that destruction is action, and that a holiday has been declared wherein we are all excused from learning our lessons. Goodness, effectiveness, and love live among particulars; hate feeds on sweeping categories.

Line 21. Doesn't really do justice to the American accent. It is something, that accent, that happens between the throat and the heart, and has to do with bourbon, or heat, or talking to farm animals, or Jacobean pronunciation. Hearing across a London hotel lobby a silver-haired Texas businessman growl "My friend" to the fastidiously recoiling desk clerk, or eavesdropping on a bus while a pair of elderly female compatriots cackle and giggle together in their strange bubbling twang, or listening to a young American talk in that soft, rather cautious drawl (a drawl just as the American walk is, compared to the British strut, a prowl), I see those breezy big kitchens, and the lawns burnt brown by August, and the twirling sprinklers and fainting skies, and wonder at the cracked tender terrible confident emptiness of it all, and wonder how it happened so quickly, in two or three centuries, and think that we are the last new race, and that we are all inside the bus now, and there is nothing to do but ride out together the billion or so years before the sun swamps the planet.

Line 22. Advice I have often given myself.

AMOR VINCIT OMNIA
AD NAUSEAM

(After Awakening from Bruno's Dream, *by Iris Murdoch,
and Falling into the Nursery)*

"Hey diddle—?"
"Diddle."
"You're thinking about God again."
It was true. She had been. The cat had been thinking about the fiddle. She had been looking at him. He had a long stringy neck and a plump brown resinous hollow body. His voice had vibrato. She had been his mistress for four years. It had been ecstatic but not extremely. She was a small-boned calico with high tender ears and a broad subdivided brow and a moist nose and an abrasive triangular tongue the color of faded drapes. She had been attracted by his voice. They had met at a benefit concert being given for churchmice. A bow had scraped him and he had sung. The cat had gone up afterwards and had rubbed herself against him and in her whiskers, so decisively parallel, he had recognized something kindred. He had sung to her of Viennese woods and she had related to him tales of her previous lovers. There had been a succession of toms behind the Bromley gasworks. They had had terrible voices. They had clawed her. They had bitten. As the palms of a religious come to be indented by stigmata so the image slowly formed itself upon her mind of a hairless toothless lover, fragile and lean. He would have resonance. He would be powerless to pounce. Her telling the fiddle all this in those days had pleased and flattered them both. That had been in those days. These were these

days. All day she took a small abrasive pleasure in licking the calico
fur of her chest with her triangular tongue while he failed to sing
but instead leaned in the corner and almost hummed. She looked
at him, his shape, his texture, his state of tension. One of her toms
had been made into a tennis racquet. Perhaps that had been the
attraction. She thought, I need a larger fate, warmer, kinder, yet
more perilous in its dimensions, coarsely infinite yet mottled like
me. Her vertically slit eyes, hoarding depths of amber, dilated at a
shadow from her barnyard days as a kitten in the straw in Surrey.
Something large had often been above her. Something smelling of
milk. It had mooed.

The cow was in love with the moon. Throughout the first
three quarters she had wept solidly, streams and streams. The moon
had become full. Tears poured down her muzzle in an invincible
tide.

"You are seeking," said the full moon, "to purify yourself by
giving rein to impossibility."

"Oh, God—I can't—I don't—"

"Go on."

"When I first saw you, you were new—a sort of weak bent
splinter of a sort of nibbled thing. How loathsome, thought I. I
think even then I was protecting myself from the truth. I believe
even then I deeply knew you were cheese. You began to grow.
Mare Serenitatis showed, and one bluish blind mad eye, and the side
of your lopsided leprous smile. At first I loved you in spite of your
leprosity. Then I loved it because it was part of *you*. Then I loved
the leprosity itself, and you because you were the vehicle whereby
it was boldly imposed upon the cold night sky. I have never known
pain so ungainsayable. I beg you, What—?"

"Jump."

"Jump?"

"*Jump*."

"Jump—"

"JUMP!"

"Imagine the moon," advised a little dog who had been eavesdropping, "as only slightly higher than the Albert Memorial. Or

consider the Albert Hall. It is round and deep and vast and many-entranced, like a woman's love. Oppositely, the Memorial is phallic. Between them there is only the Kensington Road."

The cow was jumping. Splendidly. Galaxies concentrically countervaulted. Sphere upon diamantine sphere chimed the diatonic music that mesmerized Jerusalem the Golden. Time and space were fooled at their own game. *Ab ovo*, lactogalactic. He was near, Him, ashy, awful, barren, lunar, luminous, Him. *He was Him.* They grazed. The hint of a ghost of a breath of a touch. The cow was descending. The cow was reëntering Earth's orbit. The atmosphere sizzled. The cat's eyes dilated as the shadow gathered. She felt the ponderous loved thing close and warm above her.

"Is it to be—?"

"Can't stop. Gravity."

"Oh—how *right!*" Black ecstasy flattened the cat. Her ego was, if not eliminated, expanded beyond the bounds of dissatisfaction. She was ever so utterly content. The little dog laughed to see such sport.

The fiddle cleared his long narrow throat. "Er—when you laughed like that—I, er, *twanged.* Strange to say, I love you insanely."

"Too bad," said the little dog. "I love the cow. This fact was asleep in me until I saw her jump. Christ, what an august uncanny leap that was!" He was a beagleish dog. A history of bitches had lengthened his ears and bloodied his eyes. His forepaws however had an engaging outward twist. He yapped amorously at the cow. She stepped backward into the fiddle. Her glossy hoof fragmented the ruddy wood.

"Thank you—thank you—" sobbed the fiddle. He had been excessively pampered heretofore. It was bliss to be hurt. "Of course I love *you.*" He of course meant the cow. She became haughty. Her high hot sides made a mist like fog off the Greenwich Reach. She indicated distinctly that she had consecrated herself to the memory of the cat. Or rather the cat had become the angel of death whose abiding iron presence it is the destiny of all life to worship. What else is love? Nothing else.

The little dog yowled. "I discover I was confused. It is the moon

I adore, for having permitted itself to be so splendidly jumped."
He yowled and yowled.

The moon beamed. "I love everyone. I shine on just and unjust alike. I give to all the gift of madness. That is my charm. That is my *truth*."

The fiddle lived with his wound for a fortnight, as one would live with the shifting shades and fluorescent evanescences of an unduly prolonged sunset. Then he found he could sing. He had once sung. He was again singing. He sang,

"*A questo seno, deh! vieni, idolo mio,*
Quanti timori, quante lacrime . . ."

And the dish ran away with the spoon.

CEMETERIES

"Personal relationships must have been very strange," the tall young State Department man said to me. We were speaking of Russia in the 1930's; we had just turned from the tomb of Stalin's wife, a square stone column the height of a woman, capped by a sculptured female head with something touchingly vivid about the nape of the marble neck. Along tight paths we walked among the heavy tombstones of generals, scientists, commissars, engineers. Many bore inset photographs of the departed; a miniature iron tank adorned the tomb of a tank commander famous in World War II. A ballerina's slippers had been carved on a stone block as if casually set there, creased and warm from use. It was a sunny October Sunday years before Svetlana's memoirs had clarified the mysterious death of her mother; my escort had been describing to me the rumors of poisoning, of murderous Kremlin concubinage, of intricate betrayals.

"Even more than usual," I agreed, and tried to picture men and women rearing children, honoring parents, and seeking each other's love in a decade like a low-ceilinged subway tunnel where the lights are flickering off and the air is suffocatingly stale. I couldn't picture it, life continuing, but here was proof, here were the survivors, Soviet citizens honored in death, standing erect, in close order, in the open, enjoying the pale sunshine and late flowers of the day and season. Life-sized, with faces and trinkets, the tombs conveyed a cheerful substantial impression, as if this atheist state, like ancient Egypt, considered death a short and eminently practical voyage. I felt happy here; I am usually happy in cemeteries.

＊

In Highgate Cemetery—the old, neglected section above the famous monument to Karl Marx—the English journalist asked me about oral love. He was short and middle-aged and had cleverly sensed I would like a cemetery. It was again a warm October day. Intensely green overgrowth narrowed the paths and all but smothered the tombs. Some vaults had been burst open by flourishing saplings; there was a kind of mews of tombs, an arcade of green vault doors so rusted and silted shut no Judgment Day, one felt, could ever crack them open, though there were keyholes and door-knobs and numbers and knockers, as on any genteel, if shady, street.

I discovered I had no opinion on oral love. I ventured that, all other things being equal, I was as much for it as not. In irritation the journalist tucked his notebook away and began to rail at the dead. Their pretensions to immortality enraged him. He rattled at the door of a grenadiers colonel interred in 1903 and invited me, where vandals had smashed a grating, to peer in and see how a bur-rowing creature, a rat or badger, had penetrated the coffin, adding sawdust to the rubble of bricks and powdered mortar. The pious mottoes—"From strength to strength in the everlasting," "Love shines yet more brightly above"—abraded against my escort like supercilious assertions at a party where he was socially insecure. And indeed he came, with his cleverness, from a Midlands working-class family, and the tombs represented Victorian gentry. "The fools!" he shouted. " 'Honor perisheth never.' Well, Mr. Nevil Cunninghame-Wright Esq., O.M., M.B.E., it bloody well has!" He kicked at the black drift of rustflakes and leafmold clogging the Cunninghame-Wright portal, and read the next motto. " 'Earth's shadows testify to radiance eternal.' Oh, my buggering God! Oh, my dear old Eustace Pickering, you poor old sodden mouse-nest of agglutinated bones, how do you like your radiance eternal now?"

He was most affronted by the immense mausoleum of a man called Julius Beer. Chinks in its cupola had admitted generations of pigeons; their excrement, feathers, and corpses covered the marble floor. The mosaic murals of pre-Raphaelite angels were clouded with lime. The journalist, when I had satisfied his desire that I look in, put his mouth against the crusty grating and shouted,

"*Hooh!*" Nothing happened. He bellowed louder, "HOOH!" Evidently, the pigeons were supposed to fly out. He squinted into the depths of the befouled and forgotten memorial. "Damn," he said. "I think they've cleaned it up a bit." He backed off, and his face brightened. "But can you catch that smell, that evil stench? It's a pigeon Dachau. You ass, Julius, you absolutely silly puffed-up old capitalist ass, you were so full of yourself we don't even know what you *did!*" It was true; no identification, not even dates, qualified the high carved name of Julius Beer, the emperor of doveshit.

The cemetery had been private and fashionable. An outward-spreading cypress, now obscured by deciduous trees that had grown up, was to have been the center of a symmetrical system of vault lanes and individual tombs. One tomb, of a "menagerist," had a smiling lion carved upon it. Deep in the woods—elm and oak and ailanthus that had taken root, perhaps, at the outset of World War II—a stone angel lifted her weather-blurred face, vague as Anglican theology, toward green leaves. We were far from the urban compactness of Novodyevichi Cemetery. I was impressed by England's tropical luxuriance; the force so decisively tamed in the parks was here, untended, shattering marble and swallowing crypts whole. Yet I felt that these genteel 19th-century dead, who to judge from the novels about them had loved a country wildness, were not as overthrown as my escort believed. They were merely immersed, much as the living are immersed. A wild sapling grafts onto the spirit no less snugly than a toy tank.

Both of my escorts—the State Department man tacitly, obliquely; the journalist boisterously, indignantly—disapproved of the dead, implying that they were still alive. A cemetery, which like a golf course bestows the gift of space, also touches us with the excitement, the generalized friction, of a party.

The Chemin du Puy steeply climbed the hill from Antibes and on the long gradual downslope, before the farmhouse with the sign MÉCHANTS CHIENS, passed a cemetery of bright plaster, where things twirled to discourage birds. Though lonesome, I never dared enter; the dead were speaking French.

In Mayrhofen, at Christmas, candles glowed and guttered in the snow, before strict upright stones of black marble. The faces of

Tyrolean burghers alternated with that of an anguished Jesus. *Hier ruhen in Gott*, the stones said.

And in Peredelkino, in the village graveyard where Pasternak is buried, scrolling iron crosses spoke of an Orthodox Russia where burial took place in springtime, and metal echoed the burgeoning shape of the flowers.

In Prague, the tombstones of the Jewish cemetery were squeezed together like cards, conjuring up a jumble of bodies underneath. Visitors left pebbles on them instead of flowers. Was it an ancient custom, or something forced upon the Jews by Hitler? A kind of chapel here had walls gray with the names, six hundred thousand of them, of Jews whose death-dates were 1943, 1944, 1945. Years whose smoke permanently stained the ceiling of Heaven.

And the mass graves of the Siege dead near Leningrad, acres of hummocks, like giant bulb beds in winter, marked with stone tablets 1941, 1942, 1943.

And the Pyramids, and the gaily painted corridors leading into the robbed chambers of Ramses, and the even gayer cells of the nobles, into which light is shuttled by a set of mirrors held by silent brown guides. In Cairo, the necropolis is inhabited by children and beggars, and is a slum.

The Long Island necropolis seen from an airplane: a pegboard that abruptly yields to the equally regular avenues of the living, each gray rooftop companioned by a green backyard pool, like a wide-awake eye.

Also from the air, descending I think into Cleveland, I saw a little triangular family cemetery, precious soil spared from the corner of a field, like the book page whose corner I had turned down to mark my place.

And the stingy clusters of markers, too many of them children, in rocky abandoned places once farmed, like Star Island off Portsmouth, or the mountainsides of Vermont north of Montpelier.

In Marigot, on St. Martin's, one noon, my wife and I walked a mile to a restaurant that was closed, along the shimmering white road, and came back along the beach to cool our feet, and came to a cemetery that was being nibbled away by the sea. There were no signs of an attempt to halt the gentle erosion; one tombstone was teetering, another had fallen upside down, and fragments of a third were being washed and ground into sand. We went up into the cemetery, and there, amid the French *colons* and the tessellated patterns suggestive of voodoo and the conch-shell borders and the paper flowers and the real flowers that looked like paper, my wife, starved and weary, sat on a crypt and dried her feet with her bandana and put on her shoes. I took her picture; I have the slide.

Years before, when we were at college, a girl whose major was biology and whose hobby was fungi used to make me bicycle with her to ancient burying-grounds in Cambridge and Concord. There, on the tipping old Puritan slate tombstones half sunk in the earth and sometimes wearing artfully shaped weatherproof hats of lead, she would show me lichen, in a surprising variety of colors, each round specimen, scarcely thicker than a stain, somehow an individual creature or, rather, two creatures—a fungus living symbiotically with an alga. Whitish, brownish, bluish, the lichens enforced their circles upon the incised, uniquely graceful Puritan lettering and the winged skulls which, as the 17th century softened into the 19th, became mere angels, with human faces. She was, perhaps because she majored in biology, wonderful at sex—talk of oral love!—and the lichen, the winged skulls, the sweaty ache in my calves from bicycling, and her plump cleavage as she bent low for a determined inspection and scraping all merged in a confused lazy anticipation of our return and my reward, her round mouth. Cemeteries, where women make themselves at home, are in one sense dormitories, rows of beds.

"But the *view* is so lovely," my mother said to me. We were standing on the family burial plot, in Pennsylvania. Around us, and sloping down the hill, were the red sandstone markers of planted farmers, named and dated in the innocent rectangular lettering that used to be on patent-medicine labels. My grandfather's stone, rough-hewn granite with the family name carved in the form of bent branches, did not seem very much like him. My grandmother's Christian name, cut below his, was longer and, characteristically, dominated while taking the subservient position. Elsewhere on the plot were his parents, and great-aunts and uncles I had met only at spicy-smelling funerals in my remotest childhood.

My mother paced off two yards, saying, "Here's Daddy and me. See how much room is left?"

"But she"—I didn't have to name my wife—"has never *lived* here." I was again a child at one of those dreaded family gatherings on dark holiday afternoons—awkward and stuffed and suffocating under the constant need for tact. Only in Pennsylvania, among my kin, am I pressured into such difficult dance-steps of evasion and placation. Every buried coffin was a potential hurt feeling. I tried a perky sideways jig, hopefully humorous, and added, "And the children would feel crowded and keep everybody awake."

She turned her face and gazed downward at the view—a lush valley, a whitewashed farmhouse, a straggling orchard, and curved sections of the highway leading to the city whose glistening tip, a television relay, could just be glimpsed five ridges in the distance. She had expected my evasion—she could hardly have expected me to pace off my six feet greedily and plant stakes—but had needed to bring me to it, to breast my refusal and the consequence that, upon receiving her and my father, the plot would be closed, would cease to be a working piece of land. Why is it that nothing that happens to me is as real as these dramas that my mother arranges around herself, like Titania calling Peaseblossom and Mustardseed from the air? Why is it that everyone else lacks the sanguine, corporeal, anguished reality of these farmers, these people of red sandstone? When was Pennsylvania an ocean, to lay down all this gritty rock, that stains your palms pink when you lift it?

Placatory, I agreed, "The view *is* lovely."

"Think of poor Daddy," she said, turning away, Mustardseed dismissed. "He has no sense of landscape. He says he wants to be buried under a sidewalk."

The cemetery of the town where I live, like many, has climbed a hill, and the newest graves are on the top, arranged along ample smooth roadways of asphalt. Some friends of ours have buried children here. But I had stayed away until it was time to teach my son to ride a bicycle. It is safe; on weekdays few cars visit the fresh graves, with their plastic-potted morning glories and exotic metal badges from veterans' organizations. The stones are marble, modernly glossy and simple, though I suppose that time will eventually reveal them as another fashion, dated and quaint. Now, the sod is still raw, the sutures of turf are unhealed, the earth still humped, the wreaths scarcely withered. Sometimes we see, my son and I, the strained murmurous breakup of a ceremony, or a woman in mourning emerge from an automobile and kneel, or stand nonplussed, as in a social gap. I remember my grandfather's funeral, the hurried cross of sand the minister drew on the coffin lid, the whine of the lowering straps, the lengthening, cleanly cut sides of clay, the thought of air, the lack of air forever in the close dark space lined with pink satin, the foreverness, the towering foreverness—it does not bear thinking about, it is too heavy, like my son's body as he wobbles away from me on his bicycle. "Keep moving," I shout, the words turning chalky in my mouth, as they tend to do when I seek to give instruction—"the essence of the process is to keep moving!"

LETTER FROM ANGUILLA

○

February 1968

UNTIL ITS REVOLUTION last summer, Anguilla was one of the most obscure islands in the Caribbean. A long, low coral formation of thirty-four square miles, it seems from the air a cloud shadow, or a shadow image of St. Martin, which lies twelve miles to the south and whose green mountains loom dramatically in the view from Anguilla. Whereas from St. Martin, Anguilla, at its highest elevation scarcely two hundred feet above sea level, can easily be overlooked. It is even obscure who named it "Eel"—the Spaniards, who may have cruised close enough under Columbus to call it *Anguila*, or the French, who, under Captain René Laudonnière in

1564, definitely called there, en route to Florida from Dominica, and may have bestowed the appellation *L'Anguille*. Both nations left this modest island to the British to colonize. In 1609, a Captain Harcourt, after touching at Nevis, "disembogued" on the north side of Anguilla, where "I think never Englishmen disembogued before us." Southey's history of the West Indies records under the year 1650, "The island of Anguilla, so called from its snake-like form, is said to have been discovered and colonized by the English this year; it was filled with alligators and other noxious animals, but the soil was good for raising tobacco and corn, and the cattle imported multiplied very fast. It was not colonized under any public encouragement; each planter laboured for himself, and the island was frequently plundered by marauders."

The lack of external encouragement sounds a constant note in Anguilla's history. In 1707, Captain Thomas Bolton and nine other survivors of a sunken ship, after thirty-one days adrift in a small boat, were cast up at Long Bay. His journal acknowledges that "the People were very kind to us"—"The Islanders very much bewail'd our Condition, and were ready to fight among themselves, in shewing their Eagerness to welcome us to their Houses"—but complains of their stay that "the worst was, we could not have any News from other Islands; this being an Island of little Trade, and no Shipping." J. Oldmixon's *The British Empire in America* (second edition, 1741) states that in Anguilla people lived "without Government or Religion, having no Minister nor Governor, no Magistrates, no Law, and no Property worth keeping," and adds that they "live poorly, and we might say miserably, if they were not contented." In 1825, when Henry Nelson Coleridge visited Anguilla, the people seemed "a good sort of folks, though they have been living for a long time in a curious state of suspended civilization. They acknowledge the English laws, but the climate is said to induce fits of drowsiness on them, during which Justice sleepeth, and Execution tarrieth." In 1920, Mrs. Katharine Janet Burdon, in *A Handbook of St. Kitts-Nevis*, wrote, "Strangers are so rarely seen that the last one who visited Anguilla, in 1917, an enterprising and eminent official from a neighbouring British Colony, was taken for a German spy, and greatly to his amusement was followed by the whole police force of the Island until he had presented his credentials to the Magistrate." And in 1960, when my wife, three children, and I lived for five weeks in Sandy Ground, we had the pleasure of being, for intervals, the entire tourist population of the island. I will not forget an evening spent with Mr. Vincent Lake —one of Anguilla's leading citizens, the scion of a family whose holdings in island land and cargo-carrying sloops amounted to a fortune—in which I found myself describing to him, as if to a latter-day Miranda, such commonplace wonders of the Western world as four-lane highways and skyscrapers and neon lights. He had never seen them even in a movie. In those days, when Anguilla was a British colony, a lonely generator supplied power to a telephone line serving fourteen users, most of them island officials. There was also a Social Center at the East End, with electric lights and a jukebox. Later that year, in September, the eye of Hurricane Donna passed directly over Anguilla. Miss Selma Buchanan wrote my wife, "Mrs you can only imagin what a time we had that night. . . . The Carty's house half is gone and the Cocial Centre at the east end is gone there are only two school standing on island church to flew off every boat sink in the harbour so many big trees fell what a sight to see little Anguilla." In 1968, returning, we find that the homes destroyed by Donna have been replaced, but the telephone line has not been reactivated.

Henry Nelson Coleridge's 1825 description still serves:

> Anguilla presents a very singular appearance for a West Indian island. A little wall of cliff of some forty feet in height generally rises from the beach, and when you have mounted this, the whole country lies before you, gently sloping inwards in a concave form, and sliding away, as it were, to the south where the land is only just above the level of the sea. . . . Seven-tenths of the country are entirely uncultivated; in some parts a few coppices, but more commonly a pretty species of myrtle called by the negros maiden-berry, seems to cover the whole soil: the roads are level grassy tracks over which it is most delightful to ride, and the houses and huts of the inhabitants are scattered about in so picturesque a manner that I was put in mind of many similar scenes in Kent and Devonshire. Indeed there were scarcely any of the usual features of West Indian landscape visible; neither of those prominent ones, the lively wind-

mill or the columnar palm, was to be seen, and there was a rusticity, a pastoral character on the face of the land, its roads and its vegetation, which is the exact antipode of large plantations of sugar.

The roads, at least to the driver of a rented jeep, are now quite undelightful puddings of potholes and coral protrusions, and the scanty crops of cotton and yams and sisal seem to occupy rather less than three-tenths of the soil, and a certain pastel Los Angeles look is creeping into Kent and Devonshire, but the dominant impression, of scattered homes and no windmills, remains to tell the tale: Anguilla was but lightly involved in the sugar economy. Captain Bolton in 1707, over sixty years after cultivation of sugarcane had been introduced into Barbados and the shift from tobacco to sugar had swept the Leeward Islands, found on Anguilla "2 or 300 English" engaged in the planting of tobacco, "which is highly esteem'd." Anguilla was too rocky and dry for the great mechanized plantations the sugar industry required, and hence was exempted from the full force of the social transformation whereby communities of white planter-proprietors gave way to feudal estates supporting vast slave populations. Anguilla has no equivalent of the slums of St. John's on Antigua or Basseterre on St. Kitts. As drought, piratical raids, and the abolition of slavery (in 1834) thinned the ranks of the white settlers, the ungrateful land fell by default to the Negro inhabitants. By 1847, of about twenty sugar estates once under cultivation, only three or four survived. Mrs. Burdon states that as of 1911 the population consisted "almost exclusively of peasant proprietors." She goes on, "Anguillans are a particularly sturdy, independent, intelligent type, their high character being developed by the hard school of nature in which they live, and by the system of proprietorship which has existed for generations." The island, she notes, is free of tropical diseases to a unique degree, in part because "the people of Anguilla, differing from the usual habits of the West Indian negro, build their houses some distance apart."

So nature, in neglecting Anguilla, has not been entirely unkind; nor has the neglect been total. There is good fishing. There are pockets of fertile soil, and ample pasturage for goats and sheep. Ancient wells supposedly dug by the Caribs provide fresh water for those who do not have private cisterns. The harvest of salt from the large, diked saltponds behind Sandy Ground, a peculiar industry established in the early 1800's, still goes on, generating an annual burst of employment, mostly for women. The export of Sea Island cotton, a silky, long-fiber variety used in underwear, produced for a time thousands of pounds in annual revenue and financed the construction of the island's own ginnery—now defunct. And there exists a native tradition of shipbuilding; elegant all-wood hulls, the keel timbers shaped from branched tree trunks, dot the beaches, though work on them proceeds imperceptibly, at about the speed of coral formation. Fundamentally the economy runs by remittance. Anguillan men emigrate to work in the cane fields of Jamaica, or the oil refineries of Curaçao and Aruba, or the hotels and construction crews of St. Thomas. Though the men are gone for years, money returns regularly, and across the island pleasant and sturdy houses of imported cement block slowly rise. There are few tarpaper shacks; there is no begging. Literacy is a relatively high 70 per cent. A young American resident on Anguilla in recent months analyzes last summer's upheaval as a middle-class revolution—Anguilla's refusal to join the Socialist revolution being perpetrated in Basseterre by the Labor government of Robert Bradshaw. Bradshaw is the walrus-mustachioed, dictatorial premier of the St. Kitts–Nevis–Anguilla state to which Britain granted local self-government on February 27, 1967. St. Kitts and Nevis have long been one-crop sugar islands, and the sugar depression has created problems unknown in perennially depressed Anguilla, including a drastic split between the white proprietorial class and the black laborers, and the start of political terrorism. Last August, an unnamed Anguillan was quoted in the *Times* as saying, "St. Kitts is a millstone around our necks."

Anguilla's association with St. Kitts (St. Christopher) has always been tenuous. St. Kitts is the nearest British island, but lies seventy miles to the south, beyond St. Martin/Sint Maarten (French and Dutch), St. Bart's (French), and Saba and Sint Eustatius (both Dutch). When, in 1796, a French force invaded Anguilla under orders to exterminate the English inhabitants (legend says the fishermen of Anguilla loaded their cannon with lead seine weights), help arrived not from St. Kitts but from more distant Antigua, in the form of the man-of-war *Lapwing;* the St. Kittians,

to be fair, did address to the *Lapwing* commander a letter of thanks
for his rescue of a "sister colony." In Anguilla, the laws lay dor-
mant for want of a magistrate, and not until after 1800 did the
Anguillans send a representative to the St. Kitts legislature. In lieu
of anarchy, the Anglican vestry ruled the island, headed by the
parson and the warden; until very recently, the manager of the
island's rather minimal affairs has borne the proud title of Warden.
The West Indian archives contain more than one instance of a
colonial official's shirking and bemoaning his assignment to Anguilla. "Indeed such an assignment," one penned in 1842, "is but
poor reward for a life devoted to the Service of the Crown." In
1871, when the Federal Colony of the Leeward Islands, with its
capital in Antigua, was created by Parliament, Anguilla expressed
a desire not to be lumped with St. Kitts, but Governor Benjamin
Pine, already sufficiently harassed by a plethora of presidencies
under his government, ignored the request. During the Second
World War, when St. Martin was a Vichy fuelling station for
German submarines, American soldiers built an airstrip on Anguilla
and impressed the Anguillans so favorably that as late as 1960
wistful hopes of an American takeover were still alive. One rumor
claimed that the United States had offered to forgive Great Britain
her entire lend-lease debt in exchange for Anguilla, and had been
refused. Anguilla's poor-sister status within the Leewards worsened
after the St. Kitts–Nevis–Anguilla state was granted home rule.
Anecdotes of the short shrift that Anguilla thereafter received
from the Bradshaw government have the orotund ring of legend.
For instance, when Great Britain requisitioned money for a much-
needed pier on Anguilla, where anything bigger than a sack of
wheat must be tediously rafted in, the St. Kitts government took the
money and built the pier on its own island, christening it, deadpan,
Anguilla Pier. School supplies and salaries for Anguillans were held
up. Anguillan public-works projects—such as the planting of
hundreds of unwired telephone poles along the roads—were carried forward with labor brought from St. Kitts. "Anguilla men go
all over the islands looking for work," our taxi-driver said, gestur-
ing toward these poles. "Anguilla men know enough to build big
boats and plant a sixty-foot mast when the boats sit in the water,
but Anguilla men don't know enough to dig a hole." The St.

Kittian policemen on Anguilla were not beloved. In March of 1967, their precipitate use of tear gas turned into a riot an intended demonstration at a potentially benign gathering—the contest to choose a Miss Anguilla to compete for the title of Miss Statehood. It is a parable of the slenderness of St. Kitts–Anguilla ties that when the revolution came, on May 30th last year, it consisted simply of rounding up the seventeen St. Kitts policemen, putting them into a boat, and pushing them out to sea.

Though everyone, including the Anguillans themselves, emphasizes the revolution's comic-opera episodes, bloodshed was threatened, and there was no going back. On June 11th, gunmen attacked police headquarters in Basseterre; earlier that spring, fifty shots had been fired into the lodgings of a Warden sent from St. Kitts. On June 16th, Peter Adams, who had been Anguilla's representative in the state legislature, proposed that the United States make Anguilla an American territory. His proposal was ignored in Washington. On July 11th, a popular referendum showed 1,813 to 5 for independence; Peter Adams was chosen president and asked for talks with President Johnson. Our President's response, if any, did not make the newspapers. On August 1st, under the supervision of a Caribbean Commonwealth Conference in Barbados, a reconciliation was worked out whereby Anguilla ended its secession and Bradshaw promised greatly increased financial aid. On August 4th, Anguilla deposed Peter Adams and installed as president Mr. Ronald Webster, a member of the Seventh-Day Adventist Church, one of the wealthiest men on the island, and Adams' Minister of Interior. Two days later, Jeremiah Gumbs went to the United Nations and told reporters, "The people are very aware about not losing control of their land. . . . We want to keep the island the way God made it." By the middle of August, the frigate *Lynx*, with a contingent of British Marines, moored off Blowing Point but was warned by Webster that blood would flow if a landing was attempted. (One strange tale from this period of crisis is that some Marines did land, distributed candy to the children who had gathered, and were seen off by a band playing "God Save the Queen.") By the end of August, Jamaica had refused to condone an expeditionary force from various islands that would put down the rebellion, and it became clear that Bradshaw lacked the military muscle to impose his will. On August 29th, the U.N. hearing ended, with no action advised, and a nebulous, nervous peace prevailed. Even now, an incoming tourist is sternly questioned as to what his "mission" might be, and one can see on the dirt runway of the airfield barrels and rolls of barbed wire to obstruct the landing of any planes other than the two-engine Aztecs that run daily shuttles to St. Martin and St. Thomas. Our first evening here, a British pleasure craft lowered a few female swimmers into Rendezvous Bay, and a carload of Anguillan militia rushed to investigate the invasion. Without doubt, Anguilla is under economic siege; the Bradshaw government has cut off even the island doctor's salary, and the schools and public services are kept going by infusions of private money, including tens of thousands of dollars from the pocket of Ronald Webster himself. A young man held on suspicion of murder languishes in the island's jail; not only is there no magistrate to hear his case but St. Kitts, which has the facilities to test the murder weapon for fingerprints, both refuses to do so and refuses to let the gun be examined on another island. The suspect's story is typically bizarre for these bewitched times: he was walking with one hand on a girl and the other on his bicycle when suddenly she fell down dead, a bullet in her heart.

Anguilla is currently run by a seven-man council, headed by Webster, that was elected on October 17th. The island's international status is suspended for a year under the so-called Interim Agreement forged in December by a delegation of two British Members of Parliament; under the agreement, the Anguillan government supposedly accepts the advice and counsel of a Parliamentary mission headed by Mr. Tony Lee, a distinguished veteran of the British Colonial Service and a graduate of the hard schools of Kenya and Aden. Mr. Lee, an intelligent, tall, faintly corpulent Englishman of the breed whose diffident persistence once imposed British order on a quarter of the globe, is possibly the most popular man on Anguilla. "NO COMMUNISM—NO GANGSTERISM!" proclaims a legend painted on a building next to the old Methodist church on Road Hill. "WE WANT BRITISH RULE AND DEMOCRACY. GIVE US BRITAIN!" After its initial appeal to the United States, Anguilla has placed its hopes for stability and protection upon the power that elsewhere in the world is liquidating the last scraps of its empire.

Lee's task is not easy, nor is his role clear. Even if Great Britain wished to grant Anguilla perfect independence, it is powerless to do so, for by the terms of the creation of the St. Kitts–Nevis–Anguilla state it abdicated all control over the state's internal affairs, which include secession. Lee is present on Bradshaw's sufferance as well as on Webster's, and his principal leverage in local affairs seems to be the threat to leave. As he drives about the island in his Morris Mini, the quality of the salutes he receives suggests that, in the eyes at least of the older Anguillans, who have lived most of their lives under the scarcely palpable rule of an appointed white Warden, Lee is the new Warden. But in fact Anguilla's destiny rests in the hands of Anguillans, and Lee's task may be to persuade them to take their destiny seriously.

A population of six thousand is the size of a small American town. Like small-town politics everywhere, Anguillan politics appears to an outsider an inscrutable tangle of personalities, old grudges, and bad habits. The island, for instance, is geographically divided into the East End and the West End, and white and mulatto East Enders dominated the drive for independence. Is this resented? Anguilla surely is one of the most color-blind places left in an increasingly racist world, but an egalitarian tolerance bred by centuries of colonial obscurity may well be strained by the opportunities and adversities of independence. And what of nepotism, where every third person is named Rey, Richardson, or Gumbs? We attended a political rally on the cricket field and heard a young man called Atlin Harrigan try to defend, under some vicious badgering, his newspaper, the *Beacon*, which had asked for new elections and an expanded council, and had implied graft and logrolling in the present council. "I am in a fearful bind," he said into the microphone, "for if I print half of what I know, I fear Bradshaw will use it to prove that Anguillans cannot govern themselves." In turn, a council member, Mr. Wallace Rey, rose up and claimed that it was highly improper for the *Beacon* to be printed on the Anglican Church's duplicator. This demand for separation of church and state strikes a rather new note on an island governed for generations as an adjunct of the Anglican Church, and may not be unrelated to the whiteness of the present rector. Although the crowd of several hundred acted much like any bored and amused small-town rally, two old ladies came to blows beneath a mahogany tree, and some of the speakers, including an urbane refugee from one of Bradshaw's jails, seemed all too expertly demagogic. When the council secretary spoke suavely of the council's right to secret discussion and of its wisdom of choice as to what "the people" should know, I myself, as children scampered around the mustered trucks in the tropic twilight, felt chilled by a whisper of Fascism. The crowd seemed puzzled and somewhat cynical, and voiced unity only at the mention of the hated name of Bradshaw, a bogey whose usefulness cannot be infinite.

The Anguillan national flag, designed by an American firm, shows three orange dolphins in a circle on a white field above a stripe of sea blue. The dolphins seem to be chasing each other

around and around. If one of them is Tony Lee, the representative of empire, of Britain's desire to salvage a colony she shaped, and another is Ronald Webster, the representative of independence, of Anguilla's honorable heritage of self-reliance, the third might be Jeremiah Gumbs, the representative of enterprise, which can eat up the other two. Mr. Gumbs, an energetic, bearish man who had visited the island shortly before we arrived, was enterprising enough to leave Anguilla as a youth (he was born in 1913) and become a successful fuel-oil dealer in Edison, New Jersey. It was Jere Gumbs who hired as advocate and adviser the Harvard Law School professor Roger Fisher and, with him, took Anguilla's case to the U.N. Assembly's Special Committee on Colonialism. He owns the island's only passably modern hotel, the Rendezvous Bay, which his sister Beatrice runs in a breezy American style. Jere

Gumbs has also recently bought from the Lake family Dog Island, an uninhabited but sizable satellite island, where, rumor goes, he would like to construct a convalescent home. It was Jere Gumbs who, on his flying visit, restored to workability two of the five St. Kittian bulldozers confiscated in the revolution; it was also Jere Gumbs who arranged to rent these same bulldozers, at a price thought by some to be nominal, from the public-works department for the purpose of excavating a large cistern at his own hotel.

Anguilla needs but distrusts enterprise. A new resident in the community of nations is apparently subjected to a Welcome Wagon of international opportunists: after the American flag designers and the Swiss stamp printers, come the offers to float in a gambling casino, to set up a quickie-divorce and/or abortion haven, intermixed with a trickle of utopian anarchists and political scientists preparing studies of the mini-state. Foremost among the latter has been Dr. Leopold Kohr, of the University of Puerto Rico; an admirer of the Pennsylvania Amish, Dr. Kohr advocates a world of self-sufficient agricultural villages. A San Francisco group interested in copping out of the 20th-century nexus of *Realpolitik* was actively fascinated by Anguilla last summer; they placed in *The New York Times* a slick full-page ad written by one of their number, Mr. Howard Gossage, an advertising man, asserting that Anguilla "does not want to become a nation of busboys" and impetuously offering honorary citizenships at a hundred dollars a head. More recently, a young hippie couple, penniless but equipped with a shotgun and several cameras, set up a tent on the beach near Shaddick Point and begged food from a wealthy American woman who has built a home there; after several weeks of this idyll, they were expelled back to St. Martin. Anguilla has thus far defended herself from these crude assaults, but any defense of virginity runs the risk of altogether succeeding. "ANGUILLA has been DELIBERATELY RETARDED," reads a sign nailed up on a cement-block shed near Rendezvous Bay, and the question that hovers over the island's scruffy pastures and empty beaches and minuscule taverns named Amity and Sea View and Lonely Valley and United Nation is how to bring Anguilla into the present without destroying the charm and virtue of its tardiness.

Tony Lee, in the interim year of grace, would like to see the roads improved and telephone service inaugurated, and has called in a United Nations planner to survey the island. He described to me the Christmas holidays, when over two thousand Anguillan men returned from St. Thomas and other unretarded islands, and dances were held all over Anguilla; "It's their place, you see; there aren't any big hotels they aren't allowed into. I don't know, it may be airy-fairy of me, but I think it would be nice somehow, if one could, to keep it, you know, their place." Ronald Webster, a tea-colored man with the trim, stiff carriage of a self-taught school-teacher, speaks of ten or more small hotels, one at each beach, and of Anguilla's supporting a population larger than that of St. Thomas. He gives native industry priority over the tourist trade, but though there is a young furniture factory, and an American has set up a tiny shop for the manufacture of trinket jewelry, and two indigenous airlines are operating (despite a mysterious case of arson that grounded one plane), it is difficult to imagine any appreciable industry that would not have to import all its raw materials—to an island without a pier. Nor is the limbo status of the present government, while Bradshaw in Basseterre waits for Anguilla to prove unviable, likely to attract much investment capital. Americans hoping to acquire a cheap spot in the sun will be discouraged by the high value that the "peasant proprietors" place on their land. "This is paradise," Ronald Webster said to me, with a quick, wicked smile, "and paradise is not cheap." What Jeremiah Gumbs thought was expressed by the roaring and growling of the bulldozers as they slowly scraped a long hole in the coral earth beside our room at the Rendezvous Bay Hotel. By the end of a week, one bulldozer had sprung a tread and, after futile attempts to lift it with an automobile jack, stood mired in the pit it had dug. On the other bulldozer, one of the two cables supporting the front blade had snapped. Ronald Webster thought that the first dozer had merely lost a pin; so the concern of the Anguilla Department of Public Works, and of a displeased Tony Lee, and, behind him, of the British government (two British radio operators were daily exchanging messages with Whitehall), and, behind *that*, of the brooding American hemispherical over-presence on guard against a mini-Cuba, all danced for the moment on a pin lost in the dust.

And meanwhile the patient goats are tethered to the bushes of maiden-berry, and the sun beats down, and the Methodist churches thrive, and any tourist willing to jet from the mainland to St. Martin and stay overnight in Marigot or Philipsburg and take the next morning's more-or-less-ten-o'clock, ten-minute, five-dollar flight to Anguilla's dollhouse airport can experience, as did I and my wife, the aboriginal luxury of walking barefoot along miles of soft white coral sand and encountering no footprint but one's own of the day before. It will not last forever. Transistor radios are creeping into Anguilla, conveying the Top Forty hits in the U.S.A. by way of Radio Antilles in Montserrat, and a few Americans and an Irish airline pilot have built permanent vacation homes, and Anguillans who travel, like Mr. Émile Gumbs, say that now strangers nod knowingly when told you are from Anguilla: they have heard of it. Progress will come—these are the finest undeveloped beaches in the Caribbean—but slowly, resisted, one feels, by the instincts of the Anguillans themselves. The crowd at the political rally make a happy, erect impression in their Sunday suits and chiffon dresses, with an occasional miniskirt and a few motorcyclists—the impression of a colored population free, for this interim, of anger and shame. In the West Indies as a whole, these "islands in the sun" whose history is so scored with slaughter (the first modern genocide was committed by the Spaniards on the Arawaks), with the oppression of slaves and the rebellions of slaves, with piracy and massacre and cruelty—with the rage, in short, that seems to afflict Europeans whenever they leave their own ugly climate—one now feels a benevolent remove from world conflicts and a precious possibility: the possibility that blacks, torn as slaves from their African tribes and roughly implanted with Western languages and traditions, can now construct a fresh society. One goes to the Caribbean not only for the sun but for a tone—the tone of a culture based upon negritude but as different from that of the American Negro as the blues and the desperate joy of jazz are from calypso wit and the translucent pealing of the steel band. The large number of slave revolts in the islands, as opposed to their remarkable rareness on the North American continent, is an index of how much more demoralizing our subjugation was, and how much more durable its bad effects will be. Integration in the United States must be primarily an act of the white majority; in the Caribbean, where the majority is black, integration feels closer. A backwater like Anguilla, where black and white settlers were bound together in a fraternity of poverty, seems to offer a chance of skipping several nightmare chapters of race relations and of moving rather promptly into the polyracial future.

Various quotations occur to me as I wonder about Anguilla's chances for independent survival. One of the Englishmen attached to the Parliamentary mission referred to the Anguillans as "the poor dears," and another, as we lay on the beach, in answer to my question as to what St. Kitts was like, answered, with a wave that included the immaculate beach and the turqoise sea, " 'Bout like this. A bloody 'ole." Then there is a quote from Postlethwayt's 18th-century *Dictionary of Commerce* that says, "Every man being a kind of sovereign in his own family . . . no other government there is in Anguilla." And a sentence by Aldous Huxley: "The worst enemy of life, freedom, and the common decencies is total anarchy; their second worst enemy is total efficiency." Our taxi-driver, whose name is Charlie Gumbs and who has sent his two sons to college, again gestures at the telephone poles as he drives us back to the airport. "We're waiting for them to grow branches to hang the wires from." We pass the three other earthmovers, bright yellow and motionless, that were lengthening the airstrip before the revolution. "Men from St. Kitts bring them in, have to run them themselves; Anguilla men put sixty-foot masts on boats in the water, but they don't know how to run bulldozers." He turns and grins, apparently oblivious of the fact that these machines are derelict and that the two back at the hotel are out of repair again. "Well, now we show them Anguilla men know how to run bull-dozers."

P.S.

September 1974

A YEAR AND A MONTH after the visit to Anguilla that prompted my letter, banner headlines announced to me in London that Great Britain had invaded little Anguilla: early in the morning of March

19, 1969, two frigates landed three hundred fifteen Red Devil paratroopers, forty Marines, and forty-nine London policemen, in response to a supposed insult delivered to William Whitlock, Parliamentary Under-Secretary of State for Foreign and Commonwealth Affairs, by an unruly Anguillan mob six days before. This Lilliputian exercise of gunboat diplomacy (the Anguillans, foreseeing the invasion, had buried all their guns, and not one person was injured) attracted derisive world attention and terminated Anguilla's claim to being "one of the most obscure islands in the Caribbean." Also terminated were whatever proprietary feelings I had had for her. The full Anguilla story is told, thoroughly but all too facetiously, by Donald E. Westlake, in his *Under an English Heaven* (Doubleday, 1972). The uneasy interim condition prevailing in early 1968 persisted through the year, while various raffish Americans infiltrated advice into Ronald Webster's ear and the young Anguillans of the "Defence Force" that had replaced the St. Kittian policemen grew to resemble licensed hoodlums. Our friend Tony Lee, Mr. Westlake feels, proved too airy-fairy for his responsibilities as Our Man on Anguilla, and failed as the Commissioner installed by the invasion forces. Certainly he looked very tired the last time we saw him, on page 13 of the March 23, 1969, London Sunday *Times*, beside the wrap-up headline, "BRUTE FARCE AND IGNORANCE." The British press, generally anti-Vietnam, was stridently unsympathetic with their own government's interventionism. "This 'wag the flag and flog the wog' farce," the *Evening News* termed it, and the *Times* drew the conclusion that "a British Government is still capable of replaying Suez not as tragedy but as farce."

Farce or no, reinstatement to the status of an English colony was just what the Anguillans wanted, and under subsequent Commissioners the Royal Engineers busied themselves, according to Westlake, "building schools, paving roads, starting an electrification program, studying the water table, and generally tidying up the effects of the previous three hundred years of neglect." The last of them left, to kudos from the *Beacon*, on September 14, 1971, leaving a better island than they found, a *de facto* colony still technically part of the paper federation of St. Kitts–Nevis–Anguilla. Anguilla has dropped from the news these last years, nor have we

returned to compare her with the lost world of 1960 remembered
in this poem:

> The boy who came at night
> to light the Tilly lamps
> (they hissed, too bright;
> he always looked frightened)
> in the morning dragged his bait pail
> through the beryl seawater
> sauntering barelegged
> without once looking down.
>
> The night Rebecca's—
> she lived beneath us—
> sailor lover returned from sea
> and beat her for hours,
> it was as hard to sleep as the time
> she tied a rooster
> inside an oil drum.
>
> The woman across the road,
> pregnant by an annual visit,
> cursed ungratefully, tossing rocks
> at her weeping children.
> The radio on her windowsill
> played hymns from Antigua all day.
>
> And the black children in blue
> trotted down the white-dust road
> to learn cricket and Victorian history,
> and the princesses
> balancing water drawn
> from the faucet by our porch
> held their heads at an insolent angle.
>
> The constellations
> that evaded our naming.
> The blind man. The drunk.

The albino,
his fat lips blistered by the sun.
The beaches empty of any hotel.
Dear island of such poor beauty,
meekly waiting to rebel.

FOUR INTRODUCTIONS

To Pens and Needles, *a collection of literary caricatures by David Levine* (*Gambit, 1969*)

IN 1963, when the newly founded *New York Review of Books* began to publish the drawings of David Levine, the art of caricature in America was quiescent; the theatrical cartoons of Al Frueh in *The New Yorker* had ceased, Al Hirschfeld had become primarily a decorator of advertisements, and William Auerbach-Levy, the most artful of them all, had rounded off his career with an elegant album entitled—a question he had too often heard—*Is That Me?* These men had followed the linear tradition of Ralph Barton and Max Beerbohm; economy was the soul of their wit, and their mood, as they reduced the features of this or that celebrity to a cunning black-and-white design, partook of the genial mood of showbiz.

Levine, instead, flung himself in a fury of crosshatching upon his subjects. His style looked past Beerbohm to the three-dimensional grotesques of Daumier and Tenniel. No weary pucker or complacent bulge of physiognomy could slip through the supple net of his penstrokes, and every corner of the face—that vulnerable patch between the eyebrows, the unseemly area behind the chin, the mute folds of the ears—was brought into a focus whose keenness transcended the mild demands of "humor." On the gray expanses of the *NYRB* pages his etched homunculi seemed astoundingly *there*; one wanted to pick them up and put them on the shelf. Now, in the form of this book, one can.

Our selection concentrates upon literary figures. Drawn in fortnightly installments to illustrate topical book reviews, the gallery of modern authors approaches completeness. Mann and Borges are missing, and one wonders what Levine would do with Salinger's sad handsomeness or Kierkegaard's bent beauty. But how good it is to know that Gide has no top to his head, and that Truman Capote has no chin, resting, like Baudelaire, within his bow tie like an egg in an egg cup. Levine is not so much an observer as a visionary. Working principally from photographs, he evolves a concept, a monstrous breathing idea. His grasp of this idea deepens with time; of the two versions of Malraux in this volume, the one is a caricature and the other is a caricature of a caricature. Of the three Becketts, the smallest and earliest has the innocence of wit; it puns the man and buzzard. This simile is absorbed and heightened in the alarming metaphor of the profile, with its drastically eroded cheek, its delirious pinpoint eye, its incredible chopping-knife of an ear. And the lava contours and volcanic turtle-neck of the third drawing seem gouged from chaos and quite intimidate any thought of satire. Levine's evolving style reinvents the gargoyle, that antidote to the angel and necessary adjunct to a complete humanism. All we humans, beneath the faces that would proclaim for each a separate individuality, share the worse-than-simian weirdness of thinking reeds. Mankind is a riddle it takes the Gothic style to pose.

Since Levine, as clairvoyant, has liberated himself from the physical presence of the subject, the living and the dead are the same to him, and with uncanny authority he conveys, out of fudged old portraits and stylized prints, the essence of the immortals. Take Browning's wonderfully astute, plump, and conceited left hand; or Ben Franklin's cherry-nosed, finger-snapping display of pragmatic pep; or Casanova's evidently numbing virility. The artist discovers a surprising dandyish sneer on the time-softened face of John Milton, and elicits from the noseless bust of Catullus, at the farthest rim of Caricature's reach, the agonized satyr's howl that resounds through imperial Rome. One looks forward to, yet rather dreads, Levine's inevitable cartoon of Jesus.

Our artist was born in 1926 in Brooklyn, where he still lives. He has been quoted as describing himself as "a painter supported by a hobby—satirical drawings." As a painter he is representational and has been described, by John Canaday, as "a legitimate anachronism." In his comic art also he displays somewhat anachronistic qualities. Besides offering us the delight of recognition, his drawings comfort us, in an exacerbated and potentially desperate age, with the sense of a watching presence, an eye informed by an intelligence that has not panicked, a pen ready to encapsulate the latest apparitions of publicity (Twiggy inspires a drawing too lovely to omit) as well as those historical devils who haunt our unease.

To the Czech edition of Of the Farm, *translated by Igor Hájek in 1968 and left unpublished in post-Dubček Czechoslovakia*

As I REMEMBER, I wrote *Of the Farm* (the title originally was simply *The Farm*, but this had a monumentality that seemed bogus to me, which the preposition "Of" suitably reduced; I intended to mean that the book was *about* the farm, and that the people in it belonged *to* the farm, were of the earth, earthy, mortal, fallen, and imperfect) in the late summer and early autumn of 1964, in pencilled longhand. Then I embarked on a trip through the Soviet Union and Eastern Europe that lasted six weeks; the last night of this tour, and perhaps the most pleasant and unconstrained, was spent in Prague, in the apartment of Mr. Igor Hájek, the brilliant and engaging young man then involved in translating my previous novel *The Centaur*. Upon returning to the United States, I rewrote and typed *Of the Farm*, and in due course it was published, enjoying the mild sale and mixed reviews that usually greet my productions. Now, when Eastern Europe presents an aspect more troubled yet more hopeful than four years ago, Mr. Hájek and I both find ourselves in London, and he is translating my novella. And it has amused him to point out to me that I, like Joey Robinson, now possess, if not a new wife, a Citroën station wagon. Of such circling strands are past and present, fact and fiction, woven.

Of the Farm was my first attempt at book-length fiction after the writing of *The Centaur;* it was undertaken after a long hesitant interval fruitful of short stories. Like a short story, it has a continuous action, a narrow setting, a small cast. I thought of it as chamber music, containing only four voices—the various ghosts in it do not speak, and the minister's sermon, you will notice, is delivered in close paraphrase, without the benefit of quotation marks. The voices, like musical instruments, echo each other's phrases and themes, take turns dominating, embark on brief narrative solos, and recombine in argument or harmony. The underlying thematic transaction, as I conceived it, was the mutual forgiveness of mother and son, the acceptance each of the other's guilt in taking what they had wanted, to the discomfort, respectively, of the dead father and the divorced wife.

Threads connect it to *The Centaur:* the farm is the same, and the father, even to his name, George, seems much the same in both books. Mr. Hájek has directed my attention to a strange phrase, "his humorous prancing whine," in which the prancing is purely a remnant, like a badly erased pencil line, of the half-horse half-man. In a sense this novella is *The Centaur* after the centaur has died; the mythical has fled the ethical, and a quartet of scattered survivors grope with their voices toward cohesion. And seek to give each other the stern blessing of freedom mentioned in the epigraph from Sartre.* Let us hope that all nations will in their varying languages seek to bestow this stern blessing upon one another. I am honored at this moment [that is, when the cultural liberalization under Dubček had just been crushed by Russian tanks] to be translated into Czech.

---

* "Consequently, when, in all honesty, I've recognized that man is a being in whom existence precedes essence, that he is a free being who, in various circumstances, can want only his freedom, I have at the same time recognized that I can want only the freedom of others." [*En conséquence, lorsque sur le plan d'authenticité totale, j'ai reconnu que l'homme est un être chez qui l'essence est précédée par l'existence, qu'il est un être libre qui ne peut, dans des circonstances diverses, que vouloir sa liberté, j'ai reconnu en même temps que je ne peux vouloir que la liberté des autres.*]

To
The Harvard Lampoon Centennial Celebration 1876–1973
a collection of cartoons, verse, parodies, and humor
edited by Martin Kaplan (Atlantic Monthly Press, 1937)

THERE IT STANDS, in the shadow of Adams House, where Mt. Auburn Street unaccountably branches into Bow, an unaccountable little flatiron building with Amsterdam gables and a face—two round windows that look crosseyed, a red lantern for a nose, and, above the bright bowtie of its door, an exclamatory mouth of which the upper lip is so complex it might be a mustache. A copper hardhat tassled with a cage completes the apparition. This is the Lampoon Building. One's first impression is of an extravagance, and even in the 1950's, before the national-parody money shored up the subsiding foundations and restored lustre to the furnishings, this impression was confirmed by entering the tiled, worn, odorous, festooned interior. The gorgeous playful thing was put up, as a civilized prank, by American wealth when it was untaxed and unconscience-stricken; it is a folly and a toy and a bastion, an outcropping, like the brick mass of Harvard itself, of that awful seismic force which has displaced nine-tenths of the world: Wasp Power. The Lampoon is a club and, as do all clubs, feeds on the delicious immensity of the excluded. Robert Lampoon, born Robert Stewart, lucidly advances the doctrine usually left unspoken: college men are the "highest type in the world," Harvard men are "the best of all," and Poonsters are "the cream of Harvard men." And with him we travel to an enchanted realm where young Lord Byrons, garbed as monks and nuns, are served roast pigs on platters and sit each "with a bottle of imported sherry between his knees." In 1973, sipping our bitter domestic sherry, we feel, even without John Reed and Granville Hicks to remind us, that there is a shadow side to this "Harvard of the chosen few," the underworld of callow snobbishness and automatic jokes about "Kikeland House," of arrest-exempt lawlessness and an inherited consensus of the "dull and sated and blind." To be fair, the same page which reprints this last phrase from John Reed's reminiscences also shows a Lampoon window dedicated to Reed's memory; The Lampoon, though a flower of the Establishment, is a twisted flower, stemmed from the Establishment's wise instinct to grant itself license—license to be idle and (hence) open, license to mock and hence (symbolically) to destroy. Of my uneasy year as President, I remember fondly certain moments of ecstatic, probably revolutionary confusion. Trying to deliver stern speeches about impending deadlines, I was pelted with buttered rolls. A born follower, I found myself leading a bellowed medley of preposterously obscene songs, waving my potent baton, the Presidential jester's stick donated, as I remember, by the beneficent Sadri Khan. Where is it now? Not stolen, I hope, as was my engraved mug, and my youth.

The Lampoon is saved from mere sociable fatuity by being also *The Lampoon*, a magazine. Month after month, through thin seasons and thick, it insists on coming out, even though it contain naught but hastily hustled ads and snippets of past issues scrambled together through a haze of beer and boisterous kibitzing. Along with the anarchic camaraderie of Thursday nights, I cherish those groggy Monday-morning subway rides down to the South Station stop and thence to the emporium (up several flights in a quivering elevator of Art Nouveau tracery) of Best Print, Inc., where a mild, mustached, and unblinking craftsman called Harold (Harold o' Bestprint, he was invariably called in the Common Books) relieved me of my raggedy pasted-up dummy and, unless his lawyer advised him otherwise, turned it into 1,200 (more or less) shiny magazines, with real staples, on real paper—or "stock," as we learned to term it, lisping resonant professional terms such as "pica" and "ital" and "halftone" and "mortise" and "bleed." An undergraduate magazine loses its maturest contributors every June, a fact which, combined with the distracted condition of the average collegiate head, creates a wonderfully ongoing vacuum for those few who want to fill it. Fop though it pretends to be, *The Lampoon* has apprenticed a sturdy number of professional writers and artists. It was the editorial aspect, presumably, that weighed so heavily on the young Robert Benchley as he wrote to his mother of his election as President, "It will mean a lot of work and a lot of worry and responsibility, for it is a responsible position." George Santa-

yana, a half-century earlier, even more solemnly felt the invisible
pressure of the "forthnightly edition" conjured up in "an atmosphere of respect for holy things," by young men with "literary
tastes, leaning toward the sentimental and nobly moral." The
vocabulary surprises but the reverent tone is right. Raising a smile
is a delicate piece of artistic engineering that may well prepare one
for higher things. "It's all in the execution," we used to say of some
particularly lame cartoon idea hatched in a Sanctum gag session.
That is to say, there *was* such a thing as execution; no humor is so
broad it cannot be relayed badly or ably. The suppressed *Pontoon*,
for instance (police-confiscated for reprinting Midwestern cartoons
of which my favorite showed an ovum surrounded by long-tailed
sperm one of whom was saying, "Joe sent me"—a dramatization
that would not raise an eyebrow in a high-school contraception
class now), contained much wit, where little was needed; Bink
Young's editorial, "Easy, Breezy, You'll Slide a Mile," seemed an
especial gem, and I was glad to find it in this anthology.

Martin Kaplan '71, between earning his *summa* in molecular
biology and serving as head of every undergraduate organization
but the YAF, has done a brave deed; he has descended into the
dank abyss of the archives and clambered back with a staggering
amount of Pooniana. Not only did he cull the back issues, he
spelunked past slippery stalagmites of compacted Common Books
into unthinkable caves of ancient correspondence, and even panned
the memoirs of old grads for germane nuggets. The result is a
beautiful and scholarly labor of love. Mr. Kaplan has drawn heavily
on the parodies, which makes for something of a social history as
well as a private album. He has given generous helpings of the
cartoons and light verse, wherein the jejune can shine, and skimped
mercifully on the prose. Here is nostalgia enough for anyone who
has ever gone dizzy down the Narthex stairs, and laughter enough
for any general reader. May the next ninety-seven years yield
as happy a century's harvest.

To Soundings in Satanism, *a collection of essays assembled by F. J. Sheed (Sheed and Ward, 1972)*

MOST OF THE CONTRIBUTORS to this volume are Catholic or European or both; an American Protestant feels an understandable diffidence at leading such a parade, as it confidently marches from the mustering ground of Biblical exegesis into the weird marshes of possession, exorcism, and witchcraft and onward to the familiar firm terrain of psychopathology and literary criticism. To be honest, most of us Americans who out of reasons quixotic and sentimental and inertial persist in playing disciple to Calvin and Luther and Henry VIII have trouble enough conceiving of a deity, without dabbling at diabolism. Can evil be a personal, dynamic principle? The suggestion seems clownish; instinctively we reject it. If we must have a supernatural, at the price of intellectual scandal, at least let it be a minimal supernatural, clean, monotonous, hygienic, featureless— just a *little* supernatural, as the unwed mother said of her baby. There is no doubt a primitive resonance in the notion of God battling, across the surface of the universe, with a malevolent near-equal. But can we morally tolerate the God who would permit such an opponent to arise, who would arm him with death and pain, who would allow suffering Mankind to become one huge Job, teased and tested in heavenly play? Alas, we have become, in our Protestantism, more virtuous than the myths that taught us virtue; we judge them barbaric. We resist the bloody legalities of the Redemption; we face Judgment Day, in our hearts, much as young radicals face the mundane courts—convinced that acquittal is the one just verdict. We judge our Judge; and we magnanimously grant our Creator His existence by a "leap" of our own wills, incidentally reducing His "ancient foe" to the dimensions of a bad comic strip.

Yet these grand ghosts did not arise from a vacuum; they grow (and if pruned back will sprout again) from the deep exigencies and paradoxes of the human condition. We know that we live, and know that we will die. We love the creation that upholds us and sense that it is good, yet pain and plague and destruction are everywhere. It is not my province to discuss the shadowy Old Testament Satan so well evoked by Father Valensin; nor the demons swarming through all cultures, touched upon by M. Bazin in his essay on art; nor the disturbing boundary area where sexual hysteria and Christ's ministry of healing and the (to a Protestant) incredible rite of exorcism intertwine. I would, timidly, in my capacity as feeble believer and worse scholar, open the question of the devil as metaphysical possibility, if not necessity. For the assertion "God exists" is a drastic one that imposes upon the universe a structure; given this main beam, subordinate beams and joists, if reason and logic are anything, must follow. But let a true theologian speak. Karl Barth somewhere, coping with the massive—nay, central—theological problem of evil, speaks of God "turning His back" upon a section of the cosmos. Unable to locate this frightening metaphor, I found instead, in *Church Dogmatics*, a systematic portrait of "nothingness," which I here abridge:

> Only God and His creature really and properly are. But nothingness is neither God nor His creature. . . . But it would be foolhardy to rush to the conclusion that it is therefore nothing, i.e., that it does not exist. God takes it into account. He is concerned with it. He strives against it, resists and overcomes it. . . . Nothingness is that which God does not will. It lives only by the fact that it is that which God does not will. But it does live by this fact. For not only what God wills, but what He does not will, is potent, and must have a real correspondence. . . . The character of nothingness derives from its ontic peculiarity. It is evil. What God positively wills and performs in the *opus proprium* of His election, of His creation, of His preservation and overruling rule of the creature revealed in the history of His covenant with man, is His grace. . . . What God does not will and therefore negates and rejects, what can thus be only the object of His *opus alienum*, of His jealousy, wrath and judgment, is a being that refuses and resists and therefore lacks His grace. This being which is alien and adverse to grace and therefore without it, is that of nothingness. This negation of His grace is chaos, the world which He did not choose or will, which He could not and did not create, but which, as He created the actual world, He passed over and set aside, marking and excluding it. . . . And this is evil in the Christian sense, namely, what is alien and adverse to grace, and therefore without it. In this sense nothingness is really privation, the attempt to defraud God of His honour and right and

at the same time to rob the creature of its salvation and right. For it is God's honour and right to be gracious, and this is what nothing-ness contests. . . . In this capacity it does not confront either God or the creature neutrally. It is not merely a third factor. It opposes both as an enemy, offending God and threatening His creature. From above as well as below, it is the impossible and intolerable. By reason of this character, whether in the form of sin, evil, or death, it is inexplicable as a natural process or condition. . . . It "is" only as the disorder at which this counter-offensive is aimed, only as the non-essence which it judges, only as the enemy of God and His creation. We thus affirm that it is necessary to dismiss as non-Christian all those conceptions in which its character as evil is openly or secretly, directly or indirectly, conjured away, and its reality is in some way regarded or grouped with that of God and His creature.

(*Church Dogmatics*, 3, 3)

Pantheism on one side, Manichaeanism on the other, clutch at the theologian's skirts. A potent "nothingness" was unavoidably con-jured up by God's creating *something*. The existence of something demands the existence of *something else*. And this same ontic in-evitability serves Barth to explain man's strange capacity, under God, to choose evil.

> Without this possibility of defection or of evil, creation would not be distinct from God and therefore not really His creation. The fact that the creature can fall away from God and perish does not imply any imperfection on the part of creation or the Creator. . . . A creature freed from the possibility of falling away would not really be living as a creature. It could only be a second God—and as no second God exists, it could only be God Himself.

Are there not tendencies in our private psychologies that would give these cosmic propositions credence? Is not destructiveness within us as a positive lust, an active hatred? Who does not exult in fires, collapses, the ruin and death of friends? Who has seen a baby sleeping in a crib and not wanted, for an instant of wrath that rises in the throat like vomit, to puncture such innocence? What child is not fascinated by torture and monstrosity? What man can exempt, from his purest sexual passion and most chivalrous love, the itch to defile? What man or woman does not carry within, as tempter and last resort, the thought of suicide? After satisfaction, revulsion. Into the most ample contentment rushes, not an impulse to sing gratitude, but a frightful impatience that would, like Lucifer, overthrow the tyranny of order, however benign. Indeed, the more fortunate our condition, the stronger the lure of negation, of perversity, of refusal. For the more completely order would enclose us, the greater the threat to our precious creaturely freedom, which finds self-assertion in defiance and existence in sin and dreads beyond hell a heaven of automatons forever "freed from the possibility of falling away." Thus the devil—to give "nothingness" his name—thrives in proportion, never falls hopelessly behind, is always ready to enrich the rich man with ruin, the wise man with folly, the beautiful woman with degradation, the kind average man with debauches of savagery. The world always topples. A century of progressivism bears the fruit of Hitler; our own supertechnology breeds witches and warlocks from the loins of engineers.

We resist what is good for us; humanity cannot be imagined doing otherwise and remaining human. Barth's formulas fit: man is a battlefield, and Satan at best is "behind" one. But what of creation in general? Does a black-and-white *opus proprium* and *opus alienum* really satisfy our perception of the universe as a curious explosion, a chaos wherein mathematical balances achieve momentary islands of calm? Man as organism is beset not by "nothingness" but by predators and parasites themselves obeying the Creator's command to survive and propagate. Disease is a clash of competing vitalities. And what of those shrugs, those earthquakes and floods and mudslides, whereby the Earth demonstrates her utter indifference to her little scum of life? Nature—Nature, whom we love more than our own bodies, from whose face we have extracted a thousand metaphors and affectionate messages—cares nothing for us. Is this the Satanic nothingness? In fact, it has been taken as such; the Christian West, with its myth of the devil, has taken the fight to Nature with a vengeance, has sought out the microbe and dammed the river and poisoned the mosquito in his marsh and gouged the mineral from its hidden vein and invented the machines that now threaten to scrape Nature into the infernal abyss as Lucifer's angels were scraped from Heaven. Oriental fatalism, which would see death and nothingness as limbs of God, could not have done this. Yet we wonder, as now our human species like some giant strand of bacteria fills every vacuum and re-creates chaos artificially, if this was intended. Or if the essence of our creature-hood is coöperation, with even the devil.

I do not know. I call myself Christian by defining "a Christian" as "a person willing to profess the Apostles' Creed." I am willing, unlike most of my friends—many more moral than myself—to profess it (which does not mean understand it, or fill its every syllable with the breath of sainthood), because I know of no other combination of words that gives such life, that so seeks the *crux*. The Creed asks us to believe not in Satan but only in the "Hell" into which Christ descends. That Hell, in the sense at least of a profound and desolating absence, exists I do not doubt; the news-papers give us its daily bulletins. And my sense of things, senti-mental I fear, is that wherever a church spire is raised, though dismal slums surround it and a single dazed widow kneels under it, this Hell is opposed by a rumor of good news, by an irrational confirmation of the plenitude we feel is our birthright. The instinct that life is good is where natural theology begins. The realization that life is flawed admits the possibility of a Fall, of a cause behind the Fall, of Satan. How seriously we must take this possibility, and under what forms we might imagine it, these "soundings" will elucidate.

GOLF

The First Lunar Invitational

FIVE SHORT YEARS after Alan Shepard, swinging an improvised 6-iron, took a one-handed poke at a golf ball on the moon, space suits were developed which permitted a nice full shoulder turn and the Vardon overlapping grip. The next year, 1977, the first Semi-Invitational Tournament was scheduled, under the joint sponsorship of NASA, ALCOA, M.I.T., and Bob Hope. An elimination tournament was held under simulated conditions in the Mojave Desert, and the refined field of thirty pros, plus twenty invited celebrities, was lifted from Cape Kennedy on the Monday following the Azalea Open. A maximum of three woods per bag was allowed, mallet-head putters were forbidden, and caddies were expected to double. Two modules, of the "bus" type developed by Lockheed to transport the football teams matched in the previous January's Crater Classic, cast off from the mother ship Thursday morning, for a tee-off time of 9 a.m. Players grumbled of sleeplessness and the failure of officials to provide for a practice round, but praised the dry, open fairways and evidently relished the absence of wind and water hazards. "We'll tear this sucker apart," Lee Trevino's voice crackled confidently across the vastness of space.

Robert Trent Jones, working from detailed relief maps of the lunar surface, had designed with the aid of computers in Lacus Somniorum a 42,000-yard layout, threaded among the natural outcroppings and effluvia and the debris left by previous expeditions. The cups were cut and the eighteen cores thus taken shipped back to the Manned Spacecraft Center in Houston for pulverization, analysis, and adoration. The rules committee pondered the inch or so of ubiquitous dust and suspended the law against grounding your club in a sand trap. But preferred lies were banned. One of the invited amateurs, a Texas oilman playing snugly to a handicap of 23, had brought along a piece of Astroturf to make his own lies preferable. American flags of titanium foil, battery-powered to simulate rippling, vividly signalled the pin placements. The tee markers were pineapples rocketed fresh each day from the private Dole launching pad in Oahu, at not a penny's cost to the taxpayer.

The pros quickly adjusted to the extraterrestrial conditions. The dust, for instance, was "fluffy" rather than "gritty" and the ball could be "struck" rather than "stung," as if from a lie of bedded dandelion polls; though it was hard to put enough "stop" on the ball for the rock-hard "greens" of smooth lunar gneiss. "It's a chipper's game up here," big-hitting George Archer confided to the three hundred million televiewers of the tournament. "It's like playing in a flour bin," Miller Barber observed from behind his accustomed sunglasses, and the Earthbound gallery could verify, despite the ragged television transmission, that owing to the tendency of the divots to hang cloudlike in the air the players slowly accumulated bulk, like snowmen.

Moon play had other peculiarities. Without an atmosphere, balls could not hook or slice, which licensed lashers like Arnold Palmer to overswing with impunity. Drives one mile long became standard by the second day of play. Smartly struck wedge shots, however, had a worrisome tendency to float into orbit; Jack Nicklaus lost two successive approaches to the fourth green this way, taking a humiliating eight on the hole. "It's a puncher's game," said Nicklaus. "Keep the ball low, and don't gulp oxygen." A ball lying in shadow, even a mere few inches from the razor-sharp sunlight, had to be played promptly, lest it freeze and shatter when struck. And unexplained concentrations of basalt beneath the crust played magnetic havoc on some fairways; the shortest hole on the course, a 1,000-yard cutie nestled between a lava flow and a three-billion-year-old impact crater—for most pros an easy 8-iron—was birdied only four times the first two days of play.

Toward the end of the second afternoon, as the frigid lunar dusk was tracing long shadows across the course, Spiro Agnew,* playing in a foursome with Bobby Nichols, Bob Lunn, and Robert McNamara, shanked a difficult spoon shot with such penetrating puissance that, from 900 yards away, it punctured the fuel tank of one lunar module and rendered it inoperable. The P.G.A. ruled from Palm Beach that those who failed to make the 36-hole cut should not only receive no prize money but should be the ones to stay on the moon and perish. Since this included most of the participating amateurs, several government officials demanded another ruling from the C.I.A., which refused, however, to identify itself over public networks. So the P.G.A. ruling appeared to stand. The next day, however, while the active field was playing the eleventh through fourteenth holes deep in the Taurian Highlands, the disqualified golfers commandeered the operable module and rejoined the mother ship.

"Easy as sinking a six-inch putt," comedian Jerry Lewis later confided to newsmen.

The tournament, interestingly, was played to a conclusion, though the backpack radios did not send sufficiently powerful signals to announce to Earth the winner. The Dole Company continued to rocket pineapples moonward, and the Mount Palomar Observatory reported sighting on Sunday afternoon a crisp hit to the left of the pin by a player who, judging from his restricted backswing, must have been Doug Sanders.

The participants who returned to Earth found that their ardor for the game had permanently cooled. As singer Andy Williams put it, "I don't know, it just feels down here like you're swinging underwater at lumps of putty." Plans were projected for the next year's competition, with an enlarged purse and solar-powered golf carts contributed by the Russians; but that autumn the major powers, honoring their commitments to the contending factions in the Ethiopian civil war, staged a prolonged nuclear exchange, and in the subsequent regression of technology not only was the secret of solid-fuel rockets lost but of tapered tempered-steel golf shafts as well.

---

* Still a real person as of February 1971, when this jape was composed.

Tips on a Trip

I HAVE BEEN ASKED * to write about golf as a hobby. But of course golf is not a hobby. Hobbies take place in the cellar and smell of airplane glue. Nor is golf, though some men turn it into such, meant to be a profession or a pleasure. Indeed, few sights are more odious on the golf course than a sauntering, beered-up foursome obviously having a good time. Some golfers, we are told, enjoy the landscape; but properly the landscape shrivels and compresses into the grim, surrealistically vivid patch of grass directly under the golfer's eyes as he morosely walks toward where he thinks his ball might be. We should be conscious of no more grass, the old Scots adage goes, than will cover our own graves. If neither work nor play, if more pain than pleasure but not essentially either, what, then, can golf be? Luckily, a word newly coined rings on the blank Formica of the conundrum. Golf is a *trip*.

A non-chemical hallucinogen, golf breaks the human body into components so strangely elongated and so tenuously linked, yet with anxious little bunches of hyper-consciousness and undue effort bulging here and there, along with rotating blind patches and a sort of cartilaginous euphoria—golf so transforms one's somatic sense, in short, that truth itself seems about to break through the exacerbated and as it were debunked fabric of mundane reality.

An exceedingly small ball is placed a large distance from one's face, and a silver wand curiously warped at one end is placed in one's hands. Additionally, one's head is set a-flitting with a swarm of dimly remembered "tips." Tommy Armour says to hit the ball with the right hand. Ben Hogan says to push off with the right foot. Arnold Palmer says keep your head still. Arnold Palmer has painted hands in his golf book. Gary Player says *don't* lift the left heel. There is a white circle around his heel. Dick Aultman says keep everything square, even your right foot to the line of flight. His book is full of beautiful pictures of straight lines lying along wrists like carpenter's rules on planed wood. Mindy Blake, in *his* golf book, says "square-to-square" is an evolutionary half-step on

---

* By *The New York Times Book Review*, in the summer of 1973.

the way to a stance in which both feet are skewed toward the hole and at the extremity of the backswing the angle between the left arm and the line to the target is a mere 14 degrees. Not 15 degrees. Not 13 degrees. Fourteen degrees. Jack Nicklaus, who is a big man, says you should stand up to the ball the way you'd stand around doing nothing in particular. Hogan and Player, who are small men, show a lot of strenuous arrows generating terrific torque at the hips. Player says pass the right shoulder under the chin. Somebody else says count two knuckles on the left hand at address. Somebody else says *no* knuckle should show. Which is to say nothing about knees, open or closed clubface at top of backswing, passive right side, "sitting down" to the ball, looking at the ball with the right eye—all of which are crucial.

This unpleasant paragraph above, strange to say, got me so excited I had to rush out into the yard and hit a few shots, even though it was pitch dark, and only the daffodils showed. Golf converts oddly well into words. Wodehouse's golf stories delighted me years before I touched a club. The story of Jones's Grand Slam, and Vardon's triumph over J. H. Taylor at Muirfield in 1896, and Palmer's catching Mike Souchak at Cherry Hills in 1960, are always enthralling—as is, indeed, the anecdote of the most abject duffer. For example:

Once, my head buzzing with a mess of anatomical and aeronautical information that was not relating to the golf balls I was hitting, I went to a pro and had a lesson. Put your weight on the right foot, the man told me, and then the left. "That's all?" I asked. "That's all," he said. "What about the wrists pronating?" I asked. "What about the angle of shoulder-plane vis-à-vis that of hip-plane?" "Forget them," he said. Ironically, then, in order to demonstrate to him the folly of his command (much as the Six Hundred rode into the valley of Death), I obeyed. The ball clicked into the air, soared straight as a string, and fell in a distant ecstasy of backspin. For some weeks, harboring this absurd instruction, I went around golf courses like a giant, pounding out pars, humiliating my friends. But I never could identify with my new prowess; I couldn't *internalize* it. There was an immense semi-circular area, transparent, mysterious, anesthetized, above the monotonous weight-shift of my feet. All richness had fled the game. So gradually I went back on my lessons, ignored my feet, made a number of other studied adjustments, and restored my swing to its original, fascinating *terribilità*.

Like that golf story of mine? Let me tell you another: the greatest shot of my life. It was years ago, on a little dog-leg left, downhill. Apple trees were in blossom. Or the maples were turning; I forget which. My drive was badly smothered, and after some painful wounded bounces found rest in the deep rough at the crook of the dog-leg. My second shot, a 9-iron too tensely gripped, moved a great deal of grass. The third shot, a smoother swing with the knees nicely flexed, nudged the ball a good six feet out onto the fairway. The lie was downhill. The distance to the green was perhaps 230 yards at this point. I chose (of course) a 3-wood. The lie was not only downhill but sidehill. I tried to remember some tip about sidehill lies; it was either (1) play the ball farther forward from the center of the stance, with the stance more open, or (2) play the ball farther back, off a closed stance, or (3) some combination. I compromised by swinging with locked elbows and looking up quickly, to see how it turned out. A divot the size of an undershirt was taken some 18 inches behind the ball. The ball moved a few puzzled inches. *Now here comes my great shot.* Perfectly demented by frustration, I swung as if the club were an ax with which I was reducing an orange crate to kindling wood. Emitting a sucking, oval sound, the astounded ball, smitten, soared far up the fairway, curling toward the fat part of the green with just the daintiest trace of a fade, hit once on the fringe, kicked smartly toward the flagstick, and stopped two feet from the cup. I sank the putt for what my partner justly termed a "remarkable six."

In this mystical experience, some deep golf revelation was doubtless offered me, but I have never been able to grasp it, or to duplicate the shot. In fact, the only two golf tips I have found consistently useful are these. One (from Jack Nicklaus): on long putts, think of yourself putting the ball half the distance and having it roll the rest of the way. Two (from I forget—Mac Divot?): on chip shots, to keep from underhitting, imagine yourself *throwing* the ball to the green with the right hand.

Otherwise, though once in a while a 7-iron rips off the clubface with that pleasant tearing sound, as if pulling a zipper in space, and falls toward the hole like a raindrop down a well; or a drive draws sweetly with the bend of the fairway and disappears, still rolling, far beyond the applauding sprinkler, these things happen in spite of me, and not because of me. On the golf course as nowhere else, the tyranny of causality is suspended, and men are free.

Is There Life After Golf?

GOLF IN THE KINGDOM, by Michael Murphy, 205 pp. Viking, 1972.

Like a religion, a game seeks to codify and lighten life. Played earnestly enough (spectatorship being merely a degenerate form of playing), a game can gather to itself awesome dimensions of subtlety and transcendental significance. Consult George Steiner's hymn to the fathomless wonder of chess, or Roger Angell's startlingly intense meditations upon the time-stopping, mathematical beauty of baseball. Some sports, surely, are more religious than others; ice hockey, fervent though its devotees be, retains a dross of brutal messiness, and handball, though undoubtedly it has its fine points, has not generated many holy books. Golf, on the other hand, inspires as much verbiage as astrology. In the television era, the sport has added to its antiquity and air of privilege the aura of sudden fame and fortune earned by broad-backed boys from Latrobe, Pennsylvania, and El Paso, Texas; millions now trudge out to the dawn starting lines inwardly clutching a tip from the Saturday sports page or the driving-range pro; an esoteric cult has become a mass cult while remaining esoteric. In Palmer's disastrous lapses, in Casper's persistent slump, golf reasserts its essential enigma. It is of games the most mysterious, the least earthbound, the one wherein the wall between us and the supernatural is rubbed thinnest. The exaltation of its great spaces; the eerie effortlessness of a good shot; the hellish effortfulness of a bad round; the grotesque disparity between a drive that eats up two-thirds of the fairway and the ten-yard dribble hit with an almost identical swing; the unpredictable warps and turns of fortune in the game; its tranced silences; its altering perspectives; its psychosomatic sensitivity to our interior monologue and the sway of our moods; the sullen, menacing sheen the monotonous grass can suddenly assume; the quirks of visibility; the dread of lostness; the ritual interment and resurrection of the ball at each green—such are the ingredients that make golf seem a magic mirror, an outward projection of an inner self. Even the most mechanical-minded books about golf evoke, for initiates, the game's intoxicating mysteries; Michael Murphy, in his curious and benign *Golf in the Kingdom*, takes these mysteries as his major topic.

Mr. Murphy, a Californian, is a co-founder of the Esalen Institute, described as "a research and development center established to explore those trends in the behavioral sciences, religion, and philosophy which emphasize the potentialities and values of human existence." On the back of the jacket of his book he is grinning with perfect teeth, and but for a faraway, faintly metaphysical gleam in his eyes he might be one of the interchangeable square-jawed young pros who clutter the tournament circuit with their competence. His book appears to be as open as his visage—he talks about himself as harried executive and student truth seeker; he names friends and gives dates, he describes rounds of golf we do not doubt he has played. Yet the basic autobiographical episode, involving a Scots guru/pro named Shivas Irons, is, like the name itself, frankly fantastic. The book liltingly begins:

> In Scotland, between the Firth of Forth and the Firth of Tay, lies the Kingdom of Fife—known to certain lovers of that land simply as "The Kingdom." There, on the shore of the North Sea, lies a golfing links that shimmers in my memory—an innocent stretch of heather and grassy dunes that cradled the unlikely events which grew into this book. . . . There I met Shivas Irons, introduced to me simply as a golf professional, by accident one day in June 1956. I played a round of golf with him then, joined him in a gathering of friends that evening, followed him into a ravine at midnight looking for his mysterious teacher, watched him go into ecstatic trance as the sun came up, and left for London the following afternoon—just twenty-four hours after we had met—shaken, exalted, my perception of things permanently altered.

Mr. Murphy was on his way to India, to study philosophy and practice meditation with the seer Aurobindo, and it may be that he retrospectively assigned much of what he learned there to this mythical golf instructor, who plays supernaturally well, keeps a library of the occult in his digs, and, in the dead of the night, scores a hole-in-one with a feather-stuffed ball and an antique shillelagh belonging to an immortal hermit named Seamus MacDuff. Yet the course, called Burningbush, is by its location and layout recognizably St. Andrews—golf's holy place. The book never totally strays from its base subject of golf, and it even contains some practical tips: Don't strain after a good score, play it as it lies, don't try too hard. "Let the nothingness into yer shots," Shivas tells Murphy— a memorable admonition to all of us who, not trusting the unconscious mechanics of the swing, smother the ball with too much hand-and-arm action. When Murphy tenses up on the first tee, Shivas makes a gesture that eases him "into a feeling of stomach and hips, making a center there for my swing." The well-worn advice "Hit from the inside" is metaphysicalized to "Ken the world from the inside." Warming to his theme of "true gravity," Shivas bids his pupil "feel yer inner body." Murphy, evidently a natural athlete, travels, club in hand, through a number of yoga-like states (he feels like an hourglass, then enormously tall), and sees turquoise "auras" expand and contract, and experiences other vivid intimations of "energy-dimensions" that might more distract than settle your average 20-handicapper. Unity and harmony are the goals of Shivas' instruction; imagine the ball and the "sweet spot" on the club as one, he says. Further, see and feel "the club and ball as one unbroken field." Further still, "sometimes a path appears in your mind's eye for the ball to follow: let it blend with your body." Murphy recalls a moment on Burningbush when all his senses joined: "For the moment . . . the world was a single field of music, joy, and light." Shivas has the ultimate word: "Aye ane fiedle [always one field] afore ye e're swung."

This religious bias, which would break down the opposition between game and player, between striker and thing struck, between man and landscape, comes as alien to the Occidental followers of aggressive Jahweh and tragic Jesus. This Occidental, for one, remains suspicious of a cosmic philosophy that so easily devolves into golf instruction. Murphy, drawing upon Shivas' supposed journals, has little trouble expanding the first part of his book, the golf part, into the comprehensive mysteries of the second. Because of the lightness of the golf ball (one and a half ounces), Shivas is led to conclude that the world, too, is feather-light, "an earthy nothingness." It is also "an icon of Man the Multiple Amphibian, a smaller, waffled version of the crystal ball, a mirror for the inner body; it is a lodestone, an old stone to polarize your psyche with." Its whiteness suggests (hello, Melville) the terror of the hueless void; its flight serves as "reminder of our hunting history and our future powers of astral flight." The hole is another mystery, linked to nostrils and other significant bodily apertures; Jean-Paul Sartre is called in to testify (from *Being and Nothingness*): "A good part of our life is passed in plugging up holes, in filling empty places, in realizing and symbolically establishing a plenitude." Not all such symbol-spinning is vapid, but it does border on the facile and the fanciful—less mysticism than mystchief. And it reduces, in practice, all this talk about luminous bodies and manifesting planes, about *hamartia* and *darshan*, about Agni the Primal Fire and the Net of Jewels, to something like witchcraft. The victory of Jack Fleck over Ben Hogan in the 1955 Open, for instance, is explained to have been Fleck's appropriation of Hogan's "inner body," and Murphy relates that while watching a baseball game he and his neighbors in the stands set up a "psychic fire-storm" that permanently injured the opposing pitcher's arm. Even if it works, is black magic what we need now? " 'Tis a thin line," Shivas himself says, " 'tween the madness of God and the madness of the Devil."

The Western spirit longs for a peaceable creed that would flatter the flesh instead of mortifying it, that would blur away the painful mind-body split and ease the agonies of egoism. But these wisdoms imported from the Orient have a disturbing way of melting into physical therapy—of a harmless, deep-breathing, sweet-swinging sort—and trivial spookiness. In regard to traditional Christian problems like the existence of evil and the paradoxes of ethical action, *Golf in the Kingdom* says little. During the raucous symposium that follows his round of golf with Shivas, Murphy claims, there was a "lively discussion of shanking and the problem of evil," but we never hear it. Murphy/Shivas does offer, for the length of a page, ethical distinctions between "Mind-at-Large" and "Higher Self"; it is good to know the latter before you drown in the former.

LSD is distinguished from disciplined contemplation, moral entropy from nirvana. "Ye need a solid place to swing from," Shivas says, which is half of the truth; you also need a spot to aim at. Shivas would be a complete prophet if the world were a golf course and life a game. In a game, purposes and means are indisputably ordained; in golf, rules regulate the most minute points of etiquette and equipment. A golf wherein some players were using tennis rackets and hockey pucks, some were teeing off backward from the green to the tee, and some thought the object of the game was to spear other players with the flagsticks—such a contest might produce a philosophy we could carry everywhere. As it is, analogies should be very tenderly extended outward from an island that, like golf, has been created as an artificial haven from real problems. Even within the analogy, Murphy is limited by his natural happiness at the game; for a description of the infernal misery possible *within* golf, read George Plimpton's *The Bogey Man*, especially the hideous chapter wherein Plimpton practices with four golf balls on a tinselly, night-lit par-3 course in the desert, each ball diabolically possessed of individual bad habits.

Yet there is much wit and good will in *Golf in the Kingdom*. "We are spread wide as we play, then brought to a tiny place" beautifully describes both golf and life. And why *not* make the world more of a golf course, where our acts would take validity from within, and we would replace our divots in apology for each blow, and joy would attach to the leisurely walking, the in-between times? There is a goodness in the experience of golf that may well be, as Mr. Murphy would have it, a *pitha*, "a place where something breaks into our workaday world and bothers us forevermore with the hints it gives."

Golf in the Kingdom put me in mind of another curious devotional work, William Price Fox's *Doctor Golf*, published in 1963 and long out of print. Doctor Golf, a fanatic even quainter and keener than Shivas Irons, runs a thirty-nine-member golf sanctuary in Arkansas called Eagle-Ho, refers to "young Hagen," advocates caddy-flogging, sells by mail order a clanking, cumbersome line of golf paraphernalia, and conducts a large correspondence. When one correspondent writes, "I am in my 65th year and I have been seized by golf like a mouse in the claws of a golden eagle," Doctor Golf congratulates him:

> Only after the fetters of youth have been flung aside can golf enter. Only then can the man know the folly of his adolescent belief of the swing answering to the man and perceive the joy and the truth of the complete man answering to the swing.
>
> And, as the years and the eagles cascade by, the even greater joy is realized when he stands in the bright sunlight of complete fulfillment and comes to realize that the *swing is the man.*

The swing is the man. The Dance of Shiva, Michael Murphy concludes, is at the heart of everything. Doctor Golf is more mystical still:

> The swing by its very nature transcends the human form. The swing is there when you pass on. . . . The swing, sir . . . is like the blue in the sky, immutable, eternal, indeed transcendental.

Reviews

THE FORK

THE LAST YEARS: JOURNALS 1853–1855, by Søren Kierkegaard, edited and translated by Ronald Gregor Smith. 384 pp. Harper & Row, 1965.

It is not certain that the United States needs still more translations of Kierkegaard. The Kierkegaard bibliography in this country is already amply confusing; led by the dauntless Walter Lowrie,* a campaign of translation coincident with the Second World War endowed the English-speaking world with almost all of the torrential *oeuvre* that the Danish thinker had created a century before. Eight books, including the immense *Concluding Unscientific Postscript*, were published here in 1941 alone. The current index of

---

* The reviewer, in his versifying youth, once indicted, for a threnody never finished, these lines "On the Death of Dr. Lowrie":

> The Reverend Doctor Walter Lowrie, 91, is dead.
> The *Times* of August 12th contains a picture of his head.
> I never knew the man but his translations often read.

> I never read his forty books, I never sought him whole;
> I had to pass right through him when, returning from a stroll,
> I flung myself on Kierkegaard to save my flagging soul.

> For Walter Lowrie had no peer at Englishing the Dane:
> Of twenty-six translated works, thirteen are his domain,
> And in those dreadful castles his kind heart will always reign.

> His prefaces relate the tale with modest balladry,
> Of how a tiny band—scarce more than Swensen, Dru, and he—
> Subdued a hostile continent of dark theology.

> He led them; old, a clergyman, he led. Retired, old,
> He started; goaded Swensen; wrestled *Angst*, battled *Forhold*,
> *Bestemelse*, and *Aufgehoben;* strove. The presses rolled

> At Princeton and at Oxford; the pastor's blue eyes bled
> On the thorns of an ugly language; *The Concept of Dread*
> He wept through in a month's long sitting; *inspirator*, he led.

books in print lists twenty-two Kierkegaard titles, not counting
duplications and anthologies. Distributed among a number of commercial, university, and religious presses (notably Harper, Princeton, and Augsburg) and bedevilled by overlappings and omissions
(*Stages on Life's Way* seems to be out of print, whereas some of
the *Discourses* crop up repeatedly), the list is nevertheless the
fullest outside of Germany and Denmark itself. We lack in English
only some topical and humorous trifles and the very voluminous
total of the journals and stray papers.

The Last Years: Journals 1853–1855 draws upon the papers from
1853 onward and the journals from their resumption on March 1,
1854, after a four-month gap. This material, which represents
Kierkegaard in his most haranguing and repetitious phase, is not
unknown to previous translation. The final fifty-five pages of
Alexander Dru's selection derive from the same portion of the
journals. Professor Smith, though he compiles three hundred and
forty pages, omits half of what Dru includes. Absent in Smith are
some of the most pungent entries in Dru:

> Oh, Luther, Luther; your responsibility is great indeed, for the closer
> I look the more clearly do I see that you overthrew the Pope—and
> set the public on the throne.

> Hypocrisy is quite as inseparable from being a man as sliminess is
> from being a fish.

> What could be more ridiculous than to use a jack to pick up a pin—
> or to make use of the eternal punishment of hell in order to make
> men into that half-demoralized, half-honest bagatelle which is
> roughly what it means to be a man.

Professor Smith prefers the extensive to the epigrammatic, and he
might claim that his selection emphasizes Kierkegaard's religious
thought—the ideas that were projected outward in his pamphleteer-
ing attack upon the established Christianity of Denmark. But the
pamphlets (ten in all, called *The Instant*) and the open letters that
Kierkegaard issued have been already rendered into English by
Lowrie, under the title *Attack Upon "Christendom."* This book
relates to *The Last Years* much as the outside of a sock relates to
the inside; the pattern is not identical, but the threads are the same.

After minimizing the considerable duplication, the editor of *The Last Years* justifies its publication by saying, "The last years of Kierkegaard's life saw a remarkable concentration of the motifs which controlled his whole authorship. This comes vividly to life in the present selection from the journals and papers of that time, and casts light on all that went before it." True, if "concentration" is taken to mean a narrowing. The prolix philosophizing of the "aesthetic works" and the fervent exhortation of the "religious works" have been succeeded by a third stage—an apostolic or pathological vehemence. *The Last Years* shows Kierkegaard's mind narrowed to a very hard point. More precisely, it shows his mind and life, those antagonistic twins, both narrowed to a very hard point, the point of attack, which becomes the point of vanishing.

Søren Aabye Kierkegaard (the name means "churchyard," and is pronounced "Kĕrkĕgōr") was born in Copenhagen in 1813—"the year," he was to say, "when so many worthless notes were put in circulation." His father, Michael, was a man of great force and complexity. A shepherd lad from the desolate West Jutland heath, he had become a prosperous cloth merchant and grocer in the city, only to retire at the age of forty, perhaps to devote himself to religious brooding. Within a year of his first wife's death, Michael married a household servant, Ane Lund, who bore him a child four months after their wedding. This marriage was to produce seven children, of whom Søren Aabye (as distinguished from his older brother, Søren Michael) was the last. His father was fifty-six, his mother forty-five; the advanced age of his parents accounts in part for Kierkegaard's physical frailty, and his position as the family Benjamin for his pertness and conceit. His nickname within the family was Fork—bestowed when, rebuked for shovelling food greedily at the table, he announced, "I *am* a fork, and I will stick you." Descriptions of his childhood abound in his journals:

> I was already an old man when I was born. . . . Delicate, slender, and weak, deprived of almost every condition for holding my own with other boys, or even for passing as a complete human being in comparison with others; melancholy, sick in soul, in many ways profoundly unfortunate, one thing I had: an eminently shrewd wit, given me presumably in order that I might not be defenseless.

But many weak boys with sharp tongues are born into the world, and Kierkegaard's heightened sense of himself reaches for more:

> I am in the deepest sense an unfortunate individual who has from the earliest age been nailed fast to one suffering or another, to the very verge of insanity, which may have its deeper ground in a disproportion between my soul and my body.

And in *The Last Years*, in the last entry, within a few weeks of his death, this sense of initial misfortune attains a frightening pitch:

> Through a crime I came into existence, I came into existence against God's will. The fault, which in one sense is not mine, even if it makes me a criminal in God's eyes, is to give life. The punishment fits the fault: it is to be deprived of all joy of life, to be brought to the supreme degree of disgust with life.

His adult life consisted of a series of quixotic, or expiatory, gestures. His father wanted him to study for the ministry, so he spent his youth in frivolity, drunkenness, and dandyism. His father died, so he settled down to pass the theological examination. He fell in love with and successfully courted Regine Olsen; then he broke off the engagement and buried himself in a frenetic literary activity dedicated to her. He became, under his own name and under the open secret of his pseudonyms, the most remarkable writer in Denmark, the only author above attack by the scurrilous magazine the *Corsair*; so he incited the *Corsair*, though its editor, Meïr Goldschmidt, revered him, to attack, which it did with such success that Kierkegaard's personal life was made a torment. Lastly, he who had long been on the verge of becoming a country parson mounted a savage attack upon organized Christianity, exhorting true Christians to abstain from the sin of church worship. He refused the Eucharist, since it could not be administered by a layman, on his deathbed.

Kierkegaard's American reputation was long deferred and is still esoteric, but in Denmark he was a celebrity. Indeed, he seems to have been the Benjamin of Copenhagen, the marketplace capital of a small and homogeneous country. His break with Regine was surrounded by so much gossip that it amounted to a public event. His pseudonyms, with their interlocking prefaces and compliments, must have been private jokes to a considerable group. His books, surprisingly, sold well enough to make money. During the *Corsair* persecution, his twisted back and uneven trouser legs were caricatured every week for a year, and the students at the university produced a comedy whose ridiculous hero was called Søren Kirk. Children taunted him on the streets. In his journals, he lamented, "To let oneself be trampled by geese is a slow way of dying," and complained that "when . . . I have sought recreation by driving ten or twelve miles, and my body has gradually become somewhat weak . . . when I alight from the carriage . . . there is sure to be someone at hand who is jolly enough to call me names." Astonishingly, the very name Søren, up to then the most common male baptismal name, became a byword for the ridiculous, and Danish parents, according to Lowrie, took to admonishing their children, "Don't be a Søren." Though helpless under such assault, Kierkegaard was not without power. A staunch monarchist, he was on conversational terms with King Christian VIII, and Lowrie asserts that in the relationship it was Kierkegaard who "held himself a little aloof." (In his journals, Kierkegaard dryly noted, "On the whole, Christian VIII has enriched me with many psychological observations. Perhaps psychologists ought to pay particular attention to kings, and especially to absolute monarchs; for the freer a man is, the better he can be known.") Kierkegaard's satirical pen was a feared weapon. He undoubtedly ruined the life of a former friend, P. S. Møller, with a personal attack published in the newspaper *Fatherland*. So his assault upon the ecclesiastical establishment was delivered from the strength of notoriety, and, far from being the private fulminations of an obscure aesthete and mystic, was a demagogic assault, a well-publicized uproar reverberating throughout Scandinavia. (*The Instant* was immediately translated into Swedish and, not needing translation in Norway, aroused the interest of young Ibsen, to become the basis of *Brand*.) Kierkegaard's expectation of arrest and imprisonment was not fulfilled, but at his funeral a crowd of students gathered to protest the church's appropriation of the body, and a riot was barely averted. W. H. Auden, in introducing his own Kierkegaard anthology, regards *The Attack Upon "Christendom"* as not a book but an act: "What for the author was the most important book of his life is for us, as readers, the least, for to us the important point is not what it contains, but the fact that Kierkegaard wrote it."

Certainly, the journals of *The Last Years* are difficult to enjoy. How different are, say, the *Last Diaries* of Tolstoy, wherein the old man, honored all over the world, a sacred figure to his countrymen, struggles with the naïveté of a child to become good! Kierkegaard never had Tolstoy's candid willingness to learn and grow. He was endowed from birth with a somewhat elderly mind. Though he read voraciously and could be gregarious and charming, only five people seem to have really interested him: Jesus, Socrates, Hegel, Regine Olsen, and his father. Though his ability to vary and extend his voice is marvellous, a single field of ideas appears to have been in his possession since the beginning. It remained only for him to explore it and to arrive at the ultimate conclusion. One does not find in *The Last Years* those categories— "the absurd," "the leap," "dread"—that modern Existentialism has made fashionable; they were expounded in the earlier "aesthetic works." What one does find, theologically, is a wholehearted insistence upon the inhumanity of God. Through the bitter clamor of these journals—the outrageous but telling satires on bourgeois Christianity, the complaints about priests and professors and Bishop Mynster, the searching diagnoses of Luther and Schopenhauer, the not always tender deprecations of women, the copious self-dramatization, the tedious extollation of "the individual," the slashing dismissals of "knavish religiosity," "scoundrelly posterity," and the "increasing mass of drivel which is called science"—there sounds a note that attains a crescendo in the last pages: Christianity is torture, and God a torturer:

> In Christianity God is spirit—and therefore so immensely severe, from love: for he longs for spirit from man. . . . God is never so severe with those he loves in the Old Testament as he is with the apostles, for example, whose life was sheer suffering and then a martyr's death. . . . In the Old Testament, when the prophet is in need, God always finds a way out—but as for the apostle . . . there is no talk of unexpected help which shall bring him his strictest necessities; no, God just leaves him in the lurch, leaves him to die of hunger and thirst—it can be as severe as that.

If I were a pagan and had to speak Greek, I should say that God has arranged everything for his own entertainment; he amuses himself like a man who puts a piece of bacon in a mousetrap and watches all the tricks of the mice to get the bacon out without being gripped —so God amuses himself at the leaps and springs and contortions of these millions of men to get hold of the truth without suffering.

. . . What torture! If a man is really to be the instrument of God, for the infinite will that God is, then God must first take all his will from him. What a fearful operation! And it is natural that no one knows how to examine so painfully as one who is omniscient and omnipotent. Certainly with other forms of torture there are doctors present to estimate how long the tortured man can hold out without losing his life. Yet mistakes can happen, and the tortured man can die before their eyes. This never happens with one who is omniscient.

To be a Christian is the most terrible of all torments, it is—and it must be—to have one's hell here on earth. . . . One shudders to read what an animal must suffer which is used for vivisection; yet this is only a fugitive image of the suffering involved in being a Christian—in being kept alive in the state of death.

The vision is so terrible that Kierkegaard almost relents; "What I write is from a Christian standpoint so true, so true, and from a Christian standpoint this is how I must write. And yet I can say that what I write here tortures me to produce . . . it is repugnant to me." Again: "Ah, it is with sorrow that I write this. In melancholy sympathy, though myself unhappy, I loved men and the mass of men. Their bestial conduct toward me compelled me, in order to endure it, to have more and more to do with God."

And what is the essence of God's nature, that makes "having to do" with Him so painful? Majesty:

Suffering, that there must be suffering, is connected with the majesty of God. His majesty is so infinite that it can be characterized or expressed only by a paradox; it is the paradox of the majesty which is bound to make the beloved unhappy. . . . Suffering depends on the fact that God and man are qualitatively different, and that the clash of time and eternity in time is bound to cause suffering.

A little later, the formula is given a personal turn:

O infinite majesty, even if you were not love, even if you were cold in your infinite majesty I could not cease to love you, I need something majestic to love. . . . There was and there is a need of majesty in my soul, of a majesty I can never tire of worshipping.

Yet elsewhere this majesty acquires human attributes, even weaknesses. God knows sorrow. "Alas, the more I think about it the more I come to imagine God as sitting in sorrow, for he most of all knows what sorrow is." God loves, out of need. "It is God's passion to love and to be loved, almost—infinite love!—as though he himself were bound in this passion, so that he cannot cease to love, almost as though it were a weakness. . . ." And: "I know that in love you suffer with me, more than I, infinite Love—even if you cannot change."

The paragraph preceding this last quotation is revealing:

> If my contemporaries could understand how I suffer, how Providence, if I may dare to say so, maltreats me, I am certain that they would be so profoundly moved that in human sympathy they would make an attempt (as sometimes happens with a child which is being maltreated by its parents) to wrest me free from Providence.

The hypothetical cruel parents return in another metaphor:

> As the child of a tight-rope walker is from his earliest years made supple in his back and in every muscle so that, after daily practice, he is sheer suppleness and can carry out every movement, absolutely every movement, in the most excruciating positions, yet always easily and smiling: so with prayer to the absolute majesty.

And in a third image, world history is likened to "the uproar and hubbub which children make in their playroom, instead of sitting still and reading their books (as their parents would like)." With these similes, we touch a central nerve of Kierkegaard's thought—the identification of God with his father, whom he both loved and hated, who treated him cruelly and who loved him.

Much is known of Kierkegaard's relation with his father, but more is mysterious. Kierkegaard wrote in his journals: "Perhaps I could recount the tragedy of my childhood, the fearful secret explanation of religion, suggesting an apprehensive presentiment which my imagination elaborated, my offence at religion—I could recount it in a novel entitled *The Enigmatical Family*." And another entry reads:

It is terrible whenever for a single instant I come to think of the dark background of my life, from the very earliest time. The anxious dread with which my father filled my soul, his own frightful melancholy, the many things which I cannot record—I got such a dread of Christianity, and yet I felt myself so strongly drawn to it.

A childhood classmate later wrote, "To the rest of us who led a genuinely boyish life S.K. was a stranger and an object of compassion, especially on account of his dress. . . . This [his costume, which resembled the costume of charity schools] procured him the nickname of Choirboy, which alternated with Søren Sock, in allusion to his father's previous business as hosier. S.K. was regarded by us all as one whose home was wrapped in a mysterious half-darkness of severity and oddity." And in his autobiographical *The Point of View for My Work as an Author*, Kierkegaard wrote, "As a child I was strictly and austerely brought up in Christianity; humanly speaking, crazily brought up. A child crazily travestied as a melancholy old man. Terrible!"

Yet the boy's relation to his father was also intimate and admiring. One of Kierkegaard's pseudonyms, Johannes Climacus, reminisces:

His father was a very severe man, apparently dry and prosaic, but under this rough coat he concealed a glowing imagination which even old age could not quench. When Johannes occasionally asked of him permission to go out, he generally refused to give it, though once in a while he proposed instead that Johannes should take his hand and walk back and forth in the room. . . . While they went back and forth in the room the father described all that they saw; they greeted passersby, carriages rattled past them and drowned the father's voice; the cake-woman's goodies were more enticing than ever. He described so accurately, so vividly, so explicitly even to the least details, everything that was known to Johannes and so fully and perspicuously what was unknown to him, that after half an hour of such a walk with his father he was as much overwhelmed and fatigued as if he had been a whole day out of doors. . . . To Johannes it seemed as if the world were coming into existence during the conversation, *as if the father were our Lord and he were his favorite*, who was allowed to interpose his foolish conceits as merrily as he would; for he was never repulsed, the father was never put out, he agreed to everything.

I have abbreviated this often quoted passage and italicized a signal clause. By the same light, Kierkegaard did not expect to live past the age of thirty-three (the age of Christ) and *did* expect his father, though fifty-seven years older, to outlive him (to be immortal). In fact, his father lived to the patriarchal age of eighty-two and Kierkegaard died when he was only forty-two, so the premonition was in spirit correct. There is no doubt that his father fearfully dominated the household. Incredibly, in all of Kierkegaard's writings there is not one mention of his mother. And an age that has been able to peruse Kafka's diaries need not be reminded that, severity aside, the *competence*, the very wonderfulness of a father can be felt as a crushing tyranny. "It is a fearful thing," Kierkegaard wrote, "to fall into the hands of the living God."

To all this add a precocious compassion. In his journals Kierkegaard writes of the perils of religious education:

> The most dangerous case is not when the father is a free thinker, and not even when he is a hypocrite. No, the danger is when he is a pious and God-fearing man, when the child is inwardly and deeply convinced of it, and yet in spite of all this observes that a profound unrest is deeply hidden in his soul, so that not even piety and the fear of God can bestow peace. The danger lies just here, that the child in this relationship is almost compelled to draw a conclusion about God, that after all God is not infinite love.

It does not seem to me contradictory to posit a father who appears as both God and a victim of God. Such a paradox, after all, is fundamental to Christian theology, and Kierkegaard's imagination often returns to the forsaken Christ's outcry on the Cross. Duplicity was the very engine of Kierkegaard's thought, a habit he elevated to a metaphysical principle—the principle of "indirect communication," which he found both in Socrates' intellectual midwifery and in God's decision to embody Himself in a scorned and mocked sufferer. In all Kierkegaard's production, nothing is more powerful, more beautiful and typical, than the sweeping Prelude to *Fear and Trembling*, wherein the story of Abraham and Isaac is pursued through a sequence of differing versions. All portray, in similar language, Abraham and Isaac rising in the morning, leaving Sarah, and travelling to Mount Moriah, where God has told Abraham he must sacrifice his son. In the first version, Abraham, whose face has shown sorrow and "fatherliness," turns away a moment,

> and when Isaac again saw Abraham's face it was changed, his glance was wild, his form was horror. He seized Isaac by the throat, threw him to the ground, and said, "Stupid boy, dost thou then suppose that I am thy father? I am an idolater. Dost thou suppose that this is God's bidding? No, it is my desire." Then, Isaac trembled and cried out in his terror. "O God in heaven; have compassion upon me. God of Abraham, have compassion upon me. If I have no father upon earth, be Thou my father!" But Abraham in a low voice said to himself, "O Lord in heaven, I thank Thee. After all it is better for him to believe that I am a monster, rather than that he should lose faith in Thee."

Here, in this shocking twist of a myth, that nerve is bared. Here, in this play of ironies and deceits carried out under the highest pressure of dread, we feel close to Kierkegaard's mysterious and searing experience of his father.

A specific revelation about his father troubled Kierkegaard's young manhood and was transmuted, or absorbed, into a gnawing guilt or uneasiness that he refers to in his journals as "the thorn in my flesh," which in turn seems to be synonymous with his singularity, his fate, as "the individual," to suffer a martyrdom not incomparable with Christ's. Some crucial confidence was imparted on his twenty-second birthday: "Then it was that the great earthquake occurred, the frightful upheaval which suddenly forced upon me a new infallible rule for interpreting the phenomena one and all. Then I surmised that my father's great age was not a divine blessing, but rather a curse. . . . Guilt must rest upon the whole family, a divine punishment must be impending over it." The exact nature of the "earthquake" is forever buried in the portentous secrecy Kierkegaard assigned it. Possibly the old man's confession had to do with sex. On the mere statistical records, Michael Kierkegaard seduced his housekeeper in the year of mourning his first wife, married the woman when she was five months pregnant, and fathered upon her a total of seven children, the last, Søren Aabye, being born when the parents, if not as ancient as Abraham and Sarah, were of an age when, in Lowrie's delicate phrase, "no such blessing was expected." Kierkegaard frequently speaks of his own existence as a "mistake," and in the journals of *The Last Years* this sense of himself has spread to include all humanity: "This whole human existence, dating from the Fall, and which we men are so puffed up about as a devilish *tour de force* . . . is merely the consequence of a false step." Of a hypothetical son he writes:

> Concerning himself he learns that he was conceived in sin, born in transgression—that his existence is therefore a crime, that therefore his father, in giving him life, has done something which is as far as possible from being well-pleasing to God.

His vivid, even sensual awareness of Original Sin, of life itself as a crime, may be traceable to an embarrassment he felt about being himself living proof of an elderly couple's concupiscence. He ranged from the heights of conceit to abysmal depths of shame; near the end of his life, he suffered a stroke while visiting friends and, falling helpless to the floor, rejected the attempts to lift him up by saying, "Oh, leave it [his body] until the maid clears it away in the morning." In the last journals, he thanks God "that no living being owes existence to me," urges celibacy upon all Christians, faces cheerfully the consequence that the race would die out, and asserts that "human egoism is concentrated in the sexual relation, the propagation of the species, the giving of life."

Or the "earthquake" may have been learning that his father, as a eleven-year-old boy, had cursed God. An entry in the journals of 1846 reads:

> How terrible about the man who once as a little boy, while herding the flocks on the heaths of Jutland, suffering greatly, in hunger and in want, stood upon a hill and cursed God—and the man was unable to forget it even when he was eighty-two years old.

The first editor of Kierkegaard's papers, Barfod, showed this passage to Bishop Peter Kierkegaard, the one surviving sibling, who confirmed that this was indeed his father, and that, since shortly thereafter the shepherd boy was adopted by an uncle and set on the road to prosperity, he regarded this prosperity as an inverted curse, as God's vengeance for, to quote Peter, "the sin against the

Holy Ghost which never can be forgiven." It seems likely that this, and not a sexual confession, is the matter of the "earthquake." And it seems to me, furthermore, that Kierkegaard's attack upon Christendom is a repetition of his father's curse—an attack, ostensibly directed against the Danish Protestant Church, upon God Himself, on behalf of the father who had suffered, and yet also against this same father, who had made his son suffer and bound him to Christian belief.

In 1849, Kierkegaard wrote in his journals, under the heading *Something about myself which must always be remembered:* "If, with my imagination, and with my passions, etc., I had been in any ordinary human sense a man, then I should certainly have forgotten Christianity entirely. But I am bound in agonizing misery, like a bird whose wings have been clipped, yet retaining the power of my mind undiminished, and its undoubtedly exceptional powers." And the pamphlets comprising *The Attack* have been, in every language except English, the first things by Kierkegaard to be translated, as anti-clerical, anti-Christian literature. The "Christendom" Kierkegaard denounced was popularly taken to be synonymous with Christianity, and perhaps it was. It is hard to account otherwise for the strange qualities of the attack as found in *The Instant* and in these journals. Are specific abuses, as in Luther's attack upon the Papal church, named? No: "Luther nailed up niney-five theses on the church door; that was a fight about doctrine. Nowadays one might publish one single thesis in the papers: 'Christianity does not exist;' and offer to dispute with all parsons and dons." This is from a journal of 1851; by 1854, Kierkegaard had developed a piercing critique of Luther, stated wittily as:

> Luther suffered extremely from an anxious conscience, he needed treatment. Very well: but is that a reason for completely transforming Christianity into a matter of calming anxious consciences?

Kierkegaard does not want consciences to be calmed, he wants them to be exacerbated by the truth about Christianity. "My task is to put a halt to a lying diffusion of Christianity, and to help it to shake off a mass of nominal Christians." And what is the truth about Christianity?

The ideal means hatred of man. What man naturally loves is finitude. To face him with the ideal is the most dreadful torture . . . it kills in him, in the most painful way, everything in which he really finds his life, in the most painful way it shows him his own wretchedness, it keeps him in sleepless unrest, whereas finitude lulls him into enjoyment. That is why Christianity is called, and is, hatred of man.

Now, is such advocacy not a hidden prosecution? It may be argued that harsh words were a needed corrective to an existing complacency and that the New Testament itself is sternly world-denying. But I notice that, just as liberal apologists are troubled to explain away the "hard" sayings of Jesus, Kierkegaard is embarrassed by the Gospels' softer moments—the genial miracle at the wedding of Cana, the sufferance of little children, the promise to the thief on the cross. Kierkegaard says, "Men live their life in the strength of the assurance that of such as children is the kingdom of God, and in death they look for consolation to the image of the thief. That is the whole of their Christianity, and, characteristically enough, it is a mixture of childishness and crime." Surely here he is attacking something essential to Biblical teaching—the forgivingness that balances majesty. He seems impatient with divine mercy, much as a true revolutionary despises the philanthropies whereby misery is abated and revolution delayed. The "Christendom" he attacks has strangely little substance, apart from the person of Bishop Mynster, his father's pastor, who is criticized only for his urbanity and eloquence and his refusal to confess that "what he represented was not really Christianity but a milder form of it." Indeed, the whole attack is an invitation to the Church to commit suicide: "Yes, truly, suicide, and yet an action well-pleasing to God." Any specific reform—a revival of monasteries, an abolition of "livings"—he explicitly disavows. The one concrete result he expects from his attack is his own imprisonment and death. Though the Church's functionaries barely troubled to respond even in writing, he did die. He suffered his fatal stroke while returning from the bank with the last scrap of his fortune. He had nowhere further to go, and his death, whose causes eluded diagnosis, seems willed.

In the hospital, he told his only intimate friend, the pastor Emil Boesen, "The doctors do not understand my illness; it is psychic, and they want to treat it in the ordinary medical way." His conversations with Boesen, a kind of continuation of the journals (printed as such by Dru), have a relaxed sweetness; his terrible "task" is done, and he is happy that so much in his life has "come out right" and is melancholy that he cannot share his happiness with everyone. He refuses to put flowers sent him into water: "it is the fate of flowers to blossom, smell, and die." Of *The Instant,* whose tenth number lay unpublished on his desk, he said, "You must remember that I have seen everything from the inmost center of Christianity, it is all very poor and clumsy. . . . I only said it to be rid of evil, and so to reach an Alleluia! Alleluia! Alleluia!" This "Alleluia," it may be, could be reached only through a scandal in which, alone like a shepherd boy on the Jutland heath, Kierkegaard execrated God. At any rate, with Kierkegaard, as with Proust, we feel writing as a demon—the one way to set a bent life straight.

Kierkegaard would hardly be pleased to know that more than any other thinker of the 19th century—not excluding Newman and Dostoevsky—he has made Christianity intellectually possible for the 20th. Not that the "millions of men falling away from Christianity" that he foresaw and desired has not occurred. But, by giving metaphysical dignity to "the subjective," by showing faith to be not an intellectual development but a movement of the will, by holding out for existential duality against the tide of all the monisms, materialist or mystical or political, that would absorb the individual consciousness, Kierkegaard has given Christianity new life, a handhold, the "Archimedean point." From Jaspers and Barth, Unamuno and Marcel, Heidegger and Sartre, his thought has filtered down through the seminaries to the laity. He has become, as he angrily predicted, the property of those men "more abominable and gruesome than the cannibals," professors and clergymen, and he is used, in the form of a few phrases or a bolder style, to prop up the feeble, always tottering faith of contemporary "Christians." He has become an instrument in the conspiracy to "make a fool of God." Those who read him eat the aesthetic coating and leave the religious pill, and "neo-Orthodox" Protestantism, his direct beneficiary, has accepted the antinomianism and ignored the savage austerity, the scornful authoritarianism. Yet Kierkegaard himself, this two-tined Fork with his trouser legs of unequal length, this man in love with duplicity and irony and all double-edged things, lived luxuriously to the last and is nowhere quite free of sophism and vanity. (His sermons, for example, so symphonic and ardent, somehow belong with the memorable sermons of fiction, like those of Father Mapple in *Moby Dick* and of Père Paneloux in *The Plague*.) In the journal of 1849 he reminded himself, "It must never be forgotten that Christ also succored temporal and worldly needs. One can also, untruly, make Christ so spiritual that he becomes sheer cruelty." If this is what Kierkegaard seemed to do in the end, he also remembered that infinite majesty infinitely relents. Late in *The Last Years* we find this surprising entry: "For with such clarity as I have, I must say I am not a Christian. For the situation as I see it is that in spite of the abyss of nonsense in which we are caught, we shall all alike be saved."

RELIGIOUS NOTES

On the Boundary, by Paul Tillich. 104 pp. Scribners, 1966.
The Future of Religions, by Paul Tillich. 94 pp. Harper & Row, 1966.

These two small posthumous volumes cast a sympathetic backward light upon a somewhat puzzling figure. Tillich, though possessed of a personal radiance that penetrated even the speckled fog of a television interview, seemed in his writing pervasively ambiguous and tortuously euphemistic. In *On the Boundary*, a terse autobiographical sketch, he declares that for all of his long life he considered his proper place to be on both sides of the fence. Theologian and philosopher, conservative and socialist, German and American, he felt himself a mediator in a world of fragmentation, and entertained atheism in the church parlor. It took an exceptional serenity to do this: "The man who stands on many boundaries experiences the unrest, insecurity, and inner limitation of existence in many forms." His tolerance of uncertainty and of contradiction was perhaps specifically Lutheran, and Tillich may have been the first Lutheran voice in American intellectual history. Lutheranism (existing throughout the United States in geographical enclaves whose atmosphere, oppressive and stagnant and idyllic, can be felt in the novels of Conrad Richter) is itemized by Tillich as "a consciousness of the 'corruption' of existence, a repudiation of every kind of social Utopia (including the metaphysics of progressivism), an awareness of the irrational and demonic nature of existence, an appreciation of the mystical element in religion, and a rejection of Puritanical legalism in private and corporal life." In *The Future of Religions*, which contains, amid much eulogistic padding, four short addresses, he more specifically relates Utopianism and the concept of progress to the Calvinism that has informed American ideals. On the other hand, Lutheranism, with Greek Orthodoxy, is a church of "withdrawal from history." One wonders, considering the exhaustion of the frontier, where Puritanism had point, whether the future of Christianity in America does not lie with some such withdrawal. History is proving to elude apotheosis, and Tillich's remarkable rapport with young students appears prophetic of the mystical, latitudinarian, and rather Asiatic new wave of American religious expression.

MY TRAVEL DIARY: 1936, by Paul Tillich, edited and with an introduction by Jerald C. Brauer, translated from the German by Maria Pelikan. 192 pp. Harper & Row, 1970.

The late Professor Tillich, having fled Nazi Germany in 1933, returned to Europe three years later for a round of lectures and conferences, and he mailed his wife installments of the diary he kept from April to September. Now this affectionate record has been published, and while it is neither very amusing nor very enlightening, it is something of both. Tillich's own generous and receptive nature shines through his notation of countless conversations, audiences, bottles of wine, beautiful vistas, nights of good or less good sleep. In Paris he visits night clubs featuring "very nude" girls; in Switzerland he climbs glaciers. In Scotland he is "seated at the Dean's right, next to Patterson, an old systematic theologian"; in Holland he marvels at the Rembrandts. At all stops he counsels and consoles friends he may never see again—expatriated and polarized citizens of a Europe that was on the edge of the abyss and knew it, yet was still the immemorial Europe of good food, mountain views, well-mannered prostitutes, hikes, ideas, and rain showers that enliven rather than ruin an afternoon. Though Tillich visits Barth and gossips about Heidegger, he rarely reads a book or goes to church. In a way, this is everybody's summer abroad, right down to the well-evoked days at sea, except that Hitler's handwriting is now no longer a topic of analysis, and trips to Russia are not the latest thing among the intelligentsia. This charming memento of a vanished man and era has been indifferently served by its publishers: typographical errors abound, and where contemporary photographs of the scenery would have helped, there are quite superfluous pen-and-ink scribbles (by Alfonso Ossorio) of nothing in particular.

DELIVERANCE TO THE CAPTIVES, by Karl Barth, translated from the German by Marguerite Wieser. 160 pp. Harper, 1961.

This collection of recent sermons displays the grave, generous, and—often—genial humanity of "anti-humanist" theology's living Olympian. Seekers of novelty and subtlety in philosophical accommodation should seek elsewhere; it has been Barth's work to turn the Christian field with a resharpened plow, rather than to look for new pastures or draw new boundaries. The force of these sermons lies in that—minus a few topical references and with a few adjustments of emphasis—they might have been preached any time in the last two millennia, and, but for their exceptional compactness and pertinence of expression, by a conservative clergyman anywhere. Perhaps because they were for the most part delivered to inmates of the prison in Basel, their dominant note— an unusual one in contemporary Christian literature—is of hope, of joy in the Lord, of an ardor that can assert, concerning faith, that "no human being has ever prayed for this in vain."

HOW I CHANGED MY MIND, by Karl Barth, with an introduction and epilogue by John D. Godsey. 96 pp. John Knox Press, 1966.

A bracing demi-autobiography, essentially composed of three self-descriptive articles Barth wrote for the *Christian Century* in 1938, 1948, and 1958 under the heading "How I Changed My

Mind." Actually, in the three decades considered, Barth changed his mind rather little, holding fast to his central vision of God's otherness through all political and theological storms. The dominant impression these pages leave is of Barth's heroic stubbornness, the reasoned yet pugnacious refusal to let others think for him: when political relativism was fashionable, he implacably opposed Hitler, and when political absolutism prevailed, he took a mediating attitude toward Communism. Though his theology, a virtual reinvention of Christian orthodoxy, must be described as conservative, it has been viewed by himself as a "restless" activity, a "process" in which he has been concerned "not to forfeit my freedom." What also emerges from these essays, amplified by the editor's description of a visit to Barth in 1965 and the theologian's concluding letter, is an account of the aging process as it has been experienced, with rare good grace, by a man of firm health, normal worldliness, and enviable sense of vocation.

DISCOURSE ON THINKING, by Martin Heidegger, translated from the German by John M. Anderson and E. Hans Freund. 93 pp. Harper & Row, 1966.

A small book, of which nearly half is occupied by a not very helpful introduction. The other half consists of a "Memorial Address" delivered by Heidegger in honor of the German composer Conradin Kreutzer, and a trialogue between a scientist, a scholar, and a teacher entitled "Conversation on a Country Path About Thinking." The address, with a certain donnish orotundity, lucidly sets forth the propositions that there are two kinds of thinking—calculative and meditative—and that amid the technological triumphs of calculative thinking man must survive as a meditative being. This he can do by saying both yes and no to technology, the yes being a "releasement toward things" and the no a continuing "openness to the mystery." These concepts are developed into total obscurity by the "Conversation," whose English version abounds in possibly precise but gritty equivalents like "re-present," "autochthonic," and "that-which-regions." Meditative thinking is explained as "the coming-into-the-nearness of distance," and our human position as a kind of holy "waiting"— "The relation to that-which-regions is waiting." And "That-which-regions [*die Gegnet* in German] is an abiding expanse which, gathering all, opens itself, so that in it openness is halted and held, letting everything merge in its own resting." What emerges is a humanism tied to a mysticism shorn of theology; the final coalescence of meaning is a metaphor of the night that, without seam or thread, binds the distant stars together in apparent nearness. The rarefied poetry of the discourse is made eerie by our knowledge that it was based on a conversation that really occurred, within Germany, in 1944–1945, when the anvils of Hitler's hell were beating loudest.

THE HEART PREPARED: GRACE AND CONVERSION IN PURITAN SPIRITUAL LIFE, by Norman Pettit. 252 pp. Yale, 1966.

This finely written and beautifully printed study of post-Reformation theological niceties doubles as an analysis of the infant American psyche. Zwingli and Calvin held that man in his utter depravity "could neither anticipate salvation nor look to the inner self for signs of regeneration." The English founders of Puritanism tentatively qualified the severity of predestinarian doctrine with suggestions that the heart, however unworthy, might predispose or prepare itself for the invasion of saving grace. In the theocratic communities of New England, a proclaimed inner experience of conversion became a criterion for church membership, and the "grappling with the heart" developed, notably in the discourses of Thomas Hooker, of Hartford, into a veritable poetics of introspection. Preparationism, never without its opponents, eventually succumbed to a reasserted Calvinism and to the practical problems of church enrollment, but its experiential emphasis remains a feature of American religious revivals and perhaps accounts for a Pelagian bias in our spiritual heritage. Dr. Pettit, though he traces the image of the prepared heart down to its final diffusion in Emerson, leaves to implication the present relevance of his thesis. His approach is strikingly concrete and, dealing with quibbles that might seem quaint, convincingly serious. In a prose whose clarity belies the volumes of cobwebbed tracts he has suffered through, he renders penumbral nuances of theology distinct, gives personality to a dozen divines, and somewhat sweetens our impression of the Puritan tenets.

DOSTOEVSKY

A Raw Something

THE ADOLESCENT, by Fyodor Dostoevsky, translated by Andrew R. MacAndrew. 585 pp. Doubleday, 1971.

Why a new translation? And, if a new translation, why of this novel? Written between *The Possessed* and *The Brothers Karamazov*, *The Adolescent* (entitled *A Raw Youth* in the 1916 translation by Constance Garnett) possesses the greatness of neither. The novel, though it bears many marks of Dostoevsky's devotion, and definitively enunciates some of the themes dearest to him, has that penetrating badness that casts doubt over even the peaks of an author's accomplishment—as, say, *Across the River and into the Trees* drained magic from *all* of Hemingway's headwaiters and undermined forever the consolations of café stoicism. In *The Adolescent* the frequent feverishness of Dostoevsky's characters appears compulsory and their willful, self-careless perversity seems merely automatic, an author's trick he employs in scene after scene. For once, the elements of Dostoevsky's fictional universe— the fantastically compressed action, the stunning tirades, the melodramatic welter of coincidences and encounters and incriminating documents and postponed revelations—fail to fuse into a fiery whole. Rather, a string of firecrackers goes off, some louder than others, and some so damply we turn back the pages to catch what we missed. Four novels, Dostoevsky once told his wife, fight for attention within the covers of this one; his original instinct, Mr. MacAndrew tells us in his lengthy and gossipy introduction, was to entitle the book "Disorder."

: 129 :

The hero is a young bastard, Arkady Dolgoruky. Unlike some of Dostoevsky's first-person narrators, Arkady does not conveniently vanish when the action becomes heated, but wears out several pairs of boots rushing around St. Petersburg to keep eavesdropping appointments and wears out our ears with expostulations over the difficulties of maintaining a narrative so tangled. His voice and psyche, however, are the strongest thing in the novel: a "raw youth's" passion for exploration and posturing and humiliation have rarely been more indulgently dramatized. Arkady aside, the characters seem inferior copies of characters met in the other novels—Versilov a more trivial Stavrogin, Katarina a feeble sister of *The Idiot's* Nastasia, Makar a preliminary study for Father Zosima. The plot, on a circumstantial level, absurdly revolves around a slightly embarrassing letter that rides out six hundred pages in Arkady's coat pocket; on a thematic level, it gropes toward secrets of parenthood and kinship that are firmly seized in the next novel, *The Brothers Karamazov.*

Why this novel? Perhaps, though Mr. MacAndrew does not say so, he felt it to be especially appropriate to America's present condition of self-doubt and generational estrangement. Here is the Russia of the 1870's:

> All the better people are crazy . . . only the mediocrities, the unimaginative bystanders, are having a great time. . . . Selfishness displaces the old unifying principle, and the whole system breaks up into a multitude of individuals, each with a full set of civil rights. . . . whole batches of our best people are tearing themselves away from it and lightheartedly joining the roving packs of the disorderly and the envious.

Sound familiar? Yes, but I doubt that a majority of Americans will embrace Dostoevsky's solution: "any order as long as it is our native one."

And why a new translation? Presumably because the old one, by the tireless Mrs. Garnett, was judged to be improvable. I have compared passages of Garnett vs. MacAndrew, and read the last third of the novel in alternate chapters from each; and my impression is that more has been lost than has been gained. Mr. MacAndrew's modern idiom does very well with the jerks and halts of interior monologue, and occasionally captures a precision where Mrs. Garnett either flunked the Russian or held to a Victorian middle style—"as though pouring his words through a funnel" betters "dropping out his words one by one"; "crush him until there's only a wet spot left behind" outcruels "pound him to a jelly." But more often the precision is on Garnett's side: "worldwide compassion for all" pales to "universal concern"; "she was now evil" simpers as "she was not a nice person." MacAndrew drops the patronymics, which may save some confusion but sacrifices a peculiar warmth of Russian novels, and when terms of endearment are employed he is almost helpless. Where Garnett's phrasing is moving, his is often blank tin: "They rejoiced, like birds, did not feel their ruin, and their voices were like little bells" becomes in MacAndrew's version, "They're happy like little birds and their voices sound like jingle bells." And surprisingly, the modern translator shows less feel for the philosophic checkpoints of the novel: the key concept that Garnett imaginatively renders as "seemliness" is blandly presented by MacAndrew as "beauty," in quotation marks. The most famous sentence in *A Raw Youth*—

> It always has been a mystery, and I have marvelled a thousand times at that faculty in man (and in the Russian, I believe, more especially) of cherishing in his soul his loftiest ideal side by side with the most abject baseness, and all quite sincerely—

comes out all muddled and adverbial in MacAndrew's version—

> Yes, it has always been a mystery to me and thousands of times I've stopped and marveled at man's capacity (especially a Russian's, I believe) to cherish in himself some infinitely lofty ideal alongside something unspeakably base, and all this quite openly.

Even the title feels wrong. MacAndrew has Arkady as nineteen, Garnett as twenty years old: either way, he is too old to be an "adolescent." In general, two translators being more or less competent, the one closer in time to the original is apt to be better, more instinctively sharing the author's universe. Manners and moral concerns become distant and take language with them. The characters in the Garnett translation behave bizarrely, but as foreigners do. In MacAndrew's translation they are bizarre like figures in a dream.

Polina and Aleksei and Anna and Losnitsky

THE GAMBLER, by Fyodor Dostoevski, with Polina Suslova's Dairy, translated by Victor Terras. 366 pp. University of Chicago Press, 1972.

The University of Chicago Press, which has issued, under the editorship of Edward Wasiolek, Dostoevsky's notebooks for his five major novels, has extended this valuable series with a new, complexly augmented translation of the short novel *The Gambler*. The augmentations include: letters from Dostoevsky during the hectic period of his life when he was obsessed by gambling, debts, his dying wife, his dying brother, and Polina Suslova; the diary of this same Polina Suslova, who is described by the normally unemphatic *Encyclopaedia Britannica* as a "young woman of sensual, proud, and 'demoniac' character" and who is often cited by critics as a prototype for the perverse and taunting Dostoevsky heroines; and a short story by her about a love affair between "Losnitsky" and "Anna." This bundle of interrelated materials is intelligently edited and fluently translated, though I blinked at the exclamation "Wow!!!"—the Garnett translation has "What!!!"— and regretted that the proofreaders allowed one doubled slug to slip through. And I would have been grateful for a little factual background to Polina's diary, "published here in English for the first time." Why does it begin and end so conveniently and abruptly, August 19, 1863, to November 6, 1865, in effect bracketing the European phase of her affair with Dostoevsky? Did she keep a diary only then? And the chronology of this affair is not set forward as clearly as it is in, say, Avrahm Yarmolinsky's biography.

Polina and Dostoevsky probably met, in Petersburg, before September of 1861, when a story of hers appeared in *Vremya* (*Time*), which he edited. He was forty; she was little more than half his age. They became friends and, by the time she was twenty-three, lovers. He kept the secret from his wife and made no offer to divorce her, which may have offended Polina. However, she went to Paris in the spring of 1863 with the understanding that Dostoevsky would join her there and that they would travel together in Italy. A tangle of business generated by the government's suppression of his magazine held him in Petersburg until mid-August, and en route to his mistress he stopped off at Wiesbaden and Baden-Baden to gamble—first winning, then losing. By the time he arrived in Paris, Polina had been captivated, seduced, and abandoned by Salvador, a young South American medical student, who did not love her. Dostoevsky quickly adjusted to this new embarrassment and proposed that he and Polina travel to Italy anyway, not as lovers but "remaining like brother and sister." Thus uneasily attached, they toured for two months; then Dostoevsky returned to Petersburg, to write *Notes from the Underground* and most of *Crime and Punishment*. He did not see Polina until nearly two years later, in the summer of 1865, in Wiesbaden. Though his wife (Maria Dmitrievna Isaeva, a she-devil in her own right) had died in the interim, the affair did not prosper. In the few days he and Polina were together, Dostoevsky lost his last kopeck at roulette, and proved no luckier at love. The reunion didn't rate a line in her diary, though it did elicit from him two frantic but amiable letters to her, postage due, begging for a hundred and fifty gulden. Their final encounters occurred that fall and winter, in Petersburg, to which Polina returned in November; "he has been offering me his hand and his heart," Polina wrote, "and he only makes me angry doing so." She departed three months later. He finished *Crime and Punishment* and in October of 1866 dictated *The Gambler* to a competent, patient, and smitten young stenographer, Anna Snitkina. Dostoevsky married Anna in February of 1867, and that spring, in response to a letter from Polina, informed her of his marriage and added, *"Au revoir,* my good friend forever!" He and Polina did not—if one discounts a romantic story Dostoevsky's daughter tells of a "woman in black" who called on her father in the late seventies—meet again.

Reading through *The Gambler* and its attendant documents produces several unexpected impressions—chief among them that the lovers did not much like one another. Indeed, through the mist of egoistical preoccupations they hardly *saw* each other. Polina's story "The Stranger and Her Lover" betrays no awareness that she is representing, in fictional guise, one of the century's most fascinating spirits: "He started telling her various anecdotes and stories from his own life. These tales might have been, perhaps, of some interest to other people, but Anna saw little wit, and even less refinement, about them." Once Dostoevsky returns to Russia, he drops out of her diary with scarcely a thud, to be replaced by a titillating series of (at the least) flirtations. Mr. Wasiolek, in his introduction, protests: "one is dismayed to find that it is only our interest that lifts the image of Dostoevsky in her diary from the mesh of her prosaisms." The literary scholar, necessarily in love with greatness, cannot help scolding this mediocre little blue-stocking who, awarded the living Dostoevsky's love, betrayed him with a—Wasiolek's phrase—"trivial and insensitive medical student." Worse yet, in her fictional representation Dostoevsky appears "petty, boastful, and vulgar; his only redeeming features consist in his appreciation of her majestic character and beauty, in his astonishment at having possessed her, and in his contrition at having lost her." It is true that Polina's "The Stranger and Her Lover" is pitiably inept and self-promoting; the persistently "majestic" heroine obtusely refuses to perceive that her one ticket to significance, from the standpoint of posterity, lies with this repulsive, repelled lover, whose immortal genius is never for an instant permitted to wink through the vapors of her narcissism.

But does Polina fare better in Dostoevsky's version of their affair, in the minor masterpiece *The Gambler*? Not much. The pages dealing with "Polina Aleksandrovna" and her willful abuse of the infatuated "Aleksei Ivanovich" seem rather perfunctory, as though the author were blocking out an idea instead of giving flesh to inspiration. "I simply don't understand what I find in her. All right, she is beautiful, that she is; or it seems that she is. She drives other men out of their minds, too. She is tall and slender, though very slim. It seems as if one could tie her in a knot or bend her double. Her foot is long and narrow: tormenting. Exactly so: tormenting." The focus is on the torment, not on the woman. When she dares Aleksei to insult a passing baron, the vivacity of the incident depends on his zealous willingness to play the fool; he overreacts to her, as he overreacts to the seductive spin of the roulette wheel. Her moods, indeed, have for Aleksei the blind chanciness of roulette, and they offer him the same opportunity to humiliate and impoverish himself and thereby to demonstrate his exalted Russian disregard of material consequence. Aleksei, and the author, do not attempt to discover an inner logic of Polina's behavior, because a cruel arbitrariness is what satisfies them. So Polina remains too volatile to be grasped by our imaginations; "one could tie her in a knot or bend her double." In contrast, a secondary female character, the French adventuress Blanche, is quite solid:

> She is tall, with broad, strong shoulders. Her neck and bosom are magnificent. Her complexion is a swarthy yellow, her hair raven black, and she's got a great deal of it, enough for two coiffures. Her eyes are black with yellowish whites, her look insolent, her teeth very white, and her lips always painted. Her perfume smells of musk.

This musky creature develops amusingly when Aleksei, in a feverish trance of gambling clairvoyance, wins a hundred thousand gulden; Polina, though she is deeply in debt, in good Slavic style disdains the money ("The bankroll hit me painfully in the face and scattered all over the floor"), whereupon Blanche delightedly pounces upon the fortune: "First of all, *je veux cinquante mille francs.* You will give them to me in Frankfort. *Nous allons à Paris.* We'll be living together there *et je te ferai voir des étoiles en plein jour.*" In Paris, however, instead of making him see stars in daytime, Blanche deigns to tie his necktie for him every morning and shrewdly uses his money to set herself up as a respectable person: "So now I have established myself in decent style once and for all, and nobody is going to put me out, not for a long time, at least that's the way I've got it planned." To crown her new status, she weds a useless but ornamental general, a Russian aristocrat whose mother's fortune has been disastrously depreciated at the voracious tables of "Roulettenburg." Nevertheless, Blanche will make the best of the bargain: "To begin with, he's got his pension, and second, he'll live in a back room, where he'll be perfectly happy. I shall be '*madame la Générale.*' I'll belong to a nice social set. . . . Later I'll be a Russian landowner; *j'aurai un château, des moujiks, et puis j'aurai toujours mon million.*" In this interplay between brisk French avarice and the mystical wastefulness of the Russian character, *The Gambler* finds its best comedy and its serious point, anticipating the magnificent if deluded Slavophilism of the great novels to follow. Seen, caricaturally, as a hard-headed, hard-hearted European, with her mainspring plainly diagrammed, Blanche succeeds as a character and as a lovable woman. "Blanche, it ought to be said, was indeed a very nice, good-natured girl—in her own way, of course; I did not appreciate her enough in the beginning." Whereas Polina remains mysterious, and rather unlikable, to the end.

Polina Suslova's diary explains her more sympathetically than does either work of fiction. The grandiose, ill-coordinated self-assertiveness that her own story expresses and that Dostoevsky's portrays is here muted and disclosed as fruit of a central plight: she is a woman.

> Now I feel and see clearly that I cannot live, that I cannot find happiness in the enjoyment of love, because the caresses of men will remind me of my humiliations and my sufferings.

Clinically she observes herself in love with the indifferent Salvador, transcribing each of her pleading, unanswered letters; mordantly noting the fluctuations of her disease. "Any mention of S[alvador] gives me a terrifying, painful, and sweet feeling. However, what rubbish that whole thing was, everything that happened between me and Salv[ador]." Coolly, with her nearest approaches to irony, she admires her beloved's stratagems of withdrawal while she records her own maneuvers with Dostoevsky, moderated "so that he could neither cherish hope nor be quite without it." Out of her pain, she rises to chilling heights of detachment: "Today I have been thinking a great deal, and I almost felt glad that Salvador loves me so little; it makes me freer." Freedom is what she wants and cannot attain:

> I am now thinking about my return to Russia. Where shall I go, to whom? To my brother, to my father? I will never be as free as I would like to, and to what end should I suffer this dependency? What have I in common with these people? Carry out my ideas! Stupid.

She distrusts her ideas as she distrusts her loves. In the midst of a discussion with one of her intellectual, revolutionary boy friends, she flashes out, "Why go to see a woman? There isn't much interesting about me, is there? If you are looking for intellect and erudition, you won't come here to find them." In a shocking passage, she is abruptly, without anesthesia or psychological preparation, operated upon by a doctor:

> He said, as he was putting away his instruments, that after this operation I could have children if I got married. I said that I found no comfort in this. "Why so?" he asked; "all women want to have children." "Because I don't know how to bring them up," I said. The thoughts which occurred to me in connection with this conversation made me sad and caused me to shed tears, which I did not hold back.

Polina's feminism turns her diary outward from the stifling self-concern of her fiction; her jottings abound in sharp vignettes of the life about her as she moves from Baden-Baden to Turin and Genoa and Rome, and then to Paris and Zurich and back to Petersburg. She is unself-consciously sensitive, as the pain of Salvador ebbs, to other women: waitresses, flower girls, kept women, landladies, lady novelists, countesses. Only with another woman can she relax and spill her grief: "I could not restrain myself, but dropped on my knees before her [the Countess Salias] and began to sob aloud. She was frightened and wanted to get me a glass of water. 'No, no,' I said, 'forget it; I feel good this way.'" As she receives compassion from women, so she gives it; she offers to find work for a young woman who begs for two sous on the street, and she takes note of the inequities between a young student and his mistress:

> The relationship between the student and the lady is a touching one. At table, she lets him have the choice morsels; when she pours herself some wine, she always lets him have some first.

With the same eye, she observes her feelings, in the course of her entanglements, of humiliation, disgust, and uncertainty, and the contradictory behavior these feelings engender. As she tussles with an admirer called Robescourt:

> Then there began an incoherent conversation, interrupted by kisses. He was trembling all over, and he had such a happy, smiling face. I was also feeling happy, but kept breaking off our ardent embraces, with my pleas to be left alone. I kept pushing him away, then again passionately stretched out my arms to him.

Her awareness of her own ambivalence gives some episodes the sentence-by-sentence surprisingness of the best fiction:

> I stroked his hair and kissed his forehead. We talked all kinds of light-hearted nonsense, no worries or doubts of any sort entered my mind. Then I drove over to the C[ountess's]. He accompanied me. As we were sitting in the carriage hand in hand, I felt that his love was not a good one, if this can be called love. We got up. We parted in the park. Having walked a considerable distance I 'turned around and saw him standing there, following me with his eyes, but it was a farce, and an awkward one, in fact. He came the next night. There was no limit to his rapture and passion, and I surrendered to these moments without any anxiety or doubt.
> He wanted more than that, but I wouldn't let it happen, and he saw his mistake. I said that I was leaving.

Such a passage, in which the subtle female heart begs dignity and verity of a world that offers her only motherhood and "love," illuminates from within the self-punishing, lover-punishing perversity that Dostoevsky was content to represent as an inscrutable delirium.

Yet these two people, who saw into each other so imperfectly, so carelessly, were useful to one another. Dostoevsky's "turbulent and destructive affair with Polina Suslova," as Wasiolek calls it, coincides, he admits, with the writer's final awakening, the production of two works—*Notes from the Underground* in 1864, *Crime and Punishment* in 1866—that lift him into the empyrean of Western literature, into that small circle of writers who have appreciably enlarged Man's self-knowledge. In her story, Polina has Dostoevsky's surrogate say, "You have meant a lot to me. Your love descended upon me like a gift from God, against all hope and expectation, when I was weary and desperate. This young life at my side promised me so much and has already given me so much. It has resurrected my faith and what remained of my former strength." Was this a real speech, or her own sentimental fantasy? At any rate, the heroine responds with a startlingly dry inner observation: " 'You've really put it to good use,' thought Anna, but she said nothing." This mirrors a passage in *The Gambler*, as Aleksei meditates:

She doesn't bother to hide her aversion to me at all, this I can see. But she also does not conceal from me either the fact that she needs me for some purpose and that she is saving me for some future use.

What were these uses? In Dostoevsky's case, Polina—apart from her sexual benefactions in the short period before she shut them off—helped him debase himself toward that ground of suffering nullity from which he drew creative strength. Self-humiliation is one of the writer's most useful aids; it puts him in touch with the basal humanity that dignity, honors, flattery, and prosperity would estrange him from. It frees the artist of a respectable man's baggage. Biting the dirt, he recovers the taste of comedy and dread. Among contemporary practitioners, Norman Mailer most diligently, or at least most publicly, humiliates himself, but any serious writer needs keep some access to shame and abasement. Dostoevsky's need was acute; that Polina taunted him with her lovers, banished him from her bed, ignored his immense gifts, and urged him to play the fool should not be counted against her. In her unhappiness, she had an instinct for the necessary plunge. With odd generosity, she lent Dostoevsky money for his gambling, which became to his temperament a religious trance, a frightful prostration to the divine *nihil*, a kind of induced epilepsy, a giddy descent into himself, a defiance of worldly wisdom. In his begging letters to Polina he exults in his pennilessness, in the contempt expressed by his German servants, for "there is no greater crime in the eyes of a German than to have no money." But there *is*, he announces in the next letter, food beyond bread: "I continue to go without dinner, subsisting on my morning and evening tea for the third day now, and strangely enough, I am not very hungry at all." Eventually, such a regimen kills; Dostoevsky turns from Polina and takes shelter in marriage to a kind woman.

What of Polina, though; what was Dostoevsky's use to her? Not, I suspect, as an intellectual companion. In her diary, though she mentions a healing talk with him about "the emancipation of women," it is the feline Frenchman Jean-Baptiste Gaut who manages to speak her heart's language.

> Yesterday Gaut was here and I had a sentimental discussion with him: on love, marriage, etc. . . . "And love," he said, "passion, what

are they? Just a needless scandal. Surround yourself with sensible people, that's all."

I agreed with him.

Her soul finds flattery, too, in the company of her revolutionary countrymen—Herzen, Bakunin, Luginin. Dostoevsky by this time is not even a liberal. And before she begins this diary, she has committed herself to younger lovers. Dostoevsky tells her, "You fell in love with me by mistake." But there is evidence in her diary that he did, once, perform for her the lover's essential service: he shook her up. "I hear about F[yodor] M[ikhailovich]. I simply hate him. He made me suffer so much, when it was possible not to suffer." And "As I remember what happened two years ago, I begin to hate D[ostoevsky]. He was the first to kill my faith." Yet a proud otherworldliness is perhaps what they shared. Though he accuses her, when she first refuses to sleep with him, of a "utilitarian attitude," in the end, in the last entry in the diary, all passion useless, she talks teasingly, in a vein dear to his heart: "I said that I was going to become a holy woman, that I would walk through the Kremlin gardens in Moscow in my bare feet, telling people that I was having conversations with angels."

In fact, she married, in her middle years, a much younger man who was, strangely, an ardent devotee of Dostoevsky—the critic and *littérateur* V. V. Rozanov. He grew to hate her. Her later life has the flavor of *The Possessed*. After parting with Dostoevsky, she opened a village school that the authorities closed on the grounds that she bobbed her hair, never went to church, and had consorted abroad with revolutionaries. Six years after marrying Rozanov, she fled with a young lover; when this neo-Salvador spurned her, she denounced him to the police as a revolutionary. Her husband, whom she refused to divorce, likened her to Catherine de Medici and claimed to have found a perfect description of her in Dostoevsky's *The Insulted and Injured:* a woman who "looked upon everyone with impartial severity, like the abbess of a medieval convent," yet whose "sensuality was such that even the Marquis de Sade might have taken lessons from her. . . . In the very heat of voluptuousness she would suddenly laugh like one possessed." Dostoevsky wrote the description first; then he met Polina.

KNUT HAMSUN

"My Mind Was Without a Shadow"

HUNGER, by Knut Hamsun, translated from the Norwegian by Robert
Bly. 232 pp. Farrar, Straus & Giroux, 1967.

ON OVERGROWN PATHS, by Knut Hamsun, translated from the Norwegian by Carl L. Anderson. 176 pp. Paul S. Eriksson, 1967.

Coincidence, of the rather amiable kind it amused Knut Hamsun
to record, marks the simultaneous publication in the United States
of his first novel, *Hunger*, and his last book, a memoir entitled *On
Overgrown Paths*. *Hunger* was written by a starving young man in
the late 1880's and finally published, after serialization, in 1890,
when Hamsun was thirty-one; *On Overgrown Paths* was written
by a disgraced old man, held accused of treason, in the late 1940's
and was published in 1949, when Hamsun was ninety. Sixty years
and a career that included a Nobel Prize lie between them, yet the
books are similar, and are beautiful in the same way. They are
laconic, brutal, joyous, and not quite formless. Their literary
freshness flows from a positive human quality of, to give it a negative name, *defenselessness*. The "I" of both accounts has scorned
all systems, has formed no alliances, not even with a woman;
Hamsun's wife, though she shared his ordeal of ostracism and
harassment after the war, is virtually absent from the pages of *On
Overgrown Paths*. The ratty boarding houses of *Hunger* and the
various institutions of Hamsun's internment and, for that matter,
the hunter's hut occupied by the hero of his novel *Pan* are all
temporary shelters unregretfully shed by a spirit intent upon the
inner play of mood, a rapt yet detached spirit to whom pain is

merely one of the many winds that tug and shift the soul. Such lucidity approaches madness; in the absence of all other armor, a carapace of willful eccentricity must be grown. As a young transient in this country, Hamsun began to spit blood, and countered the diagnosis of terminal tuberculosis by riding on top of a locomotive from Minneapolis to New York, gulping fresh air all the way. The cure worked; but the same headlong stubbornness also led him to support the Nazis to the end, writing, upon Hitler's death, "He was a warrior, a warrior for mankind and a prophet of the gospel of justice for all nations." At the very outset of his career, the young Hamsun undertook a lecture tour attacking the living great writers of Norway, culminating in a verbal assault upon Ibsen while Ibsen sat glowering in the front row. Hamsun was always more enthusiastically admired in Germany and Slavic Europe than in Norway itself. Of American writers, he resembles Hemingway in his estrangement from the cultural establishment, in his proud follies, in his cauterization of prose style, in the impression of lightness and transparency his pessimism produces. By this analogy, *On Overgrown Paths* is like *A Moveable Feast*—a return, after troubled middle years spent pursuing "depth" with a puerile ideology, to an instinctive youthful allegiance to surfaces and moments.

Hunger, first published in English in 1899, is flattered by its new translation and by its two introductions. In one, the Yiddish writer I. B. Singer describes, with an emphatic generosity that may surprise younger literary generations, Hamsun's importance to his own: "European writers know that he is the father of the modern school of literature in his every aspect—his subjectiveness, his fragmentariness, his use of flashbacks, his lyricism. The whole modern school of fiction in the twentieth century stems from Hamsun, just as Russian literature in the nineteenth century 'came out of Gogol's greatcoat.' . . . Hamsun belonged to that select group of writers who not only interested a reader but virtually hypnotized him." The other introduction, by the translator, Robert Bly, sensitively points up the novel's paradoxical affirmation: "The hero of *Hunger* obeys the unconscious, and remains in hunger, despite suffering, until he has lived through what he must, or learned what he had to. What seems to us catastrophe, his spirit experiences as secret victory. His anarchic inability to support himself is experienced by his spirit as obedience." This first-person narration compresses into a few months the ten years (1879–1888) Hamsun spent in extreme poverty—sporadically relieved by laborers' jobs and immigrations to the United States—in Oslo, then called Kristiania. The nameless hero seeks to make his living by writing grandiose newspaper articles that, on the rare occasions when one is accepted, each earn him about three and a half dollars. The action moves from one five-kroner windfall to the next— an article is bought, a waistcoat is pawned, a grocery clerk errs in making change, an editor or acquaintance unexpectedly proffers a loan. Between these financial peaks are long, not unhappy troughs of emptiness:

> I kept on going through streets, rambling on with no purpose in mind at all. I stopped at a corner without needing to, turned and went up small alleys without having anything to do there. I just drifted on, floating in the joyful morning, rolling along without a care among other happy people. The air was clear and bright and my mind was without a shadow.

He is unable to organize his thoughts into any plan of enterprise or escape:

> I could not sit on a park bench by myself or put my foot down anywhere without being besieged by tiny and pointless events, absurd nonsense, which forced itself into my brain and scattered my powers to the four winds. A dog that shot past me, a yellow rose in someone's lapel, could set my thoughts in motion and obsess me for hours.

His external actions, his contacts with human society appear ludicrously antic and whimsical; he spouts frenzied nonsense to strangers on the street, he attracts and then rejects a prostitute called Ylayali, he prays to and then curses God, he refuses to beg from those who might succor him. When he is miraculously granted money, he squanders it on a rich meal he instantly vomits, or gives it away to an uncomprehending old cake peddler, or hurls a ten-kroner note in the face of a landlady who has ceased to expect anything. Though the physical humiliations of starvation are fascinatingly, grindingly detailed and the hero ostensibly yearns for a respectable, normal existence ("What a marvellous sensation to be sitting in a human house again and to hear a clock tick, and to talk with a spirited young girl instead of with myself!"), his self-realization lies with "the joyful insanity hunger was."

> My hair lay on my forehead wet and cold; I sat up on my elbow and looked down at the pillow: wet hair was also lying there in small tufts. My feet had swollen during the night inside my shoes; there was no pain, but I could barely move my toes.
>
> Toward late afternoon, when it was already beginning to be dusk, I got up and started puttering about the room. I tried walking with short, deliberate steps, careful to keep my balance and spare my feet as much as I could. I was not really suffering, and I didn't cry; on the whole I wasn't even sad; I was on the contrary wonderfully at peace—the thought that anything could be any different than it was never once crossed my mind.
>
> Finally I went out.

Finally he accepts, without premeditation, employment on a Russian freighter bound for Cadiz, and *Hunger* ends.

On Overgrown Paths—a journal Hamsun kept from his arrest, on May 26th of 1945, for treasonous activities during the German occupation, to his conviction and sentencing, on Midsummer Day of 1948—shows that his willingness to embrace isolation and deprivation had survived a life of success. The prose is still swift, fitful, immediate, innocently quick to feed on trifles: "These are trifles I write about, and trifles that I write. . . . All prisoners can only write about the eternally everyday occurrences and wait for their doom." But we are all prisoners. "We are all guilty. We are legion in our guilt." We are all doomed. "Now and then there is also some one of us who dies; it cannot be avoided, but it does not make much impression on us who remain. We follow the white coffin with our eyes, but when the hearse has driven away, we turn back to ourselves again." Hamsun is apathetic, tranquil. "I am weary of myself, have no wishes, no interests, no pleasures. Four or five senses in torpor and the sixth sense [he is deaf] snatched away. . . . I have attained the condition of certain Orientals: the necessary silence. I do not even talk to myself any more, having got out of that bad habit. . . . It is three years today since I was arrested.

And here I sit. It has not mattered to me, not bothered me. It has gone by as though merely one more event."

Of the several hospitals and nursing homes where he is incarcerated, only a psychiatric clinic shatters his calm of resignation. He is unable, in this memoir, to describe his months there except by allusive fragments: "Domination over a living being, regulations lacking mercy and tact, a psychology of blank spaces and labels, a whole science bristling defiance. Others can endure that sort of torture; that is no concern of mine. For my part, I could not. Which the psychiatrist ought perhaps to have understood. I was in good health; I was turned into jelly." Only in his letter to the attorney general about this experience does Hamsun rant, and seem to deserve the official judgment of him as a person with "permanently impaired faculties." His defense, when he presents it in the form of a courtroom statement, is coherent and almost adequate: his crimes were confined to a few newspaper articles urging Norwegians not to waste their lives in futile resistance; he constantly interceded with the Germans, even with Hitler himself, for the lives of Norwegian resistance fighters; he never belonged to the Nazi Party; he scorned fleeing his native land to Sweden or England; he was captivated by the promise that Norway would occupy a high place in Hitler's Germanic empire. In short, he stands defenseless, having based his actions upon the premise that Norway was defenseless. One reads this section of the book, and the prefatory description of Hamsun's trial, with some sympathy for the predicament of governments confronted with politically aberrant great writers, and with a feeling that the Norwegian government exacted less suffering from Hamsun than the United States government did from Ezra Pound, though both eventually settled upon a factitious mental incompetence.

As Bly points out, Hamsun, the son of a farmer, unschooled and for years indigent, was alienated from the bourgeois Europe that believed in progress and social reform. His years of hunger had left him with few expectations of human society; even his lovers, such as Glahn and Edvarda in *Pan*, are whimsical and cruel. He responds only, and is ever alert, to nature—the torrential, unanswerable nature within and beyond man. "Here are only cropped hills without a flower bed. The weather is biting, the wind almost always blows; but nearby are trees and woods with songbirds aloft and all sorts of creeping things on the ground. Oh, the world is beautiful here too, and we are to be very grateful for being in it. How rich the colors are here in the very rocks and the heather, how incomparable the forms in the bracken! And the taste of a piece of wall fern that I found is still good on the tongue." We find him unaged, in these valedictory pages, his appetites still undisciplined ("But completely contrary to my good intentions to ration my reading, I fell voraciously on Topsøe's book and devoured it in one gulp"), his conversations still quixotic—talking with a lady at a bus stop, the elderly Hamsun rips off his jacket and lays it in the snow for her to sit upon. He is still fond of outcasts and still able, in the depths, to attract women who wish to minister to him and with whom he grows impatient. Irascibility remains the sign of his independent genius. Of his poetry, he admits it lacks tenderness: "And it was not only tenderness that was lacking but all too many other things as well, the whole kit and caboodle." Lacking the kit and caboodle of civilized prejudice, he was able to confront experience direct, and to convey it magically. Toward the end of this book of therapeutic jottings, his thoughts revert to his confirmation and first communion:

> The pastor put something in my mouth, and afterwards let me sip from a cup. There were many people around who watched, but they restrained themselves and did not smile.
> Why remember that now? I have no earthly use for it and there is no wisdom in it. It uplifts me merely because I am happy and am teeming.

His memory wanders on, to his "first time in America," and the sails of his artistry fill, and he embarks upon a fine funny story without a moral—"merely a series of simple experiences from day to day on foreign soil and in a little arid prairie town." On the last page he remembers a woman's hands: "Those hands astonished me; they were yellow in complexion, but very soft and fine, never having been used to do anything with, never especially clean, but so beautiful to look at." The last two phrases tell the tale—"never especially clean, but so beautiful to look at." Hamsun speaks, still freshly, to us out of the human creatureliness that knows no accountability, no ideal systems. He has not dated; his prose remains tonic. Though convicted of collaboration with a tyrant, he is in literature a democrat, in the spirit of Proust's prescription:

> The great quality of true art is that it rediscovers, grasps, and reveals to us that reality far from which we live, from which we get farther and farther away as the conventional knowledge we substitute for it becomes thicker and more impermeable, the reality that we might die without having known and which is simply our life, real life, life finally discovered and clarified, consequently the only life that has been really lived—that life which in one sense is to be found at any time in all men as well as in artists.

Half-Mad and Maddening

MYSTERIES, by Knut Hamsun, translated from the Norwegian by Gerry Bothmer. 340 pp. Farrar, Straus & Giroux, 1971.

Perhaps too furiously, *Mysteries* struggles to express most of the themes that obsessed the young Hamsun. Like *Hunger*, it has a half-mad and maddening hero; as in *Pan*, the hero kills the dog his beloved cherishes; as in *Victoria*, he saves someone from drowning and regrets it. First published in Norway in 1892, two years later than *Hunger*, this novel lacks the weird jubilation of the masterpiece, and denies us empathy with the principal figure, Nagel, who, neither impoverished nor a writer, seems in his perversity merely a prankster. He arrives abruptly in a small Norwegian coastal town, creates an air of capricious wealth, defends the town scapegoat against the town bully, falls in love with the town beauty, proposes marriage to the local spinster, astounds and affronts several gatherings of the local bourgeoisie, sheds money, spouts words, and attempts suicide, not always unsuccessfully. The laconic formal control that usually imposes crystalline dignity on Hamsun's brutal vision here slackens; the plot abounds in false hares, unsolved mysteries, and editorial digressions. The atmosphere is heavy with emotional energy that expends itself, lightning-like, in mere display. The trolls of the subconscious infest not only the characters but the narration. Nevertheless, there are some remarkably harrowing moments, frequent streaks of brilliant fancy, and always a presiding vitality. Not many books published in 1892 could make us as uncomfortable as this one.

Love as a Standoff

VICTORIA, by Knut Hamsun, translated from the Norwegian by Oliver Stallybrass. 170 pp. Farrar, Straus & Giroux, 1969.

This short novel dates from 1898, when Hamsun, though no longer young as a man, was still rather young as a writer. Perhaps Hamsun always wrote a young man's books. He was one of modern literature's great fresheners; his loyalty to the elemental, his impatience with Ibsenian social moralizing, and his expressed determination to "grant the individual soul its due" contributed to the great liberation of artistic energy in the generation succeeding his and elicited gratitude from writers as different as H.G. Wells and Thomas Mann. To mention Mann, however, and to think of Mann's own naïveté, his disarmingly material curiosity and his blunt little inventories of furniture and weather, is to remind ourselves of a certain broad, balanced, *educated* humanism that cannot be included in the considerable list of Hamsun's virtues.

Victoria seems young in its proximity to the fabulous, in the magical edge of its quick imagery—"over by the sluice the water fell sheer, like a brightly colored fabric hung out to dry." Or "Again the weeks and the months went by, and spring returned. The snow had gone: the distant roar of liberated waters gave the illusion of coming from the sun and the moon." The novel also seems young in its air of disconnectedness, of being partly hidden from the author as well as from us, of being the residue of an emotional experience more than a re-creation of one. The hero, Johannes Møller, is a miller's son (Møllerens Sønn). We meet him walking and thinking, "bursting with ideas"—"When he grew up he would work in a match factory. It would be pleasantly dangerous, and he could get sulfur on his fingers so that nobody would dare to shake hands with him." He dreams of the future, has for friends the trees and the birds and the stones in the granite quarry, and is, of course, in love with Victoria, the daughter of the Castle, the manor house near the mill. As children, they play and flirt, but as social unequals. Well, Johannes leaves home and becomes, guess what, a writer. His frenzied habits of work—every night from the evening church bells to dawn, despite the complaints of the insomniac next door—sound very like those of the hero of *Hunger*. Except that Johannes is a success, critical and commercial, from the start. He returns home educated, famous, and a man. Meanwhile, Victoria, to save the sagging Castle fortunes, has had her troth plighted for her to a caddish toff called Otto. Victoria and Johannes hold several hot-and-cold conversations establishing their love on a firmly star-crossed basis. As a consolation prize, she offers him, at her engagement party, their mutual friend little Camilla, whom our hero once saved from drowning (as a nature expert, he is amphibian; "I know the shoals," the dripping boy modestly avers), and to whom he now (and this is an honest Hamsun touch) takes enough of a shine, true love notwithstanding, to plight *his* troth. *But*, just then, what should happen but that Otto should go hunting, and—you know how sloppy caddish toffs are with guns; please don't let me spoil the story for you. Suffice to say that the lovers stay star-crossed and tuberculosis intervenes to keep the book brief.

If the plot sounds quaint and somewhat mechanically Tristan-and-Iseultish, it may be that Hamsun was masking a personal experience still puzzling to himself. Like Edvarda in *Pan*, Victoria compulsively humiliates her rustic admirer at parties. Party scenes seem to operate for Hamsun as a point of painful reference, in contrast to nature walks: love is made outdoors and destroyed indoors. Behind the vivid, cruel, hectically flushed women of his parties stands some bitter recollection. In *Victoria*, Hamsun suddenly digresses: "Watch any woman in profile when she drinks. Let her drink from a cup, a glass, anything you care to mention, but watch her in profile. It's a terrifying sight, the act she puts on. She purses up her mouth, dips only the extreme edge in the drink, and gets desperate if during the performance anybody notices her hand."

Though mutilated, as it were, by the jerky action of the puppet-theatre plot and by the pained reticences of Hamsun's memory, Victoria lives in each fragmentary glimpse of her, from the flighty but gracious child to the dying woman, still mostly a child, who writes Johannes a magnificently pathetic letter of farewell. *Victoria* adds a small portrait to literature's gallery of 19th-century women, those hapless creatures denied all rights but the right to be adored, those poor properties assigned an exclusively sexual value and given only a black market to trade it on—those scapegoats of romanticism, those saints of intrigue and dreaming who lived only in books, those oppressed innocents whose one method of protest was self-destruction.

The pride of these women, their defiant perversity and desperate gaiety, Hamsun can depict. But he is dealing here with an attenuated case. Whereas Madame Bovary, borrowing some iron from her bourgeois captors, did jimmy her way out and become for a moment that dark, sensual apparition who alarms Léon in Rouen, Victoria stands helpless and stares. The obstacles between the lovers drop away: Otto and Camilla vanish; the debt-ridden Castle and its paternalistic proprietor go up in smoke. Still, Johannes and Victoria do not move toward each other but preserve a silence one is tempted to call stubborn. They are Romeo and Juliet without the Nurse, without the night of love. The action of the book is their few conversations—they have none, except as children, that we do not overhear—and when she breaks silence for the last time, most fully, the book ends.

Stubborn silence was dear to Hamsun; he fled from publicity, played no games but solitaire, and kept silent during his trial. His laconic style feels engraved upon silence. Speech, and events in general, have a peculiar, exceptional air in his work. It is not merely that the characters do odd things—the hero of *Pan*, asked by the heroine, whom he loves, for the gift of his pet dog, shoots the dog and sends her the body; in *Victoria*, Johannes, needing a pipe cleaner, wrenches a hand from the face of a clock—but that very simple objects hop onto the page with an enigmatic, trollish wink. Victoria halts at a shopwindow and moves away; Johannes spies her and stops at the same window:

Why was she standing there? The window was a mean one, a small shop window displaying for sale a few bars of red soap, grain barley in a glass jar, a handful of cancelled postage stamps.

How oddly charged and sharp and potent is this little inventory of the inconsequential! Of Johannes' fiction we are told, "Often, his imagination played crazy tricks on him, obtruding into his book irrelevant conceits which he afterward had to strike out and throw away." For example, he imagines, "A man is at the point of death, he writes to a friend, a note, a little request. The man dies, leaving this note. It is dated and signed, it has capital letters and small letters, though the writer would die within the hour. Very strange." Later, when he receives Victoria's note, he sees that "there were capital letters and small letters, the lines were straight, and she who had written them was dead!" This interest in not merely peculiar circumstances but the *peculiarity of circumstance* deflects his prose from the path of high seriousness and rounded intention but does give it a continuous quirky life and stabs of unexpected power. In *Victoria*, a long dream is recounted to no immediate purpose but with a concrete wildness given to few dreams in fiction:

> He wades out into the ocean and dives down. He finds himself standing in front of a great doorway where he meets a huge barking fish. It has a mane on its back and barks at him like a dog. Behind the fish stands Victoria. He reaches out his hands toward her, she has no clothes on, she laughs at him and a gale blows through her hair.

Dreamlike also is Victoria's explanation of why, at the party, she rudely interrupted Johannes' speech: "All I heard was your voice. It was like an organ, and the power it had over me made me frantic." In Doris Lessing's *The Golden Notebook*, the heroine relates how as soon as she heard a certain man's voice she knew she would sleep with him. What is mere confession in a female writer amounts to intuitive genius in Hamsun.

Just as dreams and passionate impulses erupt into our conscious lives, so the flow of this novel is interrupted, at the end, by a gratuitous spate of anecdotes on the topic of love. One of them describes a cuckolded husband who knowingly returns when his wife is entertaining her lover. He knocks, the lover sneaks away, the husband enters, and a strange conversation ensues—a groping amid mutual compassion and deceit. Then:

> But suddenly he threw his arms around her, in an ironlike grip of terrifying strength, and whispered in her ear, "What do you say, shall we put horns on him . . . on the fellow who left. . . . Shall we put horns on him?"

She screams for the maid, and in the morning describes his proposal as "a very strange attack." He answers, "Yes, it's a strain being witty at my age. I'm giving it up." The entire encounter, in its comic knottiness, in the depths and turns of uxoriousness it reveals, is quite startling, and shows the degree of psychological complexity Hamsun's strange simplicity could conjure with. Strindberg and Nietzsche were his tutors, but he drew upon the Nordic cultural tradition that underlies the realism of the sagas, the anti-philosophy of Kierkegaard,* and the films of Ingmar Bergman. Like Hamsun, Bergman loves plain textures and tangled minds, renders details with surreal clarity, indulges a savage streak of fantasy, and sometimes depends ingenuously upon fable and a mysticism of brooks and saplings. Scandinavia, untouched by Hellenism and only lately and lightly submissive to Christianity, sees things in its own slant of sunlight. Platonic precedences do not obtain; the riddle and not the Idea lurks behind phenomena. The wish to "grant the individual soul its due" has roots in an ancient Germanic individualism: the 6th-century *Strategicon* says of German warriors, "Headstrong, despising strategy, precaution, or foresight, they show contempt for every tactical command." The Viking god of battle, Odin, was the god of inspiration, whether as battle frenzy, intoxication, or supernatural wisdom; Hamsun is a literary Viking whose reliance upon inspiration is his strength and his weakness. Born in a rural valley, by predilection a recluse and a farmer, he belongs in the company of those tanned, clear-eyed truants (the Basque Unamuno, the Algerian Camus, the Egyptian Cavafy, the Russian Tolstoy) who jeer into the classroom of European civilization. A heathen visionary, he sees peculiar particulars that resist being smoothed

---

* "I am anything but a devilish good fellow at philosophy . . . I am a poor, individual existing man. . . ." "[Philosophy] is disinterested; but the difficulty inherent in existence constitutes the interest of the existing individual, who is infinitely interested in existing."—*Concluding Unscientific Postscript.*

into plots, exemplary characters, or slogans to live by. The moral of *Victoria* is profferred as "There's always a catch somewhere," or "God has fashioned [love] of many kinds and seen it endure or perish." Such an inconclusive conclusion, a standoff, well caps this intensely static love story, whose characters, though immersed in bookish circumstances, proudly reject the dynamism of characters.

JOYCE AND PROUST

Questions Concerning Giacomo

WHAT IS "GIACOMO JOYCE"?

It is (a) a tiny prose work of some twenty-six hundred words, whose first sentence is interrogative—"Who?"—and whose substance is so evanescent with tentativity and mysteriousness that the reviewer, like the heroine, finds it handy to don "quizzing glasses." Variously described as a "short story" and "the notebook" and "a love poem which is never recited" and "this most delicate of novels," *Giacomo Joyce* was probably copied out, in his best schoolbook hand, by James Joyce (1882–1941) in 1914 in Trieste.

(b) It is also an elegantly produced, boxed, ten-dollar object of veneration published by Viking Press on January 1, 1968—a saint's bone whose marrow is (a) and whose surrounding calcium consists of nine pages of introduction by the foremost of American Joyce scholars, Mr. Richard Ellmann; four and a fraction pages of notes amplifying and exemplifying correspondences and echoes already noted in the introduction; and, most delightfully and luxuriantly, a photographic facsimile of the manuscript pages, two of them full size (13¼ inches by 10¼ inches) and folded quarto, the six others reduced by half but still legible.

DOES THE SUMPTUOUS FORMAT OF (B) ENTIRELY SUIT THE MODEST TEXT OF (A)?

It is a pleasure to handle, in an age when the crafts languish, so fine a piece of book production. Mr. Ellmann, as master of scholarly ceremonies, writes gracefully, employing his matchless intimacy with the Joycean universe to demonstrate how phrases from this slender text were dispersed, with surprising transmutations, through *A Portrait of the Artist as a Young Man, Exiles, Pomes Penyeach,* and *Ulysses.* The decision to print, however, this text line for line as it appears in the manuscript, with all the spaces, not only compels a rather stingy size of type but somehow weakens the voice of the prose; the sections of this notebook quoted in Ellmann's massive biography of Joyce (Oxford, 1959) and set in orthodox justified lines, read more vividly, with more of the narrative energy whose lack is the most puzzling aesthetic quality of *Giacomo Joyce.* Departing from normal typographic procedures seems chichi, since the facsimile manuscript is also bound into the volume.

The facsimile is doubly welcome, as a specimen of Joyce's fluent, lucid hand and as light upon the central riddle—of what the work wishes to *do;* we seem to draw a little closer to Joyce's intention in examining the graphic texture of these paragraphs and phrases spaced and scattered upon large sheets of art paper. There is no crossing-out or emendation, though there is some trouble with "websoft" on page 7. This indicates a fair copy from preëxistent notes, yet on some pages the tone of ink (page 10), or the size of the writing (page 15), or the speed of the penmanship (page 13) changes between paragraphs. Mr. Ellman's suggestion is that, "perhaps with Mallarmé in mind," Joyce was indicating "pauses of varying duration measured by spaces of varying length." If that is so, this pictographic intention is indifferently carried out; the amount of waste space—the lower third of the sheets is frequently blank, and some of the space gaps, as on pages 5 and 8, are huge— seems inartistic and its distribution rather random. More likely that this enterprise, whether of copying or composition, was executed at several sittings, with a mixture of purposes, among them crystallization and formal ordering for the author's own benefit, as a way of pinning these images to a surface from which they could be later plucked and employed in published works. I doubt that *Giacomo Joyce* was ever intended for print. It is too personal, too unformed and febrile; it would scarcely be published now were its author not a classic. Publication in a very private sense, however, may have been intended: these pages, one's impression grows, were copied out to be shown or given to someone, like the parchment sheets upon which Joyce five years earlier copied out the poems of *Chamber Music* as a gift for his wife.

SHOWN OR GIVEN TO WHOM?

One possibility is Italo Svevo, Joyce's fellow-author and fellow-Triestine of the time, who contributed so much information and temperament to the character of Leopold Bloom, and who had written and shown to Joyce a novel called *Senilità* (the English title, at Joyce's suggestion, became *As a Man Grows Older*), concerning a middle-aged man's love for a young woman, and who had asked Joyce, in a letter dated June 26, 1914, "When will you write an Italian work about our town? Why not?" Joyce had recently shown Svevo a typescript of the first three chapters of *Portrait of the Artist*, and *Giacomo Joyce* could be his response to Svevo's challenge. The story's complex tone, literary and personal and polyglot and arch, and its distinct Triestine locality are congenial with this thesis; any clear-cut echo of *Senilità* would be virtually clinching. But Mr. Ellmann offers none, and Svevo's elegiac and wry psychologizing belongs to a different literary era from Joyce's compacted personal imagery. The friendship between Svevo and Joyce was a curious one. The letter of June 26th, read in full, is stilted even beyond the stiltedness of Svevo's English; his inquiry in context seems more polite than spirited. Svevo was in his fifties, a prosperous and amiable businessman who had diffidently abandoned writing after two early, neglected novels; Joyce was in his early thirties, an impoverished and unamiable Berlitz instructor, full of faith in his own genius and, as his brother Stanislaus put it, "that inflexibility firmly rooted in failure." Joyce's fierce enthusiasm for Svevo's novels—tinged, perhaps, by the generosity authors feel toward non-competitors and by Svevo's usefulness to him as a hoard of Jewish lore—seems to have rather baffled the older man. They came together as student and teacher, since Svevo wanted to improve his English. His letters retain a student's shyness and tact.

A more piquant possibility is that the intended readership of one was the work's subject herself. *Giacomo Joyce* tells us that she had been shown some of *A Portrait*, including the third chapter, wherein Stephen's erotic sins are described, for "She says that, had

The Portrait of the Artist been frank only for frankness' sake, she would have asked why I had given it to her to read." On the next page the author broods, "Those quiet cold fingers have touched the pages, foul and fair, on which my shame shall glow for ever." It can be objected that within *Giacomo Joyce* its heroine is sometimes mocked and sometimes hymned in physical terms she could only have found embarrassing. But Joyce was peculiarly fond of this mode of wooing—courtship by shamelessness. He detailed to Nora Barnacle his sexual life before he met her. In the long letter of August 29, 1904, he refers to another letter, in which he dwelt on the details of their first liaison: "You have misunderstood, I think, some passages in a letter I wrote you and I have noticed a certain shyness in your manner as if the recollection of that night troubled you." And, amid that extraordinary torrent of letters he directed toward her from Dublin in 1909, while she remained in Trieste, he beseeches her, "Now, my darling Nora, I want you to read over and over all I have written to you. Some of it is ugly, obscene, and bestial, some of it is pure and holy and spiritual: all of it is myself." He dotes on the "something obscene and lecherous in the very look" of certain words, and hopes that "you too will write me letters even madder and dirtier than mine to you." It was always one of his marital sorrows that she would not read his books. Voyeurism and exhibitionism both were exercised by his performance of writing. In 1918, Joyce, seeing Martha Fleischmann on a Zurich street, sent her four ardent and presumptuous letters in French and German. In the first, he tells this unknown lady she is *"un joli* animal," likens himself to Dante espying Beatrice, and concludes by saying, in French, "I believe you are good at ——." The word, evidently obscene, was torn from the corner by the recipient. He also sent her a copy of *Chamber Music*, and Ellmann's biography describes how Joyce "from his vantage point on the street had watched her take it from the letter box and sit down with it in her front room." Among Stephen Dedalus' sins are "the foul long letters he had written in the joy of guilty confession and carried secretly for days and days only to throw them under cover of night among the grass in the corner of a field or beneath some hingeless door or in some niche in the hedges where a girl might come upon them as she walked by and read them secretly." When, in *Exiles*, Robert Hand rebukes Joyce's alter ego Richard Rowan for waking his wife from sleep and confessing the night's infidelity, Rowan answers, "She must know me as I am." But one suspects that in Joyce's case candor was an act not merely of integrity but of concupiscence. It would not have been out of character for him to display this delineation of passion to its young but intelligent and nubile object.

One is forced into these conjectures by the definite omissions of Ellmann's introduction. He tells us at the outset of the manuscript that "The present owner . . . wishes to remain anonymous." He goes on to discuss the "title" of these pages, which are "loosely held within the nondescript gray-paper covers of a school note-book. . . . On the upper left-hand corner of the front cover, the name 'Giacomo Joyce' is inscribed in another hand." Well, *whose* hand? Can no comparison be made of the handwritings of Joyce's intimates at this time? Is it a matter of indifference who was permitted to bestow this ironical title? It looks to me, assuming that the label on the Viking volume is an accurate reproduction, as if the word "Joyce" were written in the center, with a spidery "Giacomo" added above it, perhaps in the "cobweb handwriting" of the little book's heroine. Ellmann declines to speculate. And he withholds two points of information given in his biography of Joyce. "Giacomo" was Casanova's first name and "a familiar epithet in Italy for a great lover" and the lady, the young student with whom Joyce fell in love and who inspired this work, also had a name. She was Amalia Popper, the daughter of a Jewish business-man called not quite Leopold Bloom but Leopoldo Popper.

HOW MUCH—ER—ACTUAL CONTACT DID JOYCE MAKE WITH SIGNORINA POPPER?

A good question. Ellmann assumes that the affair is "of eyes rather than of bodies" and that the sexual episodes of the manu-script represent "morose delectation—diet of writers." This is not hard to believe of overheated passages like

> Soft sucking lips kiss my left armpit: a coiling kiss on myriad veins. I burn! I crumple like a burning leaf! From my right armpit a fang of flame leaps out. A starry snake has kissed me: a cold nightsnake. I am lost!

But there are quieter passages with an air of reality:

> Whirling wreaths of grey vapour upon the heath. Her face, how grey and grave! Dank matted hair. Her lips press softly, her sighing breath comes through. Kissed.

Joyce observes that "her body has no smell: an odourless flower" and describes a seduction with a soft clarity of detail that belongs either to reality or to an imagination of genius:

> I hold the websoft edges of her gown and drawing them out to hook them I see through the opening of the black veil her lithe body sheathed in an orange shift. It slips its ribbons of moorings at her shoulders and falls slowly: a lithe smooth naked body shimmering with silvery scales. It slips slowly over the slender buttocks of smooth tarnished silver and over their furrow, a tarnished silver shadow. . . .

True, Joyce was an imaginative genius. True, his adventures with women, Nora Barnacle excepted, appear to have tended toward either plain whoring or timid, voyeuristic adoration. But his attentions to Martha Fleischmann, of which only the correspondence remains, caused her lover and *Vormund*, Rudolph Hiltpold, to write Joyce (all this is confided in a note to Frank Budgen) "a threatening violent letter" leading to a "long interview" in Hiltpold's apartment with "violent gestures" on Hiltpold's part and "that timidity which yet is courage" on Joyce's, ending in a return of Martha's letters and a "*Waffenstillstand*." The photographs of these years * show a somewhat rakish dandy; in 1915, the Joyce strumming a guitar is positively handsome. Richard Rowan of *Exiles* says he has betrayed his wife "grossly and many times." The one moment of psychological tension in *Giacomo Joyce* occurs when the heroine's father tells Joyce in Italian that "My daughter has the greatest admiration for her English teacher." This assertion, whose manner purportedly combines "suspicion, naturalness, helplessness of age, confidence, frankness, urbanity, sincerity, warning," is inwardly greeted by Joyce with the exclamation "Ignatius Loyola, make haste to help me!" The girl's susceptibility is as moot

---

* Ellmann's two volumes of Joyce's letters contain many, and Viking published in 1968 a fascinatingly illustrated study, *James Joyce and His World*, by Chester G. Anderson.

as the strength of his advances. Concerning the percentage of wealthy middle-class Jewish girls seduced by their instructors in prewar Austria-Hungary, there was no Kinsey to gather statistics. The elliptical, fraught allusiveness of *Giacomo Joyce* and the powerful resonance with which the experience reverberates through Joyce's work (Signorina Popper not only is credited with being Beatrice Justice of *Exiles* and the Irish girl of the last chapter of the *Portrait* but is supposed to have contributed the something Mediterranean in the character of Molly Bloom) do seem insufficiently explained by a one-sided infatuation. The relationship, at any rate, made an impression upon Signorina Popper. Nineteen years later, in 1933, now Signora Risola of Florence, she wrote Joyce asking for permission to translate *Dubliners* into Italian. Permission was granted, and a book entitled *Araby* did appear in Italian, but the standard Italian translation was done by other hands. She died not much longer than a year ago, and perhaps her death (again we must resort to speculation) released *Giacomo Joyce* to posterity.

Is "Giacomo Joyce" good or bad art?

Difficult to answer, even discounting the extent to which it is not art at all but personal therapy and private communication. Parts of it sing with the familiar voice: "She follows her mother with ungainly grace, the mare leading her filly foal." Some images bring the heroine into good focus: "A pale face surrounded by heavy odorous furs. . . . The long eyelids beat and lift: a burning needleprick stings and quivers in the velvet iris." Other images float oddly, unattached: "Long lewdly leering lips: dark-blooded molluscs." Some of the writing is Joyce at his most palely swooning: "Her eyes have drunk my thoughts: and into the moist warm yielding welcoming darkness of her womanhood my soul, itself dissolving, has poured and flooded a liquid and abundant seed." Some of it is mere noise: "Weep not for me, O daughter of Jerusalem!" And some downright trite: "This heart is sore and sad. Crossed in love?" These many glimpses, exclamations, and parodic spurts, though anticipating, in Ellmann's happy phrase, the "clashing of dictions" that becomes the method of *Ulysses*, do not quite hang together, perhaps because they are engraved upon a personal incident that remains obscure rather than upon the mundane, mappable events of Bloomsday. *Giacomo Joyce* does point up the lack of psychological presence Joyce's characters, even in the masterworks, often have. His dialogue, for example, where it is not comic or telegraphic (and largely excepting *Dubliners*), more suggests worked-up notes than the living exchange of speech. The key utterance in *Giacomo Joyce* is Amalia's saying, "Because otherwise I could not see you," a remark which meant so much to Joyce that he gives it twice to Beatrice Justice in *Exiles;* neither here nor there does it make much sense. In both places the statement, like many things said in *Ulysses,* arrives unprepared-for, devoid of context, and without weight. Compared to Tolstoy's protagonists or those of Henry James, Joyce's characters do not take each other seriously; they seem detached, for all the formal significance arrayed behind them, from concern with their own fate, and move sluggishly beneath the semi-opaque thickness of their artistic rendering. They are the creations of an artist-God who is himself "refined out of existence, indifferent, paring his fingernails." Indeed, *Giacomo Joyce* is most interesting for its illustration of a stage of the aesthetic sequence that Stephen Dedalus expounds to Lynch in Chapter Five of *A Portrait,* which was completed later in 1914, and abounds in echoes of *Giacomo;* Stephen might well have this tiny work in mind as marking the exact point where the lyrical form—"the simplest verbal vesture of an instant of emotion"—becomes the simplest epical form, "when the artist prolongs and broods upon himself as the centre of an epical event. . . . The personality of the artist passes into the narration itself, flowing round and round the persons and the action like a vital sea." *Giacomo* anticipates not only the triumph but the limits of *Ulysses.* We do not see as well in water as in air, and the chief character Joyce's books glorify is himself, the writer as God and oceanic mind, the frail and arrogant sponger/saint with the black eye patch, holding all literature and languages inside his head, mixed with "pebbles and rubbish and broken matches and lots of glass." It is this monstrous and marvellous self-dramatization whose adventures we follow in his books, whose fanaticism transfigures gritty old photographs of Dublin and Paris, and whose relics we revere.

Remembrance of Things Past Remembered

"ONLY THREE OR FOUR BOOKS IN A LIFETIME," Swann says in *Remembrance of Things Past*, "give us anything that is of real importance." For a book to be great in a reader's life it is not enough for the book to be great; the reader must be ready. I began to read Proust the first months I lived in Manhattan, on Riverside Drive. I was twenty-three, newly a father, newly employed. Since boyhood I had wanted to live in New York. I had wanted to work for the magazine that now I did work for. I had wanted to be a writer and now a few poems and short stories were filtering into print. In this atmosphere, then, of dreams come true, I opened my wife's tattered college copy of *Swann's Way;* she used to read under a sun lamp, and the cover was stained by a spot of oil. While our baby cooed in her white, screened crib, and the evening traffic swished north on the West Side Highway, and Manhattan at my back cooled like a stone, and my young wife fussed softly in our triangular kitchen at one of the meals that, by the undeservable grace of marriage, regularly appeared, I would read:

> . . . if my aunt were feeling "upset," she would ask instead for her "tisane," and it would be my duty to shake out of the chemist's little package on to a plate the amount of lime-blossom required for infusion in boiling water. The drying of the stems had twisted them into a fantastic trellis, in whose intervals the pale flowers opened, as though a painter had arranged them there, grouping them in the most decorative poses. The leaves, which had lost or altered their own appearance, assumed those instead of the most incongruous things imaginable, as though the transparent wings of flies or the blank sides of labels or the petals of roses had been collected and pounded, or interwoven as birds weave the material for their nests. A thousand trifling little details—the charming prodigality of the chemist—details which would have been eliminated from an artificial preparation, gave me, like a book in which one is astonished to read the name of a person whom one knows, the pleasure of finding that these were indeed real lime-blossoms, like those I had seen, when coming from the train, in the Avenue de la Gare, altered, but only because they were not imitations but the very same blossoms, which had grown old. And as each new character is merely a metamorpho-

sis from something older, in these little grey balls I recognised green buds plucked before their time; but beyond all else the rosy, moony, tender glow which lit up the blossoms among the frail forest of stems from which they hung like little golden roses—marking, as the radiance upon an old wall still marks the place of a vanished fresco, the difference between those parts of the tree which had and those which had not been "in bloom"—shewed me that these were petals which, before their flowering-time, the chemist's package had embalmed on warm evenings of spring. That rosy candlelight was still their colour, but half-extinguished and deadened in the diminished life which was now theirs, and which may be called the twilight of a flower. Presently my aunt was able to dip in the boiling infusion, in which she would relish the savour of dead or faded blossom, a little madeleine, of which she would hold out a piece to me when it was sufficiently soft.*

A thousand other passages equally wonderful could be quoted from the four thousand pages of Proust's novel. Everyone knows of the madeleine from whose long-forgotten taste the whole of Combray sprang into renewed being; the paragraph I have quoted gives us the tea direct, as it was fed by Aunt Léonie to little "Marcel." Hemingway would have rendered this action in twenty words; Balzac, in a hundred and made us feel the chemist's shop, and hear the ring of francs on the counter. Proust's tendrilous sentences seek out an essence so fine the search itself is an act of faith. It was a revelation to me that words could entwine and curl so, yet keep a live crispness and the breath of utterance. I was dazzled by the witty similes—the vanished fresco, the book holding the known name—that wove art and nature into a single luminous fabric. This was not "better" writing, it was writing with a whole new nervous system.

The passage manifests the work's great theme: the metamorphoses wrought by Time. This sense of metamorphosis—tied to Proust's neurasthenically keen sense of the organic, especially of

---

* As rendered in C. K. Scott Moncrieff's very fluent and ornate translation. Looking, since, at Proust in French, I am struck by how often Proust is terse —less Proustian, indeed, than he is in English. The few proof sheets in the Harvard collection show his alterations to be often (unlike those of Joyce, who usually added) shortenings and simplifications. Yet, that Moncrieff caught the essential power and perfume I do not doubt.

botany—carries into the tragic, temporal dimension Proust's peculiar sensitivity to *changing perspectives*. Perspectives change
in space (the steeples at Martinville), in the heart (Swann's
views of Odette), in society (Mme. Verdurin's rise; Swann
as seen in Combray and in Paris). External reality is but a cluster
of moments no two of which subtend the same angle. This
is impressionism, but impressionism on the move, whether the
moving object is the narrator's life or the "little train" to Balbec:

> . . . but, the course of the line altering, the train turned, the morn-
> ing scene gave place in the frame of the window to a nocturnal
> village, its roofs still blue with moonlight, its pond encrusted with
> the opalescent nacre of night, beneath a firmament still powdered
> with all its stars, and I was lamenting the loss of my strip of pink
> sky when I caught sight of it afresh, but red this time, in the opposite
> window which it left at a second bend in the line, so that I spent
> my time running from one window to the other to reassemble, to
> collect on a single canvas the intermittent, antipodean fragments of
> my fine, scarlet, ever-changing morning, and to obtain a compre-
> hensive view of it and a continuous picture.

Einstein used moving trains to illustrate the special theory of relativity, propounded in 1905. Also in 1905, Proust's mother died, releasing him to final loneliness and earnest search for entrée into his
own endowment, his precocious powers of evocation. In his relativity Proust is a modern, though the modern most lavish with
old-fashioned virtues—characterization, ambitious scale, idealistic
rapture, stylistic confidence. *Remembrance of Things Past* is to
19th-century novels as a magic lantern is to little landscape models
with plaster hills, matchstick houses, and trees of green sponge.
Proust abolished the nagging contradiction between the author as
God and the author as nebulous character, as reader's confidant.
In Proust's cosmos, Marcel (so called only once, in an elaborately
hedged aside) is both the most supine of witnesses and the mightiest
of creators. There is no "outside" to the firmament of his skull. His
perceptions are not derived from substance; they *are* substance.
And the plot is not what connects the images and gestures and
masks; their enclosure within one field of perception *is* the plot,
the drama. Our excitement as we traverse these immensities of
prose has to do with their Providential coherence: microcosmically,

with the dissecting delicacy of each sentence and the ecology of mutual assistance the tender images extend toward one another; and macrocosmically, with the thrilling leaps of far-flung continuations (Vinteuil's manifestations, for example, or De Forcheville's reappearance after three thousand pages, to marry Odette) and a grand architectural completeness (the Swann side, in Gilberte, unites with the Guermantes side, in Saint-Loup, to produce a daughter who, we are told casually, "later on married an obscure man of letters"). As in a cathedral, organic profusion is subdued to a design. It might be said that by deviating from his original design (*circa* 1909) of two Testamental volumes—the way of innocence and the way of experience—to insert the immense dirge to Agostinelli (d. 1914) that comprises the Albertine books, Proust created a Flamboyant rather than a Romanesque cathedral. Yet, without those sometimes monotonous stretches of misty Albertine, how much would be diminished the culminating effect of vastness, of dizzying height? *Time Regained* ends with acrophobia. Like Marcel, the reader turns "giddy at seeing so many years below and in me as though I were leagues high." Among other writers only Dante lifts us to such an altitude.

Like Dante, Proust lives in one work. There is a great dropping off elsewhere. We read *Jean Santeuil* or *Contre Sainte-Beuve*, or try to, much as we read Proust's nattering letters, or criticism of him—for the lover's pleasure of being with Proust and being reminded of the raptures he has given us. No other 20th-century writer has inspired such a bulk of appreciation and analysis; the shelves at Widener Library include the bound bulletins of *La Societé des Amis de Marcel Proust et des Amis de Combray*. In English the Proust chapters by Edmund Wilson in *Axel's Castle* and by Harry Levin in *The Gates of Horn* show omnivorous critics sagaciously digesting; the small books by Howard Moss and Roger Shattuck with special affection polish and refocus some of the lenses of Proust's panopticon; and the brilliant two-volume biography by George Painter in one sense offers more adventure than *À la Recherche du Temps Perdu* itself, since in Painter's account we see Proust journeying toward the mastery that the novel possesses from the very first page. There are also Samuel Beckett's rather acerb essay and, in translation by Elsie Prell, a memoir by François Mauriac that combines a young writer's awe at the "sudden occupation of the literary heaven by the Proustain constellation," a generous appraisal from a Catholic viewpoint of the corrosion and stagnation felt to overtake the latter half of the masterpiece, and a vivid personal recollection of "that gloomy room on the rue Hamlin, that black den, that bed where an overcoat served as a blanket, that waxy mask through which it could have been said our host watched us eat, and whose hair alone seemed living." Proust is not only the greatest modern creator of characters; he is among modern authors the most amusing character, the most self-dramatizing (see his letters) and bizarre, whose cork-lined room has become the very symbol of hypertrophied aestheticism. In 1971 the hundredth anniversary of his birth was observed in the American literary press with tributes, by such writers as Melvin Maddocks and William Gass, surprisingly grudging and irritated in tone, even jeering—as if in these distributors of contemporary relevance had been reborn those *fin-de-siècle* smarts, the Comte de Montesquiou and his peers, who could not believe that "little Proust," that sickly parasite and queer half-Jew, had vaulted over them into immortality.

American readers in general, I suspect, have been put off by the unwieldy, intimidating twin-elephant Random House edition of *Remembrance of Things Past*. Better to read it in the seven Modern Library volumes, now reprinted in a Vintage paperback edition, and better still to obtain the charming twelve volumes of the English edition by Chatto & Windus (this edition has recently been disfigured by the insertion of totally insipid pencil illustrations by Philippe Jullian, but they can be excised with a razor blade). The pagination of the Chatto & Windus edition (and, but for *Swann's Way*, the Modern Library edition, which was a photograph of it) fits the extremely useful index-guide compiled by P. S. Spalding, which serves not only as a memory freshener as one reads along but as a way to extract all the references to, say, Hawthorn, Heredity, or Victor Hugo from their vast matrix.*

---

* I have been told, since writing this Proust advisory for the readers of *Horizon*, that the Spalding index is out of print. Too bad, if true.

Americans also, perhaps in their zeal for practical instruction, tend to expect too much of Proust as a social critic. Satire of snobs and anatomizing of society occur, of course, and Proust was a climber in his day; but a personal obsession should not be confused with an artistic one. He writes about aristocrats, in their banality and glamour, their vanity and gallantry, because they are there: *were* there, in the life he has ceased to live, the life that lostness has bathed in paradisiacal colors. As soon call Proust an anti-snob as a gargoyle-carver anti-devil; hatred is swallowed in an art of homage. Proust would take the entire living population of France as a *trésor trouvé,* a paleontological imprint left by the past, a clue to the central mystery of France herself, with her cathedrals, her blossoms, her place names. As the hero, aging, discovers deceit everywhere and absurdity everywhere, only two things remain worth loving: Marcel and France, which are everything. The book is not a tract but a religious travail.

In those August and September Manhattan days, themselves now paradisiacal, when I first read Proust, I also began to read Kierkegaard. College had left them out of my education; now I embraced them. I was not only a would-be writer but a would-be Christian. I was happy, but happiness, as Harold Brodkey observed in a short story from those same 1950's, makes us afraid. And Proust and Kierkegaard seemed (though both had been petite men) two giant brothers, whose bullying and showing-off I forgave because between them I could walk safely down the street, the street of my life. The remorseless pessimism of Proust's disquisitions on the heart, the abyss he makes of human motives, the finality of all our little deaths, did not appall me; morbid myself, I only trusted morbidity. In the interminable rain of his prose, I felt goodness. Proust was one of those men—increasingly rare, as faith further ebbs—who lost the consolations of belief but retained the attitudes and ambitions of a worshipper. For all his biochemistry, Proust emphasizes the medieval duality of body/spirit: "the body imprisons the spirit in a fortress." For all the disillusion and cruelty it depicts, *Remembrance of Things Past* is, like the Bible, a work of consolation. Einstein's relativity developed its formulas from the recognition of an absolute, the speed of light. Marcel, having experienced—in the madeleine, in the uneven paving stones—"a sense of eternity," vows to "leave this behind me to enrich others with my treasure." The next sentence goes on to uncover in his momentary "sense of eternity" a strangely modest secret, a kind of Godless Golden Rule and the germinating principle of art:

> My experience in the library which I wanted to preserve was that of pleasure, but not an egotistical pleasure, or at all events it was a form of egoism which is useful to others—for all the fruitful altruisms of Nature develop in an egotistical mode.

BORGES

The Author as Librarian

OTHER INQUISITIONS, 1937–1952, by Jorge Luis Borges, translated from the Spanish by Ruth L. C. Simms. 205 pp. University of Texas Press, 1964.

DREAMTIGERS, by Jorge Luis Borges, translated from the Spanish by Mildred Boyer and Harold Morland. 95 pp. University of Texas Press, 1964.

BORGES THE LABYRINTH MAKER, by Ana María Barrenechea, edited and translated from the Spanish by Robert Lima. 175 pp. New York University Press, 1965.

The belated North American acknowledgment of the genius of Jorge Luis Borges proceeds apace. The University of Texas Press last year published two volumes by this Argentine fantasist, critic, poet, and librarian. These translations, together with Grove Press's *Ficciones*, bring to three the number of complete books by Borges available in English. There is also New Directions' *Labyrinths*, a selection. And now the New York University Press has published a book *about* him.*

Four years ago, when Borges shared with Samuel Beckett the Prix International des Éditeurs, he was known here to few but Hispanic specialists. A handful of poems and short stories had appeared in scattered anthologies and magazines. I myself had read only "The Garden of the Forking Paths," originally published in

---

* In the decade since this rather pioneering piece of homage was framed, the Borges bibliography in English, with the forceful midwifery of Norman Thomas di Giovanni, has added an offspring a year, including a Personal Anthology and, that ultimate elegance, some Conversations With.

Ellery Queen's Mystery Magazine and subsequently a favorite of detective-story anthologies. Though vivid and intellectual beyond the requirements of its genre, the story can be read without awareness that its creator is a giant of world literature. I was prompted to read Borges seriously by a remark made—internationally enough—in Rumania, where, after a blanket disparagement of contemporary French and German fiction, Borges was praised by a young critic in a tone he had previously reserved for Kafka. An analogy with Kafka is inevitable, but I wonder if Borges' abrupt projection, by the university and avant-garde presses, into the bookstores will prove as momentous as Kafka's publication, by the commercial firm of Knopf, in the thirties. It is not a question of Borges' excellence. His driest paragraph is somehow compelling. His fables are written from a height of intelligence less rare in philosophy and physics than in fiction. Furthermore, he is, at least for anyone whose taste runs to puzzles or pure speculation, delightfully entertaining. The question is, I think, whether or not Borges' lifework, arriving in a lump now (he was born in 1899 and since his youth has been an active and honored figure in Argentine literature), can serve, in its gravely considered oddity, as any kind of clue to the way out of the dead-end narcissism and downright trashiness of present American fiction.

Borges' narrative innovations spring from a clear sense of technical crisis. For all his modesty and reasonableness of tone, he proposes some sort of essential revision in literature itself. The concision of his style and the comprehensiveness of his career (in addition to writing poems, essays, and stories, he has collaborated on detective novels, translated from many tongues, edited, taught, and even executed film scripts) produce a strangely terminal impression: he seems to be the man for whom literature has no future. I am haunted by knowing that this insatiable reader is now virtually blind.

A constant bookishness gives Borges' varied production an unusual consistency. His stories have the close texture of argument; his critical articles have the suspense and tension of fiction. The criticism collected in *Other Inquisitions, 1937–1952* almost all takes the form of detection, of uncovering what was secret. He looks for, and locates, the hidden pivots of history: the moment (in Iceland in 1225) when a chronicler first pays tribute to an enemy, the very line (in Chaucer in 1382) when allegory yields to naturalism. His interest gravitates toward the obscure, the forgotten: John Wilkins, the 17th-century inventor *ab nihilo* of an analytical language; J. W. Dunne, the 20th-century proponent of a grotesque theory of time; Layamon, the 13th-century poet isolated between the death of Saxon culture and the birth of the English language. Where an arcane quality does not already exist, Borges injects it. His appreciation of the classic Spanish satirist and stylist Francisco de Quevedo begins, "Like the history of the world, the history of literature abounds in enigmas. I found, and continue to find, none so disconcerting as the strange partial glory that has been accorded to Quevedo." His essay on Layamon concludes, " 'No one knows who he is,' said Léon Bloy. Of that intimate ignorance no symbol is better than this forgotten man, who abhorred his Saxon heritage with Saxon vigor, and who was the last Saxon poet and never knew it."

Implacably, Borges reduces everything to a condition of mystery. His gnomic style and encyclopedic supply of allusions generate a kind of inverse illumination, a Gothic atmosphere in which the most lucid and famous authors loom somewhat menacingly. His essay on Bernard Shaw begins, "At the end of the thirteenth century Raymond Lully (Ramón Lull) attempted to solve all the mysteries by means of a frame with unequal, revolving, concentric disks, subdivided into sectors with Latin words." It ends on an equally ominous and surprising note: "[Existentialists] may play at desperation and anguish, but at bottom they flatter the vanity; in that sense, they are immoral. Shaw's work, on the other hand, leaves an aftertaste of liberation. The taste of the doctrines of Zeno's Porch and the taste of the sagas."

Borges' harsh conjunctions and plausible paradoxes are not confined to literary matters. In "A Comment on August 23, 1944," Borges meditates on the ambivalent reaction of his Fascist friends to the Allied occupation of Paris and ends with this daring paragraph:

> I do not know whether the facts I have related require elucidation. I believe I can interpret them like this: for Europeans and

Americans, one order—and only one—is possible: it used to be called
Rome and now it is called Western Culture. To be a Nazi (to play
the game of energetic barbarism, to play at being a Viking, a Tartar,
a sixteenth-century conquistador, a Gaucho, a redskin) is, after all,
a mental and moral impossibility. Nazism suffers from unreality, like
Erigena's hells. It is uninhabitable; men can only die for it, lie for it,
kill and wound for it. No one, in the intimate depths of his being,
can wish it to triumph. I shall hazard this conjecture: *Hitler wants to
be defeated*. Hitler is collaborating blindly with the inevitable armies
that will annihilate him, as the metal vultures and the dragon (which
must not have been unaware that they were monsters) collaborated,
mysteriously, with Hercules.

The tracing of hidden resemblances, of philosophical genealogies,
is Borges' favorite mental exercise. Out of his vast reading he dis-
tills a few related images, whose parallelism, tersely presented, has
the force of a fresh thought. "Perhaps universal history is the history of a few metaphors. I should like to sketch one chapter of
that history," he writes in "Pascal's Sphere," and goes on to compile, in less than four pages, twenty-odd instances of the image
of a sphere "whose center is everywhere and whose circumference
nowhere." These references are arranged like a plot, beginning
with Xenophanes, who joyously substituted for the anthropomorphic gods of Greece a divine and eternal Sphere, and ending
with Pascal, who, in describing nature as "an infinite sphere" had
first written and then rejected the word *"effroyable"*—"a frightful sphere." Many of Borges' genealogies trace a degeneration: he
detects a similar "magnification to nothingness" in the evolutions
of theology and of Shakespeare's reputation; he watches an Indian
legend succumb, through its successive versions, to the bloating of
unreality. He follows in the works of Léon Bloy the increasingly
desperate interpretations of a single phrase in St. Paul—*"per
speculum in aenigmate"* ("through a glass darkly"). Borges himself
recurrently considers Zeno's second paradox—the never-completed
race between Achilles and the tortoise, the formal argument of
regressus in infinitum—and comes to a conclusion that is, to use
his favorite adjective, monstrous: "One concept corrupts and confuses the others. . . . I am speaking of the infinite. . . . We (the
undivided divinity that operates within us) have dreamed the
world. We have dreamed it strong, mysterious, visible, ubiquitous

in space and secure in time; but we have allowed tenuous, eternal interstices of injustice in its structure so we may know that it is false."

Borges is not an antiseptic pathologist of the irrational; he is himself susceptible to infection. His connoisseurship has in it a touch of madness. In his "Kafka and His Precursors," he discovers, in certain parables and anecdotes by Zeno, Han Yü, Kierkegaard, Browning, Bloy, and Lord Dunsany, a prefiguration of Kafka's tone. He concludes that each writer creates his own precursors: "His work modifies our conception of the past, as it will modify the future." This is sensible enough, and, indeed, has been pointed out by T. S. Eliot, whom Borges cites in a footnote. But Borges goes on: "In this correlation the identity or plurality of men matters not at all." This sentence, I believe, expresses not a thought but a *sensation* that Borges has; he describes it—a mixture of deathlike detachment and ecstatic timelessness—in his most ambitious essay, "New Refutation of Time." It is this sensation that encourages his peculiar view of human thought as the product of a single mind, and of human history as a vast magic book that can be read cabalistically. His highest praise, bestowed upon the fantastic narratives of the early H. G. Wells, is to claim that "they will be incorporated, like the fables of Theseus of Ahasuerus, into the general memory of the species and even transcend the fame of their creator or the extinction of the language in which they were written."

As a literary critic, Borges demonstrates much sensitivity and sense. The American reader of these essays will be gratified by the generous amount of space devoted to writers of the English language. Borges, from within the Spanish literary tradition of "dictionaries and rhetoric," is attracted by the oneiric and hallucinatory quality he finds in North American, German, and English writing. He values Hawthorne and Whitman for their intense unreality, and bestows special fondness upon the English writers he read in his boyhood. The *fin-de-siècle* and Edwardian giants, whose reputations are generally etiolated, excite Borges afresh each time he rereads them:

> Reading and rereading Wilde through the years, I notice something that his panegyrists do not seem to have even suspected: the provable and elementary fact that Wilde is almost always right. . . .

he was a man of the eighteenth century who sometimes condescended to play the game of symbolism. Like Gibbon, like Johnson, like Voltaire, he was an ingenious man who was also right.

Borges' tributes to Shaw and Wells have been quoted above. In connection with Wells and Henry James, it is a salutary shock to find the terms of the usual invidious comparison reversed: "the sad and labyrinthine Henry James . . . a much more complex writer than Wells, although he was less gifted with those pleasant virtues that are usually called classical." But of this generation none is dearer to Borges than Chesterton, in whom he finds, beneath the surface of dogmatic optimism, a disposition like Kafka's: "Chesterton restrained himself from being Edgar Allan Poe or Franz Kafka, but something in the makeup of his personality leaned toward the nightmarish, something secret, and blind, and central . . . the powerful work of Chesterton, the prototype of physical and moral sanity, is always on the verge of becoming a nightmare . . . he tends inevitably to revert to atrocious observations." Much in Borges' fiction that suggests Kafka in fact derives from Chesterton. As critic and artist both, Borges mediates between the post-modern present and the colorful, prolific, and neglected pre-moderns.

Of the moderns themselves, of Yeats, Eliot, and Rilke, of Proust and Joyce, he has, at least in *Other Inquisitions*, little to say. Pound and Eliot, he asserts in passing, practice "the deliberate manipulation of anachronisms to produce an appearance of eternity" (which seems, if true at all, rather incidentally so), and he admires Valéry less for his work than for his personality, "the symbol of a man who is infinitely sensitive to every fact." The essays abound in insights delivered parenthetically—"God must not theologize"; "to fall in love is to create a religion that has a fallible god"—but their texts as a whole do not open outward into enlightenment. Whereas, say, Eliot's relatively tentative considerations offer to renew a continuing tradition of literary criticism, Borges' tight arrangements seem a bizarre specialization of the tradition. His essays have a quality I can only call *sealed*. They are structured like mazes and, like mirrors, they reflect back and forth on one another. There is frequent repetition of the adjectives and phrases that denote Borges' favorite notions of mystery, of secrecy, of "intimate ignorance." From his immense reading he has distilled a fervent narrowness. The same parables, the same quotations re-cur; one lengthy passage from Chesterton is reproduced three times.

Here and there appear sentences ("One literature differs from another, either before or after it, not so much because of the text as for the manner in which it is read") that elsewhere have been developed into "fictions"; in "Pierre Menard, Author of Don Quix-ote," a modern writer as his masterwork reconstructs passages from *Don Quixote* that, though verbally identical, are read very differ-ently. This story, in fact, was, according to an interview given in Buenos Aires in 1960, the first Borges ever wrote. Long a respected poet and critic, he turned to fiction with a grim diffidence. In his words:

> I know that the least perishable part of my literary production is the narrative, yet for many years I did not dare to write stories. I thought that the paradise of the tale was forbidden to me. One day, I suffered an accident. I was in a sanitarium where I was operated upon. . . . a time I cannot recall without horror, a period of fever, insomnia, and extreme insecurity. . . . If after the operation and the extremely long convalescence I tried to write a poem or an essay and failed, I would know that I had lost . . . intellectual integrity. Thus, I decided upon another approach. I said to myself: "I am going to write a story and if I cannot do so it does not matter because I have not written one before. In any case, it will be a first attempt." Then, I began to write a story . . . which turned out rather well; this was followed by others . . . and I discovered that I had not lost my intellectual integrity and that I could now write stories. I have written many since.

Turning from Borges' criticism to his fiction, one senses the liberation he must have felt upon entering "the paradise of the tale." For there is something disturbing as well as fascinating, some-thing distorted and strained about his literary essays. His ideas border on delusions; the dark hints—of a cult of books, of a cabalistic unity hidden in history—that he so studiously develops are special to the corrupt light of libraries and might vanish out-doors. It is uncertain how seriously he intends his textual diagrams, which seem ciphers for concealed emotions. Borges crowds into the margins of others' books passion enough to fill blank pages;

his essays all tend to open inward, disclosing an obsessed imagination and a proud, Stoic, almost cruelly masculine personality.

Dreamtigers, a collection of paragraphs, sketches, poems, and apocryphal quotations titled in Spanish *El Hacedor* (*The Maker*), succeeds in time the creative period of narrative fiction his essays foreshadow. It is frankly the miscellany of an aging man, fondly dedicated to a dead enemy—the Modernist poet Leopoldo Lugones, like Borges the director of a national library.

> Leaving behind the babble of the plaza, I enter the Library. I feel, almost physically, the gravitation of the books, the enveloping serenity of order, time magically desiccated and preserved. . . . These reflections bring me to the door of your office. I go in; we exchange a few words, conventional and cordial, and I give you this book. . . . My vanity and nostalgia have set up an impossible scene. Perhaps so (I tell myself), but tomorrow I too will have died, and our times will intermingle and chronology will be lost in a sphere of symbols. And then in some way it will be right to claim that I have brought you this book, and that you have accepted it.

The epilogue repeats this prediction of his own death:

> Few things have happened to me, and I have read a great many. Or rather, few things have happened to me more worth remembering than Schopenhauer's thought or the music of England's words.
> A man sets himself the task of portraying the world. Through the years he peoples a space with images of provinces, kingdoms, mountains, bays, ships, islands, fishes, rooms, instruments, stars, horses, and people. Shortly before his death, he discovers that that patient labyrinth of lines traces the image of his face.

The book is in two parts. The first, translated by Mildred Boyer, consists of those short prose sketches, musical and firm, that Borges, unable to see to write, composes in his head. The first of these describes Homer: "Gradually now the beautiful universe was slipping away from him. A stubborn mist erased the outline of his hand, the night was no longer peopled by stars, the earth beneath his feet was unsure." In a critical essay, Borges had traced the evolution of God and Shakespeare, as reputations, from something to nothing; now this nothingness is discovered in Shakespeare himself, intimately: "There was no one in him; behind his face (which even in the poor paintings of the period is unlike any other) and his words, which were copious, imaginative, and emotional, there was nothing but a little chill, a dream not dreamed by anyone." Dante is imagined dying in Ravenna, "as unjustified and as alone as any other man." God in a dream declares to him the secret purpose of his life and his work, which is like that of the leopard who endured a caged existence so that Dante might see him and place him in the first canto of the *Inferno.* "You suffer captivity, but you will have given a word to the poem," God told the leopard, "but when he awoke, there was only a dark resignation in him; a valiant ignorance. . . ." And the illustrious Italian Giambattista Marino—"proclaimed as the new Homer and the new Dante"—dying, perceives that "the tall, proud volumes casting a golden shadow in a corner were not—as his vanity had dreamed—a mirror of the world, but rather one thing more added to the world." It is as if, in his blindness and age, the oneness of all men that Borges had so often entertained as a theory and premonition has become a fact; he *is* Homer, Shakespeare, Dante, and tastes fully the bitter emptiness of creative splendor. The usurpation of a writer's private identity by his literary one has not been more sadly, or wittily, expressed than in "Borges and I":

> It's the other one, it's Borges, that things happen to. I stroll about Buenos Aires and stop, perhaps mechanically now, to look at the arch of an entrance or an iron gate. News of Borges reaches me through the mail and I see his name on an academic ballot or in a biographical dictionary. I like hourglasses, maps, eighteenth-century typography, the taste of coffee, and Stevenson's prose. The other one shares these preferences with me, but in a vain way that converts them into the attributes of an actor.

Borges tempts one to quote him at too great length. These brief paragraphs composed in his head have an infrangible aptness. His ability to crystallize vague ideas and vaguer emotions into specific images has grown. The image of Layamon, the last Saxon poet, returns in the form of an anonymous old man, dying, unaware that he is the last man to have witnessed the worship of Woden. He lies in a stable: "Outside are the plowed fields and a deep ditch clogged with dead leaves and an occasional wolf track in the black earth at the edge of the forest." This stark sentence, with its unexpectedly vivid ditch, has in it the whole of a primitive England, and pierces us with a confused sense of elapsed time. These sketches see a diminishing of those adjectives—"mysterious," "secret," "atrocious"—with which the younger Borges insisted on his sense of strangeness. Instead, there is a delicate manipulation of the concrete—lists and catalogues in which one or two of the series seem anomalous (". . . islands, fishes, rooms, instruments, stars, horses . . .") and the application now and then of a surprising color adjective (the volumes' "golden shadow" above, "red Adam in Paradise," and, apropos of Homer, "black vessels searching the sea for a beloved isle"). Immensity is reified in terms of color: "Every hundred paces a tower cleft the air; to the eye their color was identical, yet the first of all was yellow, and the last, scarlet, so delicate were the gradations and so long the series." In this image the concept of the infinite—the concept that "corrupts and confuses the others"—is tamed into something lyrical and even pretty. One feels in *Dreamtigers* a calm, an intimation of truce, a tranquil fragility. Like so many last or near-last works—like *The Tempest*, *The Millionairess*, or "Investigations of a Dog"—*Dreamtigers* preserves the author's life-long concerns, but drained of urgency; horror has yielded to a resigned humorousness. These sketches can be read for their grace and wit but scarcely for narrative excitement; the most exciting of them, "Ragnarök," embodies Borges' most terrible vision, of an imbecilic God or body of gods. But it occurs within a dream, and ends easily: "We drew our heavy revolvers—all at once there were revolvers in the dream—and joyously put the Gods to death."

The second half of this slim volume consists of poems, late and early. Poetry was where Borges' ramifying literary career originally took root. The translations, by Harold Morland, into roughly four-beat and intermittently rhymed lines, seem sturdy and clear, and occasional stanzas must approximate very closely the felicity of the original:

> In their grave corner, the players
> Deploy the slow pieces. And the chessboard
> Detains them until dawn in its severe
> Compass in which two colors hate each other.

As a poet, Borges has some of the qualities—a meditative circularity, a heavy-lidded elegance—of Wallace Stevens:

> With slow love she looked at the scattered
> Colors of afternoon. It pleased her
> to lose herself in intricate melody
> or in the curious life of verses.

And

> We shall seek a third tiger. This
> Will be like those others a shape
> Of my dreaming, a system of words
> A man makes and not the vertebrate tiger
> That, beyond the mythologies,
> Is treading the earth.

But in English the poems are chiefly interesting for their content; they are more autobiographical and emotionally direct than Borges' prose. The first one, "Poem About Gifts," movingly portrays himself in his blindness:

> Slow in my darkness, I explore
> The hollow gloom with my hesitant stick,
> I, that used to figure Paradise
> In such a library's guise.

Thoughts anonymously cached in the maze of his fictions are enunciated in his own voice. In a fabricated encyclopedia article he describes the "philosophers of Uqbar" as believing that "Copulation and mirrors are abominable. . . . For one of those gnostics, the visible universe was an illusion or, more precisely, a sophism. Mirrors and fatherhood are abominable because they multiply it and extend it." In a poem, "Mirrors," the belief turns out to be Borges' own:

> I see them as infinite, elemental
> Executors of an ancient pact,
> To multiply the world like the act
> Of begetting. Sleepless. Bringing doom.

The profound sense of timelessness that in the prose activates so much textual apparatus becomes in verse an elementary nostalgia:

Rain is something happening in the past. . . .
And the drenched afternoon brings back the sound
How longed for, of my father's voice, not dead.

And his long poem about his childhood home at Adrogué culminates:

The ancient amazement of the elegy
Loads me down when I think of that house
And I do not understand how time goes by,
I, who am time and blood and agony.

Together, the prose and poetry of *Dreamtigers* afford some
glimpses into Borges' major obscurities—his religious concerns and
his affective life. Physical love, when it appears at all in his work,
figures as something remote, like an ancient religion. "[Shakespeare]
thought that in the exercise of an elemental human rite he might
well find what he sought, and he let himself be initiated by Anne
Hathaway one long June afternoon." And Homer remembers when
"a woman, the first the gods set aside for him, had waited for him
in the shadow of a hypogeum, and he had searched for her through
corridors that were like stone nets, along slopes that sank into
the shadow." Though *Dreamtigers* contains two fine poems addressed to women—Susana Soca and Elvira de Alvear—they are
eulogies couched in a tone of heroic affection not different from
the affection with which he writes elsewhere of male friends like
Alfonso Reyes and Macedonio Fernández. This is at the opposite
pole from homosexuality; femaleness, far from being identified
with, is felt as a local estrangement that blends with man's cosmic
estrangement. There are two prose sketches that, by another writer,
might have shown some erotic warmth, some surrender to femininity. In one, he writes of Julia, a "sombre girl" with "an un-
bending body," in whom he sensed "an intensity that was altogether
foreign to the erotic." In their walks together, he must have talked
about mirrors, for now (in 1931) he has learned that she is insane
and has draped her mirrors because she imagines that his reflection
has replaced her own. In the other, he writes of Delia Elena San
Marco, from whom he parted one day beside "a river of vehicles
and people." They did not meet again, and in a year she was dead.
From the casualness of their unwitting farewell, he concludes,

tentatively, that we are immortal. "For if souls do not die, it is right that we should not make much of saying goodbye."

It would be wrong to think that Borges dogmatically writes as an atheist. God is often invoked by him, not always in an ironical or pantheistic way.

> God has created nighttime, which he arms
> With dreams, and mirrors, to make clear
> To man he is a reflection and a mere
> Vanity.

He hopes seriously for immortality. Death is "the mirror/In which I shall see no-one or I shall see another." One of the many riddles that interest him is Christ's aspect, and he is moved by the possibility that "the profile of a Jew in the subway is perhaps the profile of Christ; perhaps the hands that give us our change at a ticket window duplicate the ones some soldiers nailed one day to the cross." But we feel that he *entertains* these possibilities, almost blasphemously; they are isolated, for him, from the corpus of ethics and argument which is historical Christianity. He dismisses the orthodox afterlife: "We distrust his intelligence, as we would distrust the intelligence of a God who maintained heavens and hells." He ransacks Christian apologetics for oddities of forced reasoning. He writes, "Those who automatically reject the supernatural (I try, always, to belong to this group). . . ." While Christianity is not dead in Borges, it *sleeps* in him, and its dreams are fitful. His ethical allegiance is to pre-Christian heroism, to Stoicism, to "the doctrines of Zeno's Porch and . . . the sagas," to the harsh gaucho ethos celebrated in the Argentine folk poem of Martín Fierro. Borges is a pre-Christian whom the memory of Christianity suffuses with premonitions and dread. He is European in everything except the detachment with which he views European civilization, as something intrinsically strange—a heap of relics, a universe of books without a central clue. This detachment must be, in part, geographical; by many devious routes he returns to the home in space and time that he finds

> in the tumbledown
> Decadence of the widespread suburbs,
> And in the thistledown that the pampas wind

Blows into the entrance hall . . .
And in a flag sort of blue and white
Over a barracks, and in unappetizing stories
Of street-corner knifings, and in the sameness
Of afternoons that are wiped out and leave us . . .

Perhaps Latin America, which has already given us the absolute skepticism of Machado de Assis, is destined to reënact the intellectual patterns of ancient Greece. Borges' voracious and vaguely idle learning, his ecumenic and problematical and unconsoling theology, his willingness to reconsider the most primitive philosophical questions, his tolerance of superstition in both himself and others, his gingerly and regretful acknowledgment of women and his disinterest in the psychological and social worlds that women dominate, his almost Oriental modesty, his final solitude, his serene pride—this constellation of Stoic attributes, mirrored in the southern hemisphere, appears inverted and frightful.

Borges the Labyrinth Maker, by Ana María Barrenechea, has for its jacket design a labyrinth from which there is no exit. I do not know whether this is intentional or a mistake in drawing. The book is a methodical and efficient arrangement of quotations from Borges in abstract categories—The Infinite, Chaos and the Cosmos, Pantheism and Personality, Time and Eternity, Idealism and Other Forms of Unreality. In a foreword, Borges says that the book "has unearthed many secret links and affinities in my own literary output of which I had been quite unaware. I thank her for those revelations of an unconscious process." Professor Barrenechea's collations, however—including many sentences and paragraphs of Borges not elsewhere translated—seem to me an admirable explication of his conscious philosophical concerns as they shape, adjective by adjective, his fiction. What is truly unconscious—the sense of life that drives him from unequivocal philosophical and critical assertion to the essential ambiguity of fiction—she scarcely touches. The labyrinth of his thought-forms is drawn without an indication of how his concrete and vigorous art has emerged. She admits this: "Only one aspect of the writer's work—the expression of irreality—has been treated; but Borges' creativity is characterized by the richness and complexity of his art."

The great achievement of his art is his short stories. To round off this review of accessory volumes, I will describe two of my favorites.

"The Waiting" is from his second major collection, *El Aleph*, and is found, translated by James E. Irby, in *Labyrinths*. It is a rarity in Borges' *oeuvre*—a story in which nothing incredible occurs. A gangster fleeing from the vengeance of another gangster seeks anonymity in a northwest part of Buenos Aires. After some weeks of solitary existence, he is discovered and killed. These events are assigned a detailed and mundane setting. The very number of the boarding house where he lives is given (4004: a Borgian formula for immensity), and the neighborhood is flatly described: "The man noted with approval the spotted plane trees, the square plot of earth at the foot of each, the respectable houses with their little balconies, the pharmacy alongside, the dull lozenges of the paint and hardware store. A long windowless hospital wall backed the sidewalk on the other side of the street; the sun reverberated, farther down, from some greenhouses." Yet much information is withheld. "The man" mistakenly gives a cabdriver a Uruguayan coin, which "had been in his pocket since that night in the hotel at Melo." What had happened that night in Melo and the nature of his offense against his enemy are not disclosed. And when the landlady—herself unnamed, and specified as having "a distracted or tired air"—asks the man his name he gives the name, Villari, of the man hunting him! He does this, Borges explains, "not as a secret challenge, not to mitigate the humiliation which actually he did not feel, but because that name troubled him, because it was impossible for him to think of any other. Certainly he was not seduced by the literary error of thinking that assumption of the enemy's name might be an astute maneuver."

Villari—Villari the hunted—is consistently prosaic, even stupid. He ventures out to the movies and, though he sees stories of the underworld that contain images of his old life, takes no notice of them, "because the idea of a coincidence between art and reality was alien to him." Reading of another underworld in Dante, "he did not judge the punishments of hell to be unbelievable or excessive." He has a toothache and is compelled to have the tooth pulled. "In this ordeal he was neither more cowardly nor more

tranquil than other people." His very will to live is couched nega-
tively: "It only wanted to endure, not to come to an end." The
next sentence, grounding the abhorrence of death upon the simplest
and mildest things, recalls Unamuno. "The taste of the maté, the
taste of black tobacco, the growing line of shadows gradually
covering the patio—these were sufficient incentives."

Unobtrusively, the reader comes to love Villari, to respect his
dull humility and to share his animal fear. Each brush with the
outer world is a touch of terror. The toothache—"an intimate discharge of pain in the back of his mouth"—has the force of a
"horrible miracle." Returning from the movies, he feels pushed,
and, turning "with anger, with indignation, with secret relief,"
he spits out "a coarse insult." The passerby and the reader are alike
startled by this glimpse into the savage criminal that Villari has
been. Each night, at dawn, he dreams of Villari—Villari the
hunter—and his accomplices overtaking him, and of shooting them
with the revolver he keeps in the drawer of the bedside table. At
last—whether betrayed by the trip to the dentist, the visits to the
movie house, or the assumption of the other's name we do not
know—he is awakened one July dawn by his pursuers:

> Tall in the shadows of the room, curiously simplified by those
> shadows (in the fearful dreams they had always been clearer), vigi-
> lant, motionless and patient, their eyes lowered as if weighted down
> by the heaviness of their weapons, Alejandro Villari and a stranger
> had overtaken him at last. With a gesture, he asked them to wait
> and turned his face to the wall, as if to resume his sleep. Did he do
> it to arouse the pity of those who killed him, or because it is less
> difficult to endure a frightful happening than to imagine it and
> endlessly await it, or—and this is perhaps most likely—so that the
> murderers would be a dream, as they had already been so many
> times, in the same place, at the same hour?

So the inner action of the narrative has been to turn the utterly
unimaginative hero into a magician. In retrospect, this conversion
has been scrupulously foreshadowed. The story, indeed, is a beautiful cinematic succession of shadows; the most beautiful are those
above, which simplify the assassins—"(in the fearful dreams they
had always been clearer)." The parenthesis of course makes a
philosophic point: it opposes the ambiguity of reality to the rela-

tive clarity and simplicity of what our minds conceive. It functions as well in the realistic level of the story, bodying forth all at once the climate, the moment of dawn, the atmosphere of the room, the sleeper's state of vision, the menace and matter-of-factness of the men, "their eyes lowered as if weighted down by the heaviness of their weapons." Working from the artificial reality of films and gangster novels, and imposing his hyper-subtle sensations of unreality on the underworld of his plot, Borges has created an episode of criminal brutality in some ways more convincing than those in Hemingway. One remembers that in "The Killers" Ole Andreson also turns his face to the wall. It is barely possible that Borges had in mind a kind of gloss of Hemingway's classic. If that is so, with superior compassion and keener attention to peripheral phenomena he has enriched the theme. In his essay on Hawthorne, Borges speaks of the Argentine literary aptitude for realism; his own florid fantasy is grafted onto that native stock.

"The Library of Babel," which appears in *Ficciones*, is wholly fantastic, yet refers to the librarian's experience of books. Anyone who has been in the stacks of a great library will recognize the emotional aura, the wearying impression of an inexhaustible and mechanically ordered chaos, that suffuses Borges' mythical universe, "composed of an indefinite, perhaps an infinite, number of hexagonal galleries, with enormous ventilation shafts in the middle, encircled by very low railings." Each hexagon contains twenty shelves, each shelf thirty-two books, each book four hundred and ten pages, each page forty lines, each line eighty letters. The arrangement of these letters is almost uniformly chaotic and formless. The nameless narrator of "The Library of Babel" sets forward, pedantically, the history of philosophical speculation by the human beings who inhabit this inflexible and inscrutable cosmos, which is equipped, apparently for their convenience, with spiral stairs, mirrors, toilets, and lamps ("The light they emit is insufficient, incessant").

This monstrous and comic model of the universe contains a full range of philosophical schools—idealism, mysticism, nihilism:

> The idealists argue that the hexagonal halls are a necessary form of absolute space, or, at least, of our intuition of space. They contend that a triangular or pentagonal hall is inconceivable.

The mystics claim that to them ecstasy reveals a round chamber containing a great book with a continuous back circling the walls of the room. . . . That cyclical book is God.

I know of a wild region whose librarians repudiate the vain super-stitious custom of seeking any sense in books and compare it to looking for meaning in dreams or in the chaotic lines of one's hands. . . . They speak (I know) of "the febrile Library, whose hazardous volumes run the constant risk of being changed into others and in which everything is affirmed, denied, and confused as by a divinity in delirium."

Though the Library appears to be eternal, the men within it are not, and they have a history punctuated by certain discoveries and certain deductions now considered axiomatic. Five hundred years ago, in an upper hexagon, two pages of homogeneous lines were discovered that within a century were identified as "a Samoyed-Lithuanian dialect of Guaraní, with classical Arabic inflections" and translated. The contents of these two pages—"notions of com-binational analysis"—led to the deduction that the Library is total; that is, its shelves contain all possible combinations of the ortho-graphic symbols:

Everything is there: the minute history of the future, the auto-biographies of the archangels, the faithful catalogue of the Library, thousands and thousands of false catalogues, a demonstration of the fallacy of these catalogues, a demonstration of the fallacy of the true catalogue, the Gnostic gospel of Basilides, the commentary on this gospel, the commentary on the commentary on this gospel, the veridical account of your death, a version of each book in all lan-guages, the interpolations of every book in all books.

Men greeted this revelation with joy; "the universe suddenly expanded to the limitless dimensions of hope." They surged onto the stairs, searching for Vindications—books that would vindicate and explain his life to each man. Sects sprang up. One used dice and metal letters in an attempt to "mimic the divine disorder" and compose by chance the canonical volumes. Another, the Purifiers, destroyed millions of books, hurling them down the air shafts. They believed in "the Crimson Hexagon: books of a smaller than ordi-nary format, omnipotent, illustrated, magical." A third sect wor-shipped the Man of the Book—a hypothetical librarian who, in some remote hexagon, must have perused a book "which is the cipher and perfect compendium of *all the rest*." This librarian is a god. "Many pilgrimages have sought Him out."

The analogies with Christianity are pursued inventively and without the tedium of satire. The narrator himself confides, "To me, it does not seem unlikely that on some shelf of the universe there lies a total book. I pray the unknown gods that some man— even if only one man, and though it have been thousands of years ago!—may have examined and read it." But in his own person he has only the "elegant hope" that the Library, if traversed far enough, would repeat itself in the same disorder, which then would constitute an order. At hand, in the illegible chaos, are only tiny rays of momentary sense, conglomerations of letters spelling *O Time your pyramids, Combed Clap of Thunder*, or *The Plaster Cramp*.

This kind of comedy and desperation, these themes of vindication and unattainability, suggest Kafka. But *The Castle* is a more human work, more personal and neurotic; the fantastic realities of Kafka's fiction are projections of the narrator-hero's anxieties, and have no communion, no interlocking structure, without him. The Library of Babel instead has an adamant solidity. Built of mathematics and science, it will certainly survive the weary voice describing it, and outlast all its librarians, already decimated, we learn in a footnote, by "suicide and pulmonary diseases." We move, with Borges, beyond psychology, beyond the human, and confront, in his work, the world atomized and vacant. Perhaps not since Lucretius has a poet so definitely felt men as incidents in space.

What are we to make of him? The economy of his prose, the tact of his imagery, the courage of his thought are there to be admired and emulated. In resounding the note of the marvellous last struck in English by Wells and Chesterton, in permitting infinity to enter and distort his imagination, he has lifted fiction away from the flat earth where most of our novels and short stories still take place. Yet discouragingly large areas of truth seem excluded from his vision. Though the population of the Library somehow replenishes itself, and "fecal necessities" are provided for, neither food nor fornication is mentioned—and in truth they are not generally seen in libraries. I feel in Borges a curious implication: the unrealities of physical science and the senseless repetitions of history have made the world outside the library an uninhabitable vacuum. Literature—that European empire augmented with translations from remote kingdoms—is now the only world capable of housing and sustaining new literature. Is this too curious? Did not Eliot recommend forty years ago, in reviewing *Ulysses*, that new novels be retellings of old myths? Is not the greatest of modern novels, *Remembrance of Things Past*, about its own inspiration? Have not many books already been written from within Homer and the Bible? Did not Cervantes write from within Ariosto and Shakespeare from within Holinshed? Borges, by predilection and by program, carries these inklings toward a logical extreme: the view of books as, in sum, an alternate creation, vast, accessible, highly colored, rich in arcana, possibly sacred. Just as physical man, in his cities, has manufactured an environment whose scope and challenge and hostility eclipse that of the natural world, so literate man has heaped up a counterfeit universe capable of supporting life. Certainly the traditional novel as a transparent imitation of human circumstance has "a distracted or tired air." Ironic and blasphemous as Borges' hidden message may seem, the texture and method of his creations, though strictly inimitable, answer to a deep need in contemporary fiction—the need to confess the fact of artifice.

Three Translations

(*with Norman Thomas di Giovanni*)

THE SEA

Before our human dream (or terror) wove
Mythologies, cosmogonies, and love,
Before time coined its substance into days,
The sea, the always sea, existed: was.
Who is the sea? Who is that violent being,
Violent and ancient, who gnaws the foundations

Of earth? He is both one and many oceans;
He is abyss and splendor, chance and wind.
Who looks on the sea sees it the first time,
Every time, with the wonder distilled
From elementary things—from beautiful
Evenings, the moon, the leap of a bonfire.
Who is the sea, and who am I? The day
That follows my last agony shall say.

THE ENIGMAS

I who am singing these lines today
Will be tomorrow the enigmatic corpse
Who dwells in a realm, magical and barren,
Without a before or a when.
So say the mystics. I say I believe
Myself undeserving of Heaven or Hell,
But make no predictions. Each man's tale
Shifts like the forms of Proteus.
What errant labyrinth, what blinding flash
Of splendor and glory shall become my fate
When the end of this adventure presents me with
The curious experience of death?
I want to drink its crystal-pure oblivion,
To be forever; but never to have been.

THE LABYRINTH

Zeus himself could not undo these nets
Of stone encircling me. My mind forgets
The persons I have been along the way,
The hated way of monotonous walls
That is my fate. The galleries seem straight
But curve furtively, forming secret circles
At the terminus of years; and the parapets
Have been worn smooth by the passage of the days.

In the tepid alabaster dust I discern
Tracks that frighten me. The hollow air
Of evening sometimes brings a bellowing,
Or the echo, desolate, of bellowing.
I know that hidden in the shadows lurks
Another, whose task it is to exhaust
The loneliness that weaves this unravelling Hell,
To crave my blood, to fatten on my death.
We seek each other. O if only this
Were the last day of our antithesis!

NABOKOV

Mnemosyne Chastened

SPEAK, MEMORY, *An Autobiography Revisited,* by Vladimir Nabokov.
316 pp. G. P. Putnam's Sons, 1966.

Alas, Nabokov doesn't want to be an American writer after all.
He has moved to Switzerland and, instead of composing the delightful, devilish, and unimaginable successor to *Pale Fire,* fusses
with backward-looking projects such as ushering his minor Russian works (*Despair, The Eye, The Waltz Invention*) into English,
defending in *Encounter* his sumptuous but ungratefully received
version of *Eugene Onegin,* and translating *Lolita* into Russian, a
virtually posthumous maneuver not likely to win much gratitude
either.

The pity is, his greatness waits here. To my taste his American
novels are his best, with a fiercer frivolity and a cruelty more
humane than in the fiction of his European decades. In America
his almost impossible style encountered, after twenty years of
hermetic exile, a subject as impossible as itself, ungainly with the
same affluence. He rediscovered our monstrosity. His fascinatingly
astigmatic stereopticon projected not only the landscape—the eerie
arboreal suburbs, the grand emptinesses, the exotic and touchingly
temporary junk of roadside America—but the wistful citizens of
a violent society desperately oversold, in the absence of other connectives, on love. If the perceiver of John Shade and Charlotte Haze
and Clare Quilty and the Waindell College that impinged on poor
Pnin devotes the rest of his days to fond rummaging in the Russian attic of his mind, the loss is national, and sadder than Sputnik.

The latest memento confided to the care of Nabokov's American public is a revision of *Speak, Memory*, whose chapters were published one by one in (mostly) *The New Yorker* from 1948 to 1950 and assembled as *Conclusive Evidence* in 1951. As readers then already know, twelve of the fifteen chapters portray an aspect of the writer's happy boyhood as the eldest son of a St. Petersburg aristocrat, and the last three, more briefly but as enchantingly, sketch his rootless years in Cambridge, Berlin, and Paris. Nabokov has never written English better than in these reminiscences; never since has he written so sweetly. With tender precision and copious wit, exploiting a vocabulary and a sensibility enriched by the methodical pursuit of lepidoptera, inspired by an atheist's faith in the magic of simile and the sacredness of lost time, Nabokov makes of his past a brilliant icon—bejewelled, perspectiveless, untouchable. While there are frequent passages of Joycean trickiness, Proust presides in the metaphorical arabesques, the floral rhythms, and the immobilized surrender to memory. Proust, however, by fictionalizing Illiers into Combray, threw his childhood open to everyone; whereas the Nabokov memoir is narrowed by its implication that only an expatriate Russian, a well-born and intellectual Russian at that, can know nostalgia so exquisite.

The revisions, which a laborious collation with the 1951 edition has bared to my scrutiny, tend to narrow the memoir further. The author, back in Europe, has consulted with his sisters and cousins, who have chastened his imperfect recollections. Much new information about the Nabokov tribe, bristling with parenthetic dates and hyphenated alliances with the Prussian nobility, has been foisted off on Chapter Three; a tidy dry biography of his father now inaugurates Chapter Nine. (Compare, invidiously, the fabulous epic of filial admiration worked into his novel *The Gift*.) Elsewhere gardeners and dachshunds have been named, tutors sorted out, and apologies delivered to his previously suppressed brother Sergey. Some of the interpolations are welcome (the family tennis game in Chapter Two, the wooing of Tamara in Chapter Twelve, the differentiated drawing masters in Chapter Four); but sentences at times limp under their new load of accuracy and the ending of one vignette, "Mademoiselle O" (Chapter Five), is quite dulled by the gratuitous postscript of some recent personal history. The additions, and the addition of pleasant but imagination-cramping photographs, make the book more of a family album and slightly less of a miracle of impressionistic recall. Very few changes are stylistic. The grand evocations of the Nord-Express and the blending parks and gardens of exile are not improved—how could they be? On page 19, "sensitive youth" becomes "young chronophobiac," and on page 284, "Dostoevskian emotion" becomes the more scornful "Dostoevskian drisk." On page 100, a rather conventional image of "that great heavenly O shining above the Russian wilderness" has very wonderfully become "the moon, fancy's rear-vision mirror." And on page 48, a burned bridge has been unkindled; Nabokov has smoothly stricken an irreverent reference to a dachshund descended from a dog of Anton Chekhov's as being "one of my few connections with the main current of Russian literature." Alas, that now seems his hope —to rejoin, by some sparkling future rivulet beyond the grim hydroelectric dam of Sovietism, that remote Zemblan current.

Mary Unrevamped

MARY, by Vladimir Nabokov, translated from the Russian by Michael Glenny in collaboration with the author. 114 pp. McGraw-Hill, 1970.

His first novel, written in 1925. Faithful Nabokovians have met Mary before; she sat for her portrait as Tamara in *Speak, Memory*, lurks near the heart of *Lolita*, and was deified in *Ada*. Here, artistically as well as chronologically young, she is the first love of the autobiographical hero, Ganin, for whom her wanton yet delicate Tartar beauty condenses into pure perfume the idyll of rural Russia and the enchantment of privileged youth. But Ganin remembers her from afar, when he is in a Berlin boarding house surrounded by other émigrés, comic and pathetic types of exile from reality—a race as of film extras, "flickering, shadowy doppelgangers, the casual Russian film extras, sold for ten marks apiece and still flitting, God knows where, across the white gleam of a screen." Ganin wakes from the shadows, from dreaming of Mary, at the end, and slopes off to his future as, it may be, an internationally renowned poet/scholar/novelist. *Mary* not only adumbrates the future of a master, it shines by its own light. From the start, Nabokov had his sharp peripheral vision, an intent deftness at netting the gaudy phrase, and the knack (crucial to novelists and chess players) of setting up combinations. Though his materials are tender, his treatment shows the good-natured toughness that gives an artist long life. Wisely, and nicely, he has spared this venerable text the—he admits—"high-handed revampments" to which his elder self is prone, and has supervised an exact, deferential translation.

The Crunch of Happiness

GLORY, by Vladimir Nabokov, translated from the Russian by Dmitri Nabokov in collaboration with the author. 205 pp. McGraw-Hill, 1971.

Here is a book that deserves not a review but a party. Let us all rejoice with Vladimir Nabokov. Before he was twenty, revolution deprived him of his Mother Russia and of an estate worth millions. When he was forty, Hitler deprived him of his second home, Europe, and of another fortune—the accumulated treasure of fiction and poetry that his pseudonym V. Sirin had composed in the Russian language, a precious *oeuvre* unpublishable in the Soviet Union and destined, it seemed, to fade into oblivion as the subnation of Russian émigrés was scattered and absorbed by the passage of time. When Nabokov landed here, in 1940, his genius had neither a visible past nor an imaginable future. However, he had known English since his boyhood, and in this second language he recast his aloofly original inspirations, reignited his singular verbal fire, and bestowed upon America a literary master it had done nothing to raise. This second career, crowned by the notorious and remunerative and splendid *Lolita*, has in its strength reached down and redeemed from limbo the substance of the first career—the novels composed by "Sirin" in Berlin between 1925 and 1937. Now, with Nabokov sailing nicely into his eighth decade, the last of these Russian novels to reach the safe haven of definitive English translation, *Glory*, has been published. The rainbow of romances (nine Russian, six American) now arches complete, from *Mary* to *Ada*, and though, along with some short stories and poems and feuilletons, a few fine vibrations have no doubt been left behind in the Russian—a fuzz of nuance and euphony as untransferable as the dust on a butterfly's wing—Nabokov's diligence and self-respect have essentially defied a cruel century's blind attempt to silence his sensibility and disarray his shelf of work.

Why *Glory* (up to now translated on bibliographical lists as *The Exploit*) waited until last must be guessed at. It was written in 1930, immediately after *The Eye;* if *The Eye* is discounted as a novella, *Glory* falls between two masterly novels—*The Defense* and *Laughter in the Dark.* By comparison, it is weak; the ending baffles, and what happens on the way to the ending occurs with a curious, rather ingratiating casualness. *Glory* never really awakens to its condition as a novel, its obligation to generate suspense. Its secondary characters—Darwin, the sanguine and gentlemanly Englishman, and Sonia, the sulky little émigrée—come into view elliptically, as if they were revolving around some other sun. The youthful hero, Martin Edelweiss, is a center of anti-gravity; we feel that things flee him. Though he is Russian, his name is Swiss, cluing some atomic split within. In one of those landlordly prefaces that slam shut the doors of unsightly closets, inveigh against the Freudian in the hall, and roughly nudge the prospective tenant toward the one window with a view, Nabokov likens the design of *Glory* to a chess problem whose crux is the impotence of the customarily high-powered Queen. The hint is helpful. In the backward look, the book's two faults, if faults they be (sleepy development, stark conclusion), do combine into a single, intended quality—a weak strength, or sad joy.

Martin is led along some of the paths of Nabokov's autobiography—the country house with its sandy *allées*, the numinous shadowy albums and tinted porch glass, the English biscuits and toothpaste imported from afar, the idyllic days in the warm Crimea while civil war rages, the improvised departure on a Black Sea freighter, the arrival in a Europe that will never shed the postcard brightness and carved-clock quaintness of a place visited, of a place that is not Russia and therefore not quite real. We have been here before, in Luzhin's boyhood and in Van Veen's private mythology and, above all, in *Speak, Memory*. Nabokov, in his role of over-solicitous proprietor, warns us away from seeking out "duplicate items or kindred scenery" in *Speak, Memory*, but who could miss the marvellous newspaper-phoenix, the sheet of the London *Times* held across the fireplace to make it draw?

> The taut sheet would grow warm and transparent, and the lines of print, mingling with the lines showing through from the reverse side, looked like the bizarre lettering of some mumbo-jumbo language. Then, as the hum and tumult of the fire increased, a fox-red, darkening spot would appear on the paper and suddenly burst through. The whole sheet, now aflame, would be instantly sucked in and sent flying up. And a belated passerby, a gowned don, could observe, through the gloom of the gothic night, a fiery-haired witch emerge from the chimney into the starry sky. Next day Martin would pay a fine.

When, a quarter of a century later, Nabokov set down in English his memories of Cambridge, this imagery returned, almost sentence by sentence: "Then the flaming sheet, with the whirr of a liberated phoenix, would fly up the chimney to join the stars. It cost one a fine of twelve shillings if that firebird was observed." In that same Chapter Thirteen of *Speak, Memory*, Nabokov states, "The story of my college years in England is really the story of my trying to become a Russian writer." Martin Edelweiss is an alter ego gutted of Nabokov's artistic vocation; this deliberate lobotomy leaves an oddly hollow protagonist, a "travelling playboy" with dreams but no ambitions, graduating from college into tennis and vagabondage and, at the end, a suicidal return to Russia. But Martin has always, come to think of it, been close to death:

> Lying in the next room and feigning to snore so his mother would not think he was awake, Martin also recalled harrowing things, also tried to comprehend his father's death and to catch a wisp of post-humous tenderness in the dark of the room.

Not only his father but friends die—contemporaries fighting with the White armies—and in the Crimea, on a dark road, he is challenged by a drunk with a gun, and in the Alps he challenges himself to venture out onto a dizzying ledge. If in retrospect the reader finds that he has failed to take these dark hints seriously enough, the reason may be that Martin is Nabokov's healthiest hero and *Glory* his sunniest book.

Page after page brims with glistening physical description:

> With the onset of summer the cross-marked sheep were herded higher into the mountains. A babbling metallic tinkling, of unknown origin and from an unknown direction, would gradually become audible. Floating nearer, it enveloped the listener, giving him an odd tickling sensation in the mouth. Then, in a cloud of dust, came flowing a gray, curly, tightly packed mass of sheep rubbing against each other, and the moist, hollow tinkle of the bells, which delighted all of one's senses, mounted, swelled so mysteriously that the dust itself seemed to be ringing as it billowed above the moving backs of the sheep.

By denying Martin any artistic or political passion while not denying him his own full complement of senses, Nabokov has released a genie rare in fiction—a robust sense of physical well-being. The sensations of vigorous tennis, of goal tending at soccer, of a bare-knuckled fistfight are in *Glory* given their due by an artist and meditator who was also an athlete; so, too, are the subtler but not less physical sensations of train travel, of pipe smoke and male companionship over tea, of "the fresh rough smell of earth and melting snow," of agriculture—"the hollowed earth would fill with bubbling brown water and, feeling in it with a spade, he mercifully softened the soil, until something gave delightfully, and the percolating water sank away, washing the roots. He felt happy he knew how to satisfy a plant's thirst." Happiness, as with an earlier Russian author, is the fragile, somehow terrible theme. Martin's sexual encounters tend to be felt in terms of the woman's fragility:

> He thought with rapt nostalgia about that amiable woman, with the touchingly hollow chest and the clear eyes, and about the way her fragile frame crunched in his embrace, causing her to say softly, "Ouch, you'll break me."

Similarly rapt, the sentences seek to embrace, with the crunch of a superb adjective, the full and fainting body of a moment.

> A wave would swell, boil with foam, and topple rotundly, spreading and running up on the shingle. Then, unable to hold fast, it would slip back to the grumbling of *awakened* pebbles.

. . . the country coolness of the rooms, so keenly perceptible after the outdoor heat; a fat bumblebee knocking against the ceiling with a *chagrined* droning; the paws of the fir trees against the blue of the sky. . . .

From that year on Martin developed a passion for trains, travels, distant lights, the heartrending wails of locomotives in the dark of night, and the *waxworks* vividness of local stations flashing by.

The author's efforts to fix the sensations, the gestures—"he would compress his thin lips, take off his pince-nez as carefully as if it were a dragonfly"—so freshly and precisely become a means whereby the third-person hero accrues moral credit, or at least a certain scrupulous stubbornness. An old man dies, and "Martin felt sorry for the originality of the deceased, who was truly ir-replaceable—his gestures, his beard, his sculpturesque wrinkles, the sudden shy smile, the jacket button that hung by a thread, and his way of licking a stamp with his entire tongue before sticking it on the envelope and banging it with his fist. In a certain sense this was all of greater value than the social merits for which there existed such easy little clichés." Martin is credited with a "medita-tive *joie de vivre*" and a search for "scintilla," but is declared untormented "by a writer's covetousness (so akin to the fear of death), by that constant state of anxiety compelling one to fix indelibly this or that evanescent trifle"; the declaration is rather formal and does have about it the cruelty of some dissecting ex-periment that permits a creature to twitch without benefit of a head. Yet it is true, as our decade has again borne witness, that youth, in the sensitivity of its animal health, tends to be artistic, and that without the task of art before it the artistic temper wastes itself in symbolic actions, in "trips" that are meaningless self-tests and whose secret destination is death. This point is contained in *Glory*, but it is not the point of the book. The point, surely, lies in its rapturous evocations and the *frissons* they give us—what Martin terms "the unexpected, sunlit clearings, where you can stretch until your joints crunch, and remain entranced," what Nabokov in his afterword to *Lolita* announces he "shall bluntly call aesthetic bliss." In its residue of bliss experienced, and in its charge of bliss conveyed, *Glory* measures up as, though the last to arrive, far from the least of this happy man's Russian novels.

Van Loves Ada, Ada Loves Van

ADA, by Vladimir Nabokov. 589 pp. McGraw-Hill, 1969.

When a book fails to agree with a reader, it is either because the author has failed to realize his intentions or because his intentions are disagreeable. Since Vladimir Nabokov is, all in all, the best-equipped writer in the English-speaking world (of which he inhabits a personal promontory by the side of Lake Geneva), the opening chapters of his giant new novel, *Ada*, must be taken as intentionally repellent. His prose has never—not even in his haughty prefaces to works resurrected from the Russian, not even in Humbert Humbert's maddest flights—menaced a cowering reader with more bristling erudition, garlicky puns, bearish parentheses, and ogreish winks. For example:

> "I can add," said the girl [Ada], "that the petal belongs to the common Butterfly Orchis; that my mother was even crazier than her sister; and that the paper flower so cavalierly dismissed is a perfectly recognizable reproduction of an early-spring sanicle that I saw in profusion on hills in coastal California last February. Dr. Krolik, our local naturalist, to whom you, Van, have referred, as Jane Austen might have phrased it, for the sake of rapid narrative information (you recall Brown, don't you, Smith?), has determined the example I brought back from Sacramento to Ardis, as the Bear-Foot, B,E,A,R, my love, not my foot or yours, or the Stabian flower girl's—an allusion, which your father, who, according to Blanche, is also mine, would understand like this (American fingersnap)."

Nor is the matter being thus roughly intruded into our consciousness of a compensating solidity or persuasive immediacy. *Ada* is subtitled "Or Ardor: A Family Chronicle," and the central family matter, not easily grasped, concerns the marriage of the two Durmanov sisters, Marina and Aqua, to two men each called Walter D. Veen, first cousins differentiated by the nicknames Red (or Dan) and Demon. Demon has an extensive love affair with Marina but marries Aqua, who readily goes insane; this unhappy marriage has one apparent offspring, Ivan, who is not to be confused with Uncle Ivan, the Durmanov sisters' short-lived brother. "Apparent," I say, because young "Van's" real mother is Marina, who, fertile as well as obliging, is also the mother of Demon's other illegitimate child, Ada, and—by her own husband, Red Veen, the well-known art dealer—another daughter, Lucette. The very incestuous ("very" because besides being ostensible first cousins and actual siblings they are also third cousins, descended from Prince Vseslav Zemski) love affair between Van and Ada preoccupies nearly six hundred rollicking pages.

The genealogical maze rests upon the unquiet geography of the planet Demonia, or Antiterra, where our homely Terra is a disconnected rumor, pieced together from the visions of madmen and "believed in," or not, like Heaven. On Antiterra, Canady and Estoty contain large French and Russian territories (much as Nabokov's memory must) and surprising sights, like "the peasant-bare footprint of Tolstoy preserved in the clay of a motor court in Utah where he had written the tale of Murat, the Navajo chieftain, a French general's bastard." Most of *Ada* occurs in the second half of Antiterra's 19th century, after the "L disaster" has caused electricity to be banned, leaving people to communicate with "dorophones," which ring by making all the toilets in the house gurgle; one answers by saying "*A l'eau!*" The atmosphere of this "distortive glass of our distorted glebe" is dreamy with the stale air of classic novels and swarms with swattable little midges like "Mr. Eliot, a Jewish businessman," "Dr. Froit of Signy-Mondieu-Mondieu," "*Les Amours du Docteur Mertvago,*" "*Collected Works of Falknermann,*" "that dislikable Norbert von Miller," and "James Jones, a formula whose complete lack of connotation made an ideal pseudonym despite its happening to be his real name."

Now, why should an author not create a "nulliverse" to represent "oneirologically" the contents of his own mind? The "L disaster," "which had the singular effect of both causing and cursing the notion of 'Terra,' " is surely the Russian Revolution, which caused such a great dislocation in Nabokov's life. The confusion of America (Estotiland) and Russia (Tartary) into one idyllic nation where everyone speaks French is, more than a joke upon Canada, a metaphor of personal history. Vain, venereal Van Veen verges on V.N.; Nabokov = Van + book. Ada (rhymes with Nevada) is ardor and art—but not, I think, the Americans for Democratic Action. She is also, in a dimension or two, Nabokov's wife Véra, his constant collaboratrice and the invariable dedicatee of his works. Ada's marginal comments on Van's manuscript, reproduced in print, are among the liveliest bits in the book, and offer an occasional check upon the author's rampaging genius. I suspect that many of the details in this novel double as personal communication between husband and wife; some of the bothersomely exact dates, for instance, must be, to use a favorite word of our author, "fatadic." I am certain that trilingual puns crowd and crawl (*"Je raffole de tout ce qui rampe"*—"I'm crazy about everything that crawls"—Ada says) beneath the surface of this novel like wood lice under the bark of an old stump. Their patient explication, and the formal arrangement of the parallels and contraries that geometricize "our rambling romance," the hurried reviewer may confidently leave to the graduate student who, between puffs of pot, while his wife strums the baby or dandles the guitar—by Log, this deadly style is infectious!—can spend many a pleasant and blameless hour unstitching the sequinned embroidery of Nabokov's five years' labor of love. He might begin with the prominently displayed anagram of "insect" ("incest," nicest," "scient"), move on to the orchid-imitating butterflies and butterfly-imitating orchids, get his feet wet in the water imagery (Aqua, Marina, *"A l'eau!"* yourself), and then do something with "cruciform," which crops up in several surprising connections, such as mounted moths, the hero's feces, and the arrangement of a mature woman's four patches of hair. Indeed, this book is Nabokov's most religious—his Testament as well as his *Tempest*—and manages several oblique squints at the Christian religion, a previous sketch of a structured supernature. *Ada* is the feminine form of the Russian "Ad," for Hades or Hell, and there is a Van in Nirvana and Heaven, for instance.

But, to answer the question posed above, one reason that an author should not create a nulliverse is that it is difficult to generate on an Antiterra the gravity that even the feeblest terrestrial tale appropriates. The details, the sometimes comical and sometimes waspish extensions of the author's prejudices and fancy, distract us from the angels and demons, who are, it turns out, meant to be human. Specifically, Ada and Van adventure amid obstacles so automatic, so confessedly retrieved from the attics of Mme. de La Fayette and Count Tolstoy, that it is hard to care about their intermittences of copulation as much as they and their creator do. In a landscape of "Ladore, Ladoga, Laguna, Lugano, and Luga," everything melts into foolery. I confess to a prejudice: fiction is earthbound, and while in decency the names of small towns and middling cities must be faked, metropolises and nations are unique and should be given their own names or none. I did not even like it when Nabokov, in *Pale Fire*, gave New York State the preëmpted appellation of Appalachia. He is, among other titles to our love, the foremost poet of Earth's geography, who in his remarkable story "Lance" saw long before the actual astronauts "the praying woman of the Baltic, and . . . the elegant Americas caught in their trapeze act, and Australia like a baby Africa lying on its side." His vision and flair are themselves so supermundane that to apply them to a fairyland is to put icing on icing. There is nothing in the landscapes of *Ada* to rank with the Russian scenery of *Speak, Memory* or the trans-American hegira of Lolita and Humbert Humbert.

As with place names, so with face names; we never get over the playful twinning of Aqua and Marina, Demon and Dan, and though Aqua's madness spins a few beautiful pages and Demon makes some noises approximating those of a flesh-and-blood father, the four remain animated anagrams, symmetrical appendages that want to be characters. To be sure, we are in a world of chrysalis and metamorphosis; as in *Invitation to a Beheading* and *Bend Sinister*, the cardboard flats and gauze trappings collapse, and the author/hero, heavy with death, lumbers toward the lip of the stage. This does happen, and the last pages of *Ada* are the best, and rank with Nabokov's best, but to get to them we traverse too wide a waste of facetious, airy, side-slipped semi-reality.

Define reality.

That which exists.

Don't you mean merely that which is perceived? Can we divide the universe, of which you seem so wholly fond, from our perception of it? And can we, more to the point, divide the reality of a book from what the author says it is? Does a "dorophone" exist less on the paper than a "telephone" because a hundred million "real" telephones echo in coarse Bakelite the latter, while the former is a unique coinage of the writer's imperious imagination? And isn't an author entitled to applause and gratitude for daring to work not in dreary Zolaesque dredging of a swampy "external world" as hallucinatory as the next but along the living rainbow edge where writer's mind meets reader's in the mist of the retreating thunderstorms of "traditional" novels, a retreat most prettily signalled by the jovial iridescence of parody? Don't you think that your plebeian cavils were anticipated and scornfully dismissed in advance by this towering, snorting wizard?

To be sure, the risks have been calculated. Some offenses are intentional. On the second page, Van disarmingly confesses his "ancestral strain of whimsical, and not seldom deplorable, taste." And defensive jabs at "cretinic critics" abound. But is it intentional that the conversations between the two lovers so stiflingly reek of mutual congratulation, that the dialogue everywhere defuses itself with quibbles and pranks, and that the hero is such a brute? When the girl who relieves him of his virginity, courteously described as "a fubsy pig-pink whorlet," tries to kiss him, Van "elbow[s] her face away." When Lucette, Ada's younger sister, falls in love with him, he drives her to suicide. When Kim, a servant boy at Ardis Hall, photographs Van and Ada making love and tries to blackmail them, Van arranges to have him blinded—"carried out of his cottage with one eye hanging on a red thread and the other drowned in its blood." Ada, bless her, now and then rebukes him for his hard-heartedness, explaining that "not everybody is as happy as we are," but Van holds aloof from "silly pity—a sentiment I rarely experience" and continues to nourish at the expense of others an ego "richer and prouder than anything those two poor worms could imagine," the two worms being two lovers of Ada whom the author dispatches before duel-crazy Van can get to them. As to Kim: " 'Amends have been made,' replied fat Van with a fat man's chuckle. 'I'm keeping Kim safe and snug in a nice Home for Disabled Professional People, where he gets from me loads of nicely brailled books on new processes in chromophotography.' " This useful therapy is cousin, presumably, to "those helpful hobbies which polio patients, lunatics, and convicts are taught by generous institutions, by enlightened administrators, by ingenious psychiatrists—such as bookbinding, or putting blue beads into the orbits of dolls made by other criminals, cripples, and madmen."

It is not always easy, but it is necessary, to distinguish between the hero's callousness and the author's zest for describing deformity and pain. Gentle Professor Pnin, we remember, was going to give someday a course on "The History of Pain." Throughout Nabokov's work, pain appears as the twin, in the physical world, of madness in the psychical. *Ada* contains a cruel vision of the afterlife: "The only consciousness that persists in the hereafter is the consciousness of pain." Little sensitive particles, a web of toothaches here, a bundle of nightmares there, cling to each other "like tiny groups of obsure refugees from some obliterated country huddling together for a little smelly warmth, for dingy charities or shared recollections of nameless tortures in Tartar camps." The fragmentation of Lucette's consciousness as she drowns ("she thought it proper to inform a series of receding Lucettes . . . that what death amounted to was only a more complete assortment of the infinite fractions of solitude") is monstrously well felt. Such sharp focus on pain, death, and madness incriminates not Van but the world. After Lucette's death, he longs in a letter for "more deeply moral worlds than this pellet of muck." Yet the phrase "pellet of muck" is a dandy's dismissal, and as Van goes about the world swaddled in his millions, exposing himself to chambermaids, feasting off of adolescent prostitutes, squashing literary critics, despising his lecture audiences, and fiercely repelling all who would trespass upon his inviolate ego and his adoration of Ada, he bares, perhaps unintentionally, a moral deformity comparable to the physical deformities that fascinate him.

Nabokov was born and reared as an aristocrat. Rich, healthy, brilliant, physically successful, he lacks the neurasthenic infirmities that gave the modernism of Proust, Joyce, Kafka, and Mann its tender underside. Asked, in a recent Japanese magazine (*The Umi*, Volume 1, No. 1), the question "What authors or works have influenced you most?" Nabokov answered serenely, "None." In truth, it is hard, in the ranks of literary genius, recruited as they are from the shabby-genteel and the bedridden, to find his aristocratic, vigorous peers. There is Tolstoy, and there is Chateaubriand. Tolstoy is much on Nabokov's mind. *Ada* begins by inverting the opening sentence of *Anna Karenina* and closes by likening itself, "in pure joyousness, and Arcadian innocence," to Tolstoy's reminiscences. It contains a Vronsky, a Kitty, a Dolly; Levin's code-word courtship of Kitty is parodied by Scrabble games between Van and Ada. The country-house atmosphere of Ardis Hall mimics yet partakes of the Tolstoyan idyll. Van's father accuses him of belonging to "the Decadent School of writing, in company of naughty old Leo and consumptive Anton," and Ada does a "clever pastiche . . . mimicking Tolstoy's paragraph rhythm and chapter closings." The list of concealed allusions and twittings could doubtless be lengthened. (Graduate student, go do it!)

But Chateaubriand, to whom the author tips his hat at half a dozen intersections, looms more fondly, as grandfathers will over fathers—and boorish, booted, crypto-Communist fathers at that. *Ada* shares with *Atala* its heroine's vowels and the setting of a fantasized America, with *René* the theme of incest, and with *Mémoires d'Outre-Tombe* its posthumous posture and an affinity of tone. Even through the brown varnish of translation, certain colors and twists in Chateaubriand's prose suggest Nabokov. In *Atala*, the Mississippi (which Chateaubriand probably never saw) is described in flood:

> But in the scenes of nature grace and magnificence always go together: while the main current drags the corpses of pines and oaks to the sea, floating islands of lotus and water-lily, their yellow blooms raised like standards, are borne upstream along either bank. Green snakes, blue herons, red flamingoes, and young crocodiles travel as passengers on these flowering boats, and each colony, spreading its golden sails to the wind, will come to rest in its own quiet backwater.

The observation of the *counter*-current, the magical precision applied to a vision, the detection of an idyll at the heart of a tumult, have a kinship with the prose flights of our Russian; Chateaubriand, too, was a survivor of revolution and a naturalist:

The scene is no less picturesque in broad daylight; for a crowd of butterflies, dragonflies, humming-birds, green parakeets, blue jays, attach themselves to these mosses, which are then like a tapestry in white wool, upon which the European craftsman has worked insects and dazzling birds.

The habit of viewing nature as an artifact blends with a trick of seeing human personality as a mechanism, wherein certain rather sad inevitabilities produce jerky effects:

Apolline de Bedée [Chateaubriand's mother] had large features and was dark, dainty, and ugly; her elegant manners and lively temperament contrasted with my father's stiffness and equanimity. As fond of society as he was of solitude, and as high-spirited and cheerful as he was cold and unemotional, she did not have a single taste which was not at variance with those of her husband. . . . Obliged to keep silent when she would have liked to speak, she found consolation in a kind of noisy sadness broken by sighs which formed the only interruption to the mute sadness of my father. In matters of piety, my mother was an angel.

Later in the *Mémoires*, Chateaubriand evokes the imaginary woman that his solitude in the château at Combourg created:

A young queen would come to me, decked in diamonds and flowers (it was my sylph). She sought me out at midnight, through gardens of orange trees . . . beneath a sky of love bathed in the light of Endymion's star; she moved forward, a living statue by Praxiteles, in the midst of motionless statues, pale pictures, and silent frescoes whitened by the moonlight . . . the silken tresses from her loosened diadem fell caressingly on my brow as she bent her sixteen-year-old head over my face, and her hands rested on my breast, throbbing with respect and desire.

This is Ada, to the diamonds and flowers, the *respect* and desire. Our sensation is confirmed that Ada is Van; that the duo is a single "A" of refracted solitude; that she is too ardent and intelligent, too *respectful*, to be external. She tells him, "All my thoughts, oh, my darling, are mimotypes of yours."

Rape is the sexual sin of the mob, adultery of the bourgeoisie, and incest of the aristocracy. Romanticism, which made of every ego an aristocrat, spawned Wordsworth and Dorothy, Byron and Augusta, and Chateaubriand and Lucile, the sister who shared his

Combourg solitude, who took on the moonlit lineaments of his "sylph," and who fled into a nunnery. "When we spoke of the world," Chateaubriand recalls, "it was of that which we carried within ourselves, a world which bore little resemblance to the real world." "Van," Ada writes in the margin of *Ada*, "I trust your taste and your talent but are we *quite sure* we should keep reverting so *zestfully* to that wicked world which after all may have existed only oneirologically, Van?" The idyll of Ardis Hall has its roots in the childhood fictionalized in the early pages of *The Gift* and *The Defense*. The idyll concerns self-discovery, the discovery of poetry, of chess, of lepidoptery (Ada's passion, not Van's), of one's own genius. *Ada* allegorizes self-love, self-respect; its spirituality (and it is a spiritual book) generates itself along the circular lines that to love one's self under the guise of a sister is to feminize one's soul, to make it other than the masculine ego, to externalize it—to give oneself, then, a soul.

The outward process is less pleasing, incestuous self-sufficiency plunging rapidly through world denigration into despair. Though Van sleeps with harlots and Ada with fools, only Lucette, their half sister, has enough precious substance to come between them; when she is drowned (as movingly as possible, from Van's rather aerial point of view), the union of Ada and Van is only a matter of time, which we are told is a motionless "grayish gauze." In a world without substance, the twinned genius-ego risks acrophobia.

CHATEAUBRIAND: I made progress in the study of languages; I became strong in mathematics, for which I have always had a pronounced leaning: I would have made a good naval officer or sapper. . . . I was good at chess, billiards, shooting, and fencing; I drew tolerably well; I would have sung well, too, if my voice had been trained.

VAN: He was ten. His father had lingered in the West where the many-colored mountains acted upon Van as they had on all young Russians of genius. He could solve an Euler-type problem or learn by heart Pushkin's "Headless Horseman" poem in less than twenty minutes.

CHATEAUBRIAND: My imagination, kindled into flame and spreading in all directions, failed to find adequate nourishment anywhere and could have devoured heaven and earth.

VAN: He had to do it his own way, but the cognac was frightful, and the history of thought bristled with clichés, and it was that history he had to surmount.

CHATEAUBRIAND: In life weighed by its light weight, measured by its short measure, and stripped of all deception, there are only two things of real value: religion married with intelligence and love married with youth . . . the rest is not worth while.

VAN: . . . this pellet of muck. . . .

CHATEAUBRIAND: Finally, one thing completed my misery: the groundless despair which I carried in the depths of my heart.

VAN: He wondered what really kept him alive on terrible Antiterra, with Terra a myth and all art a game. . . .

Is art a game? Nabokov stakes his career on it, and there exist enterprising young critics who, in replacing Proust, Joyce, and Mann with the alliterative new trinity of Beckett, Borges, and naBokov,* imply that these wonderful old fellows make fine airtight boxes, like five-foot plastic cubes in a Minimal Art show, all inner reflection and shimmer, perfectly self-contained, detached from even the language of their composition. I think not. Art is part game, part grim erotic tussle with Things As They Are; the boxes must have holes where reality can look out and readers can look in. Beckett shows us the depraved rudiments of our mortal existence; Borges opens a window on the desolation of history's maze and the tang of heroism that blows off the Argentine plain. And *Ada*, though aspiring to "an art now become pure and abstract, and therefore genuine," is full of holes, stretches and pages and phrases whose life derives from life.

Oh? Such as? Your praise-space is cramped.

(1) Ada herself. Witty and convolute *and* kind in her marginal addenda, wanly feminine in her lapses and evasions, quite lovable as a pornographic heroine progressively engaged in fancier pranks. The frontier of sexual explicitness, where *Lolita* was once an outpost, has been rolled way back; Nabokov adds a charming page

---

* "Oh, I am well aware of those commentators: slow minds, hasty typewriters! They would do better to link Beckett with Maeterlinck and Borges with Anatole France."—N., interviewed by Allene Talmey, of *Vogue*, on June 26, 1969.

(page 141) to the rapidly expanding American anthology of fellatio, and the inventory of Ada's charms beginning on page 215 is of Sapphic purity and Homeric grandeur.

(2) The essays, toward the end, on time and memory. Though his rebuttals of Freud and Einstein suggest the efforts of a very impressively costumed witch doctor to analyze an internal combustion engine in terms of mana and sympathetic magic, it is fun to watch; and his attempt, in droll lecturese, to pry open the innermost secrets of existence has the uncanny dignity of high blasphemy. Science fiction in the best sense.

(3) A thousand images and verbal moments where intelligence winks and wonder gleams. At random: the moment when Demon dorophones Marina from "a roadside booth of pure crystal still tear-stained after a tremendous thunderstorm" to beg her to come see "the daze of desert flowers that the rain had brought out."

(4) All of Part V, which is "not meant as an epilogue; it is the true introduction of my ninety-seven percent true and three percent likely, *Ada or Ardor, a family chronicle*." The author, "a crotchety gray old wordman on the edge of a hotel bed," confides to us from the height of his ninety-seven years what it is like to be old, famous, impotent, and content. He describes his medicines, including "the delightful effect of a spoonful of sodium bicarbonate dissolved in water that was sure to release three or four belches as big as the speech balloons in the 'funnies' of his boyhood." He faces death, and its preliminary pain: "A giant, with an effort-contorted face, clamping and twisting an engine of agony." He reveals that Terra and Antiterra, rather casually, have merged. Ada and Van together translate into Russian some lines of John Shade, casting the last of many backward looks into Nabokov's *oeuvre*. Then they die, "into Eden or Hades, into the prose of the book or the poetry of its blurb." The blurb ends the book. It is strange but solid; sensations close to the edge of experience have been given equivalence in print. Would that such a marriage of lovely mind and surly matter had occurred earlier in *Ada*!

Wait a minute, une petite minute, pazhalsta—*what sort of loose, not to say queasily quasi-mystical, talk is "sensations close to the edge of experience"?*

Well, a man's religious life is the last province of privacy these

days, but it is clear from *Ada* and other evidences that Nabokov
is a mystic. "You believe," Ada asks Van, "you believe in the
existence of Terra? Oh, you do!" And Nabokov, when asked by
his *Playboy* interviewer if he believed in God, answered, "I know
more than I can express in words, and the little I can express
would not have been expressed had I not known more." In the
same interview, he describes his preparations for a novel, which
consist of random jottings at the behest of a "force" like that
which makes a bird collect bits of straw and fluff in preparation for
a nest. Just as Chateaubriand found accommodation for his massive
egotism and morbidity within Catholic orthodoxy, Nabokov has
made a church for himself out of fanatic pedantry; the thousand
pages of his *Onegin* footnotes are a cathedralic structure where
even the capitals that face the wall are painstakingly carved. Chateaubriand's morose and windy communion with nature at Combourg has its counterpart in Nabokov's happier intimations at
Vyra of natural intricacy, particularly that of mimetic patterns in
lepidoptera, a mimicry whose extravagant ingenuity seems unaccountable in a mechanical scheme of evolution. His fiction, from
its punning prose and its twinning of characters to the elegance of
each tale's deceptive design, re-presents his boyhood's revelation
of art-for-art's-sake within Nature. If Nature is an artifact, however, there must be, if not an Artist, at least a kind of raw reality
beneath or behind it, and the most daring and distressing quality
of his novels is their attempt to rub themselves bare, to display their
own vestments of artifice and then to remove them. Hence the
recurrent device of the uncompleted, imperfect manuscript; this
text embodies not only Ada's marginal notes but various false paragraph starts and editor's bracketed notes of the type frequent in
proof sheets. Van says of a moment of semi-recognition, "It was
a queer feeling—as of something replayed by mistake, part of a
sentence misplaced on the proof sheet, a scene run prematurely,
a repeated blemish, a wrong turn of time." This "queer feeling" is
the sensation "close to the edge of experience" that Nabokov
seeks to embody in *Ada;* this "queer feeling" is the heart of his
artistic rapture and devotion, and also of his not always delicious
mystification, his not invariably enlightening pursuit of nuancé
inklings. In *Pale Fire*, John Shade showed a surprisingly literal

interest in the afterlife; in *Ada*, Nabokov has sought to construct, with his Hades and Nirvana, an Otherlife. Art begins with magic. Though Nabokov operates, it seems to me, without the sanctions, the charity and humility, that make a priest, he lays claim to the more ancient title of magician.

The Translucing of Hugh Person

TRANSPARENT THINGS, by Vladimir Nabokov. 104 pp. McGraw-Hill, 1972.

Confessions: I have never understood how they saw the woman in half. Any willful child can dumbfound me with card tricks learned from the back of a comic book. Mystery novelists find in me their ideal gull, obligingly misled by the fishiest red herring. In calculus, I never grasped the infinitesimal but utile distinction between dt and Δt. And I do not understand Vladimir Nabokov's new novel, *Transparent Things*. This is a confession, not a com-. plaint; the world abounds in excellent apparatuses, from automobile engines to digestive tracts, resistant to my understanding. So be it. I am grateful. I am grateful that Nabokov, at an age when most writers are content to rearrange their medals and bank their anthology royalties, rides his old hobby-horses with such tenacious mount and such jubilant tallyhos. A new book by him, any new book by him, serves as reminder that art is a holiday, however grim workdays grow in the sweatshops of reality. His exuberance is catching, as readers of this hyperbole-pocked paragraph can at a glance diagnose. Well, to work.

If the critic attempts to consider *Transparent Things* as itself transparent, he can perceive several impulses pressing their faces against the glass. One is an impulse to make the most of language: a hearty impulse, even jolly, by no means above the coarse buffoonery of pun ("Giulia . . . wore a Doppler shift over her luminous body," "An electric sign, DOPPLER, shifted to Violet") and alliteration ("ruts, rocks, and roots," "cracked that crooked

cricoid"). The language bubbles, chortles, and in its abundance
of simmering exactitude boils over into mad exhortation:

> The tap expostulated, letting forth a strong squirt of rusty water be-
> fore settling down to produce the meek normal stuff—which you
> do not appreciate sufficiently, which is a flowing mystery, and, yes,
> yes, which deserves monuments to be erected to it, cool shrines!

Transparent Things's hero, Hugh Person, is an editor of, among
other authors, one "R." (a mirroring of the Russian я, *ya*, meaning "I"), who, though more corpulent and less uxorious than
Nabokov himself, does live in Switzerland, composes "surrealistic
novels of the poetic sort," and regards the rest of the world as a
grotesquely clumsy siege upon his artistic integrity. "Our Person,
our reader, was not sure he entirely approved of R.'s luxuriant
and bastard style; yet, at its best ('the gray rainbow of a fog-
dogged moon'), it was diabolically evocative." Nabokov's is really
an amorous style—foreplay in the guise of horseplay. It yearns to
clasp diaphanous exactitude into its hairy arms. To convey a child's
nocturnal unease, it can toss off the looming metaphor "Night is
always a giant"; or with tender euphonic trippings it can limn
a woman's facial expression during intercourse as "the never deceived expectancy of the dazed ecstasy that gradually idiotized her
dear features." Such a yen to evoke, to use the full spectrum latent
in the dictionary, would teach us how to read again. If not always
a comfortable, it is surely a commendable impulse.

Less so, perhaps, the murderous impulse visible through the
workings of *Transparent Things*. Since the book is something of a
thriller, its plot should be left its secrets; but, needless to say, almost no character, major or minor, survives its last turn. Strangulation, conflagration, embolism, cancer—these are some of the
methods employed. Characters who barely appear onstage have
their offstage demises dutifully reported: a detective who researched an incidental infidelity is "at present dying in a hot dirty
hospital on Formosa," a momentary lover of the heroine is smartly
crushed under an avalanche in "Chute, Colorado." A worse than
Calvinist sense of rigor constricts the poor bright creatures into
the narrowness of the killing bottle. When Muriel Spark, another
deft dealer in fatality, conjures up a hotel fire, a building's col-

lapse, or a multiple murder, an implacable God is prefigured and the crime transcends the writer's will. Not so with Nabokov. He proposes, he disposes. A design must be completed. The sometimes touchingly vivid characters exist as spots of color bounded on all sides by a shimmering nothingness; their deaths come as a rubbing out. And the reader, too, is put in his place, exterminated by the announcement that this is all an invention—*poof!* This announcement surfaces explicitly * in *Transparent Things*, as it does in *Invitation to a Beheading* and *Bend Sinister*, but the gesture of withdrawal, of Prospero's retirement, of termination and disavowal, closes even such relatively straight fiction as *Pnin* and *Laughter in the Dark*. Here, in a book that freely uses the second person and that calls its central figure (a professional reader) Hugh, the wish to personify in order to destroy carries well out into the reader's lap. You (Hugh) person, whoever you are, are nobody (*personne*): vanish, die.

A third impulse is to formulate, at the highest level of intelligence and subtlety, some statement about space/time, death, and being. R., dying, writes to his publisher:

> I believed that treasured memories in a dying man's mind dwindled to rainbow wisps; but now I feel just the contrary: my most trivial sentiments and those of all men have acquired gigantic proportions. The entire solar system is but a reflection in the crystal of my (or your) wrist watch. . . . Total rejection of all religions ever dreamt up by man and total composure in the face of total death! If I could explain this triple totality in one big book, that would become no doubt a new bible and its author the founder of a new creed.

And Vladimir Nabokov writes, on the last page, "This is, I believe, *it*: not the crude anguish of physical death but the incomparable pangs of the mysterious mental maneuver needed to pass from one state of being to another." This at least helps explain this artificer's compulsive revelations of artifice; in the moment of a fictional world's collapse, one state of being yields to another. But are we to take this as an analogy for death? If death

---

* Though not quite so explicitly in the finished book as in the bound galley proofs, wherein the last sentence, "Easy, you know, does it, son," indented like the valediction of a letter, is followed by "Vladimir Nabokov" flush right and, flush left, "*Montreaux*/April 1, 1972." The novel as published omits these prankish proofs or spoor bestowed by the author's passing.

is total, is it a "state of being" at all? And—to examine the last sentence quoted—aren't adjectives like "incomparable" and "mysterious" the refuge of an incommunicable mysticism?

The central impulse behind the novel remains obscure. At first, it seems that the "transparency" of things refers to their dimension in time—an ordinary pencil found in a drawer is taken back to its birth as a rod of agglutinated graphite and a splinter buried in the heart of a pine tree. Then it seems that the transparency has to do with an artful overlapping of beds, bureaus, carpets catching a slant of sunshine, shuttlecocks, dogs, and so on, as Hugh Person returns several times, between the ages of eight and forty, to the Swiss village of Trux. Other things are transparent, such as book titles "that shone through the book like a watermark," and a loved one "whose image was stamped on the eye of his mind and shone through the show at various levels." But the culminating image of transparency ("the incandescence of a book or a box grown completely transparent and hollow"), though the author presents it as if it were the crown of his life's thought and passion, arrives as the answer to a conundrum that has not been posed. Alas, what we remember of *Transparent Things* are its agreeable opacities: the busy clots of choice adjectives ("frail, lax, merry America"), the erotic peculiarities of Person's charming and difficult wife, Armande (she likes to make love as fully dressed as possible, while maintaining a flow of cocktail chatter), the delicious, glacial scene of a ski resort particularized by "the glaze of the upper runs, the blue herringbones lower down, the varicolored little figures outlined by the brush of chance against the brilliant white as if by a Flemish master's hand." We close the book guiltily, having licked the sugar coating but avoided, somehow, swallowing the pill.

If an artistic life so variously productive, so self-assured, so hermetically satisfactory to its perpetrator could be said to have a failing, Nabokov has failed to get himself taken seriously enough. A sad shadow of modesty touches this narrative. "This part of our translucing is pretty boring." "Mr. R., though perhaps not a master of the very first rank. . . ." Only "some of the less demanding reviewers in his adopted country" call R. a "master stylist." The book abounds, indeed, in wry self-portraits. The heroine's perverse sexual charades, in which her excitement derives "from the contrast between the fictitious and the factual," parody Nabokov's "*it*"—the "pangs" of the "maneuver" needed to pass from one state to another. A further "maneuver" with "pangs": Armande's Russian mother sits trapped by her own bulk in a chair, waiting for the "one precise little wiggle" that will "fool gravity" and, like "the miracle of a sneeze," lift her. Nabokov's own tricky legerity discourages solemn praise; he makes his acolytes and exegetes seem ridiculous as they compile their check lists of puns and chase his butterfly allusions. His aesthetic of gravity-fooling confronts us with a fiction that purposely undervalues its own humanistic content, that openly scorns the psychology and sociology that might bring with them an unfoolable gravity. Joyce also loved puns, and Proust was as lopsided an emotional monster as Humbert Humbert. But these older writers did submit their logomachy and their maimed private lives to a kind of historical commonalty; the Europe of the epics and the cathedrals spoke through them. The impression created by Nabokov's works in Russian, I am told, differs from that given by his spectacular works in English; he can be compared to Dostoevsky and Tolstoy in a way in which he cannot be compared with Thoreau and Twain. In his post-*Lolita* novels, especially, he seems more illusionist than seer. Though he offers us sensations never before verbally induced, and performs stunts that lift him right off the page, we are more amused than convinced. The failing may be ours; we are not ready, we are too dull of ear, too slow of eye, too much in love with the stubborn muteness of the earth to read the meaning behind his magic. He mutters from his sky, this comical comet, and hints, through his masks, of "a new bible." His measure is that we hope for nothing less from him.

Motley But True

Look at the Harlequins!, by Vladimir Nabokov. 253 pp. McGraw-Hill, 1974.

Nabokov's last three novels form, in the squinting retrospect of at least this surveyor, a trilogy of sorts: one, *Ada*, is remarkably long; another, *Transparent Things*, is remarkably short; and the third, the newly published *Look at the Harlequins!*, is, like Mama Bear's bed, comfortably middle-sized. All three books feature on the jacket back (in three different tonalities, if you line them up) the same frontal, staring, intimidatingly cranial photograph of the author; and all three, composed in the sparkling and salubrious vacuum of Switzerland, are—in the nicest possible sense—narcissistic to a degree unprecedented in his other English-language fiction, where a distinct madness differentiates the narrator (Humbert Humbert, Charles Kinbote) from the author, or where at the end Nabokov himself breaks in, as if to establish that these unfortunate heroes (Krug, Pnin) are somebody else entirely. But no such disclaimer attaches to Van Veen of *Ada* or to R. of *Transparent Things*—creations that flagrantly flirt with our knowledge of their creator. And the main movement of *Look at the Harlequins!*, the core of its "combinational delight" (to quote *Pale Fire*), is the reduction to zero of the difference between the author and the apparently contrasting Russian émigré author, Vadim, whose last name we never learn, though he is nicknamed "MacNab" and receives by mistake the press clippings of a British politician called Nabarro.

Much of the fun of *Look at the Harlequins!* arises from Nabokov's apparent invention of a contemporary and peer who is nevertheless conspicuously unlike him—oft-married where Nabokov's monogamy is declared in every book's dedication to his wife, anti-athletic where Nabokov was a soccer player and a tennis instructor, dipsomaniacal where wholesome, outdoorsy ("My own life is fresh bread with country butter and Alpine honey"—interview with James Mossman of the BBC) Nabokov is satisfied with "an occasional cup of wine or a triangular gulp of canned beer" (interview with Kurt Hoffman for the *Bayerischer Rundfunk*). Nabokov provides this alter ego with a list of works—but even at first glance the master's *oeuvre* peeps through its mimotype: *Tamara* (1925) is surely *Mary* (1926); *Camera Lucida* (*Slaughter in the Sun*) replicates *Laughter in the Dark* (*Camera Obscura*); *The Dare* mistranslates *The Gift* [*Dar*]; *See under Real* and *Dr. Olga Repnin* openly conceal *The Real Life of Sebastian Knight* and *Pnin*; and *Ardis* (1970) is scarcely even a pseudonym for *Ada, or Ardor* (1969). The persona of Vadim, too, is thin to translucence, and rubs thinner as the book goes on. Though he advertises himself as "a complete non-athlete," he lapses into athletic imagery —"a crack player's brio and chalk-biting serve"—and likens his literary prowess in two languages to being "World Champion of Lawn Tennis *and* Ski." Vadim's novels as he describes them are oneiric distortions of Nabokov's own; he signs himself as "Dumbert Dumbert" in one nightmare episode of nymphetolatry, and his central psychological problem, an inability to imagine certain permutations of Space, transposes *Ada*'s elaborate speculations on Time. Rightly Vadim is haunted by "a dream feeling that my life was the non-identical twin, a parody, an inferior variant of another man's life, somewhere on this or another earth." When he comes to describe himself, his face is line for line the face on the back of the jacket. Even his three wives, so lovingly limned and so various—Iris, Annette, Louise—finally seem metamorphic phases of the nameless fourth mate, the "you" to whom this "autobiography" is addressed and who, when she enters Vadim's hospital room, is saluted as "Reality"—"I emitted a bellow of joy, and Reality entered."

Nabokov's long joust and lovefeast with reality seems notably good-humored in this novel, the best, in *my* book, of his last three. If *Transparent Things* is a splintered hand-mirror, and *Ada* cotton-candy spun to the size of sunset cumulus, *Look at the Harlequins!* is a brown briefcase, as full of compartments as a magician's sleeve and lovingly thumbed to a scuff-colored limpness. It holds, in sometimes crumpled form, all the Nabokovian themes, from ardor to Zembla, and shares with us more frankly than any book since *The Gift* his writer's bliss, "the endless re-creation of my fluid self":

> . . . I regarded Paris, with it gray-toned days and charcoal nights, merely as the chance setting for the most authentic and faithful joys of my life: the colored phrase in my mind under the drizzle, the white page under the desk lamp awaiting me in my humble home.

Describing his three wives gives Vadim a quite contagious pleasure. First, there is Iris, a petite brunette, "a suntanned beauty with a black bob and eyes like clear honey":

The moldings of her brown back, with a patch-size beauty spot below the left shoulder blade and a long spinal hollow, which redeemed all the errors of animal evolution, distracted me painfully. . . . A few aquamarines of water still glistened on the underside of her brown thighs and on her strong brown calves, and a few grains of wet gravel had stuck to her rose-brown ankles.

Then there is Annette, a Russian blonde, "with very attractive though not exceptionally pretty features":

. . . her graceful neck seemed even longer and thinner. An expression of mild melancholy lent a new, unwelcome, beauty to her Botticellian face: its hollowed outline below the zygoma was accentuated by her increasing habit of sucking in her cheeks when hesitant or pensive.

And thirdly Louise, an American, "porcelain-pretty and very fast":

She . . . pulled off her wet sweater over her tumbled chestnut-brown, violet-brown curls and naked clavicles. Artistically, strictly artistically, I daresay she was the best-looking of my three major loves. She had upward-directed thin eyebrows, sapphire eyes registering (and that's the right word) constant amazement at earth's paradise (the only one she would ever know, I'm afraid), pink-flushed cheekbones, a rosebud mouth, and a lovely concave abdomen.

The manner in which these three wives (Nabokov's three languages?) travel in fictional space, enlarging from first glimpses into love objects and marriage partners and then diminishing through disenchantment into death or abandonment, is no mean feat of projection. And the hero describes other women as well—Lolita-like creatures such as the whorish little Dolly and his own elusive daughter Bel and the schoolmate of Bel's who turns out to be "you," repulsive creatures such as the adoring but sub-brachially pungent Lyuba and the stocky, whiskery, pro-Soviet Ninella. But then Nabokov has always loved to describe women, and the landscapes of childhood, and the student chill of Cambridge, and twins, and butterflies, and insomnia, and all the gaudy mirages of "a happy expatriation that began practically on the day of my birth" (to quote a letter to *The New York Times*). But toward the end of *Look at the Harlequins!* Vadim does two things never, to our imperfect knowledge, experienced by Vladimir Nabokov: he travels to the Soviet Union, and he has a stroke.

Both episodes show an exercising of the imaginative powers that one rather wishes had not had so strenuously to vie, over Nabokov's career, with his passion for trickery and annihilation. For a rabid Soviet-hater, the imagined return is surprisingly mild and calm in tone—and, to this one-time guest of the Soviet state, surprisingly accurate, from the smells on the Aeroflot turboprop to the insolence of the hotel lift-operators and the slowness of the restaurant service to the "morose, drab, oddly old-fashioned aspect that Soviet kids have." The thrilleresque details of intrigue that get Vadim there are funny, and his conversation afterwards, in the Paris airport, with a Soviet spy who has shadowed him all the way, is hilarious:

> "*Ekh!*" he explained, "*Ekh*, Vadim Vadimovich *dorogoy* (dear), aren't you ashamed of deceiving our great warm-hearted country, our benevolent, credulous government, our overworked Intourist staff, in this nasty infantile manner! A Russian writer! Snooping! Incognito!"

The agent (himself an old émigré, turned Communist) confuses, as the conversation goes on in this bumptious style, Vadim with Nabokov, and when the elderly author (whoever he is) knocks him down, exclaims, with timeless Russian stoicism, "*Nu, dali v mordu. Nu, tak chtozh?*" ("Well, you've given me one in the mug. Well, what does it matter?"). Somehow, absurd and sketchy as it is, this episode contains a warmth, a humor and suspense, that only unguarded feeling bestows, and that are too much missing from the professedly ardent filigree of Nabokov's later fiction. The stroke, a moment of near-fatal paralysis that overtakes Vadim at the turning-point of a preprandial walk, is amazing in its authentication, in the near-mystical swoops of its inner detail:

> Speed! If I could have given my definition of death to . . . the black horses gaping at me like people with trick dentures all through my strange skimming progress, I would have cried one word: Speed! . . . Imagine me, an old gentleman, a distinguished author, gliding rapidly on my back, in the wake of my outstretched dead feet, first through that gap in the granite, then over a pinewood, then along misty water meadows, and then simply between marges of mist, on and on, imagine that sight!

Or imagine any other writer since the beginning of time providing such a blend of sensation, metaphysics, and comedy.

Oh, yes, the title. Vadim's great-aunt, when he is an impressionable seven or eight, cries out to him, "Stop moping! . . . Look at
the harlequins!"

> "What harlequins? Where?"
> "Oh, everywhere, all around you. Trees are harlequins, words are
> harlequins. So are situations and sums. Put two things together—
> jokes, images—and you get a triple harlequin. Come on! Play! Invent
> the world! Invent reality!"

Throughout the invented reality of this novel, harlequins recur,
as a butterfly glimpsed with Annette and as an Iranian circus troupe
that boards a Soviet plane, as the "motley of madness" the hero
wears and as a cunning multiplicity of lozenge-shapes, some as small
as a "sequence of suspension dots in diamond type." As the jacket
design reminds us, a harlequin's traditional lozenge-pattern is a
chessboard made oblique. Beside him on the hospital bedside table,
as Vadim/Vladimir, "paralyzed in symmetrical patches," slowly
reassembles the world, he notices "a pair of harlequin sunglasses,
which for some reason suggested not protection from a harsh light
but the masking of tear-swollen lids." Which hint of masked grief
suggests, more strongly than is his wont, why our author has so
insistently harlequinized the world and tweaked the chessboard
of reality awry.

A Tribute

Contributed to the Triquarterly, *Winter 1970, Issue,*
Celebrating Nabokov's Seventieth Birthday

YOUR INVITATION to Vladimir Nabokov's birthday party reaches
me in England, and it was in England, nearly fifteen years ago, in
Oxford, that I first read this great man: in *The New Yorker,* the
Pnin story where the pencil sharpener says *ticonderoga, ticonderoga* and Pnin bursts into tears during a flickering Russian film. It
was another fictional universe, or at least a stunning intensification of the ordinary one, and it has been one of the steadier

pleasures of the fifteen years since to catch up on the considerable amount of Nabokov then in English and to keep up with the ample installments of reincarnated Russian and newly spawned American that have been issued through an untidy assortment of publishers, ranging from the elegant Bollingen Press to a miserable little bindery called, I think, Phaedra.* Though I may have nodded here and there among the two volumes of notes to *Onegin*, I have not knowingly missed any of the rest; for Nabokov is never lazy, never ungenerous with his jewels and flourishes, and his *oeuvre* is of sufficient majesty to afford interesting perspectives even from the closets and back hallways. I have expressed in print my opinion that he is now an American writer and the best living; I have also expressed my doubt that his aesthetic models—chess puzzles and protective colorations in lepidoptera—can be very helpful ideals for the rest of us. His importance for me as a writer has been his holding high, in an age when the phrase "artistic integrity" has a somewhat paradoxical if not reactionary ring, the stony image of his self-sufficiency: perverse he can be, but not abject; prankish but not hasty; sterile but not impotent. Even the least warming aspects of his image—the implacable hatreds, the reflexive contempt —testify, like fortress walls, to the reality of the siege this strange century lays against our privacy and pride.

As a reader, I want to register my impression that Nabokov does not (as Philip Toynbee, and other critics, have claimed) lack heart. *Speak, Memory* and *Lolita* fairly bulge with heart, and even the less ingratiating works, such as *King, Queen, Knave*, show, in the interstices of their rigorous designs, a plenitude of human understanding. The ability to animate into memorability minor, disagreeable characters bespeaks a kind of love. The little prostitute that Humbert Humbert recalls undressing herself so quickly, the fatally homely daughter of John Shade, the intolerably pretentious

---

* The great man, in his peppery supplement to *Triquarterly*'s fat (371 pp.) bundle of paeans, bridled at this "harsh and contemptuous reference to a small publishing house, which brought out excellent editions of four books of mine." I have seen only three of these volumes, but they *are* miserably bound, in the sleazy pseudo-cloth of high-school yearbooks; the signature on the covers has Nabokov dotting his *i*'s with circles like Walt Disney. Of course, *nichyvo*, if the text is right. But I wish for him and his works the best of everything, from the integument in.

and sloppy-minded woman whom Pnin undyingly loves, the German street figures in *The Gift*, the extras momentarily on-screen in the American novels—all make a nick in the mind. Even characters Nabokov himself was plainly prejudiced against, like the toadlike heroine of *King, Queen, Knave*, linger vividly, with the outlines of the case they must plead on Judgment Day etched in the air; how fully we feel, for example, her descent into fever at the end. And only an artist full of emotion could make us hate the way we hate Axel Rex in *Laughter in the Dark*. If we feel that Nabokov is keeping, for all his expenditure of verbal small coin, some treasure in reserve, it is because of the riches he has revealed. Far from cold, he has access to European vaults of sentiment sealed to Americans; if he feasts the mind like a prodigal son, it is because the heart's patrimony is assured.

ENGLISH LIVES

A Short Life

A Voice Through A Cloud, by Denton Welch. 254 pp. University of
Texas Press, 1966.

"Promising" is a pale term of praise reviewers customarily employ to excuse themselves from reading closely the work at hand.
But the term applies with some force to Denton Welch, an Englishman born in 1917, severely injured in a highway accident at the
age of eighteen, and dead by 1948. In his thirteen years of pain
and invalidism, Welch composed three novels, of which the last,
entitled *A Voice Through a Cloud*, was left uncompleted at his
death. While not quite a masterpiece (not only does it not end, it
gives no sign of knowing how to end), the book is, especially in its
first half, masterly: a fine intelligence, a brave candor, a voracious
eye, and a sweet, fresh prose are exercised. Possibly these gifts,
liberated to wider use by a healthy life, would have proved equal
to many subjects. It is also possible that Welch's gifts were best
realized by the one subject he had—the effects of his absurd and
savage accident—and that nothing else would have burnt away so
much of his dilettantism or turned his somewhat sinister detachment to such good artistic account. Again, it could be argued that
save for his accident he would have outgrown the distrustful and
diffident brilliance of a schoolboy. But in the end a man is what
happens to him plus what he does. In a world aswarm with might-
have-beens, Welch took his shortened life, his remittances of pain
and fever, and delivered a unique account of shattered flesh
and refracted spirit.

This "novel," in which Welch rechristened himself Maurice

: **223** :

and presumably used the convenience of fiction to change some names and fake a few details, begins with the hero, a London art student, setting out on his bicycle for his uncle's vicarage in Surrey. The landscape and a tea shoppe are rather adjectivally evoked; the hero resumes his pleasant ride; then

> I heard a voice through a great cloud of agony and sickness. The voice was asking questions. It seemed to be opening and closing like a concertina. The words were loud, as the swelling notes of an organ, then they melted to the tiniest wiry tinkle of water in a glass.
>
> I knew that I was lying on my back on the grass; I could feel the shiny blades on my neck. I was staring at the sky and I could not move. Everything about me seemed to be reeling and breaking up. My whole body was screaming with pain, filling my head with its roaring, and my eyes were swimming in a sort of gum mucilage. . . . Bright little points glittered all down the front of the liquid man kneeling beside me. I knew at once that he was a policeman, and I thought that, in his official capacity, he was performing some ritual operation on me. There was a confusion in my mind between being brought to life—forceps, navel-cords, midwives—and being put to death—ropes, axes, and black masks; but whatever it was that was happening, I felt that all men came to this at last.

In spite of certain lazy, boyish locutions ("the tiniest," "screaming with pain," "swimming in a sort of"), a private apocalypse is rendered with icy exactness, and throughout the succeeding pages of hospital ordeal Welch does not funk his essential task—the portrayal of "the savage change from fair to dark":

> In the middle of the furnace inside me there was a clear thought like a text in cross-stitch. I wanted to warn the nurses, to tell them that nothing was real but torture. Nobody seemed to realize that this was the only thing on earth.

It is strange to realize how incidentally narrative fiction treats the physical base of human existence; food is an occasion for conversation, sleep an interval of action, elimination a joke. Bodies are felt as mobile scaffoldings for conversing sensibilities, and pain, that sensation of ultimate priority, is almost never (Tolstoy and Samuel Beckett are exceptions) rendered solidly. In Welch's narrative, agony precedes psychology; introspection takes place only as pain's monopoly loosens. The mind worms in the chinks of suffering.

> I tried to lull myself to sleep. . . . but all the pleasant things that only yesterday I liked so much rose up to haunt me. I thought of eating delicious food, wearing good clothes, feeling proud and gay, going for walks, singing and dancing alone, fencing and swimming and painting pictures with other people, reading books. And everything seemed horrible and thin and nasty as soiled paper. I wondered how I could ever have believed in these things, how I could even for a moment have thought they were real. Now I knew nothing was real but pain, heat, blood, tingling, loneliness, and sweat. I began almost to gloat on the horror of my situation and surroundings. I felt paid out, dragged down, punished finally. Never again would my own good fortune make me feel guilty. I could look any beggars, blind people in the face now. Everything I had loved was disgusting; and I was disgusting, too.
>
> As this terrible gloating unhappiness flooded over me, my head began to swim; the pain sucked me under and I wanted to die and not be tortured any more.

The action of this narrative is the narrator's recovery of the world, a recovery effected without much assistance from other people. Welch, though he can do a sketch of a doomed eccentric as well as the next literate hospital patient, is not a creator of characters. All the persons he meets are depicted flatly, on the inner walls of a neurasthenia that probably existed before his catastrophe. At the worst, other people outrage and torture him—most of the hospital attendants he met struck him as sadists—and at best they merely disappoint and irritate, like static obstructing a delicate tuning-in. Welch/Maurice seeks rapport not with any other person but with the world at large, and it is remarkable, considering that more than ten years had passed since his accident, how fully, how delicately he can conjure up the sense impressions that make this search credible:

> The bare walls [of the hospital corridor] seemed to be waiting for just another human sight or sound or smell to be swallowed up in them. They had sucked in so much hope and fear and boredom; but nothing showed. Their blank faces stared back and sinister little draughts struck against my face and ears and hair.

As he ventures into the outer world, everything is hungrily snapped up—"the leathery gray spread of the sea," "the faint gunpowdery smell of new stone," "the broad leaves in the gutter, splendid, decaying, rich, like some rare food." Returning from the verge of oblivion, he writes of familiar sights as might a visitor from another planet:

> I had not been in a night street scene for a long time. I watched the people's faces as they pushed through the theatre doors. The faces changed when they passed from the street into the building. Outside they were more hardened, more scoured and flinty, tragic too from all they had withstood. Inside they grew more cushiony and fluid; they lost the vagrant haunted look. The look of anxiety melted into the sparkling monkey, or the soft bear look. And people undid belts and buttons, loosened their hair, patted, polished, breathed out their warm breath, like animals penned together in a farmyard.

In an age quick to label any sufficiently bleak and sententious novel "existential," here is a work, by an author born again out of agony into the world, that seems to reconstitute human existence particle by particle.

Fiction captures and holds our interest with two kinds of suspense: circumstantial suspense—the lowly appetite, aroused by even comic strips, to know the outcome of an unresolved situation—and what might be called gnostic suspense, the expectation that at any moment an illumination will occur. Bald plot caters to the first; style, wit of expression, truth of observation, vivid painterliness, brooding musicality, and all the commendable rest pay court to the second. Gnostic suspense is not negligible—almost alone it moves us through those many volumes of Proust—but it stands to the other rather like charm to sex in a woman. We hope for both, and can even be more durably satisfied by charm than by sex (all animals are sad after coitus and after reading a detective story); but charm remains the ancillary and dispensable quality.

Toward the end of *A Voice Through a Cloud*, the hero acquires some use of his legs, and the plane of concern shifts from the struggle with oblivion to a search for suitable housing. The writing, though more polished than before, begins to feel aimless. Detail becomes obsessive. Maurice walks up an ordinary road of two-family dwellings: "There was something monstrous about the long avenue of coupled pink brick boxes. I felt that I was climbing up between gigantic naked Siamese twins with eyes all over their bodies." Circumstantial suspense is deliberately generated; old characters reappear and are skillfully "used." The book, as the dying author wearies, begins to act like a conventional novel. Though Welch had the abilities of a novelist, misfortune made him a kind of prophet, and it is as a prophetic document, a proclamation of our terrible fragility, that his book possesses value.

Ayrton Fecit

FABRICATIONS, by Michael Ayrton. 224 pp. Holt, Rinehart & Winston, 1972.

In 1967, the English painter and sculptor Michael Ayrton published *The Maze Maker*, one of the best of the many mythological novels written in English since 1955, when Robert Graves offered, in his two-volume Penguin *Greek Myths*, a handy compendium with-it and far-out enough to make the Hellenic legends interesting again. Mr. Ayrton's tale of Daedalus, supposedly written by Daedalus himself, picks its way nimbly among the scattered and conflicting classical references to its hero, ingeniously exploits Graves's jumbled treasure of semantic and anthropological explications, and—though the narrative turns rather mazy amid a welter of mysticism and interlocked symbols—repeatedly draws energy from the author's excitement over the art, business, and mystery of fabrication. The primitive craftsman's careful magic comes to life in a dozen procedural descriptions—how to cast bronze, how to make wings, how to counterfeit a honeycomb in gold, how to construct an artificial cow in which a real woman may enjoy intercourse with a god who has assumed the form of a bull. Daedalus gives us the book's thematic core: "Poets have much in common with heroes. They are neither of them aware of the world, of its true appearance nor its real consequence, its structure nor its marvellous imperfection. They are blind to that, and because my methods of gaining experience have been observation, deduction, and experiment, I have been no worse off and much better instructed than any poets or heroes known to me. . . . I am involved in matters which I do not wish disturbed nor interrupted by eloquent activities, the facile assumption of power, speculation on immeasurable phenomena, nor any apotheosis. What I make exists."

Fittingly, then, Mr. Ayrton's next, and present, volume of fiction is entitled *Fabrications*. Twenty-seven short prose pieces, fashioned in a variety of styles and with a variety of pictographic devices, propose to insert into the packed and stacked reality of documented history various shims of speculation and fantasy. Imaginary pages of actual memoirs are supplied. Gilles de Rais takes his part in a performance of Shaw's *Saint Joan* in wartime Southampton, and enlarges the part with a stirring self-defense. An invented Scots artist, "John Calder of Kelty," is plausibly intertwined with known facts and surviving works of 16th-century Italy. An extant 12th-century manuscript illustration is explained by a fable involving one of Mr. Ayrton's favorite themes, taurophilia. The man whose ear St. Peter sliced off lends the other to the mendacities of Flavius Josephus. And so on. The stories presuppose a reader able to delight in pedantry, with enough sense of history to find enchantment in its odd nooks and corners—Rome in 1001, Jotapata in 67. Embroidery of the archival texts is not, in this eclectic era, an unfamiliar form of art: witness the stories of Borges and Barthelme, the poems of Richard Howard and, a century ago, Robert Browning. As a cherisher of old oddities, Mr. Ayrton shows much erudition, wit, and spirit. He tells us about John Philip Sousa's novels, about the curious cookery (flourishing in the dyspeptic reign of Charles I) that incorporated consenting dwarves into large pies called "surprise pastries," and about the eerie heroic statuary of the Saluvii, a Celtic tribe that dominated the valley of the Rhone in pre-Christian times. He is especially vivid, predictably, when he deals with art. Brunelleschi and Giacometti are seen interfering with the space of their time, and Piero della Francesca and Caravaggio deliver monologues that startle with their intensity—for Mr. Ayrton, not predictably, is an excellent mimic of dead styles.

Yet, though *Fabrications* pulls us willingly along from one con-

ceit to the next, and a number seem perfect, something makes resistance all the way, and we emerge feeling that we have left the
shop not of an artist but of a hobbyist. Why is this? For one, Mr.
Ayrton's voice, when not engaged in a work of impersonation,
gravitates toward an off-putting archness:

> If I suggest that an art dealer, with whom I have for some time been
> acquainted, is exceptional even among his coevals, I might, if I
> named him here, be thought basely to seek to curry favor with him.

In flirting with clichés, he does not always avoid being seduced by
them:

> He is particularly knowledgeable about, and on the best of terms
> with some of those commanding and seminal figures whose names
> hang, in the world of art, upon every lip.
>
> . . . not without a substratum of truth to which I at least sub-
> scribe.

And, from this same unfortunate pair of pages (the first two in the
book, and we never quite trust him again), a specimen of the clarifying that stupefies:

> His later life was spent in endlessly seeking to penetrate the barrier
> and establish the spatial and human dimensions of those few
> personages whom experience had taught him he could grope truly
> to perceive when face to face with one.

More than a matter of an occasional careless or windy sentence,
it is an error of tone, this trivializing fussiness of diction. In contrast, Borges (whom Mr. Ayrton several times names, as if defying
an invidious comparison), though equally recondite in his matter,
maintains a directness and simplicity of prose that carry us into
the heart of his shadows and bestow upon *his* fabrications—his
Ficciones and *Labyrinths*—the nobility of monoliths.

Nor are Mr. Ayrton's fancies uniformly pretty. It is one thing
to bring Dionysus to modern America in search of devotees ("Cool
it, man" is the greeting he receives) and another to have Kierkegaard watch the progress of Abraham and Isaac up Mount Moriah
in an episode of a television Western. The former impossibility has
a certain pith; given the existence of gods, this is how they might
behave. The latter is merely impossible; given the existence of tele-

vision, it could not have been turned on in 1843. The incongruity seems wantonly—even, with the attendant gibes at the Dane's theology, spitefully—produced. Mr. Ayrton takes too lightly his own dreadful freedom to invent what he pleases. Some of his fabrications—"The Minocorn," "Dr. A. R. Broga"—are feeble japes, if not family jokes; others—"A Gesture of the Hand," "The Vanishing Point"—are so graphic in conception that they are too difficult, even with illustrations, to "picture." The illustrations, some of them indispensable, are not very snugly married to the text, or very sharply engraved. Indeed, and alas, the book as a whole is not very well produced. Unlikely to reach a large audience, it should have been exquisitely aimed, as a fine fabrication, at the few who would relish its dry learning and delicate mirror play. But the American publisher has imported the English edition, with its strong savor of thrift. The pages have slender upper and outside margins, matched with disproportionately wide lower and inside margins; these large margins make it possible to add illustrations here and there without the expensive trouble of resetting type around them, but they look mistaken on the pages (two out of three) that carry no illustrations or footnotes. And I have never seen a book contain, for its size, so many widows. A widow (a short line, especially one ending a paragraph, that turns up at the top of a page, where it looks bereft) can usually be avoided, either by tampering with the text or by adjusting the pagination; it is elementary book-production manners to do so. Of the first thirty-one pages in *Fabrications* that could be possibly headed by widows, seven are; a deliberate widow-maker could scarcely have contrived more. What would Daedalus have said? Daedalan strictures will seem picayune to writers of a Dionysian persuasion; and of course no story or poem is purely constructed, or purely inspired, any more than the event of sailing can be all sail or all wind. This time out, Mr. Ayrton's intricate rigging creaks, in puffs of erratic breeze.

The Mastery of Miss Warner

SWANS ON AN AUTUMN RIVER, by Sylvia Townsend Warner. 200 pp. Viking, 1966.

The stories of Sylvia Townsend Warner stick up from *The New Yorker*'s fluent fiction-stream with a certain stony air of mastery. They are granular and adamant and irregular in shape. The prose has a much-worked yet abrasive texture of minute juxtaposition and compounded accuracies. Candles are lit in an antique shop, and "The polished surfaces reflected the little flames with an intensification of their various colors—amber in satinwood, audit ale in mahogany, dragon's blood in tortoise shell." Two old ladies reminisce: "They talked untiringly about their girlhood—about the winters when they went skating, the summers when they went boating, the period when they were so very pious, the period when they were pious no longer and sent a valentine to the curate: the curate blushed, a crack rang out like a pistol shot and Hector Gillespie went through the ice, the fox terriers fought under old Mrs. Bulliver's chair, the laundry ruined the blue voile, the dentist cut his throat in Century Wood, Claude Hopkins came back from Cambridge with a motorcar and drove it at thirty miles an hour with flames shooting out behind, Addie Carew was married with a wasp under her veil." Though Miss Warner can be trivial in her effects and vague in her intentions, she rarely lacks concreteness. On every page there is something to be seen or smelled or felt.

In *Repetition*, Kierkegaard, who had considerable fabling powers, interrupted his narrative to write: "If I were to pursue in detail the moods of the young man as I learned to know them, not to speak of including in a poetical manner a multitude of irrelevant matters—salons, wearing apparel, beautiful scenery, relatives and friends—this story might be drawn out to yard lengths. That, however, I have no inclination to do. I eat lettuce, it is true, but I eat only the heart; the leaves, in my opinion, are fit for swine." Contrariwise, Miss Warner's appetite for the leaves of circumstance is excellent. One story in this collection ("An Act of Reparation") is basically a recipe for oxtail stew; several others ("Happiness," "The View of Rome") are like architectural drawings of houses with people sketched in for scale. The furniture in her fiction is always vivacious and in her stories about Mr. Edom's antique-shop, not included in this collection, *objets* dominate. The grit of factuality scintillates for her, and she inhales the world's rank melancholy as if it were ambrosial perfume. Churches especially arouse her olfactory relish:

> Candles were burning, some before this image, some before that. They gave a sort of top-dressing of warmth to the building, but basically it was as cold as river mud, and under a glazing of incense it smelt of poverty.

In another church, the preserved corpse of a local saint is wonderingly detailed:

> What extraordinary gloves—so thin that the nails, long and rather dirty, showed through. . . . She looked at the face. It had blue glass eyes, to match the blue dress. One of them projected from the face, squeezed out by the shrivelling socket into which it had been fitted. It seemed to stare at her with alarm. The other eye was still in place, and placid.

The story containing this placid glass eye, "Fenella," and others such as "Healthy Landscape with Dormouse" and "Total Loss" pursue a steadily deepening drabness with a remorseless exhilaration. The septuagenarian Miss Warner's continued health as a writer of fiction is a testimonial to her iron diet. She has the spiritual digestion of a goat, and a ravenous eye for unpleasantness.

Between her firm particulars and the overbrooding Olympian forbearance of tone there is, sometimes, an unexpected vacuum. Her sense of form, of direction, is erratic, which is to say she has no prejudices about her material. Her endings are often weak— abrupt and enigmatic ("A Stranger with a Bag," "Their Quiet Lives"), sentimental ("Happiness"), crowded and vague ("Johnnie Brewer"). Here, where an author normally gathers his matter to a point in a final phrase or word, a dominant that will reverberate backward, Miss Warner wanders off in the middle of the measure, or goes on a measure too long, or comes down hard on a note so wrong we doubt our ears. As I read these bound stories I had the impression that some were better when I first read them in *The New Yorker*. A little research proved it to be so.

"The View of Rome" is a generally charming story about an old engraver recovering from a nearly fatal illness. He is very anxious to return to his home and in order to secure early release from the hospital pretends that his cat, Hattie, is a stepniece coming from the Isle of Wight to nurse him. Though rather lightweight, the story gathers substance from the many sharp small touches ("The clock, with its light hopping gait, like a robin's, ticked on"), the persuasive portrait of a gentle old bachelor (Miss Warner makes herself quite at home in male minds), and its articulation of a kind of joy, the joy of domestic possession, not often dramatized. I enjoyed rereading it until the last sentences, which went: "God is an Oriental potentate, unaffectedly lavish and sumptuous. He would not think it extravagant to heap up all these apples into a cenotaph for a Rural Dean. Here was no need for jam pots. They could stay in the attic." The apples, we know, are lying all about, and making jam of them has preoccupied the hero in the hospital, and we have been told of the Dean who died of a wasp sting incurred at a Harvest Festival. But those last two sentences, besides choppily cutting across the preceding grand strophes about God as an Oriental potentate, bring some unlooked-for words to the fore. Jam pots? Attic? The house's attic has not been previously mentioned, and abruptly occupies the position of a keystone. It is bewildering, and dulling. *The New Yorker* version, in place of these last two sentences, has: "There was no call for jam pots here." Surely this is better: "call" for "need," "here" for "attic," and the simpler phrasing permits the potentate-lavish-extravagant-cenotaph conceit to sound the conclusive chord in this wry fugue of mortality and gratitude.

Miss Warner thought well enough of "Swans on an Autumn River" to name her collection after it. It tells of Norman Repton, overweight and sixty-nine, attending a congress of sanitary engineers in Dublin. He has never been in Ireland, though when he was young it had represented romance to him. He sightsees confusedly, overeats in a restaurant, and, while feeding bread to some swans on a river and angrily fending off hungry seagulls, dies of a heart attack. Some women waiting for a bus and a *garda* directing traffic witness his death. The book version ends with the paragraph:

> The *garda*, who had left his place amid the traffic, now came up to where Norman Repton lay motionless. After a momentary hesitation, as though he were hastily summoning up something he had learned, he knelt beside him. The women drew closer together, and one of them pulled her coat about her, as though she had suddenly become conscious of the cold. Presently the *garda* looked up. "Will one of you ladies go across to the hotel," he said, "and ask them to telephone for the ambulance?" Two women detached themselves from the group and hurried across the road, arguing in whispers.

The New Yorker version is the same, until:

> Presently, the *garda* got up from his knees. Looking gravely down at the figure on the pavement, he pulled off his cap and crossed himself. The action unloosed a flutter of hands, a murmur of sound, among those waiting for the bus, as though it had stirred a dovecote.

Now, this at least gives us a vivid image in which Ireland, an exotic Catholic land, and birds, whose aloof beauty and sordid hunger have lured the hero to his death, intersect. The ending Miss Warner has chosen to preserve in her book is totally centrifugal, a burst of irrelevancies. Of what significance is the mechanical request for an ambulance? Who are the two women who go to telephone, and what if they argue "in whispers"? Whispers have nothing to do with Norman Repton, and though neither ending is quite satisfactory, it is Miss Warner's that confirms our suspicion that this story is aimless. It is an insistently ugly story whose ugliness has not been shaped to any purpose. We do not know enough about Repton to feel his terminal fight with the seagulls as anything more than the irritable fit of a choleric man. The editorial process that brought two endings into being is not at issue; either *The New Yorker* version is the original one, later revised, or it is a revision prompted by the magazine and finally discarded. In either case, Miss Warner has expressed her old-fashioned preference for events over gestures. The two women walking across the road to the telephone, however flat and irrelevant as an image, are, as an event, more world-engaging and, as it were, negotiable. In an artistic age of credit manipulation, Miss Warner deals in quaintly hard cash.

Her stories tend to convince us in process and baffle us in conclusion; they are not rounded with meaning but lift jaggedly toward new, unseen, developments. "Healthy Landscape with Dormouse" presents with unblinking clairvoyance a miserably married and (therefore) unrepentantly mischievous young woman, Belinda. The story's locale is Belinda's consciousness, but instead of ending there the story leaps out of her head and concludes on a village street. Some suddenly introduced bus passengers have seen Belinda and her husband fight and jump into a car: "They ran to the car, leaped in, drove away. Several quick-witted voices exclaimed, 'Take the number! Take the number!' But the car went so fast, there wasn't time." It suggests a Mack Sennett comedy; it suggests furthermore an almost compulsive need, in Miss Warner's work, for witnesses. Her world is thoroughly social, like those rings of Hades where the sinners, frozen into eternal postures, must stare at each other. "A Stranger with a Bag" and "A Long Night" make the act of onlooking centrally dramatic; and the excellent "A Jump Ahead" ends with the narrator understanding what he has seen: his ex-wife preparing to die of leukemia.

The very best story in the book, thirty pages that feel as spacious as a novel, is "A Love Match." It too is a story of witnessing: a brother and sister, Justin and Celia, live incestuously in a small English town and finally, killed by a stray bomb while in bed together, are discovered. The witnesses, the men who find their bodies, agree upon a fiction:

> Then young Foe spoke out. "He must have come in to comfort her. That's my opinion." The others concurred.

This tale, with its congenial mixture of the Gothic and the pedestrian, excites the author's prose to a fine vividness:

> The rescue workers . . . followed the trail of bricks and rubble upstairs and into a bedroom whose door slanted from its hinges. A cold air met them; looking up, they saw the sky. The floor was deep in rubble; bits of broken masonry, clots of brickwork, stood up from it like rocks on a beach. A dark bulk crouched on the hearth, and was part of the chimney stack, and a torrent of slates had fallen on the bed, crushing the two bodies that lay there.

The first act of love, the initial violation of this most sacred taboo, is beautifully described and justified as an incident within the horror and fatalism and hysteria of the First World War. Their quiet life and smoldering secret allegorize England between the wars. Twenty years of truce pass in terms of private social strategies and public social movements. Justin arranges the dusty items of a dead eccentric's military collection; Celia interests herself in the poor, in Communism. They make a few friends and sometimes attend church.

> There was a nice, stuffy pitch-pine St. Cuthbert's near by, and at judicious intervals they went there for evensong—thereby renewing another bond of childhood: the pleasure of hurrying home on a cold evening to eat baked potatoes hot from the oven.

The odors and occupations ,of *inter-bella* England, evoking Miss Warner's full vocabulary of flowers and foods and architectures, are suffused with the blameless decadence of the central situation. The cozy sibling idyll of Victorian mythology has gone mad. Incest has become the civilized person's ultimate recourse:

> Loving each other criminally and sincerely, they took pains to live together happily and to safeguard their happiness from injuries of their own inflicton or from outside.

Of course, no touch of implied condemnation, or of undue compassion, intrudes upon the perfect sympathy with which this scandalous marriage is chronicled. Miss Warner's genius is an uncannily equable openness to human data, and beneath her refined witchery lies a strange freshness one can only call, in praise, primitive.

A Sere Life; or, Sprigge's Ivy

THE LIFE OF IVY COMPTON-BURNETT, by Elizabeth Sprigge. 191 pp. Braziller, 1973.

In a time of outsize literary biographies, Elizabeth Sprigge has written a pleasantly compact and understated life of Ivy Compton-Burnett, called just that. Miss Sprigge writes, her foreword tells us, "as a friend," and her book enjoys the privileged insights of close acquaintanceship, and suffers just slightly from the tactful reticence that friendship imposes. How nice it would be if, of Shakespeare, we knew details such as these of Miss Compton-Burnett: that she kept her work-in-progress stacked on one end of her living-room sofa; that when she acquired a refrigerator she "played with the new possession like a little girl with a doll's house, delighted that each time she opened it a light came on"; that she loved fires, flowers, and fruit; that the walls of her flat held almost no pictures and all the floors were covered in linoleum; that when, in the Second World War, oranges became scarce and other adults let children have their share, she kept on eating hers, saying, "My need is greater than theirs. They have that nasty yellow bottled stuff at school." Miss Sprigge shows something of her subject's mastery of indirection, for, without ever dropping her affectionate tone, she manages to let us know that Ivy Compton-Burnett was a curiously hardened specimen of humanity: forbidding in manner, fascinated by money, blind to painting, deaf to music, fierce on etiquette, and, like so many of her characters, tyrannical. Miss Sprigge sketches unendearing traits as if they were endearing:

> If a conversation took a turn alien to her, Ivy would bring it to heel. For example, one day at a friend's tea-party a number of people began discussing a Russian icon hanging on the wall. Ivy listened for a few moments abstractedly, then observed decisively, "I do like a laburnum."

This author's life was not, to use her own word, "deedy." Ivy Compton-Burnett was born on June 5, 1884, the first child of the marriage of Dr. James Compton Burnett, a homeopathic physician large in size and formidable in intellect (philology was his private passion), and Katharine Rees, a young woman of distinguished family and striking beauty—her mane of bright gold was so wonderful that even now a nephew in his eighties remembers "the glory of Aunt Katie's hair." It was not the Doctor's first marriage; fifteen years older than Miss Rees, he had had five children by his first wife, a chemist's daughter, who died when the youngest was an infant. The new bride brought a hyphen to the family name ("to make the name sound grander"; the Doctor and her stepchildren

never used it) and added to the household seven children, of whom
Ivy was the first. Four sisters and two brothers followed. (A remarkable fact, which Miss Sprigge declines to emphasize, is that *not
one* of Dr. Compton Burnett's eight daughters ever married.) Ivy
—"a small child . . . with grey-blue eyes and long fair hair which,
although lacking her mother's brilliance of colour, was very pretty"
—grew up, then, amid siblings and step-siblings, servants and tutors,
in a comfortable hubbub of charades and family prayers, of incestuous cross-currents and precocious inklings, all presided over
by a "splendid, great, bearded" father and a mother haloed by her
glorious hair. The Doctor's office was at 86, Wigmore Street, and
his immense household finally settled at 20, The Drive, an ornate
red brick mansion in Hove. Throughout her long creative life Ivy's
imagination never left that crowded, prosperous household and its
late-Victorian ambience. "I do not feel," she told an interviewer,
"that I have any real or organic knowledge of life later than about
1910. I should not write of later times with enough grasp or confidence." As with Nabokov's Russia, disaster sealed shut an enchanted cave. Both her parents died rather younger than demigods
should: her father, suddenly, at the age of sixty-one, in 1901, and
her mother, after "last sad days" that became "a sore trial to her
family," in 1911, at the age of fifty-six. Ivy, in 1902, had gone to
Royal Holloway College, founded by the manufacturer of Holloway's pills and ointments in order "to give women of the middle
and upper middle classes the educational advantages afforded by
universities to young men." She read Classics and won a scholarship. Back home at Hove, while tutoring her younger sisters, she
began to write, and in 1911 she published, to enthusiastic reviews,
her first novel, *Dolores*. Later that year, upon her mother's death,
"Ivy at the age of twenty-seven became the undisputed head of the
household." Miss Sprigge's discreet phrasing can only hint at the
ominous quality of the next years: "She enjoyed this power and
became something of a tyrant, which was difficult both for Minnie
[their old nurse] and for Ivy's sisters, particularly for Topsy and
'Baby,' who were still in their teens and far from happy." So far
from happy, indeed, that in 1916 Topsy and Baby, the younger
pair of sisters, committed suicide together, in the house to which
all four sisters, led by the older pair, Vera and Judy, had fled Ivy's

tyranny a year earlier. Vera and Judy later found a cottage in Hertfordshire, and still live there. After her sisters had revolted against her rule, there was little for Ivy to do but sell the family home and, alone in the world (her brother Guy had died, in 1904, of pneumonia, and her other brother, Noël, was killed in battle in 1916), to make herself one of a pair. Her first companion, Dorothy Beresford, was something of a tyrant herself—a vivacious, argumentative woman "determined that Ivy should not 'come the bluestocking over her.' " However, Miss Sprigge tells us, "Ivy does not appear to have resented Dorothy's tyranny," and the two shared a flat in Bayswater until Dorothy married, in 1919. That same year, Ivy began living with Margaret Jourdain, a woman of letters and furniture expert, who, like Dorothy, appeared to outsiders to be the dominant of the two. Their happy relationship continued until Miss Jourdain's death, in 1951; Ivy "could not forgive Margaret for having left her," and lived, uncompanioned, until her own death, in 1969. She had resumed writing fiction at about the time Margaret Jourdain came into her life, at the end of a decade that, if not "deedy," had seen more than its share of family tragedy. In 1925, fourteen years after the publication of *Dolores*, she began, with *Pastors and Masters*, in her mature style of scarcely adorned conversation, the succession of more or less biennial novels that were to win her her little iron niche in English literature.

This efficient and seemly book reminded me of another biography recently read—Chris Albertson's life of Bessie Smith. The two women, so unlike, were both born late in the 19th century, into large families, and after obscure, unhurried apprenticeships emerged with an artistic power so confident and pure that their lives could not trouble it. Bessie Smith was cheerfully bisexual, while Ivy Compton-Burnett dryly described herself as "neuter," and the one's alcoholic binges and Pullman-car road tours are a far cry from the other's four-o'clock teas and weekends in Dorset; but in either case a social calendar quite fails to penetrate the mystery of a consummate talent. The biography of an artist is hollow because, unlike that of a general or a billionaire, an artist's life is not the sum of its incidents. As we read about Bessie Smith, we can at least put on her records, and let her bottomless, winsome voice override the

clutter of dates and liaisons and anecdotes. With a writer, there is
no such way to apprehend simultaneously the life and the oddly
disparate thing that was made of it. Though Miss Sprigge quotes
reviews (in wise moderation) and gives us her own acute though
never critical appraisal of each novel as it comes out, only in one
place do we get Ivy, as it were, hot. That is in the interview she
concocted with Margaret Jourdain in 1944, when they were living
in the country to escape the London bombing. If Margaret Jourdain's questions were actual, she talked remarkably like a character
in a novel by I. Compton-Burnett:

> I should like to ask you one or two questions; partly my own and
> partly what several friends have asked. There is time enough and
> to spare in Lyme Regis, which is a town well-known to novelists.
> Jane Austen was here, and Miss Mitford.

The answer knits itself into place:

> And now we are here, though our presence does not seem to be
> equally felt. No notice marks our lodging. And we also differ from
> Jane Austen and Miss Mitford in being birds of passage, fleeing
> from the bombs. I have a feeling that they would both have fled,
> and felt it proper to do so, and wish that we could feel it equally
> proper.

With the same absolutely firm diffidence, the novelist turns aside a
number of common objections to her work: "I think that my writing does not seem to me as 'stylised' as it apparently is, though I do
not attempt to make my characters use the words of actual life. I
cannot tell you why I write as I do, as I do not know. I have even
tried not to do it, but find myself falling back into my own way."
To the complaint that her books contain almost no description she
replies, "However detailed such description is, I am sure that everyone forms his own conceptions, that are different from everyone
else's, including the author's." Both these responses appear to emphasize the artist's modesty, but by the end of the interview an
astonishing subordination of life to art has been proposed. To the
question of how closely she derives her characters from real people,
Ivy Compton-Burnett responds that "people in life hardly seem to
be definite enough to appear in print. They are not good or bad
enough, or clever or stupid enough or comic or pitiful enough."
Further,

As regards plots I find real life no help at all. Real life seems to have no plots. And as I think a plot desirable and almost necessary, I have this extra grudge against life.

Astonishing! Almost every other novelist in this century, noticing that life has somehow ceased to coagulate into plots, has sought to bring art into adjustment, by making novels plotless or by relocating plot among the shifts and nuances of virtually formless daily existence. Only a superb tyrant like Miss Compton-Burnett could assert that life, not art, is at fault, and could then in exercise of her grudge thereat manufacture twenty plots whose pivot points of murder, retribution, proposal, inheritance, and deception are not softened by the slightest padding of plausibility or gradualness. As a demonstration of *character*—her own—her work is grand. The perfect, relentless appositeness of her dialogue is but another way of her insisting, in the tea parlor of her *oeuvre*, that manners be observed—manners derived not from the slovenly example of reality but from the precedent of other books and the capabilities of language itself.

But, as a character in *Mother and Son* states, "we must use words as they are used, or stand aside from life." That Ivy Compton-Burnett did stand aside from life, unapologetically, was a great gesture—of greater artistic value, it may be, than the novels themselves. The most deeply felt praise of her has come from Nathalie Sarraute, at the end of the essay "Conversation and Sub-Conversation"; the writer, striving with the seriousness peculiar to the French of the fifties to analyze and solve by decree the formal crisis in fiction, takes the English spinster's shameless, hyper-articulate dialogue to be a step in the direction of her own (Sarraute's) verbal staccato of "little movements" within experience, "somewhere on the fluctuating frontier that separates conversation from sub-conversation." The tribute is strong but a shade theoretical. Reading several Compton-Burnett volumes recently, I myself was reminded of two other critical remarks, on two other writers. (1) Dr. Johnson on Shakespeare: "A quibble, poor and barren as it is, gave him such delight, that he was content to purchase it by the sacrifice of reason, propriety, and truth." (2) Clifton Fadiman on Gertrude Stein: "My notion is that Miss Stein has set herself to solve, and has succeeded in solving, the most difficult problem in prose composition—to write something that will not arrest the attention in any way, manner, shape, or form." Miss Sprigge's book quotes Pamela Hansford Johnson's opinion that Ivy Compton-Burnett's novels "have an extraordinarily good effect upon the critic, because they enforce his entire attention. It is absolutely essential to read every line . . . because to miss a single one turns the whole book gibberish." Which is a nice way of saying that the books demand a fearful effort from the reader, whose attention keeps slipping. Whole pages of malicious banter about ham fat or some microscopic impropriety slide by while the eyes mechanically shuttle. I reread the entirety of one novel without realizing, as handwritten notes in the back of the book proved, that I had read it before. Such tenuity, like life's plotlessness, may be not the artist's fault; it sometimes feels, as we read Ivy Compton-Burnett, that she is trying to force our brain to operate along entirely novel circuits, like those grammar-school penmanship teachers who wanted us to write with our forearms instead of our fingers. The last of the Victorian novelists, she makes the 19th century seem another planet—adamant, mischievous, claustrophobic, cruel— from which her messages emanate with an arresting, exasperating semi-intelligibility. Her planet is so much her own we are pleasantly surprised to read, in this biography, that for a time she inhabited ours.

Milton Adapts Genesis; Collier Adapts Milton

MILTON'S PARADISE LOST, *Screenplay for Cinema of the Mind*, by John Collier. 144 pp. Knopf, 1973.

No clue is offered, on the jacket flap or in the author's rather testy "Apology," as to what possessed John Collier to turn John Milton's *Paradise Lost* into a screenplay. Was this a commercial, practical project—after all, Cecil B. De Mille mined Exodus and Judges for a pretty penny—from whose shipwreck the writer salvaged his script? Or was it always to be a curiosity purely literary —a "Screenplay for Cinema of the Mind," as the title page advertises? Sumptuously produced by Knopf in a kind of Loew's Orpheum Art Deco, it begins as space opera, *2001*-plus: "We are moving upward into a region where the blue is lighter and clearer"; a distant star becomes a comet; the comet's tail becomes a torrent, a waterfall whose mist is bubbles, and each bubble "is made of six or eight living creatures. These are gigantic and glorious beings with beautiful, stricken faces and flying hair. They wear minimal golden armour, such as we are accustomed to associate with demigods or angels." They *are* angels, dressed like Barbarella, millions of them, and then we see them charred and writhing in a lake of lava, and Satan himself, "burned to incandescence, like a log that is red all the way through, ready to fall to pieces." But he does not fall to pieces; instead, inventing magic on the spot (one of Collier's anthropological updatings of Milton's version), he pulls himself together and then invents oratory, announcing to the lake of the tormented, "All is not lost. The unconquerable will, and study of revenge, immortal hate, and courage never to submit nor yield." These three lines from Milton are the only ones Collier quotes entire; elsewhere he resists the delicious thunder of Milton's pentameters and for cinematic speed substitutes his own tinny *vers libre*. Satan's rhetorical question in Milton

> ". . . But first whom shall we send
> In search of this new world, whom shall we find
> Sufficient? who shall tempt with wand'ring feet
> The dark unbottom'd infinite Abyss
> And through the palpable obscure find out
> His uncouth way, or spread his aery flight
> Upborne with indefatigable wings
> Over the vast abrupt, ere he arrive . . ."

becomes in Collier's script

> "Who'll fly through the night, and
> chaos and the endless void?
> And find this race called Man?
> Who'll dare?
> Who'll go?"

The loss in magnificence is well-nigh total, but Milton is already on record, and Collier is attempting a new thing.

His description of the Burning Lake and charred angels evokes Dresden, Hiroshima, and napalming; the conclave of the damned in Pandemonium draws imagery from Fascist rallies, even to a clenched-fist salute. Space flight—the fact and technics of it—infuses the heavy epic with easy momentum. In Milton, Satan's passage from Hell to earth is a sloggy business, a piece of Renaissance exploration: "the fiend / O'er bog or steep, through strait, rough, dense, or rare / With head, hands, wings, or feet pursues his way, / And swims or sinks, or wades, or creeps, or flies. . . ." In Collier, he generates speed as smoothly as an equation, and travels as a "dark ripple in space." We ride "that wave of darkness, which is Satan in flight," and, as under the eyes of our astronauts, the huge, curved horizons of earth and sun float into view. Milton, after Gabriel confronts Satan in Paradise, has Satan hide by circling the earth on the side of darkness; though the possibility fits with Newtonian astronomy, it seems farfetched and uncomfortable in the verse, mixed with antique imagery:

> . . . thrice the Equinoctial Line
> He circl'd, four times cross'd the Car of Night
> From Pole to Pole, traversing each Colure. . . .

For Collier, such an orbiting is a familiar stunt; Satan hangs in darkness "like a surfer awaiting the wave" and exultantly teases both sunset and sunrise in the course of his confident free fall. "Free Fall," for that matter, would be a pretty good title for this movie, were it ever made.

When Satan arrives in Paradise, we arrive at hackneyed territory. Mr. Collier refreshes the fable with a lot of delightfully precise botany, some clever lighting, and an attentiveness to Eve's dreams worthy of a psychoanalyst. But his retelling founders where most modern retellings do: he does not believe in God, and God is the most interesting character in the story. God has a plan and a hope; He experiences love and regret. Satan is just a successful saboteur by comparison, and Adam and Eve are a pair of gullible yokels. The God of Genesis brims with surprises; his question of Adam, "Who told you that you were naked?" has all the cunning of do-your-own-guilt paternalism since the world began. How affably, without a blink, the blame having passed from Adam to Eve to the serpent, does He curse the serpent first, and how obligingly, having delivered the curses to all three, does He squat down like a tailor and make for His two errant children, grown out of nudity, "garments of skins." Adam and Eve are banished from Paradise not spitefully, as punishment for what cannot be undone, but as a simple Self-protective measure, to prevent the created pair, who have already eaten from the tree of the knowledge of good and evil and become "like one of us," from eating now also from the tree of life and living forever; the cherubim and the flaming sword guard not the gates of Paradise but the path to the tree of life—not the way back but the way out. This pleasant plantation owner, safeguarding His prerogatives against a slave uprising, is a remote rustic ancestor of Milton's God, a defensive monarch always ready to argue the legalities of His own decisions. To "justify the ways of God to men" was Milton's announced purpose, and the thorny conundrums of Justice and Mercy, Free Will and Divine Foresight, Liberty and Order, frame the Biblical events in a continual dialetic of serious political argument. Foreseeing Man's Fall, God sends Raphael to Adam to

> ". . . advise him of his happy state,
> Happiness in his power left free to will,
> Left to his own free Will, his Will though free,
> Yet mutable; whence warn him to beware
> He swerve not too secure: tell him withal
> His danger. . . ."

Milton then assures us, "So spake th' Eternal Father, and fulfill'd / All Justice." And Adam, when Eve complains that his failure to command "absolutely" permitted her to sin, answers in echo of God:

> "I warn'd thee, I admonish'd thee, foretold
> The danger, and the lurking Enemy
> That lay in wait; beyond this had been force,
> And force upon free Will hath here no place."

Mr. Collier is a modern atheist, and will have none of this. The long middle of Milton's poem—Raphael's exposition to Adam of the Christocentric universe—he almost entirely omits. The theological reasoning that Satan was permitted to perpetrate evil "but to bring forth / Infinite goodness, grace, and mercy" elicits from Collier the scornful paraphrase "In other words, the prisoner was paroled in order that he might commit fresh crimes and incur a yet heavier sentence. Man, at the cost of death to all and damnation to many, was to serve as bait in this outrageous trap." Mr. Collier then goes on to praise Satan as morally superior to God (". . . he is the rebel against the Establishment, the defeated, the exile, the endungeoned, the resurgent, and the guerrilla. . . . We watch in vain for some example of his wickedness. . . . He inflicts no tortures"). Mr. Collier is of course entitled to his humanist pieties and left-wing wrath, but he has no artistic right to pump the Voice of God into the end of his scenario. The Voice has been labelled hollow. The plot that turns on the strictures of such a moral nonentity as Mr. Collier's God falls to nonsense. You can have a sentimental Satan, and an adorable Jungian Adam and Eve, and an apple that is all vitamins and eroticism, but you cannot have these and Jahweh too. By the time this script reaches its last shot (Satan smiling out of the screen at us, just like Walter Huston in that old Hollywood make of "The Devil and Daniel Webster"), the corniness betrays an inner chaos. The God of Genesis walking in His garden in the cool of the day had a blunt corporeal reality. The God of Milton derives actuality from the believer's tortured strenuousness. Collier's God is just a black hole in a funny old story that must (*"Must!* That's the word now," Adam says) have something profound about it.

What did attract this excellent British fantasist to *Paradise Lost?* Possibly its superficial shimmer of the fantastic, of the hallucinatory. The conceit of making it into cinema recalls an image Santayana uses, of Dante, in *Three Philosophical Poets*: after pages of praise for the medieval poet, Santayana adds the devastating demur ". . . he has no true idea either of the path to happiness or of its real conditions. His notion of nature is an inverted image of the moral world, cast like a gigantic shadow upon the sky. It is a mirage." Some such mirage-sense of Milton's poem may be at the root of the curious metamorphosis Collier has wrought. Of the assembly in Pandemonium his scenario says, "Perhaps this vast, dark sphere is Satan's brain, and the luminous seraphs are the brain cells, glowing or flashing or dimming according to the electrical impulses that pass through them." A frequent (and, I would think, technically implausible) feature of his script is the specification of elaborate trompe-l'oeil effects:

> . . . a reddish flush emanating from the maddened seraphs hangs like a luminous cloud in the centre of the vast, dark sphere. Soon it coalesces into a tangle of fuzzy, incandescent lines which form a fiery tracery, semi-abstract, showing an imagined assault on the battlements of Heaven.

Satan ruffles a tree of dark leaves with light undersides so that from a hundred yards it exactly resembles Eve; Mulciber's body goes transparent and becomes his palace; a vast horde of devils so disperses itself as to shadow forth the forms of Adam and Eve, like a marching band at halftime. What does Collier intend by such illusions except to transfer the entire cosmic epic to the realm of dream and subjective psychology? A movie screen has no substance; it exists only for our eyes, which in turn—physiologists tell us—are specialized segments of the brain, the only ones that have surfaced and protrude through our skins.

But would these grandiose tricks—mist into angels, angels into "semi-abstract" tracery—work? Much is possible to the movie camera; but it remains a camera, a mirror of the external world's texture and accidents. Though there is immense visual ambition in Mr. Collier's directives to his hypothetical technicians, there is little that is effortlessly concrete. Phantasmagoria eclipses the luminously mundane. The human protagonists, for instance, are presumably naked until the fig leaves descend, but the script never brings Eve's body to our awareness like these lines of Milton:

> . . . but Eve
> Undeckt, save with herself more lovely fair
> Than Wood-Nymph, or the fairest Goddess feign'd
> Of three that in Mount Ida naked strove,
> Stood to entertain her guest from Heav'n . . .

Collier's "Apology" announces that his hero is Eve, yet she seems more the subject of speculation than an object of vivifying love. This kind of love Milton shows her when he has Adam say:

> "Neither her out-side form'd so fair, nor aught
> In procreation common to all kinds . . .
> So much delights me, as those graceful acts,

> Those thousand decencies that daily flow
> From all her words and actions. . . ."

Collier's Adam says:

> ". . . she grew so lovely that
> all she does and says seems
> wisest and most virtuous and best."

Which is indeed bleak praise, if not blank verse. Milton has not been generally prized for the virtues of psychological tenderness or lively sensuality; Mr. Collier's script leads us to realize how much of those virtues Milton possessed. And it leads us to suspect that in a fictional universe there is no borrowed gravity; unless an author is writing for his life, images become mere "effects" and fly into space. Precision is a function of attention, and attention is a function of concern. Too diffidently Mr. Collier tells us, of the poem's Christian content, "I do not share these beliefs, and I have substituted other ideas, also not profound in themselves, but which are more in accord with those commonly held today." There are ideas here, but no possessing *idea*. Milton's God may be a tedious old bluffer, but he fascinated Milton, and aligned the poet's inspirations in one magnetic field. A phrase like "those thousand decencies that daily flow" holds a piece of felt reality up to a moral light, and transfigures all women, all wives. Mr. Collier's Eve, on the other hand, is conceived unsteadily: eating the apple on her knees like a drugged porn queen, voting for life like some vociferous Shavian heroine, snivelling like a groupie when the angelic fuzz arrives, jerked through a series of attitudes by the dead strings of Genesis 3. The screenplay ends—for this viewer, at least—as a flicker of unweighted significances and symbols. The projector throws not a beam of light but a tatter of brilliancies.

Auden Fecit

ABOUT THE HOUSE, by W. H. Auden. 84 pp. Random House, 1965.

> There are two atlases: the one
> The public space where acts are done,
> In theory common to us all,

Where we are needed and feel small . . .
The other is the inner space
Of private ownership, the place
That each of us is forced to own,
Like his own life from which it's grown,
The landscape of his will and need
Where he is sovereign indeed . . .

Thus, in his great *New Year Letter* of 1940, Auden distinguished between the two realms explored by his life-long search for "the City." As a young man, his concern was more with "public space," and he remains *the* poet of the foreboding that preceded World War II, the lucid exhausted voice of "September 1, 1939" and the elegies to Freud and Yeats, both dead in 1939. As an aging post-war man, he has turned more toward the "inner space," the landscape of his will and need and (from the same poem) "the *polis* of our friends." His latest collection, *About the House*, celebrates this intimate city, the microcosm of his privacy, in almost doting detail. But the best of the poems are redeemed from triviality by the seriousness with which Auden considers his own comfort an episode in civilization.

The first, and superior, half of the book is a sequence of twelve poems inspired by the rooms of his recently acquired house in Austria. Each poem carries a personal dedication, and though the anonymous reader may be charmed by intimations of custom-tailored pertinence (a husband and wife get the cellar and attic respectively, and Christopher Isherwood is awarded the toilet), he is more likely to feel merely excluded; what with the Kennedys, the Glasses, the Sinatra Clan, the friends of Norman Podhoretz, and the Pop-Camp-Hip crowd, there seem enough in-groups in the Western world without a formal roll-call of Auden's acquaintance-ship. Plato's vision of the Perfect City ruled by philosopher-kings seems somewhat impudently transmuted into genial snobbery:

> The houses of our City
> are real enough but they lie
> haphazardly scattered over the earth,
> and her vagabond forum
> is any space where two of us happen to meet
> who can spot a citizen
> without papers.

Technically, the sequence is marred by the erratic interruption of "Postscripts"—short poems in another meter, often in the irksome form of haiku, tacked on wherever (however vaguely) appropriate. And it must be said that Auden, in developing each room into a cosmic instance and drawing significance from every nook, does not always avoid his besetting sin of, well, silliness. The steamy bath is extolled in an uncharacteristic non-meter which he explains as a "mallarmesque / syllabic fog," and the stanzas to excrement include:

> Freud did not invent the
> Constipated miser:
> Banks have letter boxes
> Built in their facade,
> Marked *For Night Deposits*,
> Stocks are firm or liquid,
> Currencies of nations
> Either soft or hard.

But in sum the twelve poems comprise an impressive essay upon Man the domestic animal; his domesticity is felt as a consecration of his animality.

> city planners are mistaken: a pen
> for a rational animal
> is no fitting habitat for Adam's
> sovereign clone.

Precise biological terms—clone, conurbation, neotene—insist on humanity's living context. The poem on the dining-room with high wit summarizes the full organic history of dining:

> The life of plants
> is one continuous solitary meal,
> and ruminants
> hardly interrupt theirs to sleep or to mate, but most
> predators feel
> ravenous most of the time and competitive
> always, bolting such morsels as they can contrive
> to snatch from the more terrified . . .
>   Only man,
> supererogatory beast,
> Dame Kind's thoroughbred lunatic, can

                    do the honors of a feast,
                    and was doing so
                before the last Glaciation when he offered
                    mammoth-marrow
            and, perhaps, Long Pig, will continue till Doomsday
                    when at God's board
                the saints chew pickled Leviathan.

The house abounds in remembrances of human prehistory: the
cellar "Reminds our warm and windowed quarters upstairs that /
Caves water-scooped from limestone were our first dwellings";
the archetype of the poet's workroom is "Weland's Stithy"; like
the "prehistoric hearthstone, / round as a birthday-button / and
sacred to Granny," the modern kitchen is the center of the dwelling; in conclusion, "every home should be a fortress, / equipped
with all the very latest engines / for keeping Nature at bay, /
versed in all ancient magic, the arts of quelling / the Dark Lord and
his hungry / animivorous chimeras." Nor is history forgotten: the
bathroom is seen as a shrunken tepidarium; the dining table is
compared with "Christ's cenacle" and "King Arthur's rundle"; and
the peace of the living-room is felt against "History's criminal
noise." The function of each chamber is searched in such depth that
a psychological portrait of man is achieved. Auden finds in defeca-
tion the prime Art, an "ur-act of making"; in swallowing "a sign
act of reverence"; in sleeping a "switch from personage, / with a
state number, a first and family name, / to the naked Adam or Eve."
His anatomization is controlled, at times playfully, by religious
conceptions:

                then surely those in whose creed
            God is edible may call a fine
                omelette a Christian deed.

Biology tends toward theology; our personal and animal particulars are grounded in the divine ontology. Speech is "a work of
re-presenting / the true olamic silence." This sequence of poems,
entitled "Thanksgiving for a Habitat," is an essay in architecture,
which is to say the creation of a structure enabling the human organism to perform its supernaturally determined functions of praise
and service. In a faithless age, there are

> no architects, any more
> than there are heretics or bounders: to take
> umbrage at death, to construct
> a second nature of tomb and temple, lives
> must know the meaning of *If*.

While one regrets that Auden's Christian faith is so iffy, its presence has enabled him to organize his youthfully indiscriminate variety of perceptions and data into a credible humanism.

The second half of *About the House*, "In and Out" (a habitat has been previously defined as "a place / I may go both in and out of"), consists of poems, often about travelling, that are casual in tone and middling in quality. The best is the last, "Whitsunday in Kirchstetten," a kind of annex to the house poems, wherein the poet is discovered temporarily domiciled in church. In the author's favorite late style, the long lines, pedantic terms, and discursive sequiturs evoke what was rather conspicuously absent from the house sequence—a sense of the "public space," the enveloping condition of the world:

> from Loipersbach
> to the Bering Sea not a living stockbroker,
> and church attendance is frowned upon
> like visiting brothels (but the chess and physics
> are still the same). . . .
> Down a Gothic nave
> comes our Pfarrer now, blessing the West with water:
> we may go.

Again, "Hammerfest," a description of Auden's visit to Norway's northernmost township, frames within his baroque sense of lapsed time—"the glum Reptilian Empire / Or the epic journey of the Horse"—the geological innocence of a region whose "only communities . . . / Were cenobite, mosses and lichen, sworn to / Station and reticence." And of the many (too many) poems in haiku-stanzas, I liked best "Et in Arcadia Ego," a rephrasing of his habitual accusatory apostrophe to "Dame Kind"—who "Can imagine the screeching / Virago, the Amazon, / Earth Mother was?"

The poem uses the exigencies of this Japanese form to generate lines of great energy, both polysyllabic ("Her exorbitant monsters abashed") and monosyllabic ("Geese podge home").

Auden is the supreme metrical tinkerer. Haiku, canzoni, ballades, limericks, clerihews, alliterative verse (a whole eclogue's worth) —there is nothing he will not attempt and make, to some extent, pay off. His ability, as in "Tonight at Seven-Thirty," to coin an elaborate stanza-form and effortlessly to repeat it over and over, suggests the 17th-century metaphysicals and Tennyson: the latter more than the former. His technical displays cast doubt upon the urgency of his inspiration. It is one thing to sing in a form, whether it be Homeric hexameters or Popian couplets, until it becomes a natural voice; it is another to challenge your own verbal resources with insatiable experimentation. In any collection by Auden there are hardly two successive poems in the same form, which gives even his most integral sequences, such as the "Horae Canonicae" of *The Shield of Achilles*, a restless and wearing virtuosity. As a poet, his vocation begins in the joy of fabrication rather than in an impulse of celebration: in ways it is strength, enabling him to outlive his youth, to explore, to grow, to continue to think, even—blasphemous suggestion!—to believe, in order to feed the verse-making machine. He is that anachronism, the poet as maker; but he makes expressions rather than, by mimesis, men and deeds. Compared to Eliot, he has no dramatic imagination. Despite an almost desperate metrical juggling, his plays and dialogues are the monologues of one very intellectually imaginative voice. He dramatizes all sides of an issue, but lacks the modesty, the impish and casual self-forgetfulness, that tossed off Prufrock, Cousin Harriet, Sweeney, and the curiously vigorous phantoms of *The Waste Land*. If Eliot was a dramatist, Auden is an essayist, in the root sense: he will try anything, but his adventures never take him beyond the territory of the first-person singular. He is one of the few modern poets whose genius is for the long discursive poem; for all his formal invention, he has written best in two rather accommodating meters—a long, elegaic, unrhymed or loosely rhymed line less regular than pentameter, and the tetrameter quatrains or couplets associated with music hall lyrics and with light verse.

His light vein is very rich. What could be better than, say, this stanza from "On the Circuit"?—

> Since Merit but a dunghill is,
> I mount the rostrum unafraid:
> Indeed, 'twere damnable to ask
> If I am overpaid.

Or this, from "After Reading a Child's Guide to Modern Physics"?—

> Marriage is rarely bliss
> But, surely it would be worse
> As particles to pelt
> At thousands of miles per sec
> About a universe
> In which a lover's kiss
> Would either not be felt
> Or break the loved one's neck.

In his present pleasant house, to which his dream of the City has congenially dwindled, Auden portrays his workroom, "The Cave of Making," with "windows averted from plausible / videnda but admitting a light one / could mend a watch by." By such dry clear light, a dictionary at hand, he is best read—not, as he hopes, as "a minor atlantic Goethe" (the difference in generosity may be less between Goethe and himself than between Goethe's Europe and our America), but as a man who, with a childlike curiosity and a feminine fineness of perception, treats poetry as the exercise of wit. For almost always, in his verse, the oracular and ecstatic flights fail; what we keep are the fractional phrases that could be expressed in prose, but less pointedly. He defined light verse, for his anthology of it, as poetry written in the common language of men. Powerfully attracted by the aristocratic and the arcane, he has worked to preserve his democratic loyalties, his sense of poetry as a mode of discourse between civilized men. *About the House*, though it contains no single poem as fine as "Ode to Gaea" from *The Shield of Achilles*, has nothing in it as tedious as the infatuated concept-chopping of the "Dichtung und Wahrheit" interlude of *Homage to Clio;* and on the whole marks a new frankness and a new relaxation in tone. Auden remains, in the Spirit as well as by the Letter, alive.

A Messed-Up Life

GREAT TOM, *Notes Towards the Definition of T. S. Eliot*, by T. S. Matthews. 219 pp. Harper & Row, 1974.

T. S. Matthews, in *Great Tom*, gives an impressively suave and sprightly demonstration of how to write a book when the book isn't there. You begin by including in your Acknowledgments a gracious mention of "those who did not answer my letters, or who denied me access to various unpublished papers, or who refused to see me." You go on to discuss, with unabashed candor, the New York publisher who approached you to write upon a subject in which you have neither scholarly interest nor personal involvement: Mr. Matthews met Eliot on a few "widely spaced occasions," and, like Eliot, emigrated from America to England, but the publisher seemed bewitched chiefly by the congruence of their first two initials, and his excitement was further whetted by a letter from Eliot's widow and executrix flatly declining to assist in any way; "for reasons which I still fail to understand," Matthews confides, "the publisher found this letter encouraging. I did not; but by this time the idea of writing Eliot's biography had begun to appeal to me strongly. I signed a contract for the book. Was this a mistake? Some people have said so; and if they read this book perhaps they may see no reason to change their minds."

By now, the reader has been roused to a great pitch of suspense as to how the bulk of pages still unread in his hand will be filled. The suspense becomes well-nigh unbearable under a hail of goose-flesh-raising questions:

> Who *was* T. S. Eliot? Why did he want to keep his private life a secret? . . . Is there less, or more, in his poetry than meets the eye? To what extent does his poetry depend on plagiarism and parody? Did he have a "tin ear"? Was he a phony scholar? A phony saint? . . . Was he a homosexual? Did Bertrand Russell seduce Vivienne Eliot?

The Lord only knows; with the same long breath Mr. Matthews admits that, "in the pages that follow," these "awkward questions"

have to be asked, "whether or not they can be satisfactorily answered." This is indeed, as he names the genre, "a biography, of
sorts."

Well, forewarned is disarmed, and only the most impatient seeker
of truth could fail to be beguiled by the succeeding parade of
types of padding. There is the irrelevant catalogue:

> The home remedies, the lotions and standard antiseptics, tonics, and
> germicides of the day were familiar to the Eliot household and
> particularly to little Tom: peroxide, antiphlogistene, *baume anal-
> gésique*, Listerine, camphor ice, malt extract, Castoria.

The vacuous speculation:

> Of his interior life we have no record, but we know it existed and
> suspect that it was his home address. Also he was an adolescent,
> and we know, or can partly remember, what that was like.

The impudent assertion:

> Did he masturbate? Of course. And was he ashamed of it? Un-
> speakably.

The water-treading rumination:

> Who can tell what is going on in a small boy's head? The only
> witness, the child himself, is less witness than observer, most of the
> time enthralled, some of the time in flight (either from fear or
> from what he will later call boredom), and never capable of re-
> porting his observations in any form that his elders can understand.

The mystery of Eliot's early sexual attitudes and experience evokes
from Matthews the tone of a hectoring bully:

> But why, surrounded by women as he was, should his feelings about
> them have been so faint-hearted? Because his mother and his
> sisters were ladylike women, terrified of sex and disgusted by it,
> and ashamed of their female bodies. By precept and example, they
> encouraged his own shame.

Out of wholly thin air he constructs an imaginary "facts of life"
interview between Henry Eliot and his thirteen-year-old son:

> Too soon might shock the tender young mind; too late would
> find its petals browned and withering in corruption. (They really
> thought in such terms.) Henry Eliot was a man who knew his
> duty and did it. . . . The boy would have listened with half an
> ear to his father's cautious roundabouts, the customary euphemisms,

about birds and bees. . . . His father's voice overwhelmed him with the weight of Sinai, and he crept from the presence knowing in his heart that all was lost.

The primly liberated biographer unconscionably equates the Eliots' Unitarianism with Calvinism (against which it was a liberal revolt), treats St. Louis as a suburb of a cliché-Puritan Boston, and takes poetic evidence of Eliot's sensuality ("so rank a feline smell") to mean unqualified repugnance. He assures us on no given evidence that the young Eliot was chaste both at Harvard and in Paris, and, more fascinatingly but with little more substantiation, portrays his first marriage as one long sexual rejection by the clever and neurotic Vivienne. Matthews' discussion of this marriage includes the enchanting disclaimer "Here again some significant facts are available, even if we cannot always be quite certain of their significance."

As Eliot's private life moves into the relative light of printed poems and opinion, of worldwide fame and London gossip, Matthews has more material to work with. Yet he handles the *oeuvre* rather brusquely, even dismissively. Of two youthful poems of 1910: "Neither showed the slightest sign of originality or was worth preserving." Of "Mr. Eliot's Sunday Morning Service": "If this isn't showing off with a smirk and a vengeance, what on earth is it?" Of the criticism: "Eliot as critic is also Eliot at his least satisfactory and least likeable—a know-it-all who puts us in our place and keeps us there." Of *The Waste Land:* ". . . the scheme, such as it is, is mostly afterthought." Of the poet's ear: "Examples of Eliot's failure of musical ear abound in his later poems." Matthews elsewhere says generous and shrewd things of Eliot's works, but he rarely seems to examine them with any focussed concern for the life of the mind behind them. Eliot's Christianity, for instance, stimulates a long, fulminating, personal, and rather obtuse essay in which Matthews, himself an Anglo-Catholic, worries the cheap paradox that Christians have made war and inflicted cruelties upon one another. The intellectual atmosphere *de l'entre-deux-guerres*, in which Eliot's profession of faith was a shocking and, to some, an exemplary proclamation, is scanted. Throughout, the tone of the title—crass, jaunty, faintly bellicose—is sustained; one can feel Eliot's fastidious ghost wincing.

Yet the book, in part because of its breezy thinness, is easy to read. Mr. Matthews occasionally strikes off a fine phrase: "Eliot's benign, almost wordless presence seemed to have an encouraging effect on [John Hayward], like the silent flame under a singing tea kettle." He quotes some illuminating remarks: Stravinsky's saying of Eliot, "He is not the most exuberant man I have ever known, but he is one of the purest." And Eliot himself saying, "No honest poet can ever feel quite sure of the permanent value of what he has written: he may have wasted his time and messed up his life for nothing." What a beautiful sadness in this implication that a poet, an artist, "messes up" his life in the hope of producing something immortal. And how startling to know that Eliot composed his poetry standing at a typewriter! "It is a mystery to me how anyone can write poetry except on a typewriter." And how awful to imagine him, in his little office at Lloyds Bank—"a figure stooping," I. A. Richards remembered, "very like a dark bird in a feeder, over a big table covered with all sorts and sizes of foreign correspondence"—working directly under the pavement, with heels hammering on the thick green glass squares above his head all day long. And how touching, after the recent revelation that Eliot diffidently accepted almost all of Ezra Pound's cuts of The Waste Land, to read that Pound, shown the manuscript half a century later, was equally diffident about his strokes of editing genius: "He should have ignored me. Why didn't he restore some of the cancelled passages when Liveright wanted more pages?"

And, though an official biography might bring forth an abundance of the correspondence and specificity rather strikingly sparse in these "Notes," Mr. Matthews' silhouette of the life seems unlikely to change: a life disfigured by an unhappy marriage in the middle and distinguished from beginning to end by a proud industry. As a student at Harvard, Eliot compressed four years' work into three; as a graduate student, he added Sanskrit and Italian to his knowledge of French, German, Latin, and Greek; when he worked a full day in Lloyds, he would rise at five to labor at criticism; in the years he was remapping the English literary tradition, he was nursing an ill wife; he lectured; he edited Criterion for seventeen years; at both his banking and, later, publishing jobs he not only put in time but won promotions and praise from his colleagues; after his conversion, he served on many church committees and even edited an ecclesiastical publication; at an age when many men retire, he undertook to make himself into a commercially successful playwright. Through all this, the meagre, reluctant, pained trickle of poetry, aiming (in his words) at "the maximum emotional effect with the minimum verbal decoration."

No doubt the time will never return when, as in the early fifties, to those of us in college, Eliot's reputation was an encompassing gray cloud, the very atmosphere of literature. It was a remarkable looming, a matter of style as well as of content, to a generation that loved the aloof, the cryptic, the ominous, the wry, the weary. Mr. Matthews, who offers a variety of verdicts on the worth to posterity of his elusive subject, suggests that when the "emotional radioactivity" has died away all that will be left of Eliot is "a case of the dry grins." It is true that Eliot's poetry is, as was his personality, somehow transuranic, bonded together by a perilous pressure. The contemporary estimates of its worth ranged as wildly as a Geiger counter gone crazy—from R. P. Blackmur's reverence to Van Wyck Brooks's abhorrence—and an archaeologist of literature, exhuming its decayed carbon traces in the far future, may have trouble identifying it as poetry at all. It is like no other. Its droning tone underlines a confessed poverty of inspiration and vitality, yet a steady force of seriousness, of caustic austerity, engraves it on our minds. The revelation of *The Waste Land* revisions shocked us, of course, because this of all modern poems had come to seem inevitable; it feels familiar when we read it for the first time, and by the third time it feels memorized. And when we reread it after wading through *Great Tom*, we are exhilarated by its altitude; we are "In the mountains, there you feel free." Though Eliot's critical phrases ("objective correlative," "dissociation of sensibility") may no longer serve as signposts for the student, and the plays fade, as most plays do, what lines of poetry between Yeats's late poems and the verse that Roethke and Sylvia Plath wrote from within the shadow of death burn deeper, better remember themselves, than Eliot's? His will asked that no biography of himself be written; we would not be much poorer if his request had been honored.

FRENCH DEATHS

Death's Heads

THE FIRE WITHIN, by Pierre Drieu La Rochelle, translated from the French by Richard Howard. 183 pp. Knopf, 1965.

SELECTED WORKS OF ALFRED JARRY, edited by Roger Shattuck and Simon Watson Taylor, translated by many hands. 280 pp. Grove Press, 1965.

Pierre Drieu La Rochelle (1893–1945) and Alfred Jarry (1873–1907) were French men of letters whose reputations, inseparable during their lifetimes from personal notoriety, were eclipsed after their suicides (Drieu shot himself, Jarry no less deliberately drank himself to death) but have been revived in contemporary France. Drieu, a Vichy collaborator whose passionate political inconsistency antagonized all parties, has been rehabilitated from disgrace by, an article in *Le Monde* stated in 1964, "a new generation which has chosen *désengagement*, but which is attracted by his outspokenness, his elegant cynicism, his aristocratic aestheticism, and his desperate lucidity." Jarry, an undersized super-bohemian whose play *Ubu Roi* marks the birth of the avant-garde theatre, has been honored not only by continuing editions of his writings but by the founding, in 1949, of the Collège de 'Pataphysique, an eccentric and elusive pseudo-science he invented. In the United States, a book by each author has been recently published.

Drieu's *The Fire Within* is a brief, flickering novel issued in France in 1931 as *Le Feu Follet*—"playful fire," an idiom for "*ignis fatuus*," or "will-o'-the-wisp." The will-o'-the-wisp presumably is the hero himself, Alain, whose weak hold upon life finally yields to the pull of suicide. As Alain moves through his last few days vainly seeking an excuse to live, the author subjects him to a bewildering alternation of acute sympathy and stern lecturing. The sympathy probes emotional nihilism to its last dead end and self-defeating checkmate; the lecturing seems delivered from a standpoint nearly Christian:

> Alain had never looked at the sky or the housefronts or the pavements—palpitating things; he had never looked at a river or a forest; he lived in the empty rooms of this morality: "The world is imperfect, the world is bad. I disapprove, I condemn, I annihilate the world."

Yet although he scolds him as a "fetishist" and a "naïve dandy," Drieu cannot in honesty construct a fictional world that at any point substantially resists Alain's premonitions of futility. So Alain's suicide, instead of afflicting us with the dizzying impression of waste we feel in, say, *Anna Karenina* or *Appointment in Samarra*, arrives serenely, as something appropriate and slightly overdue. It is a kind of happy ending: "A revolver is solid, it's made of steel. It's an object. To touch an object at last."

Alain is much concerned with objects, and part of Drieu's appeal to the modern young must be his flat objectivity, a dispassion that reduces people to a species of object opaque in their psychology and mute even in speech. In Drieu, the tendency has not achieved the doctrinal purity of Robbe-Grillet; his flat narrative texture is bubbled by incongruous outbursts of sermonizing. But his sense of actuality rejects mankind's ancient claims of special importance, the conviction of spiritual destiny that inflames and inflates the living newspapers of Balzac and Dickens. *The Fire Within* ends a moment before death and begins a moment after coitus. The lover and beloved are discovered looking at each other with eyes dreadfully clear of illusions: "All she saw was a hairy chest, no head. It didn't matter: she had felt nothing very violent either, yet the switch had been tripped, and that was the only sensation she had ever known, not permeating but precise." *The switch had been tripped.* Drieu's mordant and entertaining characterizations—and there are many characters; the novel in form is picaresque—work to mechanize humanity, to chisel a series of hard-featured marionettes:

Mademoiselle Farnoux smiled at Alain with meagre lust. . . . She was a little girl between forty and sixty, bald, with a black wig on her bloodless skull.

The doctor was a nervous jailer. His huge round eyes swivelled above cheeks scored by the terror of losing his boarders, and the little beard that substituted for a chin trembled incessantly.

Brancion smiled. He wore his dentures with ostentation; women were not put off by them.

Even the beautiful women are rigid dolls:

[Eva] got up and slid her dress over her head. Then she pulled off her slip, her garter belt, her stockings. She was completely naked, a magnificent, bloodless plaster body.

Maria was Russian. A Russian peasant with a face and a body carved out of wood.

It is natural that Alain, who has some of the instincts of an artist, mocks this de-animated society with ironic collages and random assemblages of objects:

On the mantel, two objects: one a delicate piece of machinery, a perfectly flat platinum chronometer, the other a hideously vulgar painted plaster statuette of a naked woman that he had bought at a fair and took with him everywhere.

In his mirror he has arranged two photographs, a foreshortened man and woman, and between them "a news item pasted on the glass with four stamps reduced the human mind to two dimensions and left it no way out." The third dimension must be the supernatural.

Though *The Fire Within* takes place in Paris, its spiritual locale is the empire of disenchantment whose twin capitals are Paris and New York. The two chief women in Alain's life, his absent wife and his present mistress, are Americans, and his vices and weaknesses seem peculiarly American—drug addiction, sexual inadequacy, fear of losing his youth, a greedy awe of money, an enfeebling dependence upon women. He is described as a Puritan: "a man who saw the vices sprouting from his prejudices, but who was incapable, because of his prejudices, of enjoying his vices." He even has a psychiatrist, who sagely tells him, "A strong, healthy woman like these Americans will make you forget all this." But Americans, as represented in this book, are clearly also "a race exhausted by civilization." The only convinced spokesman for life is a scholar immersed in the study of the gods of ancient Egypt; "he would have liked to recite some of those Egyptian prayers distended with the fullness of being, in which the spiritual life, exploding, pours out all the sap of the earth." Perhaps the reason that the waning of the Christian faith is so peculiarly desolating in France and America is that in these nations the pagan gods, whether Hellenic or Teutonic, were never taken very seriously. The Christian bet was hardly hedged. Pascal and Cotton Mather alike theologize on the basis of a vast gamble, and their heirs feel cheated. "There was, after all, something of the Christian in Alain"—this something, which needs to act righteously and refuses to embrace the mediocre muddle of living, produces, with a purity coolly mathematical, his self-destruction.

The New World to the Old is a hemisphere as disappointingly empty as the heavens. Alain, seeking to save himself, flees to New York and only deepens his plight. Of course, there are differences: Paris is a "lingering, low fever," whereas "New York, at least, was an open atrocity." But the two cities, as spiritual ciphers, are interchangeable. The faddish artistic scene of post-Surrealist Paris strikingly resembles the Camp of contemporary Manhattan:

> Among other delusory projects, Alain had thought of opening a shop in Paris or New York to sell all those dated, ugly, or absurd objects which industry, hovering between the popular and the vulgar, has produced in the last fifty years.

And the lean and sketchy style of the novel itself belongs to the Franco-American world of Hammett/Simenon detective novels and Bogart/Gabin movies and their Existentially fortified *nouvelle-vague* descendants; these things are thin with the thinness that implies a background of immense loss. Drieu La Rochelle is not as cool as his material—hence his erratic imprecations, his disturbing efforts to steer his tale toward an unsighted morality. But this roughness of tone touches the narrative from a source outside itself and recalls a context beyond the mechanical and mocked world Alain haunts, a context in which his extinction can be felt, momentarily, as a waste:

For him, the world was a handful of human beings. He had never thought there could be anything more to it. He had never felt involved with anything larger than himself. He knew nothing of plants, of the stars: he knew only a few faces, and he was dying, far from those faces.

A character in *The Fire Within* is described as "admiring spontaneously only the eccentrics of the past, from Byron to Jarry." In Alfred Jarry we encounter, at the beginning of the century, a personality and an art more radical than the regretful nihilism of Drieu. The art was a copious but incidental emanation of the personality, and Roger Shattuck's chapters on Jarry himself, in *The Banquet Years*, are more readable than the *Selected Works of Alfred Jarry*, which Mr. Shattuck and Simon Watson Taylor have edited. Descriptions of Jarry's bizarre person abound. André Gide remembered him as he was around 1895:

> This plaster-faced Kobold, gotten up like a circus clown and acting a fantastic, strenuously contrived role which showed no human characteristic, exercised a remarkable fascination at the *Mercure*. Almost everyone there attempted, some more successfully than others, to imitate him, to adopt his humor; and above all his bizarre implacable accent—no inflection or nuance and equal stress on every syllable, even the silent ones. A nutcracker, if it could talk, would do no differently.

A schoolmate, C. G. Gens-d'Armes, wrote:

> When he opened the valve of his wit, he seemed to follow after the stream of his words without any control over them. It was no longer a person speaking but a machine driven by some demon. His jerky voice, metallic and nasal, his abrupt puppetlike gestures, his fixed expression, his torrential and incoherent flow of language, his grotesque or brilliant images, this synchronism which today we should compare to the movies or the phonograph—all this astonished me, amused me, irritated me, and ended by upsetting me. . . . His originality was too much like some mental anomaly.

These quotations convey the eerie mechanical quality of Jarry's personality, or, more precisely, its insane immersion in mechanism. Virtually a midget, he insisted that the theatre appropriate the rigid ultra-reality of the marionette theatre, and lived the last years of his life in a half-floor apartment where normal-sized visitors had to crouch. Fascinated by bicycles, hydrology, physical experiments, and machinery of all sorts, he fuelled himself on alcohol and ether and did not so much die as break down; friends knocked on the door of his cupboard and he could not answer because his legs no longer worked. His last request was for a tiny tool, a toothpick. The nickname given him by a hostile critic—"La Tête de Mort"—was earned. Jarry himself had christened his first apartment, a cell at the foot of a dead-end alley, "Dead Man's Calvary."

Certainly there is little life in Jarry's writings. "I imitate nothing," he once said, and his works more resemble graffiti, cartoons, technical treatises, and verbal games than novels and plays seeking to portray human life in action. He achieved fame in 1896 with *Ubu Roi*, which was derived from schoolboy skits perpetrated against an incompetent science teacher in the lycée at Rennes. Its first word is a modified obscenity, and its hurly-burly of schoolboy cruelty and Shakespeare parody (a monstrously simplified Falstaff murderously ascends to the throne of a nonexistent Poland) does not make very good reading now, especially since New Directions has seen fit to publish the play in a scribbly novelty format. *Ubu Roi*—whose first performance occasioned a riot in the audience and left a young spectator from Ireland, William Butler Yeats, to conclude momentously in his journal, "After us the Savage God"— now in its bare text wears the sadness of a faded program, a testament to vanished fireworks. *Selected Works of Alfred Jarry* begins with several sequels to *Ubu Roi*, in which Jarry exercises a more mature wit and allegorizes his instinctive anarchism with scenes such as Ubu flushing his conscience down the toilet. But the outrageousness of such farce does not liberate; rather, one feels suffocated by a stunted sensibility and an arbitrary cruelty. As with the currently admired school of neo-pornography (e.g., *Last Exit to Brooklyn*), the author's participation appears suspiciously enthusiastic. Jarry seems to be having most of the fun in passages like (from *Ubu Cocu*):

> There's nothing to be done with him. We'll have to make do with twisting the nose and nears [*sic*], with removal of the tongue and extraction of the teeth, laceration of the posterior, hacking to pieces

of the spinal marrow and the partial or total spaghettification of the brain through the heels. He shall first be impaled, then beheaded, then finally drawn and quartered. After which the gentleman will be free, through our great clemency, to go and get himself hanged anywhere he chooses.

And this repellent note of inhumanity, of frenzy, runs through Jarry's fiction as uncontrolled hyperbole. The novel *Messalina* is not meant to be absurd, but at the height of applause in a great stadium we are told that "the sound of Messalina smacking her lips dominated the uproar." While she is being impaled on a sword, a bystander behaves most strangely:

> "But it is a sword blade, carrion," slavered the freedman, "it is not a . . ."
> But it was he who then sobbed out aloud and prostrated himself as though struck down by a god; and he buried his face in the ground, biting at the flowers whose perfume throbbed with his cry:
> "But I love her! I love her!"

Purple is too pale a word for such passages. Jarry's non-fiction is better controlled: his remarks on dramaturgical science, calling for a theatre of "man-sized marionettes," are, though irascible in tone, cogent. His scientific and blasphemous essays show demonic ingenuity and humor. After reading H. G. Wells's *The Time Machine*, Jarry, with a relentless wealth of engineering detail, set down plans for one, consisting of an ebony bicycle frame mounted on three gyroscopes aligned with the three planes of Euclidean space. In "The Passion Considered as an Uphill Bicycle Race," the Cross becomes a bicycle "constructed of two tubes soldered together at right angles"—"and it is worth mentioning in this connection that Jesus rode lying flat on his back in order to reduce his air resistance." Jarry's mad hyperbolism veers close to profundity. Refuting the notion that a bicycle rider should pedal slowly to contemplate the view, he argues:

> He should . . . make use of this gear-equipped machine to scoop up forms and colors as rapidly as possible while whizzing along roadway and bicycle track; for fueling one's mind with crushed, confused fragments relieves the memory's secret dungeons of their

destructive work, and after such an assimilation the mind can more readily recreate entirely original forms and colors. We do not know how to create out of nothingness but we are capable of doing so out of chaos.

His faith in unconscious (and therefore natural) processes is serious; he describes what must have resembled his own method of composition:

> Sengle constructed his curiously and precisely equilibrated literary works by sleeping a solid fifteen hours, after eating and drinking, and then ejaculating the result in an odd half hour's scribbling. . . . Some professors of philosophy rhapsodize that this resemblance to natural processes partakes of the ultimate Masterpiece.

Although *Selected Works of Alfred Jarry* contains only a few chapters of what Professor Shattuck elsewhere calls "the best of his novels," *Les Jours et Les Nuits*, and omits entirely "the most difficult and personal of all his texts," *L'Amour Absolu*, it includes *in toto* his exasperating "neo-scientific novel" entitled *Exploits and Opinions of Doctor Faustroll, Pataphysician.* 'Pataphysics, a concept present in Jarry's earliest work, is "the science of that which is superinduced upon metaphysics," or more fully:

> 'Pataphysics is the science of imaginary solutions, which symbolically attributes the properties of objects, described by their virtuality, to their lineaments.

Faustroll grew from Jarry's planned treatise on 'pataphysics, which was modified by a desire to "create a cast of characters to incarnate, practice, and expound the new science." Professor Shattuck's description of the inchoate hybrid that resulted is usefully succinct: "Jarry's good doctor is born full-grown at the age of sixty-three, navigates unendingly across dry land in a sieve, and travels everywhere with a summons server who is trying to collect some hundred thousand francs of back rent from him." In addition to Panmuphle, the summons server, there is Bosse-de-Nage, a dog-faced baboon whose only utterance is an intermittent "Ha ha." Beginning with a replica of the summons and ending with a geometrical discourse on the "surface of God," the book follows the adventurers through several hydrological experiments, visits to many islands, each inhabited by an artistic acquaintance of Jarry's, a banquet ending in a holocaust, a succession of prose poems, Faustroll's death through drowning, and his resurrection, or unravelling, into the happy condition of Ethernity. Such a summary makes it sound more entertaining than it is. Though it contains some good metaphors and jokes, the tale is top-heavy with personal allusions and pseudo-science, clotted with obscurities, and darkened by Jarry's infantile cruelty. Here is a specimen:

> The isle of Cyril first appeared to us as the red fire of a volcano, or as the punch bowl full of blood spattered out by the fall of shooting stars. Then we saw that it was mobile, armored, and quadrangular, with a helix at the four corners, shaped like the four demi-diagonals of separate arms able to advance in any direction. We realized that we had approached within gun range when a bullet tore off Bosse-de-Nage's right ear and four of his teeth.
>
> "Ha ha!" stammered the *papio;* but the impact of a steel cylindrocone against his left zygomatic apophysis made short work of his third word.

How can one judge Jarry? Apollinaire expressed the hope that his weird works "will be the foundation of a new realism which will perhaps not be inferior to that so poetic and learned realism of ancient Greece." Gabriel Brunet explained him by saying, "Every man is capable of showing his contempt for the cruelty and stupidity of the universe by making his own life a poem of incoherence and absurdity." I think the second estimate more plausible; Jarry's life, as a defiant gesture, matters more than his works, which are largely pranks and propaganda of a rarefied sort. Compared to Jarry, most of today's so-called Black Humorists seem merely ex-admen working off their grudges in sloppy travesties of a society whose tame creatures they remain still. Though we cannot grant him the comprehensive sanity and the reverent submission to reality that produce lasting art, we must admire his soldier's courage and his fanatic's will. He made himself into a Death's Head. When Drieu's hero Alain looks into the mirror, he sees evidence of the "terrible emaciations that a year or two before had begun to carve a death mask out of the living substance." Time acts upon him; Jarry assaults time. Alain felt himself sinking in a spiritless and mechanical world, while Jarry, skimming along on his bicycle, turned himself into a machine, with a machine's hectic ferocity and—though, unlike Ubu and Faustroll, he proved destructible—a machine's self-disregard.

Albertine Disparue

THE RUNAWAY, by Albertine Sarrazin, translated from the French by Charles Lam Markmann. 480 pp. Grove Press, 1967.

ASTRAGAL, by Albertine Sarrazin, translated from the French by Patsy Southgate. 172 pp. Grove Press, 1967.

Most men are potential desperadoes; but the concept of the female criminal seems paradoxical. Laws enforce a stability whose ultimate domestic unit is the woman herself; her physiology and psychology turn on the cultivation of inner space, while the man's role calls for the conquest of outer space, for thrust and adventure, for arrowing forms of outward assertion as various as rape and theology, as admirable as scientific exploration and as deplorable as war. The most common form of female criminality—prostitution —is, however masked in toughness, an act of submission, and keeps the peace. True, the insect world (not to mention the world of literary criticism) offers striking instances of female enlargement and predation, but the unhappy history of the male praying mantis confirms that the seminal contribution to the generative process, though not negligible, is momentary and helps account for the primordial willingness of men to undergo risk. Granted that among the highest of the primates sexual instincts androgenously overlap, enough polarity remains so that we approach two autobiographical novels by a repeatedly jailed woman, billed on the dust jackets as "a female Genet," with the expectation of something monstrous, delicious, and revelatory.

Albertine Sarrazin appears in her photograph as a curly-haired, big-eyed street Arab with a wry tuck of intelligence in the corner of her mouth. The bleak jacket notes state that she was born in Algiers in 1937, and that she was an orphan. She ran away from her foster home at the age of fifteen, was placed in reform school, escaped to Paris, "drifted into a life of theft and prostitution," and spent the next nine years either in jail or in hiding. In prison she wrote two novels, *La Cavale* and *L'Astragale*, whose publication in Paris in 1965 made her famous and secured her parole. For two years she "lived quietly with her husband Julien in the south of France," and then died, after a kidney operation, a week before her thirtieth birthday. A female Genet she was not. These two novels, published simultaneously by Grove Press as *The Runaway* and *Astragal*, are not in Genet's class, either as literary creation or as self-proclamation. Though she refers to her prison guards as "angels" and invokes "St. Duty" and "St. Java," Mme. Sarrazin shows none of Genet's myth-making power or the Satanic philosophy that conceives of prison as an inverted Heaven where seraphim swirl in violent rhythms controlled by the Deity-like onanist fantasizing in his cell. This order of originality is well beyond the very young woman who has, she tells us, "only my ball-point to pull me out of the shit and the despair." Whereas Genet celebrates the brutal, homosexual microcosm of prison as his chosen universe, Mme. Sarrazin describes nothing but daily dreariness and dreams only of escape.

The Runaway is a very long piece of scarcely disguised autobiography. Its English title inadequately translates the complex associations of *cavale*, a literary word for "mare," from which has been derived the slang verb *cavaler*, meaning "to run, to decamp, to take a powder." The translator, Mr. Markmann, confronted with a slangy and idiomatic text, has responded with sprinklings of faintly obsolete and off-key terms like "yack" (for "talk") and "mitts" (for "hands") and "nut" and "noodle" (for "head") and with impossible medleys like "What vision froze the guy in his tracks?" and gauche metonymy like "I Colgate the pearly whites," to signify tooth-brushing. In fairness, nothing deteriorates quicker in passage than slang, and there is little to suggest that the original French text is very finely nuanced. The first four hundred pages are really quite dull: the housekeeping details of prison cells, a lot of tape-recorder dialogue, a hope to escape and mount the *cavale* that never comes to anything, a succession of cellmates indistinguishable except that some smell worse than others. There are patches of vivid description:

Sometimes I like to squat on the laundry steps, where the rivulets of soap and dirty water gather in a moldy coldness; motionless, slightly bent over, my head leaning toward my shoulder, I open my mouth a little and feel the breeze vibrating through my cheeks, like a cool breath of air through a harmonica; and, a little higher up, the sun explodes lightly on my eyelids and roots me in the earth, through the rotting stones and the bubbles of laundry water; sudden joy pours out of the sky and swirls round my legs, while without changing position I move forward, with a slight effort, as against a tide.

The details of note-smuggling (in candy, via vagina, from mouth to mouth during kisses) are surprising, and there are some interesting psychological touches, as when Anick, the fastidious and reclusive heroine, takes it upon herself to delouse a senile fellow-inmate. But it all comes upon the reader haphazard, worse organized than even a sociologist would do it—the objectified diary of a precocious girl who detests jail yet is unable to stay out of it, whose self-perception is barely emerged from the chaos of self-pity, whose principal activities are stamp-cadging and daydreaming, whose days ebb by amid conversations like:

"What kind of soap do you think we'll get this week? Cadum? Palmolive?"
"I wonder what view of Paris there'll be in the biscuit boxes."

To be sure, this unstinted dreariness has a mimetic effect of sorts; we become as eager to escape the book as its narrator is to escape prison.

Anick begins her story well after the middle; she is a hardened jailbird when we meet her. The turning point of her life—her falling in love with a man called Zizi during an interval of freedom, and her concomitant conversion from lesbianism—is past, and it figures in the present tense of this novel as a constant pining for him and a futile scheming to rejoin him in the life of burglary they once led. He is in another part of the prison. On his initiative, they get married, winning the privilege of meeting once a week, with glass between them. They can kiss only in the police wagon taking them to and from the interrogations preparatory to their trial. Their final sentence is severe. Zizi is more cautious than Anick, and discourages her hopes of escape. The end of the book, if I understand it, shows her joining him in resignation—"another stroke through the calendar is not so bad. Slowly the mercury is getting down to zero, and from zero you make a fresh start." Her *cavale*, her "runaway mare," has become transformed into the interior escape of imagination. The secret action of this book is the act of its own writing; what Mme. Sarrazin has described, with steadily growing conscious intent, is the process of what we on the outside would call her "rehabilitation." In the last hundred pages, the writing grows cleaner, the imagery more complex, the plot more active. Her lawyer emerges from the shadows and becomes a character. And she herself gains access to the defiant child she once was: "I try to recapture the basic savor that I found in the hole [the isolation cell] during my adolescence. . . . I had my shoulder to the wheel of hardships, I made frightening bets against myself; I fasted, I burned myself, I pricked myself. . . . The hole was a vice, as much a vice as being tattooed or masturbating, a vice that I wanted to savor while I had the chance, and, if possible, to learn to like." She tells her lawyer, "I've been asocial ever since I was born." Earlier in the book she has tersely referred to her "mother," in puzzling variance with the dust jacket's claim that she is an orphan; now she cries out, "I'm a bastard, no one's child." Though at times she prays "Let my fury never abate. Let me always keep intact my wrong, my hurtful ways," an essential perspective has been gained, and an essential peace. "Zi, my love, one day the cycle of days and nights will stop torturing us and turn kind to us again. . . . The hateful blanket in which I roll myself up will vanish like the cold, and I will gorge myself on sun." The monotonous texture of the bulk of the book yields to heartfelt exclamations, glimpses of the past, a poetry of "this golden coma of prison where nothing makes a mark." The process of rehabilitation merges with the process of learning how to write.

The second novel also, femininely, embodies a process—the process of healing. *Astragal* ("anklebone") begins with the drop from the prison wall whereby Anne, a less slangy Anick, escapes and shatters her ankle, and ends with her walking back toward prison, "hardly limping at all." In the months between, she has met Julien (the name of Albertine Sarrazin's actual husband), has been sheltered by him in a series of hideouts, has supported herself by prostitution while he is in jail, and has broken her emotional ties with Rolande, her last female lover. These months of freedom and rescue and healing are, then, the pivotal idyll remembered in *Runaway*. The writing is in every sense happier, and Patsy Southgate's translation, comparatively uncluttered by lingo, keeps pace with the brief scenes, the nice ease of prose:

> An arm went around my shoulders, another slid under my knees, I was lifted up, carried away; the man's face of a moment ago was very close, above mine, moving across the sky and the tree branches. He carried me firmly and gently, I was out of the mud and I was moving, in his arms, between the sky and the earth.

With her new virtuosity, Mme. Sarrazin has no trouble in making the injured foot both a symbolic presence—"I had a new heart in my leg, still irregular, responding inordinately to the other"— and a convincingly painful "stew of shattered bones and flesh." Though not a sensual writer compared to Violette Leduc or to Colette, she can strike off a fresh phrase quick with the life of the moment. When she and Julien are together, "the ground is under our feet like an island"; of her outgrown lesbianism she simply says, "Rolande was the night light, the daylight is here, I turn it off." And she can detect, in the classic manner of French analysis of the sentiments, small motions within herself, such as the "cruel ill will" with which she invites Jean, an unloved protector, to zip up her dress as she goes to meet Julien, so Jean will "sniff at my new skin" and "realize that I was . . . happy; and that he didn't, that he never could, have anything to do with it." True, the depths within herself are still out of reach; her recourse to streetwalking seems screened in the telling, her alcoholism can be deduced from the text but is unacknowledged by it, the will toward self-destruction is never disentangled from her wild will toward freedom, and a certain innocent egotism flattens the other characters, including and especially her hero, Julien.

These two books, for all their developing skill, exist less as literature than as life, as the record of a life that against crippling odds fought through to expression and, in its last two years, success— "she lived quietly with her husband Julien in the south of France." While the novels of Genet insist that the male criminal dwells in a world apart, with a morality and rationale of its own, Albertine Sarrazin's world is not readily distinguishable from that of respectable women: a world of momentary but keenly felt pleasures —a cigarette, a sunbath, a bowl of fruit on a linen tablecloth—in which the chief enemy is boredom rather than (as with men) defeat, in which a prevalent stoicism is qualified by fits of panic, in which a monogamous passion is qualified by phases, almost absent-minded, of wantonness, in which powerful impulses, with a reckless lightness amazing to a male, override conventions. The laws Albertine Sarrazin broke were not, one feels, real to her; only the policemen and warders were real. At the end of *Astragal*, arrest arrives with lyric suddenness, in a courteous flurry:

> I grab my bag, I open the door, I put the key outside; on the landing a man is standing, not very big, looking cheerful and gratified:
> "Hello, Anne," he says to me. "I've been looking for you for a long time, did you know that? Come on, let's get going, I'll follow you. And don't try to run away, O.K.?"
> I smile, Julien will see us go by, he'll understand that I'll be a little late and that it's not my fault.

Now she is gone, her redeemed life cut short, and again it is not her fault.

Saganland and the Back of Beyond

SCARS ON THE SOUL, by Françoise Sagan, translated from the French by Joanna Kilmartin. 141 pp. McGraw-Hill, 1974.

THE BRIDGE OF BEYOND, by Simone Schwarz-Bart, translated from the French by Barbara Bray. 246 pp. Atheneum, 1974.

In the *Herald Tribune* of April 14, 1955, under the headline " 'BONJOUR TRISTESSE' PRODIGY ARRIVES FOR 10 DAYS IN CITY," nineteen-year-old Françoise Sagan, after informing the interviewer that she wrote her sensationally successful novel in one lazy month, confided some thoughts on existentialism and then added, deferentially, "But I am no philosopher. Sometimes I think philosophical thoughts when I have nothing better to do." Well, a generation later, Mlle. Sagan evidently has nothing better to do, for her new (and eighth) novel, *Scars on the Soul*, is full of philosophizing and devoid of almost everything else. A fiction of sorts unfolds between pages of musing and self-display: two gorgeously languid characters from her play, *Castle in Sweden*, the van Milhem siblings Sebastian and Eleanor, are revived ten years later and allowed to drift through a plot whose subsidiary characters keep dropping away (one commits suicide, others are abandoned or forgotten by the author) like petals from a vase of tired roses. The plot is in fact a subplot; the real plot, and the more exciting one, traces the chic, bored, speed-crazy ex-prodigy's attempts, through Normandy vacations and automobile accidents and spells of acedia, to push this little book through to its ending. End it does, with Françoise Sagan, as a character, in the arms of her paper hero, and this bit of origami may be, in her mind, her ticket of admission to the ranks of the New Novelists. Amid her *pensées* are some sentences devoted to these now avuncular experimenters:

> This is what I have against the New Novelists. They play with blank cartridges, defused grenades, leaving their readers to create for themselves characters left undelineated between neutral words, while they, the authors, openly wash their hands of them. God knows, ellipsis is tempting . . . but it's really a little too facile, possibly even unhealthy, to make people puzzle over obscurities when there's nothing to show that they've caused the author himself any real headache.

Whereas readers of *Scars on the Soul* will put down the book convinced, if of nothing else, that it gave the author a headache to write it.

One must be fair. There is a dainty wit, a parody of decadence, in the delineation of the ethereally incestuous and cheerfully parasitical van Milhems. Not all of the author's *aperçus* are banal; she knows her world of night clubs and vacation villas and remorselessly self-conscious love. The book reads easily; it is *company*. The author's cry of personal crisis, which leads to a novel that haltingly invents itself under our eyes, feels sincere; she is honest

even in her lameness and limpness of thought, and her self-ex-
posure, as "someone tapping away at her typewriter because she's
afraid of herself and the typewriter and the mornings and the
evenings and everything else," has its fascination, as do, on this
side of the Atlantic, the lurching franknesses of Mailer and Vonnegut. However, there is about *Scars on the Soul* an arrogant flimsiness that invites a quarrel, just as the generous margins and blank
interchapter pages invite contentious jotting. "Oh, tush!" and
"Ho-hum," I discover myself to have written, respectively, beside
these pieces of Mlle. Sagan's wisdom:

> For nothing will alter my conviction that only by pursuing the
> extremes in one's nature, with all its contradictions, appetites, aver-
> sions, rages, can one hope to understand a little—oh, I admit only a
> very little—of what life is about. At any rate, my life.

> And the women who want equality with men, and the good argu-
> ments and the good faith of some and the grotesque obtuseness of
> others, human just the same and subject to the same god, the only
> god, whom they try to deny: Time. But who reads Proust?

Françoise Sagan reads Proust, is the answer. But her Proustian
meditations have an unstately way of dwindling to nothing, to a
flirtatious self-mockery:

> Since, fundamentally, the only idol, the only God I acknowledge is
> Time, it follows that I cannot experience real pleasure or pain
> except in relation to Time. I knew that this poplar would outlast
> me, that this hay, on the contrary, would wither and die before
> me; I knew I was expected at home and also that I could just as
> easily spend another hour beneath this tree. I knew that any haste
> on my part would be as stupid as any delay. And for the rest of
> my life, I knew everything. Including the fact that such knowledge
> meant nothing. Nothing but a privileged moment. The only
> authentic moments, in my view. When I say "authentic," I mean
> "instructive," which is just as silly.

Proust interweaves his speculations and confessions with the
exhaustively evoked details of a world he powerfully loves; Mlle.
Sagan has for fabric only the shreds and scraps of a world she
has come to despise. She confesses on the first page "the distaste
I now feel for a way of life that until now . . . has always attracted me." Later, she rises to the defense of her "Saganland" of

the privileged and idle and frivolous; "The majority of critics are appalling hypocrites. . . . What could be more enjoyable than to know that a whiskey on the rocks awaits you at a villa on the other side of this golf course, among people as lively as yourself, and as free from material worries?" But the defense rings hollow. The details are tired. The furniture and chitchat, the spongers and spongees of *Scars on the Soul* are dismissed in the same breath that evokes them; only the aloof weather and landscape of Normandy arouse the writer's respect, that reverence without which description is so much word-trundling. We have indeed come a long, heavy way from *Bonjour Tristesse*, with its sparkling sea and secluding woods, its animal quickness, its academically efficient plot, its heroes and heroines given the perfection of Racine personae by the young author's innocent belief in glamour. The van Milhems, those blond leeches, seem by this retrospect degenerate forms of the incestuous affection between Cecile and her father in *Bonjour Tristesse*. Incest, self-love's first venture outward, feels deliberately burlesqued; Mlle. Sagan—at this juncture in her career, at least—has ceased to love herself, and with love has lost the impetus to create a fictional world.

An abundance of love nearly overburdens *The Bridge of Beyond*, the first novel by Simone Schwarz-Bart. The novelist, a native of Guadeloupe, married to the French author of *The Last of the Just*, describes her intention in an autobiographical note: "For me, the essence of Guadeloupe will always be the most oppressed and proudest Negroes of the island, 'unbroken and unbreakable.' I early dreamed of speaking about them someday so that justice might be done for them." She has written *The Bridge of Beyond* (whose title in French is the very different *Pluie et Vent sur Télumée Miracle*) "in memory of an old peasant woman of my village who was my friend." Telumee tells her story, beginning with her genealogy; she is the daughter of the black woman Victory, who was the daughter of Queen Without a Name, who was the daughter of Minerva, who was "a fortunate woman freed by the abolition of slavery from a master notorious for cruelty and caprice." These matrilineal generations overlap those of Mme. Schwarz-Bart's husband's recent short novel, *A*

Woman Named Solitude, which brings slavery to Guadeloupe in the person of Bayangumay, a girl abducted from an African village of pre-Adamic pleasantness. Schwarz-Bart is a European Jew writing about slavery; his wife is a native Guadeloupean writing about Guadeloupe. Though the two books have a companionable closeness of tone—a kind of tranced lyricism, as if, in her phrase, "dreamed in broad daylight"—her novel is the less surreal and the more substantial, the more convincing as a testament of life. The imagery of rivers flows through it, and its radiant shimmer and feeling of unforced movement are drawn from the center of the stream. "We were steeped in day, the light came in waves through the shifting leaves, and we looked at one another astonished to be there, all three, right in the stream of life." The book takes for its theme nothing less than living: Queen Without a Name "went on doing what God had created her for—living," though she can also ask, "To see so much misery, be spat at so often, become helpless and die—is life on earth really right for man?" Her granddaughter, Telumee, who acquires the title of Miracle, searches for "the thread of [her] life" and pronounces the verdict on her life and on life simultaneously:

> We have no more marks to guide us than the bird in the air or the fish in the water, and in the midst of this uncertainty we live, and some laugh and others sing. I thought I would sleep with one man only and he abused me; I thought Amboise immortal; I believed in a little girl who left me; and yet, without quite knowing why, I don't regard any of all that as a waste of time.

The events of the book are numerous; the author follows three heroines through their lives' adventures—their children, their lovers, their shacks, their occupations on the edge of survival. It is a frontier world, this post-slavery village of Fond-Zombi, where harsh disappointments suddenly wipe out years of tranquil harvesting; the human—or, more particularly, the female—capacity to survive sorrow and reconstitute the work of cultivation is a theme illustrated several times over, always movingly. The "miracle" attached to Telumee's name and present in the French title may be that of the human spirit, with its immortal resilience, its quicksilver moods admirable even when malevolent, its—as the book puts it—*panache.* Another theme is the special shape and tactics forced upon the black spirit in a land ruled by white proprietors. Telumee is advised, "Be a fine little Negress, a real drum with two sides. Let life bang and thump, but keep the underside always intact." The word "Negro" recurs insistently, not as a demoted term of racist distinction but as a metaphor for all men who are oppressed and scant of hope. To be Negro is to be human in a heightened degree: "however beautiful other sounds may be, only Negroes are musicians." Telumee comes to understand "what a Negro is: wind and sail at the same time, at once drummer and dancer, a first-class sham, trying to collect by the basketful the sweetness that falls scattered from above, and inventing sweetness when it doesn't fall on him." We are all, this novel makes us feel, "Negroes at the back of beyond," "flat on our bellies," our main defense "the Negro's ingenuity in forging happiness in spite of everything." "What happiness!" comes as the book's concluding phrase, and if words of wisdom are spoken by too many sibylline Negresses, and a Caribbean brand of black populism pushes some passages into sentimentality, the book's gift of life is so generous, and its imagery so scintillant in the sunlight of love, that we believe every word.

In Praise of the Blind, Black God

A HAPPY DEATH, by Albert Camus, translated from the French by Richard Howard. 192 pp. Alfred A. Knopf, 1972.

Albert Camus' first novel, *A Happy Death*, which he did not allow to be published during his lifetime, has now been issued in a handsome, annotated edition. Read in conjunction with the other writings of the young Camus—the notebooks begun in 1935, the two small collections of essays *The Wrong Side and the Right Side* (1937) and *Nuptials* (1938), the play *Caligula* (composed in 1938 but not performed until 1945), and his second novel, the classic *The Stranger* (completed in 1940 and published in 1942)— his first attempt at extended fiction offers an instructive lesson in the strategies of the imagination. Though shot through with brilliant rays, *A Happy Death* is a chunky, labored work, cumbersome for all its brevity, so cluttered with false starts and halting intentions that it occludes its own themes. In Camus' published *Notebooks*, it first appears as some chapter titles listed in January of 1936, when he was twenty-two; the last relevant notation occurs in March of 1939, when work on *The Stranger* was well advanced. An entry in June of 1938—"Rewrite novel"—implies a finished draft of *A Happy Death* by that time, but a month earlier, in a sketch of a funeral in an old people's home, *The Stranger* had begun to germinate, and some months later the uncanny, chilling first sentences of the masterpiece were written out intact. During the interval when passages for both novels compete in the *Notebooks*, those relating to *A Happy Death* suffer by comparison, seeming febrile and flaccid amid the sharp glimpses of the novel eventually published. Wisely, Camus let the first novel be consumed by the second, reusing a number of descriptions, recasting the main theme (a happy death), and transforming the hero's name by the addition of a *u*—Mersault, the man of sea and sun, darkening to Meursault, with its shadow of *meurtre*, of murder. Technically, the third-person method of *A Happy Death*, frequently an awkward vehicle for alter egos (see, see the sensitive young man light his cigarette; now let's eavesdrop on his thoughts), becomes the hypnotic, unabashed first-person voice of *The Stranger*. Substantively, Camus has located, outside of autobiography, the Archimedean point wherefrom he can acquire leverage upon his world. Often in art less is more, and one must depart to arrive. In the first novel, the author fumbles, trying to pick himself up by too many handles, and growing more handles in the process; in the second, he takes a short but decisive side-step, becomes less himself, and with this achieved narrowness penetrates to the heart of his *raison d'écrire*.

The youthful Camus evidently had many attributes of a normal Algerian working-class lout. He liked soccer, girls, beachbumming, moviegoing, and idleness. He had decided, one feels, to cherish the image of himself as a citizen of the Belcourt slums, a spiritual mate to the proletariat of whom he wrote, in "Summer in Algiers":

> They start work very early, and exhaust the range of human experience in ten short years. A workingman of thirty had already

played all his cards. . . . His delights have been swift and merciless. So has his life. And you understand then that he is born in a
land where everything is given to be taken away. . . . So reflection
or self-improvement are quite irrelevant.

The Camus whose gifts for reflection and self-improvement were
early recognized and nurtured by a grade-school teacher, the
Camus who entered the *lycée* at the age of ten, who studied philosophy at the University of Algiers from 1932 to 1936, who by
the age of twenty-five was a working, travelling, published intellectual and the mastermind of a theatre group—this Camus figures
little in the early essays or in the character of Mersault. Mersault,
though his consciousness is brushed by philosophical speculation,
confesses no ambition for his future and almost never reflects on
his past.

By any standards, Camus' upbringing had been bleak. His father,
an agricultural laborer, was killed in the Battle of the Marne ten
months after Albert was born. His mother, a Spaniard, took the
infant and his older brother Lucien from the village of Mondovi
to the poor district of Algiers, where she became a cleaning
woman. Camus was raised in a ménage that included his mother,
a partially paralyzed uncle, and a domineering grandmother. These
three adults were all illiterate and, in various ways, ill. The grandmother eventually died of cancer of the liver; Camus wrote of her,
"She fainted very easily after family discussions. She also suffered
from painful vomiting caused by a liver complaint. But she showed
not the slightest discretion in the practice of her illness. Far from
shutting herself away, she would vomit noisily into the kitchen
garbage can." His mother, he wrote, "could think only with
difficulty"; deafness, a speech impediment, and a docile temper
combined to enforce a habit of silence. Camus once described his
literary career as the attempt to speak for the "silent mother"—
the inarticulate and disenfranchised of society. An early sketch
portrays a grandmother who persistently asks a child, "Whom do
you like best? Your mother or your grandmother?"

> The game was even better when the daughter was present. For the
> child would always reply: "My grandmother," with, in his heart, a
> great surge of love for his ever silent mother.

Death for a father, silence for a mother: with such a parentage, Camus would never become a fluent or frivolous creator. At the moment of beginning his first novel, what, indeed, was his artistic treasure? A good education, a normal sensuality, a fond ear for working-class dialect, a rapturous sensitivity to nature, a conviction that paganism was being reborn around him in Europeanized North Africa. "For twenty centuries, men have strived to impose decency on the insolence and simplicity of the Greeks, to diminish the flesh and elaborate our dress. Today, reaching back over this history, young men sprinting on the Mediterranean beaches are rediscovering the magnificent motions of the athletes of Delos." Two events in his early maturity urged him toward energetic use of his capabilities: in 1930 he nearly died of tuberculosis, and in 1934 he joined the Communist Party. Yet always, in the heart of this young man, coexistent with the desire to celebrate and explicate, lay an unshakable lassitude and a blankness. Caligula (a part Camus wrote for himself to act) says, "There's something deep down in me—an abyss of silence, a pool of stagnant water, rotting weeds." At the age of forty-five, great in fame and accomplishment, Camus wrote of "the profound indifference that haunts me like a natural infirmity." Around this natural infirmity, then, the novice artist must shape his strategies—no, not around it; he must point himself *into* it, for this silence is his message.

The first sketch, in the *Notebooks*, for the novel that is to become *A Happy Death* outlines, with an excessively formal scheme of alternation between past and present tense, what appears to be a story about love and jealousy among students, ending with the hero's death by disease. "Taste of death and of the sun. Love of life," reads a note for the ending, encapsulating the tensions—the sun as life-giving yet cruel, the affirmation of life in the moment of death—that Camus wished to dramatize. Violent death does not figure in this first version, though the hero (called simply Patrice) does tell "his story of the man sentenced to death: 'I can see him, he is inside me. And everything he says pierces my heart. He lives and breathes with me. He is afraid with me.'" This premonition of *The Stranger*, however, remains fallow in the notes; a year and a half later, the novel, still untitled, has become involved with an idea about a gambler and with Camus' European travels. "Theme of the revolver," however, emerges in one list of chapters, and a little later a fresh approach to the plot is indicated:

> Novel: the man who realizes that one needs to be rich in order to live, who devotes himself completely to the acquisition of money, who succeeds, lives and dies *happy*.

The italicization of "happy" signals an arrival; a month later (September of 1937), the title "La Mort Heureuse" appears. That fall, the character of "an invalid—both legs amputated" begins to talk in the notes, and before the end of the year he has his curious name, Zagreus. To this new character adheres the old "theme of the revolver," elaborated in a remarkable earlier notation about a man who plays with a loaded revolver before going to sleep: "And, as he woke up, his mouth filled with an already bitter saliva, he licked the barrel, poking his tongue into it, and with a death rattle of infinite happiness said again and again in wonder and astonishment: 'My joy is priceless.' "

The stage is at last prepared, then, for the central action of *A Happy Death*. Patrice Mersault, a poor young man, makes the acquaintance, through a mistress, of a legless invalid, Roland Zagreus, who shows him one day a safe full of money, a loaded revolver, and an undated suicide note. Some days later (in a chapter Camus transposed to the beginning of the novel), Mersault visits Zagreus, takes up the revolver, kills the cripple with it, leaves the suicide note on a table, and departs with the money. Walking away from this perfect crime, he sneezes, and the remainder of the novel traces his wandering, through a variety of countries and romantic entanglements, toward his own death, of pleurisy, chills, fever, and weak heart—a somewhat poetic syndrome. Assembled rather than conceived, the story has too many duplicating parts— too many women, too many deaths, too many meditative approaches to the lyrical riddle of "happiness." Simple problems of clarity exist. Has Zagreus deliberately invited Mersault to murder him? Why, when Mersault holds the gun to his head, doesn't Zagreus gesture or speak? "When he felt the barrel against his right temple, he did not turn away. But Patrice, watching him, saw his eyes fill with tears." These tears are given meaning not by the context but by an entry in the notebooks: "The man who doesn't

want this easy way out, and who wants to chew over and taste
all his fear. He dies without a word, his eyes full of tears." The
murder is so abruptly rendered as to seem merely sensational. Nor
do its consequences easily flow: after the murder and the theft,
Mersault does not live like a rich man; he travels thriftily in Europe
and loafs among friends. None of his pleasures are beyond the
financial reach of Camus himself at this impoverished stage of his
life. Mersault never becomes the proposed hero "who devotes
himself completely to the acquisition of money"; money never
becomes an embodied theme.

Since *A Happy Death* arrives now with an excellent critical
afterword by Jean Sarocchi, and since Camus suppressed the work,
why belabor its weaknesses? Only to marvel at how its materials
and concerns reëmerge in *The Stranger*, transformed by their new
position within a unified action. For instance, chapter two of *A
Happy Death* describes for several pages the passage of a Sunday
in Algiers as witnessed by Mersault from a window in his room.
These pages rank with the youthful essays for poetic power, and,
indeed, "Between Yes and No" shows Camus' mother thus sitting
and gazing at the street for hours. But the resonance remains private: the Sunday is no particular Sunday; it illustrates Mersault's
boredom within a somewhat formless flashback. In *The Stranger*,
however, where the passage recurs almost word for word, the
Sunday is the Sunday two days after Meursault has buried his
mother, and the very day after he has taken a beach pickup, Marie,
to a Fernandel movie and begun an affair with her; in this context,
the reused description reflects sinisterly upon him and ominously
upon life: "It occurred to me that somehow I'd got through another Sunday, that Mother now was buried, and tomorrow I'd be
going back to work as usual. Really, nothing in my life had
changed." Another instance: the "tough" characters in *A Happy
Death*—the customers in Céleste's restaurant and the barrelmaker
Cardona, who lives downstairs—provide only background; they
exist in the book because Camus, a convinced egalitarian, has invited them in. Whereas, in *The Stranger*, old Salamano and the
pimp Raymond Sintès, besides being more vivid, actively lead
Meursault into the nexus of violence that dooms him. Further, they

testify at his trial, during which Raymond's friendship is cited in proof of Meursault's criminality. All the events of *The Stranger*, indeed, are relevant at the trial; the plot's turns are cast in iron.

No amount of trimming and rearranging can counterfeit the effect of a single concept alertly pursued. How splendidly, at the center of *The Stranger*, event, symbol, and statement fuse! Camus' obsession with that harsh wonder the sun—with the "*Nada* whose birth is possible only at the sight of landscapes crushed by the sun"—creates a furnace in which existential absurdity engenders sensation and action:

> The whole world seemed to have come to a standstill on this little strip of sand between the sunlight and the sea. . . . And just then it crossed my mind that one might fire, or not fire—and it would come to absolutely the same thing. . . . But the heat was so great that it was just as bad staying where I was, under that flood of blinding light falling from the sky. To stay, or to make a move—it came to much the same. . . . The trigger gave, and the smooth underbelly of the butt jogged my palm. And so, with that crisp, whipcrack sound, it all began. I shook off my sweat and the clinging veil of light. I knew I'd shattered the balance of the day, the spacious calm of this beach on which I had been happy. But I fired four shots more into the inert body, on which they left no visible trace.

These four additional shots, fired in dazed indifference, are what condemn him to death. The inner blankness of the Camusian hero, a puzzling sullen driftingness in Mersault, Meursault proclaims as a splendid defiance. "It makes no difference, I am not interested" —such phrases, repeated in the face of society's hatred, reconfirmed in the moment of extinction, become the litany of a new kind of holiness. Before his execution, Meursault opens his heart to the "benign indifference" of the universe. Its indifference and his are akin. "To feel it so like myself, indeed, so brotherly, made me realize that I'd been happy, and that I was happy still." All that is needed to complete his happiness is the howl of execration from the mob around the guillotine. Caligula, under the swords of his assassins, "laughing and choking," cries out, "I'm still alive!" Of himself, Camus wrote, in a youthful essay, "And yet, at the very moment that the world was crumbling, he was alive." A few sentences further: "Every time it seems to me that I've grasped the deep meaning of the world, it is its simplicity that always overwhelms me. My mother, that evening, and its strange indifference." Indifference, life, simplicity, the sun, death: the concepts link up, make a circle. "There is no love of life without despair of life," an essay affirms. Love, despair, silence, mother, nature. A sentence deleted from *A Happy Death* reads, "The sun is the real mirror of the world." Blank, indifferent, merciless, the sun is in each of us, the sun is life. Instead, then, of a soul seeking reunion with God, we contain a stark reflection of "the blind, black god"—another phrase deleted from *A Happy Death*. We serve this god by pretending no more than we feel, though we feel nothing, and by accepting death in a pantheistic ecstasy that Camus called "happiness." Some of Camus' most interesting ethical precepts, as set down in *The Myth of Sisyphus*—written directly after *The Stranger*—are deliberate inversions of Christian suppositions: each man has "his irreparable innocence," "what counts is not the best living but the most living," and the heart the creator needs is "the closed heart."

But *A Happy Death*, with its half-hearted autobiography, too numerous romances, static scenery-painting, and ingenuous melodrama, could not focus this anti-theology. The images that could, however, already lay in Camus' notebook. One of the entries for January of 1936 lists six story ideas; two are "Death of the mother" and "The story of the condemned man." These two preoccupations figure marginally in much of Camus' youthful production; with *The Stranger*, for the first time he *invents* them, in the freedom of fantasy. By proposing a young man who could not shed tears at his mother's funeral and went to the movies instead of mourning, and by rendering her pauper's funeral and his daily life in the full dry light of their absurd inconsequence, Camus placed his hidden theme of blankness where no reader could avoid being challenged by it. Though of course derived from observation (impressions of a funeral occur in the notebooks, and his grandmother's death had already provided matter for an essay), the central circumstance is imagined; Camus' mother, in fact, outlived him. His essays show how deeply he loved her. But by killing her in his mind, he unlocked an essential self, Meursault the essential orphan, in all his "simplicity" and estrangement, this cool monster who is Everyman, with his casual, androgynous voice that would blow down all our castles of Christian decency and conventional delusion. And by making this hero's condemnation to death literal and legal, instead of an attenuated wasting by disease, Camus immensely heightens the pressure. He is forced, observe, by these inventions to conjure up two blank-walled interiors—the old people's home and the jail—that crystallize *Nada* better than the open landscapes he so loved to describe. And the necessary characters of the warden and the chaplain, with their tragicomic eloquence, lead his book into a dimension undeveloped in *A Happy Death*—the dimension of the political. Society acquires spokesmen, and in debate Meursault turns singular, heroic, revolutionary. The fussed-over irrelevancies of *A Happy Death* fall away. The new novel pours smooth and hot from start to finish.

Fiction must hold in healthily tense combination the mimetic and pedagogic impulses. Perhaps because kind teachers had guided his rise from poverty, Camus respected pedagogy, wished always to make things formal and clear, liked stories to have morals. He sometimes reminds us of a schoolteacher standing before us insisting that though there is no headmaster and no grading system and scarcely any blackboard, we must stay at our desks, learning virtue and happiness with the diligence of saints. We must, in short, love our mother—"The earth! . . . that great temple deserted by the gods"—even though she is silent. After *The Stranger* and *The Plague*, Camus' fiction shows more intellectual will than vital, involuntary substance. *The Fall* and the short stories of *Exile and the Kingdom* seem relatively stiff and diagrammatic. The poet stoops in his prophet's robes. *A Happy Death* shows the other extremity of this curve—the beginning, when artistry and philosophy struggled with an abundance of live impressions; the prophet had not yet been robed, the young man stood naked.

EUROPE

Two Points on a Descending Curve

MOUCHETTE, by Georges Bernanos, translated by J. C. Whitehouse. 127 pp. Holt, Rinehart & Winston, 1966.

TWO VIEWS, by Uwe Johnson, translated from the German by Richard and Clara Winston. 183 pp. Harcourt, Brace & World, 1966.

Time passes in America and Asia; in Europe, history occurs. We have this impression, perhaps, because Europe had a Middle Ages, a fusion of faith and action, politics and culture, symbol and reality, after which all things seem to disintegrate and decline. In Georges Bernanos' great sacerdotal novel, *The Diary of a Country Priest*, an old curé tells the hero, "Mind you, it's not that I'm taken in by the usual fairy-tale Middle Ages: people in the thirteenth century didn't pretend to be plaster saints. . . . But we were founding an empire, my boy, an empire that would have made the Caesars' effort look like so much mud." Further on, a soldier indicts the Church for abandoning the Middle Ages: "It was you who first pandered to the lawmakers of the Renaissance, whilst they made short work of Christian rights, and patiently constructed . . . the Pagan State: the state which knows no law but that of its own well-being—the merciless countries full of greed and pride." Medieval nostalgia, bumptiously expressed in English by Chesterton, is not confined to Roman Catholics but pervades secular Europe with a sense of loss, of a historical fall and a progressive demoralization. Modern man is man demoralized. "I'll define you a Christian people by the opposite," the curé says. "The opposite of a Christian people is a people grown sad and old." First went supernatural faith, then faith in kings, then faith in reason, then faith in nature, then faith in science, and, most lately, faith in the subconscious. The texture of prose and the art of narration have changed to fit the case; indeed, since *Don Quixote* fiction has to some extent thrived on disillusion. But in this century the minimal presupposition of human significance, the power of one human to touch another's heart, seems too much to be assumed. Love is, a current epigram* has it, "the friction of two epiderms," and, if Freud is to be believed, we spend our emotional lives vainly seeking, amid a crowd of phantoms, to placate our parent's ghosts. Such solipsism renders obsolete the interconnectedness of action that comprises "plot" and the trust in communication that gives a narration voice and pulse. Formless tales blankly told may be the end result; two recently published novels illustrate the trend.

Mouchette, Bernanos' last novel, has just been brought out. Written in 1937, it seems still older; no automobile violates the muddy roads of its Picard village, and it comes as a surprise to learn that Mouchette, the fourteen-year-old peasant outcast who is its heroine, sometimes sees the "faces of film-stars" in newspapers. The acrid rural poverty, the rain-whipped woods, the nocturnal poaching, the harsh pedantry of her school seem at least as old as Balzac, and of course Bernanos is an old-fashioned writer, Balzacian in his melodrama and in the importance he rather feverishly insists that his characters have. This quality, of feverishness, of inflamed significance, suggests unhealth, and the characters tangent to Mouchette include her bestially alcoholic father and brothers, a mother who suffocates before her eyes, an epileptic and raving poacher, and a gentle old female necrophile. Mouchette lives "on the edge of a stagnant pool," in a countryside whose sandy fields are "swarming with starving rabbits scarcely bigger than rats." The novel itself feels sinisterly underpopulated, as if a plague has passed. Yet these macabre circumstances are set forth in a vivid, even sprightly style constantly alert for telling natural details: "The soil, undermined by rabbits, gave way beneath her feet at almost every step, and if she kept to the edge of the wood, where the interlaced roots made the ground firmer, she was lashed

---

* Current but not recently coined. *"L'amour est l'assouvissement de deux désirs par le contact de deux épidermes"*—Chamfort (1741-1794).

by sodden branches." Or: "Nothing remained but the tall poplar, scarcely visible in the sky, murmuring like a spring." Gallic intelligence plays eagerly across the dismal village, scattering aphorisms on the subject of poverty:

> If the very poor could associate the various images of their poverty they would be overwhelmed by it, but their wretchedness seems to them to consist simply of an endless succession of miseries, a series of unfortunate chances.

> Lying had never seemed wrong to Mouchette, for it was the most precious—probably the only—privilege of the wretched.

> But once they have been induced to despair, the defences of the simple are irretrievably breached and their ignorance knows of no escape save suicide—the suicide of the poor, which is so like that of children.

Bernanos, as he expresses it in his terse foreword, "watched [Mouchette] live and die" with acute tenderness. Her interlude with Arsène, the poacher who shelters her from the rain, confesses to her that he has just committed murder, makes her his accomplice, and finally rapes her, is a superb scene, lit by fire and tempest and the dumb kindling of life within the girl.

> It did not occur to her to find Arsène's face handsome. It was simply that it seemed made for her, and seemed as easy and natural in her gaze as the handle of her old knife in her hand, the old knife which she had found on the road one evening, and had shown to no one, and which was the only thing in the world which she possessed. She would have liked to touch his face, but its golden color, as warm as that of bread, was enough to make her happy.

The idea of bread, beautifully transposed, echoes a few sentences later: "All the pleasure in looking at [his face] came not from him, but from the depths of herself, where it had lain hidden and germinating, like a seed of wheat beneath the snow."

In a 19th-century novel, Mouchette's encounter with Arsène would develop into a prolonged involvement, rich in recurrence and mutual reaction. It is *Mouchette*'s failure, yet also its seal of fidelity to its time, that nothing of the sort happens; the encounter leads nowhere. Arsène disappears, and Mouchette discovers that his crime was imaginary, rendering her pledge of self-sacrifice to him meaningless. Nothing connects. Moved in her extremity of misery to communicate with her mother, Mouchette confides to the deaf ear of a dead woman. The attentions of the villagers—not all of them hard-hearted—repel her exacerbated spirit; she is at last befriended by an old lady who cunningly invites her to die, to find in death the purity that the child naïvely associates with "the physical image of clear water." The image of the poplar "murmuring like a spring" returns as a tiny pool in a sand quarry, where "the water was so clear that no fish would live there." To this place Mouchette comes to terminate her brief story.

Though church bells ring in the distance, as they do in all European novels, God does not break His silence. The squalor is unredeemed. There is small trace of the author's ardent Catholicism (and where, in contemporary France, are the successors to Bernanos and Mauriac, Marcel and Maritain, Claudel and Péguy?) beyond his abrupt assurance that poverty is a "sacred sign." Mouchette's passage into despair yields no more of a moral than the slipping flight of a swallow across the smoky evening sky. Tragedy is dwindled to a mournful pang, a surrender, almost complacent, to universal indifference. Bernanos' Christianity lingers merely as a tone, as the outsize intensity with which he broods upon Mouchette's small lost soul.

This intensity is willfully absent from Uwe Johnson's *Two Views*. While *Mouchette* seems to belong to the past, *Two Views*, which takes place in the Berlin of 1961–1962, has the insubstantial quality of the future. Picardy's sodden fields have yielded to a papery world of maps (the endpapers are maps of the Berlin Wall), newspapers, passports, neon advertisements, airplane and train schedules, flimsy automobiles, and ambiguously worded love letters. The novel's structure is two-dimensional, switching in alternate chapters from the viewpoint of Dietbert, a young West German photographer, to that of Beate, an East Berlin nurse. The views and lives of both are transcribed, if the Winstons' translation is to be believed, in an intelligent but somehow preoccupied prose that hastens past crises to dwell with fond flatness upon daily routines.

Officially First Class was known as the chief's ward so that the patients in Second Class would think of it solely as the head doctor's private preserve, not a place where the patients enjoyed special privileges; unofficially, it was known simply as 1-b, after the traditional corridor whose rooms for a long time after the war had held four or five beds but by and by had been reduced once more to private or semiprivate setup.

That is Beate at work; here is Dietbert:

From a high apartment whose owner rented window places to the photographers he was able to take shots of the slender barrels which from his angle protruded over the border, with the line of battle-equipped soldiers drawn up in front of them, in the distance the conventional Soviet tanks with the white star. And if he happened to arrive when a refugee in the boundary canal had already been shot, another had already plunged to his death from a roof, he photographed the lingering crowd of onlookers, the soldiers in the cutters probing the water or the holes in the roof that the dead man had broken in the course of his fall; was able to sell these, and also the cloud of the teargas bomb that had driven the horde of photographers back from the scene. *Often he felt as if he were living in a movie.*

The pouncing italics are mine. These Iron-curtained lovers move jerkily, as if on celluloid; they seem immersed in "the gray racket of the television set." Their plight has been predigested by the voracious news media that instantly commercialize catastrophe. Furthermore, Dietbert is an indecisive blunderer, who keeps himself tranquillized with alcohol, and Beate a faintly drab prig.

Yet through this crust of inconsequence—indeed, credible because of it—eros breaks, and the perfunctory liaison and nearly accidental reunion of Dietbert and Beate serves, at least for me, as a moving parable of human love and as a sufficient indictment of the political systems that would separate us, "the merciless countries full of greed and pride." Johnson, a native of Pomerania who in 1959 became a West Berliner, does not weight the argument between East and West; Dietbert's need to acquire a fancy sports car beyond his means is as debilitating as Beate's search, in the Communist housing jungle, for a private room. The vulgar scramble of capitalism is balanced against the obstinate bureaucracy of Socialism. Beate does not wish to mingle her friends from the two

Berlins, for "the former would have ridiculed the latter for their faith in the prospects of the East German state, and the latter the former for ignorance of society and the tendency under the influence of alcohol to despair loudly and tearfully of the meaning of life." Partition is made visible as, from a West German airplane, "the transition from the small patches of color on the ground to the large fields that marked East German territory" and, from an East Berlin tram, as "the wet glittering red of neon advertising in West Berlin." If a political emotion is present, it is a Berliner's frustration over the sundering of his city, which becomes, on the human level, a need to have lovers—however mediocre, vague, and ignorant of one another—reunite. Beate's escape, whose methodical details build into a terrific cinematic suspense, is a leap of the heart, a change of angle more than of locus. From where she arrives she can see the platform from which she left. Dietbert, hastening to meet her, misses connections and winds up in a hospital, where he becomes to Beate "a patient like any other." The ending, though not what we expect, seems happy; the author, who in *Mouchette* was a grieving, helpless God, ambles into the last pages as an ordinary Berlin citizen, exuding normal human warmth. The post-apocalyptic irresolution of *Two Views* may well be where European man, after history's extravagant demands, is glad to settle.

The View from the Dental Chair

LOCAL ANAESTHETIC, by Günter Grass, translated from the German by Ralph Manheim. 284 pp. Harcourt, Brace & World, 1970.

"If you're out to buy a pig, talk about the weather." This "old peasant rule" is quoted in Günter Grass's fourth novel, *Local Anaesthetic*, and the book illustrates the tactic. As the author talks, with manic erudition and rather lumpy explicitness, about such weather as dentistry, cement, Seneca, battles, German history, and the aquarium care of guppies, the pig nearly gets away. For the first half of the novel, there are no characters one can visualize, no action one can follow, no reason to persevere, indeed, but the faith that this quirky experiment will begin to add up. And it finally does, into a well-meditated if fliply presented dialogue on the generation gap and the revolutionary urge. "Fliply"—as when one flips the channel knob on a television set. Grass's dominant metaphor and method derive from the medium of television, with its rapid intercuts, its numbing discontinuity, its ectoplasmic freedom from the laws of either truth or art. The framing conceit is this: Eberhard Starusch, a West Berlin schoolteacher, is having his toothache and life-long prognathic bite corrected by capping. His dentist, an omniscient prattler in tennis shoes, distracts his patients with a television screen, where old films and educational panels and lewd commercials and gauzy static flow indiscriminately on. Into this flow, Starusch, his mouth stoppered with cotton and aluminum, mentally hurls scenes supposedly from his life, many of which are mere fantasies. He several times murders, for instance, his ex-fiancée, the goatlike Sieglinde Krings, employing such special weapons as a bicycle chain and a swimming-pool wave-generating machine; the truth seems to be that she is alive and married to an electrician called Schlottau. Or was really named Monica Lindrath and has become a pediatrician. Similarly, Sta-rusch's career as an engineer for the Krings cement works seems a grandiose blow-up of a summer job he had, as a student, with a different company. And what of Krings, the cement-and-pumice magnate returned from prisoner-of-war captivity, the stoic ex-general who spends his dotage reconstructing old battle sites in sandboxes and refighting old defeats into victories? He, too, dissolves into shadow play. Apparitions succeed one another in segments often less than a page long. A sample:

> The soundless picture showed a clerical-looking gentleman who, it being Saturday, wished to say a word about Sunday, although this program is televised after 10 p.m. and never before the Berlin evening news: "Yes, yes, my son, I know, it hurts. But all the pain in the world is powerless to . . ."
> (His finely articulated fingers. When he raised an eyebrow in mockery. Or his delayed head-shaking: Scherbaum calls him Silvertongue.)
> Then the bells rang in Sunday: Bim!—And the pigeons rose up

in fright. Boom!—Ah, and the little tin satellites in my head that knows it all tinkled: Bim! Poom! Pumice!

Grass's shuttle of scenes becomes as fatiguing and irritating as a battery of TVs manipulated by invisible children; verily, one's teeth begin to hurt, sensitized by unsparingly dental doses of short-circuited prose:

> (Eased, tapered off, hardly to be remembered. One more twinge —but that may have been a reflex—then silence.) Outside it was snowing from left to right on Hohenzollerndamm. (Not the .TV, the street side of the office.) The screen was uninhabited. Like myself: all fuzzy and, I may as well say it, deaf. ("I'm told that anaesthetized tongues have been maimed by the experimental bites of incredulous patients.") His voice was wrapped in tinfoil. ("And now we'll take off the aluminum shells. . . .") And my question— "What do you mean, take off?"—was also muffled as it rose up to fill blubbery balloons. Not until he breathed at me from close, too close, up: "They are removed with tweezers. Kindly open wide," did I surrender and make my big Ah.

Grass's artistic temperament, from *The Tin Drum* on, has been drawn to the gritty and mechanical; even in a nostalgic idyll like *Cat and Mouse*, he devotes a disproportion of words to the mechanics of getting in and out of a sunken minesweeper and to chemical substances such as flakes of rust and gull droppings. His plots snag on small operational procedures: *The Tin Drum* opens by specifying how a woman rotates five skirts, wearing four and washing one each week. His characterizations ponderously depend on physical deformities—dwarfishness, protuberant ears, a grotesque Adam's apple. Whereas Starusch has a prognathic bite, his young antagonist, Scherbaum, turns out to have the opposite defect, a distal bite, and is last seen wearing a corrective labial bar. Grass's prose is physically encumbered, chunky, resistant. Even if we allow for the losses of rhythm and penumbral connotation inevitable in any translation, we miss the plastic ease of expression and interconnection that until recently was the common property of even mediocre European writers. The ability, preëminent in Tolstoy, to move exciting spiritual currents through masses of circumstance and sensuous detail is perhaps lost, along with the instinctive belief in the dualism of matter and spirit. Strange to say, materialism in fiction seems to reduce the vitality of physical description, to make it clot into topographic (Robbe-Grillet) or professional (Grass) detail. Compared to relatively recent masters of European humanism like Proust and Mann, Grass is hard to read, hard to "get going" in. His device of aping television, however witty and timely and rigorously exploited, feels superimposed; it is a gesture of the author rather than an outgrowth of the material. Who, we wonder as we read, really retains his life in film-clip form, who but an author at his desk would project these overanimated parables of German guilt and unease?

In an interview given a few weeks ago in New York, Grass spoke of *Mief*, of the stale air that envelops every group and gathering and conversation in the West. His narrative device of a televised, self-cancelling clutter does work as a metaphor for *Mief*, like the cement dust that grayly settles upon every leaf in Krings Park. In his obsessive sense of static, grit, and dust, this author is true to himself; he is true to himself when he moves from romantic triangles that bore him, and from echoes of the Nazi nightmare that are beginning to bore him, into political debates that, though wreathed in *Mief*, interest him. Grass's role as an active campaigner and spokesman for the Social Democratic Party finds a happy correlative in Starusch's role of schoolteacher.

Starusch wants his pupil Scherbaum to take over the school paper and run it, working toward such liberal/reformist objectives as creating a student smokers' corner. Scherbaum instead opts for the radical gesture of burning Max, his pet dachshund, alive, in the heart of cake-eating, dog-loving Berlin, as a protest against the Vietnam war. He is encouraged not only by his Maoist girl friend but by Starusch's female colleague, Irmgard Seifert, who is tormented by the guilt she incurred as a "Hitler bitch" at the age of seventeen. Starusch tries to reason the boy out of it, and, failing, offers to substitute a stray from the dog pound for Max. The boy is tempted, but Starusch then denounces his own plan as "exploitation, rank imperialism." Next, he conceives the idea of poisoning the dog, to "deprive Scherbaum of the object of his demonstration. React radically to a radical project." Throughout all this maneuvering, he confers with his dentist, who speaks suavely from the melioristic center:

"And how do you feel about napalm, Doc?"

"Well, measured against the nuclear weapons known to us, napalm must be termed relatively harmless."

"And what about the living conditions of the Iranian peasants?"

"In the light of conditions in India we can speak, with all due reserve, of a relatively progressive agrarian structure in Iran, though compared to the Sudan India may well strike us as a reformer's paradise."

"Then you see progress!"

"Within limits, my friend, within limits."

In the whirlwind of argument and gesture that surrounds the unwitting dachshund, everybody has something to say. The schoolteacher urges his students "to try to understand the world in all its variety and contradiction." Youth scorns "the daily capitulations characteristic of adults" and prescribes "spontaneous action" as the only way "to make room . . . for new foundations on which to build a pacified existence." The dentist looks toward a day of "worldwide Sickcare" and warns that "with all its display of realism, this younger generation is looking for a new myth. Watch your step!" The terms of the debate are familiar to Americans, but not explicated so many-sidedly, with the charity of humor, and with the specifically German dimension of a disastrous "transvaluation of all values" (Nietzsche's phrase) that did occur. Starusch, though with the dentist's help he seduces his pupil from caninocide, is left with a vision of the violence within himself, a desire to strangle and drown Sieglinde and to bulldoze away all the suffocating junk of industrial affluence. The very tartar on his teeth, the dentist tells him, is "petrified hatred." Seneca is the dentist's favorite philosopher, and the last sentences have a stoic ring: "Nothing lasts. There will always be pain." Grass himself, evidently, has complained that his final phrase in German—"*immer neue Schmerzen*" ("always new pains")—is more active; "new pains are always coming" might be more faithful and faintly more optimistic. Yet the difficulty is inherent; the dentist, like him or not, has the best lines, and the dust jacket, designed by Grass himself, shows a finger over a candle flame—an allusion to the most primitive dental anesthetic, which was to divide the pain by holding the patient's hand over a candle, and a symbol of all our palliations. All anesthetic is local.

Snail on the Stump

FROM THE DIARY OF A SNAIL, by Günter Grass, translated from the German by Ralph Manheim. 310 pp. Harcourt Brace Jovanovich, 1972.

Günter Grass addresses his newest book, *From the Diary of a Snail*, to his four children. The eldest of *my* four children once, under the illusion that she could turn pebbles into jewels, acquired a bright little machine that, loaded with gray sludge and plugged into a socket, revolved and tumbled to a hypothetical lustre whatever bits of the material universe were put inside. That curious device (now defunct) offers the best analogy I can think of to Grass's present authorial method. The gray sludge is *Mief* or "melancholy"—the leaden aura of staleness and inertia possessed by compromised, relative, muddled, hashed-over, snail's-pace reality. The electricity is Grass's phenomenal energy, not only intellectual but personal, soulful, human; however farfetched his fancies, Grass (like the not dissimilarly mustachioed Kurt Vonnegut) convinces us that his heart remains in the right place. The bits of rough matter are whatever obsessions he finds simultaneous within him: in this book, snails, children, hermaphroditism, Dürer's print entitled *Melencolia I*, the fate of the Danzig Jews, the suicide of Manfred Augst (real), the adventures of Hermann Ott (fictional), and the 1969 West German elections, wherein Grass contributed nearly a hundred speeches to Willy Brandt's successful campaign. While functioning, Grass's narrative engine, like the polishing machine, seems inexhaustible and distinctly unmusical, at least in translation. Though my daughter's polisher ran for days and weeks without stopping, the rocks and shards inside never shed, along with their incidental roughnesses, the core of obduracy that makes sea-smoothed stones so dryly disappointing when arranged on the summer cottage mantelpiece. And when *From the Diary of a Snail* stops shuddering and churning, what tumbles out, though of a certain sheen, is not a work of art.

Not that art is overtly aspired to. The snail's diary began as a

Sudelbuch, a scribble book, a book of jottings Grass carried with him on the campaign trail: "My entries come to me on the road. . . . I mean to speak to you by roundabout bypaths: sometimes offended and enraged, often withdrawn and hard to pin down, occasionally brimful of lies, until everything becomes plausible." Some of the notations, then, deal with the incidents of the municipal hall and the hotel room; some are comments on the author's allies in the Social Democratic Party and his enemies in the Christian Democratic Union. A portrait of Germany filters through the jottings—the Germany of the postwar economic miracle (". . . and now after twenty-five years. From rubble and ashes we. From scratch. And today we are once more"), a Germany of glimpses (". . . air shafts, garages, squares, warehouses, building sites, railroad tracks, the city park, the restored Old City: swans and shingled roofs as in the prospectus"), a Germany of little cities Grass particularizes with his nice eye for local industry:

> A small town not far from the Dutch border, which, saturated with history and swan lore, was destroyed shortly before the end of the war, and even today, rebuilt in its original small-checkered pattern, looks as if it were about to fall apart. (Little industry—children's shoes and margarine . . .). . . . Or in Bocholt, where the textile crisis (Erhard calls it a "healthy shrinkage") feeds discussion. . . . I visited a factory where stopwatches are assembled and chatted with the shop committee in a room whose walls were decorated with framed photographs of famous sprinters. . . .

"How beautiful Germany is. So transparently impenetrable. So eerily innocent. So different and the same wherever you go," Grass exclaims as he goes about speechifying, sitting in endless conferences, answering questions, coping with radical youths ("And I discover with what a prodigy of deception hate fosters beauty in youthful faces"), trying "to pull the weeds of German idealism, which spring up again as inexorably as rib grass."

Upon this campaign diary Grass permits to intrude—or has imposed in two years of revision—a number of other concerns, tales, devices, and designs. The primary conceit, which wears out before the book does, is that all this is addressed to his children (Franz, Raoul, Laura, and Bruno) as a justification of their father's long absences in what little Bruno calls the "fight with the whale" (*Walkampf* = *Wahlkampf* = election campaign). Four piping voices break into print, and the paternal author responds with a lecture, an evasion, a piece of self-portraiture, or a digression; his youth in Danzig, for instance, mushrooms into a considerable detailed history of Danzig's ten thousand Jews after the free city was incorporated into Hitler's Germany. Danzig also suggests to Grass a fictional person, a Gentile named Hermann Ott, nicknamed Doubt, who teaches in a Jewish school before the war and hides throughout the war in the cellar of a Kashubian bicycle dealer, Anton Stomma; Ott's invented story is the most characteristically Grassian, and most easily followed, thread in this tangle of motifs. An academic thread is the lecture Grass has promised to give on Dürer's dark and symbolically fraught etching *Melencolia I;* he carries a print with him on the campaign, ruminates in his *Sudelbuch* about it, attempts to see his own efforts of "talk-talktalk" in the light of an abiding opposition between Melencolia and her sister Utopia, and ends the book with the lecture itself, which is excellent and might seem even better had not its major points been several times adumbrated in the preceding pages. Another theme intrudes when, during the campaign, at an Evangelical Church congress in Stuttgart, a fifty-six-year-old man takes the microphone, delivers a jumbled harangue about fellowship, concludes, "Now I've got a provocation for you: I salute my comrades of the S.S.," sits down, drinks something, and dies. His last words are wonderful; turning to the girl student beside him, he says, "That, young lady, was cyanide." The man's name is Manfred Augst, and, though Grass feels he knows his type well—a typical German craving "annihilation and redemption"—he cannot forget the incident, and finally interviews Augst's widow and children. We also witness Grass interviewing Danzig Jews who now live in Israel, and see him taking a vacation with his family in Brittany, and are treated to several recipes and poems of his concoction, and to a rather opaque glorification of Willy Brandt as a kind of recessive Superman—"a man . . . whose loneliness draws large crowds," a man whose "slow, steady ascent" is a "snail's career." Snails, of course, are meant to be the unifying metaphor and theme of this farrago. They peep in everywhere. Hermann Ott collects snails, and a lively abundance of circumstantial snail lore is given, from the "foamy crackling" they emit in even a state of rest to the "calcareous darts (known as love arrows)" that hermaphroditic Roman snails thrust into the soles of one another's feet. The trouble is that the snail symbolizes too many things: Willy Brandt, the vagina, melancholy embodied, the human masses, moderate progressiveness, the author himself. "With my forward, inward drive, with my tendency to dwell, hesitate, and cling, with my restlessness and emotional haste, I am snail-like." Grass is one of the "progressive mobile snails," as opposed to the "conservative clinging snails"—though in the muddle of events and the fug of staleness and "talktalktalk" only an expert could tell the difference. And only a snail-lover could feel that the image is not overworked, overloaded, and harped upon with too much random ingenuity.

What we want from our great imaginers is not fuel but fire, not patterns but an action, not fragmented and interlaced accounts but a story. Amid all this personal and apologetical rubble one story moves, as follows: When Hermann Ott takes refuge in the cellar of Anton Stomma, the household includes Stomma's daughter Lisbeth. She is fair, plump, and stupefied. In the first four days of the war her Polish lover and her small son have been killed; she spends much time visiting cemeteries, and performs all her duties, which come to include sleeping with Ott, in a daze of unfeeling. "She lay mute under his thrusts, which struck the void." Further obliging, she brings him snails from her cemeteries; one day she introduces into Ott's cellar an unidentifiable purple-red slug. By accident, he discovers that when the slug is placed on her skin Lisbeth begins to stammer. Soon she is talking, then laughing; she ceases visiting cemeteries and goes instead to a hairdresser's; she awakens sexually. As her cure progresses, the snail, with each application to her flesh, becomes more discolored and hideous. "It was as though the unidentified slug had sucked up Lisbeth's melancholy, possibly her black bile." The cure is complete; as normal femininity returns to her, she becomes a normal woman—demanding, willful, squeamish. The bloated and black "suction snail" disgusts her. On the first Sunday of Advent in 1944, she steps on it. "It burst with a full-bodied report. On the inside, too, it was black." After the war, she and Ott marry, but he falls prey to melancholia and spends more and more of his time in cemeteries, searching for another of the melancholy-curing snails. Finally, Lisbeth commits him to an asylum. Now, this story is not patently edifying; mysterious and unpleasant and pessimistic, it does not tell us how to vote in the next election. But it draws resonance from an actuality beyond explanation; it objectifies the teller's feelings, sensations, and convictions so that they carry into us more penetratingly than any declarative statement. The snail Grass has from his own substance produced a love arrow. The story takes place in a chilly cellar redolent of the muddy potato lands that are this author's peculiar terrain. Imaginations seem to be as choosy as mollusks about the soil they inhabit; amid a great deal of mental travelogue, this one episode sticks fast and dankly lives.

In fairness to Grass, and with no aspersion on the efforts of Mr. Manheim, who for all I know has done the best of all possible jobs, one feels that exceptionally much has been lost in translation. The poems flung into this diary must be better than they seem. For every piece of wordplay that is explained in a footnote, there must be several too delicate to unravel. Grass's curious trick of unpunctuated word-triplets ("bitter tired finished," "went stood lay") must appear less gratuitous in German. Throughout, the skin of words feels a little raw in English, lacking its epiderm of intelligent verbal nervousness, of voiced sensitivity. And of course the many references to contemporary political figures strike chords muffled here. We do not so much read this book as overhear it: a German is speaking to Germans, intimately and urgently. For Grass, in addition to the universal duties of a writer, has the local duty, with all the German writers of his generation, of guarding and barring the path back into Hell.

Witold Who?

FERDYDURKE, by Witold Gombrowicz, translated from the Polish by Eric Mosbacher. 272 pp. Grove Press, 1967.

PORNOGRAFIA, by Witold Gombrowicz, translated by Alastair Hamilton from the French translation from the Polish by Georges Lisowski. 191 pp. Grove Press, 1967.

Witold Gombrowicz, a Polish writer born in 1904, is being set forward as a master, whose not very copious complete works, mostly composed in the obscurity of Argentine exile, are to be published in America by that zealous exhumer of overlooked classics, Grove Press. The project begins* with two novels—*Ferdydurke* and *Pornografia*. Gombrowicz's claim to be—to quote *L'Express*—"the greatest unknown writer of our time" has reached us via the French, who took him up after his triumphant but short-lived resurrection in Poland itself, during a moment (in 1957) of cultural thaw.

Ferdydurke (the word is Polish schoolboy slang meaning nothing in particular) came out, with considerable success, in 1937 but was suppressed under both the Nazis and the Communists. In Gomulka's Poland of 1957, the novel's burlesque of psychological tyrannies, its premonitions of brainwashing, and its sharp savor of the prewar avant garde must have seemed liberating. The French presumably found congenial Gombrowicz's mixture of intellection and impudence, his familiar air of knowledgeable disillusion. This country may find its own contemporary style reflected in his free-wheeling "black humor" and his avid delineation of interpersonal "games." Myself, I must register my sensation that *Ferdydurke*, a book about the imposition of form, has itself more the form— the assurance, the daring—of greatness than the substance. Beneath the energetic surface there is a static difficulty of event. The recurrent motifs seem merely curious—a strange jealousy of

---

* And evidently ended there: two promised further works, the novel *The Trans-Atlantic* and Gombrowicz's *Diary*, still await, eight years later, publication.

the young, an eccentric trick of seeing human bodies as assemblies of parts. Compared with the ideas (the recovery of time through involuntary memory, the eventual union of the paths of innocence and experience) that give momentum to Proust's masses of description, or with Kafka's intuitions of exclusion and interminability, Gombrowicz's themes are spindly, infertile, too much insisted upon, too little dramatized. There is, at least for a reader deprived of the nuances of the original Polish, not much warmth, of the kind that led Nathalie Sarraute to liken classics to furnaces still giving off the heat of their passion for reality.

In the most up-to-date manner, Gombrowicz disarms criticism by including it in his text, mocking the reader's eagerness "to evaluate and to assess, and to decide whether the work is a novel, or a book of memories, or a parody, or a lampoon, or a variation on imaginative themes, or a psychological study; and to establish its predominant characteristics; whether the whole thing is a joke, or whether its importance lies in its deeper meaning, or whether it is just irony, sarcasm, ridicule, invective, downright stupidity and nonsense, or a piece of pure leg-pulling." *Ferdydurke* is peppered with essays on itself, disarming admissions of its own confusion, invitations to "start dancing with the book instead of asking for meanings." Its author, in the preface to *Pornografia*, writes in an almost liturgical vein, "*Ferdydurke* is undoubtedly my basic work. . . . [It] is intended to reveal the Great Immaturity of humanity. Man, as he is described in this book, is an opaque and neutral being who has to express himself by certain means of behavior and therefore becomes, from outside—for others—far more definite and precise than he is for himself. Hence a tragic disproportion between his secret immaturity and the mask he assumes when he deals with other people. All he can do is to adapt himself internally to his mask, as though he really were what he appears to be." This thesis, however true (and perhaps it seemed truer in the 1930's; might not Fascism be understood as a country's attempt to become "far more definite and precise" than it feels?), is erratically borne out by the narrative, which comes to life in some areas and churns unconvincingly in others.

Ferdydurke begins with a diatribe against literary criticism, and here Gombrowicz is very funny. The narrator (named Johnnie in most places and Anton Swistak in one episode) observes that "the more inept and petty criticism is, the more constricting it is, like a tight shoe." The experience of publishing a book is "like being born in a thousand rather narrow minds." He envies men of letters whose minds move perpetually toward the heights "just as if their backsides had been pricked with a pin!" He inveighs against cultural "aunts," and creates his main comic character, the Cracow philologist Pimko, who enters the room, spots the opening pages of this novel on the desk, and cries, "Well! Well! Well! An author! Let me immediately criticize, encourage, advise!" With "masterly composure" Pimko sits and reads, while Johnnie inwardly writhes: "The minutes lasted for hours and the seconds were unnaturally extended, and I was ill at ease, like a sea that somebody was trying to suck up through a straw." Gombrowicz expresses more vividly than I have seen elsewhere the something intolerable about a literary establishment—any literary establishment. If a harsh Providence were to obliterate, say, Alfred Kazin, Richard Gilman, Stanley Kauffmann, and Irving Howe, tomorrow new critics would arise with the same worthy intelligence, the same complacently agonized humanism, the same inability to read a book except as a disappointing version of one they might have written, the same deadly "auntiness." Gombrowicz's irritation is heartfelt, and the whole style of the book— its fragmentation, its tauntingness, its serene implausibility, its violent catalogues and metaphors—sustains his protest against "being tied to the cultural aunts' apron strings."

Pimko takes the thirty-year-old narrator in hand and unaccountably but irresistibly places him in school, among cruel and obscene boys extolled for their "innocence." Two schoolmates, Mientus and Siphon, engage in a grotesque combat: "The two contestants will stand facing each other and will make a series of faces. Each and every constructive and beautiful face made by Siphon will be answered by an ugly and destructive counter-face made by Mientus. The faces made will be as personal and as wounding as possible, and the contestants will continue to make them until a final decision is reached." Mientus scowls, spits, and dips his finger into a spittoon, but Siphon implacably points at the sky; "his face became diffused with seven colors, like a rainbow after a storm, and lo! there he stood in seven colors, the Boy Scout, Purity Incarnate, the Innocent Adolescent." Defeated, Mientus shouts filth into Siphon's ears, and Siphon dies.

All encounters, for Gombrowicz, are a species of duel by gesture, a clash of impersonations. The opening episode with Pimko and the narrator is such a contest: "He remained seated, so firmly and inexorably seated that the fact of his sitting, though intolerably stupid, was nevertheless all-powerful." Into the main narrative is spliced the anecdote of "Philifor Honeycombed with Childishness," wherein two philosophers—the greatest synthesist of all time and his arch-opponent, the analyst Anti-Philifor—duel by pruning with gunfire the bodies of their wife and mistress, finally killing them both. Johnnie, still a schoolboy, goes to live with a banally "modern" family called the Youthfuls and is caught up in a fierce duel of love with Zutka, the daughter. His maneuvers grow in complexity and ferocity and finally plunge the Youthfuls, plus Pimko, plus a schoolmate, into a lunatic melee, freeing the hero to launch himself into "Asphalt. Emptiness. Dew. Nothing." An antic essay interposes, and a shaggy-dog story symmetrically titled "Philimor Honeycombed with Childishness." The narrative moves to the country estate of Johnnie's rich aunt and Mientus' struggle to fraternize with a stableboy. The consequent duel of class consciousness and physical abuse culminates in yet another, crueller fray. At the end, Johnnie abducts his cousin Isabel, and then flees the blackmail of compliments and kisses ("I writhed under the blows of her admiration as under Satan's whip") that passes, in the Gombrowiczian universe, for heterosexual love.

What is the core of this repetitive whirligig of pretense, bluff, and annihilation? At one point in the country house, four men find themselves in total darkness, standing paralyzed by fear within inches of one another, unable to move, and Johnnie experiences "a sense of becoming enormous, gigantic and simultaneously a sense of growing smaller, shrinking and stiffening, a sense of escape and at the same time a kind of general and particular impoverishment, a sense of paralysing tension and tense paralysis, of being hung by a tense thread, as well as of being converted and changed into something, a sense of transmutation and also of relapse into a kind

of accumulating and mounting mechanism." In this frozen moment
of overwhelming, contradictory sensation, we seem close to Gombrowicz's central inkling—the duel between consciousness and
will. Awareness mocks and clogs and warps action. From our
sticky web of apprehension, sporadic and incongruous deeds
shake loose. The narrator, "while suspense and repetition still
remained ceaselessly at work," abruptly moves: "Suddenly I
insolently moved and stepped behind the curtain." In the context
of these pages even such a small exercise of volition is intensely
dramatic. Perhaps the composition of *Ferdydurke* can be understood as another such act, a random, twitched escape from paralysis. Hence the book's flaws of flimsiness and centrifugality, hence
the monotonous mood of wry nervousness. Gombrowicz has made
his move, but he is not yet at home behind the curtain.

Pornografia, written twenty years later, is a more conventional
and integrated work, perfectly shaped and thoroughly sinister.
Set in the Nazi-occupied Poland of 1943 (where Gombrowicz
never was), "at the depths of the *fait accompli*," the novel tells
of the hyper-subtle corruption worked upon an adolescent boy and
girl by a pair of middle-aged Warsaw intellectuals, one of whom
is Gombrowicz himself. He narrates the story in accents grimmer
and neater than the quirky pellmell of *Ferdydurke*. Compare a
landscape from each of these novels:

> Overhead there were fat little reddish, bluish, and whitish clouds,
> which looked as if they were made of silk paper, sorry and senti-
> mental-looking. Everything was so vague and confused in outline,
> so silent, so chaste, so full of waiting, so unborn and undefined, that
> in reality nothing was separate or distinct from anything else;
> on the contrary, everything was connected with everything else
> in the bosom of a single, thick, whitish and silent, extinguished
> mass. Tenuous little brooks murmured, wetted the earth, vaporized
> or bubbled. And this world dwindled and seemed to shrink, and
> as it shrank it seemed to tighten, to close round your throat, like
> a delicate cord strangling you.

> We reached the top of the hill and were confronted with the
> unaltered view: the earth rising in hills, swollen in a motionless
> surge in the slanting light which here and there pierced the clouds.

The first is a wordy conjuration of vagueness whose gaiety tugs strangely against the metaphor of strangulation with which it is clinched. The second, also vague, needs no specification of the emotion it is meant to arouse; there is no doubt that we are in the drab reaches of rural Poland, in a sordid trough of history. "An oppressive smell of iniquity permeated this landscape," the author observes, and, in town, on the next page, notices that "something was missing—there were no Jews." Jews are not mentioned again, and Germans are hardly ever seen. The thematic and metaphoric furniture of *Pornografia* is as economically distributed as the personnel of its plot; the rabid envy of young people, for instance, which seemed eccentric in the thirtyish author of *Ferdydurke*, comes plausibly from a fifty-year-old man "already poisoned by death." The duels—between a Catholic and an atheist, between a panicked resistance leader and a household—cluster tightly around the core struggle of the two adolescents and the two old men, who are themselves involved in a duel of implication and avoidance. The gratuitous, sudden actions—a boy pulling up an old woman's skirt, an old woman attacking and biting a boy—all serve to advance the action by enlarging the possibilities of depravity, and to enforce the image of man as "an angelic and demonic abyss, steeper than a mirror!" The notion of "form" has been reduced to a biting Dostoevskian essence: "There are certain human deeds which seem totally senseless, but which are necessary for man because they define him." The notion of "youth" has succinctly become: "After the age of thirty men lapse into monstrosity." All mutual existence is mutual blackmail. Inexorably the elements of *Pornografia* combine, in its less than two hundred pages, to transmute the most delicate and obscurely felt interrelations into a climax of multiple murder. The book has the clean cruelty of *Laughter in the Dark*, without Nabokov's playful puppetry; it has the moral pessimism of *Les Liaisons Dangereuses*, without de Laclos' peremptory restoration of virtue.

In short, Gombrowicz, an apostle of immaturity, has maturely subdued his formal preoccupations and instinctive obsessions to the principles of art and created, in his own prefatory words, "a noble, a classical novel . . . a sensually metaphysical novel." Is this victory at all Pyrrhic? Have the determined insights and dramatic thrust of *Pornografia* been obtained at the cost of a certain honesty present in the confusions of *Ferdydurke?* For in penetrating the imaginative curtain separating him from wartime Poland, and in creating behind it a coherent "classical" action, he in a sense hides; a book like *Ferdydurke* exists as a fantastical gloss upon the real world, whereas *Pornografia* is a small world complete in itself and sealed by its own completeness as if in cellophane. Its consummate finish deprives it of osmotic margins; it becomes an object we can turn our backs on, having experienced its catharsis, its systematic arousal and relief of suspense. Does the world require many more such novels? Or does history insist that the writer abolish, by exhortation and trickery, the glaring edge that divides the proscenium novel from its audience of readers? Ask Dr. Pimko, or some other kindly aunt.

Inward and Onward

THE INWARD TURN OF NARRATIVE, by Erich Kahler, translated by Richard and Clara Winston. 216 pp. Princeton, 1973.

Erich Kahler, the late literary philosopher and polymath, published some fifteen years ago, in the *Neue Rundschau*, two long essays on the development of narrative technique and perspective which have now been published in the Bollingen series as *The Inward Turn of Narrative*. Kahler's thesis is more easily stated than grasped. His first sentence proposes "to show the vast changes in the modern novel as the consequence of a process that has been at work throughout the whole history of Western man," and this process seems simply the development of consciousness: "Literary history will be considered here as an aspect of the history of consciousness." The "inward turn" of narrative is in fact an outward envelopment, our mental incorporation of more and more of the outer world: "Man constantly draws outer space into his inner space, into an inner space newly created by consciousness. The world is integrated into the ego, into the illuminated self." This grand one-way process (Kahler speaks of "advancing conscious-

ness" with the confident progressivism of a 19th-century coloni-
alist) finds literary reflection in surprising proportions. Three
brisk sentences, and all of primitive narrative sweeps by:

> Initially, the process of internalization of narrative consists in
> gradually bringing the narrated material down to earth and breath-
> ing into it a human soul. Narrative begins with cosmogonies and
> theogonies. Slowly, then, the themes descend to the level of annals
> and chronicles, to the recording of specific earthly events.

The reader takes this "slowly" on faith, for very rapidly, in
Kahler's exposition, we arrive at Homer and the Old Testament,
narratives of pronounced sophistication and "humanness." Of pre-
Homeric tales, the only example discussed is the fragmentary
Babylonian epic of Gilgamesh, which, though "still entirely within
the primal mythic chaos," does present, in the friendship between
Gilgamesh and Enkidu, an "impulse to attain humanity"; "in it
man is increasingly brought down to earth, is liberated from his
primal link with the elemental powers." More seems meant than
demythicization of experience; as the gods recede into a distinctly
separate realm, feeling arises out of the "internalization of raw
event. By stirring the imagination narration itself—in contradis-
tinction to mere chronicle—provokes feeling." When we arrive,
with Homer, at the threshold of Western literature, the gap between "chronicle" and imaginative "narration" has already been
crossed.

> There can be no doubt that the articulation of human experience
> in the Homeric epic is far beyond that of the Babylonian epic. . . .
> In the Old Testament, finally, complete humanness is revealed.

What remains, humanness revealed, is relatively a matter of detail,
and of increasingly detailed description of masterpieces. With
Virgil's *Aeneid* deliberate artistic construction appears in the epic
form. Early in the Christian era, "novelty itself, the novella," adds
to the telling of acts of heroism and martyrdom "the relation
of curious incidents, preferably spiced with eroticism." Then
"Christian influence [leaves] a new residue in narrative: deliberate,
imposed meaning." With the Renaissance dawns individual psychology; from Boccaccio on, narration becomes "entirely a psychological process." The rise of cities generates a sharp contrast

between town and nature, burgher and knight; from this contrast arises what Kahler calls "the romantic situation": on the one hand, the burgher's illicit impulses and fantasies find embodiment in the obsolete figure of the knight, and, on the other, the "new objectifying awareness of nature" produces sensuous natural description and a complementary realism in the depiction of social classes. Milieu deepens its substance; "perspectivistic narrative" arrives, somewhat later than perspectivistic painting. Of this "baroque" period's masterworks—Cervantes' *Don Quixote*, Grimelshausen's *Simplicissimus*, Rabelais' *Pantagruel* and *Gargantua*—*Don Quixote* is especially momentous, because it supplies the first fully realized instance of "ascending symbolism"; that is, symbolism which proceeds from an individual instance to supra-individual significance entirely within a human world created by the artist, rather than the "descending symbolism" of the Greeks and Dante, wherein the signification descends upon the individual from a higher reality—a divine or mythic entity. From Cervantes on, the writer builds the symbolic structure out of himself, and the reader extracts it *for* himself. This immense "internalization" achieved, little distance remains to modern narrative. Milton, intending to portray the Christian cosmos, unwittingly dramatizes instead the "vast, immeasurable Abyss" opened to view by the new astronomy, and man's dreadful, defiant autonomy within it. First-person narratives such as those of Marivaux, Defoe, and Richardson move the narrator's observation post deeper into the interior of the confessing ego. Eighteenth-century poets, under the influence of deism, for the first time make nature an independent object of observation. As the invention of the microscope opens on the other side of man an infinity as daunting as that revealed through the telescope, Swift, in *Gulliver's Travels*, rings a number of changes on the theme of relativity and arrives at an absolute condemnation of man. And in *Tristram Shandy*—"an end and a beginning, a harvest and a new sowing"—Sterne, making narrative entirely willful and sequence and time dependent upon the narrator's whim, so imbues reality "with the patterns, structures, and techniques of consciousness that the creatively working consciousness finds itself face to face with its own image."

This complex world, which already includes the phenomena of cognition and imagination—this already half-internalized world— becomes the raw material which is handed on to Romanticism as its reality.

There Kahler ends, having surprised us as much with what he dwells upon as with what he skimps. Even in the sparest summary, the book's scope and strength of synthesizing vision must be apparent. Many passing critical felicities adorn the exposition: Milton's Hell, he says, becomes "almost a colony of paradise"; Pope's linguistic wit "is constantly overflowing and leaving no room to breathe." The critic's essential service of *recommending* is enthusiastically performed; I can hardly wait to read *Clarissa* and *Simplicissimus*. The translators append their regret that Kahler did not live to revise his German articles for publication in English, but the translation reads well, and such imbalances toward the German as exist—conspicuously, the lengthy quotation from the poet Barthold Heinrich Brockes—are rather refreshing. Kahler was unaffectedly erudite in at least three European literatures, and the reader of English can only be pleased by the importance assigned Chaucer, Milton, James Thomson, Defoe, Swift, Richardson, Fielding, and Sterne. Amazing how much these Europeans can read into offhand British scribbling!

To Kahler's generosity of spirit and shared learning, reservations must attach apologetically, like limpets to the back of a sleeping walrus. But *The Inward Turn of Narrative* in its sweep describes a bigger circle than it seems to fill. If we are to examine the evolution—the inward turn—of narrative, then we need to grasp primordial narrative at some point deeper than the Gilgamesh epic, which Dr. Albert Lord, in his class in Oral Epic Tradition, used to classify with the "sophisticated" specimens of epic form. Ancient though the Babylonian fragments are, they represent the end of a development whose earlier stages have analogues in the tales collected by anthropology. The world does not (as Kahler implies) age all in one piece; Stone Age cultures survive to this day, and among them the scholar might find clues to the embryology of this mysterious art called narration. Kahler considers a series of forms without searching out the question of *function*.

Why do we harken to stories? What instinct do they arouse and satisfy? What is *happening* between writer and reader? Is the tribal tale-teller in the same relation to his audience as James Joyce to his? Are a medieval allegory, a dirty joke, and a Chekhov short story any more similar *in intent* than an icon, a comic book, and a Cézanne? Kahler does touch upon the issue of audience, provocatively but briefly:

> Early, naïve storytelling proceeded from a rather unsubtle narrator to a ubiquitous and tangible listener. Serious, weightier narrative, which begins in the eighteenth century, involves a personal relationship between a narrator who steps forth in his subjectivity and a virtually individualized specific listener whom the author holds by the lapel, so to speak. The later modern narrator is an impersonally objectified artistic consciousness caught up in the labor of expression. . . . The work requires, demands, and shapes its own ideal recipient.

The progression from "naïve" to "weightier," from "unsubtle" to "ideal," is not so much demonstrated as assumed. Indeed, an almost blithe assumption of progress pervades the book. Repeatedly, Kahler has to explain away some Hellenic anticipation of a post-Renaissance "advance": "The art of classical antiquity often came to the verge of modern achievements—but stopped short at certain limits. Developmental processes do not proceed in a straight line. Rather, they occur in waves, or, if we prefer a three-dimensional image, in ever-widening spirals." But art moves, surely, as often by regression and setting-aside as by any kind of accumulation. Hemingway and Pound said *no* to the elaborate genteel art prevailing around them; Cervantes, Fielding, even Jane Austen began with parody, in a spirit of deflation. Kahler instinctively sees human progress as the dethroning of the gods: "Man has liberated himself from his primordial entanglement with mythic powers." The two-thousand-year episode of Christendom, then, lies rather athwart his synopsis. The narratives of the Middle Ages rate less than a paragraph. Whereas Malraux, in his *Voices of Silence*, persuades us that the portal statuary of Chartres and Rheims expressed something missing from the blank-faced marbles of Greece and Rome, the best Kahler can make of Christian influence on narrative is the "residue" that remains once stories are "freed from their didactic purposes." Milton's conscious purposes (and the overt deism of the nature poets) are brushed aside as transitional illusions: "This wide-ranging epic was inherently contradictory and uncontrolled, a transitional opus expressing the rift that had developed between science and Biblical orthodoxy."

In a footnote, Kahler criticizes Erich Auerbach's *Mimesis* for its "fundamental error in assuming that reality is a stable thing, always the same for all ages and persons," and adds that "different writers have merely approached it in different ways. In fact, the reality of any given period is the product of struggling and advancing consciousness." But Kahler's attempt to formulate his sensation that reality is constantly expanding, and literature with it, produces labored prose:

> In considering the reciprocal creation of consciousness and reality, it is difficult to gauge what share the arts in particular have had in changing reality. The same process of reciprocal effects takes place in several fields: between historical event and historical consciousness (a question which deserves special study); between philosophical, political, and socio-economic theories and the corresponding realities; and of course in the natural sciences, where change in the real environment shows up most distinctly, although these changes are not necessarily the most profound. All these elements coalesce and affect each other.

What does this say but that things are all mixed up? Auerbach's stately and relatively static series of panels, each treating in great detail a lengthy quotation from successive literary epochs, manages not only to register a more sensitive impression of each masterpiece but to convey the feel of evolutionary movement more convincingly than Kahler. For what *is* "advancing consciousness"? Aristotle carried as many pieces of baggage, as many thoughts and facts, in his inner space as any modern savant. True, most of his baggage is now considered nonsense, but so will our baggage be. Does consciousness advance or merely shift its ground? What of the worlds of lore and observation lost to urban civilization? The Eskimos have a hundred words for snow, and the Bedouins as many for camel dung; is not the great poetry of snow and camel dung certainly behind us? How many of the three and a half billion persons living now, on the very frontier of the advance of consciousness, have appropriated more of the real world to their inner space than, say, a Carolingian serf? To most American housewives, electricity is as magical as mana to a Polynesian. The present young generation, steeped in technology, shows an astonishing willingness to live by astrology and diabolism, not to mention hallucinogens and Krishna. Are the fundamentals of human existence amid the wonders and menaces of advanced industrialism much different from the situation of Cro-Magnon man amid the wonders and menaces of untamed nature? All of recorded history has occurred in too brief a span for any evolutionary change; we confront life with the brains of cavemen. A mother suckles us; a joy of the senses crystallizes; alien shapes loom to block our desires; some desires are granted satisfaction; most are not; we age; we die. How has the drama of European cultural history, played on a little forestage of a continent by a cast of characters that was never more than a fraction of the population of the world, affected any of this? More specifically, how does modern narrative, of which *Tristram Shandy* in its self-conscious self-pleasing may be taken as the first instance, change "reality"? Picasso and Pollock turn up on fabric designs, but what happens to the modern masters of narrative? Indeed, the penetration of art into men's lives would seem, by some equation Kahler never suspects, proportional to the strength of its alliance with religion. Compared to the age of the cathedrals, we live remote from our art. Religion and technology are alike at least in that both attempt to cope directly with the pain of our existence: the first by offering us a supernatural consolation, and the second by dealing with our diseases and difficulties piecemeal. In comparison, modern art offers only distraction, sublimation, and a kind of empathy with the mental and spiritual aristocrats who are artists. The "patterns, structures, and techniques of consciousness" are of little profit to the run of men, and as overpopulation and diminishing natural resources reduce the margin of play in the world, refined literary art may be squeezed out even from the colleges.

What *is* "internalization"? There is no doubt that science accumulates, and human life is changed by its expanding discoveries. But culture may "internalize" new knowledge in the sense that the body internalizes the tip of a splinter; that is, cushions and anesthetizes it to make it ignorable. Kahler gives us a lively example of culture at work. The microscope was developed more gradually than the telescope, and the public was slow to grasp its implications. Suddenly, however, late in the 17th century, "observations with the microscope became a fashionable pastime in English society. Amateur experimenters of both sexes ('virtuosos' and 'virtuosas') became curiosity collectors and went about with pocket microscopes as some people do today with Geiger counters, looking for Leeuwenhoek's 'animalcules' in whatever came their way. They found tiny 'water flyes' and 'water lice,' 'eels' and 'worms' in blood and saliva. . . . English literature of the period reacted . . . with satires upon this fad." Are not we, in a world so out of our ken and our control, all "virtuosos" and "virtuosas" running about trying to tame the truth by turning it into group fun, into a fad? What was Pop Art but a way of subduing to fun the frightful raw trashiness of our man-made wilderness? And is the process so different from that whereby the first paintings, of bison and antelope, subdued to an appearance of control the terrible uncertainties of the hunt? Does art, then, operate as a progressive force or as a reactionary one, not to advance consciousness but to lull and muffle it—to make consciousness, indeed, passably bearable?

Some of these questions may be quibbles. Others may be riddles. They arise in response to an elegant and piquing book.

AFRICA

Out of the Glum Continent

BOUND TO VIOLENCE, by Yambo Ouologuem, translated from the French by Ralph Manheim. 182 pp. Harcourt Brace Jovanovich, 1971.

THIS EARTH, MY BROTHER . . . , by Kofi Awoonor. 232 pp. Doubleday, 1971.

THE WANDERERS, by Ezekiel Mphahlele. 351 pp. Macmillan, 1971.

The art of fiction, our beleaguered heroine, glances desperately about for rescue. Perhaps Africa will save her. Has not black music, via jazz and rock, transformed the ears of the world? Did not African masks inspire Cubism and destroy forever the sweet face that had reigned in European art from Giotto to Renoir? More to the point, have not rural societies, such as Russia, Ireland, and the American South, historically poured fresh vernacular energy and heroic simplicity into Europe's tired mainstream of literature? And has not sub-Saharan Africa already figured vividly, in the fiction of Conrad and Greene, Rider Haggard and Joyce Cary, as a skein of exotic color and a "heart" of primal mystery? So might we not expect, as the post-colonial African generations take their place among the world bourgeoisie, a passionate intelligentsia to arise and enunciate native truths, to embody in renewed fictional forms a living reality that has hitherto been seen only through white eyes?

The publication, a dozen years ago, of Chinua Achebe's *Things Fall Apart* gave plausibility to high hopes. Writing with a beautiful economy, Achebe seized the basic African subject—the breakup, under colonialism, of tribal society—so firmly and fairly

that the book's tragedy, like Greek tragedy, felt tonic; a space
had been cleared, an understanding had been achieved, a new beginning was implied. Now, in an Africa rid of overt European
domination, the artist inherits the confusions of anti-climax, of
conflicts grounded not in the grand encounter of two cultures
but in petty self-interest, leading to tangled catastrophes like the
destruction of Mr. Achebe's fellow-Ibos in Biafra. For all their
tenderness and brilliance, three recent novels by young Africans
—Yambo Ouologuem of Mali, Kofi Awoonor of Ghana, and
Ezekiel Mphahlele of South Africa—left this reader in the mood
for gloomy generalizations. Myopic lumping being one of the
white West's affronts, however, let each book speak.

Yambo Ouologuem's *Bound to Violence*, written in French,
interspersed with Arab and Bantu exclamations, conveys, through
Ralph Manheim's translation, a startling energy of language. It
begins:

> Our eyes drink the brightness of the sun and, overcome, marvel
> at their tears. *Mashallah! wa bismillah!* . . . To recount the bloody
> adventure of the niggertrash—shame to the worthless paupers!—
> there would be no need to go back beyond the present century; but
> the true history of the Blacks begins much earlier, with the Saifs,
> in the year 1202 of our era, in the African Empire of Nakem south
> of Fezzan, long after the conquests of Okba ben Nafi al-Fitri.

Ouologuem writes as a *griot*—"a troubadour, member of a heredi-
tary caste whose function it is to celebrate the great events of history and to uphold the God-given traditions." He tells, or sings,
the story of Nakem, an African state much like Mali: bordering
the Sahara, watered by the Niger (called here the Yame), ruled
since the Middle Ages by a Muslim dynasty called the Saifs. The
book's heroic subject, on the public level, is the Saif rule, the
cunning and ruthlessness that enable these Berber and Jewish
chieftains to subjugate by terror and division the tribes of "niggertrash" and then to outwit the white conquerors when they come,
using the colonial officials as a mask for their own continuous, corrupt, and refulgent power. On the private level, the book's hero
is Raymond-Spartacus Kassoumi, the son of a slave cook and a
serving woman, educated in mission schools and in Paris, and

returned to Nakem in hollow triumph as the "man of the hour," the winner of a popular election that is merely Saif rule in yet another guise. The author, however, is often distracted from the relatively domestic events of Kassoumi's progress by gaudy, curiously noisy images of physical violence:

> Saif howled as though wounded and at the same time threw something into Chevalier's eye, which it penetrated with a splashing sound punctuated by a cry.

> His knife whirled, twice he planted it in her left breast, slitted her belly from top to bottom. Suddenly expelled, her pink viscera crackled.

A hyperbolic violence also drives Ouologuem's poetry into absurdity—"I regale the air with the idiotic laugh of my gums undermined by the caries of twenty centuries of history"—and pushes his satire into jubilation. Of Raymond-Spartacus, it is said, "His academic success in the land of the Flencessi [the French] had been bruited among the people, who declared that he was better educated than the best educated of white men—after God, by golly: *o djangui koié!* Wasn't it true that in homage to his science a white woman had savored the ecstatic felicity of marrying Raymond the illustrious builder, for—*tjok!*—he spouted mathematics and physics as easily as his mother had shelled peanuts." Though a Christian missionary is sympathetically presented, Ouologuem mocks mercilessly the pro-African aestheticism of the "Shrobeniusologists," who find in the bloody empires of the African Middle Ages "a society marked by wisdom, beauty, prosperity, order, nonviolence, and humanism." Hoodwinked by fake artifacts hastily planted in the marshes and mud, the Shrobenius family in turn hoodwinks Europe with "a cult of the good nigger," "a philistine Negromania without obligation or sanction." Such romanticism Ouologuem sternly mocks, insisting, "Prehistory in a tailcoat: there stands the African."

The intelligence expressed by this book seems all too withering, all too Gallic. The last chapter is an arch dialogue between the Christian Bishop Henry and the reigning Saif, suddenly as dialectical as Sartre himself: "Destiny never wearies of forgiving, by proxy. How could it weary? If it did, would it not know Tedium, the empty consciousness of a time without content?" The point of the debate, and of the novel, seems to be that

> violence, vibrant in its unconditional submission to the will of power, becomes a prophetic illumination, a manner of questioning and answering, a dialogue, a tension, an oscillation, which from murder to murder makes the possibilities respond to each other, complete or contradict each other. The outcome is uncertainty.

The Bishop and the Saif fall to playing chess, cozy in the certainty that rulers like the Saif will be "forever reborn to history beneath the hot ashes of more than thirty African republics" and that "such was the earth of men that the balance between air, water, and fire was no more than a game."

Such refined and utter pessimism may be necessary to surmount a heritage so despairingly seen. But while Ouologuem senses a "gigantic hunger for self-destruction" in the world, he also admits and particularizes "the intoxication of feeling alive"; though no political solution can be envisioned, the woeful history of Nakem is indignantly felt. For all the book's incongruities as it leaps from idiom to idiom, it delivers on its opening promise of intensity; its furniture is incandescent. Without any note of sentimentality, apology, or excuse, a fully literate African has opened himself, and us, to modes of human existence prior to civilization:

> Her head was turned toward Yame and her body in tears was covered with watery suns.

> The silence sleeps, dreaming of the sky where the clouds envy the moon. Here's the bank of the Yame River, with its black swell, its dampness. The river. Southward. Southward. I've got to. They're expecting me. Why sleep? Maybe I've arrived. I run to catch myself, I follow myself at a gallop. I stop, body erect, arms stretched forward. I'm like a lemon without juice. I can't see myself anymore. Neither my hands nor my limbs. Sleep. I'm afraid of the snakes. Sleep. Dream. Sleep. I'm afraid of the red ants. I don't want to be eaten. I wish I could turn into an animal and survive this menacing forest, its mosquitoes, its flies, those black things that crawl out of its belly in the darkness. Fire. I want fire. With fire I'll fear nothing. The snakes will go away. The rabbits will go away. The monkeys will chatter. The animals will think I'm armed. I'll be saved. I'll wait till daylight. Only then will I sleep.

*

This Earth, My Brother . . . , by Kofi Awoonor, is a more amiable work, just as Mr. Awoonor's contemplative gaze from his jacket photograph is more amiable than Mr. Ouologuem's flash-lit stare. The jacket and title page insist that the book be called "An Allegorical Tale of Africa," though it seems no more allegorical than any novel is; i.e., its hero represents many men and his plight illustrates an aspect of the human condition. The hero, Amamu, is a young Ghanian lawyer, who, through the alternation of objective and introspective chapters (set, I think too fussily, in different sizes of type), proceeds to nervous breakdown and death. The stress he suffers is presumably the inordinate gap (and here the typographic device may have a point) between his primitive, hopeful, partially idyllic past and the mediocre, nagging, disappointed present of his life in an African metropolis no better able to cope with corruption and pollution and poverty than any other modern city. While a desert glitter and an imperial past lend fiendish glamour to Ouologuem's Mali/Nakem, Awoonor's Ghana is familiarly dismal, except that all the faces are black and the problems of overdevelopment experienced in America are matched by the not dissimilar embarrassments of underdevelopment. Amamu is a thorough bourgeois male—uneasy in his work, a witness to injustice yet a professional participant in it, a citizen perpetually testifying, inwardly, to his own puzzling incrimination in the venal, weary workings of a mercenary society:

> The Lebanese merchants are bargaining away native lands; even a government that proclaims socialism—a confusion of ideas, beliefs, and magic—cannot provide the answer. So the children turn beggars in the market place, as the eminent men play golf on the Achimota course. The best golf course in the country.
> In the Senior Common Room, the scholars of the land are debating international communism, and providing new arguments for Fabianism that died in its country of origin. . . .

> The beer is good; there are two excellent breweries and one is soon to be built in the Western Provinces to brew wholesome beer for the people.
> Meanwhile, drinking water is short in the north and in the Ewe country.

On the private level, Amamu's binds are the familiar ones of the bourgeois male: the boyhood/manhood bind, the wife/mistress bind. The mistress, Adisa, a warm and servile whore, merges with boyhood loves and visions—"the woman of the sea, his cousin love of those years long long ago rising from the sea. She rose slowly, head first, adorned with sapphires, corals, and all the ancient beads her mother left for her pubertal rites. She rose slowly from a dream sea." And this vision of Mother Africa merges in the currents of Amamu's nostalgia with the Britannia who ruled the waves. Christian hymns haunt his walks and reveries; he remembers the Empire Days, held on Queen Victoria's birthday—the uniformed dark children singing songs freshly learned, "miniature Union Jacks stuck in their shirt pockets"; the handsome mustached officers; the speeches proclaiming, "To be true imperialists, we must maintain unshaken our faith in God, in the Empire, and in ourselves. God bless you all." With the recession of the Empire, this faith has faded, leaving nothing but empty revolutions. "All revolutions must go astray. That is divine justice." Nkrumah Circle is renamed National Liberation Circle; that is modern Ghanian history.

> It is a land of laughing people, very hospitable people. That's what the tourist posters proclaim. They forgot to add that pussy is cheap here, the liquor is indifferent, and the people suffer from a thousand diseases.

The novel itself struggles against the soggy atmosphere of lassitude. The chapters of interior soliloquy lapse into an unlikely literariness:

> The flash point of creation, birth before birth long tunnels tunnels roads of womb darkness stilled the mind's eye cannot behold, prescience prenativity of total darkness, the foreknowledge of the grave the exhilaration and impatience of the emergence.

Awoonor does not have Ouologuem's access to savagery. Instead of glorying in the sun and the tears it forces upon us, Awoonor's hero says he hates the sun, and finds ease in images of spooky shelter: "Darkness peopled by ghosts in purple velvets shrieks abandoned by fireplaces by the eaves of the thatched hut in rain falling falling falling as the water whitened by cornflour is poured on the sogged earth for the benevolent ones to drink to quench their thirst in the land beyond the field where trees are green and the grove is dark." The interior monologues put us in mind of Eliot's remark (apropos of *Ulysses*) that "this new method of giving the psychology . . . doesn't tell as much as some casual glance from outside often tells." Viewed externally, Amamu is not very impressive or dynamic, and his fate is less tragic than damply sad, a shadow melting back into shadows. Yet the novel's strength is its refusal to be spectacular, to feign anger it doesn't feel, or to present Ghanian life as anything much more than a fumbling, disheartened extension of colonial rule, a blurred carbon. Humanity is not, as it rather is in *Bound to Violence*, locked out; there are pages of faithful, inconsequential dialogue, with a lilt never heard in the West, and perhaps it is this sense of voice and voices that makes *This Earth, My Brother* . . . amiable, despite its allegorical grimace.

Ezekiel Mphahlele's *The Wanderers* is the longest and least sophisticated novel of the three. His English is not always sure. His characters say unsayable things to each other, like "Aren't we happier when our love activates things in people than when it founders on passive ground?" Some sentences are untidy wastebaskets overflowing with words:

> Maybe all these factors checked the downhill thump and roll and leap of the boulder of passion before it could plunge into the placid fountain down there with a horrendous splash before anchoring under its own weight, for good or for bad.

On the other hand, there are some lucky hits a more practiced writer wouldn't have brought off:

> Always for that distance, one's mind seemed to see things in blue and yellow: colors that seemed to have been yoked violently together by some inevitable force that wanted to have fun.

Her figure was the kind that never looked overripe or bitten into. The language adequately moves its freight—an ambitious panoramic story of wandering exiles, black and white, from South Africa. The South African episodes are the most vivid and affectionate; the polychrome peculiarities of this deplorable state, with its "colored" and Indian minorities as well as blacks, are rendered in a sharp sequence of vignettes and accents. Mr. Mphahlele, whose black characters talk a little like stage Englishmen, hears peculiar speech everywhere. Here is an Indian shopkeeper:

> "What you peepel want prom Hindians, eh? Ewery person in dis worl' sweat to eat. . . . It is not enough we Hindians we are removed by gowermint out of town and we looss too much property too much bissness and den you peepel put our shops on pire?"

Here is an Afrikaans woman, at a Promethean extreme of racism:

> "Look at me. You lucky you can see your god like me and Master and Master Van Zyl. I cannot see my god, I cannot reach him he is far, far away. Sometime I t'ink he does not listen. But I only know he is listening and he knows dat the government is doing everyt'ing right to make you heppy, like dey are your fathers and mothers. . . . You heppy, not like ourself, the white people beecoss we have to look after both ourself and you. You know sometime the father and mother must be unheppy so that their children are heppy. I am right, eh? You must keep laughing."

When Timi Tabane, a black schoolteacher exiled for writing newspaper articles about a slave system of penal labor, travels to London, the colony of exiled South Africans there seems to him pathetic; the "South African English accent the whites spoke . . . irritated him as it had never done in his home country." And in Nigeria, after his initial exhilaration at being freed from South Africa's tyranny of passbooks and police, he is irritated by the effeminate way Nigerians slap at each other, and urges them to hit with fists, in good South African style. Prostitution and idleness are also new to him. One of the friends he makes there, in a small circle of intellectuals and mixed marriages, is named Awoonor (another is "an American historian, John Galbraith"), and, whether or not this means Kofi Awoonor, *The Wanderers* moves into the dispirited terrain of *This Earth, My Brother*. . . . Timi's problems become those of the free: a sense of futility, elusive responsibilities, a meagre security. He and his wife agonize over the ethics of hiring a servant. Awoonor lectures them on the duties of mastership. "You see, you have to be a master or none at all, you must be seen to be one. You've got to talk like one. If you're soft, a steward thinks Ah, na he be tenth-rate master. He wants a first-rate master." Morally compromised, unhappy among the post-colonial anti-climaxes of Nigeria and Kenya, they are faced with that ultimate Western luxury, a generation gap. Their son, Felang, after obstinately non-coöperating with the Anglophile school establishment, runs away, joins an African nationalist guerrilla army, and is fed to crocodiles by white farmers.

Where can the Timi Tabanes of the world turn? Tabane rejects the Christianity that enveloped his education. He speaks of "African humanism," but the African wisdom he cites is a Stone Age survival manual: nothing belongs to you but what you have eaten, food is nothing but decayed matter that sticks in the teeth, a woman is like a calabash—do not kick it around. For soul comfort, Tabane turns to his American records, to the music of John Coltrane and Big Bill Broonzy, of Lionel Hampton and Duke Ellington. He asks, "How can I make my children understand we have all wandered away from something—all of us blacks," and gets no answer. He laughs when an elderly white Kenyan says he is going back to Canada: "I've done Africa—eighteen years now—and I must think of my children's future. Africa's no more for us whites." Africa is no more for whites, yet not yet for blacks. Tabane tells himself, "We must move. . . . Where to? Certainly out of Africa, stay out until we can feel needed. . . . I love Africa but . . . I'll serve the country that needs me—more than that, *wants* me." The jacket flap states that Mr. Mphahlele now lives in the United States, an associate professor of English at the University of Denver. Whereas Kofi Awoonor teaches African literature at the Stony Brook campus of the State University of New York. Yambo Ouologuem makes his home in Paris.

Now, the generalizations. Africa is enormous and pluralistic. Muslimized, impoverished Mali is a continent removed from the many-layered, prosperous police state of South Africa. Even between Nigeria and Kenya *The Wanderers* notes significant differences in tone, prospects, and make-up. So expectations of an "African" literary mode are perhaps as fatuous as talk of an "American" literature that would include, along with the United States' classics, the annals of the conquistadors, Hawaiian war chants, and the cosmopolitan avant gardes of Mexico City and Buenos Aires. Indeed, these three African novels show a deficiency not only of continental self-consciousness but of national identification; the governments, white or black, are uniformly deplored, even if Ouologuem does, perversely, seek illumination in the centuries-long bloodbath of Saif rule. Timi Tabane and Amamu feel homesick for narrow scenes—a riverside, a crowded courtyard. Modernism, while it has crushed the tribes, has not produced an emotionally credible substitute.

Of the three novels, only *The Wanderers* demonstrates any pronounced resentment of white colonialism. *Bound to Violence* presents the white colonialists as dupes, along with the "niggertrash," of the demonic Nakem nobility. *This Earth, My Brother* . . . remembers colonial rule with a kind of numb affection. And even *The Wanderers* shows the English-speaking whites (but not the Afrikaners) as people who, like the blacks, are unequally matched against the vast, murderous inertia that is Africa. Steve Cartwright, for instance, Timi's best white friend, is killed, a few pages after Felang himself is killed, in another squalid skirmish. Naledi, Steve's widow, a black woman, announces in the novel's last paragraph her intention to stay in London and study nutrition, supported by her white father-in-law. The book's last word is "sympathy." There is less Fanonesque fury in these novels than one might expect; if their authors are a fair sampling, young Africans do not share their American brothers' sensation of a magical white omnipotence malevolently applied to ring them in. Rather, there is bewilderment at vastness, a sense of ungraspable forces and inutile liberty, reminiscent of New World fiction from Fenimore Cooper to Faulkner.

Un-New World, however, is the dispirited air of these novels. The African bourgeoisie, and the intellectual class within it, seem to have been born discouraged; they have inherited Western consciousness on the downswing. The otherworldly faiths have faded, and the earthly paradises—of Marxism, of industrial capitalism—have been debunked by partially coming true. Modernity's birthday party is over. At the dedication of a new hospital, pagan dancers from the highland make music with tin cans and stones; all Timi Tabane hears is the "grim note of defeat"—"like the doleful song of southern black warriors when they have lost the battle." True, what is there to do but build hospitals, import technology, invent constitutions, mitigate corruption and poverty, take wives and betray them, raise children and lose them—to play the sedulous ape, in short, to the West's aging, diseased Faust? Of course literature can afford to be cynical. It generally is. Our own first masterpiece, *The Scarlet Letter*, is scarcely a paean to the past, and *Moby Dick* shares with *Bound to Violence* a rococo pessimism. Yet one listens in vain in these African works for an echo of Emerson's and Whitman's confident sense of national audience. For whom are these works written, in the languages of departed occupiers? Not for the "niggertrash" still sunk in the tribal dream and the struggle for sustenance. Or for the African whites, ever more anachronistically clinging to their plantations and prerogatives and the 19th-century credos that justified them. At the moment, the black African artist, from his niche in American colleges or continental salons, seems a voice without an auditorium, a sensibility between worlds.

Shades of Black

THE GREAT PONDS, by Elechi Amadi. 217 pp. John Day, 1973.

IN THE FOG OF THE SEASON'S END, by Alex La Guma. 181 pp. The Third Press, 1973.

AGATHA MOUDIO'S SON, by Francis Bebey, translated from the French by Joyce A. Hutchison. 154 pp. Lawrence Hill, 1973.

Three novels from Africa, all now published in the United States, suggest, without being especially long or ambitious, that certain artistic advantages reside with the writers of that continent, in comparison with their overpublicized and overprogrammed counterparts in the West. *The Great Ponds*, by Elechi Amadi, not only gives a Homeric nobility to the tiny war between two Nigerian villages but recovers, in its acceptance of magic as a fact, the power the Greek dramatists had—of making mental acts seem momentous. *In the Fog of the Season's End*, by the exiled South African Alex La Guma, delivers, through its portrait of a few hunted blacks attempting to subvert the brutal regime of apartheid, a social protest reminiscent, in its closely detailed texture and level indignation, of Dreiser and Zola. And *Agatha Moudio's Son*, by the Cameroonian Francis Bebey, gracefully propounds an all but forgotten equation—that between the spirit of comedy and the spirit of forgiveness.

The black African moved to literary expression confronts choices a Westerner need not make. First, he must choose his language—the European language, with its alien tradition and colonial associations, or the tribal language, with its oral tradition and minuscule reading audience. Unless his mother and father came from different tribes and used a European tongue as the lingua franca of the home, his heart first learned to listen in the tribal language, which will forever then be more pungent and nuancé; but English and French command the far broader audience, across Africa and throughout the world. So he must choose his audience: foreigners and the minority of his countrymen educated in white ways, or the majority of his fellow-tribesmen, who can be addressed chiefly through recited poetry and theatrical performance. Television, of course, somewhat widens this latter possibility, and a good deal of the intellectual energy of Ghana goes into it, publication in this impoverished, politically edgy country being practically limited to Nkrumah's bound works. In all of equatorial Africa, only the market towns of Nigeria and Ghana provide enough audience for written English to engender a popular literature—Christian melodramas and self-help fables not much different from the penny dreadfuls consumed by the urban masses of London and New York a century ago. The sales of a classic like Chinua Achebe's *Things Fall Apart* lean preponderantly on the schools, which use it as a text for the teaching of English. And these texts arrive by way of English publishing houses, whose editors and readers can scarcely help prizing an "Africanness" of exotic primitivism and docile quaintness. Hence, in reaction, the aggressive sophistication and anti-"negritude" of such creative black expatriates as Yambo Ouologuem and Wole

Soyinka. The African writer must consciously choose not only his language, audience, and tone but his reality. A village-born, mission-taught, Oxford-anointed African has lived a synopsis of human history. He has outgrown prehistory so quickly that nothing has had time to die; the village gods, the Christian God, and the modern absence of God coexist in him, along with several languages and the madly multiplied number of styles, truths, slants, and stances that the global compression brings tangent to an alert mind. What is truth? At a symposium in Lagos a year ago, I heard a dazzling variety of literary tactics enunciated by a dozen Nigerian writers and critics. Elechi Amadi (addressed as "Captain Amadi," in deference to the Army years of his varied career) put forward with an arresting earnestness the opinion that supernatural reality should play its part in a narrative whose characters believe in magic.* The first question from the audience challenged this notion, or, rather, asked that it be clarified to mean that such belief should be shown to be *subjectively* influencing the characters. Captain Amadi, a slender, gracious, and handsome figure in a white robe, appeared to consent to the modification, there in the juju-proof setting of the university auditorium, amid the steel chairs and the flex-necked microphones and the beaming pink faces of U.S.I.S. officials, with the metropolis of Lagos clattering beyond the windows. But it seemed to me that Captain Amadi did not in fact mean anything quite so reasonable as the proposition that believers believe, but something more supernatural, and his novel confirms my impression.

The Great Ponds tells, in a fine quick style airy with unadorned dialogue, of the contest between two villages, Chiolu and Aliakoro, over fishing rights in the Great Ponds, particularly the very rich Pond of Wagabe. The last of a series of wars evidently settled the ownership in favor of Chiolu, but Aliakoro maintains that it possesses a still older claim, and for years its men have poached unchallenged. Now a party of poachers is ambushed, and several of them are held for ransom. In retaliation, Aliakoro kidnaps several Chiolu women, and the conflict escalates to total predation and terror on both sides:

---

* See "Excerpts from a Symposium," following.

Death lurked behind every bush. At night the pale moonlight cast dubious shadows which none but the brave dared investigate. When there was no moon the curtain of charcoal-black darkness instilled as much fear into people's minds as if it was one vast insubstantial ubiquitous enemy ready to slay any who left the security of the closely guarded houses.

Even animals began to feel the effects of the deadly conflict. No longer was the arena strewn with white drowsy sheep lured by the moonlight. . . . Every path was watched by men whose one desire was to kill. . . . There were no children playing anywhere. Reception halls, the haunts of old men, were deserted; the empty three-legged chairs in them seemed to stare back . . . in protest.

The ceremonious parleys and judicious assemblies whereby this disastrous condition is achieved are related with humorous care and an eye, certainly, on the global wars of the century. Timeless is the mechanism whereby honorable men acting measuredly in what they construe to be self-defense perpetrate ruin. The warfare, performed with arrows and with machetes that behead an enemy at a stroke, is described as in the old chronicles, with a simplicity that leaves the sufferer some dignity without excusing us from fear and pity:

Sparks flew from their knives as they parried each other's blows. Ikechi did not seem to care much for his safety. The possibility of dying did not occur to him. He fought relentlessly with the singleness of purpose of a child. He exhibited the carelessness of inexperience too, now and then leaving openings which might have been fatal if his opponent had been strong enough to exploit them. But he was not. He was a middle-aged man and he weakened under the remorseless attacks of his much younger assailant. His knees began to wobble, his eyes grew dim as he panted. Now there was a plea in his eyes, but he had no breath to translate this plea into words.

Ikechi, unseeing in his mad fury, did not heed this plea as his able hands worked his machete this way and that. Parrying a particularly heavy blow the man sank to his knees. Before he could recover it was all over with him.

There are no bad men in this story, only men. Though the reader is placed nearer in sympathy to the village of Chiolu, Aliakoro is visited, and its *eze* (chief), its *dibia* (medicine man), and its foremost warrior are characterized as interestingly as their opposite

numbers in Chiolu. Indeed, Wago "the leopard-killer," the Aliakoro
warrior who is fanatical about the ponds, and Igwu the reluctant
magic-worker, who is indifferent about the ponds but who is
pushed by his villagers into the most demonic kind of sorcery,
are rather *more* interesting than their Chiolu counterparts, Olumba
and Achichi; Captain Amadi imitates Homer in making the Tro-
jans loom in a way that the Greeks do not. His dozens of characters within the two villages are all distinct. As the war becomes
devastating, the book's microcosm expands, and an intercessory
force is revealed: the entire Erekwi clan, whose villages are now
threatened by the breach of peace. All the *ezes* meet in splendid
panoply and put the dispute up to the gods; a representative from
one warring village is to "swear." Olumba of Chiolu volunteers,
and the elders of Aliakoro nominate the god Ogbunabali, the god
of night. The "swearing" is a simple rite; Olumba recites:

> "I swear by Ogbunabali the god of the night that the Pond of
> Wagaba belongs to Chiolu.
> "If this is not true let me die within six months;
> "If true, let me live and prosper."

The novel then shifts from the social realm to the psychological;
Olumba, the strongest man of his village, struggles with the invisible. Though elaborate precautions hem in his activity, he
impulsively climbs a palm tree, is stung by wasps, falls, and nearly
dies. The event is revealed to be the result of a spell Igwu has
cast in Aliakoro; a counter-spell, cast by the consulting *dibia*
Anwuanwu, saves his life. But as the weeks of his six months drag
by, the impalpable weight of the god Ogbunabali preys on the
warrior's mind and wastes him to apathy:

> He was like a man swimming against a strong current. By frantic
> efforts he could gain short distances, but invariably the current
> swept him back, draining energy and confidence out of him . . .
> Olumba was a shadow of his former self. Emaciated and haggard he
> shuffled about with hunched shoulders. His hollow eye-sockets
> could hold a cup of water each. Looking at him people feared he
> would collapse any moment and die.

The suspense of Olumba's struggle not to die is frightful. The
motions of his morale feel immense. We see life as pre-scientific
man saw it—as a spiritual liquid easily spilled. The invisible forces

pressing upon Olumba are totally plausible. The novel treats magic respectfully, as something that usually works. The recipes of witchery are matter-of-factly detailed, as are the fevers and divinations they inarguably produce. But Olumba's heroic battle is against a force deeper than magic—the death wish itself, the urge toward osmotic reabsorption into the encircling ocean of darkness wherein life is a precarious, thin-walled epiphenomenon. Ogbunabali has no shrine in Chiolu; he is "therefore non-directional, distant, menacing, ubiquitous." His silence and neutrality are uncanny and invincible. Ogbunabali is not evil, or even especially concerned; "the gods would rather have fun than run after us." He is simply Ogbunabali.

As Olumba is about to succumb, a second intercession occurs: others in the village begin mysteriously to die. Olumba's fighting spirit returns: "His private fears vanished in the face of the village-wide consternation." *Wonjo*, the coughing sickness, carries off one of his wives and imperils his only son. Nevertheless, as the sixth new moon shines down upon the decimated village, Olumba still lives. And yet, in this defeat, Wago the leopard-killer finds a way to deprive Chiolu of the Pond of Wagaba; the war is carried to a fiendish end, though Aliakoro, too, has been ravaged by *wonjo*. Is *wonjo* the wrath of Ogbunabali, taking vengeance for the impiety of war? The villagers think so, but Captain Amadi tells us, in a last sentence like the lifting of a vast curtain, that

> *Wonjo*, as the villagers called the Great Influenza of 1918, was to claim a grand total of some twenty million lives all over the world.

One world indeed. Until this sentence, the apparent isolation of the Erekwi villages has been total and pure; this novel, so revelatory of the human condition both inward and outward, contains no trace of the world of white men save a few old Portuguese swords worn as adornment.

In Alex La Guma's novel of South Africa, white men are everywhere, "pink and smooth as strawberry jelly." They function as bosses, owners, policemen, and torturers. *In the Fog of the Season's End* has a setting as thoroughly urban as that of *The Great Ponds* is rural:

The suburbs passed quickly and the city skimmed into sight: a serrated horizon of office blocks with rows of parking meters like regiments of armless robots in front of them.

There is cosmopolitan glitter for whites:

> the clink of glasses; a woman's voice saying nasally, " . . . must come to Los Angeles some day . . . " soft music from the dim futuristic cocktail lounge where the Indian stewards moved skillfully among the tables . . .

and ghetto squalor for blacks:

> On the narrow, torrid staircase the smell of urine and old cooking hung on the stale, thick, groping air that touched exposed skin with a hot caress.

Through this crowded, active, bipartite cityscape (Cape Town, though not named as such) moves our hero, Beukes, "a brown man in a brown suit." He works for "the movement," and in the course of the novel goes about distributing incendiary leaflets, meeting varieties of coöperation and distrust among his fellow black Africans, catching odd hours of sleep in borrowed rooms, reminiscing about his life and his love, Frances, whom we never meet. At the end, the Security Police surround a tin shack where he is conferring with Elias Tekwane, an older revolutionary; Beukes escapes, but Tekwane is captured and tortured to death. The last scene shows three young blacks being smuggled north to join the army of freedom fighters while Beukes stands in the brightening sunlight and thinks, "They have gone to war in the name of a suffering people. . . . What we see now is only the tip of an iceberg of resentment against an ignoble regime, the tortured victims of hatred and humiliation."

Mr. La Guma is not, then, one to let his message slip by unnoticed, nor is his descriptive prose shy of insistence. Similes proliferate; at their best they quicken their referent:

> She was small and fine-boned and pretty as a garden snake.

> . . . the dark-skinned children staring out over fences like shabby glove-puppets . . .

and at their worse smother it beneath a clumsy muchness:

Here and there tiny cafés clung to precarious business with the fingernails of hope, like the foxholes of a last-ditch stand, dust gathering on the stale menu cards.

Faces especially excite the author to a viscous overflow of imagery:

The Sergeant had a flabby, wrinkled face over hard bone, as if a loose, flexible rubber mask had been hastily dropped over a smaller wig-stand.

. . . a woman with tired, bleached hair and the face of a painted waxed doll accidentally left near a fire, then hastily retrieved . . .

. . . a squat man with a face like a badly formed and stale chéese . . .

. . . a small man with bad teeth and a big smile that split his face like a blotched melon.

The writing does, however, convey a jumbled, sweaty sensation not inappropriate to the subject—the human jungle the white man has imposed upon the South African black. And when La Guma's prose connects directly to outrage—as when Tekwane is tortured by two tweedy policemen, or when the maze of permits the police state has created is dramatized—the fuzz of overwriting burns away. As a thriller, *In the Fog of the Season's End* suffers not only from its chosen interweave of flashbacks but from a certain languid futility in its basic mission; the risk Beukes runs distributing the leaflets seems far greater than any possible effect they can have. As political description, the book is less strident than its metaphors. The black population Beukes moves through is represented, in what feel to be fair proportions, as amused, threatened, or inspired by him and his cause. Personal friendship among these oppressed counts for more than political commitment. We are aware how far we have come from the villages of *The Great Ponds* when a character responds, "Strangers? I dunno. I reckon there's always strangers hanging about like. People you don' know." In Chiolu and Aliakoro, there are no people you don't know. In a modern state, strangers are the rule, and Beukes more than once reminds himself of the uncomfortable, comforting fact that he is anonymous while, with his carton of pamphlets addressed to the faceless masses, he dodges from one island of acquaintanceship to another. I have heard it observed that among black Africans South African exiles invariably stand out as the most dynamic. Perhaps "dynamic" should be read as "best able to deal with strangers." The people in La Guma's world are fighting for identity; Amadi's villagers have had theirs bestowed upon them —in their kinship, in their nicknames, in their hierarchical roles. Dragging its captive blacks in the ruck, the South African state has nevertheless dragged them into modernity, into the post-tribal impersonality that makes it necessary for the narrative artist to particularize every face. The need to describe, excessively felt in *In the Fog of the Season's End*, arises when teller and listener no longer share a common reality.

As protest, La Guma's cry from this particular underworld has a value that transcends its artistic faults—a special value, it may be, to Americans. For at this distance it is easy to be complacent or forgetful about South Africa, which sends us only its admirable white athletes and, with less publicity, its pleasant investment dividends. Perhaps one has to visit black Africa to realize how automatically is assumed the complicity of the United States in the continued white rule of that continent's rich southern third. The Portuguese supposedly fight with weapons we supply them through NATO; the Afrikaners buttress their tyranny with our capital; our new Vietnam will (supposedly) come here. *In the Fog of the Season's End* contains only the occasional overheard invitation to Los Angeles, the glimpsed Coca-Cola billboard. But the glistening white world that hangs above the black townships like a forbidden paradise does have a familiar air. We live there.

Agatha Moudio's Son takes place in an agreeable intermediate climate: its Cameroonian fishing village is intact but not untouched. White power has planted a public fountain in the center of the village and run a paved highway through it. A party of hunters comes on Sundays to shoot monkeys in the forest—an intrusion considered "picturesque." They are admired as exotic creatures:

> There were three white men and their two white women. . . .
> The two ladies always wore trousers: what kind of woman was
> this . . . ? One of the men was very rich, at least we thought
> so every time he opened his mouth to speak, for he had replaced

the two rows of ivory that Heaven must surely have given him at birth with two sparkling rows of gold. He was tall and strong and ugly. . . . The children were looking at these men and these women with curiosity and admiration, especially the man with the gold-filled mouth, in spite of his strange ugliness. But why on earth weren't they black, like us?

More admired still, however, is the striding Scotsman on the whiskey bottle—"blessed be thou, oh bottle manufactured by the whites." Another bracing import is law and order, which sends almost all the male villagers to jail for four years. Unlike Beukes, they accept fatalistically these strangers "who rule us, you, me, all the villagers, just as they rule our forest, our stream, our river, and all the animals and fish that live in them." They are puzzled only by how their first set of white masters, the Germans, who drank from mugs, could have been defeated by the French, who drink from "dolls' glasses."

Francis Bebey writes with the lightness and irreverence and affectionate thoughtfulness that the patterns of acculturation have bestowed upon the literature of Francophone Africa. Magic, so deadly in Amadi's Nigerian fastness, is here playful and amorous: a woman throws salt on a fire to bring on a rainstorm that will protect her and her lover from interruption; in the figure of Mother Evil-Eye the witch and midwife merge. The frightful silence of Ogbunabali becomes the kindly silence of the dead, giving assent to the living:

> We waited a few seconds for a possible manifestation. It did not come; nothing moved in the room, neither the door, nor the single window with its scanty light, which was covered by a little rectangular mat of woven raffia; we heard nothing, not even a step on the freshly beaten earth of the floor. Nothing: my father was giving us a free hand.

Even when ritual turns lethal and heaps rocks upon a culprit's head, his neck by a droll miracle refuses to break. The elaborate parleys, which in *The Great Ponds* present a worthy analogue to the discourse of nations, are here portrayed satirically; venerable formulas mask haggling greed as a bride price is agreed upon. Religion has ebbed, leaving a fertile wash of credulity. Little myths sprout into instant being; a stray frog hiding in a sleeve becomes in the telling a devil, and a young wrestler feels himself "in the process of gradually becoming a legend." Darkness, a death-concealing curtain in Chiolu, in this Cameroonian village panders to lovers, covering their comings and goings and even permitting the whispering visits of a white man on a bicycle.

The hero of *The Great Ponds*, Olumba, agonizes between life and death; Mbenda, the hero of *Agatha Moudio's Son*, vacillates between two women and solves his problem, in the way of his ancestors, by marrying them both. Though both present him with illegitimate children, the triangle is essentially amiable—Fanny, the wife whom the village has chosen for him, urges him to marry as well Agatha, the woman his heart has chosen, though she is a white man's tart and with time his desire for her has so cooled that she seems "very little different from any other woman." The novel brims with the village's most precious gift—its bestowal of value upon every life within it. An illegitimate child, far from unwelcome, "prospered and was the sun of our village." Uncle Big-Heart, upon whose head the stones are heaped, is deplored because he "had not acted in a brotherly way" toward his fellow-villagers: "After all, just because Uncle Big-Heart could read and write and talk to foreigners, he had no right to neglect his brothers." And eventually he comes to repentance, appearing at a wedding and announcing, "I was born in this village. I shall stay here all my life, and I don't intend to be ignored at moments as important as this one." All forgive him his cheating them, and he forgives their trying to break his neck, and the men imprisoned because of this escapade forgive him their term in jail.

Mbenda, as he narrates these events in a sidling, unpredictable manner, seems ambiguously situated both within and outside the village. He is a fisherman in love with the fisherman's life, with the "fraternity, solidarity, the sky, the sea, men, men lost in this overwhelming natural setting, simple men living to sea's rhythm" and solidly of the village. Yet he looks back upon it from a mysterious distance: "Happy life, what would I give to return to you again." He alludes to intervening experiences not described within the novel's compass: "Today, time and mixing with people who 'know about life' have given my arguments a certain measure of 'civilization.'" The reader expects, then, a scene of severance from this village recalled through a shimmer of nostalgia. It never comes; Mbenda never leaves. The author, however, the jacket tells us, after being born in Douala, Cameroon, studied at the Sorbonne and has been a "composer, guitarist, broadcaster, and journalist," and has given recitals "throughout Africa, in Paris, and New York." The awkwardly obtrusive narrator consciousness, with its unresolved double focus, is the only stammer in this confidently relaxed novel, and is probably symptomatic of an African unease with the device, so natural to the West, of confession, of the narrator as hero. I recall—to be personal once more—a student in Nairobi explaining her aversion to reading novels by saying they were "too much showing off." Mbenda, in one of his philosophical asides, analyzes his own distrust of books: a book is, "fundamentally, the most indiscreet of friends. . . . In our society, we had preserved the ancestral custom of communicating things only to those we loved, and with the certainty that they would make good use of our information."

Agatha Moudio's Son culminates, as the title foretells, in the birth of a boy. He is born oddly pale, with straight hair. Mbenda tells himself, "Most black children are born white, and only take on . . . local colour a few days after coming into the world." He waits. "You will understand why this child, neither flesh nor fowl, which had just been born, made me so thoughtful, when I tell you the truth: the colour of my own skin is like the deepest shades of ebony. . . . As for Agatha Moudio, very pretty as you know, she too was quite black, from head to foot. . . . I kept on hoping for a whole month after the birth of the little boy, but his milk-chocolate complexion barely changed, or so little as to be barely noticeable." At last, Mother Evil-Eye announces the obvious truth:

> "Perhaps," she said, "perhaps this child will one day have a mouthful of gold, like its father. . . ."
> I rushed to a mirror, on hearing this, and bared my teeth: two rows of ivory, clean and white beyond reproach.

But this, too, is in time forgiven—forgiven Agatha, and forgiven her white son, who as he grows and plays in the village with the other children "looks like a child come from afar." Mbenda, abruptly older, meditates, "When all's said and done, Agatha's son expects from me not the wicked and stupid sneer of a man deceived by fate but the parental advice which will bring him happiness in the strange adventure of life as a man." And he remembers Mother Evil-Eye's predicting to him, of Agatha, "She'll lead you a fine dance till you can't tell black from white." Speed the day.

Addendum: Excerpts from a Symposium

HELD ON January 26, 1973, at the University of Lagos. Text edited by Dr. Theophilus Vincent of the University Department of English and published by the United States Information Service.

"The author is faced with this difficulty. He has to write on a private level, on the social level and on this other level which, for want of a better word, we may call the supernatural. So you may find things happening in the African novel which normally would be quite untenable from the Western point of view. Why should a man die because some gods are angry? It is rubbish, it is childish, it doesn't happen. . . . And yet, down in the village, this is the reality. If someone is sick in the village it is not enough for the medicine man or even for the doctor to give him an injection. It may be a purely organic disease, so he gets this injection. Now if he has not lost his innocence, you will find that he will not recover until he has also satisfied his gods. In other words this emotional aspect of the thing is very much tied up with his illness. Even now in the village you find a relation of yours falls ill and then there is the usual divination. With your sophistication and Western education, you say, 'Look, mommy, this is trash. I will take you to the doctor; you will be all right.' Then you bundle the old lady to the doctor and the doctor does his bit and she does not recover, even with all the drugs. Now she has to go back and, if she believes strongly in this thing, and most of them do, the native doctor is called in, he does his bit and then she recovers.

This is the reality of the African situation. We have not lost all our innocence and if we try to lose it, I think we would be losing a very great deal. So we have to write in three dimensions. . . . One may ask: is this not perpetrating something which really ought to be done away with? Why resurrect all this stuff of the gods and the supernatural and so on? Well, my answer is: we really do not know—I mean, there is so much about nature that we do not know. Nowadays hypnotism is standard practice in psychotherapy. When Mesmer was exploring this art, he was dubbed a quack and he was abused and mesmerism was very much in disrepute. But today, hypnotism is an accepted part of psychotherapy. People are researching in telepathy and gathering evidence every day on this. In other words, we do not really know much about nature and it may well be that the ignorant villagers are right after all."

—CAPTAIN ELECHI AMADI, *novelist*

". . . The old forms, which Capt. Elichi Amadi says we have to bring in, like the fisherman who wants fish and has to go through the gods, are changing. If I want fish I have to go to the water and get the fish and not try to go through some gods. These things are changing. I mean this now and what happens every day. People want fish, they want money from it. They are not going to consult somebody who will get in their nets and make sure it works very well. If they are going to use poison for the fish, they throw it into the water and wait for the fish to die and collect them. The old forms are going to die. The new forms of doing things have not yet taken hold on us, so we are in a society which is in flux and is changing."

—KOLE OMOTOSO, *novelist*

". . . satire has the value of working like an invocation. In traditional society as our fathers have told us, the best way to disarm a baleful influence, an evil spirit, is to call it by its name, that is, evoke it. You can stare this baleful influence in the face and so it becomes powerless. I think this is exactly what satire is doing. . . . Who are the audience of the African writers? I think at this stage of our development the power is not really with the common people. We may deceive ourselves with socialist slogans about power to the masses. The power is in the hands of the few elite who are going to determine the future of the country, and it is among these few that you get the intelligent ones who will read the novels. I do not think it matters very much that the novel is not accessible to the ordinary person. . . ."

—D. S. Izevbaye, *critic and scholar*

". . . what our writers are tracing, what they have been charting, is a kind of moral decline due to the shock of the colonizer, the breakdown in values, the incoherence that was sort of an aftermath of our colonial experience which has produced the present situation in which we are living. The writers have always been present to report on this, to tell us about this, to write about this. They have never, it seems to me, abdicated this particular responsibility. So this moral concern may be taken as something that distinguishes the African novel today."

—F. A. Irele, *critic and scholar*

". . . It should not really matter whether these things get read and understood in America or Europe. I think first our writers should aim at getting their works read locally. This is part of what I see as the failure of works like *The Interpreters*, not only because as some people might say it is faulty in its form, but because it is not really there—it does not belong to the society. That is why works like *Things Fall Apart* get read much more widely; they are directed to a certain simple but literate audience, such as school girls. . . . I think that within the reality of African life and African tradition there is a certain kind of sacredness which even the writer must respect, however iconoclastic he wants to be. There is a certain sacredness bound up with our spirituality. . . . This is the dimension which I would like to add to this discussion."

—Ime Ikeddeh, *critic, scholar, editor*

"It seems to me that the suggestion has been made that the African artist lives in a world of his own and that the nature of his own type of reality must necessarily and artistically be different from the nature of European reality. . . . I think we should always look on the African artist or the African writer as belonging to a certain community that speaks generally to humanity. . . . the really solid thing about the good African novel is that it is a novel whose realities have not been so exclusively culturally bound as the topic of this symposium would seem to suggest."

—THEOPHILUS VINCENT, *critic and scholar*

"In this country we have a class of people who are known as poltergeist, medicine men or even rain doctors as they call them— who use incantations, incantations and so forth. That is all oral poetry; and all that the Yoruba praise singers who sing on festive days the praises of chiefs and recall past events and so forth, sing, is poetry. . . . Everybody enjoys and admires these praise singers, these priests; that is everybody in the rural areas. Everybody admires the rain doctor. Why is he so admired? Because his poetry is functional. The poetry tries to change some form of the human condition. If a threatened calamity, say, famine or problem of epidemic rages somewhere, they all crowd to this medicine man. . . . He manipulates words and sounds and appears to change the human condition. . . . He satisfies the demands of the community."

—GABRIEL OKARA, *poet*

". . . if the writer were accepted in African society he would be rather like the bird in the folk-tale that always appears on the wall and pipes a particular tune. When you hear that tune you know that there is tragedy somewhere; someone has died or something quite serious is happening. The bird disappears and within a moment you get the illumination of the bird's visit. The writer is this kind of bird. He pipes the tune which gives the warning."

—CYPRIAN EKWENSI, *novelist, short story writer*

Through a Continent, Darkly

WHICH TRIBE DO YOU BELONG TO?, by Alberto Moravia, translated from the Italian by Angus Davidson. 218 pp. Farrar, Straus and Giroux, 1974.

BY THE EVIDENCE, by L. S. B. Leakey. 276 pp. Harcourt Brace Jovanovich, 1974.

ALPHABETICAL AFRICA, by Walter Abish. 152 pp. New Directions, 1974.

"Africa, that repetitive, bewildering continent in which everything is reiterated until one's ordinary sense of reality reels and one is thrown into stupefied, visionary states of mind"—thus Alberto Moravia describes the geographical enigma that, over nine years' time, beguiled him into making five sub-Saharan journeys, which produced thirty-eight journalistic essays now collected under the too perky title of *Which Tribe Do You Belong To?* The first trip, taking him across Central Africa from Accra to Nairobi in the spring and summer of 1963, produced the most exhilarating impressions and most sweeping theories; the second, during which he was attached to a crew making a film on Tanzania for Italian television, encountered more misadventures (thefts, delays, quarrels with the natives, perilous plane landings) and evoked essays more disgruntled and problematical; the third, fourth, and fifth, touring the hinterlands of black Africa in the early seventies, show considerable traveller's fatigue and exasperation with the monotony, the impoverished sameness, the "oppressive and melancholy" lakes, the "tangled, evil bush country," the "red, obscene cones of anthills," the fleas, the bribes, "the wide prairies enlivened by the despairing gestures of dropsical baobabs." By the book's last incident (Moravia photographs some "truly peculiar women" in Chad and is scolded by "three young men, probably students, reproaching us with nationalist severity"), the impressionable fancy of this highly alert traveller seems defeated by the inexhaustible drabness of what he sees. Moravia, who has composed a fresh, even impudent book about his tour of Red China, is one of the best travel writers in the world; in English only V. S.

Pritchett can match his sharpness of phrase and flair for generalization. Before the muddled, stubborn refusal by everything save the
animals to be picturesque gets to him, he says a number of beautiful things about the Dark Continent and its inhabitants:

> The Africans walk; for their long, indefatigable legs space is
> needed.

> Indeed, all these Africans who were hurrying in small groups
> toward the market seemed already to be having a foretaste of the
> moment when they would plunge into the crowd and, mingling
> with a great number of others in the clouds of dust, in the sweat
> and the noise, would rid themselves of the unstable, troublesome
> superfluity of individual difference.

> . . . the African is the only one among the so-called primitives
> who is capable of fitting happily—in fact actually by dancing—
> into modern industrial civilization.

> The African, in point of fact, does not know what awaits him in
> his dance, just as, in general, we do not know what awaits us in
> life.

> [Of a masked dancer] This mask, in fact, was not intended to
> arouse fear; it *was* fear. . . . The face, enclosed in the stocking and
> covered with shells like a reef under the sea, was an allusion to the
> inability of man to show his face in competition with prolific, over-
> powering nature.

Anthropologically unprejudiced as only a European confident
in his superiority could be, Moravia finds what is specifically
African in the thinly populated immensity, in the landscapes that
repeat "a single theme or motif [such as the acacia tree] to the
point of terror," in the transnational tribalism centering on the
market towns, in the "frenzy for trading" that makes Africans
"one of the most contriving races in the world," in the African's
unique success at "becoming a modern man while still preserving
intact his original dancing capacity," and in the fact—apparent,
as of 1963, in the shining and incongruous commercial buildings of
the African cities—"that, whereas the red star of Communism
shines over Asia, it is . . . the white star of neo-capitalism that
gleams over Africa."

The crisp first impressions lose some starch in the later travels.

Moravia's initial sense that Africa, "a great natural space, swarming with tribes but devoid of nationality," is destined to become one of "the great continental countries such as India, China, the United States, or the Soviet Union" runs up against the obstinate fact that the Africans cling to the institutions and arbitrary national boundaries created in Europe. The Nigerian civil war of 1967–70 represents for Moravia "a symbolic contest . . . between two different conceptions of nationality, the one previous to colonialism, the other subsequent to it. The defeat of Biafra was the defeat of the tribal conception." And he admits to difficulty, as he moves through the open market of Fort Lamy, in imagining the traders "no longer unoccupied and on the alert but efficient and rational, sitting at European desks in bureaucratic offices." Some of Moravia's perceptions, like the things perceived, repeat to the point of monotony; the image of a red-dirt road as a bloody wound recurs close to a dozen times. But his eye remains basically attentive, his attention basically loving; some of the best pieces (few more than six pages long) are among the last, as he wanders from Timbuktu to the Mountains of the Moon. He combines the passive, even dazed traveller's receptivity to random detail with the thinker's determination to *see through*—to observe, as it were, aggressively. His essays not only describe to us wonders we will never visit, they tell some of us who were there what it is we saw.

Sitting in a posh hotel in Mombasa, Moravia observes across the dining room a tableful of specimens of "homo Victorianus"—a species extinct in Europe but surviving in Kenya:

> The English today rarely have those big, slightly bandy legs, those monumental thighs, those bellies as tight as drums, those muscular chests and massive napes to their necks, those prominent chins and toothbrush moustaches.

To a passing traveller, the late Louis S. B. Leakey might have seemed such—one of those white men whose whiteness, in the Kenyan highlands, had become self-cherishing, muscular, clever, and brutal. His memoir *By the Evidence* savors of the satisfied adventurer, of spacious opportunities ingeniously and unapologetically seized. It was Leakey, of course, who perceived the depth of human prehistory that lay beneath the sunstruck gorges and dried lake beds of East Africa, and who seized the opportunity to verify Darwin's intuition that Africa had been the cradle of humankind. With his discovery, in 1959, of the Zinjanthropus skull, a hominid fragment nearly two million years old, Leakey became the most famous paleoanthropologist of his time. *By the Evidence* is subtitled *Memoirs, 1932–51,* and was meant to be the middle volume of an autobiographical trilogy. The initial installment was *White African*—published in England in 1937, in the United States in 1966. The third volume, because of Leakey's death, of a heart attack the very day after he had completed *By the Evidence,* is now never to be written. The book in hand tells, then, of neither his epochal, career-vindicating discovery nor of his extraordinary African upbringing. *By the Evidence* chronicles his settled middle years, between the ages of thirty and fifty. Too much of it is concerned with the organizational trivia surrounding such promotional triumphs as the 1947 Pan-African Congress of Prehistory; Leakey kept a journal, and our passage through his days sometimes plods. On the other hand, he is intriguingly terse on personal matters; his marriage to Frida Avern, he tells us, literally in parenthesis, "had, regrettably, broken up" while he was roughing it in the bush with Mary Nicol, who becomes Mary Leakey a few pages later. There is more revealed of the man in *White African*—regarded by the author, too lightly, as a "potboiler."

Leakey was born, his first memoir tells us, in 1903 of missionary parents in a mud-and-thatch hut in Kabete, eight miles from Nairobi, then itself "little more than a scattered collection of corrugated-iron bungalows, and offices, gathered for convenience round the railway station." Born prematurely, he was swathed in cotton wool, and had to be kept dry not only from rain leaking through the thatch but from the saliva of Kikuyu visitors, who believed spitting to be an anti-curse courtesy. In the isolated mission outpost, Leakey and his siblings learned Kikuyu along with English, and all his life he dreamed in Kikuyu. He was initiated into the tribe, with full rites, as "Wakaruigi, son of the Sparrowhawk." His playmates, the games they played, the bedtime stories he heard, were all African. Though his family several times made the long trip back to England, the boy found himself, when he entered British public school, in 1919, painfully disadvantaged—unfamiliar with cricket, accustomed to playing football barefooted, incapable of swimming (crocodiles discourage this recreation in Africa), innocent of Greek and of firsthand encounter with the theatre, yet habituated to an independence improper for English schoolboys: at the age of thirteen, in accordance with Kikuyu custom, he had built himself a house and begun to live in it alone; at English boarding school he was required to get permission to go shopping, and to wear a straw hat and dark suit on a Sunday country walk. So his outlook was biased rather differently from the conventional "homo Victorianus," colonial subspecies; on his digs he insisted, to the scandal of Kenyan white settlers, on both digging beside his "boys" and carrying water with them. His imperfect indoctrination into European ways not only made his schooling awkward (at Cambridge he was rebuked for playing tennis in shorts and a sort of bush jacket) but may account for an abrasiveness that rubs through the memoirist's civil manners, for his unseemly delight in academic contests, which he always wins, and for the earthiness and voracity of his scientific approach.

For instance, in *By the Evidence* he heartily advises all would-be zoologists, "Always, as a matter of routine, examine the stomach contents of any dead animal to which you have access," and by way of illustration relates with a zest not quite infectious his own delighted discoveries of "a mass of water beetles" in the stomach of a giant pangolin, of millipedes and centipedes inside a civet, of cucumber seeds and red biting ants in an aardvark, and of "bracelets, beads, necklaces, and many other indisputable indications of the human meals that had been eaten" inside a crocodile he has shot. There is something savage about Leakey's resourcefulness—he tells us how to replace a broken car spring with strips of green hardwood and freshly skinned goat hide—and uncanny about his luck. "Leakey's luck" was a phrase coined by his rival prehistorians. On holiday in England, he was approached by a neighbor about some flakes of flint in one of his fields; though the spot had been snubbed by British archaeologists, Leakey opportunely dug, and uncovered, he tells us, "an example of the earliest known dwelling anywhere in England." The casual skills proclaimed in this volume range from dog judging to handwriting analysis, of both the English and the Gujarati scripts. He displays by his own account authoritative expertness in museum curatorship, ornithology, the care of sick animals, the primitive art of string figures. During the war he functions as spy, broadcaster in African languages, graphologist, even footprint castmaker. Some of his sentences are downright comic in their bustle of enterprise:

> As well as gathering valuable information by chatting with the local people while I watched the Verreaux's eagles, I also located a series of Late Stone Age living sites belonging to the Kenya Wilton culture.

> I could look back on the previous eighteen months as having been very rewarding. I had written three books, *White African, Stone Age Africa,* and *Kenya: Contrasts and Problems.* I had also almost completed the research necessary for my first book on Olduvai Gorge and had undertaken some exciting studies of pygmy chimpanzee skulls.

But there was nothing comic, or especially lucky, about the archaeological discoveries that are Leakey's main accomplishment. From the age of twelve, when he began to collect obsidian arrowheads lying about Kabete, he had a passionate, rather patriotic faith in East Africa's richness for the study of Man's prehistory. The Zinjanthropus skull came to light after thirty years, off and on, of "crawling up and down . . . with eyes barely inches from the ground." The spot in the Olduvai Gorge where Zinjanthropus was found is marked by a plaque, and can be reached through a little detour off the main road from the Serengeti Plain to the Ngorongoro Crater; it has become a tourist spot. But even now it seems lonely and barren and strange; a few orange-cloaked Masai herdsmen wander in the middle distance as if the immensities of African space were still untroubled. The great, lovable antagonist of Leakey's memoirs (and the first volume more vividly conveys this than does the second) is African space. The difficulty of getting there, of nursing machines through roadless terrain, of locating water sources in a geologically parching land, of finding a significant bone in an ocean of rubble—against such odds Leakey, no mere scientist, looms as a hero.

*

African space of another kind, and patience of a more literary sort, figure in Walter Abish's remarkable, ludicrously programmatic novel *Alphabetical Africa*. The adventure Mr. Abish has set himself is to compose a novel of twice twenty-six chapters, of which the first employs only words beginning with "A," the second words beginning with "A" and "B," and so on up to "Z," by which time the full lexical possibilities of the English language are available; then, from "Z" to "A," he moves back down the alphabet, subtracting letters one by one until the last chapter, like the first, is composed entirely of words beginning with "A." The hardships of such a journey should not be underestimated; "A" brings with it a handy number of articles and connectives, but not until "H" is reached can the pronoun "he" and the helper verb "have" be used, and for all but the fourteen chapters between "T" and "T" such virtually indispensable formations as "the," "to," "they,' "their," and "this" must be dispensed with. A character called Queen Quat cannot appear until after the middle of the ascending alphabet is reached, and must perish on the downhill side when her letter vanishes. Fortunately, Mr. Abish's style, even when unhampered by artificial constraints, is rather chastened and elliptic, so his fettered progress is steadier than you might imagine. Here is a paragraph from the first chapter:

> Africa again: Antelopes, alligators, ants and attractive Alva, are arousing all angular Africans, also arousing author's analytically aggressive anticipations, again and again. Anyhow author apprehends Alva anatomically, affirmatively, and also accurately.

By the time his verbal safari reaches "G," Abish can make, at length and almost fluently, observations reminiscent of Moravia's:

> Genuine gestures are African gestures, because Africans can by a few gestures demonstrate a deep and abiding affection between altogether different foreign bodies, each clap, each groan, each facial gesture conveying a convincingly eternal dramatic African confusion and also a fusion of bodies, as bodies explore boundaries, generously emitting a fresh African ecstasy . . .

"I" releases the possibility of self-exposition, "M" brings with it the themes of memory and money and murder, and by "S" only an alerted eye and hypersensitive ear would notice that a quarter of the dictionary is still being abjured:

Summarizing Africa: I can speak more freely. I find fewer and fewer impediments. Soon I'll reach my destination. Soon I'll also complete my documentation and my book. Daily Africa is shrinking from extreme heat and fatigue, as rebels in bush battle African armies led by foreigners.

The attainment, long anticipated by the alphabet-battered reader, of "Z"'s total freedom brings a disappointingly short chapter, written in the cramped, clicking tone of the others:

Zambia helps fill our zoos, and our doubts, and our extrawide screens as we sit back. Each year we zigzag between the cages, prodding the alligators, the antelopes, the giant ants, just to see them move about a bit, just to make our life more authentic . . .

Each chapter, as it possesses another letter, celebrates its acquisition with a burst of alliteration, so our knowledge of systematic expansion is aurally emphasized; this subtly joyous undertone of organic growth is lost in the book's second half, wherein the subtraction of letters echoes supposed land shrinkage ("Africa's gradual deterioration and Africa's decreasing area"), and some violent events on Zanzibar swallow up Queen Quat (who has painted Tanzania orange to match the maps) and squeeze the novel's protagonists—Alex, Allen, and Alva—into a climax of betrothal. The extremely silly plot begins as a jewel robbery in Antibes and a consequent flight to Angola, Burundi, Chad, etc., and culminates in a kind of people's uprising by the Vietcong-like army ants: "All complain close-by artillery barrage battered beautiful city, battered beautiful avenues, all because ants continue advance, continue creeping along, carving a continent." Though the tale is murky as well as absurd, one is tempted to concede that Mr. Abish has performed as well as anyone could, given such extravagant handicaps. "A masterpiece of its kind" does not seem too strong an accolade for a book apt to be the only one of its kind.

And there is a nice rightness to setting such a work in Africa, where incantations are still potent and national boundaries slice across tribal realities as arbitrarily as the alphabet schematizes language. Teeming yet vacant, mysterious yet monotonous, Africa permits this literary experiment. *Alphabetical Asia* would not have been so funny, *Alphabetical America* would have been cluttered with reality, *Alphabetical Antarctica* would have been blank. "Africa is a favorite topic in literature, it gives license to so much excess," the author explains, and confesses, of his old bush jacket, that it "fed my imagination long before I ever set foot on this continent." Mr. Abish is pictured on the dust jacket wearing this bush jacket, and a romantic black eye patch, in a studio containing African sculptures. For the Western mind, art and fancy and travellers' accounts form Africa's body. Though *Alphabetical Africa* gives some evidence that the author has visited the continent, it was not necessary; his Swahili dictionary and a four-color map took him where he wanted to go. Setting out with his elaborate impedimenta, he chose the mental milieu that offered him the most license and sport. Africa, explored and excavated and neo-capitalized as it now is, remains—for Mr. Abish as for Moravia, as it was for Leakey and Livingstone, for Gide and Hemingway, for Rider Haggard and Edgar Rice Burroughs, for Burton and Speke and Mungo Park and Prince Henry the Navigator—an invitation to the imagination.

THE AVANT GARDE

Grove Is My Press, and Avant My Garde

LA MAISON DE RENDEZ-VOUS, by Alain Robbe-Grillet, translated from the French by Richard Howard. 154 pp. Grove Press, 1966.

MIRACLE OF THE ROSE, by Jean Genet, translated from the French by Bernard Frechtman. 344 pp. Grove Press, 1966.

THE INQUISITORY, by Robert Pinget, translated from the French by Donald Watson. 399 pp. Grove Press, 1966.

Grove Press, that happy caterer to our prurience and our progressivism, continues to nourish the illusion of a literary avant garde by dishing up hitherto obscure modern masters (Borges, Gombrowicz), pornography with a taint of sociological or psychological interest (*My Secret Life, The Story of O*), native scatwriting (LeRoi Jones, William Burroughs), and such imported delicacies as the three French novels about to be savored. The *smörgåsbord* is mixed but not to be sniffed at. On balance, Grove Press has been the one post-war publishing house to show a personality and mission of its own, to serve the fifties and sixties as New Directions served the thirties and forties. Its courage has preceded its commercialism; it pioneered in the territory it now so cheerfully exploits with its black-mass version of the Book-of-the-Month Club, its roguish get-with-the-sexual-revolution ads, its stable of Ph.D.s willing to preface the latest "curious" memoir or "underground" classic with admonitory sermons on the righteousness of fornication. And if Grove Press's best American author remains Eric Berne, its Art Nouveau jackets have enfolded many foreign titles for whose translation the conscientious reader should be grateful.

It is surprising, for instance, that no more orthodox publisher undertook to make the works of Alain Robbe-Grillet available in this country. Robbe-Grillet is the leading theoretician of the *nouveau roman;* he coined the phrase and composed the first example —*The Erasers* (1953). If American writers, and loud worriers like Susan Sontag ("The novel is probably the most rear-guard art form today. . . . Most critically respectable novels . . . are, I think, essentially journalistic in conception. . . . [American novelists] are not essentially concerned with the novel as a work of art in the sense that most other art forms are today . . ."), imagine that progress is being made elsewhere, Robbe-Grillet's astute propagandizing is a prime cause. The tired cry "Make it new" has become new in his essays, and before the consideration of his fifth and most recent novel, his program should be summarized. The first major manifesto, "A Fresh Start for Fiction" (1956), announced:

> The world is neither significant nor absurd. It *is*, quite simply. That, in any case, is the most remarkable thing about it. . . . Around us, defying the mob of our animistic or protective adjectives, the things *are there*. Their surfaces are clear and smooth, *intact*, neither dubiously glittering, nor transparent. All our literature has not yet succeeded in penetrating their smallest corner, in softening their slightest curve.
>
> Instead of . . . "signification" (psychological, social, functional), we must try to construct a world both more solid and more immediate. Let it be first of all by their *presence* that objects and gestures impose themselves, and let this presence continue to make itself felt beyond all explanatory theory that might try to enclose it in some system of reference, whether sentimental, sociological, Freudian, or metaphysical. In this future universe of the novel, gestures and objects will be "there" before being "something," and they will still be there afterward, hard, unalterable, eternally present, mocking their own meaning, which tries in vain to reduce them to the role of precarious tools. . . . Thus objects will little by little lose their inconsistency and their secrets; will renounce their false mystery, that suspect interiority which Roland Barthes has called the "romantic 'heart' of things."

A later essay, "Nature, Humanism, Tragedy" (1958), develops these ideas into a stylistic purge. Metaphor is the villain, weaving a complicity between humanity and the alien world of "things"; metaphor—a concept including all adjectives with moral or anthropocentric coloring—implies a general myth of *depth*, humanizing nature, cheating it of its essential otherness. The categories of the "tragic" and the "absurd" are oblique maneuvers of this persistent humanism, this "bridge of souls thrown between man and things." The task, then, is to "scour" descriptive prose of any "analogical vocabulary" and to restore "things" to "themselves," cleansed of any hint of profundity or preëstablished order. In this scouring, the sense of sight occupies a privileged position, as the sense that measures distances—"our best weapon, especially if it keeps exclusively to outlines." And in a still later essay, "Time and Description in Fiction Today" (1963), Robbe-Grillet adds to the priority of visual precision "the breaks of cutting, the repetitions of scene, the contradictions, the characters suddenly paralyzed as in amateur photographs" that in fact do distinguish his later novels and his films alike. The purpose of these devices is to "afford this perpetual present [of the cinema, of the *nouveau roman*] all its force, all its violence." Temporal and spatial discontinuity, a present that never accumulates, are employed to dissolve "the trap of the anecdote." The thereness of things emerges from their dissolution.

Robbe-Grillet's theories constitute the most ambitious aesthetic program since Surrealism. My summary necessarily has skimped much: his reasoning is close; his remarks upon other writers, including the classics of the bourgeois novel, are reverent and lively. Because of his training as an agronomist, his understanding of science and of how its truths subvert our workaday assumptions exceeds that of most writers. His pronouncements do catch at something—a texture, an austerity—already present in other, often older French novelists, such as Nathalie Sarraute. To an American, however, there is a hollow ring of Thomism. Robbe-Grillet's concept of thereness looks like the medieval *quidditas;* the attempt to treat existence itself as a quality that can be artistically emphasized seems a formal confusion, a scholastic bottling of the wind. Robbe-Grillet's key concept—of "purely external and superficial" things —takes no account of the vast area of mobile and animate phenomena that mediate between *Homo sapiens* and inert matter, or of the difference between raw material and artifacts already imbued with human intention, or of the fact that to one man another is as much a "thing" as a chair or waterfall. In making his cleavage between "humanity" and "things," is he not guilty of a kind of humanism, elevating men into a glorious concept—Man? The real split, surely, is between the single ego and the external world—which would take us back into psychology, where Robbe-Grillet does not want to go. There is a forced naïveté in his vision, and a strange inversion of the pathetic fallacy he detests, for in artistic practice his concern with the inviolable otherness of things charges them, saturates them, with a menace and hostility as distortive of their null inner being as an imagined sympathy. One's reservations about Robbe-Grillet's formulations come down to the discrepancy between his description of what happens in his fiction and what actually happens. Far from striking us with their unsullied thereness, the "things" in his novels are implicated in the pervasive flimsiness and inconsequence.

La Maison de Rendez-Vous could have been translated as *The House of Assignation* or *The Blue Villa* or even *Up at Lady Ava's*. It tells of, or circles around, a night at the elegant brothel run by Lady Ava, or Eva, or Eve, in Hong Kong. There is a police raid, and an American, or Englishman, named Ralph or Sir Ralph Johnson or Jonestone, in love with a prostitute called Lauren, and the murder of a man called Edouard Manneret and of another named Georges Marchat or Marchant or Marchand, and several ferry rides to Kowloon, and a fluctuating penumbra of dope smuggling and white slavery and Cold War intrigue. Above it all is an "old mad king" pounding an iron-tipped cane on the floor and insomniacally rocking in a rocking chair; his name is given as King Boris, but he strongly resembles Manneret. The other presiding presence is a narrator who confesses to being constantly beset by images of female flesh and who sometimes inhabits Johnson's body or partakes of his adventures. Through this fog of events, or anti-events ("What does all that matter? What does it matter?" the book asks itself, answering, "All this comes to the same thing"), rotates a constellation of repeated and refracted images—a broken champagne glass, an envelope containing sand or heroin or documents, a scrap of paper illustrating the evils of drugs or else pushing them, a ubiquitous rickshaw driver, the slit hobble skirt of several interchangeable Eurasian beauties who are also mannequins in shop-windows. True to Robbe-Grillet's credo, the present never ac-cumulates; rather, it unravels. There is a studied false numerical precision. A hand is "about eight or twelve" inches from a serving tray; forty pages later, the distance is given as six inches. Man-neret's apartment is on the third floor, or the fifth, or the sixth, or the eighth. Different characters relive the same adventures; a play within the action becomes the action; and twin servant girls have the same name, "pronounced quite similarly, the difference im-perceptible except to a Chinese ear." The ingenuity behind all this doubling and shuffling is considerable. The writing is clean and deft and even entertaining, though the reader's interest tends to cling, pathetically, to the excitements of the hackneyed tale of exotic intrigue that is being parodied, fragmented, and systemati-cally frustrated. The popular adventure form underlying the sophisticated *nouveau roman* rises up and revenges itself by im-posing upon the book a cliché ending of double-cross and a flat last sentence: "And there is nothing in her eyes." But there has never been anything in her eyes. Upon the basis, I think, of false analogies, Robbe-Grillet has already dissolved, with his "descriptions whose movement destroys all confidence in the things described," the credibility as elemental to the art of narrative as the solidity of stone or metal is to sculpture.

The analogies are with the cinema and modern painting. The 20th-century novelist finds himself in competition with a mode of storytelling—motion pictures—that is astonishing in the directness with which it presents and manipulates imagery and virtually tyrannical in its possession of the viewer's attention and in its power to compel emotion. The novel, rooted in the historical past tense of the histories, legends, journals, and epistles from which it is descended, cannot but envy this constant present that does not tell but simply *is*, dancing and slicing through space, juxtaposing in montage landscapes and faces, swords and roses, violence and stasis—a new poetry, a wordless vocabulary that engulfs us like an environment. *Ulysses* was one of the first attempts, and remains the noblest, to appropriate to prose fiction some of the new medium's properties—the simultaneous intimacy and impersonality, the abrupt shifts from close-up to boom shot, the electric shuttle of scenes. Joyce immerses these effects in an orgy of literariness; Robbe-Grillet's fiction is almost exclusively cinematic. *La Maison de Rendez-Vous* is not so much written as scripted: "The scene which then takes place lacks clarity," "Then the images follow one another very rapidly," "Now we see the young Eurasian girl backed into the corner of a luxurious room, near a lacquer chest whose lines are emphasized by bronze ornaments, all escape cut off by a man in a carefully trimmed gray goatee who is towering over her." The full syntax of splicing, blurring, stop-action, enlargement, panning, and fade-out is employed; the book lacks only camera tracks and a union member operating the dolly. The trouble is that prose does not inherently possess the luminous thereness of a projected image, and all of Robbe-Grillet's montages, visual particularization, careful distinctions between right and left, and so on do not induce the kind of participation imposed by, say, his real movie *Last Year at Marienbad*. A man sitting with a book in his lap is a creature quite different from a man sitting hypnotized in a dark theatre. The mind translates verbal imagery into familiar images innocent of a photograph's staring actuality; it seizes on a single detail and enshrouds it in vague memories from real life. An image, to have more than this hazy recollective vitality, must be weighted with a momentum beyond itself, by that movement of merged relevance that Aristotle called an "action."

For this movement, and the accumulating emotion and concern around the things described, Robbe-Grillet, in his essay "Time and Description in Fiction Today," offers to substitute "the very movement of the description." Here we have the second false analogy—with painting. The practitioners of literature can hardly escape the impression that painting is the century's heroic, dominant art, the art that has won the allegiance of the rich, the art most productive of manifestos, credos, saintliness, and fresh waves of innovation. Above all, it is painting that has purified itself of content; with Cézanne, the canvas ceases to be a window and becomes a flat field whereupon a drama has occurred—the oranges or Mont Sainte-Victoire or Mme. Cézanne serving as a mere excuse. Abstraction eliminates even the excuse. Naturally, novelists seek to attain to this lordly independence of circumstance, this sacerdotal self-sufficiency. As early as 1861, Flaubert was assuring the Goncourt brothers that "The story, the plot of a novel is of no interest to me. When I write a novel I aim at rendering a color, a shade. For instance, in my Carthaginian novel, I want to do something purple. . . . In *Madame Bovary*, all I wanted to do was to render a gray color, the mouldy color of a wood louse's existence. The story of the novel mattered so little to me that a few days before starting on it I still had in mind a very different Madame Bovary from the one I created. . . . she was to have been a chaste and devout old maid." Flaubert's claim seems wistful; he sounds like an Impressionist, and the Impressionists were still short of the final liberation, insofar as their brushwork recalls the beauty of *real* water lilies, sunshine, haystacks. A page of print can never, like a rectangle of paint, lift free of all reference to real objects; it cannot but be some kind of shadow. Further, a painting is from the painter's hand, whereas a book has passed through a mechanical process that erases all the handwriting and crossing-out that would declare the author's presence and effort. Robbe-Grillet's off-center duplications, subtle inaccuracies, and cubistic fragmentation do not convey "the very movement of the description." They instead seem mannered devices intended to give unsubstantial materials an interesting surface.

Compare Kafka's truncated chapters and warps of narrative. They rise, we feel, from within, *in spite of* the author's pained sincerity and conscientious prose; they are neurotic in nature. And a neurosis is a profounder product of a culture than a theory. Robbe-Grillet does have instincts, tropisms toward certain styles of experience; his first novel, *The Erasers*, a coherent detective story, shows the same surveyor's eye, the same fondness for duplication and stalled motion, as does his last. But between the two there has been a buildup of theory, a stylization of intuition. *La Maison de Rendez-Vous* is less a work of art than an objet d'art, shiny with its appliqué of progressive post-Existential thought; it has a fragile air of mere up-to-dateness, of chic.

Whereas *Miracle of the Rose*, by Jean Genet, is as subjective and compulsive as one could wish. This, his second novel, was written in the prisons of La Santé and Tourelles, in 1943, on the pieces of white paper supplied to the convicts for the making of paper bags. Any hope of publication must have been desperate. His first novel, *Our Lady of the Flowers*, written in 1942, proclaims itself, and is acclaimed by Sartre in his introduction, as a jailbird's masturbatory fantasies. *Miracle of the Rose* springs, as it were, from the same aesthetic: "I carried Bulkaen off in the depths of my heart. I went back to my cell, and the abandoned habit of my abandoned childhood took hold of me: the rest of the day and all night long I built an imaginary life of which Bulkaen was the center, and I always gave that life, which was begun over and over and was transformed a dozen times, a violent end: murder, hanging, or beheading." Reality and fantasy are inextricable. *Miracle of the Rose* seems slightly more earthbound than *Our Lady of the Flowers*—a touch less brilliant and soaring, a shade more plausible and didactic. Genet's own person emerges somewhat more solidly; while the earlier novel made the reader marvel that a criminal had become a writer, now it seems stranger that such a writer became a criminal. We are permitted glimpses—in categorical phrases like "a region to which irony has no access," in a critical disquisition on the vulgarity of placing slang words in quotation marks—of a depraved man whose vocation, nevertheless, from boyhood on has been literary. As a thief, he stole books!—"books with heraldic bindings, the Japanese vellum of deluxe editions, the long-grained moroccan copies."

As in *Our Lady*, the story line of *Miracle of the Rose*, obeying no known gravitational laws, flies back and forth among the men Genet loves: Harcamone, the condemned man invisible in the death cell; Bulkaen, the young weakling covered even to his eyelids with tattoos; Villeroy, the big shot whose chicken Genet becomes at the boys' reformatory of Mettray; Divers, Villeroy's successor, who marries Genet in a mock ceremony and reappears fifteen years later, at the state prison of Fontevrault, and again possesses his bride. An occasional physical description or snatch of dialogue reveals the lustreless thugs beneath the extraordinary flowers of metaphor in which they are garlanded, but these pimps and crashers, big shots and chickens, exist primarily as angels and archangels in the inverted heaven of Genet's dreaming. The prison Fontevrault was once a monastery; when Genet arrives, manacled, the doorways are lit up as if for Christmas. Christianity permeates his confinement there. He suffers a series of mystic visions centered upon Harcamone, and indeed the prison world, "the eternal gray season in which I am trapped," does approximate the religious view of the world. Abasement gives rise to transcendent consolations: "And as our life is without external hope, it turns its desires inward. I cannot believe that the Prison is not a mystic community," "Your pride must be able to undergo shame in order to attain glory," "One is a saint by the force of circumstances which is the force of God! . . . I loved Bulkaen for his ignominy." These testimonies, obtained under pressures of deprivation comparable to the oppression in which primitive Christianity thrived, cannot be dismissed as blasphemous any more than the pervasive erotic content can be dismissed as "homosexual." Genet is one of the few writers to make homosexual love credible, both in concrete detail—"Our shaved heads rolled around each other, with our rough cheeks scraping"—and in inner essence, in the tenderness and hysteria it shares with all sex.

Some months ago, the Reverend Tom Driver, writing in the *Saturday Review*, admired *Miracle of the Rose* for showing Genet's transformation from a passive, "female" homosexual, the concubine of Villeroy, into an aggressive "male" one, the assaulter of Bulkaen. The improvement, to Driver, seemed self-evident, but three angry letters responded, one refusing to renew a subscription, another deploring "the literary morass of this decade," and a third likening Genet to the Nazis. Indeed, Genet, whose wartime efforts consisted of weaving, while in prison, camouflage nets for the Germans, does write kindly of the occupation forces: "When it was reported that the Germans were preparing to leave, France realized, in losing the rigidity they had imposed on her, that she had loved them." It must be admitted, especially by those of us admiring of his rhetoric, that Genet, in his submission to rigidity and his quest for the resplendence of emotional extremes, is led into a moral realm where no conventional liberal, or even civilized person, can follow. "War was beautiful in the past because in shedding blood it produced glory. It is even more beautiful now because it creates pain, violence, and despair. . . . I love the war that devoured my handsomest friends. . . . Novels are not humanitarian reports. Indeed, let us be thankful that there remains sufficient cruelty, without which beauty would not be." He worships Harcamone, who gratuitously murders a guard at Fontevrault; at Mettray, he admires Van Roy, who betrays an escape plot and thereby has "dared make a terrible gesture" demonstrating that "the strongest big shots were squealers." He is nostalgic for the superior—compared to mature criminals—ferocity of adolescents and remembers his own cruelty: "My cruelty, when I was sixteen, made me stab the left eye of a child who, frightened by my pitiless stare and realizing that his eye attracted me, tried to save it by putting his fist to it." Consistent with this savagery toward others is a fervent death wish: "My love of beauty (which desired so ardently that my life be crowned with a violent, in fact bloody, death) . . . made me secretly choose decapitation." Genet's outlawry is more thorough than de Sade's, who at least blamed God for the existence of pain; Genet says, "God is good. . . . He strews so many traps along our path." Only the desert saints of early Christianity, perhaps, would so blithely have burned the world to produce visions.

Is *Miracle of the Rose* an avant-garde novel? Genet does not claim it to be: "If I were writing a novel, there might be a point in describing the gestures I made, but the aim of this book is only to relate the experience of freeing myself from a state of painful torpor, from a low, shameful life taken up with prostitution and begging." Certainly it lacks description in the sense of giving persons and objects an appearance of autonomy. The characters, apart from their names, are no more distinguishable than the mosaic figures aligned within a Byzantine dome. The dome is Genet's skull: he is absolute Creator within this universe, not only of persons but of the laws that control their motions. The humanization of nature, which Robbe-Grillet would eliminate from fiction, here operates with a vengeance; everything is transmuted into metaphor, nothing is more than what it means to Genet. The very prison melts so that, at the book's climax, Genet can mystically join Harcamone on his walk to the guillotine. The novel is a loose form, but *Miracle of the Rose* seems to me to fall outside it and to belong rather to that older stream of French literature, contributory to the novel, of essay and *pensée*, memoir and letter, confession and self-revelation. "We belonged to the Middle Ages," Genet says of his fellow-convicts, and when he writes of entering through

Harcamone's gullet a country landscape detailed down to "the remains of a country fair: a spangled jersey, the ashes of a camp-fire, a circus whip," his untrammelled hyperbole belongs—in defiance of intervening centuries of bourgeois empiricism and objectivity—to Rabelais.

Robert Pinget is not as yet well known on this side of the Atlantic. *The Inquisitory* was originally published in 1962; from the jacket copy, and a laudatory review of some earlier novels printed among Robbe-Grillet's essays, I gather that since his first book, a collection of stories entitled *Entre Fantoine et Agapa*, Pinget's fiction has explored an imaginary provincial region between Fantoine and Agapa, a Gallic Yoknapatawpha County—an "absurd suburb of reality," in Robbe-Grillet's phrase. Certainly *The Inquisitory*, which won the Prix des Critiques, abounds with circumstantial information. Thirty pages are devoted to a description, shop by shop, of the main square of the village of Sirancy; the street geography of the town of Agapa is exhaustively examined; eleven pages call the roll of furnishings in the drawing room of a château, which is eventually inventoried from cellar to attic; and an attentive reader with pencil in hand could probably draw, from the various textual indications, a map of the entire region. Now, such feats of particularization demand more patience than passion from writer and reader alike, but the end result is the kind of trust-worthiness absent, for different reasons, from both *La Maison de Rendez-Vous* and *Miracle of the Rose*. *The Inquisitory* is of the three by far the best novel, if by novel we understand an imitation of reality rather than a spurning of it.

Not that Pinget is old-fashioned; he has put himself to school with Robbe-Grillet and Beckett. The novel's premise is a Beckettian stripped situation: an infinitely garrulous old château servant is being quizzed by an infinitely curious investigator. Both are nameless. Punctuation marks are abjured. A shadowy secretary is in the room, typing up all three hundred and ninety-nine pages of meandering testimony. The object of the investigation—the disappearance of the château secretary—is never clarified. The dialogue, initially full to bursting of visual measurement and *quidditas*, ebbs into a fatigued exchange, laconic and baffled. All this circumstantiality protests against circumstantiality, both as an adjunct of the novel and as the illusory stuff of life: "Another twenty rooms and then there'll still be more and you'll tell me to describe them, and more and more kitchens servants tell-tale tittle-tattle secrets of the bedchamber families mile upon mile of streets and stairs and lumber-rooms and junk-shops of antique-dealers grocers butchers of skimping and scraping everywhere in our heads how dreary it all is always starting all over again why." The investigator is in a sense the all too ideal reader, asking again and again, "Go on," begging, "Describe the longest route." And the answerer, with his omnivorous memory and solipsistic deafness —the questions put to him must be written on slips of paper—is the aboriginal storyteller, whose enterprise is essentially one of understanding:

> . . . we're bound to understand in the end
> Understand what
> The rest what one's forgotten sometimes I tell myself
> Explain
> Perhaps that's the answer that does the least harm
> What answer
> Understanding what one's forgotten
> What
> It seems so to me unless I'm talking nonsense. . . .

Pinget's very avant-garde novel of the absurd incorporates the full French novelistic tradition. Like Proust, he has a curé who dabbles in the etymology of place names; like Balzac, he avidly traces the fortunes of little provincial shops through all the ups and downs that gossip traces. The number of anecdotes, of minia-ture novels, caught in his nets of description cannot be counted; presumably some are expanded elsewhere in Pinget's *oeuvre*. In this book, the curve of interest moves through the château itself (the two "gentlemen" who own it, their wealth, their homo-sexuality, their fussiness, their decadence, all implied by lengthy humorous descriptions of their house-furnishings), and then out into the social and geographical composition of the region as a whole ("The main resources of the district are in the soil and al-ways will be"), and finally into the character and philosophy of the narrator himself. He has lost a wife and child; he is immensely lonely; he believes in diabolism and locates direct access to Hell in a quarry region called Vaguemort. Heaven's counterpart appears with the revelation that in the medieval section of the château lives a third employer, Monsieur Pierre—"a few intimate friends used to call them the Holy Trinity but to be frank the only holy man is Monsieur Pierre"—who is a hermit and an astronomer. So by the novel's end this district, into which enough historical allusion has been insinuated to render it an analogue of France, serves as a model of the world, with all human possibilities somewhere touched upon. Grove Press will, I hope, publish more of Pinget's work, which seems not only highly accomplished but thoroughly masculine, quite without the eunuchoid air of distress with which too much modern fiction confronts its bride the world.

All praise conceded, it remains to confess that none of these three books was hard to put down and that it is hard to imagine very many Americans, except for reviewers and students of the "art of the novel," reading them. All partake of that resistant modern motionlessness, so different from the lightning speed of Biblical chronicle or the tidal roll of Homeric narrative or the bustling forward march of the 19th-century novel—a motionlessness present in the circular structures of *Finnegans Wake* and *Remembrance of Things Past*, in the unconquerable distances of Kafka and the unconscionable length of Bloom's day, in the final "Let's go" of *Waiting for Godot*, followed by the stage direction "(*They do not move*)." The avant-garde novel itself has been saying "Let's go" for forty years, and has not outdistanced Joyce or left Kafka behind. There is an enfeebling doubt as to *ends:* Do stories end? Do novels have an end, a purpose? To entertain? To educate? To exasperate? To dehumanize literary idiom? To facilitate the author's onanism? The characteristic movement of modern narrative is of prolongation, of postponement. Novels end but do not *have* an end.

> Yes or no answer
> I'm tired

Thus *The Inquisitory* concludes. It is an honest, inconclusive conclusion. In an age of waiting (of, Christian eschatology would have it, a between-times), we find our loss of teleological sense reflected in books whose intricate energy, like that of barbarian designs, is essentially static.

Infante Terrible

THREE TRAPPED TIGERS, by G. Cabrera Infante, translated from the Spanish by Donald Gardner and Suzanne Jill Levine. 487 pp. Harper & Row, 1971.

Some things are more lost in translation than others; jokes and Racine, for instance, lose more than newspapers and de Maupassant. In its original Spanish, *Tres Tristes Tigres*, by G. Cabrera Infante, won the Biblioteca Breve and contended for the Formentor Prize; in French, it won the Prix du Meilleur Livre Étranger. In English, however, as *Three Trapped Tigers*, the novel comes over as a tedious, verbose, jejune, self-delighting mess, and unless the publisher decides to distribute good-sportsmanship awards to those few readers who persevere to the end it should generate no prizes. One can deduce that the life of *Three Trapped* (though "sad" is what they originally were) *Tigers* lay in its skin of Spanish, and that a creature so ectomorphic, so narrowly vital, was bound to perish away from the nurture of its native climate. Or one might, less kindly, conclude that the novel was derivative, that its excitement derived from the translation of the methods of *Ulysses* into Cuban idiom, and that, restored to Joyce's mother tongue, it shows up as a tired copy.

Three Trapped Tigers offers to do for the Havana of 1958 what *Ulysses* did for the Dublin of 1904: wandering itineraries are mapped street by street, minor characters reappear in a studied interweave, a variety of voices abruptly soliloquize, a kind of "Oxen of the Sun" procession of literary parodies is worked on the theme of Trotsky's assassination, an endless "Nighttown" drunkenness episode picks up the deliberate hungover banality of the Eumaeus sequence, and a female interior monologue closes the book. Unlike Joyce, however, Cabrera Infante packs most of his pyrotechnics and montage into the novel's first half and winds down into a more natural narrative tone. And, instead of attentive, soft-spoken, gradually solidifying Bloom, *Three Trapped Tigers* has for its hero an insubstantial, logomaniacal trio of would-be writers—Arsenio Cué, Bustrófedon (who is dead), and the principal narrator, Silvestre. As these three compile reams of undergraduate gags ("*Crime and Puns,* by Bustrófedor Dostowhiskey," "*Under the Lorry,* by Malcolm Volcano," "*In Caldo Brodo,* by Truman Capone," "*The Company She Peeps,* by Merrimac Arty," etc., etc.) and tootle around Havana in a convertible (Bustrófedon is there in spirit, like the Paraclete, or—as Infante might say— Parakeats), they make little significant contact with the nonverbal world around them. Havana of this era was notoriously full of prostitution and pickups, but the only instance of achieved intercourse throughout four hundred and eighty-seven pages occurs in some *tableaux vivants* staged for tourists. There is a good deal of partial undressing, and the work of one long night of seduction does jimmy a girl loose from her underpants, "*but,* BUT, where old Hitch would have cut to insert and intercut of fireworks, I'll give it to you straight—I didn't get any further than that." Later, Silvestre and Cué pick up two street flowers and proceed to bore them silly with puns and nonsense. One of the girls at last cries out, "Youse weird. You say real strange things. Both of you say the same strange things. Youse like twins, youse somethin' else. Whew! And you talk and talk and talk. Whaddya talk so much for?" To which the reader says, "Amen," and to which the author says, "Could she be a literary critic in disguise?"

A fearful air of congestion, of unconsummation, hangs over this book. Which may be deliberate: Batista's Havana is about to go under to revolution. Cabrera Infante, we are told by the dust jacket, served Castro's government as head of the Council of Culture, as a director of the Film Institute, as editor of a weekly magazine called *Lunes de Revolución,* and as a staff member of the Cuban Embassy in Brussels; in 1965, after returning to Havana, he "decided to leave Cuba," and he now lives in London. So his involvement was not trivial, and his viewpoint cannot be simple. Yet the coming storm impinges on the action of *Three Trapped Tigers* only once, when Cué drunkenly announces his intention to "join

Fffidel." Silvestre argues that he is crazy, it's like joining the Foreign Legion. "Nashional," Cué answers. "The National Leshion."
The topic is then dropped, and the two spend another hundred
pages driving and drinking and punning and remembering the
palindromes of Bustrófedon. An American reader, especially now
that Cuba is remoter than China, longs for a more anatomical portrait of this Havana that has vanished. In the first pages, such a
portrait—a cross-section of corrupted and dissatisfied lives—seems
to be promised. A sharp imitation of a night-club m.c.'s bilingual
prattle lifts the curtain on some monologues by a kept woman, a
movie-struck child, an underpaid printer. We read a letter written
back to her village by a recent emigrant to the city; we eavesdrop
on a psychiatric session that reappears throughout the book. Silvestre introduces himself:

> I am. a press photographer and my work at that time involved
> taking shots of singers and people of the *farándula*, which means
> not only show business but limelights and night life as well. So I
> spent all my time in cabarets, night clubs, strip joints, bars, *barras*,
> *boîtes*, dives, saloons, *cantinas*, *cuevas*, *caves* or caves. . . . Some-
> times, when I had nothing to do after work at three or four in the
> morning I would make my way to El Sierra or Las Vegas or El
> Nacional, the night club I mean not the hotel, to talk to a friend
> who's the emcee there or look at the chorus flesh or listen to the
> singers, but also to poison my lungs with smoke and stale air and
> alcohol fumes and be blinded forever by the darkness. That's how
> I used to live and love that life and there was nobody or nothing
> that could change me.

O.K., fine; rather lengthily said, but we obediently settle down
for a tour of tropical night life. We meet a bongo drummer; we
don't quite catch his name, but it doesn't matter, since he talks in
Silvestre's voice, though he seems to be hung up on a little gringo
chick called Vivian Smith-Corona, whereas Silvestre is hung up
on Cuba Venegas, a local singer who looks better than she sings.
We go back to Silvestre, who is trying to tell us about a great
Negro singer, La Estrella, but the story keeps unravelling on him
—maybe because this is "an island of double and triple entendres
told by a drunk idiot signifying everything." Our eyes begin to
sting in the smoke and stale air. Now an American tourist, a writer
called Campbell, writes a funny story about a walking stick he

bought fresh off the ferry from Miami, and about taking another off an outraged native because he thinks it's his, and then his wife produces *her* version of what happened, and he rewrites it (or perhaps this is meant to be a translation by somebody called Rine), and the wife does a second version, and then we get pages of the anti-works of the late Bustrófedon, and the above-mentioned parodies of Cuban authors on Trotsky's assassination, which might be the best part of the book if you're Cuban (it seems funny even in English), but by now Arsenio Cué is revving up his convertible, and we blearily realize that, whatever happened in Havana in 1958, this book isn't going to tell us. "Mare Metaphor is loosed upon the world. Rhetoric of the nation?" Cabrera Infante asks, as if hopeful that his stream of literary consciousness will somehow apply to Cuba. He applies it, but it doesn't stick. Though his translators work furiously to shore up the slippage, throwing in anachronisms like space-shot terminology, the slang word "gig," and "Agnewsticism," they can't keep the gobbets of "Esperanglish" and the limp avant gardisms and the liquorish 4 a.m. foolery from pulling loose from any reality we care to recognize or consent to care about.

The eclectic culture of Americanized Havana, Cabrera Infante seems to be saying, deserves an eclectic novel as its nostalgic monument. But eclecticism is itself a borrowed method by now. *Ulysses*, static and claustrophobic enough, is energized throughout by the tactful, evocative prose of a master short-story writer, and it draws for its allusions upon the immense perspective of European culture since Homer. Cabrera Infante writes run-on, like Faulkner but without Faulkner's intensity of self-hypnosis, and his perspective extends little farther than the mass culture of the giant nation to the north; the horizon of felt history for him appears to be Trotsky's murder in 1940. The book crucially lacks tact—the tension and economy that enforce themselves when method and material are in close touch. A mass of memories and a heap of verbal invention have been hopefully tossed toward one another, but confusion isn't fusion.

That Latin America can produce adventurously original novels has been shown many times over, from Machado de Assiz on. A recent striking instance, and an instructive contrast to *Three*

Trapped Tigers, is Gabriel García Márquez's *One Hundred Years of Solitude.* Here an array of fantastic premises (substantial ghosts, everyday miracles, magic that works, a village so isolated only gypsies can find it, a man tattooed on every inch of his skin, a man who fathers seventeen sons by seventeen women, a family of repeating names and insatiable incest) is breezily set forth by topic sentences that seem jokes, and then maintained with an iron consistency and kept rolling until the amusing becomes the magnificent—a magnificent symbolic contraption expressing a family's fate, a continent's experience, and Time's impenetration of humanity. The novel's Olympian ease and its catholic acceptance of horror and splendor as they arise in this our "paradise of misery" could not have been achieved in the United States, and no European novel would contain its joyous emptiness, its awed memory of a world "so recent that many things lacked names, and in order to indicate them it was necessary to point." The book even has a texture all its own: a dense translucence, a flow of long paragraphs that yet do not linger, that feel laconic, like stories the teller and listener already obscurely share and that are being not so much invented as called from the shadows. Such a novel, unlike Infante's sophomoric farrago, has learned from other novels how to become itself.

Satire Without Serifs

PATRIOTISM, INC. *and Other Tales,* by Paul van Ostaijen, edited and translated from the Dutch by E. M. Beekman. 170 pp. University of Massachusetts Press, 1971.

THE ADVENTURES OF MAO ON THE LONG MARCH, by Frederic Tuten. 121 pp. Citadel, 1971.

Sans-serif type belongs to one of those futures that never occurred. Elegantly simple, jauntily functional, it was everything the Bauhaus thought modernity should be, yet except in posters and telephone books it never really caught on. As with so many oddities a revolution would sweep away, serifs exist for a purpose:

they help the eye pick up the shape of the letter. Piquant in little amounts, sans-serif in page-size sheets repels readership as wax paper repels water; it has a sleazy, cloudy look. Yet now we have two works of fiction so printed—the first in a 9-point sans fainter than sandpiper tracks, and the other in a narrow-column boldface sans that fairly stamps itself on the retina. What is being signalled? A defiant chic, a refreshing change.

By printing Paul van Ostaijen's *Patriotism, Inc., and Other Tales*, the University of Massachusetts Press, itself obscure enough, has rescued a poet, proseur, and seer of the twenties from obscurity. E. M. Beekman, the translator, in his rather defensive and fancy introduction, blames van Ostaijen's obscurity on his writing in "Dutch, that poor relation of Northern European languages." He adds, "Van Ostaijen's work is an indictment of the Monroe Doctrine in the world of literature." This false hare (the implication that American foreign policy of some sort has kept the Dutch language down) is but one of several that Mr. Beekman starts; in the high-flown style of easy indignation associated with "black humor" and its apologists, he terms this century "the fool of history." "Never before has there been such an unrelenting succession of absurdities. . . . When a pertinaciously sensitive and sensible mind encounters such a world he is horrified and terror-stricken." Supposedly, however, the century has, in compensation, produced "a flowering of satiric literature" that includes such rich-relation-language types as Mann, Joyce, Gide, Brecht, Beckett, Grass, Nabokov, and Bruce Jay Friedman. Defining satire, Mr. Beekman asserts:

> To expose an ulcerous growth the surgeon must be dextrous with his scalpel. A hatchet job does little to relieve pathology. But control, skill, and a passionate immunity to suffering can chance to alleviate the pains of man. Confronted by an ailing society these authors dissect in order to heal.

This trite opposition between a sick society and a dexterous, anti-septic-handed satirist/doctor does not do justice to the complexity of the humorous impulse. I doubt that many satirists since Voltaire have hoped to change the world even a bit. If a satirist is an entertainer, he is gunning for laughs, in those target areas just to one side of the audience's really sensitive spots; if the satirist is an artist, he is venting a disgust mixed with love, a scorn hard to distinguish from fascination, an indictment that includes himself. Satire less than this is one-dimensional journalism that cannot outlive its object; L. B. J.'s retirement turns *MacBird!* into trash, or, rather, reveals it as the trash it always was. Nineteenth-century America was prolific of vitriolic lampoons, yet the one book with verifiable political repercussions was a sentimental melodrama, *Uncle Tom's Cabin.* Mr. Beekman is wrong to call the satirist "kin to the ideal revolutionary." The ideal revolutionary—Washington, Robespierre, Lenin—is humorless. Illusions are destroyed not by ridicule but by better, more fiercely held illusions. Indeed, insofar as satire fosters the impression of an enemy met and dealt with, it reinforces, like philanthropy, the status quo; an abundance of satire typifies a reactionary and helpless society, such as imperial Rome. In all times, humor is a form of resignation; in modern times, it comes peculiarly charged with self-doubt and moral ambiguity. Kafka can be said to satirize the Austro-Hungarian bureaucracy as something frozen, ornate, inscrutable, and cruel. But his art begins, not ends, there; satire is the mere crust of his real matter—his own confession of incapacity, his heroes' lust for punishment and their pathetic willingness to enlist, if they can find the right official, in the workings of an absurd universe. Society is sick, no doubt, but only the coarsest modern writer would exempt himself as healthy.

Mr. Beekman does, later in his introduction, place satire in the right focus: "Its intention is to cut the reader into awareness." This seems to me excellent, and all that any art should be asked to do. Also excellent, at a guess, is Mr. Beekman's translation from the Dutch; at any rate, van Ostaijen's prose comes over as elliptical and limpid and unlike Mr. Beekman's own overwrought English.

Van Ostaijen is principally renowned in his native Belgium as a poet; his prose pieces, which he called "grotesques," were written after two books of verse had made him a conspicuous presence on the Flemish literary scene, and were not published until after his death, at the age of thirty-two, in 1928. Much of his short life was spent in circumstances of constraint: he began his career in the blockaded port of Antwerp, fled to Berlin in 1919 to escape imprisonment for political offenses against the Walloons, returned to Antwerp only to be drafted and sent back to Germany in the occupation forces, and, after a few years spent struggling with poverty and an addiction to cocaine, died in a Belgian tuberculosis sanitorium. His "grotesques" were mostly written in the Berlin years (1919–1921), and they illumine a bizarre Weimar world of huge inflation and savage political competition, of brothels and cafés, of Dada and jazz, of Dietrich bluebirds singing to Grosz audiences. Van Ostaijen worked for a time in Antwerp's city administration, and the theme of corporate organization runs through his work: "The City of Builders" describes a city where ordinances foster a mad accumulation of buildings; "The Lost House Key" shows a thriving "free city" where syphilis has become the *sine qua non* of citizenship; "Ika Loch's Brothel" and "Hierarchy" are concerned with the organization of whorehouses; "The General" proposes organizing armies by sexual character, in battalions of sadists, masochists, homosexuals, fetishists, and so on; and "Patriotism, Inc." imagines an international conspiracy, among the conservative parties of Teutonia and Fochany, to rig provocative incidents in each other's countries and thereby promote mutual chauvinism. Though politically obsessed and a convicted activist, van Ostaijen did not think of his satire as social therapy; in a Berlin letter he noted, "Wrote a novella in which I try to make monkeys of people. Positive criticism: baloney. . . . People aren't worth criticising. Only material for burlesque novellas."

All these stories are rather schematically developed, with few sensual details and turns of characterization. Though resembling Kafka in his obsession with officialdom, van Ostaijen is incapable of such a passage as this:

> I was not at all certain whether I had any advocates, I could not find out anything definite about it, every face was unfriendly, most people who came toward me and whom I kept meeting in the corridors looked like fat old women; they had huge blue and white striped aprons covering their entire bodies, kept stroking their stomachs and swaying awkwardly to and fro. I could not even find out whether we were in a law court. Some facts spoke for it, others against.

Here are a deep, puzzled humor, vivid particularization, and incalculable, dreamlike turns. Van Ostaijen's mind, at least in his fiction, tends to travel straight to the mark. His pages yield a harvest of acute if dispiriting epigrams:

> For values are only safe when he who is entrusted with their preservation stands above them, when the preserver is not a dupe at the same time.

> Hypochondria is eroticism in atrophied form.

> Do not forget that masculine eroticism has an undertone of melancholy, even when this masculine eroticism is heterosexual. If it is homosexual, however, then the melancholy is both in the object and in the subject.

Expatiating on the subject of war in the persona of "The General," van Ostaijen teems with dark ideas:

> War is the clashing of two parties with the goal of separating the conqueror from the conquered. There is no significant child's game that does not spring from the love of war. Nonsense to believe that we suggest the idea of war to children. A warlike element resides in the sperm.

> The most meaningful and universal trait of humanity, more so than love, is the urge for battle. . . . The essence of every law is to aspire to curb instinct. Instinct wants to kill. Clearly.

> The British psyche . . . has conquered its warlike instinct with a rationally individualistic philosophy of life. They don't know what war is. They only know plunder.

> Actual wars are a cheapening of the ideal war. . . . Actual wars are a test of economic conditions, not of martialism.

With striking contemporaneity, van Ostaijen finds the alternative to war in drugs. "When negotiating for peace," the General tells us, "narcotics are unquestionably important. The so-called primitive peoples have already taught us this. . . . The chieftains gather together and immediately a pipe with opium or Indian hemp is passed from man to man. A peaceful mood cannot be far behind. . . . Next to war, gentle peace is therefore dearest to me. And so I am willing to smoke the opium pipe. And so will all those others who have only waged war to actualize the personality they contemplated."

"To actualize the personality they contemplated"—this is the talk not of a satirist but of a visionary. Van Ostaijen is fascinated by organization because he detests it. Ika Loch, the proprietress of a brothel, is a play on the Dutch *logika* (logic), and her authoritarian mismatching of customer and whore results in the murder of the lovely Promethea, who symbolizes art; the scandal enhances the fame of Ika's establishment. Though in "questions of business management" Ika possesses "a real talent for organization," she cannot perceive that "a head and a neck, as a totality, are still not the same thing as the sum of the two parts."

In the short prose poems, van Ostaijen projects synthesis out of derangement. A cocaine user, he writes out of "that peace of heart and tranquillity of spirit [that] could be his only after his retina became threadbare from the maddest realities of light." He writes sometimes in the texture of a drug trip:

> You must lie on the ground. Thus, across the ground, past much ochre and brown, past much green, your eye gains the bark and again the green, the old and the young and finally this gray, this crazy gray green, which is so exhausting that your eye flees to earth and slowly, only slowly, awakens to the motion of a brown hay wagon in the midst of the yellow-brown bed of needles.

And in "Bankruptcy Jazz," an electric confusion of phrases, placards, scenes, and oddly hydraulic jazz (*The jazz overflows into the street*, one direction reads) sums up an era when wheelbarrowloads of inflated currency were trundled along Europe's cobblestoned squares, between the Gothic cathedrals and the rococo city halls, when Charlie Chaplin might as well have been the government, when jazz tumbled everywhere and Dada took upon itself the slogans of salvation: "DADA is universal reason which the superidiocy of everybody can attain," "DADA is not an artistic Business, but the FORMULA of BANKRUPTCY," "JOIN DADA." The scenario, in its sans-serif spasms, has the fluttering fury of a moth beating against a street lamp. This volume of prose affords glimpses of a poetic genius, and we put it down hoping that soon Mr. Beekman and the University of Massachusetts Press will give us, in a slightly darker and bigger typeface, van Ostaijen's poetry.

*

If Dada was, as "Bankruptcy Jazz" proclaims, Nietzsche Without Nietzsche, a definition of Pop could be Mao Without Mao. *The Adventures of Mao on the Long March*, by Frederic Tuten, wears a nice comic-book jacket by Roy Lichtenstein and is described by Susan Sontag on the inside flap as "soda pop, a cold towel, or a shady spot under a tree for culture-clogged footsoldiers on the American long march." Broken into components, the hundred and twenty-one pages of Mr. Tuten's opus consist of (1) twenty-seven pages of straight history of the Long March (October 1934–October 1935), done in a neutral, factual tone, as by a fellow-travelling *Reader's Digest;* (2) thirty-six and a half pages of quotations in quotation marks, from unidentified sources (such as, diligent research discovers, Hawthorne's *Marble Faun*, Walter Pater's *Marius the Epicurean*, and Engels' *Origin of the Family, Private Property, and the State*); (3) twelve and a half pages of parody, of Faulkner, Hemingway, Kerouac, the Steinbeck/Farrell school, the Malamud/Bellow school, and of modern-art criticism in numerous schools; (4) nineteen pages of a supposed interview with Chairman Mao in 1968, in which the Chairman reveals himself as an avid subscriber to American highbrow periodicals and a keen devotee of Godard films and Minimal Art; (5) twenty-six pages of what might be considered normal novelistic substance —imaginary encounters and conversations. For an example of (5): Chairman Mao is alone in his tent, after the strain of the Tatu campaign. He hears the rumble of a tank :

> A tank, covered with peonies and laurel, advances toward him. Mao thinks the tank will crush him, but it presently clanks to a halt. The turret rises, hesitantly. Greta Garbo, dressed in red sealskin boots, red railway-man's cap, and red satin coveralls, emerges. She speaks: "Mao, I have been bad in Moscow and wicked in Paris, I have been loved in every capital, but I have never met a MAN whom I could love. That man is you Mao, Mao mine."
> Mao considers this dialectically. The woman is clearly mad. Yet she is beautiful and the tank seems to work. How did she get through the sentries? Didn't the noise of the clanking tank treads wake the entire camp? Where is everyone?
> Mao realizes the camp is empty. He is alone with Garbo. But Mao has always been more attracted to Harlow than to Garbo. What should he do not to break her romantic little heart?

"Madame, I have work to do," says Mao gently.

"It can wait till tomorrow, my love," she answers, unzipping her coveralls.

Mao thinks: "After all, I have worked hard and do deserve a rest." But an internal voice answers him: "Rest only after socialism."

"My Mao, this is no way to treat a woman who has made a long journey to be with you."

"But what of my wife?"

"Ah, that is an old bourgeois ploy, Mao mine."

Mao succumbs, and in the tent recites to her the entirety of the famous conclusion to Pater's *The Renaissance*, wherein we are entreated to "burn always with this hard, gemlike flame."

The whole episode is, like others in the book, charming, and it illustrates how well Mr. Tuten handles deadpan fantasy; except for a rare smirk like "her romantic little heart," a chaste solemnity rules the book. The tone is hard-edged, straight, dry, lyrical—anything but facetious. The tone, and the pamphlet-like type, smooth the different textures of this outrageous collage into an oddly reasonable unity. We never doubt that a lucid intelligence is in control; unlike many experiments of fictional assemblage, *The Adventures of Mao* never sinks into self-display, never becomes the mounted Kleenexes and tangerine peels of an author's private life. Mr. Tuten, in his jacket photograph, is looking not at us but at the flame of a match that is about to light his cigarette; he is wearing long hair and a wristwatch and has no biography. The contents of his book reveal nothing of him but his attitude.

And what is that attitude? What is *The Adventures of Mao* saying? Is it satirical? In general, when confronted with, say, a giant toothpaste tube of sewn canvas or a silkscreen of soup cans, we are predisposed to assume satiric content; our liberal prejudices and romantic aesthetics (in favor of trees, naked women, sunsets, and bowls of fruit) can accept any number of wry putdowns of our comfortably deplorable mass-trash society. But works viewed this way need only a glance. The more rewarding and plausible assumption, I think, is that the artist was obscurely delighted—"turned on"—by toothpaste tubes and soup cans, and that the ancient impulse of mimesis has led him to lift these things from the flow of transient impressions and to cast them into enduring form.

Mr. Tuten *likes* Chairman Mao, is the first message of the novel. The schoolbook account of the Long March inspires admiration on the flat level of propaganda. Sub-heroically (as Homer dimples Hector's heroism with glimpses of the private man), Mr. Tuten portrays Mao as sensitive to criticism of his poetry, as self-doubting and diffident and erotically wistful. In one of the funniest episodes, Mao lies awake coveting Eva Braun and Mussolini's mistress ("Claretta, what was the marvellous creature but the Mediterranean itself") but *not* Mrs. Roosevelt and Señora Franco ("a rosary-kissing midget, as sexy as a decayed turnip"). Mr. Tuten seems to be confessing that his Mao is a figment, a poster personality in a whimsical canon; he likes him as the author of the Gospel of John liked Jesus, but with the difference that he knows the Logos is a myth. Still, this is not satire, and in Mao's spirited championing of the bourgeois avant garde we reach a level of serious statement:

> "Pragmatically speaking, I like the opulent severity of this art, Minimal or ABC, because it both fills the imagination with the baroque by way of dialectical reaction to the absolute starkness of the object, and denudes the false in art and in life. [Such] work is like the Long March, a victory over space and time, a triumph of the necessary over the unnecessary, and, above all, it is like Marxism, or should I say like Heraclitus."

The American interviewer finds this enthusiasm "astonishing" and the Chinese interpreter exclaims, "To be honest, Chairman Mao, hearing all this talk from you confuses and disturbs me." It is, of course, impossible for Mao to be saying these things, but not—and herein the interest, the seriousness—implausible. When, in the same interview, he asserts that

> "youth is never reactionary; youth is progressive in time and hence always in the avant-garde, hence never wrong in spirit, hence *never* to be satirized,"

the statement originates from a profound depth, where the Free World's youth-proud greening merges with the mind that unleashed the Red Guards upon the entrenched Establishment of Communist China. We are confronted, in this elevation of youngness to a moral absolute, in this denial of any possibility of venerable wisdom and selective conservation, with something truly *other* than the reasonable liberalism and sentimental romanticism that have shaped our radically imperfect world.

The ideological fabric of *The Adventures of Mao* is deliciously complicated by Mr. Tuten's heavy reliance, for authority in aesthetic matters, upon fusty old wizards like Hawthorne and Pater —and Pater, it should be said, holds up nobly in this curious context. Another complication is that while the battles of the Long March are presented with the heroic generality of a newspaper recap, vivid and bloody and inglorious episodes of our own Civil War, as described in Whitman's *Specimen Days* and John William De Forest's *Miss Ravenel's Conversion*, are interspersed. The warrior Mao, whose revolution, after all, was bought with millions of lives, is thus displaced, along with the Mao who, on cultural matters, declared (at Yenan in 1942):

> There is in fact no such thing as art for art's sake, art that stands above classes, art that is detached from or independent of politics. Proletarian literature and art are part of the whole proletarian revolutionary cause; they are, as Lenin said, cogs and wheels in the whole revolutionary machine.

For this implacable and dynamic dogmatism Mr. Tuten substitutes a "longing for the great simple primeval things." Mao's interviewer tells him, "All your thoughts have given me the desire to be inert." Tuten's Mao is a suave decadent, whose languor, nevertheless, has a certain appositeness to revolution. The book's last sentence (quoted from Oscar Wilde's *De Profundis*) sounds a call for purification: "I feel sure that in elemental forces there is purification, and I want to go back to them and live in their presence."

So, in part, was Dada a call for purification—a purgation of cant through nonsense. Like Pop, it embraced its age's random materials with a frantic hug that transcended criticism, cynicism, or satire. Such violent gestures seem to ask for revolution in human consciousness; what they achieve is, more modestly, a refreshing of conventional artistic forms. *The Adventures of Mao on the Long March* provides an intelligent, taut, and entertaining change from conventional novels. Its substance is satisfyingly solid and satisfyingly mysterious. Like any work of art, it could not be mindlessly replicated; a sequel might slip into being a mere anthology. Nor would it be easy to locate another symbolic person as fabulous and germane as Mao. As is, Mr. Tuten's studied scrapbook, like van Ostaijen's precipitous scenario, contains the live motion of a novel within a jagged form that does "cut the reader into awareness."

Bombs Made Out of Leftovers

BAD NEWS, by Paul Spike. 152 pp. Holt, Rinehart & Winston, 1971.

BEING THERE, by Jerzy Kosinski. 142 pp. Harcourt Brace Jovanovich, 1971.

THE BARK TREE, by Raymond Queneau, translated from the French by Barbara Wright. 281 pp. New Directions, 1971.

We have with us this week three, ah, experimental works of fiction. In our struggles to understand them, we shall depend heavily on the dust jackets. The jacket of the first, *Bad News*, by Paul Spike (jacket by Push Pin Studios), tells us that the author, "a member of our youngest generation of fiction writers," was born in 1947 and that his work, published mostly in the *Columbia Review*, "could be classified as 'experimental' à la Borges or Pynchon"—though it is not Borges or Pynchon who comes handsomely through with a puff but William Burroughs, to wit: ". . . at once a beautiful and disquieting book, in which seemingly commonplace happenings suddenly open into other planetary perspectives."

Though the jacket is at some pains to avoid creating the (correct) impression that this is a collection of short pieces, it does let slip the word "stories," and stories they are—nine of them. They do, however, contain recurring characters, and they are wired for cross-currents, and some are so episodic that they might have been sliced another way and still be "stories." After O. Henry came the epiphany, the kind of short fiction that an irreverent friend of mine use to call the "so what?" story. Now comes its successor, the "so nothing" story. Mr. Spike owes more to Barthelme than to Borges; the "other planetary" perspectives intrude upon a this-planetary texture of *blague* and *Dreck*, of parody and an unimpeachably deadpan tone, of obscene technology and mechanical sex, of stillborn indignations and friendly puzzlements and, at the end, a curt, fishy-eyed stare, as from a cocktail-party companion upon whom one has, with some sudden warmth of interest or desire, unwittingly presumed. Not that Mr. Spike's cool is perfected yet; there is still something collegiate in his fascination with smelly socks and the word "mess," in his unfeigned delight at cooking up sexual descriptions, in his imperfectly concealed worry that prose fiction ought to amount to more than nervous anti-silence, like the overlapping crackle of a radio tuned between stations. Certain persistent messages want to break through the static. Mr. Spike's generation is one born to riot, and the telegraphy of social concern comes naturally to him:

> "Calcutta has an epidemic and the guerillas won't pump out the Pittsburgh enclave for months, which directly affects all of the East Coast. How about this submarine highway in the Pacific?"
> "You agreed to leave that route for Russia, a token perhaps, they'll go for it. The American government will iron that out."

Certain public events—nothing, naturally, prior to 1947, or even 1957—have sunk into his generation's consciousness, and they surface with symbolic portent; assassination is a recurring trauma. "Okay then I'm paranoid but maybe if the Kennedy family had been a little more paranoid? . . . The DIC is responsible for those assassinations, that's my opinion. . . . In November, 1963, over 400 New Yorkers fell down with 'speck attack' raging in their chests." And our accursed affluence, of course, takes its licks:

> Comfort is a surface, a straight line. The emptiness of comfort astounds man. It is like the world's most powerful ray gun.

Unexpectedly, the "emptiness that comes in the world's biggest ice-cream cone" includes the sexual wealth that the post-Korea generation has created:

> Nikolaus thought how odd it was that now that he could have all the sex he wanted, the world was becoming more and more messy.

The medicine of love unsettlingly merges with the diseases of pollution and aggression:

Man is the dirtiest animal. His pollution is driving him to look for an edge of the world which he can fall off. Yet he loves like no other animal. . . . And his love and beauty, in a sense, are a pollution to the world. They spray emotion into green vegetation.

But these thematic glimpses are mere footsteps in the underbrush of verbal celebration, a young man's luxuriant revenge on the media that have nearly driven him mad. His gifts of mimicry are keen. They range from college-humor jesting ("The Conference Man") to mock letters ("Box 456") and memorabilia ("The Diary of Noel Wells") and computer tapes ("Multi") to a fluid, sprightly Surrealism ("Specks Saga," "A Good Revolution"). The manner of presentation amounts to more than the things presented; the most tactile imagery, apart from the bodies of the young ladies who are handled, comes in the inventory of the hardware store where one of the young heroes works. The language, especially in the takeoffs of detective fiction, drolly bursts with exasperation at saying, after trillions of words of written English, anything at all:

> His hands ticked away in his pockets now. A pink rash surfaced lightly across the top of his pectorals.

> The sun is beginning to boil the atmosphere into a tight grease.

> Her face was reminiscent of a pile of gears softly rounded into one another and covered with dreadful calm.

Bad News is as much a protest against fiction as it is fiction, and since it lacks pitiable characters, a sustained action, and an earnestly felt theme, we do not wish it—as Dr. Johnson said of *Paradise Lost* —longer than it is. Yet it has its poetry and its fidelity to the discontinuous, overpackaged, pre-trivialized way we live now. "The problem is," Spike himself explains, intruding to discourse with one of his characters, "there is a bomb here made out of leftovers." The character responds, "I have nothing to do." "Right" is Spike's answer. "But there is something here," the character insists. Such an affirmation is even weaker than that of Beckett's minimal pilgrims. News is what fiction—nouvelles, novels—once was; Mr. Spike's title implies that since "good" (coherent, morally convinced) stories are impossible, bad news is better than none.

*

The dust jacket of *Being There* tells us that the author, Jerzy Kosinski, was born in Poland in 1933, and that the first of his two earlier novels, *The Painted Bird*, has been translated into thirty-two languages, and the second, *Steps*, into twenty-nine. One wonders what the missing three are—Urdu? Korean? Arawak? *Being There*, simultaneously with its American publication, is being published in England, Holland, Germany, and France, and the flap copy, with its promise of a "modern parable" and a "quintessential anti-hero," seems to be warming up an international audience in easy Esperanto. The description of the book, however, is twelve lines shorter than the description of the author, and, bizarrely, at the end of the novel the typography suggests that Kosinski's biography is the last chapter—two pages' worth of his degrees, his fellowships, his professorships, his awards, his translations. In short, the author, not the novel, is the product being pushed. Which is shrewd, since the novel, like its hero, barely exists.

The hero is called Chance. He is an illiterate foundling kept by a rich old man known, with a simplicity too ominous, as the Old Man. Chance has two activities: he tends the Old Man's garden (Madam, I'm Adam) and watches television. After the Old Man dies, lawyers discover that Chance's existence has generated no external evidence—no driver's license, no credit cards, no tax records, not even dental records. He is cast out of the garden, and instantly encounters (hello, Eve) EE, the wife of another very rich old man, Rand. Everywhere, Chance creates an excellent impression, and he comports himself very well; gardening and television-watching seem to be at least as adequate a preparation for adult life as a college education. Though he doesn't know how to read or make love beyond the preliminaries shown on the idiot box, he can make speeches that win the heart not only of EE but of the President of the United States. As the saga ends, Chance, a total nonentity four days before, has the Vice-Presidential nomination in his pocket. No doubt there is a lot in this, from political satire (Chance = Agnew) to philosophical allegory ("being there" = Heidegger's *Dasein*). Also, there is some kind of joke on McLuhanite coolness; Chance is a walking television screen: people "began to exist, as on TV, when one turned one's eyes on them. . . . The same was true of him." The dust jacket, helpful to a fault, calls Chance "prelapsarian man" and asks, "Is Chance the technocrat of the future? . . . Or is he Rousseauesque, with a touch of natural goodness to which men respond?" Tune in next parable. Myself, I prefer to see him as the blind Chance that rules the universe, into which people touchingly read omniscience and benevolence and anthropomorphic Divinity.

All this symbolic superstructure rests on a realistic base less substantial than sand. Rand has one amusing, almost lifelike speech. Chance's sensations when he appears on television, "the cameras . . . licking up the image of his body," can be felt. There is one sharp image, of "frosty sculptures," in rooms of vague furniture. Otherwise, the texture of events is thin, thin, preposterously thin. The rich and powerful may be stupid, but they would not mistake a comatose illiterate for a financial wizard. A hermit might be innocent, but his body would know how to achieve an erection. Fortune may be arbitrary in bestowing her favors, but she is not totally berserk. When a character in the book expresses incredulity at Chance's abrupt and baseless fame, he is appealing to laws of probability that have been suspended. There is not enough leverage even to spring a laugh. No two things are incongruous, because hardly anything in *Being There* is *there*.

You could say that this is an immigrant's impression of America, an "other planetary perspective." But compare Nabokov; also an immigrant, from the same Slavic hemisphere as Kosinski, he assiduously put himself to school with American particulars and came up with a portrait—not only in *Lolita* but in the background of *Pnin* and the poem "Pale Fire"—of the United States grotesquely and tellingly acute in its details. Mr. Kosinski's portrait expresses little but the portraitist's diffident contempt for his subject—the American financial and political Establishment. He does not enough hate it to look hard at it; the result is not even a cartoon. Stylized also were the nameless villages of the Polish marsh in *The Painted Bird*, but those scenes were in Kosinski's blood, and the plausibility gaps were filled with an experienced terror that redeemed the parade of Grand Guignol episodes from being· merely sensational. In *Steps*, an adult man's erotic explorations were interwoven with these same horrific villages, and incriminated in the same sinister cruelty. Perhaps the intention of

Being There was to transfer this sinisterness to an America be-fogged by media and ruled by stuffed shirts. The result is feebly pleasant—a dim and truncated television version of those old Hollywood comedies wherein a handsome bumpkin charms the swells and makes good. Unlike Kosinski's other novels, *Being There* is not painful to read, which in his special case is not a virtue.

Raymond Queneau was born in 1903, in Le Havre; his first novel, *Le Chiendent*, published in 1933, has now been translated into English, by Barbara Wright, as *The Bark Tree*. The dust jacket tells us that Robbe-Grillet has "hailed" this book as "a new-wave novel twenty years ahead of its time," and the translator's intro-duction presents further testimonials, accrediting *The Bark Tree* as a classic and Queneau as a giant in the generation of modernists that succeeded Proust and Joyce. The book, we are told, evolved from Queneau's attempt to translate Descartes' *Discourse on Method* into French as it is really spoken, dismissing the "con-ventions of style, spelling, and vocabulary that date from the grammarians of the sixteenth century and the poets of the seven-teenth." On the other hand, Queneau, a mathematician and a pedant, chose to regulate his excursion into demotic philosophy—which became a novel—with rules as strict as those of a ballade or rondeau; seven chapters, each of thirteen sections, observe within themselves the classical unities of place, time, and action. In ad-dition, there are repetitions of image and phrase planted for the author's personal pleasure, and the reader can subliminally sense a high degree of coherence and consistency beneath the surface of this rather sprawling and absurd tale.

The main plot concerns Étienne Marcel, a Parisian bank em-ployee who lives in the suburb of Obonne, as he is observed by Pierre Le Grand, a speculative member of the idle rich, while Étienne makes the transition from flat silhouette to substantial human existence and back to flat silhouette. Étienne is the Cartesian man: when he begins to think (he suddenly notices in a store window two rubber ducks floating in a hat to advertise that the hat is waterproof), he is. From the window of his commuting train, he then observes a tiny sign advertising "CHIPS" and determines, as an *acte gratuit*, to visit this place, in the factory slum of Blagny; thereby he puts himself, and his observer, Pierre, and his son, Théo, and his wife, Alberte, and his wife's admirer, Narcense, in touch with a raffish crowd that includes a concierge, an abortionist, a magician, a sailor, an old junk dealer, and a remarkably presumptuous dwarf. This impinging activates a rumor that the junk dealer, Old Taupe, is a rich miser, and a set of frantic schemes to appropriate his fortune, mainly by means of his marriage to a young waitress, Ernestine, who unaccountably dies during a wedding feast that reminded this dazed reader of the Babar books. And there are love affairs and hangings and dreams and dialogues about the meaning of nothing and, for a climax, a war between the French and the Etruscans.

The Bark Tree is full, like *Bad News*, of nonsense and, like *Being There*, of naked contrivance. It is superior to both these books in the rigor of its pattern and in the richness of its matter. A palpable Paris takes shape through a multiplicity of fine strokes:

> Four, five, six drops of water. Some people, anxious about their straw hats, raise their noses. Description of a storm in Paris. In summer. The timid take to their heels; others raise the collars of their jackets, which gives them an air of bravado. It begins to smell of mud. Many people prudently look for shelter, and when the rain is at its height, all that can be seen are blackish groups, clustered around doorways, like mussels around the pile of a pier.

Queneau's wonderful gift for simile tempts one to compile a list:

> His nose has taken on the fiery color of Campari and his eyes are sparkling like lemonade.

> They plunge into their reciprocal destinies, like shrimps into the sand. . . .

> They fill the glasses with wine, which glasses take on the joyous appearance of druggists' display bottles.

> The horizon, that universal castrator . . .

> Bits of vegetables or meat, which had jumped out of the dishes like absurd acrobats, were scattered all over [the table], wilting in little pools of gravy.

And above these odd events, these overanimated souls and artifacts, a real humanity presides; Queneau not only permits each character the dignity of eloquence but rises himself to a fury of sarcasm when he contemplates the chauvinistic farce of the "Etruscan" war: "even the strategists . . . said they'd never seen a simpler, easier, more amusing war."

Queneau's sympathy peculiarly falls upon the banal—upon the empty routines, that is, whereby human ordinariness propels itself along the quotidian. He says of certain conventional greetings that "their apparent complexity concealed a profound simplicity." Pierre, overhearing some clichés about the weather, "notes with some bitterness that these banalities correspond perfectly to reality." Perhaps, since Flaubert, banality is *the* challenge to serious novelists: the gales of romance have died, and the novelist is a sailor on a close reach, trying to use the constant wind of ordinary living to make some kind of headway against it. The melodrama of Queneau's plot is manufactured by the characters, as a vacation from boredom; his own vacation comes in the intervals of metaphysical speculation, and these—though he would not have written the book without them—seem rather mannered and pat. When Pierre talks to the reader about his boredom and his masks, or when Étienne drops the aphorism that "there isn't any gospel, there are only works of fiction," we are aware of an author pressing his claims upon our intelligence; when Ernestine, dying, formulates death as the disappearance of "the little voice that talks in your head when you're by yourself," we are in the presence of human experience and shared terror. Gertrude Stein said it: literature isn't remarks. What we want from fiction, and what fiction is increasingly loath to give us, is vicarious experience. Exiled from the great naïveté that nurtured the 19th-century masterworks of the novel, Queneau yet is old enough—humane enough—to spin, amid a metaphysics of relativity and uncertainty, affectionate images of human life in its curiosity, rapacity, and fragility. Compared to Queneau, our two other authors seem tired; a distance that cannot be exactly measured in generations or wars separates them from an instinctive belief that men are significant and that art must embody enduring principles.

A note on the translation: Barbara Wright did not set herself an easy task, and her version does permit us to glimpse an original whose prose has not only a poetic economy but, in dialogue, a slangy, punning richness. However, either this text was carelessly proofread or some of her renderings are too subtle by half. "Squite" (for "it's quite"), "wz" and "shdve" (for "was" and "should have"), "etxras" (for "extras"), and "sore span" (for "saucepan") are doubtless intentional equivalents of delicate audial distortions in the French; but what about "fairtish," "neved," and "everwhere"? These occur in dialogue, and "aand" appears in expository prose, and "becaues" in a letter in which nothing else is misspelled. Something wrong here?

A note on the price: the dust jacket calmly asks nine dollars and fifty cents for *The Bark Tree*. It is two hundred and eighty-one pages long. The Novel may or may not be dead; soon we won't be able to buy into its casket and see.

Mortal Games

THE FLIGHT OF ICARUS, by Raymond Queneau, translated from the French by Barbara Wright. 192 pp. New Directions, 1973.

ALL FIRES THE FIRE *and Other Stories*, by Julio Cortázar, translated from the Spanish by Suzanne Jill Levine. 152 pp. Pantheon, 1973.

Modernism, we are told, is passé; the Harvard English Department lists a course, "American Modernism," that treats of "American writing from 1900 to 1930," and another, "The Modern Period," that is "an introduction to the poetry, fiction, intellectual prose, and criticism of the period from 1899 to 1939." But what has come after? What now? In the uncertain twilight, where the avant garde has become the rear guard, strange loomings and mistaken perspectives bemuse us. Surely, we suppose, Raymond Queneau, a modern whose masterpiece *The Bark Tree* appeared in 1933, is dead and silent. Not so, for here is a lively new novel, *The Flight of Icarus*. And surely Julio Cortázar, the Brussels-born, Paris-dwelling Argentine expatriate who contrived such frolicsome experiments as *Hopscotch* and *62: A Model Kit*, is, as his handsome jacket photograph attests, a young man. Not so, for from the back flap of his latest book to appear in the United States, *All Fires the*

Fire and Other Stories, we learn that Sr. Cortázar, with his turned-up raincoat collar and his downy cheeks, was born in 1914. So he, scarcely less than Queneau, harks back to the brave first third of this century, when Literature hobnobbed with Life as an equal, when young Dedaluses set forth to forge in their souls' smithies the uncreated consciences of their respective races, when innovations in fictional technique could be dubbed "revolutionary," and when artistic, cerebral excitement carbonated a page of prose so that it tingled in the reader like champagne. The late Pablo Neruda, puffing Cortázar's stories, describes them as "fabrications, myths, contradictions, and mortal games." The final phrase puts well the tension between an earnest sense of reality and a playful sense of active mind that modernism brought to such a fine and precarious pitch—especially precarious in this country, where naturalism tends to breed sprawling verbal slums and, in reaction, anti-naturalists of the most antic, heedless, and dandyish sort.

Queneau, in *The Flight of Icarus*, is something of a dandy himself. The novel, written in the attenuated form of a play containing no fewer than seventy-four short scenes, takes place in Paris in 1895, when absinthe is still drunk, the bicycle and the "automobile carriage" are freshly in motion, Reason rules a feast of gourmet dining, and authors busily function as a superior type of tradesman. Icarus, our hero, escapes from a novel being written by Hubert Lubert, "a novelist by profession, by vocation, even, and . . . of some renown." Lubert, suspecting a character-napping by his rival Surget, hires the farcically inept detective Morcol ("The man who follows adulterous women and finds lost sheep. He has appeared in many novels under different names. A second Vidocq. A second Lecoq"). Morcol makes a number of brilliant deductions but nevertheless lets the escapee remain undetected under his very nose. Icarus has drifted into a low-life café and, having taken his first "flight" on absinthe, is—so appealingly has Lubert designed him—taken in and supported by a prostitute identified as LN. The plot spins faster: other characters escape from other works in progress; their frantic creators fight duels amongst themselves; Icarus buys from a bookstall by the Seine *The Principles of Mechanics* ("the less he understood it the more he enjoyed it") and goes to work for the mechanic M. Berrrier (*sic*), while LN

turns from prostitution to the production of bicycle bloomers;
Morcol retires, though the lost-character business is booming;
most of the fictional escapees creep back into their books, or somebody else's; Icarus and LN attempt flight in a giant kite, and fall.
"Everything happened as was anticipated," Lubert assures us at
the end, shutting his manuscript complacently.

It is hard to imagine a novel lighter than this that would significantly engage the mind. Yet *The Flight of Icarus*, though it is
continuously absurd, never strikes us as silly. The style is chaste
and swift, ornamented with inventions translated as "obnubilat-
ing," "spondulics," "ostreophagists," "petroliphagious," "cantharo-
drome." The many threads of the cat's-cradle plot are complicated
and regathered with an impressive efficiency. The literary satire is
sharp though good-humored; Robbe-Grillet especially seems the
butt of such speculations as

> Perhaps that is how it will be for all of us, one day. We won't have
> any more characters. . . . The novel will perhaps not be dead, but
> it won't have characters in it anymore. Difficult to imagine, a novel
> without characters. But isn't all progress, if progress exists, difficult
> to imagine?

Queneau's own characters are more or less aware that they are
caught in a novel. Lubert is preparing for Icarus a "melancholy
existence": "I want him to like moonlight, fairy roses, the exotic
types of nostalgia, the languors of Spring, fin-de-siècle neuroses—
all things that I personally abhor, but which go down well in the
present-day novel." Icarus, however, cries, "A fig for the neuras-
thenias, the neuroses, and the nostalgias of our contemporary
writers!" And, escaping the "dismal or disappointing love affairs,
with sessions in cosy, dusty apartments" that his author would have
arranged for him, he opts for technology: "personally, I'm much
more interested in theoretical mechanics, from the fall of heavy
bodies to the mechanism of a lock." Not only Icarus acknowledges
the matrix of novelistic cliché and melodrama; a waiter, observing
him and LN in a cafe, predicts (incorrectly) their fate, assuring
himself, "I've read a great many novels and I know what happens
next." And while the "fictional" characters are attempting, like
bumpkins in from the provinces, to make a go of it in mercantile

Paris, one "real" woman volunteers to become the heroine of a romantic novel. The confusion is slight. Objecting to the plot's basic fantasy, the reader might say that one does not meet fictional characters on the street; the answer would be that one is not on the street but reading a book, where one meets fictional characters all the time. The reader's demand, that is, for reality is turned back upon itself. The characters are uniformly real, "characters" or not. And the milieu is perfectly convincing. We have been there before, in the bicycle-obsessed frenzies of Jarry, in those enchanted pages of Proust where Marcel becomes an Adam among the fresh creations of the telephone, the automobile, the camera. Something in the French spirit embraced with special innocence and energy the inventions—toylike in their first forms—that equip and distinguish the modern age. The same spirit, perhaps traceable to a peculiar delight in Reason and its works, permits the French, uniquely, to produce works of art as intellectual, spare, and impudent as this, as spindly and nakedly theoretical as a primitive machine yet undeniably serious, even majestic.

Julio Cortázar is not so engaging a spirit as Queneau, and the eight pieces in *All Fires the Fire* suffer, in the way of collections, from comparison with one another—the story "Meeting" is less stunning than the title piece, and "Instructions for John Howell" ends less satisfyingly than "The Island at Noon." But in sum these eight "mortal games" correct this reviewer's previous impression (gained by that most thrifty of methods, bookstore perusal) that Cortázar was a decadent avant gardist, a rather desperate innovator snipping autobiography into eye-catching shapes. True, he cannot get started without a gimmick: there is always a fantastic premise or a startling formalistic deviation, and he does not have Borges' power of persuading us that the strangeness flows from the superior vision of a drastically refined sensibility. But, once the trick is established (and no two devices are alike in this set of eight), Cortázar pushes beyond it with surprising powers of realistic development. The first story, "The Southern Thruway," supposes that a traffic jam on the Sunday-night rush back to Paris is truly —as traffic jams often feel—of days and months in duration. The same little locality of cars inches forward together a few yards a day; a community develops. Food is shared, leaders emerge, the girl in the Dauphine sleeps with the engineer in the Peugeot and becomes pregnant by him, the man in the Caravelle behind the engineer commits suicide, a Porsche and a Mercury (the characters take on the names of their cars) peddle black-market provisions through the stalled lines, and so on. The conceit is fleshed out with so many solid details that in the end, when the jam mysteriously breaks and the cars, accelerating, separate, the reader feels as well as comprehends the allegorical meaning—the loss of community in this modern "mad race in the night among unknown cars, where no one knew anything about the others, where everyone looked straight ahead, only ahead."

The next story, "The Health of the Sick," supposes, far from incredibly, that a large family in Buenos Aires, to spare Mama the news that her son Alejandro has been killed in Montevideo, fabricates letters from him, and then invents an attendant string of lies and impostures as his absence lengthens into years, Mama's expected death being slow to arrive. A situation that could be broadly comedic, or politically satirical about the self-delusions of the bourgeoisie, instead deepens in a rather poignant direction: Mama, dying at last, reveals, as the reader has guessed some pages before, that she knows the truth and has been herself protecting the protective perpetrators of the illusion. The survivors then, receiving the last of the forged letters from the phantom Alejandro, find themselves wondering how they can break to him the news that Mama is dead. So something rather tender as well as eerie has been said about the fond and prevalent deceits of family life. Cortázar, though his methods can be jagged, is not mordant. "Nurse Cora," with its initially exasperating device of an interior monologue that shifts from person to person without so much as a paragraph indentation to signal transitions, in the end quite movingly portrays the death, in a hospital, of an adolescent boy as refracted through other minds (his nurse, his mother, his doctor) and reflected in the boy's own subtly traced surrender of pride, desire, and vitality. Another kind of dying concerns "Meeting," wherein the interior soliloquy of Che Guevara is imagined during the rebel invasion of Cuba; all seems lost, and the hopes of the revolution, the music of Mozart's "Hunt" Quartet, and the interweave of tree branches meet in the resigned mind of the exhausted revolutionary: "But it was enough to look at the treetop to feel that the will again put its chaos to order, imposed on it the sketch of the adagio that would someday pass into the final allegro and accede to a reality worthy of that name."

Juxtaposition is Sr. Cortázar's creative habit, and perhaps he is most himself when the juxtaposition is most harsh and least explained; an abyss, narrow as a black knife, gleams in the schizoid split. In "The Other Heaven," a man evidently walks back and forth between his stockbroker's job in Buenos Aires and a sinister arcade district of Paris. In "All Fires the Fire" (and there must be a better way of translating this), without even the rationale of daydream, a Roman gladiatorial fight and the breakup of a modern affair are alternately, accurately described; both events involve a sexual triangle and the cool cruelty of hedonism, and both end in a conflagration, as if a spark had leaped from the striking together of these two flinty worlds. There is also a third world—a far-off voice overheard during the telephone conversation of the modern couple, a "distant, monotonous voice" dictating numbers to "someone who doesn't speak." This little cross-connection reaches our own inner ear with the penetration of a symbolic detail (numbers, minutes, time is the final consuming fire) that is first of all a recognizable, common experience. Cortázar, sparing with his imagery, can achieve masterstrokes of sensation, especially when the sensation involves a gulf. In "Instructions for John Howell," a member of a theatre audience is suddenly enlisted as an actor in the play; a moment before he is pushed onstage, he feels to his left "the great cavern, something like a gigantic contained breath, which, after all, was the real world, where white shirt fronts and perhaps hats or upsweeps were gradually taking shape." And in "The Island at Noon" an airline steward, Marini, every other day at noon on the Rome–Teheran run looks down upon a little Greek island, Xiros, shaped like "a turtle whose paws were barely out of the water." The island becomes an obsession; "everything . . . was blurred and easy and stupid until it was time to lean toward the tail window, to feel the cold crystal like the boundary of an aquarium, where the golden turtle slowly moved in the thick blue." The sensation of looking down from a jet cannot be more beautifully described than that; the serene terror of jet travel—a tubular sample of the cheerful, plasticized mundane floats apparently motionless above an actual *mundus* reduced to the scale of a map and viewed from the top of a towering transparency that is, potentially, death—finds its fable here. And at his most intense Cortázar floods the gaps and mysteries of his tricky structures with a potent negativity—death, that invisible possibility, made electric and palpable, like the atmosphere before lightning. Whereas a curious immortality, the eternal sprightliness of pure mind, fills the airy spaces of Queneau. Both men convince us that surrealism has been elicited from them by the extremity of their ardor for reality—"the reality," Nathalie Sarraute has written, "to which we always return, in spite of our momentary betrayals and deviations, thus proving that, when all is said and done, we . . . prize it above all else." Their games repay our playing.

YOUNG AMERICANS

If at First You Do Succeed, Try, Try Again

DANCE THE EAGLE TO SLEEP, by Marge Piercy. 232 pp. Doubleday, 1970.

SINGLE FILE, by Norman Fruchter. 177 pp. Knopf, 1970.

"First Novels" are almost a genre to themselves; *Time* used to refer solemnly to a "First Novelist" with the same capitalization it employed for "First Lady" and "First Baseman." Second novels lack this irksome mystique; they are just supposed to be not as good—scrimped follow-ups of that first furious spending, strained variations on what came naturally. And, true, the two second novels at hand do seem less assured, less exuberantly annunciatory, than the first productions of their gifted young authors. Yet the flaws and deformities show stress *in a direction* and hint at why, in a historical moment when private concerns have lost moral priority to public awareness, it is difficult for an earnest spirit to write novels at all.

Marge Piercy's *Dance the Eagle to Sleep* describes—through the experiences of four major characters—the birth, short and somewhat blissful life, and violent death of a youth movement that one might call a nightmare version of S.D.S. The Piercy group is named the Indians, and early this year Bernardine Dohrn issued from the happy hunting ground of her hiding a proclamation "to express ourselves . . . as tribes at council." Miss Piercy places her history in a futuristic time (there has been a government shelling of Bedford-Stuyvesant, a President called the King of Clubs has been succeeded by one called the White Knight, a compulsory period of national service called the Nineteenth Year of Servitude has ben initiated), but the styles and equipment and brand names are all of our time, and at one point the author specifies that for "twenty-five years" the American people "had been sold a crusader's world of Armed Might Versus the Red Hordes." Twenty-five plus 1945 equals 1970. No matter. The futuristic conceit frees her to work on a large scale, to set her characters in the context of armies and headlines and—crucial to public-spirited agonists—*publicity*. The novel as the saga of private lives, soul journeys invisibly pursued under the heel of power (a tradition that Erich Auerbach's *Mimesis* sees originate in the anecdotes of the Gospels), does not suit our Roman times, when only kings and gods matter. Miss Piercy's heroes would be kings; that attempt failing, she caricatures them as gods. "Shawn felt useless and yet full of energy and light, a turned-on bulb, a ridiculous helium-taut balloon." "The blade hit [Corey] with its dull weight, making him fall. As it rolled over him smashing his bones, his heart burst free like a rising crow, and he fainted."

Shawn has been a member of a screamingly successful rock group. Corey is the part-Indian founder of the Indians; his pilgrimage begins with a vision of a buffalo who tells him (I drastically abridge this bisonian peroration):

> "I was the bread of your people. . . . Your people lived on me as on a mountain. The grass waved and I ate it as far as the clean fresh wind blew. Then I was burnt and left to rot. . . . I became garbage. It had been beautiful, the world made out of my flesh and my bone, my hide and my sinews. The people danced each season on my back. . . . The word was real, and every man had his own poem to connect him to himself. Now what is there? . . . Now there are people in boxes, their heads full of noise, their lungs full of smoke and poison, their bellies full, but their flesh sour. They do what they are told. . . . At the top are a handful of men who buy and sell the mountains and the rivers, who pollute and explode and set aside as preserves all the lands of the earth. The people. . . . are chained together and crippled by shame. They cannot dance. Only the young are alive a little while to dance and feel and touch each other."

The movement thus inspired begins by seizing a high school somewhere in the Midwest and progresses to rioting in Manhattan.

It achieves publicity: "The media discovered them . . . *Esquire* put Shawn's face on the cover in feathered headdress, and inside had a snotty article heavily laden with psychoanalytical insights." These insights, unlike the buffalo's, are not quoted. *Dance the Eagle to Sleep* fails as a novel of ideas because "the system" is never allowed to have a cogent, let alone persuasive, spokesman. The policemen are uniformly faceless and brutal, the schoolteachers are all "frustrated, embittered lumps." The adults in the book are either venal or oppressed—Brand X and Brand Y of the system, summarily dismissed in the very tone of presentation. "His father was a partner in a prestigious Philadelphia law firm. His mother owned buildings, had studied psychology and been analyzed by Jung, and was still beautiful in a gaunt silvery way." Or: "His father was a pale gray drag. Started out as a high-school math teacher and ended up as a middle-echelon man in a company specializing in auto insurance." Anything genial in middle-class life is dismissed as "co-optative softness." Fascinating suggestions pass unchallenged: research scientists have no alternative to participation in nerve-gas projects, Che and Mao will deliver us from toilet training, all people over twenty-five hate all people under twenty-five because television commercials present youthful beauty as an ideal. The actions of the government, as it blitzkriegs the movement into smithereens, pretend to no rationale beyond the author's desire to allegorize the Vietnam war. Comic-book heroes like Captain Marvel and Plastic Man are frequently invoked, and the climactic chapters strongly savor of comic-book art; one can almost see BLAM and RATATATAT in jagged balloons, and (when Corey is hyper-symbolically crushed by a bulldozer) AEEIIII trailing off into the next panel. The government becomes one of those almost omnipotent syndicates of evil that Superman did battle with. No mitigating circumstances are allowed in the Piercy condemnation—no historical causality, no suspicion that the system is a self-admittedly imperfect patchwork of changeable human devices, no comparison with other systems, living or dead. The system is never seen in operation; nobody functioning within it has any reality. This is not true of Miss Piercy's first novel, *Going Down Fast*, wherein some of the manipulators of an urban-renewal boondoggle are substantially, if unsympathetically, realized. It is even less true of—to cite a masterpiece, as magnanimous as it is devastating, of political disaffection—Solzhenitsyn's *The First Circle;* here the author's compassion moves outward from the jailed to the jailers and does not exclude even the ultimate jailer, Stalin, as he scuttles through his suite of cells beneath the Kremlin, beset by dogma and paranoia.

Yet, in another way, Miss Piercy's second novel does reveal a (let us call it) Christian sense of human fallibility. As an anti-utopian novel, a study of the breakup of a visionary movement into doctrinaire factions, *Dance the Eagle to Sleep* has a credible complexity. It is *Lord of the Flies* with girls on the island. The warrior spirit is here embodied in the Piggy figure, the fat bright boy with glasses, now called Billy Batson. Corey, the Indian chief, remains a mystic theorist. The debates within the councils of the young are vigorous and subtle; Miss Piercy follows the cruel exigencies of the social contract as they arise in the tribe with just the sympathetic understanding she denies the enclosing society. "We were right and wrong," Shawn admits in the end, without surrendering his faith that "the system is all wrong."

Where *did* the Indians go wrong? In a sense, by biting the fruit of the Tree of Knowledge. At first "there were almost no tools available in the tribe to communicate political values, but only to embody them. Which worked, sort of." Then communication becomes all too practiced: "Councils tended to turn into sharp debates now between different sides gathered around leaders who could argue a position and put others down. . . . The louder got louder still. . . . But somehow they were not getting any better at talking to people who were not yet Indians." Marcus, the Negro to whom the mantle of wisdom descends after Corey's death, says, "We thought guns made us real, but it was people, and we didn't have them." (Bernardine Dohrn's statement says, "We became aware that a group of outlaws . . . cannot develop strategies that grow to include large numbers of people.") The delusion that better communication would win "the people" seems shared by the author; her novel leaves us with the impression that the movement's only fault was not being strong enough. In the last chapter, a girl, Ginny, cries out in childbirth, "I thought I was stronger than I am." Marcus' answer comes back: "Human beings aren't

naturally strong enough or nasty enough to live in this world."
So even labor pains seem to be allied with the evils of "the system."
What did the Indians want? For a time they live in a New Jersey
farm commune, and their idyll centers upon a brown hardness of
body, which they gain through the outdoor labor that millions of
their ancestors hastened to escape. Joanna, the heroine, is always
"tough" and "skinny." When she turns traitor and sides with the
system, the first thing Corey notices is that she has put on weight.
She is "a robot that looked a little like Joanna. A plastic doll with
rubbery skin and a smell of plastics about it." In short, the system
—substitute "history" or "technology" or "overpopulation"—has
alienated us from Nature. As in the original myth of Eden, there
is in *Dance the Eagle to Sleep* a suggestion that sex is behind the
Fall. Joanna, once a blithely promiscuous runaway, becomes
Corey's mate, then betrays him with Shawn. Yet this event, though
much discussed, does not offend the sexual code of the tribe or
bear upon its military defeat. Indeed, by this time the reader has
become enough of an Indian himself, having witnessed so much
random and inconsequential copulation, that he cannot give the
incident the emotional significance it would have in a conventional,
bourgeois novel. Shawn himself says it:

> "Don't you think it's strange. We're running for our lives.
> There's a battle going on down below. Maybe it's all over for us.
> Our home is gone. Maybe our tribe is destroyed. And we're analyz-
> ing the subtleties of a love affair."

This confessed awkwardness and the curious failure of Joanna,
though she is the most vividly realized character, to be anything
but a pendant upon the book's essential action finger one crisis in
the novel form. Is sex in the shape of "romantic interest" subject
enough? If sexual "possession" is scorned as part of the hated
private-property bag, fidelity becomes meaningless and betrayal
impossible. Joanna tries to make it possible again; she tells Corey,
"I'm not liberated. . . . I'm your private property." And later,
more wifely still: "I was trying to castrate you." Corey despises
her new psychoanalytical vocabulary as part of her sellout, but
does not answer her questioning of the "freedom" he and his
desperate revolution offer. "I've got a scholarship to a decent

school. I'm going to be a teacher. I'm going to be something on my own"—is the reader meant to scorn, with Corey, her moderate hope? In this ambiguity Miss Piercy uncovers a private feminine theme within the mighty masculine one of social rebirth. Just as the old novels etched the tragedies of private persons within the gray revolution of industry and technology, new ones may trace the personal liabilities of the anti-Establishment Establishment.

Single File, by Norman Fruchter, presents a texture much different from *Dance the Eagle to Sleep*. Whereas Miss Piercy's prose crackles like a comb being hastily pulled through rather tangled hair, Mr. Fruchter's glints like fragments of a mirror. While Miss Piercy, in her haste to get on with it, is not fastidious about clichés, resorts to a hurried sociological tone, makes people talk like press handouts, and declines to linger upon sensual details, Mr. Fruchter deals in the exquisitely concrete:

> Wet white bones, glistening like licked fingernails. Tooth-white. Fleshy hunks that evaded Negrone's knife, clung stubbornly to white bone. Tougher than chicken bone, sharp enough to cut and sting—cross-hatchings of scars creased Negrone's wrist up to his elbow, a foot above the cuff of his rubber gloves. Carp skeletons stacked, moist rattles, in Negrone's brine-soaked buckets.

After Miss Piercy's editorializing, it is a relief to read through the hard news Mr. Fruchter has assembled: mock documents, interior soliloquies, street sayings, descriptions clean as ice chips, dialogue better than tape-recorded, all of it smartly shuffled and laid before our eyes in a fancy typographic dress of ragged-right margins, italics, play format, and an intermittent left-hand hairline. The conceit is that all this heterogeneous material exists in a single file of welfare casework, but my one complaint about this book is that its excessive "interestingness," its continual declaration of itself as a literary object, insulates the reader (whom Miss Piercy does engage in argument, however feverish) from the shocking substance. For this is a novel of the urban humiliated and oppressed, a novel rich far beyond its modest bulk with the sights and smells and processes of present-day city life. In content, indeed, it is more radical than *Dance the Eagle to Sleep*, which deals with middle-class teen-agers and ends with the hoariest of sentimental affirmations—the birth of a baby. Not since Steinbeck and Algren has a writer of Mr. Fruchter's skill demonstrated such unforced love for the proletariat, entered so willingly into their cramped lives, and found so much room for drama and mystery in the cabins of desire, scruple, and frustration that confine their freedom of choice.

Two clusters of days in April and July of 1965 are interwoven to form the plot. In April, Dutch Matto, an illiterate Italian laborer, limps with his mangled, infected knee from a nameless city hospital through the vacantly sociable routines of his utter solitude—pain and memories crowding upon him—to his destiny: at 5:21 a.m., "with the only pure motion of his life," he goes upstairs to where a black woman is pounding on the radiator for heat and "sweeps the pan's handle from her startled fingers and swings it through an arc which, completed, smashes her skull." In July, in the same lower West Side neighborhood, a welfare worker called only "the kid" suffers a rude ending to his affair with Angie, a Puerto Rican woman downstairs: she kicks him out and then piles the sheets he has soiled into the arms of his wife. Matto's memories and "the kid's" casebook amplify this double strand of action outward into a wilderness of other lives, and for each brief scene Mr. Fruchter finds the exact accent, the one poetic yet honest image that might filter through Matto's stupidity or the bleakness of bureaucratic notation. An uptown poolroom, a Chinese man's "bare room that smelled of scalding tea-kettle water dousing already spotless surfaces," a weekend on the water with sunburned call girls, the ins and outs of robbing trailer trucks —no corner of metropolitan existence evades the light of the author's imagining; the many vignettes expand and merge into one large landscape of impoverishment and confusion, individual egos and libidos winking like phosphorescent animalcula in a sea of despair. The "system" is seen functioning in its lowest forms (the neurotic, uncertain, well-intentioned welfare worker; the tired, tough, racist, grudgingly conscientious cop), where it intertwines with the "victims" (the ignorant laborer, the sexy, angry, helpless young hooker and her child). The policeman, Sal, lives with Angie while she is also accommodating "the kid," and he is in on Matto's arrest. Sal and the neighborhood itself are the definite links between the two strands of the novel; the indefinite link, which binds them into a "single file," I take to be a verdict—scarcely audible in its irony—of guilty on the book itself.

That is, "the kid," if not quite the author, is the assembler of these fragments. His interest in Matto's act of murder generates the vivid re-creation of Matto that is set before us; his affair with Angie, his affectionate word-portraits of his welfare cases, his willingness to stretch and overlook regulations for them all stem from a "romantic interest" in the poor. Yet the depth of the poverty he sees swallows and exhausts him. Sal dislikes his type ("I knew the kid was bad news first morning I met him, sipping Angie's coffee. . . . Department was dying for staff, but he hadda pretend he was on a mission!"), and his wife, Laurie, begs him to quit ("You know why you went to work there and it hasn't worked out. . . . It's another one of those private notions you have, nobody's keeping score"). "The kid" pretends to acquiesce, pleasantly envisions returning to college, but then sinks back into his "squalid anemia of the soul." In a world so radically awry, no effort is enough. One man goes upstairs to murder a woman, another man goes downstairs to fornicate with a woman; it equals out, it is the same. A possible response lies outside reality, in art, but his own work of art Mr. Fruchter has enigmatically fractured as if with the blow of a fist.

Both authors offer to tell us about sections of American society —the revolutionary young, the urban poor—more frequently met in the newspapers than in prose fiction. Need it be argued that the novel form accommodates some kinds of people better than others? Lively dialogue, for instance, assumes a degree of articulate self-consciousness beyond the Dutch Mattos of this world. Indoor actions like domestic quarrels are easier to diagram than outdoor actions like the street war of *Dance the Eagle to Sleep*. Secretive sufferers like Matto and Sal, vision-possessed youths like Corey and Billy, behave uncomfortably in the living-rooms of fiction, whereas on the basis of previous acquaintance very marginal figures like "the kid's" wife and Shawn's parents call out heartily to the reader. Good, greedy, guilty, quasi-Christian people: without them, where are the moral tension, the irony, the retribution that give a novel its tug and design? Mr. Fruchter's first novel, *Coat Upon a Stick*, showing the same clairvoyance and the same fascination with the humble and even the same trick of inserted monologue, dealt with an area of urban experience, the Jewish, already under cultivation; while striking his own note firmly, the young author yet based his precocious achievement upon a literary tradition. And the personae of Miss Piercy's first novel were also familiar—young bohemians and small cultural operators, their traditional absorption in sex and art wrenched toward political commitment by a not yet overt streak of demagoguery in the author. These second novels move further from bourgeois conventions.

The bourgeois novel is inherently erotic, just as the basic unit of bourgeois order—the family unit built upon the marriage contract—is erotic. Who loves whom? Once this question seems less than urgent, new kinds of novels must be written, or none at all. If domestic stability and personal salvation are at issue, acts of sexual conquest and surrender are important. If the issue is an economic reordering, and social control of the means of production, then sexual attachments are as they are in Mao's China— irrelevant, and the fewer the better. Vast portions of the world have always lain beyond the boundaries of bourgeois arrangements, and a sizable new population is in conscious revolt against them; the novel, moving into this territory of subject matter, encounters resistance. Sex figures in *Dance the Eagle to Sleep* as a puzzled promiscuity, and in *Single File* as a squalid menace. Yet neither author could quite do without it; indeed, against the grain of their prophetic purposes, it threatens to dominate their narratives, as something inchoate, unchannelled, mysterious. Both second novels —in contrast to the first novels—show people removed from the context of families. In one case, parents have been rejected; in the other, urban pressure has broken families down. Without the multiple perspectives of a family, Miss Piercy's portrait of youth rampant is a lopsided cartoon; writing about city dwellers interconnected with an extreme of tenuousness, Mr. Fruchter has compiled a scrupulous brochure of fragments. Loss of perspective, however, is where vision often begins, and less, in the case of these second novels, may be more.

From Dyna Domes to Turkey-Pressing

DIVINE RIGHT'S TRIP, by Gurney Norman. 302 pp. Dial Press, 1972.

GERONIMO REX, by Barry Hannah. 337 pp. Viking, 1972.

"We *are* as gods and might as well get good at it," announced page 1 of *The Last Whole Earth Catalog*, that mind-blowing, prize-winning compendium of hardware, natural foods, aerial photographs, cosmological tracts, and a thousand and one other handy aids to good-god-making. On the right-hand side of many of the pages, and identified by the device of a dragon, ran a narrative called *Divine Right's Trip*, written by one of the editors, Gurney Norman; this novel has now been published separately, in hard-cover by the Dial Press and as a paperback by Bantam. Though the text is little changed, and has even kept its dragons, it reads very differently out of the *Catalog*'s farraginous, clangorous context; there, competing with advertisements for Synectics and Dyna Domes and Kama Sutra Oil, Norman's episodes appeared slier and more shardlike than they now turn out to be. Within covers of its own, *Divine Right's Trip* shows itself to be a subtly written and morally passionate epic of the counter-culture, a fictional explication of the hopeful new consciousness come to birth—midwifed by hallucinogens—amid the communes and rock concerts of the sixties.

The story is simple: D(ivine) R(ight) (for David Ray) Davenport, stoned crazy, makes his way in a VW bus called Urge, with a girl called Estelle, from the West Coast to his home territory of Appalachian Kentucky, where he finds peace and purpose in soil reclamation by means of rabbit manure. Along the way, he meets a number of more or less allegorical Americans, such as the Lone Outdoorsman, and a garageman who says, "All of you, come back and see us, you hear?" and a Greek who believes the world can be cleansed of mucus by adherence to the walnut diet of the ancient Sumerians, and St. Louis dope dealers, and an Indiana talk-show host, and a Cincinnati housewife who is also Divine Right's sister. D.R.'s favorite accolade is "far out," and all the types he

encounters dissolve into harmlessness under his guileless appreciation. Sheer good-heartedness rather saps the saga of tension. The
Lone Outdoorsman, for instance, has many ingredients of a villain:
an "absurdly handsome" face on a stubby body, a fastidious armor
of camping gear, a hard-hatted interior monologue. But, the author
reassures us,

> The Lone Outdoorsman is far from your ordinary, everyday one-
> dimensional heavy: the thing that redeems the Lone Outdoorsman
> is a refreshing mental complexity of a kind you don't ordinarily
> run into in folk tales. All mixed in with his gory mental images of
> bullet-riddled bodies and heroic assaults upon beachheads was a
> commendable impulse to be nice to these kids, to befriend them
> and hopefully influence them in some constructive way.

Having spied D.R. and Estelle copulating in the woods, he debates
shooting them, and decides instead to feed them steaks. And D.R.'s
sister's husband, Doyle, a Cincinnati mechanic, feeds the young
tripper at his table, freakiness be damned. "Doyle understood that
his brother-in-law was some sort of mild outlaw. But . . . it never
occurred to any of them to withdraw their affection just because
the kid was in a phase." Doyle himself had been a maverick when
he was young, and even today—"Doyle was thirty-four now, but
as he bit down on his food the tendons in his big jaw flexed beneath
his skin, and for a second the old toughness, and even meanness, of
his youth was restored to his face, and for some reason D.R. found
that very moving. He loved Doyle." D.R.'s America, indeed, is a
web of such benevolent recognitions; nothing is too banal for him
to dig, nothing too weird to merit respectful attention. If it is a
land despoiled by strip mining and studded with importuning bill-
boards, it is also a land of daily magic, where a credit card fuels a
hegira, and collect phone calls bind together a freemasonry of
friends, and a West Coast Prospero called the Anaheim Flash foots
all bills and mends all missed connections and arrives in backwoods
Kentucky in a silver Lotus to conduct a wedding in a silver jumpsuit.

No, the only real dragon our knight errant encounters is himself
—one half of himself, when, in an extraordinary episode, he splits,
under stress of long drug use, into two persons: D.R. and David.

Surprisingly, D.R., the stoned new-consciousness half, remains our hero, and the dragon is pure, rational David:

> There is David, lurking in the shadows of the ledge. He pulls my flesh around and makes me see his eyes shining in the murky darkness of his lair. My stomach turns, my hair feels wild, but my adoration of the light remains serene. It's only David's eyes, and lower forehead. The rest is monster, the mouth of dragon teeth, the chin and jaws receding to a short, thick neck and back of horns and scales and fur.
> Oh, it's true all right.
> He's the monster-guardian of the light.

The descriptions throughout *Divine Right's Trip* of drug experience, in its range of revelation and nightmare, its jerkiness, its comically bent perspectives, and its atrocious cumulative fatigue, bear comparison with Malcolm Lowry's descriptions of drunken states in *Under the Volcano*. In both books, an inflamed mind enlarges the universe, dyes it deeper, forces its petals wider. Yet Lowry's Consul is a pathological case, a sick man even in his own judgment, whereas to a young man of D.R.'s cultural conditioning experience normally arrives as a "trip," a "hit," a "flash," a "rush." An image that frequently recurs is of the mind as a movie screen. "As D.R. drove on through the night to Cincinnati he entertained a very complex little drama in his mind, rather like a movie an airline might show its passengers while in flight." Telephoning, he fantasizes that the transparent walls of the booth are "just bad movies projected from somewhere on the other side." The television shows D.R. sees are described as circumstantially as "real" encounters. Reality, the implication is, has lost its objective backbone; inner space is the only space. Living has become continuous spectatorship. This generation was zonked on television before it zonked itself on drugs. What but an ingrained disregard for the workaday, empirical world could breed the swarm of superstitions, such as astrology and the *I Ching*, that distinguish the counter-culture, and that in this novel aid D.R.'s pathetic search for "balance," for harmony with a world drained of substance.

Gurney Norman and Divine Right were born and raised in rural Kentucky, and this regional reality does offer an outer space they can trust. When, midway through, *Divine Right's Trip* hits Kentucky, the book sheds its shimmering snakeskin of fantasy and becomes a stout celebration of the clan, of native soil and hard work and pastoral goodness. Yet it rings less true than in the first, weirder half. Not that the Kentucky voices are not lovingly and amusingly rendered; not that the blasted coal land isn't a cunningly appropriate territory for D.R.'s Dark Passage and Recovery of the Grail. The trouble is the marriage that Mr. Norman wishes to occur, and makes occur, between the rural proletariat of Trace Fork and the young would-be gods of the dome communes. The idyll becomes cute:

> "I think ginseng is the answer to about half of mankind's problems," the freak said.
> "Shoot," said Elmer. "My daddy picked 'sang for a living, when I was a boy. It's as native to these hills as it is to over yonder in China."

The author names all of his friends, hill folk and dome folk, tobacco chewers and cocaine sniffers, and has them all dance round and square to a new sound "dubbed Hillbilly Hindu Rock." And the bride and groom, D.R. and Estelle, take their vows wearing coonskin and gingham, and the Anaheim Flash in his silver jumpsuit pronounces "everybody at this wedding hereby married to one another." Just so, *The Last Whole Earth Catalog* married Buckminster Fuller to L. L. Bean and pronounced the spirits of Buddha and Henry Ford one.

Well, let's not have any dry eyes at the wedding. But a doubt remains whether D.R.'s love affair with rabbit dung and the blisters that come with digging fence-post holes amounts to much more than another "trip." Is Estelle in gingham sufficiently different from Marie Antoinette in the garb of a shepherdess? Can the sated and disgusted offspring of middle-class urban and suburban homes ever do more than condescend, with however good a will, to the remnants of rural America? Agriculture, after all, is not an intrinsically virtuous enterprise. Those who are good at it are capitalists like any other, paying their Chicano fruit pickers no more than they must, manipulating their acreages and machinery and tax loopholes toward the highest profit. Those who are not so good at it hasten (as they have done ever since the first American communes, the Puritan villages, were broken up by entrepreneurism) to the cities, to get the soft desk jobs and the middleman's cut. The counter-culture's return to the soil is a luxurious gesture, financed by the Anaheim Flash and other such imps of industrial affluence.

Divine Right's Trip in book form is subtitled "A Folktale"; its subtitle in *The Last Whole Earth Catalog* was "Our story thus far"—more modest and more accurate. A folktale must be made by the folk, "the gathered people" mentioned in the novel's last words. But the folk are slow to speak, and in this country, even as the costumes and mores and prejudices of the once radical young gain wider acceptance each year, the folk are not yet ready to yield their suffrage to D.R. and his friends. Mickey Mouse and Archie Bunker are truer folk heroes, and will probably be re-elected.* But Divine Right *is* bigger than life, and in giving the story thus far of a segment of his generation, in prose nicely threaded between the vernacular and the symbolic, Gurney Norman has shown a noble reach and a healthy grasp.

Although Barry Hannah, the author of *Geronimo Rex*, is several years younger than Mr. Norman, his novel belongs to an older tradition—the whining-adolescent novel of the fifties. The action begins in 1950, when the hero, Harry Monroe, is eight years old, and ends in the middle sixties, when he is married and a graduate student of English at the University of Arkansas. America broke in two in those years, when Johnson committed the half-million troops to Vietnam, and the new consciousness at the heart of *Divine Right's Trip* figures in *Geronimo Rex* as a bleak dawn, an irony heavily in hock to despair, an accelerating incoherence in the never very tightly woven events that make up the novel's action. These events, though they fill three hundred and thirty-seven large pages, are adequately adumbrated by the author's bio note on the jacket flap: born down South, educated here and there,

---

* Which they were, by a landslide. Only to resign, separately, in a devastating self-defeat. Of recent American mysteries, none more needfully awaits its sensitive biochemist than, in the years 1972–1974, the simultaneous and evidently symbiotic extermination of all honor in the highest places and the drying-up of the counter-culture, as if astonished to death by the super-vindication of its protests.

"plays the trumpet," took detours into "such odd work as a research assistant in pharmacology or trouble-shooter in a turkey-
pressing plant," married, "presently makes his home" someplace,
"where he is at work on his second novel." The major weakness of
a first novel like this is its limp susceptibility to autobiographical
accident; its vitality must lie not in the shaping but in the language
of the telling, and here Mr. Hannah is no mean performer. His
whine is full-throated:

> The old man had a Buick. He liked to wheel it up our brick drive,
> which was bordered by a dense cane patch. He was one of these
> magazine handsomes who was turning gray in the hair at forty-five;
> the gray strands were flames from a hot and ancient mental life,
> or so he thought. His mental life was always the great fake of the
> household. He had three years at L.S.U., makes sixty thousand a
> year, has the name of a bayou poet—Ode Elann Monroe—and has
> read a book or two over above what he was assigned as a sopho-
> more. So he's a snob, and goes about faking an abundant mental
> life. He always had this special kind of bewrenched and evaporated
> tiredness when he came home from the factory.

With the verve of the young Bellow but with little of Bellow's
love, Mr. Hannah can seize a person and hurl him into print:

> Perrino, still sporting his horseshoe beard and instructing trumpets,
> was odd. Eastman had given him license. He came to us wailing;
> he had his hands over his head, and you could see written back in
> his eyes that he had obtained some ruinous Ph.D. from somewhere.
> His tie knot waggled down on his open collar, and his clothes were
> like bandages coming apart over a horrid wound to his chest and
> soul. He wore sandals over black socks, which seemed to represent
> the same anguish at his feet. He was slightly chubby, with bags
> under his eyes like rotting bananas, and behaved as if he were the
> last gasp of Italianism in America.

The author does not shy from pushing an image into absurdity,
and pulling it out on the other side:

> [My father] engaged me in a sort of contest at milk-drinking
> while we waited for the answers to come out. It all ended with
> our drinking so much milk we were ready to puke; the old man
> churning himself into a dull butter of meditation about my life.

Some of the metaphors carry the shock of real poetry:

My youth was an old sick pirate; there was a boy back there lying on the reefs, bleeding. The lad's throat had been cut. I had cut it.

All this energy of expression, however, adorns a listless and ugly tale whose dominant mood is funk. "He wondered . . . if he could get over this period, this hump, which was not a hump really but a whole range of dismal mountains of funk." Harry's father is the third-richest man in Dream of Pines, a Louisiana papermaking town with a pervasive miasma and the cultural scope of a broom closet. Off-hours from the mattress factory he owns, he doodles in his study with the fantasy of being an author; his son flavors boredom with raptures over music. The Dream of Pines Colored High School has funnelled its meagre resources into a crack marching band, "that played Sousa marches and made the sky bang together"; this flare of excellence lights up the sodden mediocrity of all else. Dream of Pines public education is detailed with morbid zest, and the Mississippi college that enrolls Harry seems even more ill-tuned to his inner melody. Nothing links up; Harry keeps dropping things halfway through, including an inspired jazz solo and several instances of sexual intercourse. He tends to see all women as "roaches." The males he knows are possessed of isolating visions: Harley Butte, his mulatto friend, by a passion for John Philip Sousa; Bobby Dove Fleece, his roommate, by a lavishly verbalized obsession with sex; Whitfield Peter Lepoyster, his enemy, by a demented racism; Dr. Lariat, his professor, by a sterile cynicism. And in his own head Harry is Geronimo, the savage Indian rebel, at war with all society.

The youth of the fifties were not, as is sometimes implied, complacent; their contempt for the institutions around them was paralyzingly thorough. Salinger's Holden Caulfield, Keith Waterhouse's Billy Liar saw right through everything, and were too savvy to believe things could ever be otherwise. The vision of becoming as gods, of a neo-primitivist life style alternative to an ironical conformism, of a hot connection between private emotion and public policy, had to wait for a wave of desperation prefigured in *Geronimo Rex* by an unconvincing turn toward violence. This caustic small-town boyhood becomes, finally, a hollow shootout, with real bullets and blood if not real reverberations. Granted, guns seem standard equipment down South, and craziness does sometimes out. But—as in another Louisiana novel with a humid flamboyance, Robert Stone's *A Hall of Mirrors*—the violence feels dreamy, and too much the author's; the plot does not produce the violence as a tree produces fruit, but ends in it as a car ride sometimes ends in an accident. The author loses empathy with the hero. Harry's boyish infatuation with a sluttish millworker is movingly explored, but his later affair with Lepoyster's niece Catherine is nearly inexplicable, and his abrupt marriage to sixteen-year-old Prissy Lombardo totally so. The book ends on a sour note of putdown; Dr. Lariat, the professor of literature, tells Harry Monroe, the budding practitioner of it, that they're in the "wrong field." Music is the one.

Still, after *Divine Right's Trip*, in which America and its general populace form a backdrop for young tourists trailing their roots in some nirvana between here and Mars, it is salutary to read a novel in which the young and the middle-aged are interlocked, albeit in gruesome struggle. To judge by *Geronimo Rex*, young men like Bobby Dove Fleece still writhe and tremble under the old religious taboos; girls like Sylvia Wyche still struggle to save their hymens for their fiancés; instructors like Dr. Perrino still think they have something to teach; and all generations are mired equally in the squalid but substantial provincial ambience. Father and son, in this novel, lust after the same slut and the same muse. Mr. Hannah is nowhere better than he is in showing the complex currents of parent-child sympathy that swirl around acts of overt rebellion. Perhaps the South has a certain retarded solidarity; certainly Gurney Norman's pageant of reconciliation occurs more plausibly in Kentucky than on an Iowa corn farm or in a California orchard. Perhaps, too, the art of fiction is intrinsically mediating and anti-propagandistic; it reduces general issues to the faceted confusion of private lives, with their undoctrinaire mixing of personal quirk, conscious intention, and elementary biology. Of these two novels, Mr. Norman's is winged with surer purpose and Mr. Hannah's has the richer sense of circumstance. One rather skims, the other wallows; both give a fresh angle on the great American subject of Growing Up, and both offer the same American advice: Don't do it until you must.

Jong Love

FEAR OF FLYING, by Erica Jong. 340 pp. Holt, Rinehart & Winston, 1973.

Erica Jong's first novel feels like a winner. It has class and sass, brightness and bite. Containing all the cracked eggs of the feminist litany, her soufflé rises with a poet's afflatus. She sprinkles on the four-letter words as if women had invented them; her cheerful sexual frankness brings a new flavor to female prose. Mrs. Jong's heroine, Isadora Wing, surveying the "shy, shrinking, schizoid" array of women writers in English, asks, "Where was the female Chaucer?" and the Wife of Bath, were she young and gorgeous, neurotic and Jewish, urban and contemporary, might have written like this. *Fear of Flying* not only stands as a notably luxuriant and glowing bloom in the sometimes thistly garden of "raised" feminine consciousness but belongs to, and hilariously extends, the tradition of *Catcher in the Rye* and *Portnoy's Complaint*—that of the New York voice on the couch, the smart kid's lament. Though Isadora Wing, as shamelessly and obsessively as Alexander Portnoy, rubs the reader's nose in the fantasies and phobias and family slapstick of growing up, and masturbates as often, she avoids the solipsism that turns Roth's hero unwittingly cruel; nor does she, like Holden Caulfield, though no less sensitive to phoniness, make of innocence an ideal. She remains alert to this world.

> How little our happiness depends on: an open drugstore, an unstolen suitcase, a cup of cappuccino! Suddenly I was acutely aware of all the small pleasures of being alive. The superb taste of the coffee, the sunlight streaming down, the people posing on street corners for you to admire them.

Admiring she is even of the impotence, madness, and defective hygiene of her many awful lovers. A feminist since birth (she says), radicalized at the age of thirteen "on the I.R.T. subway when the moronic Horace Mann boy who was my date asked me if I planned to be a secretary," Isadora Wing nevertheless has more kind words for the male body than any author since the penning of *Fanny Hill:*

> He was so beautiful lying there and his body smelled so good. I thought of all those centuries in which men adored women for their bodies while they despised their minds. . . . That was how I so often felt about men. Their minds were hopelessly befuddled, but their bodies were so nice. Their ideas were intolerable, but their penises were silky.

Her account of her travails among these silken creatures, while not exactly a flag of truce in the war between the sexes, does hold out some hope of renewed negotiations.

The second of four daughters of a would-be paintress and a father who designed "ice buckets which looked like beer steins and beer steins which looked like ice buckets," Isadora grew up in a fourteen-room apartment on Central Park West. She heavy-pets (let's call it) at thirteen, remorsefully tries to starve herself at fourteen, embarks upon a series of psychiatrists (the first is Dr. Schrift; he's short, of course, and tells her, "Ackzept being a vohman"), enters Barnard at seventeen, meets the brilliant Brian Stollerman when she is a freshman, seduces him and puts her virginity out of its misery, marries Brian after graduation, endures his swelling madness while she attends graduate school, commits and divorces him at twenty-two, takes up with an unwashed, musical loser called Charlie Fielding, is betrayed by him, embarks upon a swinging tour of Europe with a girl friend at the age of twenty-three, returns to New York, meets a silent thirty-one-year-old Chinese Freudian named Bennett Wing, marries him, and now, five years later, at the age of twenty-nine in 1971, attends with her husband an international congress of psychoanalysts in Vienna, where she meets, loves at first sight, and runs away with an English Laingian psychiatrist called (yes) Adrian Goodlove. This life history is scattered carefreely backward and forward throughout three hundred and forty pages that should be read, one sometimes suspects, in fifty-minute sessions. A pattern and a person emerge, amid the wisecracks, postcards ("Vienna. The very name is like a waltz. But I never could stand the place. It seemed dead to me. Embalmed"), and reflections upon the hard and curious lot of Woman. Intellectual condescension, physical intimidation, deodorant-selling insinuation—women suffer them all. The case for marriage is nailed in a sentence: "Being unmarried in a man's world was such a hassle that *any*thing had to be better." Motherhood is another distrusted institution: "Basically, I think, I was furious with my mother for not teaching me how to be a woman, for not teaching me how to make peace between the raging hunger in my cunt and the hunger in my head." Her mother, a frustrated artist, is full of "misplaced artistic aggression," and Isadora thinks sadly of young wives "making babies out of their loneliness and boredom and not knowing why." The smaller discomforts of femininity are vividly, comically detailed, from the presence of a heavy suitcase to the absence of a needed Tampax; females, we are told, are even at a disadvantage making water by the roadside, tending to piss in their shoes. The one female complaint not registered, surprisingly, is the one most conspicuous in seriously sexy male fiction, such as Mailer's "The Time of Her Time." However adverse her circumstances, Isadora Wing seems to have no trouble attaining orgasm. And maybe this is what makes her saga so uncranky, for all its intelligent pain, and lends its prose a spun-sugar halo of wonder and fun, and gives its conclusion the smug snap of a shopping expedition satisfactorily completed:

> I looked down at my body. The same. The pink V of my thighs, the triangle of curly hair, the Tampax string fishing the water like a Hemingway hero, the white belly, the breasts half floating, the nipples flushed and rosy from the steamy water. A nice body. Mine. I decided to keep it.

The male reviewer, grateful to be served this lovable, delicious novel (each chapter garnished with epigraphs), embarrasses himself with digestive rumblings. While intimacy with Isadora Wing is maintained, the reader accepts the value she puts on her own story: a reconciliation of the hunger at the poles of her being, a triumph, if precarious, over aerophobia and the socially conditioned guilt and slavishness that lie beneath it. At a little remove, however, the story can be viewed as that of a spoiled young woman who after some adventures firmly resolves to keep on spoiling herself. She bounces about on a ubiquitous padding of money: her parents were well-to-do; her first husband's parents were able to pay for private treatment of his madness "fees [of] about $2,000 a month," Charlie Fielding lived on a trust fund, both her present lover and husband are psychiatrists, with the subliminal affluence of that priestly profession. To be sure, the middle class has problems, too, and most novels are written about them, but as an instance of sexist oppression Isadora Wing should be recognized as a privileged case, with no substantial economic barriers between her and liberation, and—by her own choice— no children, either. Edna Pontellier, the heroine of Kate Chopin's elegiac novel of female revolt, *The Awakening*, was a mother as well as a wife, and drowned herself to escape the impasse between her personal, artistic identity and her maternal obligations. Childless, with an American Express card as escort on her pilgrimage, and with a professional forgiver as a husband, Isadora Wing, for all her terrors, is the heroine of a comedy.

On the back jacket flap, Mrs. Jong, with perfect teeth and cascading blond hair, is magnificently laughing, in contrast to the sombre portrait that adorns her two collections of poetry. Rather disconcertingly, not only does Isadora Wing, like Erica Jong, write poetry but she writes Mrs. Jong's poetry, two samples of which are included in this book. And the reader of *Fruits & Vegetables* (1971) and *Half-Lives* (1973) has already encountered Isadora Wing's fractured leg and her burgeoning crow's-feet, her multi-colored notes to herself and the trail of sequins one of her gowns leaves, her mother's avocado tree behind her mother's avocado-colored couch, her mad first husband and her fondness for likening human cheeks to willow tips for softness, her irritated observation of Braque and Utrillo prints in psychiatrists' offices, and her quotation of Sylvia Plath's question "Is there no way out of the mind?" In some of the poems of *Half-Lives*, the husband and the lover of *Fear of Flying* are distinctly silhouetted, and in the earlier collection the sequence entitled "Flying You Home" presents the removal of "Brian Stollerman" to a California hospital in a slightly different light—more moving and ominous than what we find in the corresponding chapter of the novel, where the incident seems one more of the long string of zany mishaps that comprise Isadora Wing's amorous education. *Fear of Flying* wears its gossamer disguise as fiction with a breathtaking impudence; the difference between "The Green Hornet" and the "Blue Wasp series for radio" appears about the thickness of it. Adrian and Isadora playfully discuss how he will be portrayed in the book she will presumably write about their affair, and the sister whose husband later attempts sodomy on Isadora screams at her, "Well, I won't have you putting me and my husband and my children in your filthy writing—do you hear me? I'll kill you if you mention me in any way at all." The disinterested reader, of course, need not tremble, but the flashback sections about romances past do feel more spilled than told, and there is something a shade archetypical about the heroine: for all the times she looks at herself nude, she remains visually misty, and the author's nimble recourse to cultural and psychoanalytical tags verges on nervous patter. As a creator of scenes and characters, Mrs. Jong is at her best in the present—that is, at the Vienna Congress of 1971, with Isadora running back and forth between her husband and her new lover, getting their inexhaustible and incompatible analyses of what is happening. Here, comedy becomes satire and distress becomes drama. The prose flies. Throughout, the poet's verbal keenness rarely snags the flow of breathy vernacular; a few false shifts of tone, an occasional automatism of phrase ("intensely interested," "poring over books," "clutching my baby" within six lines), a few clammy touches of jargon insignificantly mar a joyously extended performance. The novel is so full, indeed, that one wonders whether the author has enough leftover life for another novel. Fearless and fresh, tender and exact, Mrs. Jong has arrived nonstop at the point of being a literary personality; may she now travel on, toward Canterbury.

OLDER AMERICANS

Indifference

Morning Noon and Night, by James Gould Cozzens. 408 pp. Harcourt, Brace & World, 1968.

Beginning, forty years ago, with a style of sober purity, James Gould Cozzens has purposefully evolved a prose unique in its mannered ugliness, a monstrous mix of Sir Thomas Browne, legalese, and Best-Remembered Quotations. The opening chapter of his new novel, *Morning Noon and Night*, cloudy as a polluted pond, swarms with verbal organisms of his strange engendering. As Cozzensologists before me have discovered, there is no substitute for the tabulated list. We have the Unresisted Cliché:

> Here are clouds of witnesses, faces and forms in serried ranks . . .

> I don't intend here any telling in mournful numbers.

> Simply, the wood is not to be seen for the trees.

The Lame Echo:

> To be sure, in this distraction of the mind, as through a glass darkly . . .

> You have not world enough and time. . . .

> I feel it leaves man as much as before the glory, jest, and riddle of the world.

The False Precision, the Legal "Or":

> . . . to inform yourself of any peculiarities or limitations of his that could have affected his observation or could now be coloring his report.

. . . what they seem in our work or practice. I am not suggesting that I feel we are or ever could be ethically obligated. . . .

. . . by elements of lust whether loving or unloving, a catalog longer or shorter of women . . .

The Vapid Expansion:

What used to be, not just well enough, but often very good indeed, must be left religiously alone.

The Inversion Frightful, Capped by Cute Periphrasis:

In eating employed now are partial dental prosthetic devices.

Be that how it may, Nancy, as friends call her, will not refuse the rites mysterious of connubial love.

The Gratuitous Scientism:

Penetrated, the microscopic cell is fertilized (in accepted language of the process, two gametes fuse to form a zygote). .

The Infatuated Sonority:

His course of ripe and ripe is running, and the rot and rot won't fail to follow. . . .

Multitudinous as these remembered works of Nature may be, more multitudinous still, and by far, must be remembered works of man.

What Cozzens has set himself to achieve, and has, as he might say, so regrettably succeeded in achieving, is the literary equivalent for or capture of the all too veritably human quality of *stuffiness*. In tone and tedium, *Morning Noon and Night* is a four-hundred-page-long after-dinner speech.

The speaker is Henry Dodd Worthington; the dinner has been his life. Born at the turn of the century as the son of a small-college English professor, the narrator of this novel, after an acceptable education at an unnamed prep school and Harvard, and after shrugging off both teaching and writing as possible careers, drifted into employment with a Boston collection agency, and from this indifferent beginning rose to found Henry Worthington Associates, a management-consultant firm of prestige so immense that both he and the reader find it implausible. He has been twice married: his first wife, Judith, cuckolded and divorced him; his second, Charlotte, committed suicide. Violence, indeed, has made rather free with his relatives; his parents were asphyxiated in a hotel fire, and his two grandchildren were killed in the crash of a plane. Henry (or "our Hank," as he jocosely calls himself) is of genteel Protestant background, an indirect descendant of President Franklin Pierce; during the Second World War he served as an Air Forces major, mostly in the Pentagon; his present preoccupations are the unhappiness of his daughter Elaine, now on her third divorce, and the composition of this memoir. The events of his life are not related consecutively but emerge as his memory rambles over the past; he ruminates at length upon such diverse matters as his grandfather's feud with the early Freudians, the tricks of management consultation, the technique of running an antiques shop, the sinking of the *Titanic*, the vagaries of chance, the nature of the Puritan heritage, the ups and downs and ins and outs of sexual "appetency," and (an unexpected obsession) the shabbiness of the literary world. Many of these essays, once the muddled sonority of the style is tuned out, possess interest, even a certain surly brilliance, but as a life the book lacks what it must have—life.

Elaine is the only character other than the narrator allowed to have any kind of a say; the novel's keystone scene is an interview between the distressed daughter and the stiff but sorry father, held in the courtyard of H.W. Associates' posh new suburban plant. But when, after seventy solid pages of authorial discourse, quotation marks appear amid the print and Elaine breaks into speech, she talks just like a little Henry, or (since without a doubt our Hank is pretty much our Jim) a little Cozzens. Listen to her:

> "So when Wilfred deflowered me I was pretty much, as the books say, unawakened."

> "You know; lovely Sue makes like softly panting while the geranium tree is planting. And doesn't that show what's up for grabs here is love forever true, and oughtn't he to latch onto it?"

> "You bet! Moving finger writes. Correct. And all my tears, or such as I've let drip, don't wash out a word."

Embarrassed, apparently, by her own wealth of literary tags, she admonishes her father, "Don't forget the expensive liberal-arts education you bought me. When it pays to, I can sound tolerably literate." But it doesn't pay; their conversation is lumpy with false wit and stilted slang and brittle with a supervisory knowingness— not a dramatization of her plight but an awkward exposition of it. So it is with the entire book. Henry's marriage to Judith, by all indications the deepest relationship of his life, is represented by some mocking paragraphs on newlywed lust, a potentially poignant but skimped account of their courtship, an unskimped theory as to how her father's anti-sexual High Anglicanism drove her decades later to promiscuity, a few cursory references to their divorce, a full exposition of Henry's financial advice to the antiques business she sets up in, and a glancing admission that now she is dying. She hardly speaks a sentence; for her one moment onstage, she is seen through her daughter's eyes distantly on a beach, coupling with a lover. Charlotte, the second wife, appears in Henry's account as a suicide note, as a glimpse of her in the shower (heavily misted by panting references to David and Bathsheba), and as an equable compliment to her secretarial ability. All the characters—wives, friends, business associates, service colleagues—are immersed, mute and all but immobile, in the tyrannous flow of Henry Worthington's disquisitional lava.

Now, to what extent does the author stand apart from his persona, as, say, John Marquand does from George Apley? How much of Henry's stuffiness is intentional caricature? Is his sluggish eclipse of the life he has lived a novelistic defect or an ironical comment? Mockery there is in abundance: Henry mocks his youthful ardor, his elderly dignity, his riskless wartime career, the little shams and maneuvers of his trade. His memory seeks out low moments: "mean actions of mine; uglinesses of greed or lust; shameful exhibitions of ignorance; deserved humiliations; mortifying follies and defeats." And the epigraph from Shakespeare's Sonnet 94, describing those who, "moving others, are themselves as stone," suggests that a self-portrait of a type of man and an implicit judgment were intended. But Marquand, even in his later novels, maintained an outsider's perspective on his Brahmins, whereas Worthington's voice and Cozzens' are indistinguishable, and the opinions of author and character merge in a ponderous, pessimistic morass of self-distrust and weary puzzlement.

Having troubled to invent a business profession for his alter ego, and having supplied a convincing amount of data and theory, Cozzens compulsively reverts throughout his narrative to the problems of the literary practitioner, to attacks upon "half-writer pretenders" and "liberal intellectuals." He includes a coy reference to the minor American writer Frederick Cozzens. He gives Henry, the supposed author of a million memos and directives, his own preposterously pedantic style, including the obligatory exotic words—*inappetency, erethism, furibund, condign, innominate, muliebrity, deontology.* Frequently heard is the rumble of hobby-horses being ridden by that ultra-conservative Cozzens displayed years ago in *Time*—a kind of male Ayn Rand who in this book must dote upon a fictional bank's status "in the best financial circles" as being "better regarded than the latter-day not always prudent House of Morgan," who speaks of Roosevelt's "near-senile megalomania" and the Kremlin's "dupes" and "expert perfidies and duplicities," and who seems pleasurably smitten by the speculation that a typhoon would have wiped out our scheduled invasion of the Japanese home islands had not the war been ended by the atomic bombs, which in passing are viewed as the "means to right a ceaselessly growing imbalance in Nature, to solve quickly and easily theretofore insoluble problems of excess population."

Not that political conservatives should be barred from the halls of fiction; rather, they should be better represented there, to relieve the present rather shrill unanimity on the left. Nor is author/alter-ego closeness an intrinsic handicap; *Herzog*, for example, is an excellent novel. Its superiority to *Morning Noon and Night* lies not only in Bellow's far livelier gift for conjuring up personalities but in his, and Herzog's, belief that a better world somewhere exists, that improvement can be sought and choices can be made. The illusion of free will, illusion or not, is necessary to a novel; excitement and import derive from the reality of human decision. As Henry Dodd Worthington describes himself, he has been always a product, a zygote formed by two fused gametes, in the grip, successively and simultaneously, of biology, heredity, social usage, sexual impulse, chance, and inertia. The turning points of his life—his marriage to Judith, his entry into the world of business, his enlistment in the Army Air Forces, his divorce and remarriage—are all seen as uncaused drift, "little governed by logic or demonstrable cause and effect." Herzog, at the end, can stop writing letters and set the table for a tryst, whereas Henry can only conclude that he knows nothing, that his life has been a "wandering directionless," a game of "blindman's buff—now sightlessly bumping into things, now surprised by sportive unreturnable blows." His memories—in the book's last, best flight of imagery—are seen as ruined fragments and, far off, "a dozen or more aqueduct arches, commencing suddenly, suddenly ending, coming now from nowhere, now going nowhere." There is "thin final sunlight," and then "the child must soon be taken away to bed." A child is someone who lacks responsibility and power of choice; Henry Dodd Worthington, adviser to big business, labels himself as one. This vision of helpless, pointless process is at the heart of the novel's profound inaction, of its analyzed but unrealized events, and even of its reactionary style, seeping backward to include all those tired mottoes and phrases and clichés as if wryly to admit that nothing new can be said. Resigned pessimism is a defensible philosophy, and may be the natural end of American enterprise, but it makes for very dull fiction.

Piqued by this book's curious badness, I turned to Cozzens' first full-length novel, *The Last Adam*. Though a trifle slick, with its climactic town meeting and its magnificent starring role for an aging screen idol (it *was* made into a movie, *Dr. Bull*, starring Will Rogers), it holds up well; the evocation of the Connecticut town of New Winton, the tight knit of weather and geography and people into a plot, the particularity and immediacy of every scene all show a mastery remarkable in a man of thirty. Cozzens then had more grasp of ordinary, middling America—or at least more willingness to transmute his grasp into art—than Hemingway and Fitzgerald ever showed. The hero of the novel, Dr. Bull, is sixty-seven, just about Henry Worthington's age, and he remembers the sentence from the Psalmist with which Henry begins his memoir: "I have been young and now am old." And cosmic nullity is present in both books: "Left to herself [a telephone operator in *The Last Adam*], and to what she could see of the universe, real and ideal were lost together in an indifference so colossal, so utterly indifferent, that there was no defining it." This colossal indifference, this abyss beneath society and conventional success, has always been with Cozzens, but as a threat, as a defining darkness, not as an all-swallowing enemy. From *The Last Adam* to *Morning Noon and Night*, the broad social scene of New Winton, primarily Protestant, has dwindled to one member of the Puritan aristocracy; class consciousness has narrowed to class loyalty. Cozzens has become like a Yale undergraduate in the earlier book: "He knew by now that he and his more intimate friends were right; or, at any rate, he could easily see that people who differed conspicuously in dress or behavior, in ideals or attitudes, were, as far as his college was concerned, wrong. His gray eyes considered all those in error with a level, complete indifference." Arthur Winner, of *By Love Possessed*, gave those not of his sort short shrift. Henry Worthington doesn't see them at all, they are squeezed into the remotest margins of his memoir, and there is nowhere to stand to see *him*, to judge him. Only the bitter vacuity of his conclusions betrays the possibility that somewhere along the way he went wrong.

Papa's Sad Testament

ISLANDS IN THE STREAM, by Ernest Hemingway. 466 pp. Scribner's, 1970.

This book consists of material that the author during his lifetime did not see fit to publish; therefore it should not be held against him. That parts of it are good is entirely to his credit; that other parts are puerile and, in a pained way, aimless testifies to the odds against which Hemingway, in the last two decades of his life, brought anything to completion. It is, I think, to the discredit of his publishers that no introduction * offers to describe from what stage of Hemingway's tormented later career *Islands in the Stream* was salvaged, or to estimate what its completed design might have been, or to confess what editorial choices were exercised in the preparation of this manuscript. Rather, a gallant wreck of a novel is paraded as the real thing, as if the public are such fools as to imagine a great writer's ghost is handing down books intact from Heaven.

So we are left to perform the elementary scholarly decencies ourselves. Carlos Baker's biography speaks of a trilogy about the sea that Hemingway, amid the distractions of Cuba, the cockfights and double Daiquiris and proliferating hangers-on, carried forward with enthusiasm in late 1950 and early 1951. The third item of the trilogy, "The Sea in Being," was separately, and triumphantly, published as *The Old Man and the Sea*. The first part, "The Sea When Young," seems to have been an abridgment of an earlier, disastrously long and gauche novel called *Garden of Eden*. The middle section, "The Sea When Absent," has for its hero an American painter named Thomas Hudson and, in the form that Hemingway announced as "finished" by Christmas of 1950, answers the description of the section entitled "Cuba" in the present book. "The Island and the Stream" (*sic*) had become, by mid-1951, the working title of the first section, presumably the revamped *Garden of Eden*. Baker says: "It contains 'wonderful parts' that he hated to cut out, but he was now clear that it must be reshaped to the style and tempo of the other three sections." Of the "other three," one is the story of Santiago that would soon be a separate novel, one is the "Cuba" mentioned above, and the third is "the sea-chase story," which, in Hemingway's opinion, was "impregnable to criticism" and was almost published in *Cosmopolitan*, in two installments. In the book Scribner's has published, this sea-chase is the third section, "At Sea," and the first section, whose adjusted title now does for the whole, is entitled "Bimini."

What we have, then, is a trio of large fragments crudely unified

---

* Mary Hemingway's 53-word Note scarcely counts; it admits to "some cuts" and correction of spelling and punctuation and that is all.

by a Caribbean setting and the nominal presence of Thomas
Hudson. "Bimini" is a collection of episodes that show only a
groping acquaintance with one another; "Cuba" is a lively but
meandering excursion in local color that, when the painter's first
wife materializes, bizarrely veers into a dark and private region;
and "At Sea" is an adventure story of ersatz intensity. Hudson, if
taken sequentially, does not grow but dwindles, from an affectionate and baffled father and artist into a rather too expertly raffish
waterfront character into a bleak manhunter, a comic-book super-
human containing unlooked-for bubbles of stoic meditation and
personal sorrow. Some conscious attempt is made to interlock
the characterizations—the manhunter remembers that he is a
painter, and gives us some hard-edged seascapes to prove it; the
bar clown intermittently recalls that he is drowning his grief at
the death of a son—but the real congruence of these masks is
involuntary: all fit the face of Ernest Hemingway.

Whereas an achieved novel, however autobiographical, dissolves
the author and directs our attention beyond him, *Islands in the
Stream*, even where most effective, inspires us with a worried
concern for the celebrity who wrote it. His famous drinking, his
methodical artistic devotions, his dawn awakenings, his women,
his cats, even his mail (what painter gets anything like a writer's
burdensome, fascinating mail?) are all there, mixed with less easily
publicized strains, dark currents that welled into headlines with
his last illnesses and shocking suicide. The need to prove himself
implacably drives Thomas Hudson toward violence and death. His
enemy, pain, has become an object of infatuation. Even in the
first, most lyric passages, when he is visited on Bimini by his three
sons, what lives for the father-narrator are scenes of savagery—
the machine-gunning of a shark and a boy's day-long wrestle with
a huge swordfish. The child, bent double, bleeding in hands and
feet, is held fast to the fighting chair by the surrounding men, his
guardians, so that he can experience "love":

> "Well," David said with his eyes tight shut. "In the worst parts,
> when I was the tiredest I couldn't tell which was him and which
> was me."
> "I understand," Roger said.
> "Then I began to love him more than anything on earth."

As if to insulate his fatherhood from his dreadful passion for violence, Hemingway creates in this section (never to reappear) another alter ego, a brawling, brooding writer named Roger Davis, and thrusts upon him a gratuitously brutal fistfight, as well as a number of reckless and self-destructive traits that the placid morning painter Thomas Hudson has supposedly outgrown. But in "Cuba," Hyde has been reunited with Jekyll, and Hudson—always a fond describer of guns, and a lover of blood sports—seems right at home among drinking companions who cheerfully remark, of prostitutes who gave imperfect service, "We ought to have poured gasoline on them and set them on fire." Later, Hudson himself, asked by his wife if their only son is dead, answers with the amazing monosyllable, "Sure." The final episode, "At Sea," sees Hudson's fulfillment as a killer, and Hemingway's as an addict of the casually cruel touch. A large "obscenely white" crab offends Hudson: "the man shot him between his eyes and the crab disintegrated." Removing a bullet from a sun-dried corpse is "like cutting into a pie." A grenade eliminates a wounded German: "How is the Kraut in the bow?" "He's a mess." Truly Hudson tells himself, "The horrors were what you won in the big crap game that they run." Well, the author is helping run this crap game, and it takes a little disintegration to keep him happy; unable to decide which of the hero's three boys to kill, he kills them all, two in one section and the third, with comic rigor, in the next.

Hemingway of course did not invent the world, nor pain, mutilation, and death. In his earlier work his harsh obsessions seem honorable and necessary; an entire generation of American men learned to speak in the accents of Hemingway's stoicism. But here, the tension of art has been snapped and the line between sensitive vision and psychopathy has been crossed. The "sea-chase story" is in many ways excellent, but it has the falsity of the episode in Hemingway's real life upon which it was based. In the early days of World War II, he persuaded his friends in the Havana Embassy to let him equip his private fishing launch the *Pilar* as a Q-boat, with bazookas, grenades, bombs, and machine guns. His dream was to lure a Nazi submarine close enough to toss a bomb down the hatch. He staffed the *Pilar* with cronies and, fruitlessly, but displaying much real courage and stamina, cruised the Cuban coast. Everything in "At Sea" is true, except the encounter with Germans and the imperatives of the mission, which was not demanded from above but invented and propelled from within. Such bravery is not grace under pressure but pressure forced in the hope of inducing Grace.

And even love becomes a species of cruelty, which divides women into whores and bitches on the one hand and on the other a single icy-perfect adored. Some reviewers have complained that the first wife is unreal: to me she has that hard reality of a movie star (which in the book she is), a star on the screen, with "the magic rolling line of the hair that was the same silvery ripe-wheat color as always." But it is an easy transition from the image of this beloved and lost woman, this enforcer of proud loneliness, to the cool gray pistols Hudson sleeps with:

> "How long have you been my girl?" he said to the pistol. "Don't answer," he said to the pistol. "Lie there good and I will see you kill something better than land crabs when the time comes."

Love and death: fused complements in Hemingway's universe. Yet he never formulated the laws that bind them, never dared depart from the knightly code and poser's armor he forged against the towering impressions of suffering received at his father's side in the Michigan woods.

> "Is dying hard, Daddy?"
> "No, I think it's pretty easy, Nick. It all depends."
> . . . In the early morning on the lake sitting in the stern of the boat with his father rowing, he felt quite sure that he would never die.

Sure of certain things, he never achieved the step away from himself, of irony and appraisal. He wanted to; he tried; this book opens in a mood of tonic breadth and humor, and closes with a beatific vision of Hudson dying and beloved:

> "I think I understand, Willie," he said.
> "Oh shit," Willie said. "You never understand anybody that loves you."

The new generations, my impression is, want to abolish both war and love, not love as a physical act but love as a religion, a creed to help us suffer better. The sacred necessity of suffering no longer

seems sacred or necessary, and Hemingway speaks across the
Sixties as strangely as a medieval saint; I suspect few readers
younger than myself could believe, from this sad broken testament, how we *did* love Hemingway and, pity feeling impudent,
love him still.

And Yet Again Wonderful

BULLET PARK, by John Cheever. 245 pp. Knopf, 1969.

In the coining of images and incidents, John Cheever has no
peer among contemporary American fiction writers. His short
stories dance, skid, twirl, and soar on the strength of his abundant
invention; his novels tend to fly apart under its impact. His first,
The Wapshot Chronicle, was unified by a pervading nostalgia and
a magnificent old man's journal; his second, *The Wapshot Scandal*,
amounted to a debris of brilliant short stories. *Bullet Park*, his
third, holds together but just barely, by the thinnest of threads.
It begins with an evocation of Bullet Park, a more ominously
named version of the suburban essence Cheever used to call Shady
Hill:

> The stranger might observe that the place seems very quiet; they
> seem to have come inland from the sounds of wilderness—gulls,
> trains, cries of pain and love, creaking things, hammerings, gunfire—
> not even a child practices the piano in this precinct of disinfected
> acoustics.

At church one Sunday, Eliot Nailles, our hero, meets Paul Hammer, our other hero. Not unnaturally, they, and we, are roused
to foreboding by the coincidence of their names, but for the bulk
of the book they merely glimpse one another; their fates intertwine only at the end.

The first half of the novel tells Nailles's story: he is, as male
suburbanites go, uxorious and cheerful, but his seventeen-year-old
son Tony in a spell of despair takes to his bed, inaccessible to
mother, father, and psychiatrist. At last a Negro guru from the
town's little ghetto coaxes him, with repetitions of the magic-word

"Love," back into the American Way of Life. The second half of
Bullet Park shows Hammer, a wealthy bastard (literally), being
chased from hotel to hotel in both hemispheres by a melancholy-
inducing *cafard;* his temporary occupation of a yellow room where
he feels at peace leads to his marriage to a wood-nymph who, once
wed, becomes a bitch (figuratively). In the end, Hammer goes
mad, decides to crucify Tony, kidnaps the boy, and is overtaken
in that Episcopalian church by Nailles armed with a power saw—
events almost redeemed from implausibility by the bravura speed
of their telling.

The book's broad streak of the fantastic has been deplored by
some critics—the same critics, I suspect, who readily grant emancipation from the probable to younger, overtly "experimental"
novelists like John Hawkes and James Purdy. A more serious
weakness lies in the similarity of the two heroes; though intended,
perhaps, to be contrasting polarities of the American psyche,
Hammer and Nailles are in fact much alike—decent hard-drinking
hommes moyens sensuels oppressed by a shapeless smog of anxiety.
Tony is headed the same way, and the author, in the askew irony
of his upbeat conclusion, with its quartet of "wonderfuls," * seems
to be shrugging off his own *cafard*. The tender, twinkling prose
has an undercurrent of distraction and impatience.

Bullet Park succeeds, I think, as a slowly revolving mobile of
marvellously poeticized moments—the portrait of the hungover
party couple the Wickwires as they struggle to rise on Monday
morning; Hammer's mother's detection of symphonies in the roar
of various airplane motors; Nailles's wife's visit to an off-off-Broad-
way play and her subsequent haunting by a nude actor, "his thick
pubic brush from which hung, like a discouraged and unwatered
flower, his principal member." America's urban hell presses hard
upon the suburbia that was meant to be paradise. Cheever maintains his loyalty to the middling and the decent, but speaks increasingly in the accents of a visionary.

---

* "Tony went back to school on Monday and Nailles—drugged—went off
to work and everything was as wonderful, wonderful, wonderful, wonderful
as it had been." Cf. *As You Like It,* act III, scene ii, Celia saying: "O wonderful, wonderful, and most wonderful wonderful! and yet again wonderful,
and after that, out of all whooping!"

Talk of a Tired Town

THE LONG-WINDED LADY, *Notes from The New Yorker*, by Maeve Brennan. 237 pp. Morrow, 1969.

The New Yorker's "Talk of the Town" department, a space set aside when Ross founded the magazine as a smart-aleck local, survives as a vacuum maintained in case someone has something to say.* When, a dozen years ago, I served on the large team that labored to fill each week this frontal void (a task that White and Thurber had performed with the aid of a few legmen), the problem was to perpetuate a cozy tone about a city that had ceased to seem cozy. We were, we "Talk of the Town" reporters, a sallow crew-cut brigade fresh from Cornell or Harvard, sent forth into the mirthless gray canyons to attend a mechanical promotional exhibit or p.r.-pushed pseudo-event, battering out upon our return six or seven yellow pages of rough copy to be honed into eight hundred gay, excited, factually flawless words by veteran martyrs like John McCarten and Brendan Gill. Some of us did not even live in the city, but had already established families and golf memberships in Bronxville or Rye, and even those who, like myself, did live in Manhattan had their hearts set on the green pastures of Fiction and the absentee ownership of Literary Glory. We were not avid to extract from the Eisenhowered, sullen if not apocalyptic metropolis of those years the enchantment of the Baghdad-on-the-Subway celebrated by O. Henry, by Scott Fitzgerald and Edna Millay, by Dorothy Parker and Benchley and Woollcott—whose chairs were still warm in the Algonquin lobby. It is to Maeve Brennan's credit that she, with the device of her letters from "the long-winded lady," has helped put New York back into *The New Yorker*, and has written about the city of the Sixties with both honesty and affection.

---

* My smart-aleck characterization of course pre-dates the politicization of the magazine's conscience, as expressed in its front columns, by such fiery unsigned editorialists as Jonathan Schell and Richard Harris, who have so much to say the space fairly groans.

Not that the pieces, as collected here, without most of the italics that gave them on first printing a comic breathlessness, entirely escape the "Talk of the Town's" way of making too much of too little and of being complacently, exhaustedly flat. She gives us John D. Rockefeller, Jr.'s entire credo as chiseled into Rockefeller Center, and the menus of a lot of meals she happens to eat, and the names of everyone present at a New Year's party at the Adano Restaurant. And the long-winded lady, read in bulk, reveals certain personal eccentricities. She tends to rise at dawn, to read while she eats, to like street music, to liken real streets to stage sets, to plug her favorite restaurants, to be threatened by large people and animals and loud noises—we deduce that she is small. She walks a lot but her range is curiously restricted; she never strays south of the Village, north of the eighties, and rarely east of Madison Avenue. Her favorite region, dismally enough, is the West Forties, those half-demolished blocks of small hotels and cellar restaurants and old coin shops between Fifth and Eighth Avenue; she most frequently strolls on Sixth, which she never calls the Avenue of the Americas.

Within these limitations she is constantly alert, sharp-eyed as a sparrow for the crumbs of human event, the overheard and the glimpsed and the guessed at, that form the solitary city person's least expensive amusement. A little boy crying, a bigger boy greeting his father, a young man courting over the telephone, a middle-aged couple enacting their estrangement across a restaurant table, an old lady flipping the pages of a letter from her hotel window as she reads—these vignettes are well realized, and need only a touch of padding and bluff to make them short stories. Miss Brennan does not blink when, surveying the cityscape, she sees drunks and crazy men and prostitutes with "the eyes of satisfied furies or unsatisfied prison wardresses," costumed in miniskirts "designed to show even more leg than they had." She is an unfussy but formidable phrase-maker, as in her long poem to the ailanthus (which she never calls the tree of heaven) or in her image of "daylight streaming like cold water" over the curved staircases and papered walls of roofless brownstones. A melancholy picture of New York's streets accumulates:

The night view up Sixth Avenue is eerie now that the blocks on the west side of the avenue are half broken down and half gone.

[Charles] is an attractive street, except that, like all small New York streets, it takes on a dead, menacing air at night, because of the lines and lines of cars that are parked along its sidewalks—cars jammed together, bumper to bumper, stealing all the life and space out of the place.

Broadway is dying, but the big street still looks much as it has looked for some time now—a garish architectural shambles with cheap shop fronts and a few movie houses.

At the moment, the dark shadow in New York is cast not by the past but by the future, and too many streets wear a dull air of "What's the use?"

Our cities, not too long ago the farm boy's dream and the place where every girl with a straight nose was advised to find her fortune, have become the national disgrace, the huge proofs of our native greed and haste. Who wants to live in them? The long-winded lady admits, "New York City is not hospitable. She is very big and she has no heart. She is not charming. She is not sympathetic. She is rushed and noisy and unkempt, a hard, ambitious, irresolute place, not very lively, and never gay." Yet she has lived there, during this slum of a decade, and also testifies, "In fact this is a wonderful city. It is always giving me something to think about."

His Own Horn

THE TRUMPET OF THE SWAN, by E. B. White. 210 pp. Harper & Row, 1970.

E. B. White's third novel for children joins the two others on the shelf for classics. While not quite so sprightly as *Stuart Little*, and less rich in personalities and incident than *Charlotte's Web*— that paean to barnyard life by a city humorist turned farmer—*The Trumpet of the Swan* has superior qualities of its own; it is the most spacious and serene of the three, the one most imbued with the author's sense of the precious instinctual heritage represented by wild nature. Its story persuasively offers itself to children as a parable of growing, yet does not lack the inimitable tone of the two earlier works—the simplicity that never condescends, the straight and earnest telling that happens upon (rather then veers into) comedy, the "grace and humor and praise of life and the good backbone of succinctness" that Eudora Welty noted nearly twenty years ago, reviewing *Charlotte's Web*.

At first glance, one's heart a little falls to see that wash drawings by Edward Frascino have replaced Garth Williams' finely furry pen-and-ink illustrations, which are wedded to White's other children's texts as intimately as Tenniel's to *Alice* and Shepard's to the Pooh books. From the jacket flap we learn that the tale, daring the obvious, tells of a Trumpeter Swan that learns to play the trumpet. More daringly still, he is called Louis. And in the first chapter we meet Sam Beaver, an eleven-year-old boy who, but for the dark touch of Indian about him, is too reminiscent of the many other bland, "interested" boy-heroes of books that bid us crouch behind the tall grass and spy out the wonder in a swan's nest. Yet soon White's love of natural detail lifts the prose into felicity, and the father and mother swan begin to talk to each other with a surprising animation, and the reader settles to a joy-ride through the rolling terrain of the highly unlikely. Louis discovers himself to be mute, an inconvenience during childhood but downright agony during the mating season. Louis' father, a bombastic old cob, gets him a trumpet, and to pay for it Louis turns professional. How does Louis' father acquire the trumpet? Why, by diving through the display window of a music store in Billings, Montana, and carrying the instrument off through a hail of shards and buckshot. How does Louis pack his trumpet, and the slate upon which he learns to write, and the lifesaving medal he wins, and the purse of money he makes? All are attached by strings around his neck, flapping and clanking together whenever he flies. How does he carve out his career? First, as a bugler in a boys' camp; next, as accompanist, swimming one-footed, to the swan-boats in the Boston Public Garden; last, as a night-club performer in Philadelphia, operating out of a pond in the city zoo.

If the author once winked during this accumulation of pre-posterous particulars, it would all turn flimsy and come tumbling down. But White never forgets that he is telling about serious mat-ters: the overcoming of a handicap, and the joys of music, and the need for creatures to find a mate, and the survival of a beauti-ful species of swan. When Louis realizes that he must graduate from the bugle to the trumpet with its three finger-operated valves, he unflinchingly asks Sam Beaver to slit the webbing of his right foot. The boy does, not omitting to point out that henceforth the swan will tend to swim in circles. What other writer, in such a work of fancy, would not have contrived to omit this homely, even repellent, bit of surgery?

White's concreteness holds the door open for unpleasantness and also engenders textures of small surprise and delightful right-ness. In one chapter Louis spends the night at the Ritz in Boston. He orders a dozen watercress sandwiches for dinner and then puts himself to bed in the bathtub. "Then he turned out the lights, climbed into the tub, curved his long neck around to the right, rested his head on his back, tucked his bill under his wing, and lay there, floating on the water, his head cradled softly in his feathers." The large bird's calm and successful attempt to cope with an un-familiar environment has a benedictory charm. This is how an in-telligent swan of good will behaves in a hotel room; it is also how a child feels, and indeed how we all feel, enchanted out of our ordinary selves by rented solitude.

The world of E. B. White's children's books is eminently a reasonable one. Nature serves as a reservoir of common sense. No-body panics, and catastrophes are taken in stride. When Mr. Brickle, the director of Camp Kookooskoos, is sprayed by a skunk, he does not do the slow or fast burn a meaner comic spirit would conjure up; he announces that the camp has been given "a delicious dash of wild perfume" and that "A swim will clear the air." Simi-larly, in *Stuart Little*, when a mouse instead of a baby is born to human parents, they promptly improvise for him a "tiny bed out of four clothespins and a cigarette box." Not birth nor death is meant to dismay us. When, in *Charlotte's Web*, the pig squeals "I don't want to die!" the spider says, "I can't stand hysterics," and eschews hysteria when her own death draws near. Her death-web speech is memorable: "After all, what's a life, anyway? We're born, we live a little while, we die. A spider's life can't help being something of a mess, with all this trapping and eating flies."

Near the end of *The Trumpet of the Swan*, Louis' father faces death with a grandiloquent soliloquy: ". . . Man, in his folly, has given me a mortal wound. The red blood flows in a steady trickle from my veins. My strength fails. . . . Good-bye, life! Good-bye, beautiful world! Good-bye, little lakes in the north! Farewell, springtimes I have known, with their passion and ardor!" The rhetoric is comic, but the tribute is sincere. *The Trumpet of the Swan* glows with the primal ecstasies of space and flight, of night and day, of nurturing and maturing, of courtship and art. On the last page Louis thinks of "how lucky he was to inhabit such a beautiful earth, how lucky he had been to solve his problems with music." How rare that word "lucky" has become! The universe remains chancy, but no one admits to having good luck. We and our children are lucky to have this book.

Remarks

on the Occasion of E. B. White's Receiving the 1971 National Medal for Literature on December 2, 1971

A GOOD WRITER is hard to talk about, since he has already, directly or by implication, said everything about himself that should be said. In the case of E. B. White, a consummate literary tact and a powerful capacity for reticence further intimidate the would-be eulogist. And indeed where would eulogy begin? E. B. White's *oeuvre*, though not very wide on the shelf, is far-flung in its variety; it is a nation gaily built on scattered islands, and the mind moves retrospectively through it as if sailing in a flirtatious wind. Letters arrive from all points of the compass; peaks glisten in unexpected places; sunny slopes conceal tunnels of anonymity; a graceful giddiness alternates as swiftly as cloud shadows with sombre sense; darkness threatens; and but for the

North Star of the writer's voice, his unflickering tone of truth, we would not know where we are. White's works range from some of the noblest essays of the century to the most famous cartoon caption of the Thirties, the one that goes,

"It's broccoli, dear."
"I say it's spinach and I say to hell with it."

He broke into print as a poet and has most recently triumphed, for the third time, as the author of a novel for children. Along the line he edited and augmented what has become a standard college textbook on English style and usage. He has been associated with *The New Yorker* for almost all of the magazine's life, and indeed he has demonstrated mastery of every kind of thing *The New Yorker* prints, from poetry to fiction to the quips that cap other publications' typographical errors. But also he wrote the grave and graceful essays of *One Man's Meat* for *Harper's Magazine*, and *Holiday* elicited from him his beautiful tribute, *This Is New York*. Daunted, then, by this body of work so polymorphously expressing concern, wit, and love, I will, as writers tend to when confronted with a subject too big for them, take refuge in the more manageable topic of myself. My life and E. B. White.

After reading White's essays in *Harper's* throughout World War II, my mother in 1945 bought a farm and moved her family to it. It is one of the few authenticated cases of literature influencing life. White's adventures in Maine, rather than Thoreau's recourse to the Concord woods or Louis Bromfield's *Malabar Farm* (a book White reviewed in the last verse review I have seen anywhere), gave my mother the necessary courage to buy eighty rundown acres of Pennsylvania loam and turned me overnight into a rural creature, clad in muddy shoes, a cloak of loneliness, and a clinging aura of apples.

Oddly, I sought the antidote for my plight in the poison that had produced it, and devoured the work of White, of Thurber, Benchley, Perelman, Sullivan, and all those other names evocative of the urban romance that not so long ago attached to New York City, the innocent longing for sophistication that focussed here. When, infrequently, my parents brought me to New York, I always imagined I would see E. B. White in Grand Central Station.

I never did, but the wish in its intensity gouged a distinct memory imprint, delicate as a leaf sedimentized in limestone, of White's dapper, crinkled-haired, rather heavy-lidded countenance, that I had studied on book flaps and in caricatures, superimposed upon those caramel-colored walls. I still never enter the station without looking for him. For me, he *was* the city, and I wonder, will anybody ever again love this city, and poeticize it, as he did, when, to quote one of his poems,

> In the days of my youth, in the days of my youth,
> I lay in West Twelfth Street, writhing with Truth.
> I died in Jones Street, dallying with pain,
> And flashed up Sixth Avenue, risen again.

I did at last meet White, an ocean away, in Oxford. He and his wife Katharine came through the door of our basement flat on Iffley Road. E. B. White himself! It was an experience that had all the qualities of a nightmare, except that it was not unpleasant. He spoke; he actually uttered words, and they were so appropriate, so neutral and natural yet—in that unique way of his—so *trim*, so well designed to put me at ease, that I have quite forgotten what they were.

A consequence of that awesome visit was employment of sorts; while working on West 43rd Street, I would see White in the halls and what struck me in his walk, in the encouraging memos he once or twice sent me, and in the editorial notes that in lucky weeks headed up the magazine, was how much more fun he had in him than us younger residents of those halls. Not loud or obvious fun, but contained, inturning fun, shaped like a mainspring. I dealt mainly with Mrs. White, I want to add, and what a fine warm mentor she was!—a formidable woman, an editor of the magazine before White was a contributor, gifted with that terrible clear vision some women have—the difference between a good story and a bad one loomed like a canyon in her vision— yet not burdened by it, rather, rejoicing in it, and modest and humorous in her firmness, so that she makes her appearances in White's accounts as a comic heroine, a good sport helping him dispose of their surplus eggs by hurling them against the barn wall.

After I quit my job and the city, my encounters with White became purely those of a reader—a reader to myself, and a reader aloud, to my children. When I asked my ten-year-old girl if I could say today that *Charlotte's Web* was her favorite book, she said, "No, tell them *Stuart Little* is."

Eulogy is disarmed. White has figured in my life the way an author should figure, coming at me from different directions with a nudge, a reminder, a good example. I am not alone in feeling grateful, or he would not be winning this prize. For three generations he has reinforced our hopeful sense that the kingdom of letters is a fiefdom of the kingdom of man. He writes as one among us, not above us, a man pulling his mortal weight while keeping a level head and now and then letting loose with a song.

A Citation

*Composed for the Awarding of
the 1968 National Book Award for Fiction
to* The Eighth Day, *by Thornton Wilder* *

THROUGH THE LENS of a turn-of-the-century murder mystery, Mr. Wilder surveys a world that is both vanished and coming to birth; in a clean gay prose sharp with aphoristic wit and the sense and scent of Midwestern America and Andean Chile, he takes us on a chase of Providence and delivers us, exhilarated and edified, into the care of an ambiguous conclusion.

An Unpublished Book Note

THE ARMIES OF THE NIGHT, by Norman Mailer. 288 pp. New American Library, 1968.

A fascinating, if hysterically high-flown, account of the October 1967 protest march on the Pentagon, by one of its participants. Mailer's lust for self-display has cast off whatever tenuous tram-

---

* The other judges were Granville Hicks and the late Josephine Herbst. We having made, not too contentiously, our decision, they invited me to write the citation, and I scratched this off. They had no suggestions for its improvement; otherwise I would not thus include it as my work.

mels have hitherto restrained it, and his description of his deplorably drunken speechifying on Friday night, and his headachy jockeying for literary position with Robert Lowell during the next day's march, are fearlessly frank, and funny indeed. Less funny, but the best narrative stretch in the book, is his account of arrest and the twenty-four hours soberingly spent in jail, before being handed an unexpectedly severe sentence. His sociological/ historical analysis of the forces behind the protest goes from the farcical to the brilliant; he proposes no measuring tool but his own hyperbolic sensibility. The Vietnam involvement becomes unremitting Reichian melodrama, where any flash of color will do for an insight, and any aesthetic irritation serves the most sweeping diagnostic purposes. The book's strength—until the vilely written last pages, a post-midnight collapse into bathos—is this finagling author's capacity for awe, for giving his enemies his avid attention, and giving events, in this era of humorless propaganda, a decent, sensual complexity. A good rush job.

An Interesting Emendation

in the Text of Mr. Sammler's Planet, by Saul Bellow

TOWARD THE END of the *Atlantic Monthly*'s two-part serialization of *Mr. Sammler's Planet*, the hero, calling upon his dying nephew, Dr. Elya Gruner, in the hospital, sits in the waiting room next to Gruner's daughter Angela, and thinks,

> There was no odor of Arabian musk, her favorite perfume. Instead her female effluence was very strong today, a salt odor, something from inside the woman. Elya's bitter words had had their effect on Sammler. He could not look at her eyes without thinking of her father's words, imagining her in bed, and—a worse fancy—the white of semen on her mouth. But these were, curiously, images nearly devoid of prejudice. Or very nearly. One must change one's outlook. The past perhaps exaggerated the seriousness of these things.

In the hardcover edition (Viking, 1970), the entire episode has been rewritten, with a freedom and renewed inspiration that speak well for Bellow's venturesome, perfectionistic art—though the changes are not all inarguably for the better. The sentences equivalent for those above read:

> Sitting near her, Sammler could not smell the usual Arabian musk. Instead her female effluence was very strong, a salt odor, similar to tears or tidewater, something from within the woman. Elya's words had taken effect strongly—his "Too much sex." Even the white lipstick suggested perversion. But this was curiously without prejudice. Sammler felt no prejudice about perversion, about sexual matters. Nothing. It was too late in the day for that.

The entire long paragraph containing this passage has been strenuously, anxiously revised; the second version is choppier. Details of Angela's costume (large gold earrings, a miniskirt) have been rearranged, her idol-like immobility has been charged with a certain choked anger, Elya's words are specified. Most interestingly, the vivid "white of semen on her mouth" has been softened to "white lipstick" suggesting "perversion." Why? It is as if Bellow were embarrassed by his own revulsion, and backed away from it, in the same motion as his elderly, fastidious hero moves from being "nearly devoid of prejudice" on the matter to feeling absolutely "no prejudice about perversion, about sexual matters."

Yet what people put into their mouths *does* interest us, as it interested the Biblical Jews. Philip Roth's Alexander Portnoy ragefully marvels at the *goyim*, "these imbecilic eaters of the execrable":

> Let the *goyim* sink *their* teeth into whatever lowly creature crawls and grunts across the face of the dirty earth, we will not contaminate our humanity thus. Let *them* (if you know who I mean) gorge themselves upon anything and everything that moves, no matter how odious and abject the animal, no matter how grotesque or *shmutzig* or dumb the creature in question happens to be. Let them eat eels and frogs and pigs and crabs and lobsters; let them eat vulture, let them eat ape-meat and skunk if they like. . . . They will eat *anything*, anything they can get their big *goy* hands on! And the terrifying corollary, *they will do anything as well*. Deer eat what deer eat, and Jews eat what Jews eat, but not these

goyim. Crawling animals, wallowing animals, leaping and angelic animals—it makes no difference to them— . . .

In the next paragraph, he confesses to sucking on a lobster claw and the same night, an hour later, aiming his erect penis at a *shikse* on a Public Service bus. This at age fifteen; a few years later, Portnoy makes closer but still mostly spiritual contact with one of these legendary *"shikses* Who Will Do Anything," a Catholic Gentile, Bubbles Girardi, who has blown a friend ("And does she suck on it, or does she blow on it, or somehow is it that she does *both?* Oh, God, Ba-ba-lu, did you shoot in her mouth? Oh my God! And did she swallow it right down, or spit it out, or get mad—tell me! what did she do with your hot come!"), and, more than a few years (he is now thirty-two) later, Portnoy finds the real McCoy in the West Virginia hillbilly (the quintessential Protestant Gentile) nicknamed ("let them eat ape-meat") The Monkey—"What a find, I thought, she takes it right down to the root! What a mouth I have fallen into!" Their romance begins with his inspired offer to "eat your pussy, baby" at their first meeting and ends with her complaint that "you care more about the niggers in Harlem that you don't even know, than you do about me, who's been sucking you off for a solid year!" The characters are not unimpressed with their own orality:

> A Jewish man, who cared about the welfare of the poor of the City of New York, was eating her pussy! Someone who had appeared on educational TV was shooting off into her mouth!

Nor does all this delightful uncleanness go unpunished: Portnoy, after a triadic bout with The Monkey and an Italian whore, throws up, and the undiscriminating Bubbles Girardi is killed while consorting with Negroes:

> There's a case of cause and effect that confirms my ideas about human consequence! Bad enough, rotten enough, and you get your cock-sucking head blown off by boogies. Now that's the way the world's supposed to be run!

Bellow is comparatively disingenuous: in the revised paragraph, he quotes Elya as blaming Angela for simply "too much sex," whereas what Elya had really said earlier, which her eyes recall to Sammler, is: "You see a woman who has done it in too many ways with too many men. By now she probably doesn't know the name of the man between her legs. And she looks. . . . Her eyes —she has fucked-out eyes." *Too many ways:* not quantity but the posture is crucial; Elya fears she is around the corner "Frenching an orderly," and her brother Wallace tells Sammler that "she let that twerp in Mexico ball her fore and aft in front of Wharton, with who-knows-what-else thrown in free by her." Sammler's moral dignity at times seems to consist solely of suffering witness to the sexuality of this woman "who was also something good to eat," who nevertheless had once studied Hebrew.

"You were quite studious. I was impressed that you were studying Hebrew."

"Just a front, Uncle. I was a dirty little bitch, really."

How dirty, and why dirty, are the nervous questions that lie behind Bellow's emendation, and much of the novel's moral discussion. Is sex innocent and fulfilling fun in any position, as contemporary culture would teach us, or is it, as the Judaeo-Christian tradition instructs, a fixed and solemn performance devoted to procreation? Specifically, is the eating of semen a natural kiss, caress, and engulfment of the beloved, or a perverse defilement? Recent American fiction traces a swift secularization of this magical act since the days, scarcely more than a decade ago, when the young author of *Rabbit, Run* reverently, reluctantly reduced Ruth to her knees and Nabokov, his flamboyant archness making virtue of the necessity for euphemism, had Lolita pronounce "in all insouciance really, a disgusting slang term which, in a literal French translation, would be *souffler*."

With what a thrill did one read, in the days when Henry Miller was contraband, such direct and insouciant descriptions as, from *Sexus:*

I awakened gradually, dimly conscious that my prick was in Elsie's mouth.

I stood up and unbuttoned my fly. In a jiffy [Ida] had it out and in her mouth. Gobble, gobble, like a hungry buzzard. I came in her mouth.

> Suddenly [a nameless switchboard operator] unclasped her hands and with wet fingers she unbuttoned my fly, took my prick out and made a dive for it with her mouth. She went at it like a professional, teasing it, worrying it, fluting her lips, then choking on it. I came off in her mouth; she swallowed it as if it were nectar and ambrosia.

But, as descriptions of fellatio pass from the literary underground to middle-class fiction, and from the male to the female point of view, the ambrosia takes on another taste. From Lois Gould's lengthy treatment in *Such Good Friends* (1970):

> I was down on my knees, struggling with a stuck zipper. Timmy's fly zipper! On my knees trying to take my medicine like a big girl. See? Same old Julie, washing down the nasty stuff with more nasty stuff. I can take it; I'm *supposed* to take it. . . . Okay, but I wasn't dismissed yet. He wanted me to kneel slightly higher for leverage. (When I was eight I'd talked the pediatrician out of using a tongue depressor to examine my sore throat. "Please, the wood makes me gag—see, I can open wide enough. *Ah.*" "Very good, but I still need to insert the stick—just for a minute now. There." "*Ahgh!*" "See, that wasn't so bad." Yes, it was. Yes, it is.) . . . Time for our medicine now—here it comes. Let's see it all go down in one big gulp. No, you can't have water with it; I said you're a big girl now. Don't cry. I said *don't cry*, or we'll hold you down on the bed and paint your throat with Argyrol. Whatever happened to painting your throat with Argyrol?
> Wait—he's taking it away. All gone. I called up to him, up over the dreary miles of shirtfront, a sterile snowy field with a neatly planted single row of buttons.

At least the lady protests, if too much. In a novel three years deeper into the Seventies, Erica Jong's *Fear of Flying*, the penis in the mouth has lost its power to stand and make the throat ache with indignation; it is just one wan item in a rather tender catalogue:

> His broad neck, which was sunburned. His chest, covered with curly reddish hair. His belly, a bit paunchy—unlike Bennett's brown leanness. His curled pink penis which tasted faintly of urine and refused to stand up in my mouth. His very pink and hairy balls which I took in my mouth one at a time. His muscular thighs. His sunburned knees. His feet.

With the matter-of-factly noted lingering taste of urine, all mystery has fled. Fellatio has become hardly worth describing. Alan Lelchuk, in his novel of the same year, *American Mischief*, seeks, like a pornographic film maker (*cf.* the delicious triadic scene in *The Devil in Miss Jones*) to stir us with visible sperm and lesbian voracity:

> The climax embarrassed me as much as it thrilled me. With moans and shrieks and body English growing more frenzied, I began finally coming into Gwen's mouth. But suddenly she maneuvered away so that I was lathering her face with the white sperm. Whereupon Angie, bellowing like a cow in heat, suddenly dove down upon that face and began lapping it up. Incredible. The denseness of appetites was so thick by then, the flow of juices and secretions and passions so rich, that it was like being at a feast of cannibals. I tell you, those girls would have eaten anything, anything!

But the episode feels exaggerated—more trash than truth, more exploitation than exploration. The frontier has moved on, to buggery, where sex can still touch the forbidden, the religious, the diabolical. Rojak, buggering the German maid in *An American Dream*, sees her as a Nazi, comes to her "cry of rage," and feels he has "come to the Devil a fraction too late." For an age which lusted, as did the late Sixties, for revolution, buggery is the fit deviation; it runs counter to the channels of production, whereas ejaculation into the throat conforms to them, like the liberal variations within the capitalist system. Fellatio feeds; buggery violates.

In these accelerated times, the frontier fills rapidly; Terry Andrews' novel *The Story of Harold* (1974) centers its mystique on "fist-fucking" and the brave new world beyond the anus:

> I described this whole thing to a friend afterwards . . . and he asked . . . "But wasn't it just like sticking your hand in a bowl of spaghetti?" And the answer is no—oh no, not a bit! It's like putting your fingers in fold upon fold of hot, wet velvet, some fabric never felt before, that contains a living pulse within it. For you do feel the life. There are arteries, major blood vessels, along which a human existence trills. And they can be played with and plucked and bowed like the strings of a living violin.

And here, like Mr. Sammler before he was emended, I feel not quite devoid of prejudice. This trans-anal passage tells me more than I want to know; it has the frightful melancholy of the purely physical; I can hardly bear to read it. I flinch, as Bellow (evidently) flinched at his own phrase, as some readers may have flinched at my above oral anthology. Where we draw back varies; but our sexual natures, even in this age of competitive license and Freudian sanction, do ask limits, for their own protection. The angel of disgust guards the seeds of life. Sexual excitement arises from an arcanum; some stimuli must be kept in safe deposit. Just as moral prohibitions have as their end our own safety, some boundary to the exploration of the bodies of others, some economy in knowledge, is asked for, that potency be conserved.

Phantom Life

WEST OF THE ROCKIES, by Daniel Fuchs. 166 pp. Knopf, 1971.

Nobody else writes like Daniel Fuchs:

> All right, then. Munves pressed her tightly to him and shivered. Ooooh, it felt good. Soft, soft. Women were originally built like a jackknife, like a Westchester roll, all one short round lump, he was thinking, and when God opened them up straight, the body protruded in round curved masses. He hugged her tighter and tighter, his skinny arm on her shoulders aching.

That is a young man learning to dance, in *Homage to Blenholt*, the middle novel of the three Fuchs published, quickly and obscurely, in the middle Thirties. When they were reprinted, in 1961, Fuchs wrote, "The books didn't sell—400 copies, 400, 1200. The reviews were scanty, immaterial. The books became odious to me." He goes on to describe his turning to short stories: "I was in the middle of a fourth novel but broke it up and swiftly turned it into three or four short stories. I worked away all spring, one story after the other—perhaps a dozen or fifteen in all. I rested. It was July. Nothing happened." He and his young wife made money by going out to the race track and betting. "I had visions of spending the rest of our lives at the races, travelling from track to track with the seasons. Suddenly I heard from my agent. The editors had simply been away on their summer vacations, that was all. They took the stories, all of them—one afternoon three acceptances in the same mail. I had my racetrack winnings in cash all over me in different pockets; I had checks from the magazines laid away in envelopes." It is a typically happy Fuchs story, and it is how I think of him—as a natural winner, a poet who never had to strain after a poetic effect, a writer so blithely blessed by the gods he never got dug in properly. He gave up short stories in turn and went to Hollywood.

Now, out of Hollywood, after more than three decades in the desert, comes the fourth Fuchs novel: *West of the Rockies*. It is shorter than the others—scenario-length, with odd blank or hurried patches, perhaps for the director to fill in. In his prose of glimmering diffidence, Fuchs tells the story of Adele Hogue, a movie star, and Burt Claris, a handsome nobody who works for her talent agency. The beginning of their romance is tersely sketched indeed: "He had taken up with her, had gotten into her good graces, slept with her. Claris was no better than most. She was accessible." (One of the book's incidental mirages is that Fuchs always refers to the hero as "Claris," which sounds feminine, and often to the heroine as "Hogue," which seems masculine.) The novel centers upon a Palm Springs resort to which Adele Hogue has fled after bolting the set of a movie in production; Burt Claris, on behalf of the agency, has chased her there. The action generally observes the unities of this place in these few days of crisis; as a result, Fuchs spends a high proportion of his pages filling us in—on Adele's old romance with Harry Case, a racketeer whose ex-wife, Fannie, runs the resort; on Adele's recent disastrous fling with the international jet set and an aristocratic English husband who has bankrupted her; on Burt's marriage to an immature young heiress; on the ins and outs of motion-picture financing and the ruin facing the producer, Robert Wigler, who is present, in "the great 117-degree afternoon desert heat," along with Burt's skirt-chasing superior at the talent agency, and the three children the actress has spawned in the course of her marriages, and a hungry host of reporters, and the perennial resort guests, the sun-bathing, well-preserved "second and third wives of men who made big money in meat, oil, or textiles." Even when the action is before his eyes, the author's tone is one of reverie:

> She held her shoulders straight, carrying her body with that clear-striding, forthright sexual quality they had and which they knew they had. It was the way they were put together; it was the bones in them. It was a readiness or acquiescence to use the body for all the pleasure it could give, a readiness they picked up from their mothers, in the Hollywood malt shops, out of the air.

Constructions involving "or" and "way" recur—"either because she considered him of no account or because she was too care-worn or because it was her way," "in the ways they had," "whether it was for this reason or because of some other mental quirk"—as if Fuchs were groping through a dream that puzzles him, dazzles him. The blinding California brightness seems pre-smog, and in the end the reader is told that all this slice of "phantom life" happened "some twelve years ago, when television was comparatively new and the big picture studios still throbbed, the collapse yet to come."

What might be faults in another novel feed this one's dreamlike, movie-like glow. Gentle improbabilities hurry events along. Servants are remarkably obliging: a Filipino hotel steward volunteers his room as a love nest, and a baby's nurse spontaneously tells Burt where his wife has hidden her love letters. The imperfectly guessed motives and sketchily summarized lives give a mysterious largeness to the world beyond the plot's circumference. Los Angeles becomes a nostalgic presence: "It had been another time, everything closer to the studios in those days, the Los Angeles area still spread thin and relatively undeveloped, a third of what it was to become. . . . The wide boulevards with sandy, neglected islands in the middle of them, the sun pouring down, so still and breathtakingly brilliant, as it was in those earlier years."

This tone is far from the self-promoting satire and rage usually offered by "Hollywood novels." Yet the reality to which Fuchs lends his love is recognizably cruel. A jam halts traffic on the desert thruway: "Claris looked down and saw the hard, murderous grain of the pavement concrete, the slits and abrasions, the concrete suddenly stationary and as if magnified." Contracts, erotic as well as financial, take effect in an arid atmosphere purged of any Old World notions of honor or noblesse oblige. The dreams of success and love are acted out against a hard awareness of the "they" who control destinies—the bankers, the gangsters, as implacable and irrational as Greek deities. The women who populate Palm Springs form an ominous chorus of Furies. They lie in the sun discussing girdles and beauty operations, they make love with necklaces on, they fly decorators in from New York and Texas, they are not unkind, having "all been in the business at one time or another, as stand-ins or stock girls," but with men their ardor is "overwhelmingly tender and solicitous and at the same time impersonal, a kindness which they could discontinue seemingly without an instant's feeling or trace of remembrance": they are all, Wigler tells Burt Claris, "secret agents." They have all made their "adjustments," and in this they differ from Adele Hogue.

Fuchs's portrait of a star is masterly. He seems to do everything to diminish her. She appears frightened, sick, vulgar, and foolish, callous to her children and destructive wherever she can reach. Even her body is seen sadly: "Claris saw the roundness at the upper arms and shoulders, the weight taking hold there, packing in; he saw the slack, plump roll of the belly, the widening at the waist—that thickening which, it had been surveyed and studied in the business, the young people in the movie houses spotted and resented." And when this Venus does her thing and makes love, the prose plunges into melancholy:

> She opened her arms to him, embraced and clasped him to her, taking him on. . . . Claris responded to the pressure, winding through the ritual, the kisses, the fondling, the contriving of an illusion of love—that knavish, coward's thing people relentlessly do with one another.

The weight of Hogue's mortal envelope is frightful: "Claris wondered . . . at the mauling she had absorbed in her time—the curettages, the operations, the bad operation . . . the brutal intensive reducing regimens, when . . . she installed herself in the hospital and they systematically sloughed the weight off her so that she herself came to view her body with a sick distaste." Since neither beauty nor skill ("She didn't know anything about acting, never had, would be the first to say so") has lifted her up from the high-school malt shops through the petty prostitutions and mismarriages and neurotic ailments into stardom, what has? Fuchs answers, "Fanatic energy." Adele explains it to herself: "Her special effectiveness with the audience was spontaneous, something organic, beyond control. She believed it was the product of the nervous system you were endowed with, and she was convinced her nerves were used up, that you were given just so much." So "star quality" exacts an exceptional toll, and reader and author and lover together come to adore anew this exasperating and worse-than-average woman. Using as his material the shabbiest truths, Fuchs rebuilds the Hollywood myth; a happy ending evolves in an atmosphere of exhausted illusion. When, at the end, Adele Hogue stands with Burt on the edge of a marital partnership perhaps—who knows?—as profitable as that of Doris Day and Marty Melcher, and turns to him in the mass of reporters and mouths "I love you" as if on a sound stage, her sincerity is beyond gauging; we are dazzled by her courage, her real will to go on living her life of unreality.

NON-FICTION

Black Suicide

BLACK SUICIDE, by Herbert Hendin. 176 pp. Basic Books, 1969.

Suicide, that most absolute of acts, is yet relative and can serve as a window into the peculiar stresses of a cultural group. In support of this thesis, Herbert Hendin, a professor at the Columbia University Psychoanalytic Clinic, has produced two books: his well-known, well-applauded study *Suicide and Scandinavia* (1964) and an equally fascinating and surpassingly relevant, though largely ignored, volume, *Black Suicide*. Dr. Hendin proposes, and demonstrates, that suicide is different things in different places. In Denmark, it is commonly an attempt to inflict guilt upon others or to rejoin a loved one in a sentimentally conceived hereafter. In Sweden, suicide tends to be of a "performance" rather than a "dependency" type; the self-hatred of a competitive failure, however, is deepened by a peculiar Swedish coldness that emphasizes emotional control and erects between the sexes a wall of frozen silence. In the black ghettos of America, suicide is one face of a rage that, though ultimately caused by the Negro's frustrating position in the society, originates for almost every individual in maternal rejection.

Not that uniformity prevails in Dr. Hendin's cross section of twenty-five suicide attempts admitted to the Harlem Hospital. Four older men attempted suicide after professional reverses, suggesting the "performance" motive common in Sweden—but with the difference that not so much a rigid achievement standard as an adaptive pattern fragilely based upon outward compliance and contained anger had broken down. These Uncle Toms, after lifetimes spent pushing brooms or hand trucks, found themselves still economically defenseless, and, having been taught docile compliance as a mode of goodness, construed their adaptive failure in moral terms and sought to take their lives in atonement. Again, many of the females included in this study attempted suicide after abandonment by a husband or lover—but there is a radical difference between the Danish matrix of interdependence and the sorry turmoil of abandonment, violence, foster parentage, and neglect that has served black females as models of family life.

The interviews and life histories presented in *Black Suicide* do not bear out the notion that the black female is relatively insulated from the effects of racial discrimination.

> The most disastrous impact of racial institutions seems to be felt so early in life and so overwhelmingly that the plight of the female seems as bad as that of the male. Frustration, rage, and violence already characterize the lives of both sexes when they are teenagers, and there is little difference between men and women in the degree of despair that is so often present by the time they are young adults.

Given a set of tests called the Buss-Durkee Hostility Inventory, the women in this group of would-be suicides scored higher than the men, and in the "assault category" two females—called "Ina Tracy" and "Agnes Carreth"—obtained perfect scores of ten. Ina Tracy, a tall woman of thirty-one who lived in Alabama until she was twenty, describes one of her frequent fights with friends: "I beat her as long as she moved. As long as she moved I kicked her. Blood both frightens and excites me." Of her childhood, she says, "My mother once told me that she wished I had been born dead or that she had gotten rid of me. The way things worked out, I wished it too. . . . My mother would make me break a branch and she'd beat me with it—hit me wherever it landed. I wanted to take her and choke her to death. Wished that I would die or she would." Yet her mother's desires appear to have controlled her behavior; teased for tallness at school, she was not much of a fighter until, running from another girl one day, she saw her mother, "who she knew would be furious at her running away." Similarly: "At seventeen she told her mother she had never liked boys. When her mother replied that she should, she decided to have sexual relations with the first boy who was willing and soon after became pregnant." Ina left the child with her mother a few years afterward and came to New York alone. Her first suicide attempt came a year later. A recurrent nightmare involves a "very large man who had been dead a long time, so long that one could smell him." This image seems the only peaceful one in the frenzied alternation of her homicidal and suicidal fantasies.

"Louise Greene," an attractive and engagingly childlike woman of twenty-six, scored low on the hostility tests, yet a legacy of maternal rejection also perpetuates itself through her. She was raised by her grandparents in Georgia, and did not meet her mother until the age of twelve, when a woman suddenly appeared and demanded that Louise, her first-born, come live with her and care for the younger children she had had by a variety of men. Though compelled to obey, Louise frequently ran off back to her grandparents, and after one fight was prevented from taking rat poison. She has had two children, by two men, neither of whom she wished to marry; when she did marry, she and her husband quarreled over her refusal to quit her job and stay home with the one child that was, for an interval, living with her. When this man died, under violent circumstances she never investigated, Louise came to New York, where she works as a drugstore waitress. She sends part of her salary south for the care of her children, who live with her aunt and uncle; she insists—even in her suicide note—on her love for her children. Hendin concludes: "Louise feels too keenly her position as a rejected daughter to be able to see herself as a mother. . . . Furious with her mother for abandoning her and for not providing her with a father, Louise is following in her mother's footsteps in having children with various fathers and then rejecting them."

Another type of casualty inflicted by the black home is illustrated by four male homosexuals who turned up among the twelve male suicide attempts—a surprising incidence; among male white suicides fewer than one in twelve is a homosexual. In the homes of these men—and though the statistical sample of homosexuals is small, it has been augmented by six other non-suicidal cases—a father was usually present, but so violent toward mother and son that heterosexuality became intimidating. Also, the boys were disturbed by their mothers' extramarital sexual activities. "Benjamin

Ellis" remembers discovering his mother in bed with a man and says, "It jarred me so much I wept." The violent father and promiscuous mother curiously reverse the typical recessive father and non-sexual mother of white homosexuals. Curious, too, is the usual preference of black homosexuals for white partners: a tragic indication of an unconfessed racial shame. "Andrew Vallen" insists he is proud to be a Negro but wants to have an operation to make his thick lips thinner. "Leroi Nifson," a medium-brown offspring of a black father and a Syrian mother, when asked why he confined his homosexual contacts to whites and Puerto Ricans, answered that he considered himself Arabic, "a white man sympathetic to the Negro cause." Benjamin Ellis, the oldest of the three, and the only one who achieved a high guilt rating in the psychological tests, associates dirt, masculinity, and blackness—"I do things with men, don't with women because men are dirty anyhow. The man was Negro and not as clean as he could be"—but also says, "White men don't care what they do. They'll do anything. Negroes have limitations. If it lowers their pride, they won't do it." His double need to be degraded and to be protected is best served by a white lover.

Black Suicide began as an investigation of the anomaly that, though the overall Negro rate of suicide is lower in this country than the white rate, between the ages of twenty and thirty-five *twice* as many black males as white males kill themselves in New York City. The Negro homicide rate is in all age groups higher than the white rate. The interweave of destructiveness and self-destruction in black ghetto life is everywhere bared by Dr. Hendin's case histories. "Peter Churney," who has been thinking of suicide since the age of twelve, and at nineteen has survived three attempts, was present at his father's violent death.

> [Peter's father's] suspicions that Peter's mother was having affairs led him to jealous rages. One night when he was beating her in a particularly savage way, the police were called. When they arrived, his father began shooting at them. Peter, who was seven at the time, was trapped in the room with his father, who had five guns and, although wounded, continued to fire until he was killed. . . . [Peter] was quite taken aback, however, at the suggestion that his father's death might have been a form of suicide.

Peter, whose IQ is high for this group, admired Hitler as a boy and "says he had the idea of going on a rooftop and shooting people but adds lightly that this was before 'that guy in Dallas' did it." His fantasies of mass murder, however, give him less pleasure now; Peter feels he is on a suicide course and nothing can stop him. "Harrison Eliot," a man of thirty-three, lost his mother, "whose strictness and severe beatings he still recalls," at the age of twelve; his father, a railroad chef, was robbed and beaten to death when Harrison was four. He has a savage temper, and twice has served jail sentences for fighting with policemen. He dreams of murdering his former wife and her boy friend, and drowns his rage in drink. "He mentions that several of his friends drank themselves to death but does not seem to be aware that he is following in their footsteps." "Eddie Marker," a boy of eighteen, is working toward the same goal via drugs; he is a forty-five-dollar-a-day heroin user who must rob to support his habit. A year ago his twenty-two-year-old sister killed his father, who she felt was trying to harm her baby. "Eddie does not believe in death, and thinks his father is alive and that he will meet him someday. . . . He has no plans for the future after he gets out of jail. . . . When Eddie was asked about his getting into so much trouble, he replied, 'No more than most of the people I know. . . .' Eddie uses his Muslim beliefs not simply to deny death but to deny the reality of life as he experiences it."

What, then, the white reader may well ask himself as he gazes into this snake pit of lost lives, is to be done? First he might wonder how accurate a microcosm of Negro life in America these twenty-five failed suicides afford. Certainly this is a disadvantaged group within a disadvantaged group. Seven of the twenty to whom IQ tests were administered scored in the seventies, or on the border line of effective intelligence, and only four (including the wild Ina Tracy) above the standard median of 100. On the other hand, the geographic narrowness of the sample is more apparent than real; many of these Harlemites were born and raised in the South and experienced their formative traumas there. And a look at the graphs in the appendix discovers little change in violence statistics since the 1920's; proportionally as many Negroes were killing themselves and each other in the days of Amos 'n' Andy and the

Cotton Club as in these days of summer riots and the Black Panthers. The birth dates of Hendin's subjects span fifty years; after reading their histories one feels that Negro life in America has changed sadly little except that drugs have replaced drink as the cop-out, and that Islam and paranoid politics now share with Christianity the effort to restrain despair and institutionalize self-respect.

Three conclusions of Hendin's study bear emphasis:

1. The black female, far from being a secondary victim of white racism, bears the brunt of it. As a girl she is exposed equally with her brothers to the psychological injuries inflicted by absentee or distracted parents; from her teens on she is vulnerable to pregnancy; as a woman she is the first and nearest recipient of the black man's anger. And not merely in the form of beatings:

> One senses that for many black men sex serves a double purpose. The children they father serve as living proof of their potency and also as a mark of their anger. Their abandonment of women, often when they are in the most helpless of conditions, may be a way of striking back at their mothers who rejected them or the succession of aunts, grandmothers, or cousins who raised them; of figuratively screwing womankind and lodging a protest against their own lives.

Biology appoints the black woman custodian of order in a subsociety that has no great stake in order. As a mother, then, she transmits to her children her burden of shame, inadequacy, frustration, and fury. Dr. Hendin touches on the thesis, put forward by two black psychiatrists, that "black mothers reject and castrate their sons in order to prepare them better for the life they will encounter in a white world." These same psychiatrists, William H. Grier and Price M. Cobbs (in *Black Rage*) go on to recommend a psychological shift of anger from black mothers to white society. Hendin does not think much either of diagnosis or of remedy. While conceding a limited "useful social purpose" to identifying the institutional sources of black frustration and channelling rage toward corrective action, he insists that black mothers rear their children badly because they were reared badly. "Like all other children, those black children who have experienced the least rejection are best prepared to deal with the world, black or white."

2. Racial discrimination inflicts its worst psychological damage out of sight of the white world, in the heart of the black family.

White people are strangely absent from these narrated lives. The policemen with whom Harrison Eliot battles, and the employer of whom "Jean Wayne" complains, "He didn't care how I am," may be white; but the only white people given any individuality at all are Leroi Nifson's Syrian mother and "Roger," Benjamin Ellis' Jewish lover. Racial self-consciousness seems remarkably faint; of the fifteen patients who executed drawings of human figures, none indicated skin color, and only one determinedly attempted to portray Negroid features—and he, "Owen James," had the special problem of being so pale that all his life other Negroes had picked upon him as a white. But Dr. Hendin does not conclude from the rarity of an overt black self-image—as did an earlier investigator, Charles Prudhomme—that race is not a factor in black suicide.

> The Negro usually needs to repress an awareness that he has so blanketed his entire race with his own self-hatred that he loathes all the characteristics of blackness. Over and over the subjects in this study try to deny racial motivations for their feelings or behavior, though such motives are apparent. Even the man who insisted on having an operation to make his lips thinner denied that he in any way connected the size of his lips with being black. In their most repetitive self-images the patients saw themselves as black bugs or black rats. While these images were often dreamed of as symbols linking sexuality, destructiveness, and blackness, it is no accident that the symbols that come to them originate in the most despised and unwanted living things in the Harlem tenements—the rats and the roaches.

3. Black poverty includes a poverty of motivational fantasy. Along with the low self-esteem goes an inability to imagine successful achievement. One looks almost in vain among the testimony of the young men for instances of heroes. "Luke Dellins," a promising and athletic boy cruelly maimed by hospital maltreatment, has become a bitter black nationalist and admires only Jomo Kenyatta. Peter Churney, whose fascination with Hitler has been noted, wanted to be an archaeologist and now wishes he could make movies like Sergei Eisenstein. And when one tries to imagine how a ghetto child whose father was shot before his eyes is going to become an Eisenstein, or a Hitchcock, or a Mike Nichols, the plausibility of low aspirations sinks in.

In America the rate of white suicide continues to rise after the age of forty-five, and overtakes and exceeds the black rate. Hendin's explanation for this is elegant and eloquent: the white person encounters, in late middle age, the certainty of failure and disappointed hope that his black fellow citizen encountered in the prime of life. Luke Owens, at the age of twenty-nine, has concluded: "There is no place in the world for a fellow like me. I'll always be on the same level; I'll get nowheres."

Little hope can be held for most of the subjects of this study. Yet Dr. Hendin's description of the general black plight in this country is not entirely dispiriting. For one thing, it makes intelligible, as nothing else I have read does, the vehemence of black liberation rhetoric. The roaches and rats that run through these suicides' dreams are close to such images as this one, dictated into a tape recorder by Eldridge Cleaver upon the death of Martin Luther King: "I think that America has already committed suicide and we who now thrash within its dead body are also dead in part and parcel of the corpse. America is truly a disgusting burden upon this planet."

For another, Dr. Hendin's book locates the need for *revolution* within the black psyche. I italicize this alarming and prevalent word because it is a stumbling block. Granted that the unmitigated capitalism special to America has at repeated historical moments—on the large plantations, during the North's post-Reconstruction abandonment of the freedmen, in present-day technology's devaluation of untrained labor—worked to sever the Negro from the general economic evolution, it is difficult to conceive an "overthrow" of the "system" that would not prove counterproductive for all races. Rather, the challenge to the white-dominated system would seem to be merely to make good the numerous statutes and public resolutions that already exist. But there can be no denying that the self-hatred impressed on the black man by three centuries of rope and shackle, low wages, and social insult must be overthrown. And, for all the recalcitrance of private neuroses, psychic revolutions can occur rather quickly, as one generation replaces another. Although it is tempting, as the abysmal statistics from the ghetto mount, to dismiss symbolic triumphs, what value can be given to, say, the disappearance of "conking" or the widespread use of black models in television commercials? Or to the appearance in the streets of African costumes? That whites ape such fashions and commercialize them seems to me the opposite of disheartening: it is one more step toward America's recovery of what it early lost, a sense of itself as a multiracial nation, rather than as a white nation "holding" colored minorities.

The black race presently exists in America as a sunken, underdeveloped other country, exasperated and mocked by the highly developed country that surrounds and permeates it with its imagery of affluence and opportunity. As W. E. B. Du Bois wrote in 1903, "To be a poor man is hard, but to be a poor race in a land of dollars is the very bottom of hardships." No number of damage-mending programs from the white world can lift this black nation as a dead weight. Ambition and righteous pride must be ignited within the black community, and black artists, it seems to me, have an enviable part to play. In an art situation that is generally modish and frivolously nihilistic, the black artist (and the playwright, that natural didact, seems to be foremost) has a work of genuine resurrection before him, of supplying a self-image that though angry is also potent—of generating "motivational fantasies" to which the white world, of course, helps lend substance. As long as young black men cannot "envisage a future in which their situation would improve through work," the black race draws nearer to being the instrument whereby, in Cleaver's metaphor, America commits suicide.

Fool's Gold

THE LOSS OF EL DORADO, by V. S. Naipaul. 335 pp. Knopf, 1970.

Never ask an artist to do the ordinary. Some time ago, an American publisher asked V. S. Naipaul, the Anglo-Indian novelist from Trinidad, to write the Port of Spain volume in a series of historical handbooks on cities of the world. Naipaul produced a masterly anomaly that, under the title *The Loss of El Dorado*, has been brought out, garlanded with British praise, by another American publisher. The book, though minutely researched and presented in a factual prose that verges on the dry, seems less a work of history than a piece of poetry, a rather fevered meditation, a hypnotized concentration upon two focal points in Trinidad's history: the founding of St. Joseph and its port, "which they call of Spain," in 1592 by the "dispossessed conquistador" Antonio de Berrio; and, two hundred years later, the six-year rule of the city and the island by its first British governor, Thomas Picton, a blithe brute who was to die a hero at Waterloo. Both men suggest legendary figures: like Don Quixote, Berrio was old, tough, gallant, and bewitched; while Picton's career seems a shadow of Wellingon's and his final reputation has been "absorbed in Wellington's more complex, nation-building myth." Indeed, it was Wellington who pronounced Picton's epitaph: "A rough foul-mouthed devil as ever lived." Naipaul's portraiture, closely based upon historical records hitherto scarcely tapped, mixes irony and sympathy somewhat enigmatically, yet he does seem to grant Berrio and Picton the stature of founders and a certain tenacity of purpose. In counterpoint stand his portraits of Sir Walter Raleigh and Francisco Miranda, two engaging and intelligent adventurers whom he condemns as—in the end—ineffectual and, oddly, quiescent; both ended in prison, and "prison was perhaps the setting that Miranda, like Raleigh, subconsciously required." Behind these principal actors a host of lesser ones come swarming forward out of the colonial archives: henchmen and buccaneers, Spanish soldiers and French planters and English administrators, lawyers and torturers, agitators, mulattoes, and slaves. The richly detailed episodes of West Indian history hover, however, in a virtual vacuum; the matrix of world circumstances—not only the power struggles on the Continent but even the events on nearby islands—is so lightly indicated that the machinations on Trinidad appear as eerie as the motions of a sleepwalker. This quality would be a fault were it not at the heart of Mr. Naipaul's attempt. He wishes, using his native Trinidad as a microcosm, to uncover the something strange in the entire New World, the something futile and cruel and—to use a word he repeatedly uses, as if recoined with a more sinister meaning—"simple."

There are many surprising facts, fascinating stories, and shrewd epigrammatic thrusts in these pages. Naipaul is very good on the Spaniards—their egoistic "simplicity," the unreality to them of everything but God and gold, their disastrous inability to plant crops, the abstract accounts they left of their marvellous journeys ("The conquistador who found nothing had nothing to report. Believing in wonders, he had no gift of wonder"), their superstitious and murderous abhorrence of the heathen Indian, the mild legalism of their slave code. They experienced the New World as a "medieval adventure." Antonio de Berrio became the last and least of the conquistadors. His wife, whom he married late, was the niece of one of the great ones, Gonzalo Jiménez de Quesada. Quesada had marched into the Colombian plateau, conquered the Chibcha Indians, and founded at Bogotá the kingdom of New Granada—an achievement sufficient to make him rich but not content. He wished to discover another Mexico or Peru and to become, after Cortés and Pizarro, the third marquis of the New World. The rumor of El Dorado—a tale the jungle Indians told, a confusion of the ritual gilding of a Chibchan chieftain with the opulent Inca empire the Spaniards had already seized—drew Quesada into the swamps of the Orinoco River; of the two thousand men in this expedition, twenty-five returned. When, some years later, Quesada died, his nephew-in-law inherited his fortune and his quest. The one consumed the other. Berrio, an old soldier of sixty, came from Spain to the Indies and for fifteen years devoted himself to the search for the gilded man and the city of gold. A collection of straw huts in Trinidad served as the capital of a jungle territory—Trinidad, Guiana, and eastern Venezuela—that for many decades was known in the Spanish colonial records as "these provinces of El Dorado." The tangle of ruinous expeditions and English raids and Indian massacres defies summary; by one of those ironies whereby literature wags history, it was Sir Walter Raleigh —a timid cutthroat, in Naipaul's narrative—who captured the El Dorado legend from its leading devotee, Berrio, by writing a book, *The Discovery of the Large, Rich, and Beautiful Empire of Guiana.* Though "really the story of a defeat and of a nervous six-day journey of exploration," the book "catches part of the New World at that moment between the unseeing brutality of the discovery and conquest and the later brutality of colonization. It was the swiftly passing moment when romance could be apprehended." Berrio's own story has an end worthy not of romance but of an anti-romantic novel. After seizure and release by Raleigh, Berrio, now seventy-five and probably lunatic, was stranded, with a dozen men, on an island in the Orinoco. Meanwhile, Domingo de Vera, his "campmaster for El Dorado," had wangled from the chronically bankrupt Spanish king a support expedition of twenty-eight ships and perhaps two thousand men and women. The New World was not ready to support such a population; unsheltered, unfed, cannibalized by Caribs, the expedition disintegrated and became, in the Spanish Indies, a "folk memory of horror." And Berrio, when Vera got to him on his island, was not grateful. He said (and these are the only spoken words of his that have been recorded), "We are trying to do too much. If we try to do too much we will end by doing nothing at all." So Don Quixote, invited to rise from his deathbed and resume the search for Dulcinea, replied, "No more of that, I beseech you. All the use I shall make of these follies at present is to heighten my repentance." The New World as medieval adventure had ended.

After a brief section on Trinidad's two hundred years as a "ghost province" within the Spanish Empire, and on its sudden, bloodless surrender to the British in 1797, *The Loss of El Dorado* concentrates upon Trinidad as an outpost in the young British Empire and upon the rule, disgrace, and final glory of Thomas Picton. If the collapse of Vera's relief force epitomizes the Spanish quest, the basic symbol of the British establishment is Vallot's jail. Jean-Baptiste Vallot, the conscientious, amiable, tirelessly cruel jailer of Port of Spain, is one of Naipaul's prime catches in the sea of forgotten documents. Vallot, who was paid by fees for each flogging, ear-clipping, and torture by suspension, and Begorrat, the chief magistrate, who prescribed the tortures and punishments, were both French; in Spanish times, Trinidad had suffered an influx of French planters and their slaves from the more turbulent islands of Santo Domingo and Martinique. The planters had brought with them their skill at "the management of Negroes."

> . . . the Negro called Pierre François had been ordered to fall on his knees to hear his sentence. He was then taken to the church. He was not baptized; he was already a Christian. Prayers were read to

him. He was then "heavily ironed" and the soldiers led him to where Bouqui's headless body was tied to the stake. [Bouqui was a previously executed Negro.] Many Negroes watched. Some of Vallot's jail Negroes were waiting with faggots. Pierre François was chained to the stake with the headless body. He was made to put on a shirt. The shirt was filled with sulphur. The jail Negroes built up the faggots. The executioner lit the fire. . . . The smell of sulphur and the two burning bodies drove many people out of their houses and there were some whites who feared a massacre. Begorrat and the French planters had devised the punishment and the ritual. They said afterwards it was what they used to do in Martinique.

Picton brought to his post no aversion to brutality. Instant hangings and fatal lashings were the first order of his new establishment. He signed all of Begorrat's torture orders. The growing agitation of the "radical" English-born artisans and merchants in Port of Spain, and the intervention of Colonel William Fullarton, one of two commissioners appointed to mitigate Picton's one-man rule, succeeded in having him brought to trial in London for a relatively innocent act—signing the order to torture Luisa Calderon, a young free mulatto accused by her lover of theft. Picton's two trials consumed five years. Luisa and the Negro policeman who testified with her had time to learn English between the first and the second. At the first, Picton was technically convicted, on the basis that torture was illegal under the Spanish law that still obtained in Trinidad; at the second, he was acquitted. Meanwhile, Fullarton—who, a spendthrift as well as a humanitarian, had squandered the treasury surplus accumulated under Picton's hard-headed management—fell into disfavor and died. Back in Port of Spain, Vallot's jail, with its torture chambers, its tiny, stinking cells, its *cachots brûlants* (windowless hotboxes), was pulled down by Picton's friends. No plan of it remains. Vallot disappeared; Begorrat remained a prominent planter into the 1830's; Picton's destiny took him into the peninsular campaign with Wellington, storming and sacking Badajoz, and on to Waterloo and a valorous death and a memorial statue at Carmarthen and the immortal good name enshrined, if you look him up, in the *Encyclopaedia Britannica*.

The Loss of El Dorado concludes with a summary of Trinidad's next hundred and fifty years, as a "ghost province" now of the British Empire, and touches on Mr. Naipaul's childhood in Port of

Spain, when it seemed "a place at the rim of the world." Then, in the 1940's, "Picton was the name of a street; no one knew more. History was a fairy tale about Columbus. . . . History was also a fairy tale not so much about slavery as about its abolition." These two impressions, of history as layers of fantasy and of Trinidad as a place on the rim of the world, animate Naipaul's zealous and intricate work of research and lurk behind his curious thesis that the New World is hopelessly "simple" and unreal. Himself a resident of England for twenty years, Naipaul voices this thesis, or suspicion, through the exiled revolutionary Miranda. "After the years in Europe, the books, pictures, and study, after the talk of liberty and constitutions, the colonial world remained, still knowing only about blood and money, cacao and tobacco, the management of Negroes and shops. . . . Miranda was applying the concepts of Europe as words alone, accurate but misleading, to a simpler world: the Negro-worked plantations of Venezuela, the low wooden houses of Port of Spain, the muddy shore, the rough Spanish shops, the one printery." The reader puzzles over this "deeper colonial deprivation, the sense of the missing real world." Is it that Europe has no muddy shores? Is greater length of history the token of superiority? Another exile, the Venezuelan lawyer Level de Goda, in Spain, is excited "to be close for the first time to the real world and real events, to be in a country that could support classical illusion." Illusion or allusion? Naipaul's indictment is slow to form. "It wasn't only that the wines, the manners and the graces, the books and the art and the ideas of a living culture came from outside. The simple society bred simple people" —"too simple for lasting causes," so simple that their revolutions are "second-hand," "with energy but without principles," "the imperfectly constituted society decaying into minute egoisms." And what is the cause of this decay, which turned the Spaniards feckless, which made Frenchmen into monsters of cruelty, which sapped British liveliness and idealism? Slavery. "In the slave society . . . this liveliness began to be perverted and then to fade, and the English saw their preëminence, more simply, as a type of racial magic." Inhumane laws are enacted by people "who have ceased to assess themselves by the standards of the metropolis and now measure their eminence only by their distance, economic and racial, from their Negroes."

> This was what stalled and perverted every stated metropolitan principle, French, Spanish, English, of revolution, intellectual advance, law, social drive, justice and freedom: race, the taint of slavery: it helped to make the colonial society simple.

If for "colonial" we substitute "southern," the situation, and the truth of the charge, become recognizable. There is no denying the evidence Naipaul has resurrected concerning the cruelty and folly enacted in the provinces of El Dorado, where slaves poisoned each other to destroy the master's wealth and ate dirt to destroy themselves. Naipaul's sense of an evil unreality presiding over the New World makes it possible for him to sympathize on all sides, to bring into rounded life his great variety of doomed actors. "Fantasy," with "simple," is a recurrent word: there was the fantasy of a city of gold, and the fantasy of the underground slave life of voodoo and midnight courts, and the fantasy of bookish revolutionaries like Miranda, and the fantasy of the British that they could manipulate South American revolutions to serve their economic ends. But in viewing an entire hemisphere as a corrupted dream, Naipaul dissolves what realities there were. *The Loss of El Dorado* rests upon an unexamined assumption, of metropolitan superiority. In this it is like Naipaul's last, fine but cold novel, *The Mimic Men*, which presented the men of the West Indies as poor imitations of Europeans. Yet were the conquistadors more fanatic and quixotic than the captains of the Thirty Years' War? Were the English planters more rapacious and callous than the mill-owners of Lancashire? Were the South American revolutionaries more deluded or ineffectual than the French prototypes, who slew each other and prepared the way for Napoleon? Was the cruelty of slavery not an extension of the cruelty already present on the African continent? Does not the collapse of "metropolitan" values amid "simpler" conditions demonstrate their own frailty and unreality? For the fallacy of the primitive paradise, it seems to me, Mr. Naipaul wants to exchange that of the metropolitan paradise. This desire gives *The Loss of El Dorado* its bleak and caustic tone, yet also its persuasive sadness and the power of poetry.

Sons of Slaves

THE SULTANS, by Noel Barber. 304 pp. Simon & Schuster, 1973.

THE SULTAN: *The Life of Abdul Hamid II*, by Joan Haslip. 309 pp. Holt, Rinehart & Winston, 1973.

It is a pity that Noel Barber, in writing *The Sultans*, could not muster more of the prose-empurpling zest of an Edgar Saltus, who found the follies and atrocities of the Caesars and of the Czars so perversely enchanting; for Mr. Barber tells the supreme saga of decadent misrule in an efficient journalistic manner that in the end seems rather overwhelmed and wan, and he leaves us with no moral beyond the implication that all Turks are crazy. Perhaps it would take a Beelzebub drunk on blood to sing with appropriate inspiration the annals of the royal descendants of Othman and the Magnificent Suleiman. Mr. Barber is a reasonable modern man, who, with the cumulative numbingness of the *Guinness Book of World Records*, sets down the odd facts as one more madman, imbecile, sot, and terror-stricken impotent succeeds another on the throne of the Shadow of God on Earth. Selim II (who reigned as Sultan from 1566 to 1574) laid siege to Cyprus—a siege in which thirty thousand Christians were massacred in Nicosia alone—to ensure himself a steady supply of Cyprian wine. Mahomet III (r. 1595–1603) had his nineteen brothers strangled upon his accession to the throne. Osman II (r. 1618–1622) practiced archery upon live targets, and used his own page boys when the supply of prisoners of war gave out. It amused Murad IV (r. 1623–1640) to pick off his hapless subjects with an arquebus from a corner of the Seraglio wall, "exercising the royal prerogative of taking ten innocent lives a day"; a sultan of action, he executed twenty-five thousand suspected malefactors in one year, beheaded his chief musician for playing a Persian air, and sank a boatload of women that drifted within range of his palace cannon. Ibrahim (r. 1640–1648), perhaps the maddest of the lot (though the 19th-century Abdul Aziz is an impressive contender), adorned his beard with diamonds and raped the daughter of the Mufti and drowned his entire harem on the suspicion that one concubine was conducting a romance. Not all the excesses were of cruelty: Ahmed III (r. 1703–1730) admired tulips (from the Turkish *tulbend*, meaning "turban") to such an extent that he was deposed for the extravagance of his moonlit tulip fêtes; Osman III (r. 1754–1757) in his obsession with food prowled Istanbul by night to sample the city's eating houses. Abdul Mejid (r. 1839–1861) built a palace, Dolmabache, that incorporated fourteen tons of gold leaf, the biggest mirrors in the world, and a bed of solid silver for himself; when one of his daughters married, he spent forty million francs on her trousseau and the wedding breakfast, which lasted one week. Abdul Aziz, his brother and successor, expanded the harem to nine hundred women, fed three hundred dinner guests most evenings, bought locomotives from Britain though there were no tracks to run them on, sometimes refused to sign any documents written in black ink, played soldiers with real soldiers, and bestowed upon cocks and chickens the Ottoman Empire's highest decorations for gallantry.

One does not need to be Dr. Spock to be reminded, by such behavior, of insanely indulged children begging for someone to set "limits." The sultans fascinate, indeed, as examples of how far human appetite will go when no obstacle to its satisfaction is posed. They are a spectacle to comfort the average deprived man. Several of them, early given the run of a harem, developed impotence; a surprising number, in a teetotalling culture, drank themselves to death. Over *half* of the sultans after 1600 had to be deposed! Mr. Barber, though his energetic scholarship displays itself in pages of colorful details, does not seize the opportunity to analyze the peculiarities of Ottoman kingship that shaped so preponderantly ineffective a dynasty. Rather, he offers the dark suggestion that the "unbroken line of weaklings" after Suleiman were not Othmans at all but sprang from a coupling between Suleiman's empress Roxelana and an unknown lover. Yet the background of Barber's perhaps too sensational and anecdotal chronicle of the sultanate contains more sociological reasons for its uncorrected debilitation. The Sultan was not only the administrator of a terrestrial empire but a holy man, the Caliph of Islam, and as such (though the claim to the caliphate was shadowy and emphasized chiefly in the latter centuries of the sultans) he enjoyed among the Muslim masses a religious prestige impervious to mortal shenanigans. Though the sultans' extravagance and the corruption they fostered sorely burdened the empire, the need for *a* sultan was never questioned, and except in cases of blatant imbecility the rules of succession were followed. A second insulating factor was these rules of succession, whereby not the son but the eldest male in the family inherited the throne; the welter of intrigue this invited was combatted, initially, by the extraordinary sanction of fratricide that Ottoman law offered to the newly enthroned—"the right to execute their brothers, in order to ensure the peace of the world"—and then, in a humane modification that proved surpassingly disastrous to the health of the sultanate, by the institution of the *Kafes*, the Cage, a two-storied building, within the Seraglio, set aside by Ahmed I in 1603 for the perpetual confinement of the heirs to the throne. High walls surrounded it; the ground floor was windowless; here, with no company but that of deaf-mutes and sterilized concubines, the sultans' brothers and sons awaited either the silken bowstring of assassination or the call to supreme power. Mustafa I, the first alumnus of the Cage, emerged demented; Ibrahim, who had spent twenty-two of his first twenty-four years there, proved a monster of debauchery; and Suleiman II, who logged the record of forty-five years in the Cage, had, when at last he was proclaimed Sultan, "all but lost the power of speech." Has any other nation ever so devalued human personality as to immure its future rulers in total isolation from the workings of the world? The Ottoman Empire gave an extraordinary centrality to the institution of slavery. The Sultan was the only free Turk in the government; the rest were all his personal slaves, often converted Christians from the European realms of the empire. The Janissaries, his personal troops, were impressed Christian boys; an Albanian father and son, the Kuprilis, served as highly effective grand viziers for some of the Cage-crazed sultans; two of the most powerful of the sultanas who dominated events from the harem were the Russian Roxelana and Aimée Dubucq de Rivery, a convent girl captured by Barbary pirates. (The melodramatic annals of the Seraglio contain few incidents as tender* as the summons of Mahmud II, Aimée's son, for

---

* Or as indubitably fictitious, several correspondents have assured me.

a Catholic priest to absolve his dying mother in her native faith.)
Every sultan was the son of a slave; and the dehumanizing designs
of slavery are felt everywhere, from the rigor of the pageantry to
such animate constructs as the black eunuch and the deaf-mute
assassin—his eardrums broken, his tongue slit, and his life consecrated to the use of the bowstring, as that of the concubine was
consecrated to a call from the imperial bed which often never
came. In his world of slaves the Sultan found little resistance to his
fantasies and little helpful advice. Of Abdul Hamid II, the last of
the absolute monarchs and one of the few with some gift for government, Mr. Barber says, "As his terror bore increasing signs of
madness, he chose the most incredible characters to guide him. His
advisers included a slave he had bought in the market, a circus
clown whose act he admired, the son of one of his cooks, a Punch
and Judy performer, and a bootblack." Everything, in short, but
a graduate of Whittier High School.

Yet one wonders if even a continuous line of philosopher-kings
or elected charismatics could have kept the Ottoman Empire from
shrinking. Its reduction, in any case, was less rapid than that of the
British Empire, and, unlike that of Rome, left the heartland un-
conquered. Even after generations and generations of being "sick,"
Turkey proved capable of the heroics of Plevna. The reader, grateful for so much that Mr. Barber has unearthed from the archives
of this curious despotism, regrets that he did not choose to meditate upon his basic subject—that of decadence. Do extravagance
and obtuseness in high circles significantly affect the human tides
that Tolstoy saw mysteriously sweeping back and forth across the
surface of the globe? Or do the expansion and contraction of empires have to do simply with the technology of warfare: the Ot-
tomans organized the first standing army in Europe and developed
an artillery that, in the words of Gibbon, "surpassed whatever had
yet appeared in the world." To what extent does this kind of military vitality reflect spiritual vigor or efficacious political institutions? The Ottoman bureaucracy of slaves, a model of efficiency
in the short run, proved cumbersome and unresponsive in the long.
But what possible administrative magic could have enabled the
Caliph of Islam to rule forever over the Christian peoples of the
Balkans as Christian Europe waxed mighty? The wonder is that

the Turkish "yoke" lasted so long. One would like to know in what ways Turkish rule impinged upon the subject peoples—if present-day America is taken as an empire, would the analogy be with Puerto Rico or South Vietnam?—and, for that matter, what the sultans *did* all day, aside from playing pranks on their harem and holding hieratically formal audiences, throughout which the audient's arms were pinned by two stout pashas as a safeguard against assassination.

Joan Haslip, in *The Sultan*, gives a portrait of Abdul Hamid II considerably more sympathetic than that of Mr. Barber, who makes the last of the all-powerful sultans a maze-loving paranoid surrounded by "incredible characters" and the drab tatters of an outlandish panoply. Miss Haslip sees him as an agile and prescient statesman, able, for the more than three decades of his reign, to play the European powers off against each other and safeguard Turkey's survival without the entangling alliances that, once he fell, drew the Young Turks into the First World War. A runty younger brother placed on the throne by his sibling's insanity, Abdul Hamid had some experience of cosmopolitan Europe, more knowledge of history than any sultan before him, a flair for mathematics and carpentry, an engaging fondness for the tales of Sherlock Holmes. He had in his youth enjoyed a bourgeois liaison with a woman not of the harem, a Belgian shopkeeper called Flora Cordier, and even in his reactionary old age his conservatism had the rationale of a Pan-Islamic vision, a sound instinct to salvage the empire's Muslim East and to let the European fragments go. Abdul Hamid had the self-knowledge to exclaim, in discourse with an English businessman, "What can you expect of us, the children of slaves brought up by eunuchs?" But his story, so respectfully told by Miss Haslip, who even takes the Sultan's side against the massacred Armenians, is a dreary one, of a devious holding action against a desperate need for reform. It is, furthermore, mere history, full of problematical conferences and détentes and peoples' uprisings, and tells us little more than the morning's newspaper. Whereas Mr. Barber's less solid survey, with its idiots turned sultan and its convent girls turned into complacent concubines and its claustrophobic sense of an entire empire being crushed into a few terror-filled tiled halls, has the enigmatic depth of a dream, a dream that could tell us some truth about our natures, could we but fathom the symbols.

Coffee-Table Books for High Coffee Tables

EROTIC ART OF THE EAST, by Philip Rawson. Introduction by Alex Comfort. 380 pp. G. P. Putnam's Sons, 1968.

PRIMITIVE EROTIC ART, edited by Philip Rawson. 310 pp. G. P. Putnam's Sons, 1973.

EROTIC ART OF THE WEST, by Robert Melville. With a Short History of Erotic Art by Simon Wilson. 318 pp. G. P. Putnam's Sons, 1973.

Here we have a new genre: the coffee-table book that should be kept out of the reach of the children. Higher coffee tables would seem to be the answer; but the Japanese are using all our tall lumber to make bowling alleys with. So the alternative is to raise a generation for whom there is no pudendum, and that can call a vulva a ——. That generation is here, leaning on my coffee table, and when it takes over I fear G. P. Putnam's Sons will go begging for buyers as avid as I to wallow in the formerly forbidden delights (1,001 pages, more or less) of their so-called World History of Erotic Art.

These three compendia have texts that, though beside the selling point, in decency should be reviewed. The oldest publication, dating back to staid old 1968, is *Erotic Art of the East.* Dr. Alex Comfort, well known to loving couples as the master chef stirring the stew of *The Joy of Sex,* was announced as general editor and contributed an introduction regretting the "Victorian *terror sexualis*" and our present lack of "a technology of the emotions." Philip Rawson then, in his long chapter on Indian erotic art, described an elaborate technology based on the notion that semen is a divine substance which prolonged intercourse without orgasm will force up the spinal column into the head, producing enlightenment. By way of technical illustration, there were many tinted depictions of a rubbery prince squatting *en face* with his smiling, netherly ex-

posed lady, his lingam thrust into her yoni as patiently as the little
Dutch boy's finger in the dike. The Chinese, a later chapter told
us, took this Tantric principle—copulation without male consum-
mation—a Confucian step further by making their supreme sex
symbol the ancient sage; his longevity and spiritual well-being bore
witness to a lifetime of absorbing concubines' beneficial *yin* without surrendering any considerable portion of his precious *yang*.
The Chinese, incidently, considered jade congealed dragon semen.
Whatever the cosmological delusions behind them, the Asian doctrines of sexual conduct did place value, Rawson argued, on the
gratification of the female. And it is true, the women in these rep-
resentations look much less alarmed than those in Western erotica.
This volume was rounded out by David James's game plea for the
skimpy amorous art of iconophobic, homosexual Islam, and by
Richard Lane's fussy monograph on *shunga*—Japanese "spring
pictures," pictures of sexual activity traditionally part of the print-
master's production and often given as wedding presents. The shy-
est bride, after studying the monstrously exaggerated genitals that
shunga shows, could only be relieved at the sight of her husband's.

Five years later, Dr. Comfort has vanished as general editor and
two new volumes sumptuously appear. *Primitive Erotic Art*, edited
by Rawson and written by a variety of hands, suffers from the
disparity of material included under "primitive" and from what I
take to be some undue haste in the assembling. Rawson's opening
essay, on early sexual art, is excellent, once he has given the Christian missionaries and Western sexual neuroses their compulsory
lumps. He takes art to be at the very beginning erotic—a descent,
via sinuous caves, into the womb of Mother Earth, there to stimu-
late her, with rites that included drawings, to continue her generation of the wildlife that fed a hunting society. Primitive magic,
Rawson feels, should be understood less as a mechanistic effort to
cause a result than an effort of identification and possession through
analogy and symbol; rite and its attendant art "exalt the sense of
life, and elaborate a mystery-cult to conserve and renew it." The
feminine sex of the earth was the first metaphor; the first works of
art appear to be vulva-like cups gouged on the underside of a
tomb slab. The maze, as visual pattern or narrative theme, betokens

the mystery of the female innards. Until the rise of agricultural society, generic energy was identified as female; with seed-sowing came phallic art. Rawson, as he pursues analogies through pre-history, seems sometimes too agile to be true: "It is not at all diffi-cult to associate these objects both with the feathered phalli painted in the Palaeolithic caves and with the bunched besoms which the medieval witches were supposed to straddle and ride to the Sabbat; supposed examples of witch-besoms even have handles carved as penises. The bunch attached to the end must be a graphic image for the seminal jet, a plastic analogue to the colored water sprayed about at the Indian Holi procession and the rice or confetti thrown at modern Western weddings." Well, maybe so; but a cigar, as Freud said, can be just a cigar.

By comparison, the following essays on Celtic, Indian, African, and Pacific art seem plodding and bereft of a thesis. Tom Har-rison's account of Borneo and New Guinea has the strength of testimony from the field, mixing art objects with anecdotes and with artifacts like the all-too-vividly-depicted penis bar. Cottie Burland on sub-Saharan Africa, on the other hand, seems rattled by the richness of his vast topic, grateful for all signs of "restraint" from the frequently "violent" artists, and prone to take refuge in the undefined concept of "naturalness" and "close to nature." Very bothersomely, the plates, many of them beautiful, are not well re-lated to the texts. Though the two other books in the series usefully key the plates to the discussion by means of numbers in the broad margin, this device is not employed here; nor are the plates in-cluded in the index. There are almost as many pictures without explanation as there are descriptions without illustration. The tribal name "Colima" identifies eight of the American pottery pieces, in-cluding one on the cover, yet the word doesn't occur in the index or, that I can find, in the text. An editorial disservice has been done to both the scholarly authors and the compilers of the photographs: they should have been introduced to each other.

Erotic Art of the West, however, is a singular production. Rob-ert Melville, art editor of the *New Statesman*, has not so much written a history of erotic art in the West as he has threaded an essay on eroticism through a personal anthology of works of art.

Medieval to modern illustrations range unchronologically under chapter heads like "The Toilet," "Violence and Violation," and "Treatment of the Parts"; sensitive and lively explications of visual images mingle with startlingly physical speculations—"few men could honestly claim that they have not at some time or another desired to urinate inside the beloved." Melville has an engaging way of concerning himself with the physical comfort of the figures in Renaissance tableaux, nude on their sometimes awkwardly placed pillows. He rarely says too much, though his eye sees worlds, and his sense of flaws is as keen as his warmth of response—Renoir's later nudes became "a kind of slow-breathing earthenware," the uneasy perspective in Vermeer's *At the Procuress's* betrays that the "real psychological situation is between the woman in the yellow bodice and the painter." His discourse on the ways and parts of love touches on a number of works that, by the standards of the Asian book, are not erotic at all; indeed, one of the fascinations for the reader, if he looks at the pictures first, is to discover how the author will work each one of them in. To be sure, Melville's fine fancy can become merely tricksome—William Copley's women "come forth in their bras and suspender belts as the issue of a drop of sperm that fell on to an advertisement in a woman's magazine" —and even for a personal anthology, the choice of reproductions seem unbalanced. There are seven Hans Bellmers but not one George Grosz; seven Dalis but none of Arp's or Moore's suggestive biomorphs; no Bonnard, though there is a section devoted to "The Bath"; no Courbet, though his nudes are described as revolutionary and (figuratively) seminal; no obscene or priapic Gothic gargoyles or miserichords, though many exist; and no modern pornography, though Victorian, 18th-century, and Renaissance examples are given. A British bias shows, I think, in the generous sampling of post-war English painters (plus Jim Dine, who lives in London) and the almost total ignoring of American Pop Art, which reeks of sex as heavily as Art Nouveau. The entire New York Pop scene, indeed, is represented only by one rather bland Marisol—better, for this book, her slyly ithyphallic "Guy" or the Coke-bottle fellatio of "Amor."

Yet Melville has made a book to please himself, that begins and ends in air (with a quote from Henry James that means as near nothing as grammatical English can) and that by its very blitheness somewhat refutes the imputations of Western anti-sexuality made by the exponents of primitive and Asian art. Broadly, one might say that the purpose of primitive erotic art is to participate (in the processes of vitality; an art whose phallic emblems double as initiatory dildoes), that of Asian erotic art is to show (as marriage manual, as religious illustration), and that of Western civilization seems to be to divulge, to confess, to expose. The resonances of a shared mythology are replaced by those of private psychology; from Bosch and Botticelli on, personal meanings subvert and super-charge overt symbolism. The atmosphere of Western erotic art is relatively "anxious," to use Alex Comfort's word; the very surface of many paintings feels tangled and restless. Whatever the lovers are portrayed together or one is the rendered model and the other the unseen artist, a dimension of individual psychological invasion has been added to sexual possession. The faces, even in ecstasy, are not masks. Melville's book, at least to this Westerner, never is monotonous in the way the other two are. A variety of blind men have touched the sexual elephant standing in our midst; here are their impressions. If a spirit of anthropological dispassion is to be applied consistently, the repressions that Christianity and then in-dustrialism asked of the West need be no more deplored than the genital mutilations common in primitive societies or the cruel rigidity of Oriental social structures. Nowhere is love free, any more than men are free, even in a wilderness. The beautiful whores of the Hindu temple "heaven-bands" smile out at us from a his-torical remission that ended; Moslem Puritans came and mutilated them. Now we stand in a moment when again sex seems worth studying and celebrating. More, it now appears our last uncon-taminated act, the sinuous passageway down into the womb where worship is possible, in a unifying darkness of instinctive purpose. In this sexiest of times, as a tug of reaction begins to be felt, our set of three volumes offers us a comradely perspective, as wide as the world and deep as history, into the erotic images with which other men have sought "to exalt the sense of life." "Exaltation," indeed, in the sense of lifting high into visibility, describes the crudest lavatory graffito as well as the noblest nude.

*

And what of these pictures themselves? Having passed my eyes over so many images of copulation, flirtation, erection, and excitation, I feel as if, like the weary headmaster surveying his June ocean of unruly eternal youth, I should bestow a few prizes. *Best Phallus:* Aubrey Beardsley. *Best Vulva:* Hokusai (*shunga* tradition generally leaves the lovers clothed; the heads show and, at an often unlikely remove, the cloth parts to reveal genitalia like hairy actors on a puppet-stage). *Erotica with Least Hang-ups:* Mochica (Peru) pottery vessels (produced, surely, in a joking spirit, as are the obscene Cherokee pipes "smoker" jokes). *Nicest Couple:* a very dearly drawn Chinese pair, from a 19th-century album, he with a dark but honest penis, she with a bib and bound feet, both with tiny, utterly kindly smiles. *Most Repulsive Couple:* four-armed goddess with Shiva in two aspects, 20th-century Bengal painting. *Most Disturbing Artist:* Hans Bellmer, who combines pornographic fury with linear facility; can erotic art have any further to go? *Best Venus:* Lucas Cranach. *Masterwork Most Missed:* Popeye, Olive Oyl, and Wimpy fellating and gamahuching one another, in comic book circulating in southeastern Pennsylvania in the late 1940's.

Before the Sky Collapses

XINGU: THE INDIANS, THEIR MYTHS, by Orlando Villas Boas and Claudio Villas Boas, translated from the Portuguese by Susana Hertelendy Rudge. 270 pp. Farrar, Straus & Giroux, 1974.

Xingu: The Indians, Their Myths is certainly one of the best books of 1974 whose title begins with"X." The volume shows love, from the publisher's handsome two-color printing job to the lifetimes of service the authors have devoted to the Brazilian Indians. Since 1946, the Boas brothers (a third brother, Leonardo, died in 1961) have dwelt with small intermission among the dozen or so tribes that live in villages along the Rio Xingu and its tributaries, in virtual isolation from the modern civilization that dominates and threatens them. This book, edited from the brothers' journals by

Kenneth S. Brecher, an American anthropologist who himself spent two years among the Xinguanos, consists in the main of thirty-one tales, or "myths," transcribed from oral narrations in, evidently, the rough Portuguese of bilingual Indians. The Boases state, in their introduction, "There were no pressures of time; instead, our interest was to transmit with the greatest possible accuracy everything heard and understood over . . . twenty-five years of daily, hourly, and minute-by-minute communal living with the Indians." The stories are shared, with some exceptions, among the tribes, and they are prefaced by a brief but affecting description of the region's geography and fauna and climate and history. Affecting, that is, in its sense of achieved intimacy with the alien, of modern men willfully dissolving their calendars and chronometers in the joyous cycles of the natural year:

> In April the rains taper off and the waters recede. . . . The clouds turn white and vaporous and are propelled by cold gusts of wind coming from the south and the southeast. It is the beginning of "summer."
>
> At this time of the year, it is common to see birds flying across the skies, beautiful formations of jabiru storks, flocks of white herons, and pairs of colhereiros in search of lagoons and *igapós*.
>
> As the waters recede from the shores, gulls, *bacuraus de coleira branca*, ducks, and marrecãos fly in. The *tracajas* [fresh-water turtles] and small alligators, who at flood time had clung to floating tree trunks, search for sandy shores to enjoy the heat of the sun.

There are worlds sequestered from our world; there is a history remote from our history:

> As a result of violent attacks unleashed on them by a nation called Aussumadí, who invaded their lands, the Trumái decided to move. Under the leadership of two great chieftains, Auaturí and Jaquanarí, they headed for "where the sun sets." After trekking through extensive forests, they arrived at the banks of a river that they said was the Kuluene (the Xingu, in our nomenclature).

Amid our human multitudes, how much such history has been hidden and lost! Even within the microcosm of the Xingu, there are mysteries, problematical events just beyond the reach of memory, and tribes that are "hostile" or "asocial"; they have the vividness of the half-seen:

In temperament, the Txikão are nervous and restless, reacting to any novel stimulus or situation that crops up. This trait, very pronounced in them, may be a natural result of the isolation in which they live.

Isolation within isolation. More exotic still are the reports of the Minatá-Karaiá. In a bygone time, a legend among the Kamaiurá tribe runs, some of their men, travelling, heard a whistling sound:

> Curious to know what it was, they walked in the direction the sound was coming from. After a while, they reached the village, which belonged to the Minatá-Karaiá. The village was full of people, and the men had a hole in the top of their heads that produced the whistle the Kamaiurá had heard from far away. The Minatá-Karaiá had another peculiarity: from underneath their armpits bunches of *minatás* [coconuts] grew, and they were constantly snatching the fruits off, breaking them against their heads, and eating them.

What the Boas brothers in their introduction call "the human mind's natural penchant for the marvellous" does become, as the white introducers yield to the Indian tellers of the thirty-one tales, wearing. These myths make stiff reading. Some of the fault, perhaps, belongs to the translator. There seems an unnecessary plethora of italicized un-English terms; in the passages already quoted, why not simply say "turtles" and "coconuts" instead of "*tracajas* [fresh-water turtles]" and "*minatás* [coconuts]"? Is there *no* sufficiently accurate English equivalent of *jakuí, püa, itóto, irracuitáp, imurá, tucunaré-aruiáp, moinrucú*, etc., etc.? A conscientious, if not ideal, reader of this volume would be turning to the glossary several times for every page. An ideal reader would know Portuguese and the relevant Indian languages and would have already read the Boas journals in the original. While an excessive verbal pedantry constantly pricks the eye, footnotes are rigorously excluded, where a clarifying note on ritual, or animal habits, or Xingu customs would often be helpful. And though the original was probably not a masterpiece of style, does the English have to be quite so flat, colorless, and arhythmic? "The Jurana had everything when the waters began to grow with the rains." Was there no more concrete way of putting that? "She had plunged into a murky part of the woods, and finding the ladder by way of a shortcut, she climbed up and was gone." Is "by way of a shortcut" really the thought? For me, it imposes upon the murky part of the wood a suddenly urban pedestrian, saving valuable seconds on the way to an appointment on an upper floor.

But the mind meets resistance in the texture of these tales mostly, I think, because they are indeed primitive, and not only is the milieu an alien one but the habits of narration are different. The laconic closeness of event, no doubt relieved in oral rendition by pause and gesture, tests the attention of a modern reader. One can skim a paragraph by Henry James, get the general picture, and either go back for the furniture and nuance or get on with the story. Skim a paragraph of these myths, and one is lost:

> When the boys fell, the tapir went around stepping on them and burying them with his foot. The tapir, after killing and burying the boys, went a long way away. After a while the boys in the ground began to be born, some in the form of little turtles, others as real people. The one up in the tree said to the others down below, "How are you doing down there?"

A relatively transparent passage. But this reviewer's mind—after trying to imagine how to bury boys with a tapir's foot, where "a long way away" is, why the dead boys so easily begin to resurrect, and why some only make it "in the form of little turtles"—is too boggled to recall that one boy, the paragraph before, had managed, despite the kicking of the wicked tapir's foot, to stay up in the genipap tree, whence he calls down his cheery and—considering the circumstances—rather bland greeting. The story continues (in case you've been gripped) with the boys following their murderer by interrogating successively warmer piles of excrement and killing him when he is asleep; then, "seeing that they had come a long way, the boys decided to climb up to the sky," where they casually turn into stars.

A modern story, however fabulous, proceeds subject to the discipline of some reality-derived premises; these Brazilian Indian narratives seem closer to the flow of dreams, wherein nothing is questioned. The sheer authority of the narrator is justification enough for any turn of event. His own decisiveness is echoed in the decisiveness of his characters: the boys decide to climb the sky; and, in one of the more vivid openings, "There once was an old man who wanted to get married, but no woman wanted to marry him. He was very ugly. Saddened by this, he decided to die."

As the distinctions between animals and men, the living and the dead, earth and sky are vaguely felt, so is the opposition between the inner will and the outer world. Things happen easily; in "The Origin of the Twins Sun and Moon," an old jaguar, "very angry, peeled a piece off her fingernail and threw it at her daughter-in-law, cutting her head off." Beheaded by a fingernail, the daughter-in-law thrashes, is referred to as now "dead," now "dying," has vitality enough to give birth to twin boys, the Sun (Rit) and the Moon (Une), and, pages later, after the sons have grown and avenged her by killing their wicked grandmother, still seems to be alive, and talking. A Western reader might expect from the title (imposed, I suspect, by the anthropologists) a coherent if fanciful account of cosmic origins, but this story takes place in an already created cosmos, wherein the growth of the twin Sun and Moon is measured in moons. The twins figure in many of the stories, yet with hardly a trace of celestial grandeur; they are often victimized, sometimes impotent, and rarely luminary. The elemental connection between the Sun and daylight is curiously grasped; in one myth, day is stolen by Sun from a village of vultures. Another story is reminiscent of the Greek myth of Phaëthon. The Sun has been slain (by a bunch of coconuts!), and his widow, seeing the world lost in the ensuing darkness, persuades her three sons to don their father's headdress of feathers. Two of them find the headdress too hot, and come down from the sky; the third manages to wear it across the firmament, but runs. When he learns to walk, he becomes the Sun, and his mother weeps, knowing he can never return home. The weeping mother is also the motif of the Xingu equivalent of the Adam myth, so brief that it can be quoted entire:

> In the beginning there was only Mavutsinim. No one lived with him. He had no wife. He had no son, nor did he have any relatives. He was all alone.
> One day he turned a shell into a woman, and he married her. When his son was born, he asked his wife, "Is it a man or a woman?"
> "It is a man "
> "I'll take him with me."
> When he left, the boy's mother cried and went back to her village, the lagoon, where she turned into a shell again.
> "We are the grandchildren of Mavutsinim's son," say the Indians.

The Judaic differentiation of man and God has not yet occurred; Mavutsinim is both. Metamorphosis, in this slippery Amazon world, is no miracle but a mere matter of wishing. The heroes, animal and human, are not agonists, struggling to allocate eternally the one life that is theirs, but spirits, with something of the spirit world's playful elasticity. The lack of final moral consequence encourages a kind of teeming nastiness absent from Biblical legends. "Kanaratê and Karanavarê" is an Abel-and-Cain story in which Abel keeps "messing around" with his brother's wives and Cain keeps botching the attempt at murder by such tortuous methods as scarification and starvation, but Abel at last slays *him*, and inherits his wives. The moral: "Now it will always be this way. Husband will be jealous of wife and brother will fight with brother." A kind act is as rare in these tales as a logical progression. If any moral principle emerges, it is that sexual relations with women interfere with a warrior's hardness. Though there are glimmers of humor, of earthy wisdom, of a quickening sympathy with animal life, this is a low-ceilinged world, murky and mean; the myths seem drained of religion, perhaps by an unacknowledged awareness on the part of the Xinguanos that they are, as a culture if not as a population, doomed. Though presented as if timelessly isolated, they were visited by a German ethnologist as long ago as 1887 and have ever since been subject to infiltration by white adventurers, predators, missionaries, and saintly anthropologists. *Xingu*, as a presentation of a cultural situation, is deficient just where Lévi-Strauss's *Tristes Tropiques,* describing not dissimilar primitive societies in the Mato Grosso, is rich: in the sense of cultural interplay. Humanity, from Lévi-Strauss's ironical self-portrait to the half-caste adventurers living on the margins of Indian territory to the forlorn Indians themselves, presents itself as a giant weave nowhere totally broken. In one of the book's many beautifully melancholy passages, Lévi-Strauss, emerging onto the Amazon and the outposts of white civilization, witnessed (or thought he witnessed) a tribe, the Tupi-Kawahibs, in the process of liquidating itself, in November of 1938. There, on the banks of the upper Machado, as the departing anthropologist hastened "to reconstruct from its last fragments a culture which had fascinated Europe," the Tupi-Kawahibs prepared also to depart, and to sink the remnants of their tribe into a stronger one. At this juncture, one night, the chief, Taperahi, startled Lévi-Strauss by rising from the hammock of apathy and singing a song, a many-voiced dramatization that, in the summary, sounds like a lot of the stories collected in *Xingu*—the farcical adventurers of a *japim* bird amid talking jaguars, tapirs, lizards, and spirits. In the myth that concludes *Xingu*, the Godlike Sinaa (who becomes "young again each time he took a bath, pulling his skin off over his head like a sack") shows us the forked stick that supports the sky and says, "The day our people die out entirely, I will pull this down, and the sky will collapse, and all people will disappear."

The forked stick in this case is the so-called Xingu National Park, set up, at the urging of the Boas brothers, by the Brazilian government in 1961 and now gnawed at, if not yet knocked aside, by the trans-Amazon highway. Of course, honor is due the effort of human preservation—by legislation as long as the needs of the powerful allow it, and by museums and literature afterward. One regrets of this book that the fragments were not given a context to enhance their value. Much that seems incongruous or unintelligible must allude to circumstantial details that could have been specified. Parallels with other myths and fables, especially those of other American Indians, might have highlighted the seldom memorable flux of incident. How many primitive peoples, for instance, have, like the Xinguanos, coined myths to explain the invention of the anus and the origins of toothache? Beneath the muddy surface of these tales, the deeper significances swim unfished-for, while on the surface dance wonderfully spindly and clear-eyed drawings of animals and artifacts by Wacupiá, a Waura tribesman who had never before put pen to paper. Including them as illustrations was a happy editorial stroke; they bring one Xinguano as close to us as Picasso and Klee, and brighten an otherwise rather tristful volume.

A New Meliorism

THE LIVES OF A CELL: *Notes of a Biology Watcher*, by Lewis Thomas.
153 pp. Viking, 1974.

Who dares now doubt that empirical science is the only legally
licensed hunter of truth and the one legitimate dispenser of information about reality? Yet who but the scientists themselves can
comprehend what science is saying? So a class of essayists has
grown up—they are almost the only surviving specimens of that
delicate breed—that seeks to acquaint us with the astonishing facts
revealed by research and to place them in a perspective that we
might call philosophical, did not the word itself embarrass us.
Loren Eiseley, Desmond Morris, Annie Dillard, Joseph Wood
Krutch, H. G. Wells—each of these, with his own special tone
and own field of specialized knowledge, makes "sense" of the surreal scientific facts that loom beyond our lives like Oz, a benevolent
kingdom ever receding into strangeness, but one that now and then
deigns to send us, in whimsical emission, a new immunity, or
photographs of other planets. Dr. Lewis Thomas, whose essays
for *The New England Journal of Medicine* have been collected as
The Lives of a Cell: Notes of a Biology Watcher, is by profession a
pathologist, by position the president of the Memorial Sloan-Ket-
tering Cancer Center in New York City, and by avocation a lively,
thoughtful writer. His field of expert knowledge, and of meditation, is the microcosm within the cell, but he also draws thoughts
from entomology and etymology, and believes that the best thing
about the human race so far is Johann Sebastian Bach. Writing for
his fellow physicians and researchers, Dr. Thomas does not trouble
to spare them hard words like "haptene," "eukaryotic," and "myxotricha." In several essays he deals candidly with the practice of
medicine. ("The great secret, known to internists and learned
early in marriage by internists' wives, but still hidden from the
general public, is that most things get better by themselves.") In
other essays, he twits the anthropologist C. M. Turnbull's dire report on the Ik, ruminates about computers, dotes with a hobbyist's

fervor on the intricacies of word derivations, and pays tribute to the Woods Hole Marine Biological Laboratory. But the collection as a whole is by no means random; it has a voice—awed yet optimistic, with little of Loren Eiseley's melancholy sense of inhuman vastness—and a theme. The theme is, in a word, symbiosis.

The first essay states, and several others remark upon, the fact that has impressed Dr. Thomas most:

> At the interior of our cells, driving them, providing the oxidative energy that sends us out for the improvement of each shining day, are the mitochondria, and in a strict sense they are not ours. They turn out to be little creatures, the colonial posterity of migrant prokaryocytes, probably primitive bacteria that swam into ancestral precursors of our eukaryotic cells and stayed there. Ever since, they have maintained themselves and their ways, replicating in their own fashion, privately, with their own DNA and RNA quite different from ours. They are as much symbionts as the rhizobial bacteria in the roots of beans.

Similarly, chloroplasts in plants are "independent and self-replicating lodgers"; the flagellae that propel myxotricha turn out to be fully formed spirochetes that have tidily attached themselves; the enzyme-producing colonies in the digestive tracts of many animals illustrate "meticulously symmetrical symbiosis"; giant clams possess small lenses in their tissue that focus sunlight for the engulfed, symbiotic algae. The moral seems plain: "There is a tendency for living things to join up, establish linkages, live inside each other, return to earlier arrangements, get along, whenever possible. This is the way of the world." Most diseases result from overreaction on the part of the body's defenders, "a biologic misinterpretation of borders." Apparently malevolent microörganisms "turn out on close examination to be rather more like bystanders." "Pathogenicity is not the rule. . . . There is nothing to be gained, in an evolutionary sense, by the capacity to cause illness or death." What a benevolent world the microscope reveals! "Most bacteria are totally preoccupied with browsing," just like cows. Subtle and harmonious arrangements abound: insects, harboring beneficent bacteria in their tissues, coöperate to build cathedral-like anthills and beehives; apparent adversaries among living things are "usually [in] a standoff relation, with one party issuing signals, warnings, flagging the other off"; animals and human beings are interconnected by codes of sound and odors and "chemotactic" "vibes"; the very atmosphere of our Earth, the sky, is "the grandest product of collaboration in all of nature." Benevolent coöperation reigns from top to bottom of at least this terrestrial sphere; "nature red in tooth and claw" has been transfigured by the "something intrinsically good-natured about all symbiotic relations." Small wonder that Dr. Thomas' perky, compact essays usually end on the upbeat—even his pages on death, which bid us take comfort "in the recognition of synchrony, in the information that we all go down together, in the best of company."

The marvels of symbiotic interconnection intoxicate this scientist and lead him into flights of what must be fantasy: "Any word you speak this afternoon will radiate out in all directions, around town before tomorrow, out and around the world before Tuesday, accelerating to the speed of light, modulating as it goes, shaping new and unexpected messages, emerging at the end as an enormously funny Hungarian joke, a fluctuation in the money market, a poem, or simply a long pause in someone's conversation in Brazil." Is this meant literally? The image of the joke returns later: "Maybe the thoughts we generate today and flick around from mind to mind, like the jokes that turn up simultaneously at dinner parties in Hong Kong and Boston . . . are the primitive precursors of more complicated, polymerized structures that will come later, analogous to the prokaryotic cells that drifted through shallow pools in the early days of biological evolution. Later, when the time is right, there may be fusion and symbiosis among the bits." Such identity between molecules and ideas seems more mystical than demonstrable. Dr. Thomas has the mystic's urge toward total unity. He views the Earth as a single cell in its membrane of atmosphere. He quotes approvingly the 14th-century hermitess Julian of Norwich, who saw "all that is made" in "a little thing, the quantity of an hazelnut." He rejoices, in good mystic fashion, in the dissolution of the Self: "The whole dear notion of one's own Self—marvellous old free-willed, free-enterprising, autonomous, independent, isolated island of a Self—is a myth." Not that he professes any use for old-fashioned supernaturalistic religion. Yet his doctrine of universal symbiosis soars with an evangelical exaltation, and it is interesting that even his careful prose lapses into the grammar of teleology:

> There is an underlying force that drives together the several creatures comprising myxotricha, and then drives the assemblage into union with the termite.

> [Dying] is, after all, the most ancient and fundamental of biologic functions, with its mechanisms worked out with the same attention to detail, the same provision for the advantage of the organism . . . that we have long since become accustomed to finding in all the crucial acts of living.

> To assure themselves the longest possible run, [mitochondria] got themselves inside all the rest of us.

> A framework for meaning is somehow built into our minds at birth.

Whence the underlying force? Why the attentive "provision for the advantage of the organism"? What do mindless mitochondria care about the "longest possible run"? How the "somehow"? Not that Dr. Thomas is obliged to solve all biological riddles, or that the teleological fallacy (as, say, Jacques Monod would view it) can be easily erased from language attempting to describe intricate phenomena. But Dr. Thomas' celebration of symbiotic relationships does seem tinged by the antique notion of Providence, rechristened "luck": "There may have been elements of luck in the emergence of chloroplasts." "It is another illustration of our fantastic luck that oxygen filters out the very bands of ultraviolet light that are most devastating for nucleic acids and proteins." Without exactly stating that this is the best of all possible worlds, Dr. Thomas approaches a kind of biochemical Leibnizism. His willingness to see possibility where others see only doom is, like McLuhan's, tonic and welcome. Yet his announcement that the adversary system is obsolete in nature feels premature. Every day, my well-fed cat brings as tribute to my back porch the mauled body of a field mouse or baby rabbit; one wonders how complacently the little corpses submitted to their part in our triune symbiosis. One does not have to live very close to nature to cringe at all the carnage and waste it contains. That our cells harbor useful aliens, that ants perform miracles of coöperation, that we are all more sensitive and permeable than we know—this is sheer observed fact, and provocative as such. On the other hand, Dr. Thomas' shimmering vision of a "fusion around the earth" that will spring from "more crowding, more unrestrained and obsessive communication" seems less a prognosis than a hope defiant of much we *can* observe about our increasingly crowded, irritable, depleted, de-institutionalized, and cannibalistic world.

Alive and Free from Employment

My Days, by R. K. Narayan. 186 pp. Viking, 1974.

The autobiography of a writer of fiction is generally superfluous, since he has already, in rearrangement and disguise, written out the material of his life many times. A novel like *The Man-Eater of Malgudi*, though its hero, Nataraj, and its author, Narayan, are not to be confused, tells us more about the India that R. K. Narayan inhabits, and more explicitly animates his opinion of what he sees, than his recent brief memoir, *My Days*. Not that Mr. Narayan's mischievous modesty does not lend an agreeable tone to this account of his rather uneventful life. Nor are his delightful gifts of caricature entirely inhibited by factuality. In *My Days*, as in his novels, one meets men so absorbed in self-interest that they become grotesque and emblematic: the young Narayan, seeking employment, grooms himself smartly to meet a prospective employer, who comes onto his veranda "bare-bodied and glisten[ing] with an oil-coating, as he prepared himself for a massage; he blinked several times to make me out, as oil had dripped over his eyes and blurred his vision. . . . All my best efforts at grooming were wasted, for I must have looked to him like a photograph taken with a shivering hand." The man barks a rebuff of the boy, and then paces "like a greasy bear in its cage." This sense of imprisonment within character, of each person energetically if ruinously fulfilling his dharma—his vocation, a Christian might say —reached its peak in English fiction with Dickens, and perhaps requires a religious basis. In the liberal view, character is significantly malleable, whereas the traditional character-creators fatalistically look into men for a fixed posture, an irrevocable passion. Narayan tells us that another uncle served as "an inescapable model for me—his approach to other human beings, his aggressive talk wherever he went, his dash and recklessness . . . his abandon to alcohol in every form all through the day. (I portrayed him as Kailas, in *The Bachelor of Arts,* and he provided all the substance whenever I had to portray a drunken character.)" Few writers since Dickens can match the effect of colorful teeming that Narayan's fictional city of Malgudi conveys; its population is as sharply chiselled as a temple frieze, and as endless, with always, one feels, more characters around the corner.

Yet the creator's life, as described in *My Days,* begins in loneliness. A little boy, living with his grandmother and uncle, has only pets for company, and the pets all die. He goes to school, and hates it. "On the first day I wept in fear. The sight of my classmates shook my nerves." He cannot shape clay, and his slate is always smudged. Throughout his schooling, though he toughens into an athletic child of the streets, he remains difficult, intractable, uninspired. "I was opposed to the system of being prescribed a set of books by an anonymous soulless body of textbook-prescribers, and of being stamped good or bad as a result of such studies. . . . I liked to be free to read what I pleased and not be examined at all." Taking his university entrance examinations, he flunks English —his best subject. And in the idle year this gives him, he begins to discover his own dharma—the vocation of a writer.

An aspect of this vocation, one feels after reading Mr. Narayan's fascinating middle chapters, is to have no other. His interviews for employment in business are humorous disasters; his enrollment as a teacher in the school where his father had been headmaster, a plausible route to respectability, is sabotaged by Narayan himself with the manic pugnacity of one of his own characters. His chapter describing the regimented foolishness of schoolteaching and his repeated escape from it approaches vehemence; the chapters following drop in emotional temperature, and trace a slow climb to success, contentment already achieved.

> That settled it. After the final and irrevocable stand I took [not to be a teacher], I felt lighter and happier. I did not encourage anyone to comment on my deed or involve myself in any discussion. I

sensed that I was respected for it. At least there was an appreciation of the fact that I knew my mind. I went through my day in a businesslike manner, with a serious face. Soon after my morning coffee and bath I took my umbrella and started out for a walk. I needed the umbrella to protect my head from the sun. Sometimes I carried a pen and pad and sat down under the shade of a tree at the foot of Chamundi Hill and wrote. Some days I took out a cycle and rode ten miles along the Karapur Forest Road, sat on a wayside culvert, and wrote or brooded over life and literature, watching some peasant ploughing his field, with a canal flowing glitteringly in the sun. My needs were nil, I did not have plans, there was a delight in being just alive and free from employment.

It speaks well, I think, of the Indian society of the early Thirties that it allowed, after due resistance, this prospectless young man's rebellion against gainful employment; a contemporaneous American family might have driven such a child to France, or into bohemia—altogether out, in any case, of the home environment that has continuously nurtured Narayan's creativity. Madras, where he was raised, and Mysore, where he came to live, spontaneously fostered a fictional city: "On a certain day in September, selected by my grandmother for its auspiciousness, I bought an exercise book and wrote the first line of a novel; as I sat in a room nibbling my pen and wondering what to write, Malgudi with its little railway station swam into view, all ready-made. . . ." This novel, under the title of *Swami and Friends*, was finally published in England.

The literary London of Shaw and Wells, Conan Doyle and Wodehouse, the *Strand* and the *Mercury* had been brought, via magazines subscribed to by his father's school, into the center of Narayan's boyhood, and colonial India abounded in English-language journalism, though of a threadbare sort. (This reviewer once had the opportunity to ask Mr. Narayan if present, nationalist India, which has discouraged the teaching of English, would produce any more masters of the language like himself; his answer was affable but not affirmative.) In his first year of free-lance writing, Narayan earned nine rupees and twelve annas (about a dollar and a quarter); the second year, a short story sold for eighteen rupees; in the third, a children's tale brought thirty. He labored as the Mysore correspondent for the Madras *Justice;*

Graham Greene became his champion in England, and found a fresh publisher for each of his earlier novels, which were critical successes merely. The author married, and his beloved wife's sudden death from typhoid, and his own slow recovery from sorrow via psychic communication with her, form the only significantly adverse incident in his gradual progress from journalistic piecework to international distinction, movie deals, and—crown of crowns—a travel grant from the Rockefeller Foundation. In prosperity and fame, his imagination seems to work as fluently as when Malgudi with its railway station swam into view: "During my travels in America, the idea [of *The Guide*] crystallized in my mind. I stopped in Berkeley for three months, took a hotel room, and wrote my novel."

Narayan's few revelations about his practice of writing heighten the value of this memoir. His desire to write in English was born of an early infatuation with English novels, beginning with Scott and Dickens ("I . . . loved his London and the queer personalities therein") and going on to the romanticism of Rider Haggard and Marie Corelli and Mrs. Henry Wood ("I looked for books that would leave me crushed at the end"). When he turned from mystical poems to his first novel, he let the incidents invent themselves: "Each day as I sat down to write, I had no notion of what would be coming. All that I could be certain of was the central character." The tale-teller, that is, is nearer the tale-hearer, in his openness to surprise, than college instructors of plot mechanics may know. "The pure delight of watching a novel grow can never be duplicated by any other experience." But Narayan's fertility would be tedious without his control and economy; he goes on to describe how his days of pure delight were followed by nights of "corrections, revisions, and tightening up of sentences" so that a "real, final version could emerge . . . between the original lines and then again in what developed in the jumble of rewritten lines." His one confessed doctrinal resolve, as he set out, was "to see if other subjects than love . . . could be written about. I wished to attack the tyranny of Love and see if Life could offer other values than the inevitable Man-Woman relationship to a writer." The predominantly masculine interplay of his novels develops, one feels, from street life, from the skein of casual and passing conver-

sation that he alludes to lovingly more than once. His days of journalistic news-gathering no doubt reinforced his habit of sociable
curiosity, but the impulse perhaps dates back to the time when, an
only child in his grandmother's house, he found it "exciting, one
day, to be asked to go with my uncle to the street of shops." His
days as a writer customarily began with a walk:

> All morning I wandered. At every turn I found a character fit to
> go into a story. While walking, ideas were conceived and developed,
> or sometimes lost through the interludes on the way. One could not
> traverse the main artery of Mysore, Sayyaji Rao Road, without
> stopping every few steps to talk to a friend. Mysore is not only
> reminiscent of an old Greek city in its physical features, but the
> habits of its citizens are also very Hellenic. Vital issues, including
> philosophical and political analyses, were examined and settled by
> people (at least in those days) on the promenades of Mysore.

Narayan is one of a vanishing breed—the writer as citizen. His
citizenship extends to calling up municipal officials about inadequate street lighting, to "dashing off virulent letters to newspapers
about corruption and inefficiency." Such protests do not feel, as
with so much American social consciousness, forced—a covert bid
for power and self-justification. "If I have to worry, it's about
things outside me, mostly not concerning me." What a wealth of
material becomes accessible to a writer who can so simply proclaim a sense of community! We have writers willing to be mayor
but not many excited to be citizens. We have writers as confessors,
shackled to their personal lives, and writers as researchers, hanging
their sheets of information from a bloodless story line. But of
writers immersed in their material, and enabled to draw tales from
a community of neighbors, Faulkner was our last great example.
An instinctive, respectful identification with the people of one's
locale comes hard now, in the menacing cities or disposable suburbs, yet without it a genuine belief in the significance of humanity, in humane significances, comes not at all.

APPENDIX

One Big Interview

The interviewers are as follows:

Samuels: Charles Thomas Samuels, who taped our conversations for several days in August 1968 on Martha's Vineyard, and permitted me to revise the transcript for publication in the *Paris Review* the following winter as "The Art of Fiction XLIII."

Rhode: Eric Rhode, whose radio dialogue with me for the BBC Third Programme was published in *The Listener* on June 19, 1969.

Gado: Frank Gado, professor of English at Union, Schenectady, New York; for simplicity's sake I have identified with his name not only his own questions but a few from his students, whose taped session with me in the winter of 1971 was printed as a special issue of *The Idol*, that spring.

Buckingham: Hugh Buckingham, a poet and critic then teaching at Harvard, who came and talked to me about *Bech: A Book;* the transcribed interview appeared in the Sunday *Herald-Traveler* (Boston) Books Guide supplement for January 19, 1971. His machine failed to record our first take; the second lacked much of the sparkle of the irrecoverable first.

Sragow: Michael Sragow, an undergraduate reporter for the Harvard *Crimson*, where this interview appeared on February 2, 1972, having been taped in Cambridge the preceding December.

Ogle: Jane Ogle, of *Harper's Bazaar*, whose written questions about *Buchanan Dying* were answered by me, in exceptionally lavish detail, on December 18, 1972, on the typewriter, and were never published.

Howard: Jane Howard, who spent three days in Ipswich with the Updikes in September 1966, and whose sprightly and courteous account, under the somewhat discouraging title "Can a Nice Novelist Finish First?" appeared in the November 4, 1966, issue of *Life*.

ONE BIG INTERVIEW

SAMUELS: *You've treated your early years fictionally and have discussed them in interviews, but you haven't said much about your time at Harvard. I wonder what effect you think it had.*

My time at Harvard, once I got by the compression bends of the freshman year, was idyllic enough, and as they say successful; but I felt toward those years, while they were happening, the resentment a caterpillar must feel while his somatic cells are shifting all around to make him a butterfly. I remember the glow of the Fogg Museum windows, and my wife-to-be pushing her singing bicycle through the snowy Yard, and the smell of wet old magazines that arose from the cellar of the Lampoon and hit your nostrils when you entered the narthex, and numerous grateful revelations in classrooms—all of it haunted, though, by knowledge of the many others who had passed this way and felt the venerable glory of it all more warmly than I, and written sufficiently about it. All that I seem able to preserve of the Harvard experience is in one short story, "The Christian Roommates." There was another, "Homage to Paul Klee," that has been printed in *The Liberal Context* but not in a book. Foxy Whitman, in *Couples*, remembers some of the things I do. Like me, she feels obscurely hoodwinked, pacified, by the process of becoming nice. I distrust, perhaps, hallowed, very O.K. places. Harvard has enough panegyrists without me.

SAMUELS: *After graduating from Harvard you served as a* New Yorker *staff writer for two years. What sort of work did you do?*

I was a "Talk of the Town" writer, which means that I both did the legwork and the finished product. An exalted position! It was playful work that opened the city to me. I was the man who went to boating or electronic exhibits in the Coliseum and tried to make poems of the objects and overheard conversations.

SAMUELS: *How do you feel about being associated with that magazine?*

Very happy. From the age of twelve when my aunt gave us a subscription for Christmas, *The New Yorker* has seemed to me the best of possible magazines, and their acceptance of a poem and a story by me in June of 1954 remains the ecstatic breakthrough of my literary life. Their editorial care, and their gratitude for a piece of work they like, are incomparable. And I love the format—the signature at the end, everybody the same size, and the battered title type, evocative of the Twenties and Persia and the future all at once.

SAMUELS: *You seem to shun literary society. Why?*

I don't, do I? Here I am, talking to you. In leaving New York in 1957, I did leave without regret the literary demimonde of agents and would-be's and with-it non-participants; this world seemed unnutritious and interfering. Hemingway described literary New York as a bottle full of tapeworms trying to feed on each other. When I write, I aim in my mind not toward New York but toward a vague spot a little to the east of Kansas. I think of the books on library shelves, without their jackets, years old, and a countryish teen-aged boy finding them, and having them speak to him. The reviews, the stacks in Brentano's, are just hurdles to get over, to place the books on that shelf. Anyway, in 1957, I was full of a Pennsylvania thing I wanted to say, and Ipswich gave me the space in which to say it, and in which to live modestly, raise my children, and have friends on the basis of what I did in person rather than what I did in print.

RHODE: *I don't see any affiliation in your work to the French idea of experiment, or indeed to the kinds of experiment that go on in the States. It seems to me that you are much closer to the English novel: there is a very strong sense of the domestic in your work— of the world as it is.* [A pause.]

I'm just trying to think of the word "domestic." I suppose this is true. It may be less a matter of conscious choice than of the fact that I seem to be a domestic creature. My first novel, *The Poorhouse Fair*, was, at least in my mind, something of a *nouvelle vague* book, particularly in the ending: that is, I tried to create a pattern of tension and then, instead of resolving it, dissolved it. It ended with a kind of brainless fair: people come to a fair and you hear their voices and it all dissolves. In my mind it was a somewhat experimental book, and my publishers then, Harper, seemed to think it was, because the ending puzzled them so much that I took it away from them and went to Knopf, where I've been happy ever since. In each of the books there has been, in my mind at least, a different experiment, an adventure: in *Rabbit, Run* the present tense may seem a mild adventure. It's more and more used now, but at that time it wasn't.

RHODE: *Coming back to* The Poorhouse Fair, *the most striking thing there, I think, is the fact that you have so clearly kept yourself out of the book, that you have created these very old men and women. This is an act entirely of the imagination, or so it feels. In fact Mary McCarthy said that she finds it a rather spooky accomplishment—like those boy actors who play old men—that you have created these characters so credibly. How far was it based on actuality?*

Not very. There was indeed a poorhouse a couple of blocks from where I grew up, but I very rarely went into it, and there was a fair that must have impressed me as a child. I had written prior to this, while living in New York City, a six-hundred-page novel, called *Home* and more or less about myself and my family up to the age of sixteen or so. It had been a good exercise to write it and I later used some of the material in short stories, but it really felt like a very heavy bundle of yellow paper, and I realized that this was not going to be my first novel—it had too many of the traits of a first novel. I did not publish it, but I thought it was time for me to write a novel. I was—what?—twenty-five, twenty-six. Getting to be an old man, as writers go in America. They were tearing the poorhouse down in Shillington, and I went over and looked at the shell. My grandfather, who is somewhat like John Hook in that book, was recently dead, and so the idea of some kind of memorial gesture, embodying what seems to have been on my part a very strong sense of national decay, crystallized in this novel. I wrote it in three months and then rewrote it in three months. It was my first real venture into what you might call novelistic space and it was very exciting. I haven't read it since the last set of proofs, but I'd like to think that there was some love, and hence some life and blood, in these old people.

SAMUELS: *But if I'm not mistaken, you once expressed a desire to write for the films and I think* Rabbit, Run, *in particular, is quite a cinematic novel. Do you have any such plans now?*

Rabbit, Run was subtitled originally "A Movie." The present tense was in part meant to be an equivalent of the cinematic mode of narration. The opening bit of the boys playing basketball was visualized to be taking place under the titles and credits. This doesn't mean, though, that I really wanted to write for the movies. It meant I wanted to make a movie. I could come closer by writing it in my own book than by attempting to get through to Hollywood.

GADO: *How do you react to the idea of a film being made of one of your books?*

I had the eerie experience the other day of sitting in an empty theatre looking at a movie made from *Rabbit, Run.* The picture fails in a number of ways, but one of the ways was in trying to be faithful to the book. They'd been faithful to it in a literal-minded way, but by not being so to the underlying spirit, they produced an enigmatic version of what is very clear in the book.

And yet certain things, like the furniture in the people's apartments, had been done with a richness that I had never even approached. I couldn't have imagined all these things they found to put in those sets: these identifying kinds of calendars, the style of furniture, all just for a few seconds on the screen. How incomparably more solid and entertaining the physical environment became, and yet, curiously, the inner story of the book became thin and even nonsensical.

Funnily enough, when they made a movie out of this book, they didn't see that it was written as a film in my mind. They didn't put the titles over the opening with the kids playing basketball. Instead they made a little box out of it and surrounded it with the titles. The big hands, the ball bouncing on the ground—it would have been a natural thing for an overlay. Which goes to show. . . .

GADO: *Haven't I read that someone is making a movie from* Couples?

I doubt if he'll ever do anything with it. An enterprising fellow called Wolper, who made a good thing of various television documentaries, got hold of *Couples.* He had quite ambitious plans for it. In writing to me, he kept using the word "important" all the time. "Most important book," and then, "Make an important movie."

At one point, I intended to say to him, "Would you like me to come out to Hollywood and write the movie for you?" I can see it as a film, and I know I could do it. I understand the book; I understand that it is a romantic book, a book written by a boy who went to a lot of movies. It has a happy ending. It's about a guy meeting a girl and the guy getting the girl. But I know that they don't see it that way. You know, they were talking about it as satire! Satire—this elegiac story. It's a loving portrait of life in America. No, I don't think I will write the screenplay, even if they were to ask me out there. They'd just break my heart.

One of the advantages of the kind of writing I do is that you are your own boss. You shoot your own stock, choose all the scenes, cast all the characters. You're your own everything really—and the product, then, is yours. If it plays, great—and if it doesn't, there are no alibis.

SAMUELS: *Why do you write so much about what most people take to be your own adolescence and family? Numerous critics, for example, have pointed to similarities between* Of the Farm, The Centaur, *and stories like "My Grandmother's Thimble." "Flight," for example, seems an earlier version of* Of the Farm.

I suppose there's no avoiding it—my adolescence seemed interesting to me. In a sense my mother and father, considerable actors both, were dramatizing my youth as I was having it, so that I arrived as an adult with some burden of material already half-formed. There is, true, a submerged thread connecting certain of the fictions, and I guess the submerged thread is the autobiography. That is, in *Of the Farm*, although the last name is not the name of the people in *The Centaur*, the geography is not appreciably changed, and the man in each case is called George. *Of the Farm* was in part a look at the world of *The Centaur* after the centaur had indeed died. By the way, I must repeat that I didn't mean Caldwell to die in *The Centaur;* he dies in the sense of living, of going back to work, of being a shelter for his son. But by the time Joey Robinson is thirty-five his father is dead. Also, there's the curious touch of the Running Horse River in *Rabbit, Run* which returns in the Alton of *The Centaur*. And somehow that Running Horse bridges both the books, connects them. But apart from the somewhat teasing little connections, there is in these three novels and the short stories of *Pigeon Feathers* a central image of flight or escape or loss, the way we flee from the past, a sense of guilt which I tried to express in the story, the triptych with the long title, "The Blessed Man of Boston, My Grandmother's Thimble, and Fanning Island," wherein the narrator becomes a Polynesian pushing off into a void. The sense that in time as well as space we leave people as if by volition and thereby incur guilt and thereby owe them, the dead, the forsaken, at least the homage of rendering them. The trauma or message that I acquired in Olinger had to do with suppressed pain, with the amount of sacrifice, I suppose, that middle-class life demands, and by that I guess I mean civilized life. The father, whatever his name, is sacrificing freedom of motion, and the mother is sacrificing in a way—oh, sexual richness, I guess; they're all stuck, and when I think back over these stories (and you know, they *are* dear to me and if I had to give anybody one book of me it would be the Vintage *Olinger Stories*) I think especially of that moment in "Flight" when the boy, chafing to escape, fresh from his encounter with Molly Bingaman and a bit more of a man but not enough quite, finds the mother lying there buried in her own peculiar messages from far away, the New Orleans jazz, and then the grandfather's voice comes tumbling down the stairs singing "There is a happy land, far, far away." This is the way it was, is. There has never been anything in my life quite as compressed, simultaneously as communicative to me of my own power and worth and of the irremediable grief in just living, in just going on.

RHODE: *I wonder, in the case of* The Centaur, *why you related the immediate experience of the schoolmaster to myth.*

It seemed to me that there was something mythical about the events. It's an experiment very unlike that of *Ulysses*, where the myth lurks beneath the surface of the natural events. In a way, the natural events in my book are meant to be a kind of mask for the myth. The genesis of it was reading in an old book of my wife's this footnote to the Hercules legend. It is part of the comedy of Chiron's plight that he is living in a town full of gods, and he's not quite a god himself, hence this failure of communication all the time. In fact, my father, who came from New Jersey, *did* have this feeling about Pennsylvania, that he wasn't quite clued in about what was going on. Secondly, there is a way in which to a child everything is myth-size: people are enormous and ominous and have great backlogs of mysterious information and of a life lived that you lack. I don't think that without the myth you'd have a book. It seemed to me to fit a kind of experience that I'd had: my father's immersion in the world of Christian morality, in trying to do the right thing and constantly sacrificing himself, always going off to church meetings, and yet complaining about it all the time. There was an ambivalence that seemed to make him very centaur-like. I think that initially art was tied in with theology and has to do with an ideal world: the artist is in some way a middleman between the ideal world and this, even though our sense of the ideal—and I'm speaking really of our gut sense, regardless of what we think we believe—is at present fairly dim. It may not always be so. And I find I can not imagine being a writer without wanting somehow to play, to make these patterns, to insert these secrets into my books, and to spin out this music that has its formal side.

RHODE: *Do you improvise or do you plot things out very carefully beforehand?*

I really begin with some kind of solid, coherent image, some notion of the shape of the book and even of its texture. *The Poorhouse Fair* was meant to have a sort of Y shape. *Rabbit, Run* was a kind of zig-zag. *The Centaur* was sort of a sandwich. I can't begin until I know the beginning and have some sense of what's going to happen between. There are some hinges, but really a novel, even quite a bulky one—you think of Henry James's eight hundred pages—has only a few hinges. I don't make an outline or anything. I figure that I can hold the events in my head and then hope that things will happen which will surprise me, that the characters will take on life and talk. I keep a kind of loose rein on the book. I would not begin a book, I would not advise people to begin a book, without knowing where it's going.

RHODE: *This image of the book that you have in mind is in fact a rather geometric image. It's not, say, a visual image, an image of events in the book which you're leading up to.*

It's sort of an abstract sensation, but of course you have to have a lot of other things to begin a book. You have to have at least some of the people and have to be in some ways stirred by the central people. The main motive force behind *The Centaur* would be some wish to make a record of my father. For fifteen years I'd watched a normal, good-doing Protestant man suffering in a kind of comic but real way. I think it left me rather angry. There is a lot of anger in my books, really. Their secret ingredient.

SAMUELS: *If I'm right in regarding* [The Centaur] *as formally uncharacteristic, I wonder why you prefer it to your other novels?*

Well, it seems in memory my gayest and truest book; I pick it up, and read a few pages, in which Caldwell is insisting on flattering a moth-eaten bum, who is really the god Dionysus, and I began laughing. . . . The mythology answers to my sensation that the people we meet are *guises*, do conceal something mythic, perhaps prototypes or longings in our minds. We love some women more than others by predetermination, it seems to me.

SAMUELS: *Why haven't you done more work in this mode?*

But I *have* worked elsewhere in a mythic mode. Apart from my short story about Tristan and Iseult, there is the St. Stephen story underlying *The Poorhouse Fair*, and Peter Rabbit under *Rabbit, Run*. Sometimes it is semi-conscious; for example, only lately do I see that Brewer, the city of brick painted the color of flowerpots, is the flowerpot that Mr. McGregor slips over Peter Rabbit. And in *Couples*, Piet is not only Hanema/anima/Life, he is Lot, the man with two virgin daughters, who flees Sodom, and leaves his wife behind.

SAMUELS: *Let's turn from myth to history. You have indicated a desire to write about President Buchanan. Yet, so far as I can see, American history is normally absent from your work.*

Not so; quite the contrary. In each of my novels, a precise year is given and a President reigns; *The Centaur* is distinctly a Truman book, and *Rabbit, Run* an Eisenhower one. *Couples* could have taken place only under Kennedy; the social currents it traces are as specific to those years as flowers in a meadow are to their moment of summer. Even *The Poorhouse Fair* has a President, President Lowenstein, and if one is not named in *Of the Farm* it may be because that book, in an odd way, also takes place in the future, though a future only a year or so in advance of the writing—a future now in the past. Hook, Caldwell, the Applesmiths, all talk about history, and the quotidian is littered with newspaper headlines, striking the consciousness of the characters obliquely and subliminally but firmly enough: Piet's first step at seducing Foxy is clearly in part motivated by the death of the Kennedy infant. And the atmosphere of fright permeating *The Centaur* is to an indicated extent early Cold-War nerves. My fiction about the daily doings of ordinary people has more history in it than history books, just as there is more breathing history in archaeology than in a list of declared wars and changes of government.

SAMUELS: *What about violence? Many critics complain that this is absent from your work—reprehensibly, because it is so present in the world. Why is there so little in your pages?*

There has been so little in my life. I have fought in no wars, and engaged in few fistfights. I do not think a man pacifist in his life should pretend to violence in fiction; I feel a tenderness toward my characters that forbids making violent use of them. In general, the North American continent in this century has been a place where catastrophe has held off, and likewise the lives I have witnessed have staved off real death. All my novels end with a false death, partial death. If, as may be, the holocausts at the rim of possibility do soon visit us, I am confident my capacities for expression can rise, if I live, to the occasion. In the meantime let's all of us with some access to a printing press not abuse our privilege with fashionable fantasies.

RHODE: *You are religious yourself?*

I'd say, yes, I try to be. I think I do tend to see the world as layered, and as there being something up there; certainly in *Couples* it would seem to be God who in a certain sense destroys that inoffensive Congregationalist church. My books are all meant to be moral debates with the reader, and if they seem pointless—I'm speaking hopefully—it's because the reader has not been engaged in the debate. The question is usually, "What is a good man?" or "What is goodness?" and in all the books an issue is examined. Take Harry Angstrom in *Rabbit, Run:* there is a case to be made for running away from your wife. In the late Fifties beatniks were preaching transcontinental travelling as the answer to man's disquiet. And I was just trying to say: "Yes, there is certainly that, but then there are all these other people who seem to get hurt." That qualification is meant to frame a moral dilemma.

RHODE: *You see the institution of marriage, the institution of the Church, as something that carries you back to the past, which I think again is very important in your books. For instance, in* The Poorhouse Fair *the one moment that I felt that you emerged as a person was close to the end when you say something about how we go backwards, how we become our father's opinions, and eventually our grandfather's.*

True enough, there is this interest in the past, but in a way the past is all we have. The present is very thin, it's less than a second wide, and the future doesn't exist. I think that *Of the Farm*, say, is about moral readjustment, and the readjustment is of course in terms of harsh deeds done in the past; the mother and boy need, in a way, to excuse each other, or somehow to give a blessing. It's a little hard for me to see my work from the outside, as it were, but I do notice a recurrence of the concept of a blessing, of approval, or forgiveness. The basic problem may be simply one of encouragement, because of the failure of nerve, the lassitude and despair, the sense that we've gone to the end of the corridor and found it blank. So the characters beneath the surface are exhorting each other to action. In *Couples* Piet is quite a modern man in that he really can't act for himself because he's overwhelmed by the moral implications of any act—leaving his wife, staying with her. While the women in that book are less sensitive perhaps to this oppressive quality, of cosmic blackness, and it is the women who do almost all of the acting. I don't want to say that being passive, being inactive, being paralyzed, is wrong in an era when so much action is crass and murderous. I do feel that in the generations that I've had a glimpse of—I can see my grandfather at one end, and I can see my boys coming up—there has been a perceptible loss of the sense of righteousness. But many evils are done in the name of righteousness, so perhaps one doesn't want it back. Nevertheless, I suspect that the vitality of women now, the way many of us lean on them, is not an eternal phenomenon but a historical one, and fairly recent.

SAMUELS: *In an interview you gave* Life *you expressed some regret at the "yes, but" attitude critics have taken toward it.* Did the common complaint that you had ducked large subjects lead to the writing of* Couples?

No, I meant my *work* says "yes, but." Yes, in *Rabbit, Run*, to our urgent inner whispers, but—the social fabric collapses disastrously. Yes, in *The Centaur*, to self-sacrifice and duty, but—what of a man's private agony and dwindling? No, in *The Poorhouse Fair*, to social homogenization and loss of faith, but—listen to the voices, the joy of persistent existence. No, in *Couples*, to a religious community founded on physical and psychical interpenetration, but—what else shall we do, as God destroys our churches? I cannot greatly care what critics say of my work; if it is good, it will come to the surface in a generation or two and float, and if not, it will sink, having in the meantime provided me with a living, the opportunities of leisure, and a craftsman's intimate satisfactions. I wrote *Couples* because the rhythm of my life and my *oeuvre* demanded it, not to placate hallucinatory critical voices.

---

* What I had said to Jane Howard, as quoted, was: "There's a 'yes-but' quality about my writing that evades entirely pleasing anybody. It seems to me that critics get increasingly querulous and impatient for madder music and stronger wine, when what we need is a greater respect for reality, its secrecy, its music. Too many people are studying maps and not enough are visiting places."

SAMUELS: *What do you mean by attributing the setting up of religious communities in* Couples *to God's destruction of our churches?*

I guess the noun "God" appears in two totally different senses, the God in the first instance being the one worshipped within this nice white church, the more or less watered-down Puritan God; and then God in the second sense means ultimate power. I've never really understood theologies which would absolve God of earthquakes and typhoons, of children starving. A god who is not God the Creator is not very real to me, so that, yes, it certainly *is* God who throws the lightning bolt and this God is above the nice god, above the god we can worship and empathize with. I guess I'm saying there's a fierce God above the kind God and he's the one Piet believes in. At any rate, when the church is burned, Piet is relieved of morality, and can choose Foxy—or can accept the choice made for him by Foxy and Angela operating in unison—can move out of the paralysis of guilt into what after all is a kind of freedom. He divorces the supernatural to marry the natural. I wanted the loss of Angela to be felt as a real loss—Angela is nicer than Foxy—nevertheless it is Foxy that he most deeply wants, it is Foxy who in some obscure way was turned on the lathe for him. So that the book does have a happy ending. There's also a way, though, I should say (speaking of "yes, but") in which, with the destruction of the church, with the removal of his guilt, he becomes insignificant. He becomes merely a name in the last paragraph: he becomes a satisfied person and in a sense dies. In other words, a person who has what he wants, a satisfied person, a content person, ceases to be a person. Unfallen Adam is an ape. Yes, I guess I do feel that. I feel that to be a person is to be in a situation of tension, is to be in a dialectical situation. A truly adjusted person is not a person at all—just an animal with clothes on. So that it's a happy ending, with this "but" at the end.

SAMUELS: *I was impressed by the contrast between the presentation of oral-genital contacts in* Couples *and its single appearance in* Rabbit, Run.

Well, *Couples*, in part, is about the change in sexual deportment that has occurred since the publication of *Rabbit, Run*, which came out late in '59; shortly thereafter we had *Lady Chatterley* and the first Henry Miller books, and now you can't walk into a grocery store without seeing pornography on the rack. Remember Piet lying in Freddy's bed admiring Freddy's collection of Grove Press books? In *Rabbit, Run* what is demanded, in *Couples* is freely given. What else? It's a way of eating, eating the apple, of knowing. It's nostalgic for them, for Piet of Annabelle Vojt and for Foxy of the Jew. In de Rougement's book on Tristan and Iseult he speaks of the sterility of the lovers, and Piet and Foxy are sterile vis-à-vis each other. Lastly, I was struck, talking to a biochemist friend of mine, how he emphasized not only the chemical composition of enzymes but their structure; it matters, among my humans, not only what they're made of, but exactly how they attach to each other. So much for oral-genital contacts.

RHODE: *We're talking about* Couples *as a book about sex. It's something quite different, isn't it? What astonishes me is that these descriptions are written with extraordinary delicacy and tact. You must have found them very hard to write.*

They were no harder than landscapes and a little more interesting. It's wonderful the way people in bed talk, the sense of voices and the sense of warmth, so that as a writer you become kind of warm also. The book is, of course, not about sex as such: It's about sex as the emergent religion, as the only thing left.

BUCKINGHAM: *I believe that one of the chapters of* Bech *originally appeared as a short story.*

Several did.

BUCKINGHAM: *Does that mean the book was conceived piecemeal?*

It was indeed conceived piecemeal. When I returned from the Soviet Union and Eastern Europe in '64 I had a number of impressions that only a writer could have collected. So, in trying to utilize some of them I invented Henry Bech, just to serve as a vehicle for my own impressions in a story entitled "The Bulgarian Poetess."

Distrusting writers as heroes, I made Bech as unlike myself as I could. Instead of being married with four children, he's a bachelor; instead of being a Gentile, he's a Jew—of course, a Jewish writer is almost as inevitable as an Italian gangster. I made him somewhat older than myself and gave him, sketchily, a career; the book

Travel Light was his initial success—probably I had most in mind Jack Kerouac's *On the Road*.

O.K., so there Henry Bech sat in this story, which *The New Yorker* took and published; and to my surprise the story had a degree of success. Friends said they liked it, and it got the first O. Henry Award of that year. So, never wanting to let a good thing go unflogged, I wrote another story, about Rumania this time, and made a third attempt, a story about Russia. I wrote a long journal, Henry Bech's Russian Journal, which didn't work out, though I salvaged parts of it for an appendix in the book. The little story "Rich in Russia" was done later—the bigger the country, the smaller the story, somehow.

Then out of quite a different set of memories or impressions I wrote "Bech Takes Pot Luck," which is an American story and takes place on an island a touch like Martha's Vineyard. (Is this boring you? How to build a coffin, nail by nail.) At this point I began to think that they might be a book. I wrote the London story and it was quite important that it work out—by working out I mean that *The New Yorker* take it. It did. And then I wrote two more, one to wind the book up and the other to sort of make a bridge—that is, "Bech Panics" takes us from the Bech of the Vineyard story to the somewhat older and rather hallucinating writer of London. And that's how you cook up a book.

BUCKINGHAM: *When did you do the fake bibliographies and things? They're great fun.*

They were kind of fun. Of course, the preface is very short, even though it took Bech eight days to write it.

BUCKINGHAM: *And you?*

It took me a day.

GADO: *At the end of* Bech, *you supplied the reader with bibliographical appendices. I tried to make some sense of them but couldn't. Is there a key? Or was it just the vestigial gagster in you wanting to play games with the magazines, critics, and writers?*

It was meant two ways: first, as a light-hearted attempt to give Bech a concrete bibliographical existence as a writer; second, as a means of reëstablishing a distance between Bech and myself. He's nine years older than I, and partly for that reason, his career is quite different from mine. In this respect, the bibliography was intended to be a specimen history of an American literary career of the period. He began as a kind of war correspondent, a soldier who wrote stories with gung-ho titles for magazines like *Liberty* and *Collier's*. He was intellectualized in New York in the post-war period. And now he has fallen into silence. There are careers like this. Salinger? Irwin Shaw?

To be candid, the bibliography was also a matter of working off various grudges, a way of purging my system. I've never been warmly treated by the *Commentary* crowd—insofar as it is a crowd—and so I made Bech its darling.

And then, I don't know, it just seemed to help make it a book.

BUCKINGHAM: *You say Bech was written piecemeal, not on firmly drawn lines like* Couples?

Mm hmm.

BUCKINGHAM: *And yet at the end I find the final chapter just as serious, as poetic, just as heavyweight.*

I'm always at the same weight; I mean, I may be groggier some days than others, but I tend to be equally serious about everything. Of course, *Bech* is a serious book. I never thought of it as satirical, really; it was never really a concern of mine to poke fun at the Jewish writer, or the New York-Jewish literary establishment in this country. I hope I always gave Bech my full sympathy, my full empathy.

BUCKINGHAM: *What drove him toward the literary life, that gallery of immortals?*

In the London story he has this hope that one more woman, one more leap up the falls, will bring him safe into that high, calm pool of immortality where Proust and Hawthorne and Catullus float, glassy-eyed and belly-up. (I love that sentence.) He wants to be lifted out of flux, the way that literary immortals are. Also, Bech is one of the last "moderns." He believes in Eliot and Valéry and Joyce and Rilke and those others who were convinced of the sacred importance of the written word. They believed themselves custodians of the language and therefore of the values of their society.

I think we're all attracted toward excellence of this sort, wishing to associate this very mixed deteriorating bag of our physical and egotistical selves with something fine, and Bech was drawn to literature out of that, and for a while found it, perhaps, but his success has thrown him into a very baffling world of the wrong kind of praise, or being used by younger people as in the London story, or being asked to join dead people, as in the last story, or of women constantly trying to lure him out of his monkhood. . . . It's all rather sad. Think of Mailer. He began as a war novelist, a novelist in the Steinbeck sense; and so he arrives and finds the party is breaking up. The novel couldn't be for his generation what it was for the generation of Hemingway and Fitzgerald. We're not going to get anybody like Hemingway for a while, who so intensely and instinctively cared about language. When he died there was nobody around who cared so much, cared so much he killed himself because he couldn't do it as finely as he thought it should be done. Instead you get showmen and professors. Bech becomes a showman against his will. A display piece. A toy.

SRAGOW: [Rabbit Redux] *has been hailed for its portrait of "Middle America." Did the necessity to get that close to a man who is inarticulate and guided by mass culture to as great a degree as Rabbit require a . . . leap?*

Intellectually, I'm not essentially advanced over Harry Angstrom. I went to Harvard, it's true, and wasn't much good at basketball; other than that we're rather similar. I quite understand both his anger and passivity, and feeling of the whole Vietnam involvement as a puzzle, that something strange has gone wrong; but it's no great leap of the imagination to do *that*.

There may be something also in the novelist's trade which shades you towards conservatism. Things exist because they evolved to that condition; they cannot be lightly or easily altered. It is my general sense of human institutions that they are outcroppings of human nature, that human nature is slow to change, that in general when you destroy one set of institutions you get something worse.

SRAGOW: *You've written that "an easy humanism" pervades the land. Given the fact that you deal on a very personal basis with human stress, how do your distinguish your . . .*

Difficult humanism? I feel that, as a writer, I put into practice a set of democratic assumptions. Just as in a democracy anybody can be president, so anyone can be a character in a novel, at least in one by me. Every human being who is more than a moron is the locus of certain violent tensions that come with having a brain. In fact there is an easy humanism that insists that man is an animal which feeds and sleeps and defecates and makes love and isn't that nice and natural and let's all have more of that. But this is omitting intrinsic stresses in the human condition—you foresee things, for example, you foresee your own death. You have really been locked out of the animal paradise of unthinking natural reflex.

You are born into one political contract or another, whose terms, though they sit very lightly at first, eventually, in the form of the draft, or taxes, begin to make very heavy demands on you. The general social contract—living with other people, driving cars on highways—all this is difficult, it's painful. It's a kind of agony really—the agony vents itself in ulcers internally, rage externally. . . . In short, all of our institutions—of marriage, the family, your driver's license—everything is kind of precarious, and maintained at a cost of tension.

SRAGOW: *Easy humanism, then, lies in the belief that these individual problems can be ignored for the sake of larger panaceas.*

Or taking humanity as some kind of moral index, saying that to be human is to be good and our problems all arise from not being human enough. I think I take a rather darker view. We must of necessity lose our humanity all the time.

When asked about what my philosophy was I tried to write it down in *Midpoint* in handy couplets and discovered that of all my books it is the least read, and it was hardly reviewed at all. I concluded that nobody really cared what my philosophy was. That's all right. The novelist is of interest only for what he does through empathy and image-producing, image-arranging; the more consciously a theorist he is the more apt he is to become impotent or cranky or both. Like Harry, I try to remain open. Revolt, rebellion, violence, disgust are themselves there for a reason, they too are organically evolved out of a distinct reality, and must be considered respectfully. I try to love both the redneck and the flower child, the anarchist bomb-thrower. People are basically very anarchistic. Harry's search for infinite freedom—that's anarchy too. He loves destruction. Who doesn't?

SRAGOW: *At the end of* Rabbit Redux, *Rabbit talks of going back to a farm. Are you thinking of bringing him back again?*

I left the book open, I even dangled a few threads that could be picked up. Janice talks about how he never should have had that awful indoor job. I already have a title—*Rural Rabbit*. That's going to be their next stage. I couldn't write that book now. Maybe in 1979 enough will have happened to both him and me that I can, but if it doesn't, that's all right. Maybe I should stop while I'm ahead—at least as far as *The Times Book Review* goes.

These two complement each other well enough. Anybody who really cared could get some interesting formal things out of the two books together. Certainly Janice bringing Stavros back to life is some kind of counterweight to the baby's death in the first book. She too had to make a passage—go through something to return. All that's there, I'm not sure that a third book could do it again. It would have to be a different kind of a book—a short book, a pastoral book, an eclogue.

[*The interview with Sragow transpired before I broke my leg in December of 1971, as the handsome full-length photograph in the Harvard* Crimson *attests. After my release from the hospital, Lee Wohlfert of* Women's Wear Daily *gouged from me the following drug-dazed utterances:*] "Like Harry, I'm hog fat, reactionary, passive. I'm a plugger. Even the way Rabbit sits in front of his Linotype machine day after day reminded me of myself, of the way I sit in front of the typewriter. . . . I decided to write it a while back when I couldn't get started on another book I was trying to write and the Sixties pressed heavily upon me. And I got sick of people talking about Rabbit, sick of them asking me what happened to him. So I decided to revisit my old friend. . . . [I appeared surprised that among the critics] no one's given serious consideration to the idea that Skeeter, the angry black, might *be* Jesus. He *says* he is. I think probably he might be. And if that's so, then people *ought* to be very nice to him."

*

OGLE: *You describe* Buchanan Dying *as a final homage to Pennsylvania, whose "mild, misty doughy middleness, between dangerous norths and souths," remains "your first taste of life, the authentic taste." Do you think of Buchanan as a typical Pennsylvanian?*

Well, yes, indeed I do, insofar as this large area, transected by the Alleghenies and ranging from Philadelphia to Pittsburgh, would admit of having a state character. In his fondness for good living and his distrust of radical solutions, in a certain comfortable fudging talkativeness, he seems familiar to me. Buchanan must have also seemed to his contemporaries representative, for he never lost a state election, and his Presidential victory hinged on his carrying the Keystone State. He could have been governor, also, but that his advisers, John Slidell foremost, felt that the governorship would have forced upon him a stand vis-à-vis slavery that would have marred the perfect ambiguity that did, in the end, win him the Presidency. My own muddled, middly sense of the metaphysical essence of Pennsylvania-ness has been often expressed in my fiction, and indeed is evoked one more time in my Afterword. I have often wanted to write about Wallace Stevens and John O'Hara, as Pennsylvania artists; their work, in some ways so different, shares a splendid leafiness, no? You may say that Thaddeus Stevens, the super-radical Representative, was a fellow-Lancastrian and nodding acquaintance of Buchanan's; my answer would be that Stevens came from Vermont, and was a New Englander at core. The only other President with claim to be a Pennsylvanian was, of course, Dwight Eisenhower, another lover of the middle way and the opportune evasion. Pennsylvanians tend to take the fascinating form of clouds. If the Middle Atlantic states have a psycho-history, it is that Puritanism skipped over them on its way west.

OGLE: *In recent years, there has been a lot of controversy about Presidential powers and how they are used. Are there any similarities or dissimilarities between Buchanan's Presidency and Nixon's that strike you?*

Both men were on surest ground in foreign affairs, both were surrounded by subordinates who committed dubious acts, neither projected much moral authority or personal charisma. The Covode

Investigation of 1860 bears some resemblance to the Watergate inquiry of today; and the shadow of impeachment hung over Buchanan also, as the letters of the youthful Henry Adams jubilantly confirm—though why Adams would have wanted John C. Breckinridge in the Presidential chair instead, I can't imagine. But for me the parallels run out there: Nixon is decried for riding roughshod (and blindly) over the Constitution; the main criticism of Buchanan was that he took the Constitution too seriously, and too circumspectly argued the exact limits of his powers and of such legalities as slaveholders' property rights and the federal government's right of coercion. He was too much the lawyer and conciliator, Nixon is too much the loner. Buchanan's White House was the most socially brilliant and active it had been since the days of Madison; contrast that with today's Kremlin on Pennsylvania Avenue. Most crucially, Buchanan's crisis, whatever he made of it, was a mighty and genuine one, it was the divergence between North and South that had been growing upon the nation since 1820; whereas this Watergate mess is thoroughly petty, comic opera with some sinister bass notes. It is a crisis strikingly devoid of tragic inevitability. A more worthy analogy to Buchanan's travail would be Johnson's Vietnam. But the correct spirit of historical inquiry and dramatization, surely, is one that seeks out, not facile analogies or contrasts, but what was unique to this moment, this predicament, this set of decisions, this man. My play is not about the Presidency but about a man who was President for four of his seventy-seven years. In attempting to understand him sympathetically, to a degree I attempted sympathetic understanding of every President, including the present beleaguered specimen.

OGLE: *Buchanan seems to have gotten a raw deal from at least some historians. Would you say that Lincoln has been correspondingly overrated?*

Not overrated, but deified. The accident of his assassination, and the happy chance of his literary genius, ennobles him beyond appraisal, at least in the popular impression. We are taught that he freed the slaves, without being reminded that the Emancipation Proclamation was a military maneuver, or that the slaveholding states on the Union side were exempted. And we are invited to invest the cause of the "Union" with the mysticism of war propaganda, without inspecting the legal case for secession, or weighing how much cosmic virtue resides in the determination to keep a big country big. In the crucial four months between Lincoln's election and his inauguration, while Buchanan desperately sought to prevent war, Lincoln himself said nothing, either in the way of reassurance to the border states or by way of warning to the seceding states. Demagoguery and fear went their way unchallenged, and while the Lincoln administration, once in office, heaped blame upon its predecessor, it initially pursued identical policies. But my purpose, insofar as it is historical, is not to bury the immortal Lincoln, but to revive the forgotten Buchanan.

OGLE: *Do you think the Civil War might have been avoided if Buchanan had followed a different course in 1860 and early in 1861?*

Allan Nevins, by no means pro-Buchanan, in his history of this period says that a show of force or punitive threat against South Carolina would have precipitated civil war, rather than cow the Palmetto State as Jackson did in 1833. Earlier in 1860, Buchanan possibly might have exerted his leverage as titular head of the Democratic Party to urge a single nominee (Douglas?) upon the Charlestown Convention. But, even if this unlikely work of compromise were achieved, an analysis of the voting in that fall's election suggests that Lincoln would have won even had his opposition been one united party instead of three splinters. And would another Democratic President have succeeded, more than Pierce and Buchanan, in reconciling irreconcilables, in solving the unsolvable question of fugitive slaves and making sense of the nonsensical question of the territories? It's hard to imagine how. Would the North, growing in power and population, have indefinitely accepted a Washington controlled by Southerners and doughfaces? My point (which I make in the play, and giving it a human context I cannot give here in these answers) is that time was on the side of the North, and that by buying time Buchanan did all that the Union could ask.

OGLE: *Some passages in the play suggest that Buchanan, despite charges of rakery, might be called* The Virgin President. *Was he?*

In my play I say he was. I would bow to contrary evidence if there were any. The availability of sex in the 19th century is a mysterious variable. Since no rumors of his rakery ever developed substance, his enemies developed the opposite line, that of impotence, of an androgynous fussiness. He was surely not a rake; he was a gallant, very fond of female company in the ballroom and parlor.

OGLE: *Buchanan is a great quoter of La Rochefoucauld's maxims in the original French. Is this historically correct or are you just very fond of La Rochefoucauld yourself?*

Buchanan learned French for his mission to the court of St. Petersburg as American ambassador (1832–1833), and he kept up a reading acquaintance with French the rest of his life. In a letter to Harriet from London, on January 25th, 1856, as strong indications of his nomination as President were coming to him, he wrote, ". . . I feel quite indifferent. There is profound wisdom in a remark of Rochefoucauld with which I met the other day:—'*Les choses que nous desirons n'arrivent pas, ou, si elles arrivent, ce n'est, ni dans le temps, ni de la manière que nous auraient fait le plus de plaisir.*' "

Strange to say, in the edition of *Maximes* out of which I supplied other aphorisms to put into the mouth of Buchanan's stage persona, I was not able to locate this particular saying. If any reader of *Harper's Bazaar* can help me here, I would be grateful.

[Stranger to say, the readers of *Harper's Bazaar* never saw any of these painstakingly composed answers. However, Ms. Ogle herself supplied the correct source of the quotation—La Bruyère (1645–1696). I feel adequately recompensed.]

SAMUELS: *I wonder why, with few exceptions, you only write light verse.*

I began with light verse, a kind of cartooning in print, and except for one stretch of a few years, in which I wrote most of the serious poems in *Telephone Poles*, I feel uncertain away from rhyme, to which something comic adheres. Bergson's mechanical encrusted upon the organic. But the light verse poems putting into rhyme and jaunty metrics some scientific discovery have a serious point—the universe science discloses to us is farcically unrelated to what our primitive senses report—and I have, when such poems go well, a pleasure and satisfaction not lower than in any other form of literary activity. Indeed my old poems give me more re-reading pleasure than anything I have written. Especially the little ones—"Nutcracker," with the word "nut" in boldface, seems to me as good as George Herbert's angel-wings.

GADO: *Who are your contemporaries in terms of fiction?*

It's in Salinger that I first heard, as a college student in the early Fifties, the tone that spoke to my condition. I had a writing teacher, Kenneth Kempton, who read aloud to us some of Salinger's stories as they appeared in *The New Yorker*. They seemed to me to say something about the energies of people and the ways they encounter each other that I did not find in the short stories of Hemingway or John O'Hara or Dorothy Parker or any of that "wised-up" style of short-story writing. Salinger's stories were not wised up. They were very open to tender invasions. Also they possessed a refreshing formlessness which, of course, he came to push to an extreme, as real artists tend to do. However, in those early short stories there's a marvellous tension between rather random, "soft" little events which pulls the whole story together into the final image of, say, a dead Easter chick in a wastebasket.

GADO: *Are there others you regard as contemporaries?*

Some, about my age, are not very well known: Harold Brodkey, a writer who is a little more than a year older than I, is a contemporary. His writing seems to go deeper into certain kinds of emotional interplay than the things written by older writers. Were I to try to make all this into an essay, I'm sure that I could find more ways in which writers now in their thirties and forties resemble each other.

Kerouac I would also claim as a contemporary. Clearly, he is not a man of Salinger's intelligence, but there is something benign, sentimentally benign, in his work. He attempted to grab it all; somehow, to grab it all. I like him.

GADO: *That's strange. Kerouac and Updike! I couldn't propose two writers who I thought were more unalike in their approach to literary art. Kerouac, with his binges at the typewriter, dumping the words down onto a continuous roll of teletype paper and leaving the cutting of it into pages to a more sombre moment. . . . That's not the picture I had of you at work at all.*

No, I don't agree. I don't use teletype paper, but there isn't an awful lot of revision when I'm writing—things either grind to a halt or they keep on moving. I think he was right. Kerouac was right in emphasizing a certain flow, a certain ease. Wasn't he saying, after all, what the surrealists said? That if you do it very fast without thinking, something will get in that wouldn't ordinarily. I think one tends to spoil not only the thing at hand, but the whole art form, by taking too much thought, by trying to assert too much control.

SAMUELS: *What is it that you think gets into sloppy writing that eludes more careful prose?*

It comes down to, What is language? Up to now, until this age of mass literacy, language has been something spoken. In utterance there's a minimum of slowness. In trying to treat words as chisel strokes you run the risk of losing the quality of utterance, the rhythm of utterance, the happiness. A phrase out of Mark Twain— he describes a raft hitting a bridge and says that it "went all to smash and scatteration like a box of matches struck by lightning." The beauty of "scatteration" could only have occurred to a talkative man, a man who had been brought up among people who were talking and who loved to talk himself. I'm aware myself of a certain dryness of this reservoir, this backlog of spoken talk. A Rumanian once said to me that Americans are always telling stories. I'm not sure this is as true as it once was. Where we once used to spin yarns, now we sit in front of the TV and receive pictures. I'm not sure the younger generation even knows how to gossip. But, as for a writer, if he has something to tell, he should perhaps type it almost as fast as he could talk it. We must look to the organic world, not the inorganic world, for models; and just as the organic world has periods of repose and periods of great speed and exercise, so I think the writer's process should be organically varied. But there's a kind of tautness that you should feel within yourself no matter how slow or fast you're spinning out the reel.

SAMUELS: *I'd like to ask a bit about your work habits if I may. What sort of schedule do you follow?*

I write every weekday morning. I try to vary what I am doing, and my verse, or poetry, is a help here. Embarked on a long project, I try to stay with it even on dull days. For every novel, however, that I have published, there has been one unfinished or scrapped. Some short stories—I think offhand of "Lifeguard," "The Taste of Metal," "My Grandmother's Thimble"—are fragments salvaged and reshaped. Most came right the first time—rode on their own melting, as Frost said of his poems. If there is no melting, if the story keeps sticking, better stop and look around. In the execution there has to be a "happiness" that can't be willed or foreordained. It has to sing, click, something. I try instantly to set in motion a certain forward tilt of suspense or curiosity, and at the end of the story or novel to rectify the tilt, to complete the motion.

SAMUELS: *As a technician, how unconventional would you say you were?*

As unconventional as I need to be. An absolute freedom exists on the blank page, so let's use it. I have from the start been wary of the fake, the automatic. I tried not to subdue my sense of life as many-layered and ambiguous, while keeping in mind some sense of transaction, of a bargain struck, between me and the ideal reader. Domestic fierceness within the middle class, sex and death as riddles for the thinking animal, social existence as sacrifice, unexpected pleasures and rewards, corruption as a kind of evolution—these are some of the themes. My work is meditation, not pontification.

SAMUELS: *Are you bothered by having to write for a living?*

No, I always wanted to draw or write for a living. Teaching, the customary alternative, seemed truly depleting and confusing. I have been able to support myself by and large with the more respectable forms—poetry, short stories, novels—but what journalism I have done has been useful. I would write ads for deodorants or labels for catsup bottles if I had to. The miracle of turning inklings into thoughts and thoughts into words and words into metal and print and ink never palls for me; the technical aspects of bookmaking, from type font to binding glue, all interest me. The distinction between a thing well done and a thing done ill obtains everywhere—in all circles of Paradise and Inferno.

SAMUELS: *In "The Sea's Green Sameness" you deny that characterization and psychology are primary goals of fiction. What do you think is more important?*

I wrote "The Sea's Green Sameness" years ago and meant, I believe, that narratives should not be *primarily* packages for psychological insights, though they can contain them, like raisins in buns. But the substance is the dough, which feeds the storytelling appetite, the appetite for motion, for suspense, for resolution. The author's deepest pride, as I have experienced it, is not in his incidental wisdom but in his ability to keep an organized mass of images moving forward, to feel life engendering itself under his hands. But no doubt fiction is also a mode of spying; we read it as we look in windows or listen to gossip, to learn what other people *do*. Insights of all kinds are welcome; but no wisdom will substitute for an instinct for action and pattern, and a perhaps savage wish to hold, through your voice, another soul in thrall.

SAYINGS

(taken mostly from Jane Howard's article in Life)

There is a great deal to be said about almost anything. Everything can be as interesting as every other thing. An old milk carton is worth a rose; a trolley car has as much right to be there, in terms of aesthetics, as a tree.

*

Everything is infinitely fine and any opinion is coarser than reality.

*

I've never much enjoyed going to plays. The unreality of painted people standing on a platform saying things they've said to each other for months is more than I can overlook.

*

The idea of a hero is aristocratic. You cared about Oedipus and Hamlet because they were noble and you were a groundling. Now either nobody is a hero or everyone is. I vote for everyone.

*

[My characters] go back to work; that's the real way that people die.

*

We do survive every moment, after all, except the last one.

*

A man has to build his life outward from a job he can do. Once he finds one he's got eight hours of the day licked, and if he sleeps eight more, he's two-thirds golden.

*

My own sense of childhood doesn't come from being a father, it comes from having been a child. We're all so curiously alone. But it's important to keep making signals through the glass.

*

I've touched a kind of bottom, when I've felt that existence itself was an affront to be forgiven.

*

You can't be satirical at the expense of fictional characters, because they're your creatures. You must only love them.

*

My life is, in a sense, trash; my life is only that of which the residue is my writing.

*

HOWARD: *If you could be an animal, which would you be?*
A turtle. Turtles live quite long and can retreat immediately, and live very close to the grass, the smell of which I've always liked. I also like the sound of the rain on the roof, which a turtle must get quite a lot of.

Index

A Note About the Author

JOHN UPDIKE was born in 1932 in Shillington, Pennslyvania, which he has described as "a square mile of middle-class homes physically distinguished by a bend in the central avenue that compels some side streets to deviate from the grid pattern." His father was a high-school mathematics teacher and his mother a writer. He graduated *summa cum laude* from Harvard in 1954, and spent a year in England on the Knox Fellowship, at the Ruskin School of Drawing and Fine Art in Oxford. From 1955 to 1957 he was a member of the staff of *The New Yorker*, to which he has contributed short stories, poems, humor, and, since 1960, book reviews. His own books include seven novels, five short-story collections, three volumes of poetry, a play, and a previous miscellany, *Assorted Prose*. In 1964 his novel *The Centaur* won the National Book Award for Fiction, and that same year he was elected to the National Institute of Arts and Letters. His short stories have won eight O. Henry Awards, including a first prize in 1966; in 1971 he received the Signet Society Medal for Achievement in the Arts. Updike has lectured in the Soviet Union, Africa, Australia, Korea, and Venezuela. The father of two sons and two daughters, he has lived since 1957 in Massachusetts.

A Note on the Type

The text of this book was set on the Linotype in Janson, a recutting made directly from type cast from matrices long thought to have been made by the Dutchman Anton Janson, who was a practicing type founder in Leipzig during the years 1668–1687. However, it has been conclusively demonstrated that these types are actually the work of Nicholas Kis (1650–1702), a Hungarian, who most probably learned his trade from the master Dutch type founder Dirk Voskens. The type is an excellent example of the influential and sturdy Dutch types that prevailed in England up to the time William Caslon developed his own incomparable designs from them.

The book was composed, printed, and bound by Kingsport Press, Inc., Kingsport, Tennessee.

Though
WATERS ROAR

**Center Point
Large Print**

**This Large Print Book carries the
Seal of Approval of N.A.V.H.**

Though WATERS ROAR

LYNN AUSTIN

CENTER POINT PUBLISHING
THORNDIKE, MAINE

This Center Point Large Print edition
is published in the year 2009 by arrangement with
Bethany House Publishers,
a division of Baker Publishing Group.

Unless otherwise identified, Scripture quotations are
from the King James Version of the Bible.
Scripture quotations identified NIV are from the HOLY
BIBLE, NEW INTERNATIONAL VERSION.®
Copyright © 1973, 1978, 1984 by International Bible
Society. Used by permission of Zondervan Publishing
House. All rights reserved.
The text of this Large Print edition is unabridged.
In other aspects, this book may vary
from the original edition.
Printed in the United States of America.
Set in 16-point Times New Roman type.

ISBN: 978-1-60285-566-3

Library of Congress Cataloging-in-Publication Data

Austin, Lynn N.
  Through waters roar / Lynn Austin.
    p. cm.
  ISBN 978-1-60285-566-3 (library binding : alk. paper)
  1. Women--Family relationships--Fiction. 2. Social justice--Fiction.
    3. Large type books. I. Title.

PS3551.U839T47 2009b
813'.54--dc22

2009027272

To my husband
Ken
and my children,
Joshua, Vanessa, Benjamin, Maya, and Snir
with love

God is our refuge and strength,
an ever-present help in trouble.
Therefore we will not fear,
though the earth give way
and the mountains fall into the heart of the sea,
though its waters roar and foam
and the mountains quake with their surging.

Psalm 46:1–3

CHAPTER
1

It was ironic.

I lay in my jail cell on a squeaky iron bunk, gazing at the stained mattress above me, and I remembered the day I first understood the meaning of the word *ironic*. I couldn't help smiling at . . . well, at the irony of it. The meaning had become clear to me ten years ago on the day my grandmother, Beatrice Monroe Garner, was arrested.

That day had also been a Saturday—just like today. Mother had been distressed because Grandma Bebe, as we called her, would miss church services tomorrow if Father didn't go down to the jailhouse and bail her out.

"She can't spend the Sabbath in prison!" Mother had wailed. "Please, John. We have to get her out of there!"

I was going to miss church services tomorrow, too, come to think of it. Who would teach my Sunday school class of ten-year-old girls? As my father undoubtedly would have pointed out: "Perhaps you should have considered their welfare before getting yourself arrested in the first place, Harriet."

I had been the same age as my Sunday school girls when Grandma Bebe landed in jail that day. My sister, Alice, and I had been eating breakfast with our parents when the telephone rang. The device was brand-spanking-new back then in 1910, and we all stopped eating, listening to see if it would chime our party line exchange of three short rings. When it did, Mother unhooked the earphone and cupped it to her ear, standing on tiptoes to speak into the little cone-shaped mouthpiece. She burst into tears the moment she replaced the receiver.

"That . . . that was . . . the police!" she managed to tell us through her sobs. "They arrested my mother last night and . . . and . . . she's in jail!"

My older sister gasped. She was the feminine, fluttery type of girl who did a great deal of gasping. "Arrested! But why? What did Grandma do?"

"Oh, how could they do such a thing to her?" Mother cried. "She isn't a criminal!"

"Is there any more coffee?" my father asked calmly. "I would like another cup, if you don't mind."

"Oh, John! How can you drink coffee at a time like this? Don't you care?"

"Beatrice Garner cares nothing at all for her family's reputation, so why should I care what happens to her? She knew the consequences when she and that temperance gang of hers started running around smashing whiskey barrels. She made her bed when she decided to become another Carrie Nation, and now she'll have to lie in it."

This brought another cloudburst of weeping from Mother. Alice rose from the table to comfort her. Father sighed and handed me his empty cup. "Fill this for me, would you, Harriet? That's a good girl." Our hired girl had the morning off, so I obediently took his cup to the kitchen to refill it, then sat down and waited for act two of this drama.

"Please, John. I'm begging you," Mother said. "Please get her out of that terrible place."

"And that's another thing," Father said. "What kind of an example is she setting for our daughters?" He poured cream into the coffee I'd brought him and slowly stirred it as if not expecting a reply.

Aside from begging and weeping, my mother could do nothing to help Grandma Bebe—which was ironic, since Grandma was working hard to give women more power in this world. And Grandma Bebe despised tears. *"Women should never use them as weapons,"* she always insisted, *"especially to prevail upon a man to change his mind."* Yet, ironically, my mother had resorted to tears in order to persuade my father. Grandma Bebe would not have approved.

But Grandma was in jail.

And tears were ultimately what convinced Father to go downtown and bail her out. Alice had joined the deluge of weeping, and Father wasn't strong enough to stop the flood or stand firm against it. No man was. My sister's heart was as soft and gooey as oatmeal. She could turn her tears on and off like a modern-day plumbing faucet and was capable of unleashing buckets of them.

Alice was sixteen and so beautiful that brilliant men became stupid whenever they were around her. The moment her wide, blue eyes welled up, every man in sight would pull out a white handkerchief and offer it to her as if waving in surrender. Grandma Bebe had no patience with her.

"Your sister could do a great deal of good for the cause," she once told me. "Alice is the kind of woman who men go to war over—like Helen of Troy. But she'll squander it all, I'm sorry to say. She'll surrender to the first humbug who dishes her a little sweet-talk. Women like her always do. It's too bad," Grandma said with a sigh. "Your sister believes the lie that women are the weaker sex. Her prodigious use of tears perpetuates that myth. . . . But there's hope for you, Harriet," Grandma Bebe added. Whenever the subject of Alice's amazing beauty arose, Grandma would pat my unruly brown hair and say, "Thank goodness you're such a plain child. You'll have to rely on your wits."

The fact that Alice came to Grandma's rescue with tears is ironic, isn't it? I didn't join the torrent of weeping that morning. I didn't want to let Grandma down.

I loved my grandmother, and I greatly admired her ferocity and passion. Mind you, these weren't qualities that polite society· admired in women, but they fascinated me. Even so, I didn't want to be like my fiery grandmother and end up in jail, any more than I wanted to be a dutiful wife like Mother or a virtuous siren like Alice. But how was I supposed to live as a modern woman, born just before the dawn of the twentieth century? What other choices did I have? That's the question I was endeavoring to answer when I ended up in jail.

But I was only ten that fateful day when Grandma got arrested and still young enough to be ignored most of the time unless Father needed more coffee. I was a keen observer, however, absorbing everything that went on around me as I began drawing a map for my life. Grandma Bebe told me that everyone's life led somewhere, and so I needed to have a plan.

"Grip the rudder and steer, Harriet. Don't just drift gently down the stream. If you don't have a map, you might run aground somewhere or end up crushed against the rocks. Always know where you're headed."

She had given up on coaching Mother and Alice—her current saviors, ironically—and had begun putting all of her effort into shaping me. She made that decision after she saw me kick Tommy O'Reilly in the shin one day when he tried to bully me into giving him my candy. Tommy was the constable's son, and he bullied all the kids in town. But that day I took a step toward him as if about to give him a cinnamon stick and kicked his bony shin, instead.

"You, my dear, have potential!" Grandma said as Tommy hopped around on one leg, howling. "You'll never float downstream, Harriet. You know how to paddle!"

My map was still just a pencil sketch, to be sure. In later years I would embellish it as each new experience added details to the picture. In time, I would carefully identify all of the dangers to avoid, all of the pitfalls to be wary of. I was trying to heed Grandma's advice, you see, but had she heeded her own? Had she deliberately steered her way into the town jail, or had she let go of the rudder? Or misplaced her map? If she ever got out of jail again, I intended to ask her.

"Please, Father, please!" Alice begged, kneeling at his feet like someone out of the Bible. "Please don't leave Grandma there forever!" Alice had worked herself into such a frenzy that she was about to faint. She was a champion at swooning— another womanly trait Grandma loathed. All Alice had to do was lift her dainty hand to her brow and flutter her eyelashes, and every man in sight would race to catch her before she fell.

Father set down his coffee cup and turned to me. "Get the smelling salts, Harriet. That's a good girl."

Alice was still kneeling, so at least she didn't have too far to fall this time. As I sprinted upstairs to retrieve the vial of ammonia salts, I heard Father say, "Oh, very well. You can stop all the cater-wauling. I'll go down and bail Beatrice out of jail."

I didn't blame Father for wanting to flee from the rising floodwaters. I raced back to the kitchen and pulled the cork on the smelling salts, then shoved them under Alice's dainty nose. When order was restored, I followed my father out to the front hallway.

"May I go with you to rescue Grandma?"

"Certainly not! Jail is no place for a delicate young lady."

Back then I didn't believe him, but the truth of his statement was now quite clear to me as I lay in my own jail cell.

Father plucked his duster and driving gloves from the hallstand and stuffed his hat on his balding head, muttering darkly about Grandma Bebe as he headed out the door. I skipped along beside him, nodding in support. Together we started up the Model-T Ford, and I jumped into the passenger seat. The car rattled and coughed all the way to the end of the block before he realized I was still there.

"Wait! Harriet . . . what . . . you can't come along!"

I didn't argue or weep. I simply looked up at him, eye to eye, jutting out my chin a little. That's how I faced Tommy O'Reilly whenever he tried to bully me at school—I would stare silently back at him, arms crossed, my foot aimed at his shin. The stare I gave Father wasn't quite as defiant as the one I used on Tommy, but it had the same effect.

"Oh, bother it all, Harriet! I suppose you're already here . . ." Father turned his attention back to the car as it sputtered and nearly died.

"It needs more throttle," I said, pulling out the lever. "Advance the spark a little."

"But you aren't coming inside, Harriet. I mean it. Jail isn't the sort of place . . . and your grand-mother has no business . . ."

I nodded dutifully—and followed him inside the police station just the same. Father went straight in to see the constable, Thomas O'Reilly, Sr. He told us that Grandma Bebe had been arrested after trying to close down a saloon last night. Most of the other members of the Women's Christian Temperance Union had gone home peacefully once the police arrived to break up the protest, but not Grandma. She had refused to give up the fight against the evils of Demon Rum.

"And I'm afraid we had to confiscate her axe," he finished.

Father nodded and paid her fine. In no time at all, Grandma Bebe was liberated from jail. We heard her shouting all the way down the hall as a policeman tried to lead her out of the cell.

"No, wait! Unhand me this instant! I'm not ready to leave! This jail is filled with drunkards—the very people I'm trying to rescue."

Constable O'Reilly rolled his eyes. "It's been a very long night, John. Get her out of here. Please."

"Did you know," Grandma continued as the police handed back her purse and coat, "that there is one saloon for every three hundred people in this country? There are more saloons than there are schools, libraries, hospitals, theaters, or parks—and certainly more saloons than churches."

We drove Grandma home.

Like the brave soldiers who had gone to war forty-five years earlier to battle the evils of slavery, my grandmother was willing to sacrifice her own liberty, if necessary, to set men free from slavery to alcohol. And that was the ultimate irony, I thought, as I lay on the lumpy jail cot pondering my own arrest and imprisonment. You see, Grandma Bebe had recently won the war against Demon Rum. The Eighteenth Amendment to the United States' Constitution had become law a few months ago on January 29, 1920, making the manufacture, sale, and transportation of all alcoholic beverages strictly prohibited.

And I was in jail for defying it.

Yes, I found my situation very ironic. There would be no tears of sympathy for me from Mother or Alice—much less Grandma Bebe. And Father would undoubtedly say, "You made your bed, Harriet, and now you'll have to lie in it."

So how did I end up becoming a criminal? I've been pondering that question all night. Perhaps the best way to search for an answer is to start at the very beginning.

CHAPTER
2

My grandmother was young, once, and not altogether sure of herself. I find this unbelievable, knowing the woman she has become, but she has sworn that it's true and my grandmother doesn't lie. "Any assuredness that I now possess, Harriet, has been acquired out of necessity," she insisted. "I was born with no degree of confidence whatsoever. In fact, quite the opposite is true."

She was born in the northeastern corner of Pennsylvania on her parents' farm, nestled in a valley in the Pocono Mountains. Beatrice Aurelia Monroe arrived on the same day, month, and year that the first Women's Rights Convention was held: July 19, 1848. Of course she was too young on the day of her birth to realize what a portentous coincidence this was, but she would later declare her birthday a sign from Providence.

While Elizabeth Cady Stanton, Lucretia Mott, and the rest of that august group of women were signing "The Declaration of Sentiments and Resolutions" in Seneca Falls, New York, and firing the first shot in the battle for women's rights, Great Grandma Hannah Monroe was also doing battle as she labored to give birth to Grandma Bebe—who had the audacity to come out backward. Bebe was destined to do everything in life unconventionally, so arriving feet-first was only the beginning. She also had the audacity to be a girl. Her father, Henry Monroe, had directed his wife to produce a boy—which seems a bit selfish to me, seeing as he already had four sons: James, age nine, William, seven, Joseph, five, and Franklin, who was three.

"What do you mean he's a girl?" an indignant Henry asked the midwife when she told him the news. He stomped into the bedroom in his work boots and peeked into the baby's diaper, convinced that the midwife had missed an important detail. When it was obvious that she hadn't, he handed the howling bundle back to his wife. "This was supposed to be a boy, Hannah. A man can never have too many sons to help him out."

"I know, my dear," she said gently, "but the Good Lord has seen fit to bless us with a girl this time."

Perhaps the Good Lord realized that Hannah also could use some help around the farm, feeding and clothing her strapping husband and four growing sons. That's how Hannah chose to view her little daughter—as God's good gift. She gazed down at the baby and smiled as Henry tromped out of the room. "Don't mind him, my little one. He always gets testy when his dinner is late."

Dinner was late that day on account of Beatrice coming out backward and taking more time to arrive than she should have. But Hannah was a devout Christian woman, and as soon as the midwife spread the news of the baby's arrival throughout the little farming community of New Canaan, Pennsylvania, the other church women quickly drove out to share portions of their own dinners with Hannah's disgruntled husband and four hungry sons. Of course the pantry was filled with the provisions that Hannah had prepared for her time of confinement, but Henry and the boys were incapable of crossing into such feminine territory as the pantry to forage for their own food. They were even less capable of reheating any of it on the stove.

Once Henry's belly was filled, his attitude toward his new daughter did seem to soften, slightly. "I suppose we can learn to make the best of it," he grumbled as he removed his boots at the end of the day and climbed into bed beside his wife. "There's always next time."

Hannah swallowed a rash reply at the mention of "next time," the memory of her harrowing breech labor still fresh in her mind. She whispered a swift, silent prayer to the Almighty, instead. Then she rested her hand on her husband's arm and said, "She's a beautiful, healthy baby—thanks be to God. I would like to christen her Beatrice, if it's all the same to you. Beatrice Aurelia Monroe."

Henry didn't reply to Hannah's request until after she'd finished cooking his breakfast the next morning and had set it on the table in front of him.

He crunched into a piece of bacon and said, "That name would be acceptable, I suppose."

Hannah had learned patience during her ten years of marriage. She hadn't expected a reply any sooner than noon. Henry required a sufficient amount of time to pray about such matters and didn't like to be rushed. Three-year-old Franklin, who couldn't pronounce "Beatrice," shortened the baby's name to Bebe. The name stuck, and my sister and I still call her Grandma Bebe seventy-two years later.

The first few years of Grandma's life passed uneventfully, by her account. She grew to be a quiet, nervous child, which was understandable since everyone else on the farm was bigger and louder and stronger than she was. With four older brothers to dodge—along with a team of horses, a pair of oxen, and a herd of milk cows—at times it felt as though there were a conspiracy to trample poor Bebe underfoot. The first useful phrase she comprehended as a toddler was, "Get out of the way, Bebe!"

"I was a skittish child," she told me, "perhaps because I spent a great deal of time skittering out of danger. And so shy! I would cry at the drop of a hat—and there were plenty of hats to drop, not to mention hoes and hay bales, wheels and winches, boots, buckets, and butcher blocks."

I tried to imagine growing up in a home that had butcher blocks dropping from above, and I cringed involuntarily. When I questioned Grandma about it, she laughed and said, "Don't ask, Harriet! The butcher-block incident was my brother William's doing. He was always into some sort of mischief, risking life and limb. That's why it surprised all of us when it was Joseph who lost his life and Franklin who lost a limb. Of course those tragedies happened *years* after the butcher-block episode, but we all remembered it."

Grandma Bebe never did tell a story in a straight line. In order to make any sense of her life, I've had to piece together all of her astounding statements as if working a huge jigsaw puzzle. But I happen to have a lot of spare time as I languish in this jail cell, and her peculiar stories are beginning to make sense to me as I endeavor to figure out how I got here—and what to do about it.

Bebe's brothers were wild, uninhibited boys who took great delight in risking their lives each day in newer and more creative ways. One summer they tied a rope from a branch of the tall oak tree that stood near the river on the edge of their farm. They drilled a hole through an old plank and threaded the fraying rope through the center of it, knotting it beneath the plank to form a seat. Bebe watched from a safe distance as they took turns swinging wildly from it, pumping higher and higher, sometimes falling off and skinning their knees, adding more lumps to their knobby heads. She wondered what it would feel like to fly freely through the air on that swing, the blue sky above her, the wind in her hair. But even though she longed to try it, fear always stopped her.

One day when it was hot enough to roast the chickens right on their roosts, William decided to sail out over the river on the swing and let go of the rope, splashing into the water some twelve feet below, oblivious to the unforgiving rocks. Rain had fallen for weeks that spring and the rushing river looked eager for a victim to drown. But when William bobbed safely to the surface, Bebe's other brothers followed his example, leaping into the water as if eager to meet Jesus. Bebe watched from the side of the path, wary of the snakes that lived in the tall grass near the river. James and Joseph had once caught a thick, glossy black snake three feet long and had scared Bebe half to death with it as they whooped into the barnyard, dangling their prize from the tines of a pitchfork.

After the first five years of Grandma Bebe's jittery life had passed, a momentous change occurred. Harriet Beecher Stowe had published her book *Uncle Tom's Cabin; or Life Among the Lowly* in 1852, and when it made it's way to New Canaan, the ladies from church passed around a well-worn copy of it. Hannah read it by lamplight in the farmhouse parlor and wept. Bebe had never seen her sturdy, devout mother cry before, and she quickly hurried over to comfort her.

"What's wrong, Mama?"

"It's this book I'm reading, Beatrice dear. It describes the daily lives of slaves in our country, and it's simply horrifying. Imagine being *owned* by someone! Just think how horrible it would be to be considered someone's property and thought of as inferior. Imagine having no life of your own, forced to do someone's bidding day and night, body and soul, with no power and no voice."

Hannah talked about the plight of the slaves continually for the next few months as she and Bebe kneaded bread and plucked chickens and scrubbed laundry. She spoke as they weeded the garden and peeled potatoes and mopped the floors and sewed new clothes for the family.

"I believe the Almighty is calling me to do something to help those poor, pitiful people," Hannah decided one fall afternoon while rendering fat to make soap for her household. With her conscience as her guide, she gathered all of the other women who'd read the book and held a meeting in the village church. They decided to form a local chapter of the Anti-Slavery Society. Henry sympathized with the cause after reading the book himself. He even allowed Hannah to hitch the team to the wagon if he wasn't using it and drive into town for the society meetings. Bebe accompanied her mother, watching and listening.

At first the anti-slavery meetings resembled a Sunday church service with lots of praying and hymn singing. But then the women devised a plan,

from the brim. "I'm glad you recognized me. It makes my request that much easier. You see, I have a . . . a package . . . that I need to deliver to one of the stations in this area. I understand that you are a stockholder in our railroad, Mrs. Monroe?"

Henry stared at Mr. Smith as if he regretted his decision to open the door. But Bebe, who was wide awake now, had attended enough anti-slavery meetings to know exactly what Mr. Smith was talking about. He must be a conductor on the so-called Underground Railroad. The "package" was an escaped slave who needed refuge in a safe house or "station" on the invisible line. Anyone who had contributed money or goods to the effort, as Hannah and her friends had, was known as a stockholder.

"Yes, that's right, Mr. Smith. I am a stock-holder," Hannah said with a smile. "Henry, you'd better put our guest's horse in the barn, out of the rain. This might take a while. I'll light a fire and put on some coffee."

Henry grabbed his overcoat and trudged outside with Mr. Smith. Bebe followed her mother into the kitchen and watched as she lit a lamp and gathered kindling and stoked the fire. Hannah didn't seem to notice Bebe until she bumped into her on her way out of the pantry.

"Beatrice, dear, why don't you go back to bed," she said, stroking her hair. "The storm is over for the most part."

Lightning still flashed even though the thunder was only a distant rumble among the hills. Bebe heard the rain hammering on the back porch roof and knew that her father was going to get soaked as he walked from the house to the barn. "I want to help, Mama."

She meant that she wanted to help with the "package," but her mother misunderstood. "Well . . . get out a bowl and some cups, then. Perhaps Mr. Smith would like a little soup to help him warm up."

A fire blazed in the stove by the time the men returned. Hannah hung their coats behind it to dry, filling the kitchen with the sour smell of wet wool. Stripped of his bulky overcoat, Mr. Smith turned out to be a slightly built man, dressed in a city suit and fine leather shoes. He dropped onto a kitchen chair, looking as limp and pale as a plucked pullet. Bebe watched the color slowly return to his pallid skin as he gulped his coffee and ate a bowl of left-over soup. His yellow hair curled into delicate ringlets as it dried.

"What can you tell us about this package?" Hannah asked. "When might it arrive?"

"Well, first I should explain that we don't usually send packages to stations where young children live." He glanced at Bebe. "Ever since the Fugitive Slave Law went into effect, this business has become much too dangerous to risk innocent young lives. If a package is discovered in your possession—"

"The Good Lord can protect my children and me," Hannah interrupted. "We must obey God, not an unjust law. The Bible says we are to feed the hungry and clothe the naked and rescue the perishing."

The stranger smiled slightly. "I'm glad you feel that way, Mrs. Monroe." He wrapped his fingers around his coffee cup to warm them.

"What brings you out our way, Mr. Smith?" she asked. "I didn't think the Underground Railroad passed through New Canaan."

"It doesn't, but we're in a difficult situation. Bounty hunters have discovered our usual rail lines, and our safe houses simply aren't safe anymore. We've been forced to expand the railroad into new territory, and we recalled what a faithful chapter your local society has been in the past. I spoke with your pastor, and he felt that our package would be safer out here on your farm than in town, where the wrong person might accidentally see it. It's so hard to know whom to trust, you see."

"You may trust us completely," Hannah said. "How can we help?"

"All that's required is a temporary place to rest, eat, and hide until the way is clear to the next station. I don't know how long that might be. We're asking you to take an enormous risk, as you probably know. If you get caught you could be fined as much as one thousand dollars and face six months in jail. But if you're willing to help, we would be very grateful. We simply must get our package to Canada. It has traveled so far already."

"I'll need to pray about it," Henry Monroe said. He stood abruptly as if heading to the celestial throne room to consult with the Almighty. "Can you wait for my answer?"

"Certainly. I understand. I'll wait."

But Bebe wondered if the stranger really knew how long it usually took her father to pray about something and make up his mind. Mr. Smith might well be waiting until after the next litter of hogs were born, fattened, butchered, and turned into bacon.

"I'll fix a bed for you, Mr. Smith," Hannah offered. "You should try to get a little sleep. It will still be a few more hours until dawn."

"I don't want to trouble you."

Hannah shook her head. "It's no trouble at all."

"Well, if you're certain. I have been riding all night. . . ."

Hannah evicted William from his warm bed and tucked him in with James and Franklin to make room for the stranger. Bebe crawled back into her own bed, but she had trouble falling asleep. A real live escaped slave might be sent here to hide, in her very own house! She felt scared yet excited.

Bebe had first seen a person with black skin at one of her mother's Anti-Slavery Society meetings. The man's face and arms were the color of dark, rich molasses, and she thought he must have fallen into a vat of blackberries. Her mother told her that the color wouldn't wash off, even if the man scrubbed and scrubbed with lye soap.

"People have made the Negro race into slaves, Beatrice, just because their skin is a different color than ours," she had explained. "But the Bible says that God is no respecter of persons. Man looks at the outward things, but God looks at our hearts."

"Is the man's heart as black as his skin?"

"No, his heart isn't black at all because he knows Jesus. Our sins are what turn our hearts black, but Jesus can wash each heart as white as snow." The conversation left Bebe confused. She wondered why Jesus didn't wash the slave's skin white along with his heart, so he wouldn't have to be a slave anymore. She had never forgotten the beautiful color of that man's skin—and now a slave just like him was coming to her farm.

The next morning when Bebe peeked into her brothers' room to see if Mr. Smith was still asleep, all of the beds were empty. He wasn't downstairs in the kitchen, either. "Did Mr. Smith go—?"

Hannah shushed her. Her father and brothers were tramping indoors after their morning chores, bringing mud, fresh milk, and the scent of cows with them. "We'll talk later," Hannah said. "Sit down and eat your biscuits."

The boys ate breakfast, too, then left for school. While Bebe helped her mother wash and dry the

29

dishes, Hannah explained that Mr. Smith had left at dawn.

"Did Papa decide about the package?"

Hannah nodded. "It will arrive in a few days."

The news astounded Bebe. She had never known her father to make up his mind so quickly. He always emphasized the need to "wait on the Lord" for any answers to prayer, and waiting usually took a very long time. The Lord must have let Henry go straight to the front of the line for an answer this time.

"But listen to me, Beatrice. This is very important." Hannah crouched down so she could look right into Bebe's eyes as she gripped her thin shoulders. "Your papa and I have decided not to tell your brothers about Mr. Smith or the package. The more people who know about it, the more dangerous it will be for that poor soul who is trying to escape. If one of your brothers should happen to have a slip of the tongue and accidentally tell someone at school, we could all be in danger. Do you understand?"

Bebe nodded soberly.

"Promise you won't say a word? To anyone?"

"I promise." No one had ever entrusted her with such an important secret before—and the fact that her brothers didn't know about it made her smile on the inside.

"You aren't frightened, are you, Beatrice?"

"No."

Bebe was terrified.

CHAPTER
3

The package arrived three days later in the middle of the night while Bebe slept. She had no idea it was there. The next morning she watched her mother prepare a second breakfast of bacon and eggs and biscuits after the boys left for school and wondered why. When Bebe asked her about it, Hannah smiled and said, "We have company."

Bebe looked all around, wondering if the package was as invisible as the railroad. Hannah carefully tucked the plates of food inside a basket along with some cups, knives, and forks, then covered everything with a clean towel. She handed Bebe a container filled with fresh milk.

"Will you help me carry this, Beatrice? Be careful not to spill any."

"Are we going down to the root cellar?" She was afraid that her mother had hidden the visitor underground, since that's where the invisible railroad was. Bebe hated the damp, spidery cellar. It smelled like the graveyard on a rainy day, and the crumbling dirt walls always seemed to close in on her.

"No, we're not going down to the root cellar."

Bebe followed her mother upstairs instead, then watched as Hannah retrieved a chair from Bebe's room and moved it into place below the opening to the attic. Hannah climbed up first, pushing the trapdoor aside and carefully lifting the basket up to the attic floor. She reached down to take the container of milk from Bebe and set it on the attic floor, too, then stood on tiptoes and hoisted herself up and out of sight. Bebe scrambled onto the chair to see where her mother had gone, but she was too short to see into the dark hole.

"Mama? Where are you?" she called, her voice quivering. Hannah's face reappeared above her.

"Do you want to come up, Beatrice? Stretch out your arms, and I'll pull you up."

The thought of being hauled up into the unknown void frightened Bebe more than descending into the root cellar had. But she knew her mother was strong and completely trustworthy. Bebe raised her arms above her head and allowed Hannah to grip her wrists and pull her up into the cool, dusty attic.

Dried herbs hung from the rafters along with garlands of cobwebs. Discarded chairs, an old dresser, and a battered steamer trunk lay scattered across the floorboards. Bebe worried about spiders. And mice. And bats. In the middle of the floor lay a heap of bedding, covered with one of Hannah's good winter quilts.

"Good morning," Hannah called into the still, dead air. "I brought you some breakfast."

Bebe's heart raced as the lump beneath the quilt stirred and pushed the blanket aside. When the real live escaped slave sat up, Bebe gaped in surprise. It was a woman! Bebe never imagined that an escaped slave might be a woman. All the slaves she had seen at the society meetings had been men.

The quilt shifted again and a second figure sat up—another woman, younger than the first. The two "packages" who peered at Bebe with dark, frightened eyes were the most exotically beautiful people she had ever seen. With their dark brown skin and woolly black hair, they seemed like little more than shadows in the dusky attic.

"Don't be afraid," Hannah told the pair. "My daughter, Beatrice, and I brought you some food."

Bebe stayed close beside her mother as she inched across the dusty floor on her hands and knees, dragging the basket. The attic was too cramped for Hannah to stand upright except in the very center beneath the ridge beam, but Bebe could easily stand.

"Beatrice, our new friend's name is Mary," Hannah told her. "And her daughter's name is Katie."

Bebe knew it was rude to stare, but she couldn't help it. The younger slave, Katie, was not much older than Bebe's brother William, who was twelve. Mary looked much too young to be her mother. She smoothed back her sleep-tousled hair as if wanting to make a good impression.

"We appreciate your help," she said softly. She

started to crawl forward, but Hannah stopped her.

"No, sit still, Mary. I'll bring it to you. I know you must be exhausted after walking all that way in the middle of the night." Hannah spread the dishtowel on the floor like a little tablecloth, then removed the plates from the basket and placed them on it. She had even packed two napkins.

Tears glistened in young Katie's eyes as she examined the bounty. "All this food for us?"

"Yes, it's all for you," Hannah replied. "We've already eaten our breakfast. And if you're still hungry, let me know and I'll fix more. We have plenty."

Katie scrambled forward to grab her plate. "Ain't you forgetting something?" Mary asked. Katie glanced at her mother, then set down the plate and folded her hands. Both women bowed their heads as Mary prayed. "Lord, we so grateful for these kind people and for all this food they fixing for us. Please bless them, Lord. This a good thing they doing. Amen."

Bebe watched Katie gobble her food, shoveling it down the same way her brothers did after baling hay. If any mice did inhabit the attic, the women weren't leaving them a crumb. When Mary and Katie finished eating, Hannah packed everything back into the basket.

"Please, ma'am . . . I need the privy," Katie whispered.

"Of course," Hannah replied. "Follow me downstairs and I'll show you the way. And I have plenty of hot water if you'd like to wash up."

"You don't need to be waiting on us this-a-way," Mary said. "But we surely do thank the Lord for your kindness."

Hannah lowered herself through the attic opening first, and Bebe had a moment of panic when she realized she would have to drop down into her mother's arms. But she made it safely, followed by Katie and Mary. Bebe offered to show them the way to the privy. Both women followed her cautiously, as if expecting someone to jump out of hiding and pounce on them, the way Bebe's brothers did when playing hide-and-seek. She thought the two women were right behind her as she stepped out the back door, but they had halted before venturing outside, gazing all around, eyes wide and alert.

"Ain't no paddyrollers round here, is there?" Mary asked.

"What's a paddyroller?"

"They the white men on horses who chasing after us. They wanting to take us back to our massa's place, but I sooner die than go back down there." Her words made Bebe shudder, reminding her of the risk they all were taking.

"I haven't seen any," Bebe replied. "Besides, we'd hear them coming up the road a long way off."

The women sat outside on the back steps after

they finished washing up, warming their faces in the thin spring sunlight. A grove of fruit trees ruffled with blossoms hid the back of the house from view. A cowbell jangled dully as Henry's cows headed down the path to the pasture.

"It's nice here," Mary said quietly. "But why ain't anybody working all this land?"

"What do you mean?" Hannah asked.

"I ain't never seen a farm that didn't need slaves to keep it going. This late in the morning, we'd already be out there sweating and straining, with the overseer's whip just a cracking on our backs. Sometimes we'd have to start in singing just to keep our spirits up."

"People around here don't farm more land than the family can handle by themselves," Hannah said. "My husband does all of the work with the help of our four sons."

In the peaceful silence of the morning, Bebe heard a crow cawing from the pine tree, a blue jay scolding its mate, a woodpecker hammering into a fence post near the barn.

Mary sighed again. "It's so peaceful here. I wish we could stay."

"I wish you could, too," Hannah said. "I think you're the most courageous women I've ever met."

Mary wrapped one arm around her daughter and pulled her close. "It ain't courage making me do this, it's fear. If I stay down there, I lose my child.

Lizzy, up in the big house, say Massa be selling my Katie to another massa—and he planning to use my girl for hisself."

Hannah glanced at Bebe as she patted Mary's shoulder. "There, there . . . I understand." Several years would pass before Bebe understood what Mary had meant—and when Bebe finally did comprehend, she was outraged.

"My Katie is already bought and paid for, so now both our massas is chasing us."

"Well, with the Good Lord's help you'll make it all the way to Canada, where you'll be free," Hannah said.

The women climbed back up to the attic to hide before Bebe's brothers arrived home from school. Hannah repacked the basket with food and water for their supper and sent it up with them, along with a chamber pot. That night Bebe and her brothers slept in their bedrooms beneath the attic as usual, but Mary and Katie were quieter than a pair of mice. They never squeaked a single floorboard. Their lives depended on silence. Bebe listened to her brothers laughing and scuffling as they dressed for school the next morning and smiled to herself. They had no idea that two escaped slaves were hiding right above their heads.

On the third day, as Bebe and her mother packed the breakfast basket, they heard horses trotting up the road to their farm. "Go look out the front window, Beatrice, and see who's coming."

Bebe ran to the front room and peeked through the curtain just as two men on horseback drew to a stop in front of the house. She hurried back to the kitchen. "It's two men, but I don't know them, Mama. Should I let them in?"

"No, stay inside. Your father will talk to them."

"Are they the bad men who are chasing—?"

"They might be."

What had Mary called them? *Paddyrollers.* Bebe ran into the parlor and peered through the window again as Hannah hurried upstairs to deliver the women's breakfast and to warn them to stay hidden. Bebe's father ambled out from the barn with a shovel in his hand and stood talking with the men for a while as if chatting about nothing more important than the weather. When Hannah returned, she took Bebe's hand and led her away to the kitchen.

"Help me wash the eggs, Beatrice. I want to take them into town to sell later this week." Hannah put the basket of eggs they had collected that morning on the table, along with a basin of warm water. Bebe dampened a rag to clean them, careful not to break the delicate shells.

"Mama, I know Papa would never tell a lie. But what if they ask him about—?"

"Your father can honestly say that he hasn't seen any escaped slaves because he hasn't. That's why you and I always bring the food upstairs—and why we can't go outside right now."

"Will we have to hide if Papa invites the men inside?"

"He won't invite them into our home if they're bounty hunters."

Bebe waited in the kitchen with her mother for a very long time. She never knew that her heart could beat so hard and not give out. At last she heard the horses ride away again, but Mary and Katie stayed hidden in the attic all day.

"What did those men want?" Hannah asked when she and Bebe brought Henry's lunch outside to him.

"Claimed they were looking for two escaped slaves. Two women. Showed me a wanted poster and everything. Said there's a reward for finding them."

"I never heard of bounty hunters coming all the way out here. Have you?"

"Greed, Hannah. Men will do anything for selfish greed."

Bebe's brothers arrived home from school that afternoon whooping with excitement and jostling each other as they competed to share their news. "Two strangers on horseback showed up at school today," William said, outshouting the others.

"And guess what they asked us?" Joseph said.

James elbowed him aside. "They wanted to know if we'd seen any Negroes hiding around here."

"My goodness," Hannah murmured. "Imagine that."

"The men said they would give us candy and other treats if we showed them where the Negroes were hiding," Joseph added.

"One of the men had a shiny new silver dollar that he kept flipping up in the air and catching." William tossed an imaginary coin to demonstrate. "He said we could have it if we helped him."

Bebe feared she might burst. Keeping a secret was such a hard thing to do. But her mother crouched beside her and pulled her close, the same way Mary had pulled Katie to her side the other morning. Bebe felt Hannah's courage flowing into her.

"My friend Louis told the strangers that he'd seen Negroes in New Canaan," James continued, "but he was talking about the meetings at church that you and his mama go to sometimes."

"The man gave him a stick of licorice anyway, just for helping," Joseph said. "So then all the other kids started telling stories, too."

"You seen any Negroes around here, Pa?" William asked as their father tromped in from the back porch.

"Who's asking?"

"Two strangers showed up outside the school today and—"

"Oh, them," Henry said with a grunt. "They came out here and asked me the same question. I told them I haven't seen any Negroes. But even if I had, why would I tell some stranger about it?"

"They'll give you a whole dollar, Pa, that's why." Franklin hopped up and down as if he needed the privy. "A whole dollar!"

Their father frowned. "Sure, you would get a dollar. And you know what those poor Negroes would get? Forty lashes with a bullwhip." Franklin took a step backward as if fearing the lash himself. "Then those men would carry the slaves down south again, where they're treated worse than animals. Don't you boys get mixed up with those strangers, you hear?"

"Yes, Pa." Their enthusiasm vanished like a gopher down a hole.

"If you want candy and treats and such, then earn the money the honest way by working for it, not by selling another human being into slavery."

Bebe thought of Mary and Katie, hidden beneath a quilt in her attic, and knew she wouldn't hand them over for all the licorice in the world. She felt like she had grown three years older in the last three days.

On market day, Bebe and her mother drove into town to make their weekly egg delivery and to pick up a few things at the general store. One of their egg customers, the minister's wife, invited them into her parlor for coffee. Reverend Webster himself joined them, which seemed highly unusual to Bebe. He surprised her even more by speaking in a near whisper instead of the booming voice he always used on Sunday mornings. In fact, Bebe had to lean close to hear what he was saying.

"I don't know how to advise you, Mrs. Monroe. It's too dangerous for your visitors to stay and it's even more dangerous for them to leave. Packages usually travel at night, on foot, but the bounty hunters must have tracked them this far because they're hanging around town, waiting for someone to slip up. They take turns patrolling the roads, day and night. They even have dogs on the scent."

"How far is it to the next station?"

"About sixteen miles. It would take the better part of the night to walk that far."

Hannah set down her coffee cup and stared at her hands, folded in her lap. She seemed to be thinking—or maybe praying. "Can you send word to the next station for me, Reverend?" she asked at last. "Tell them I'll deliver the package myself, tomorrow morning. I'll hide our friends in my wagon—"

"In broad daylight?"

"Yes, sir, in broad daylight. Beatrice will come with me, won't you, dear?"

Bebe wanted to say, "No!" but not a sound came from her throat.

CHAPTER
4

On Friday morning, before Bebe's brothers left for school, their father ordered them to pitch a load of firewood into the back of the farm wagon. "Who is all this wood for, Pa?" William asked.

"Someone in need. Hurry up now or you'll be late for school."

Henry moved some of the wood aside after the boys were gone and hoisted a small coffin-like box that he'd built onto the wagon bed. Mary and Katie would ride to the next station in this secret hiding place, buried beneath the wood. Before the women climbed into it, Hannah gave them a map she'd drawn.

"It's always best to know exactly where you're headed," she told them. "You can't get anywhere in life without a map. I'll drive you to the next station, but if you find yourself off course after that, you can always look for the landmarks I've drawn."

"I don't know how we can ever thank you," Mary said.

"There's no need." Hannah surprised her with an embrace. "And now I think we should pray and ask the Lord for His protection."

The women joined hands and bowed their heads. Bebe's stomach cramped as if she'd eaten too many green apples as she held on to Katie's and Hannah's hands. She didn't close her eyes. Instead, she watched her mother's face as she prayed.

"Lord, please send your angels to surround us, to guard us and guide us on our way today. Blind our enemies' eyes, Lord, as you did for your servants in times past, so they don't see these precious daughters of yours. We ask you to protect Mary and Katie on their journey and help them reach freedom in Canada. In Jesus' name, amen."

The prayer didn't make the sick feeling in Bebe's stomach go away. Her heart thudded as she watched the women crawl inside the tiny space. Then her father buried the little box beneath the pile of firewood. "Can you breathe in there?" he asked.

"We're fine," came the muffled reply.

Henry helped Hannah climb onto the wagon seat, then handed her the reins. Last of all, he lifted Bebe up beside her. The wagon started with a jolt.

New leaves sprouted from the trees along the way as the countryside burst into life after the long, cold winter. The creaking wheels and plodding horse hooves drowned out the birdsong as the wagon traveled on, but Bebe could hear her mother humming softly as they rode.

"Can God really make our enemies go blind, Mama?" she asked, remembering Hannah's prayer.

"The Bible says that He can. When the prophet Elisha was surrounded by a huge army with soldiers and horses and chariots, he said to the Lord, 'Smite this people, I pray thee, with blindness,' and God did just that. He blinded the enemies' eyes to what they were really seeing, so that Elisha could lead them far away to another place. In the New Testament, Paul and Barnabas were on one of their missionary journeys when an evil sorcerer tried to stop their work. Paul prayed and the sorcerer was temporarily struck blind."

Bebe had heard of Jesus giving sight to blind people, but she'd never known that it worked in reverse. Even so, she hoped they didn't meet any enemies along the way. She would hate for her mother to be responsible for making anyone blind.

A little while later they reached a fork in the road, but instead of turning toward New Canaan as usual, Hannah steered the horses down the other road, toward the distant hills. Bebe had never been this way before. She looked around at the unfamiliar scenery and remembered another part of Hannah's prayer.

"I don't see any angels around us, Mama."

"They're here with us, just the same, dear."

"I wish I could see them." Maybe the sick feeling in her stomach would go away if she could glimpse a halo or two. "Are you scared, Mama?"

"Of course I'm scared. It's only natural. But I've decided to trust God and to follow my conscience. I believe that the Good Lord wants me to help our new friends."

"I heard Mr. Smith say you could go to jail."

"Well, if I have to go to jail for helping Mary and Katie, then so be it. I'm sure God will have a purpose for sending me there, and He'll be with me in jail, too."

Bebe swallowed. "Will I have to go with you?"

"No, you're much too young, dear. But someday when you're all grown up, God is going to give you a task to do in your own time and place. Then you'll have to put your faith in Him as you follow your conscience. That's why I wanted you to come with me today. We grow stronger every time our faith is tested. That's how we learn to trust Him."

Bebe knew that her mother was trustworthy—but her mother was sitting right beside her. It was much harder to trust a God she couldn't see.

There was very little shade along the road, and the sun grew hot as they traveled. Bebe's hair felt sweaty beneath her bonnet. Buried beneath all that wood, Mary and Katie must feel like two loaves of bread baking in the oven. Bebe turned around to see if she could glimpse them between the logs, and her heart seemed to stop beating when she noticed a dark silhouette in the middle of the road on the horizon behind them. She watched it for a moment, and the shape seemed to grow larger—which meant that it was moving closer, catching up to them.

She tugged at Hannah's sleeve. "Mama, someone's following us."

Hannah glanced over her shoulder. "Yes, I see. Don't worry, dear. Let's recite a psalm together. 'God is our refuge and strength, a very present help in trouble . . .'"

Bebe tried to do what her mother said and not worry, but it was impossible. She kept her gaze straight ahead, watching the horses' rumps until she could no longer stand the suspense. When she turned around again, the shape had split into two figures. They rode horseback and were galloping toward the wagon, quickly closing the gap. Bebe felt like throwing up.

"They're coming closer, Mama. Two of them."

"Can you tell who they are, dear?"

She turned to look behind her again. "I think . . . th-they look like the two men who talked with Papa the other day! Hurry, Mama. Go faster!"

She wanted her mother to lay the lash to the horses and try to outrun the men. Instead, Hannah drew the team to a halt and waited for the riders to catch up. When they finally did, the bounty hunters had rifles strapped to their saddles. Three dogs bounded out of the bushes alongside the road and pranced around the horses, barking at the wagon. Bebe huddled beside her mother in fear.

"Good afternoon. Are you gentlemen lost?" Hannah asked above the clamor.

"Quiet!" one of the men shouted. The barking stopped.

"We're looking for a pair of escaped slaves,

47

ma'am. They're very valuable. We're offering a reward for information."

The dogs circled the wagon while the man talked, sniffing loudly enough for Bebe to hear them. The biggest dog stood on his hind legs with his front feet propped on the tailgate and sniffed the wood. He looked as though he might jump up. Bebe began to cry.

"Would you kindly control your dogs?" Hannah asked. "My little girl is frightened."

The man whistled and all three dogs ran over to him. "Have you seen two Negro women anywhere around here?" he asked again.

"I wouldn't tell you even if I had seen them," Hannah said quietly.

The man stared at her in surprise. He removed his hat and wiped his brow with his forearm. "Well, according to the law, you're required to hand over fugitive slaves."

"I know. But according to the Bible I'm commanded not to. It says in Deuteronomy chapter twenty-three, verse fifteen, 'Thou shalt not deliver unto his master the servant which is escaped from his master unto thee.' So tell me, whose law do you think I should obey, yours or God's?"

"Listen, ma'am—"

"No, you listen. What you're doing is wrong. You're disobeying God's Word."

"We're just trying to make a living."

"Will that be your defense on Judgment Day

when you stand before the Almighty to give an accounting of your life?"

The man's face turned red. He looked very angry, but he pressed his lips together and didn't reply.

"If you repent and ask the Lord to forgive you, He surely will," Hannah continued. "I would be happy to pray with you right here and now, if you would like me to."

The men looked at each other, then turned their horses around and trotted back the way they'd come. The dogs followed, noses to the ground, sniffing eagerly. As the dust settled around the wagon again, Bebe buried her face in her mother's lap and sobbed. She had been certain that she and her mother and the two slaves were all going to jail, and the relief she now felt was as real as if the jailer had unlocked the door and set her free.

Hannah flicked the reins to start the horses moving, then wrapped one arm around Bebe to comfort her. "You don't need to be afraid, Beatrice."

"Why did you talk to them, Mama? I was so afraid they would find—"

"Hush now. You learned a valuable lesson today. When you obey the Lord, He will always be with you, no matter what happens. Even if I had gone to jail, the Good Lord would be there, too. As the psalmist wrote, 'The Lord is on my side; I will not fear: what can man do unto me?'"

Bebe thought of several things the men could have done, but she didn't say them out loud. Instead, she wiped her tears with the heels of her hands and decided that she didn't want to be a coward anymore. She would ask God to help her be a woman of faith like Hannah; a woman of courage like the two slaves hiding beneath the firewood. She never wanted to feel afraid again.

A few hours later they arrived at a farm that was much like Bebe's. Hannah helped the elderly farmer push aside the firewood to set Katie and Mary free. The two women were so drenched with sweat they looked as though they had stood outside in a rainstorm. The farmer's wife—a woman with gray hair and a bent spine—made the slaves hurry inside her house to hide.

"Good-bye," Hannah called to Mary and Katie. "Godspeed!" When she told the farmer about the bounty hunters, they decided that he should keep the firewood in case Hannah encountered the men on the return trip. Bebe helped her mother and the man unload it, tossing down one log at a time until her arms and shoulders ached and splinters pricked her fingers.

Late that afternoon, Bebe and Hannah returned home again. As soon as the wagon stopped, Bebe jumped off and ran down the path that led to the river, feeling as though she could draw a full, deep breath for the first time all day. She halted by her brothers' rope swing. It looked inviting as it swayed gently in the wind. Bebe glanced all around, then lifted her calico skirt to climb onto the swing for the very first time.

She had watched her brothers kick with their feet, then lift up their legs, pumping higher and higher in the air, but her legs were much shorter than theirs were and her feet barely reached the ground. She closed her eyes and let the wind twirl her gently on the breeze. She had been right about riding on the swing—the wind did feel nice on her face. She held tightly to the rope and tilted her head back to look up at the sky, her feet out-stretched. She wondered what it would feel like to soar high in the air—not too high, not with abandon the way her brothers did, and certainly not out over the river—but high enough to feel as if she were flying. She imagined that she would feel the same way she had when the paddyrollers had turned around and trotted away. She lifted her face to the sky and tasted freedom.

I had thought of Grandma Bebe's story last night as I set out on my own secret errand. Like Great-Grandma Hannah and the prophet Elisha, I also prayed that the Lord would blind my enemies' eyes so they wouldn't see the cargo I was carrying.

When the patrol car stopped me, I tried to act calm even though my entire body was trembling. Much to my surprise, the officer who stepped up to my car window was Tommy O'Reilly—the constable's son and notorious bully, the boy who had made my school days miserable. Of all the policemen who patrolled our town, why did he have to be on duty last night?

"Would you step out of the car, please?" he asked.

I could barely stand. I had to lean against the fender for support. Tommy looked into the back seat, which was filled with cases of bootleg liquor, and his eyes grew very wide. He stared and stared, blinking in amazement as if he had been struck blind and couldn't quite make out what he was seeing. I thought God surely had answered my prayer. Then Tommy uncorked one of the bottles and sniffed, and I knew I was in trouble. Why hadn't I prayed that his sense of smell would be taken away along with his eyesight?

"I'm going to have to arrest you, Harriet." He seemed truly surprised.

Reasoning with him had been a waste of time last night, just as it had been for as long as I'd known him. I didn't think a kick in the shins would accomplish anything, either. He put me in the back seat of his patrol car and drove me to the police station.

So here I was, in jail. I had remembered to pray before venturing out with my hidden cargo just as Hannah had. I had been convinced that I was doing the right thing for all the right reasons—just like Grandma Bebe.

Now I stared up at the sagging bunk above me and wondered where I had gone wrong. How had I ended up here, so far from where I thought I was headed? And how was I going to find my way back to where I should be?

CHAPTER
5

Grandma Bebe's attic became a refuge for runaway slaves at least half a dozen times that she could remember. "My mother may have sheltered a good many more runaways that I never knew about," Grandma told me years later. She and I had been talking about slavery as we sat on her porch swing one sticky summer night when I was eleven, gently rocking back and forth, sipping lemonade and swatting mosquitoes. "I think my mother stopped confiding in me once I started going to school all day," Grandma said with a sigh.

I pushed my foot against the porch floor to keep the swing moving. Grandma was so short her feet barely reached the floor. "Did your brothers ever find out about the runaway slaves?" I asked.

"No, they did not." Grandma grinned as if she were still a small girl keeping a very big secret. Her dark eyes gleamed. "My brothers thought they were so smart—and to this day it tickles me to think they had no idea what Mama and I were up to."

We were looking through Grandma's box of keepsakes, and she showed me a photograph of her father and mother. They sat side-by-side, their shoulders barely touching, Henry's huge farmer hands splayed on his thighs like a pair of shovels. He wore one of those silly beards that covered his chin and the sides of his face, but without the mustache. Great-Grandpa Henry's wide, generous mouth and full lower lip looked exactly like Grandma Bebe's—although she smiled all the time, and he looked as though he didn't know how to smile. He appeared to be so uncomfortable in his ill-fitting suit and lopsided bow tie that he might have been sitting barelegged in a patch of nettles.

"The suit and tie weren't his," Grandma explained. "The traveling photographer provided a rackful of clothing that you could borrow to get your picture taken."

The photo of Great-Grandmother Hannah intrigued me after hearing so much about her. No one would ever guess from the calm, serene look on her face that she was capable of facing down a pair of armed bounty hunters. Her hands rested on her lap as if they had no bones in them, and there was such an expression of meekness in her pale eyes and faint smile that I thought she probably spoke no louder than a whisper.

I searched her face for any resemblance to my own, hoping I might have inherited some of her fine moral qualities too, but to be honest I didn't see any. I didn't resemble Grandma Bebe either, nor did I look like my beautiful socialite mother, who might have sprung to life and fluttered off one of the pages of the fashion magazines she read so religiously. I not only looked plain and ordinary, but I worried that my life would be ordinary, as well. I wasn't brave and hardworking like Hannah, and I didn't have Grandma Bebe's passion for fighting injustice, and I certainly didn't want to inherit my mother's useless life, even if I did turn out to be as beautiful as she was. I couldn't figure out who I was and how I would ever fit into my illustrious family's story.

"Don't worry dear, I've been a misfit all my life," Grandma said. "I'm sure you'll do just fine. At least you have pluck and spunk. When I was your age I was as jumpy as a baby rabbit and twice as shy." She showed me a photograph of two dozen children lined up outside her one-room schoolhouse and asked me to guess which one she was. I spotted Grandma Bebe easily. Not only was she the shortest child, but with her shoulders hunched and her head lowered, she looked as though she was trying to disappear.

"Going to school with a bunch of prankster-prone farm boys added to my fears," she said, "making me even more timid than I already was. My goal of becoming a woman of faith like my mother Hannah seemed as distant and unreachable as Canada. . . ."

• • •

By the time Bebe turned thirteen in July of 1861, the issue of slavery had become a huge, boiling cauldron that finally grew so hot it overflowed. War broke out between the states. As soon as Bebe's three oldest brothers finished harvesting the fall crops, they marched off to fight. James was twenty-two, William was twenty, and Joseph was eighteen.

"We'll lick those Rebels and be home by Christmastime," William promised as he waved good-bye. All three of Bebe's brothers displayed the same courage and bravado they'd shown as boys, making the Rebels seem like nothing more than a nest of black snakes hiding in the grass.

In a way, Bebe envied her brothers' adventures as they marched off to war. What would it be like to travel beyond the farm and visit new places? But a much wiser part of her thanked God that in His wisdom He had seen fit to make her a girl. She never could have summoned the courage to stand shoulder to shoulder in a line of soldiers and calmly aim her rifle as a horde of angry Rebels charged toward her with bayonets fixed. Bebe had prayed for courage, but so far God hadn't given her any.

With the three oldest boys gone, only sixteen-year-old Franklin remained behind to help Henry with the farm work. And Bebe, of course. The day after her brothers marched away, her father shook her awake before dawn.

"Get up. It's time for you boys to do your chores." He seemed to have forgotten that she was a girl.

"You mean . . . *me*, Papa?"

"Yes, you. Now hurry up. The cows are waiting to be milked." Bebe rolled out of bed and marched out to the barn to do her part, telling herself that the war would be over soon and her brothers would return. Everyone had agreed that the Rebels would be beaten in no time.

Everyone was wrong.

Six months later, when spring came around again, Bebe had all but forgotten that she was a girl, too. Meanwhile, her brothers were on their way to Virginia to conquer the Rebel capital of Richmond.

"Wish I were fighting with them," Franklin said as he and Bebe pitched a load of newly cut hay into the barn loft.

"You don't mean that."

"Sure do."

Bebe paused to lean against her pitchfork. "Aren't you reading their letters, Franklin? All they do is complain about the rain and the mud and the mosquitoes. The food is bad, everyone has a fever, and the Rebels have real bullets in their guns. Why would you want to be a part of that?"

"At least it's something new. I don't want to stay here, pitching hay and milking cows forever. Don't you ever get sick of this place?"

She could only stare at him. Why would he want to go anyplace else?

"Oh, that's right, you're a girl," he said after a moment. "I keep forgetting. Girls can't move around from place to place whenever they feel like it."

Bebe lifted her pitchfork and stabbed it deeper into the hay. "Can to! I just don't feel like it, that's all."

Franklin shook his head. "That's not how it works for women. First you need to find a husband. Then you have to move to wherever he wants to live."

"Who says?"

"Everyone says! That's just the way the world is. Don't you ever pay attention to these things?"

She returned to her work with a fury she didn't understand, stabbing the hay and hurling it aloft. Stubble rained down on her, sticking in her hair and dropping down the neck of her blouse until her body felt as prickly as her mood.

When the last of the hay was loaded off the flatbed wagon, Franklin grabbed Bebe's pitchfork and leaned it against the barn wall beside his. "Come on, let's go jump in the river and cool off."

"But Papa said—"

"He won't know we're finished. Come on! One quick swim before dinner."

Franklin shed his scratchy shirt, shoes, and socks on the way to the tree swing, dumping them in a heap beside the path. With a whoop of pure joy, he swung out over the river and dropped into the water below.

"Come on in, Bebe! It feels great!" he hollered up to her.

Bebe hadn't felt so hot and itchy since she'd had the chicken pox. She caught the dangling rope in her hand and sat down on the board. She was finally tall enough for her feet to touch the ground. But even though she longed for the cooling relief of the water, she simply couldn't bring herself to leap from the swing and drop all that way down into the river. She twirled in half-hearted circles for a few minutes, then got off the swing and picked her way carefully down the path to the river, still wearing her shoes in case of snakes.

"Why don't you jump in?" Franklin called to her. He floated on his back a few feet away, his bare toes sticking out of the water.

"I can't swim." Nor could she take off her clothes as Franklin had done. She was a girl.

Bebe sat down on the riverbank and dribbled water through her fingers, splashing it on her face and neck, aware for the first time of her limitations. She was still hot and prickly, while Franklin floated with the current, cool and refreshed. Bebe was forced to do the same work as a boy, but she couldn't have fun like a boy or travel wherever she wanted. It didn't seem fair. She stood and started hiking up the path away from the river, back toward home.

By the time summer ended, her brothers had marched close enough to Richmond to hear the church bells tolling, but the Union generals made them turn around and march all the way back down the Virginia peninsula to where they'd started. Bebe couldn't believe it. It seemed like the war was going to go on forever. She helped her father and Franklin bring in the harvest and slaughter the hogs. Winter came again.

Bebe rose before dawn on a frigid Sunday morning in 1863 and put on an overcoat that Franklin had outgrown and a pair of his worn-out boots and followed him and her father out to the barn through fresh shin-deep snow. The farmyard looked beautiful in the predawn light, buried beneath a sparkling blanket of pristine snow, unmarred by footprints or wagon tracks. Her breath hung in the air in front of her, as if she could grab it and put it in her pocket.

Warmth from the cows raised the temperature in the barn a few degrees, but by the time Bebe finished her chores and returned to the house, she felt as cold and stiff as a brass weather vane. She had often complained while scrubbing laundry and washing dishes with her mother, but she wished she were helping in the warm, cozy kitchen again. She missed her quiet conversations with Hannah.

"Can you stoke the fire a little hotter, Mama?"

she asked as she dumped an extra armload of firewood into the kitchen woodbox. "I'm so frozen I can barely move." Her hair crackled and sparked as she pulled off her woolen hat and shook her long braids free.

Franklin tromped through the door behind her and snatched up his plate, piling on eggs and bacon and biscuits from the warming oven. He was taking more than his fair share, from what Bebe could see. She quickly grabbed her own plate and shoved Franklin aside with her hip.

"Hey, move over. Some of this food is for me, you know."

Franklin laughed and shoved her in return, tussling with her the way her brothers used to wrestle with each other, even though the top of Bebe's head barely reached Franklin's shoulders. At fourteen, she was still as tiny as a ten-year-old, although her back had grown strong during the past two years and her rock-rough hands were callused from wielding pitchforks and shovels and scythes.

"I'm not only frozen, I'm starved!" she said, shoving a warm biscuit into her mouth. Any ladylike manners she once might have possessed had deteriorated significantly since the war began. She didn't care.

"I can't help thinking of James and William and Joseph," Hannah said as she put more wood in the stove. "Imagine eating hardtack and sleeping outside in tents on the cold, hard ground . . . I hope they've found someplace to attend church this morning."

The thought of going outside again made Bebe shiver. "Do we have to go to church?" she asked. "Can't we just stay home and read the Bible here, for once? It's too cold to ride all the way into town—and I could use a rest. Papa thinks we're his slaves."

"You don't know what slavery is," Hannah said gently. "You should thank God every day that you don't have an evil overseer standing behind you with a whip like those poor slaves down South do. And thank God we have the freedom to attend church."

"Well, I'm going to pray that this war ends soon so the boys can come home and do their own work."

Franklin nudged her with his elbow, frowning. "Don't do that. I don't want the war to end yet. I want my turn to fight."

Bebe stared at her brother. His cheeks were still red from the cold, his sweaty hair mashed flat from his stocking cap. She suddenly realized how much she would miss Franklin if he went off to war, too. The bond between them had grown strong as they'd worked together every day, and Franklin no longer treated her like a pesky little sister the way her other brothers had. She didn't know what she would do if she ever saw his name on the list posted at the general store of all the local boys who had been killed or wounded in battle. But Bebe didn't know how to explain her reasons to Franklin. Instead, she slid the rest of her bacon onto his plate.

"Here . . . I took too much." She lifted one of her biscuits onto his plate, too.

The kitchen door opened and their father came inside, trailing powdery snow from his boots and sending a shiver of cold air down Bebe's neck. "Which one of you boys left my axe lying on the ground?"

"I guess I did," Bebe said meekly. "Sorry . . . I had to use it to chop the ice out of the watering troughs."

"I've told you boys a hundred times to take care of my tools. That axe will be no good to anyone if it rusts."

"Sorry . . . And I'm a girl, Papa, not a boy." Henry didn't acknowledge the correction.

Bebe gulped down the rest of her food and quickly changed into her Sunday clothes, tying a bonnet over her unruly hair. Hannah had warmed bricks in the oven so Bebe could thaw out her frozen feet on the trip to town. She still felt grumpy as she sat down in the church pew between Franklin and her father, fuming about the endless war that might take Franklin away from her, and certain that she smelled as strongly of manure as they did, even though she had washed and changed her clothes and shoes. She barely paid attention to Reverend Webster's sermon until she noticed that an unusual hush had fallen over the congregation. She uncrossed her arms and sat up to listen.

"And so our prayers have been answered," he was saying. "According to the latest news, President Lincoln has signed an Emancipation Proclamation, which means that every slave in every rebellious state is now a free man!"

For a moment, the silence in the church was absolute. Bebe tried to imagine what it would feel like to suddenly be granted her freedom after a lifetime of slavery. Probably even better than if her brothers came home. Then one of the elders began to sing the doxology in a wavering baritone, and one by one the other members of the congregation joined in.

Praise God from Whom all blessings flow
Praise Him all creatures here below
Praise Him above ye Heavenly Host.
Praise Father, Son and Holy Ghost . . . Amen.

Bebe recalled the feeling of joy and relief she'd felt on that long-ago day when the bounty hunters had turned their horses around and trotted away from the farm wagon, and she felt guilty for complaining about the farm work. She had read the tattered copy of *Uncle Tom's Cabin* with its pages falling out and its back cover missing, and she felt the rightness of the abolition movement with every ounce of her strength.

"God heard the slaves' groaning," Pastor Webster continued, "just as He once heard the cries of the slaves in Egypt. He heard our congregation's prayers, and now He has answered them. But the slaves will still be in bondage until the war is over and liberation comes—which is all the more reason for us to keep praying for our soldiers and leaders, keep praying for the war to end soon. And when peace returns to our land once again, imagine all the other things we can accomplish if we continue to work together as God's people to further His kingdom."

Bebe was quiet for most of the ride home until the wagon reached the fork in the road, reminding her as it always did of the day she and her mother had helped Mary and Katie escape. "Wasn't that wonderful news we heard today about the slaves?" she asked.

"God is so good," Hannah murmured.

Bebe glanced down the other road and remembered the bounty hunters sitting astride their powerful horses. She remembered their hunting dogs jostling and sniffing as they approached the wagon. And she remembered the two brave women huddled beneath the firewood, holding their breath. That's why her brothers were fighting this war. Sometimes it was so hard to take her mind off the daily aches and pains and so easy to lose sight of the bigger goal.

As her farmhouse came into view beyond the turn in the road, Bebe vowed to pray every day for the war to end. And though she knew it was selfish of her, she wanted it to end for her own freedom as much as for the slaves.

CHAPTER
6

Morning comes very early when you're locked in a jail cell. The high, barred windows had no curtains, so I awakened with the sunrise. I sat up, rubbing my eyes with my fists to get out the jail dust, then smoothed my hair off my face. The cell had no mirror, so I could only imagine how disheveled I must look.

Even in the best of times I was never fastidious with my hair and clothing. I had much more important things to attend to than brushing my hair for one hundred strokes or taking hours to pin it up in a fashionable Gibson girl style or applying layers of cosmetics to my cheeks. I wore my hair bobbed, and I purchased clothing that was "serviceable," much to my mother's dismay. I couldn't be bothered with lace that could be torn or silk that would catch and shred easily.

After my wild car ride last evening, and a long uncomfortable night on a lumpy mattress, I figured

I must look like Longfellow's *The Wreck of the Hesperus*. I found myself wishing for a hairbrush. And a toothbrush. Never in my life have I slept in my clothes. Mother would be appalled, I'm sure.

There is an old adage that says, "You can't make a silk purse out of a sow's ear," but that didn't stop my mother from trying hard over the years, to transform me into a silk purse. As I lay down on my jailhouse bunk again, trying in vain to go back to sleep, I recalled one of her more memorable attempts. It was during the summer of 1910, when I was a wild and wiry child with scrawny legs and a rat's nest of brown hair . . .

"Harriet, it's time you learned to be more lady-like." My mother made the pronouncement with a firm voice and a determined nod of her stately blond head.

"But I'm not a lady," I argued. "I'm only ten!" I rose from my seat at the breakfast table and began backing slowly from the room, trying to make my escape.

"Halt!" Mother said. "I mean it, Harriet. Your manners are atrocious, and I don't know where to begin to describe your lack of concern for your appearance."

In truth, my appearance was hopeless, so why be concerned? I was mousy and plain, and no amount of wishing would ever transform me into a beauty like my sister, Alice. Or my mother for that matter, who was an older, more elegant version of my sister. God had abundantly blessed both of them with delicate features, golden hair, and alabaster skin. Both had the dainty upturned nose, pointed chin, and mysterious, haughty demeanor of a Gibson girl. Men's heads turned when Mother and Alice sashayed past. Men probably averted their gazes when I did.

"I've let you run wild for much too long," Mother continued. "But starting today that's all going to change."

I gulped. I glanced at Alice and saw her nodding in agreement. I was doomed.

"Mother and I have decided to plan a garden luncheon," Alice said gleefully. "We're going to invite all of our friends—and yours too, Harriet. Won't it be fun?"

"I would sooner be stuck on a spit and roasted over a fire."

"Why must you say such outrageous things?" Mother asked. "Honestly, I never know what's going to come out of your mouth. Perhaps that should be our first task, Alice, teaching the girl to hold her tongue."

I was tempted to stick out said tongue at them, but I knew it would get me into worse trouble. Mother made me sit down at the table again. "And please pay attention to your posture, Harriet. Don't slouch. If you're ever going to learn grace and poise, you'll need to begin with a straight spine."

I listened in horror as they spelled out their plans for me, conspiring to outfit me in a frilly white dress complete with lace and bows. I had no desire to turn all feminine and fluttery. My short, skinny body still resembled a child's, which was fine with me. I wanted no part of womanhood.

But after breakfast Mother and Alice marched me down to Daddy's department store against my will, then stood around my dressing room door *ooh*ing and *ahh*ing and telling me how pretty I looked as I tried on scratchy dresses with lots of ruffles and flounces and frills. "I look like a stray dog trying to fit into a party dress," I told them.

Alice bounced on her toes and clapped her pretty hands. "No you don't, Harriet, you look sweet."

I made a face. The last thing I wanted to be was sweet. "I hope you're not going to buy me a vial of smelling salts and a crochet-edged handkerchief, too," I grumbled.

As soon as we returned home, I bolted away as if my bloomers were on fire and ran straight to Grandma Bebe's house to tell her the terrible news.

"Mercy me, Harriet, who's chasing you?" she asked as I burst through her door, panting like a hound dog. Grandma sat at her dining room table, which was piled high, as usual, with letters and envelopes and copies of the temperance paper, *The Union Signal*. As far as I could recall, I had never actually seen the top of her dining room table—much less eaten a meal on it.

69

"Grandma?" I asked breathlessly, "I'm not going to start growing all soft and lumpy like Alice, am I?"

"Not within the next few minutes, I shouldn't think. Sit down, dear. Tell me what's wrong."

"Mother is trying to make me wear frilly dresses and go to tea parties, and I don't want to. I don't want to look like Alice, I want to look like you."

"Horrors! Why would you wish for such a thing? I've never grown any bigger than a ten-year-old. Of course, I always blamed my stunted growth on all of the farm work I had to endure while my brothers were away at war, but—"

"Can farm work really stunt your growth?" I was ready to hop on the first hay wagon if it meant avoiding a figure like Alice's and all the attention that came with it.

"I'm not really sure if it can," Grandma replied, "but I always figured that since my father needed another son so badly, my body simply complied. Will you be staying long, Harriet dear? I could use some help with these envelopes."

Grandma was always doing something for "the cause," and I was willing to help her as long as it didn't involve going to jail. After my father bailed her out a few months earlier, I'd heard him say that if she got arrested again she would just have to stay there, no matter how many tears Alice shed.

"How's your tongue, Harriet? Can you lick some envelopes for me?"

"I guess so." Licking envelopes was much better than sipping tea and acting all ladylike. Grandma brought me a glass of water to "wet my whistle."

"I wish I were a boy," I said with a sigh. "Did you hate being a girl, too, Grandma?"

"I didn't know what I wanted to be when I was your age," she replied. "I hated doing my brothers' chores while they were away at war, but I wasn't sure I wanted to be a woman, either. It seemed to me that boys had more interesting opportunities than girls did."

"But isn't that why the suffragettes are marching? So women will have more opportunities?"

"I suppose that's one of the things they're trying to change. But back then I didn't know what I wanted. If you had asked me, I would have told you that I hated doing my brothers' chores, but I didn't necessarily want to do housework, either. That nasty war dragged on and on until I didn't think my life could possibly get any worse—and then it did. . . ."

Spring came early in 1863, and as the weather grew warmer, Bebe steeled herself for another season of work. Last spring she'd held on to the hope that the war would end soon. Now she knew better. In March, when she and her father drove into town one morning to pick up supplies from Harrison's General Store, the shopkeeper had more bad news for them.

"How old is your boy now, Henry?" Mr. Harrison asked as he weighed out two pounds of sugar.

Henry gestured to Bebe with his thumb. "You mean this one?"

"I'm a girl, Papa," she said, in case he'd forgotten.

"No, your youngest boy . . . the one who isn't fighting yet."

Bebe's father looked to her for the answer. "Franklin is eighteen," she told them.

Mr. Harrison shook his head. "That's hard luck for you, Henry. Looks like he'll be leaving for the war, too, before long."

"Leaving!" Bebe stared at Mr. Harrison, waiting for him to break into a grin and tell her that it had all been a joke. He was known to be a big kidder. But his expression never changed as he slid the sack of sugar across the counter.

"Yup. Just got word that Congress has passed a new draft law. They're conscripting boys from age eighteen on up—which means my boy will have to go, too." He twirled the ends of his handlebar mustache and shook his head. "Seems the Union army needs more soldiers—which is hardly surprising the way our generals have been sacrificing them left and right. I'm guessing there'll be a lot of folks needing farm help this summer. Don't know how I'll manage the store shorthanded."

Henry scooped up the parcel of sugar and pointed to the shelf behind Mr. Harrison's head. "I'll take some of that lamp oil, too, Herbert."

Bebe stared at her father. How could he remain so calm after hearing the news? She wanted to scream. "What are we going to do if Franklin has to go away?" she asked on the way home.

"One day at a time," her father murmured. "One day at a time."

Franklin's draft notice arrived in the mail a few weeks later. Bebe sat at the dinner table with her family that evening waiting to hear what he and her father planned to do about it. Franklin was the only one who seemed cheerful about the situation. Bebe tried to be patient, waiting until the chicken and potatoes and carrots were all eaten and the rhubarb pie was cut and served, but no one seemed willing to discuss the matter. She cleared her throat, taking it upon herself to start the conversation.

"People in town are saying you can pay three hundred dollars to hire a substitute and get out of fighting in the war," she said. "That's what Mr. Harrison down at the store might do so his son won't have to go."

Henry frowned. "We don't have three hundred dollars."

"Besides, I want to go," Franklin added.

Bebe could no longer sit quietly. She pushed her chair away from the table and sprang to her feet.

73

"You can't let him leave, Papa! How will we ever manage this farm all by ourselves?"

Hannah laid her hand on Bebe's arm. "Hush, Beatrice. We'll be fine." She would never dream of telling her husband what he could or couldn't do.

"But I'll be the only one left, Mama, and I'm a girl! I can't do all the work that needs to be done around here without Franklin."

"Hush now," Hannah soothed. "With the Lord's help, we can do anything. God is asking the men to do their part to help free the slaves, and we need to do ours."

"Well, I can't do it! I won't!" Bebe ran from the house, past the vegetable garden and through the barnyard, wishing she could run all the way to Canada like the other escaped slaves. That's how she thought of herself—as a slave, forced to labor against her will.

Milkweed and chicory whipped against her legs as she sprinted across the pasture behind the barn. Mud clung to the bottoms of her shoes, but she didn't stop running until she reached her brothers' swing near the river, out of breath and out of tears. She straddled the seat and backed up to push off with her feet. She wished she could make it go as high as her brothers used to go.

It wasn't fair! She wouldn't mind doing some-thing noble and brave, like hiding slaves or fighting a battle, but why was she stuck doing farm work? Endless farm work. She dangled uselessly from the swing, kicking at the dirt and feeling sorry for herself for nearly half an hour before Franklin came looking for her.

"You're not swinging very high, Bebe. Need a push?" He grabbed her from behind and pulled the swing back as far as he could, then let go. Each time Bebe swung back, Franklin gave her another push until she was soaring higher than ever before. The rope creaked as it rubbed against the tree branch and her stomach dropped every time the swing did. Her eyes watered in the wind. She felt like she was flying.

Franklin stopped pushing after a while and sank down on the ground with a sigh. He tore out a wide blade of grass and stretched it between his thumbs to whistle through it—a feat that Bebe had never been able to do. "You have to pump with your legs if you want to keep going," he told her. "Stretch out your legs every time you go forward, then try to scoop air with them on the way back."

Bebe tried it, pouring all of her anger into the task as she reached and stretched, remembering how her brothers used to do it. When she felt the swing respond, she pumped harder, going higher.

"That's it! . . . I think you've got it!" Franklin called.

Bebe pumped as hard as she could, no longer afraid of falling, wishing she never had to stop. "I don't want you to go!" she shouted.

"I know," he said quietly. "But I have to.

Somebody needs to lick those Rebels once and for all." She looked down at him, lounging on the grass, and knew that what Franklin faced was much worse than what she did. He could be killed. She stopped pumping and allowed the swing to slow, dragging her feet in the dirt.

"Are you scared, Franklin? Tell me the truth."

"I've decided not to think about it. I'm just going to do what I have to do and take it one day at a time." That was what their father always said— "one day at a time." But those days had already added up to more than two years.

"I'll knit you some socks," Bebe said suddenly.

"Ha!" Franklin laughed. "You hate to knit."

"I know. But you'll need them to keep your feet warm." She pushed off with her feet and began to pump again, going higher, faster.

"I think you've got the hang of it, Bebe." He gave another piercing whistle, then tossed the piece of grass aside. "We'll be fine, both of us. We'll do what we have to do, and we'll be fine."

When the day finally came for Franklin to leave, Bebe couldn't bear to watch him go. She hugged him tightly, then ran upstairs to her bedroom, stuffing her fingers in her ears so she wouldn't have to hear the wagon driving away. She forced herself not to cry as she wandered into her brothers' room and gazed around at their empty beds. Franklin had left his bureau drawer open, and one leg of his work trousers hung out of it. Bebe started to tuck it inside and close the drawer, then changed her mind. She pulled out the overalls and held them up in front of her. They were miles too long for her, but if she hiked up the straps and rolled up the legs she could make them fit.

"Beatrice, what in the world are you wearing?" Hannah asked when Bebe came downstairs a while later.

"I've decided to borrow Franklin's overalls until he gets back. It'll be easier to do his chores."

"They look quite unbecoming on you. And the Bible says that it's wrong for women to wear men's clothing."

Bebe felt a surge of anger. "The Bible also says not to kill people, and everyone is killing each other, aren't they?"

"Beatrice . . ."

She crossed her arms and lifted her chin. "And what does the Bible say about women doing men's work?"

Hannah displayed relentless patience. "God's Word says that whatever your hands find to do, do it with all your heart as unto the Lord."

"Well then, I don't see why the Lord would care if I did what I have to do in a pair of pants."

Even in trousers, Bebe found it difficult to do her work "as unto the Lord," especially when her father demanded that it be done his way. Before long, the only time Bebe wore a dress was when she went to church on Sunday. That's where she was when she heard the news that General Lee and his Rebel army had defeated the Union forces at Winchester, Virginia, and had now crossed the border into her state, Pennsylvania. The townswomen were all aflutter about it after the service.

"We need to make preparations," Mrs. Harrison told the gathered group of women, "or the Rebels will take all of our food and ravish our daughters."

Bebe wasn't worried about being "ravished"— how would anyone even know she was a girl, dressed in Franklin's clothes and smelling of manure? But she would fight to the death before she'd let those Rebels steal one morsel of the food she had labored so hard to grow.

"We need to buy some extra gunpowder for Papa's shotgun," she told Hannah as they walked back to their wagon. "I'm going to shoot those dirty Rebels if they come near our farm."

Hannah's habitually mild expression grew stern. "Now, listen to me, Beatrice. It's bad enough that my sons are forced to kill—I won't have my daughter killing, as well."

"But what if they try to take our food?"

"Jesus says that if someone asks for your cloak, you should give him your coat also. If the Rebels need our food that badly, we'll let them have it."

"Mama, no! Not after all my hard work! I'm not going to let anyone have it!"

Hannah smoothed back Bebe's hair and caressed her cheek. "Don't borrow trouble by worrying about something that may never happen. 'Sufficient unto the day is the evil thereof.'"

Bebe wondered if she really could kill a Rebel soldier. Two weeks later on her fifteenth birthday, she thought that perhaps she could. On her family's weekly trip to town, she found all of her neighbors talking about the series of battles that had been fought near the village of Gettysburg, Pennsylvania. Her parents found a telegram waiting for them in Harrison's General Store. Hannah's hands trembled as she tore open the envelope. Bebe watched her face turn pale as she read it.

"What happened?" Bebe asked. "What does it say?"

Hannah choked out the words as if wringing them from her heart. "Your brother Joseph has been killed in battle."

Grief settled over Bebe's household like deep snow, bringing life on the farm to a suffocating standstill and chilling everyone's soul. The neighbors brought food but no one felt like eating it. As Bebe lay awake in her bedroom at night, she heard the floors creaking downstairs as her father paced sleeplessly. She remembered Joseph's wide grin and joyous laughter and wanted to kill a hundred Rebels in retaliation.

"How could God let this happen?" she asked her

mother. "We've been praying and asking Him to protect the boys."

"God isn't causing this war, Beatrice, people are."

"Well, why doesn't He stop us?" For once, her mother had no answer.

Bebe never did see her father weep, but he attacked his chores with a ferocity that frightened her. Hannah grieved quietly for her son, allowing her tears to fall silently as she went about her work. But Bebe railed at God, alternating between fits of anger and fits of tears until a day came when she was so hot and weary from the unending work, so feverish with rage, that she dropped her father's hoe in the middle of the vegetable patch and sprinted across the pasture toward the river. When she reached the swing she climbed onto it, remembering the day that Franklin had taught her to pump; remembering Joseph whooping for joy as he'd leaped from the swing into the river.

Bebe started swinging parallel to the river as she always had, then changed her mind. She twisted around on the wooden plank and backed up, preparing to swing out over the river for the first time. The rope creaked against the tree branch as she pumped higher and higher, and she wondered if it might be so rotten after all these years that it would break from the strain. She decided that she didn't care. Even if it snapped off while she was in midair and she tumbled to the ground and broke every bone in her body, she couldn't possibly feel any more pain than she already did.

At first Bebe clenched her eyes tightly shut, afraid to look down at the river as the swing carried her out over it. But the July day was so hot, her smoldering anger so intense, that without thinking she abruptly released the rope and dropped through the air into the river.

Bebe realized her mistake the moment her body plunged beneath the surface. She couldn't swim! Her skin tingled all over from the water's cruel slap, and she felt as if she had awakened for the first time in her life. She opened her eyes beneath the murky river and feared she was about to die— and she didn't want to die.

Somehow, she rose to the surface, coughing and sputtering for air. The shore looked a long way off. Bebe had just enough time to draw a quick breath before the water washed over her head and pulled her under again. The current gripped her as if it were a living thing, and she struggled against it with all her might, flailing and kicking as she tried to fight her way to the top for another gulp of air. Each time her head emerged, she heard birds singing and cattle lowing in the distance. Each time she went under, the growling river muffled the sounds as it tried to hold her down and pin her beneath the surface.

Bebe knew there was no one to save her. If she

yielded to the current and allowed it to carry her downstream, she would die. If she wanted to survive, she would have to fight to stay afloat, then fight her way to the riverbank. Bebe made up her mind to fight.

Franklin's heavy work boots felt like rocks tied to her ankles, so she kicked them off, then slipped the straps of his overalls from her shoulders and wiggled out of them. Freed from her cumbersome clothing, she bobbed above the surface again, long enough to drag more air into her lungs, long enough to catch a glimpse of the distant shore. Then she went under.

Bebe fought with all her might until her limbs felt leaden with fatigue. Her stomach ached from swallowing gallons of water. She could feel the current carrying her downstream, but at the same time her efforts were gradually moving her closer to shore. After what seemed like hours, Bebe's feet touched the rocky bottom. She could stand. She struggled upright, sharp stones jabbing her feet, and walked toward the shore as the river tried to drag her under one last time. At last she flopped down on dry land, collapsing with relief. She gazed up at the blue sky and white clouds and realized that in all of her struggles, it had never occurred to her to pray.

Bebe walked through the kitchen door a while later, still dripping wet, wearing only her socks, pantaloons and calico blouse.

"Beatrice, what happened to you?" Hannah said when she saw her. "Where are your clothes?"

"I jumped off the boys' swing into the river."

Hannah stared at her.

"I can't go on much longer, Mama. I hate this ugly war. Why can't things be the way they were three years ago?"

Hannah sighed and drew Bebe into her arms, even though the water from Bebe's clothing soaked through to hers. "Never forget, Beatrice, that the greater goal is to win freedom for the slaves. That's what we've been praying for and working for all this time. That's what Joseph gave his life for. If we ask the Lord to give us love and compassion for those poor souls, then we'll be willing to make any sacrifice."

"But Joseph is gone and . . . and I don't want to lose the other boys, too. When is this war going to end?"

"Do you want to know the secret of contentment, Beatrice?" Hannah released her and stepped back to hold Bebe's water-shriveled hands in her own. A damp spot now darkened the front of Hannah's apron. "We need to live each day as if it was a gift. God gives us that gift every morning when the sun rises, like the tickets they give out when you ride on the train."

"I've never been on a train," Bebe said, sulking.

"That ticket is only good for today. Yesterday is gone and that ticket is used up. We don't have a ticket for tomorrow because life has no guarantees.

Each day is a gift. When the sun comes up, we need to ask the Lord, 'What would you like me to do for you today?' That's how you'll find contentment."

"But . . . didn't you always say that we should have a plan so we'd know exactly where we're headed? You said we wouldn't get anywhere in life without a map."

"That's true. But we need to let God draw the map for us, then follow it in faith."

Bebe stared at the floor. She knew that her feeble faith fell far short of her mother's. "I can't do that," she mumbled.

"You're not willing to give your life to Him each day?"

Bebe thought of how she had nearly drowned and how she had saved herself. She shook her head. "If this is what He's going to do with my life . . . then I guess not."

She endured another summer, another harvest—this time without Franklin's help. Another winter arrived, and she learned to split wood and shovel snow. In the spring she watched four new baby calves come into the world and helped her father plant corn and cut hay. And just when it seemed as though the war would never end, it did.

"I wish I could dress up in boys' clothes like you did," I said when Grandma Bebe finished her story. The envelopes were all licked, my water glass was empty, and my tongue felt as raspy as a cat's.

Grandma shook her head. "No, don't wish for that. Those heavy old boots and baggy overalls were nearly the death of me." She tilted her head to one side as she studied me. I loved the way my grandmother looked at me, as if I were a treasure chest filled with glittering gold and precious jewels.

"Harriet, don't give your mother a hard time about the party dress. Let her go ahead and decorate the outside of you. She can't change what's on the inside, you know—and that's the most important part of you. Only God can change you on the inside."

"How does He do that?"

"Sometimes through suffering," she said quietly. Her gaze got all soft and blurry-eyed as she continued to look at me. "I didn't know during those war years that God was preparing me for the future, but He was. He knew that I would need to be strong in order to get through what lay ahead."

"Why, Grandma? What happened?"

I wanted to hear the rest of the story, but Grandma shook her head. "That's a tale for another day." She stood and smoothed the wrinkles from her skirt. "Thanks for your help, dear, but you'd better run along home. And make sure you enjoy that tea party, you hear?"

I made a face. "You can lead a horse to water," I grumbled, "but you can't make him drink."

Grandma's laughter followed me out the door.

CHAPTER
7

My jailhouse breakfast, when it finally arrived, was a terrible disappointment. It consisted of lumpy oatmeal and dry toast. The coffee tasted as though it had been sitting on the back of the stove for the past month, boiling continuously. None of the meal was palatable, so I set the tray on the floor and leaned against the brick wall again to do some more thinking. When you have nothing else to do except think, a lot of strange memories come to mind. One of them featured Grandma Bebe's brother, Franklin.

I had heard stories about him over the years, but I finally met him in person on Decoration Day in 1911, when I was eleven years old. Grandma had purchased her own car by then, much to my mother's dismay. "There's no telling how much trouble she'll get into now that she can drive her own car," my mother said, so she asked me to tag along and keep Grandma out of mischief. Little did Mother know that I was an eager partner in Grandma's mischief, and that I had no intention of keeping her out of it. In fact, Grandma was secretly teaching me how to drive on the dirt roads outside of town now that my legs were long enough to reach the pedals. I couldn't wait for another driving lesson that day.

We left early in the morning and traveled out of town, enjoying the drive through the rolling farmland, admiring the misty forests of the Appalachian Mountains in the distance. Grandma let me slide behind the wheel and practice driving for a few miles as soon as we reached the countryside. She didn't say where we were going, but I hoped she was taking me to one of her temperance rallies and that we'd be pelted with eggs and spoiled tomatoes. Grandma had shown me a story in the newspaper about a saloon owner who had captured several skunks and set them loose on a group of temperance women who were protesting outside his saloon. Since I was all prepared for some excitement, I was a little disappointed when Grandma motored into a village I'd never visited before and parked her car in a cemetery, of all places.

"What are we doing here?" I asked as we removed our driving gloves and dusters and tossed them onto the seat. "Did someone die?"

"Of course, Harriet—*thousands* of people died!" She spread her hands and stared at me in exasperation as if her reply should make perfect sense. "It's Decoration Day!"

"Oh . . ." I still didn't understand, but she linked arms with me and towed me over to a raggedy group of ancient soldiers who were milling around a Civil War monument. They were all holding miniature American flags and waiting for the ceremony to begin. I had seen Grand Army of the Republic veterans before, marching in Fourth of July parades in our hometown, but I had never gotten close enough to see how tattered and moth-eaten their uniforms were after forty-six years. Or how ill-fitting. The passing years were unkind to people's bodies, expanding them in some places, contracting them in others. I gazed around at these somber men, with their aged faces and gray hair, and I tried to imagine them as young men, their uniforms new, their bodies fit and hearty as they bravely marched off to fight a war that would change them forever. I saw a well-deserved pride in their tired expressions, an awareness that they had courageously stepped forward when their country needed them. They had a right to be proud of their accomplishments.

Grandma halted beside a tall, gaunt soldier who looked like the grim reaper in an army uniform. "Harriet, I'd like you to meet my brother, Franklin."

I thought she was joking. The tops of our heads barely reached to his armpits. He didn't resemble Grandma Bebe in the least, and his startling white hair made him look old enough to be her father. But Franklin turned to her with a wide, warm smile that took twenty years off his age.

"Hey, good to see you, Bebe." He wrapped his arm around her neck and pulled her close, kissing the top of her head.

"Franklin, this is Harriet—the granddaughter I've told you so much about."

"Pleased to meet you," I said as we appraised each other. I wondered what she had been saying about me.

"She looks just like you, Bebe, when you were her age."

"Stop it, Franklin. You'll give the girl nightmares." He laughed, and the sound reminded me of a car engine trying to turn over and start.

The ceremony, once it finally began, would have been humorous if it hadn't been so poignant. The pompous officials took turns posing for the news photographer, sucking in their paunches and gripping their lapels, their chins and jowls thrust forward. The mayor sputtered and flapped and tried not to curse after stepping backward into a mud puddle. He stammered his way through a flowery, incomprehensible speech. The next official accidentally dropped the memorial wreath facedown in the same mud puddle that the mayor had stepped in, and half of the flowers fell out of it. When he finally propped up the wreath on the metal stand, it looked as bedraggled and woebegone as the veterans.

The bugler, who looked old enough to have fought in the Revolution, played a barely recognizable rendition of taps. Uncle Franklin closed his eyes while the commander of the local GAR post spoke about sacrifice and duty and freedom, and I wondered if he was dozing or reminiscing. I saw several old veterans wipe their eyes.

After the minister pronounced the benediction, my uncle limped around the cemetery with the other old men, placing flags and GAR stars on various graves. He used an ebony cane with a silver handle, and moved very stiffly, lurching across the lumpy ground as if it pained him to move. The final grave, where he and Grandma lingered the longest, belonged to their brother Joseph.

"What a pity," Grandma murmured.

"Joe deserved better," Franklin sighed. I subtracted the dates on the grave marker while I waited. My great-uncle Joseph had died at the age of twenty—only two years older than my sister Alice was at that time.

Afterward, Grandma and I drove across town to a leafy park, following Uncle Franklin and the other veterans. A Grand Army of the Republic reunion picnic was getting under way, and my great-uncle's spirits brightened considerably as he beckoned to us. "Come on over here, ladies. Sadie and I saved you a place at our table."

Grandma halted, her arms crossed like an Indian chief. "Now, Franklin. There aren't going to be any alcoholic beverages at this shindig, are there?"

"No, ma'am," he said with a grin. "Alcohol is strictly prohibited on village property—thanks to you and the other temperance gals." I didn't tell Grandma, but I saw some of the old soldiers—

including Uncle Franklin—taking furtive sips from silver pocket flasks. The laughter grew louder as the afternoon progressed, the veterans' steps more tentative as if the ground had begun to move like ocean waves.

We sat at wooden picnic tables beneath tall pine trees, and the warm air that blew over us was scented with pine and woodsmoke. The ladies unpacked their picnic baskets and the feast began as everyone shared their bounty with one another. Uncle Franklin's wife, Sadie, brought out pickles and potato salad and cold fried chicken. Someone sliced into a watermelon, and Grandma and I had one of our spitting contests to see who could make the seeds go the farthest. I never have been able to beat her.

"How did you learn to spit so good?" I asked.

"As a matter of fact, Franklin taught me."

He turned around when he heard his name. "What'd you say?"

She held out a slice of watermelon. "Care to give it a try, Franklin? I'll bet I can still beat you."

He laughed and lifted his hands in surrender. "Aw, you're so full of spit and vinegar, Bebe, nobody can beat you."

Late in the afternoon, Uncle Franklin turned to me and pinched my cheek. "Say, there aren't any woodpeckers hiding around here, are there?" he asked.

"Um . . . I don't know . . ."

"Listen, Harriet, I'll pay you two bits if you keep an eye out for them. They might come looking for me, you know."

"Woodpeckers? Are you pulling my leg, Uncle Franklin?"

"No, no!" His laugh sounded more like a cough. "They're not after your leg, they're after mine." He rapped his cane against his calf and it sounded like he had thumped it against the table leg. I thought it was a trick, but he grinned and pulled up his pant leg and thumped it again. "It's made of wood, don't you see?"

I turned to my grandmother for confirmation, and she nodded. "If it weren't for your uncle Franklin, you wouldn't be here, Harriet."

"You mean at the picnic?"

"No, here in this world! I'm talking about the fact that you're alive, dear. It's all thanks to Franklin and his wooden leg."

I had no idea what she meant, and her astounding statement raised a lot of questions in my overactive imagination. But someone announced that the ice cream was ready, and I was swept away in the melee of adults, talking and laughing and enjoying the reunion. Grandma didn't have a chance to explain how Uncle Franklin and his wooden leg were responsible for my existence until the day ended and we were driving home in the car.

"Why did you say that if it weren't for Uncle Franklin, I wouldn't be here?" I asked with a yawn. "And how did his leg get turned into wood?"

"A minie ball shattered it just below the knee, and the army doctors had to cut it off with a hacksaw."

Grandma's grisly description should have repulsed me, but it didn't. I sat up straight, fascinated. "What's a minie ball?"

"It's like a bullet—only bigger." She made a circle the size of a nickel with her thumb and forefinger. "Once a minie ball rips through flesh and bone, there's no saving that limb. It happened on April 2, 1865, during the Union breakthrough into Petersburg. By the time we received word that Franklin had been wounded, the war was over. General Lee had surrendered at Appomattox Courthouse on April ninth, one week after that fateful battle. A few days later, President Lincoln was dead."

"My goodness," I murmured. I never paid much attention during history lessons, but this was my great-uncle we were talking about, a man I'd just met.

Grandma gazed at the road ahead of us as she drove, her chin level with the top of the steering wheel. "For years I wondered why God couldn't manage to keep Franklin safe for seven more days—seven days, Harriet! Especially after everything else my brothers had endured during the war."

"Did God ever give you a reason?" I remembered some of Grandma's other stories, such as the time God had kept her safe while she helped the slaves escape.

"Well, if God did have a reason, He never breathed a word of it to me." She concentrated on her driving for a moment, changing gears as the car chugged uphill. A moment later we flew over the summit and started down again, leaving my stomach on the floorboards. "I've composed a long list of questions to ask God when I arrive in heaven," Grandma continued. "It's nearly as long as a book, by now—and the mystery of Franklin's leg is high on that list."

Before I had a chance to remind her of my original question, she said, "And another thing I would very much like to ask is why I never grew into a properly proportioned woman. Look at me—I'm still built like a ten-year-old boy!"

I rolled my eyes at her oft-said words. "You look fine to me, Grandma."

"No offense, dear, but you're hardly one to judge. You're built like a ten-year-old boy, yourself—in case you haven't noticed."

"Good! I don't ever want to look like a woman! Or be one. Ever since Alice got all 'girly,' she's been impossible to live with. That's why I wanted to come with you today. It's sickening the way her beaux gather around on our front porch every night like flies around a peach pie."

"Well, whether you want to become a woman or not is beside the point. Believe me, it will happen. Although if that war had gone on much longer, I might have completely forgotten that I'd been born a girl. My mother reminded me, just in time when—"

"Wait a minute, Grandma. You still haven't explained how Uncle Franklin was responsible for my existence."

"But that's exactly what I'm about to tell you, Harriet, if you'd just stop interrupting and listen. . . ."

The war ended for Bebe on the day that James and William arrived home. From then on, she never had to do their farm chores again. She had been helping her father smear axle grease on the wagon wheels when she looked up and saw her brothers hiking up the road toward home. She wiped her hands on an empty burlap sack and ran toward them, her oversized boots kicking up little clouds of dust. Her brothers laughed when they saw her.

"I thought we left a little sister behind," William exclaimed. "Where did this scruffy fellow come from?"

"And what happened to little Bebe?" James asked.

Indeed, what had happened? The war had not only changed her, but James and William, as well. The lanky, teasing boys who had marched away four years earlier were grown men now with creased faces and wooly beards. They had arrived unexpectedly, just before lunchtime, and Hannah quickly conscripted Bebe to help out in the kitchen.

"Run upstairs and change into clean clothes, Beatrice. I'm going to prepare a proper feast for my boys, and I'll need your help."

Bebe had never been as close to her older brothers as she was to Franklin, so she eagerly awaited his homecoming, too. The army had sent a letter with the news that he'd been wounded, then another one that said he was convalescing in a hospital in Philadelphia. As the weeks passed with still no sign of him, Bebe began to worry. Franklin wasn't answering anyone's letters. Hannah finally wrote directly to the hospital administrator for news.

"I'm sorry to say that your son Franklin's condition is showing no improvement," one of the nurses wrote in reply. *"He is very depressed about losing his leg and has very little appetite. As a result, he has become quite frail and his wound isn't healing properly. Anything you could do to cheer him would help considerably."*

"I've been praying about Franklin's condition," Hannah told Bebe a few days later, "and I believe God has told me what to do. Franklin needs a loved one to take care of him, and you are the best person to do that. I want you to visit him in

Philadelphia and help him get well. Bring him home to us again."

"You want me to travel all that way? All alone? It's more than one hundred miles from here."

"You won't be alone. God will be with you."

Bebe bit her lip to avoid voicing her skepticism about having God for a traveling companion. It would only shock her mother. "What am I supposed to do once I get there?"

"Cheer Franklin up, remind him of home, make him laugh."

"Why can't you go, Mama?"

"Someone has to cook for your father and the boys. Besides, I thought you would enjoy a break from the farm."

"I would, but . . ." Bebe had never gone anywhere alone in her life.

On their next trip to town for market day, Hannah made all of the arrangements. Pastor Webster's wife often visited her sister in Philadelphia, and she agreed to let Bebe travel there with her by train. Bebe would stay with Mrs. Webster's sister and brother-in-law, the Yeagers, while she was there.

When everything was arranged, Hannah took Bebe to Harrison's General Store and picked out lace and yard goods and cotton thread. "We're going to sew new under-sleeves for your Sunday dress," Hannah explained, "and let out the bodice to accommodate your developing bosom."

"Shh! Mother!" Bebe whispered in embarrassment. But it was true. Her womanly figure finally had begun to sprout.

"If we add a new ruffle on the skirt, it will cover up the worn hemline," Hannah continued. "And I do believe you've grown an inch or two since we sewed that dress."

Their final purchase was a new pair of shoes, which were the most uncomfortable things Bebe had ever worn, especially after traipsing around in her brothers' old boots for the past year.

"I don't understand all the fuss and bother with new clothes and shoes," Bebe said that evening. She stood on a milking stool, trying to be patient while Hannah pinned up her hem. The full skirt felt bulky after wearing trousers for the past year, but thank goodness hoops had gone out of style. "What difference does it make what I look like? Franklin won't care. He won't even notice."

Hannah removed the pins from her mouth and stuck them in a pincushion. "Listen, Beatrice. Franklin and the other boys need to see something beautiful again and be reminded of the life that's waiting for them back home. They've witnessed too much horror these past few years."

"But I can't—"

"You did the farm work, now you can do this."

Bebe wasn't convinced.

On the night before Bebe left for Philadelphia, her mother made her take a bath. Bebe tried to back out of the door when she saw Hannah preparing the tub. "You don't need to bother with that, Mama, I can wash off in the river—"

"Oh no, you don't." Hannah snagged Bebe's arm and pulled her back into the room. "You need a proper bath in warm water. And you need to wash your hair. You can't travel to Philadelphia with your hair in braids and smelling like manure and hay. You're a young woman now, and a very pretty one. I'll put some rose water in the tub."

"Rose water!" Bebe wrinkled her nose. "What for?"

"So that you'll smell nice."

Hannah scrubbed so hard Bebe thought all of her skin would come off. Her mother inspected her from head to toe as she helped her dry off. "We have to do something about the dirt beneath your fingernails."

Bebe stared at her hands. They hadn't come clean. "I think the dirt has been there since the Rebels fired on Fort Sumter."

"Well, I have a pair of crocheted gloves you can borrow."

Hannah trimmed off the scraggly ends of Bebe's hair and brushed it until it shone. It was long and dark and thick, with a natural wave in it. Hannah taught her how to part it down the middle and sweep it up on her head, securing it with the new hairpins and fancy tortoiseshell combs they had purchased in town.

Early the next morning, Bebe put on her newly remade dress, fixed her hair, and packed her clothes and toiletries in a carpetbag. Hannah fetched the mirror that Henry and the boys used for shaving and held it up in front of her. "Look at yourself, Beatrice."

She didn't recognize the person she saw in the mirror. She had transformed into a woman—at least on the outside—with a slender waist and a pretty face and thick, luxurious hair. If only she felt like a woman on the inside, too.

"You look beautiful," Hannah murmured.

"I look so . . . different."

"Remember how life changed when the war started and the boys left? And how it changed again when Franklin had to leave? Life is like that, Beatrice—always changing, always flowing forward like a stream. Things never stay the same. And we have to move on and change, too."

Bebe glanced around at her familiar bedroom, then at her image in the mirror again. "What if I don't want things to change?"

"You can't fight against the current. You're no longer a little girl, Beatrice, you're a grown woman. I married your father when I was just a little older than you are. And that's what's next for you—marriage and a home of your own."

She couldn't imagine it. "But I don't want to leave home."

"Nevertheless, you need to trust God and be prepared for wherever the river of life will take you next."

Bebe clutched her carpetbag and a basket of homemade baked goods for Franklin. She felt a mixture of excitement and fear as she began her journey and realized, as she hugged Hannah good-bye, that she had never been separated from her mother before. Panic made it difficult to breathe.

"Mama, I—"

"I'm counting on you to help Franklin get well."

"But I can't…"

"With God, all things are possible."

Bebe nodded and struggled to control her tears. She had longed to do something courageous and meaningful throughout the war, so maybe this was her opportunity. She would be brave for Franklin's sake.

"Don't forget to attend to your appearance, dear. Look in a mirror once in a while and fix your hair. And keep your dress tidy."

Bebe made a face. "It still doesn't feel right to wear a dress all day."

"I know. But you look lovely in one. Don't be surprised if men start looking at you and tipping their hats. They take notice of pretty girls."

Bebe had never ridden on a train before, and when the monstrous thing finally arrived, rumbling into the station with its whistle shrieking, belching smoke and cinders, she walked toward it on trembling legs.

"Ready?" Reverend Webster asked as he prepared to help her climb aboard. The locomotive hissed at her like an angry barn cat. Bebe nodded. The minister had recently preached on Jesus' command to "fear not," so she was embarrassed to admit her fear.

The train chugged out of the station like an old man wheezing for air, but once it built up speed it traveled so fast Bebe feared it would fly right off the narrow rails. Scenery whipped past her window at a frantic rate. Any minute now, her heart would simply hammer itself to death. Surely there was a less frightening way to travel. She was wondering how long it would take her and Franklin to walk home from Philadelphia, when she remembered his missing leg.

They traveled south to Stroudsburg, then to Allentown, where they changed trains. Late that afternoon the view of Pennsylvania farmland gave way to jumbled buildings and smoking factories as the train neared Philadelphia. The city was a huge, bustling place bursting with people, and more horses and carriages than Bebe had ever imagined. She inched closer to Mrs. Webster, feeling lost and out of place.

Mrs. Yeager met them at the train station and led them to her waiting carriage.

Everywhere Bebe looked she saw soldiers in blue uniforms, and she searched their faces as if expecting one of them to be Franklin. She longed for the peace and quiet of her farm and hoped to convince Franklin to come home with her on the very next train so she wouldn't have to spend a single night in this frightening city.

"Would you like to get settled at home, first?" Mrs. Yeager asked. "Maybe freshen up from your trip?"

Bebe had no idea what "freshen up" meant or how she would go about it. "I'd rather go to the hospital and see my brother, if you don't mind."

"Of course," Mrs. Yeager said. "You must be anxious to see him. The hospital isn't far." And it wasn't. The carriage halted in front of a large red-brick building before Bebe had time to figure out what to say to Franklin.

"I'll have my driver come back for you in an hour. Will that be enough time?" Mrs. Yeager asked.

"Yes. Thank you." Bebe climbed from the carriage and walked toward the hospital's entrance, where a group of men stood smoking cigarettes. Every one of them had an arm or a hand or a leg that ended abruptly in a bandaged stump. Bebe quickly turned away.

She couldn't do this. The sight of those mangled, wounded men—the sight of her own brother Franklin without his leg—was too awful to contemplate. She had tried not to imagine what his missing limb would look like as she'd planned her trip, and now she couldn't face him. How could she cheer him up when even these strangers' wounds horrified her?

She hurried toward the street, waving her arms and calling to the departing carriage, "Wait! Come back!" But it drove away. Bebe could either stand here on the curb in the hot sun for an hour, or go inside the hospital. She drew a deep breath and turned back toward the entrance. The gathered men had stopped talking. They were watching her. She tried to speak but nothing came out. Then one of them snatched off his hat and gave a little bow.

"Good afternoon, miss." The rest of the men quickly did the same.

"Howdy, miss."

"Ain't you a beautiful sight?"

"Need help with that basket?"

They broke into wide grins as they looked her up and down. Bebe gripped the basket handle. "No, thank you." Her cheeks burned.

One of the men held the door open for her and she scurried inside. A nurse in a white uniform greeted her. "May I help you?"

Bebe's words came out like questions. "I-I'm Beatrice Monroe? I'm here to see my brother? Franklin Monroe?"

"Oh yes. He'll be so glad you've come, Miss Monroe. Follow me, please."

Bebe stared at the floor as she followed the nurse into a long, narrow room. It smelled of iodine and illness. Rows of beds lined the walls on both sides, and Bebe glimpsed white sheets and white faces and a blue uniform or two. She had the uncomfortable feeling that the men in the beds were watching her. Except for the occasional cough, it seemed unnaturally quiet. Halfway down the length of the room, the nurse halted at the foot of a bed.

"You have a visitor, Mr. Monroe."

Bebe never would have recognized her brother if the nurse hadn't led her to him. The sturdy, carefree boy who had marched away a year ago had become a withered old man with a gray face and a shrunken body. The dazed look in his eyes reminded her of the stuffed deer head that hung above the door in Harrison's General Store. Thankfully, a sheet covered Franklin's legs. She smiled as best she could and walked to his side, resting her hand on his arm.

"Hello, Franklin."

He didn't seem to recognize her either, at first. Then his eyes filled with tears. "Bebe? Is it really you?"

She nodded and set the basket down on the floor so she could embrace him. The last time she had hugged her brother was before he'd marched away, and he had nearly crushed her in his arms. Now she was the stronger of the two. She clung to his frail body and asked God to forgive her for complaining about doing farm work.

When they finally pulled apart, Franklin turned his face away to wipe his eyes, embarrassed by his tears. Bebe let hers flow. They were the first tears in four years that she hadn't shed in self-pity or exhaustion. She kissed his whiskered cheek.

"What are you doing here, Bebe? How'd you get here?"

"I came on the train. Mama sent you some food." She lifted the basket and set it on the bed beside him. "She sent me to take care of you until you're well enough to come home."

"I don't think I'll be coming home—unless you mean home to heaven."

His words made her stomach roll over. He looked as though he was knocking on the pearly gates already and St. Peter was about to open them.

"Of course that's not what I mean! You're coming home to the farm, Franklin. I'm tired of doing all your chores."

He shook his head. "I'm worthless now. They should have let me die."

"Don't say that!" Bebe shoved his bony shoulder. "Losing Joseph was bad enough."

"He's better off . . ."

"Stop it, Franklin. Mama grieved something awful for Joseph. Don't you dare let her lose you, too." His self-pity reminded her of her own these past few years. She drew a breath and started again. "James and William came home a few weeks ago. It's wonderful to have them back. Mama is so happy."

"You left her there all alone? Who's helping her in the kitchen?"

"She insisted that I come. She was so glad to have the boys back that she's been cooking enough food for an army. She sent some for you, too."

He shook his head and closed his eyes. "Go away."

Bebe had never felt ill at ease with Franklin before, but she did now. She had no idea what to say to him or how to cheer him up. She was searching for ideas when another patient limped over, leaning on an ebony cane with an engraved silver handle. The bed squeaked when he sat down on the end of it.

"Hey, Franklin. You never told me you had a girlfriend."

Franklin slowly opened his eyes. "She's not my girlfriend; she's my kid sister, Bebe."

"You never told me your sister was beautiful."

"She was just a kid when I left."

"Well, she isn't a kid anymore. A rose would wither in despair if forced to compete with such beauty and grace."

Bebe glanced around, wondering who the man was referring to. When she realized that he meant her, her heart began to pound the same way it had when the enormous locomotive had rumbled into the station. She had no idea why.

"I'm very pleased to make your acquaintance, Miss Monroe," he continued. "It's not every day that I have the good fortune to meet such a lovely young woman. My name is Horatio Garner, by the way."

Mr. Garner had hair the color of mown hay and the palest blue eyes Bebe had ever seen. His mustache and beard were sprinkled with red as if he'd dusted his face with copper shavings instead of talcum powder. Something about the tilt of his chin and the confident, laughing way that he spoke made him seem very self-assured. The simple folk back home would call him a "dandy," with his fancy cane and flowery words, but Bebe was intrigued.

"Your brother and I have had the good fortune to march side by side since the day we reported for duty, isn't that right, Franklin? He used to read your lovely letters out loud to me—so often, in fact, that I feel I already know you. But he never breathed a word about your matchless charms. How old are you, Miss Monroe, if you don't mind my asking? I'm twenty-two, by the way."

Bebe couldn't speak. She wished she had a fan she could unfurl to cool her burning cheeks. The changes Mama had talked about seemed to be coming much too fast, as if the river of life was at flood stage. She'd barely had time to adjust to being a woman, much less learn how to respond to a handsome man's advances.

"Are you always this quiet?" Mr. Garner asked when she didn't reply.

Franklin nudged her. "Answer the man, Bebe. Where's your manners?"

"I-I haven't needed any manners for the last four years. The cows and chickens didn't care about them, and there was no one else on our farm to impress." Mr. Garner laughed as if she'd said something very witty. "But to answer your question, I'm seventeen."

"How lovely. Seventeen . . . As fate would have it, your brother and I were wounded on the same day in the same battle—isn't that right, Franklin? Although I have to admit that the nature of his wounds was much more grievous than mine. The doctors have informed me that my foot has healed, and they have declared me well enough to return home, but I've been hesitant to leave Franklin this way. I'm worried about him, Miss Monroe. I've been trying to cheer him up, but I haven't been very successful. I'm pleased to see that you've arrived to help me. By the way, what did you bring in that basket, if I may be so bold as to ask?"

Bebe folded back the napkin, grateful to have something simple to talk about. "Um . . . there's some of Mama's sourdough bread—she baked it for Franklin this morning. And a jar of that rhubarb jam he always liked . . . and fry cakes. Would you like one?"

The hour passed quickly, with Mr. Garner doing most of the talking. He was a very cheerful fellow and quite interesting to listen to, but Franklin's glum expression never changed. Bebe felt like a failure. She would have to do better tomorrow.

"I need to go," she told Franklin when the hour was up, "but I'll be back in the morning. In the meantime, please eat some of this food so you'll get your strength back. Mama is expecting you to come home with me." She bent and kissed his forehead.

"Well, would you look at that?" Mr. Garner said.

Bebe glanced up. "Look at what, Mr. Garner?"

"I do believe that's the first smile I've seen on Franklin's face in a good long while. Your kiss is like sunshine melting away the frost."

Bebe stared at the floor, embarrassed by his flowery words. "Good-bye for now," she said. "It was nice meeting you, Mr. Garner."

"Wait." He stuck out his cane to block her path. "I won't let you leave until you promise to call me Horatio."

"Very well . . . Horatio. I'll be back tomorrow."

His grin could have lit up a root cellar. "I can hardly wait, fair Beatrice."

CHAPTER
8

Bebe took great care getting dressed and fixing her hair the following morning, hoping she would see Mr. Garner at the hospital when she visited Franklin. She had loved listening to the smooth, eloquent flow of Horatio's words—he had called her beautiful. But when she arrived, she was very disappointed to learn that he was no longer a patient.

"The doctors discharged him earlier this morning," Franklin told her. "He didn't lose his leg the way I did."

Bebe heard the bitterness in Franklin's tone and struggled for a way to cheer him. Nothing came to mind. "Listen," she finally said. "Mama sent me here to help you get well, and to be honest with you, I don't know how to do that. I thought about it all last night, and . . . and I think that the only person who can help you get well is yourself. You have to want to get better and come home, but for some reason you've given up."

He flung back the sheet to expose the stump of his leg. "Look at me, Bebe! Would you want to live with this?"

The sight shocked her, and she averted her gaze. When she faced him again, the pain she saw in Franklin's eyes made her angry with herself for flinching.

"I can't stand to see people turn away from me like you just did. Or even worse, to look at me with pity."

"Franklin, I'm sorry—"

"Why? It's not your fault that you couldn't stand the sight of me. I'm not a whole person anymore, Bebe. There's part of me missing . . . and I don't want to live this way." He pulled the sheet over his leg to hide it, but Bebe yanked off the cover again.

"Part of you is missing, yes. But back home, *all* of you is missing. We feel that loss the same way you feel this one. Joseph is gone, and it's horrible to see his empty chair at the table and his empty bed upstairs. Losing you would be even worse for me. You're not just my brother, you're my friend." She saw his jaw quiver as he struggled with his emotions. "I missed you so much after you left home, Franklin, and not just because I had to do all of your work. If you died I would miss you forever. Yes, they cut off your leg—but it will heal if you let it. Don't cut yourself out of my life. That wound will never heal."

"Don't you get it, Bebe? I'm useless this way. How can I work on the farm?"

"We'll figure something out. Remember how useless I was with the chores at first? But we made adjustments for the fact that I was smaller and weaker, and eventually things got done. You can adjust, too, Franklin—if not to farm work, then you'll find something else to do. Your family doesn't love you for the work you do, but because you're our brother. You mean so much to us. I don't know how else to say it, but I love you and I want you to come home!"

She bent to embrace him and felt his weaker hug in return. At last she pulled away. They both wiped away tears.

"Listen, I'm going to get you well enough to come home if it's the last thing I do." She set the basket of food on his bed and began rummaging through it. "Mama made you some apple turnovers, and I want you to eat one right now!"

"Better do what the pretty little lady says, Franklin. I think she means business."

Bebe looked up, surprised to see Horatio Garner limping toward them, leaning on his cane. "What are you doing here? I thought you went home, Mr. Garner." She saw the wry, admonishing smile on his face and quickly corrected herself. "I-I mean Horatio."

He grinned. "Ah, how sweet my name sounds when it flows from such sweet lips. But to answer your question, Miss Monroe, I've decided not to go home until Franklin does. We started out in this war together, we were wounded together, and it's only fitting that we leave here together. And so I pledge to partner with you, fair lady, for as long as it takes. I place myself at your service." He ended with a bow and a little flourish that made Bebe laugh.

She had never met anyone like Horatio, and she wanted to know all about him. He obliged by freely talking about himself, filling the long hours at Franklin's bedside by telling stories. Horatio described the modestly sized town of Roseton where he'd grown up, not far from the state capital of Harrisburg. He talked about the home he'd shared with his parents and his staff of servants, and the leather factory his family owned. He told tales of the two years he'd attended Dickinson College in Carlisle, Pennsylvania—and how a draft notice had ended his education.

"Why didn't your father pay the three hundred dollars to hire a substitute?" Bebe asked.

He stared at his feet as if suddenly bashful. "It was his wish to do so—but it wasn't mine. I felt it was my duty to serve my country."

By the end of the week, Bebe was smitten with Horatio Garner. She hurried through breakfast every day, impatient to get to the hospital to see him. Mrs. Webster stopped her with an invitation one morning as Bebe was about to leave the house.

"Beatrice, it must be tiresome to spend all day at the hospital. My sister and I are planning to attend a very interesting anti-slavery meeting this afternoon, and we would love to have you join us. We could pick you up at the hospital on our way."

"Um . . . Thank you very much, but I think I should stay with Franklin. I do believe he is making some progress."

"He wouldn't mind if you were to come with us, would he? Just for one hour? I believe the lecture would be of great interest to a young woman like you."

Bebe thought that nothing in the world could be more interesting than listening to Horatio Garner, but she didn't say so out loud. "Thank you, Mrs.

Webster, but my mother is counting on me to attend to my brother."

Bebe arrived at the hospital before Horatio did and couldn't help glancing at the door while she waited, watching for him. As she cajoled Franklin into eating everything on his breakfast tray, she felt light-headed and a little breathless. She used to get this same shaky, stomach-reeling sensation when she was starved for food after working in the fields all day, only now she was starved for Horatio.

"Ah, good morning, my dear friends!" he finally called out in greeting. His warm smile made Bebe smile in return. "Franklin, you're looking hale and hearty today. I do believe your charming sister is better for your health than a hundred nurses."

Bebe loved the way Horatio's eyes would soften each time he looked at her—even though she knew it could be nothing more than sisterly affection. The differences between them were much too great for it to be anything else. She was the timid daughter of a simple farmer, he the gregarious son of a well-to-do factory owner.

But the biggest obstacle as far as Bebe was concerned was the fact that the woman Horatio had met was a fraud. He saw a cleaned up, dressed up, sweet-smelling version of her, while the real Bebe had only recently changed out of men's overalls and work boots and put away her manure shovel. The real Bebe still had dirt beneath her fingernails, hidden under a pair of scratchy crocheted gloves that she wished she could yank off and toss into the trash. Her own father kept mistaking her for a boy, yet Horatio thought she was the epitome of womanhood.

"I have never met a more selfless, caring woman," he told her. "Imagine, traveling all this way to help your brother with his convalescence. What a brave, devoted woman you are."

"Um . . . but you see, Mr. Garner, the truth is—"

"Say no more. I see that blush of modesty, and I am moved by your humility."

Indeed, she was a fraud.

It hadn't been her idea to come to Philadelphia to take care of Franklin. She hadn't been the least bit brave about it. And now that she was there, she had no idea how to nurture him or anyone else back to good health. The Beatrice that Horatio Garner saw was a creation of his own flowery imagination and her mother's frugal grooming. She would have told him the truth if he had asked—or if he had let her get a word in edgewise—but Horatio never stopped talking. And, oh, how she loved to hear him talk. His words sounded just like poetry.

Little by little, Bebe's feelings for Horatio Garner began to grow and bud and blossom until she was certain she resembled one of her father's apple trees in full, glorious bloom. And little by little, the food she'd brought from home, and the laughter she shared with Horatio and Franklin, coaxed life and health back into her brother. By the end of the second week, Franklin was eating like a farmer again, and the color had returned to his cheeks. Bebe and Horatio managed to convince him to take a few hobbling steps on a pair of crutches. When he could limp as far as the front door, Horatio boosted him into a hired carriage and the three of them toured Philadelphia. The carriage rides soon became daily ventures. Sitting close to Horatio gave Bebe the same dizzy, giddy feeling she'd had when soaring through the air on the swing. She tried to forget that they soon would have to go their separate ways, certain it would feel much like the shock of plunging into the river when she had let go of the rope.

All the while, Bebe's hostess continued to invite her to attend the anti-slavery meetings. "They have such wonderful speakers—you really should hear them, Beatrice." Bebe made excuses, but truthfully she didn't want to give up a single moment of time with her new friend.

It took a month for Franklin to regain his health, but at last he was strong enough to go home. Bebe knew it had very little to do with her influence and everything to do with Horatio Garner's. The day of Franklin's discharge was a bittersweet one. Bebe was elated for her brother, who had learned to maneuver quite well on his crutches, but devastated to have to say good-bye to Horatio. He drove them to the train station, making sure Franklin's bags were loaded on board and that the porters were well compensated. And just before saying farewell, he presented his ebony and silver cane to Franklin, holding it out to him like a medieval king bestowing a great honor on his knight.

"This is for you, my friend. I want you to keep it as a token to remember me by."

Franklin scowled. "I can't use that. I need two crutches to get around."

"Only for now, my good man, only for now. I've heard there is a doctor here in Philadelphia who can outfit you with a fine wooden leg when you're ready. By this time next year you'll be running relay races."

Franklin mumbled his thanks and gave the cane to Bebe to carry. Horatio turned to her next. "Before we part, may I ask a very special favor, Beatrice?"

"Of course."

"On the day you arrived, you graced your brother with a kiss, and it was like watching the sunshine melt the frost. Would you favor me with one farewell kiss before we part? It would mean so much to me . . . I don't know when I might meet another woman as beautiful and kind as you are."

"You must have a sweetheart back home. . . ."

"No, I have no one." He leaned toward her and pointed to his cheek. "Please?"

Bebe had never kissed anyone who wasn't a family member. Tears filled her eyes as she stood on tiptoes and briefly pressed her lips to Horatio's cheek. His ruddy beard felt soft, not scratchy as she had supposed. His warm, rich scent smelled like something she would eat for dessert.

"Thank you," he said softly. He took her hand in both of his and pressed it to his heart, then raised it to his lips. "Before you came to Philadelphia I had forgotten how sweet and good a woman smells, how soft her skin feels. Tenderness . . . gentleness . . . beauty . . . I've missed those things these long, dark months when I've been surrounded by death. But a woman is made for life. How beautiful that reminder is to me." He gave her captive hand a gentle squeeze and released it.

"Good-bye," she murmured. "I'll never forget you."

Horatio helped her and Franklin climb aboard, then waved to them from the platform. Bebe waved back, her heart aching. Horatio had filled her life with laughter and delight these past few weeks, and now she would never see him again. Their parting had been inevitable. She wasn't the vision of loveliness and gentility that he imagined her to be. The rose water that had provided her with the sweet fragrance he'd admired belonged to Bebe's mother. From now on, Bebe was much more likely to smell like the bacon that she fried for breakfast every morning rather than rose water. She leaned out the window, watching until the train station—and Horatio—disappeared from sight.

"Why are you crying?" Franklin asked when he saw her tears.

She quickly dabbed her eyes with her handkerchief and forced a smile. "I'm so happy that you're finally coming home, Franklin." It wasn't a lie.

Philadelphia had seemed like a strange, foreign place when Bebe had first arrived, but after being away from home for a month, the village of New Canaan now seemed like a foreign place to her, shabby and colorless after the glittery bustle of the city. Each day on the farm moved as sluggishly as mud as she settled back into her daily routine. For Bebe, the river of life had dwindled down to a trickle, and the most she could hope for was to cool her toes in its shallows. She wondered if her brothers felt as restless and bored as she did. After all, she'd spent only a month in Philadelphia and they had marched all over the country for the past few years, seeing new things and meeting new people. She remembered complaining to her mother about not liking change, but now she longed for it.

Then one Sunday morning Mrs. Webster stopped to speak with Bebe and her mother after church. "I have good news, ladies. Our local chapter of the Anti-Slavery Society has decided to hold meetings again. We have a speaker coming from Philadelphia on Wednesday evening, and I just know you'll be fascinated when you hear what she has to say. You remember one of our society's most outstanding proponents, Mrs. Lucretia Mott, don't you? Well, she's coming to speak to our organization, Hannah. Do you think you and Beatrice might attend?"

"We'll see," Hannah replied.

Bebe hated it when her mother said, "We'll see." It usually meant "no." Bebe remembered attending meetings before the war, and although they hadn't been very exciting, hiding the occasional slave in the attic had been. She couldn't imagine what work the society would do now that all the slaves were free, but she was curious—and more than a little bored. She decided that she would go, with or without her mother.

"I would like very much to go into town for a meeting on Wednesday evening," she told her father on the drive home. "May I please borrow the wagon?"

"Is it a prayer meeting?"

"No . . . it's for the Anti-Slavery Society."

The horses traveled a full quarter of a mile before Henry said, "Seems to me the abolition people got what they wanted, didn't they? Didn't Mr. Lincoln free the slaves?"

"Yes . . ."

"Then why are the abolitionists still meeting?"

"I don't know, Papa. I guess there must be other things they would like to accomplish. May I please go and find out?"

Her father began shaking his head, his expression already warning her that he was about to say no. Surprisingly, Hannah intervened.

"Let her go, Henry . . . please."

He drove all the way home in silence. He remained silent on the subject throughout the afternoon and into the evening hours. Bebe didn't know how her mother could be so patient with such a taciturn man. She thought of Horatio Garner—as she had every day since leaving Philadelphia—and wished he were there to fill the silences in her life with his ever-flowing words.

As Henry rose from his customary chair in the parlor at bedtime, he turned to Bebe and said, "You may go, but you'll have to take care of the horse and wagon yourself." She would have hugged him, but her father never had cared much for affectionate displays.

Bebe rushed through her chores on Wednesday evening, then hitched one of the horses to the wagon for the long, dusty drive into town. Only a handful of women had gathered at the church for the meeting, and Bebe was the youngest. Several of them took out their knitting as they sat in a circle, waiting to hear what Mrs. Webster and her guest had to say.

"Like all of you, I thought our work for the society was finished," Mrs. Webster began. "I'm sure you recall the many meetings we held before the war, and all the prayers we offered up to heaven in order to end slavery here in America.

The Scriptures say, 'The effectual fervent prayer of a righteous man availeth much.' And I do believe that the same can be said about the fervent prayers of women. We all thank God that He heard our prayers and freed the slaves. But while visiting with my sister in Philadelphia recently, I became aware that there is still more work to be done. Ladies, I would like to introduce our special guest this evening, Mrs. Lucretia Mott, who is going to explain what our next task must be."

Mrs. Mott looked like a peacock among hens in her fashionable city clothes. She wore her hair coiled in an elaborate knot that Bebe wished she could copy. Her alert, observant expression told Bebe she was very intelligent, yet she seemed to have the same kind, gentle nature that Bebe always admired in her mother, Hannah. Mrs. Mott waved away the spattering of applause and remained seated as she began to speak.

"It's clear that women like us, united for a heavenly cause, can accomplish great things. Let the men shoot it out on the battlefield or argue politics; women fight best on their knees.

"Our United States Constitution has now been amended to grant Negro slaves their freedom, which is what we've been praying for. Soon another amendment will grant civil rights to those former slaves, but only to the men. That means that half of the population of America—its women—are still denied the basic rights of our Constitution.

Ladies, this simply isn't fair. Shouldn't the women who worked so hard on behalf of the slaves be accorded the same civil rights that they now will enjoy?"

Bebe glanced around at the others as Mrs. Mott paused and noticed that the ladies had stopped knitting. Everyone gazed intently at her, waiting to hear more.

"We were the force who, through our prayers and hard work, won freedom for them. We are all educated, literate women, while the vast majority of Negroes are illiterate. Yet those uneducated men will now be allowed to vote while we will be denied. Is it fair, I ask, that those of us who've worked so hard to see the Negroes raised to a position of equality—and Negro men have been so raised—is it fair that the very women who've helped raise them are still considered inferior?"

Bebe could barely sit still. She wanted to leap up and shout, "No! It isn't fair!" Mrs. Mott's cheeks flushed with passion as she continued.

"If I were to go around this circle and ask each of you to describe the sacrifices you've made for the cause of abolition and for the recent war, I believe I would hear tales of great courage and devotion. Many of you risked your own freedom to help slaves escape on the Underground Railroad. Others supported the cause with your time and donations. And you continued your volunteer work during the war, sending packages to our soldiers, and supplying the army hospitals with nurses and food and bandages. You took over your families' farms and businesses when the men marched off to fight, and sat at the bedsides of wounded loved ones when they needed you. Some of you paid the ultimate price, losing a loved one on the battlefield for the cause of freedom.

"In light of all these sacrifices and accomplishments, don't we deserve to be counted as full citizens? After everything that we have done during the war, haven't we proven our equality?"

Once again Bebe longed to shout, *"Yes!"* She had worked just as hard as her brothers had, so why should she be treated differently? Lucretia Mott's speech made sense to her, and she wanted to send up a cheer. The other townswomen sat so quietly that it was impossible to tell what they were thinking. Mrs. Webster, the minister's wife, glanced around at the ladies, and seemed surprised that no one had responded. She turned to Mrs. Harrison, who was seated alongside her.

"Tell me, Grace. Don't you work just as hard in the store as your husband does? I've seen you waiting on customers and making change and ordering goods—then you have to go home and cook dinner and clean house. And all you other women, didn't you take over a great deal of the work when your sons and husbands were away?"

"I did," Bebe said—but she didn't say it nearly

as loudly or forcefully as she would have liked to. Mrs. Webster smiled at her.

"Yes, Beatrice. You took over for all four of your brothers and helped raise the food that fed the armies."

Mrs. Morgan, the doctor's wife, lifted her hand for a chance to speak. "But if the government does grant us equality with men, might we also be required to take up arms and fight in the event of another war? I, for one, am grateful that I didn't have to fight in the recent conflict. I wouldn't care at all for equality if that were to be the case."

Bebe pictured the rows and rows of wounded men she'd seen in the hospital and had to agree with Mrs. Morgan on this point. She turned back to Mrs. Mott in confusion.

"It's true that women currently aren't required to fight," Mrs. Mott quickly replied. "Thank goodness for that. Our gentler, more tender natures don't equip us for the rigors of battle. Our soldiers displayed outstanding courage during the recent war—but who was responsible for shaping those young men's characters so that they developed the necessary courage to fight? Their mothers, of course—women like all of us. Is the task of molding and nurturing the next generation of leaders any lesser of a role, deserving lesser rights? Of course not. If we are the ones who help mold our future leaders, why shouldn't we be granted the right to help choose those leaders?"

When no one else challenged her, Mrs. Mott continued. "We need a plan, ladies. Winning civil rights for women is the next logical step. In the past, we used prayer, petitions, and pamphlets for the cause of abolition—now we will use those same methods to accomplish this new goal. Those of you who disagree"—she smiled pleasantly at Mrs. Morgan—"are of course free to engage in other work. But if you believe, as I do, that 'there is neither bond nor free, there is neither male nor female,' as the Scriptures say, 'for ye are all one in Christ Jesus,' then let's get to work tonight."

Bebe needed no further convincing. She already had proven her equality with her brothers. She would join the cause. She would give it her all.

CHAPTER
9

As I said before, Grandma Bebe never did tell a story in a straight line like the chapters in a book. Following the thread of her sagas was like chasing a startled rabbit through the woods—you never knew when it was going to turn and head in a new direction. I hated to interrupt her, but we were more than halfway home from the picnic that Decoration Day, and if she veered off the path of Horatio's story, I was afraid she would never find her way back to it. Grandma had wandered in a new direction with Lucretia Mott, and while I'm sure her story would be very interesting, I was losing patience with this new rabbit trail.

"Um . . . Grandma Bebe?" I said when she paused for a moment. "Could you go back to the story of—?"

I never finished my sentence. We heard a *bang!* that was as loud and explosive as a gunshot, and it scared the thoughts right out of my head.

Grandma hit the brakes and gripped the steering wheel with both hands to control the car's sudden swerving. "Hang on tight, Harriet! We've had a blowout!"

I've watched my father struggle to wrestle his car into submission after a blown tire, and I was pretty amazed that my tiny grandmother could manage to control her behemoth of a car. I was also glad that I hadn't been driving at the time. The sound the ruined tire made as it slapped against the roadbed was like a dozen maidservants beating carpets on a clothesline. The car came to a halt at last on the side of the road, enveloped in a great cloud of dust.

"Well!" Grandma said with a sigh. "Don't you hate when that happens?"

We climbed out of the car and walked around it to look at the rear tire. There must have been a pond nearby, because I could hear frogs *thrump-thrump*ing in the distance. I looked around for a farmhouse, but the only light I saw came from the moon high above us. We seemed to be on a desolate stretch of road, surrounded by forested hills. I hoped there weren't any hungry bears in those woods.

"Now what?" I asked. "I suppose we'll have to wait for another car to come by and rescue us?" I shivered and folded my arms tightly against my chest. The air in that mountain hollow felt as damp as the inside of a cave.

"Nonsense!" Grandma replied. "Only women in fairy tales wait to be rescued." She twisted the handle on the trunk, and it opened with a squeak. She had to raise her voice to be heard above the clamor that she made as she rooted through the shadowy bin. "No, Harriet, I made up my mind when I bought this car that if I was responsible for driving it, then I should be responsible for fixing it when something went wrong. Here, hold these . . ." She handed me a car jack and a tire pump, then disappeared into the trunk again. She emerged a moment later, waving a rubber inner tube in the air like a deflated black snake. "Always carry a spare, dear."

I watched in awe as Grandma crouched down and wedged the jack under the car frame as expertly as my father did. Her driving gloves were getting greasy and the front of her duster was smudged with dirt, but she didn't care one whit. I wanted to be just like her.

"Let me do that, Grandma," I said as I knelt

beside her. "I want to learn how." She taught me to change an automobile tire that day, step by step, and I wished the boys from school could have been there to watch me work. They thought all girls were helpless and empty-headed like my sister, Alice. I would have loved to show them how wrong they were. Grandma was right—why wait to be rescued when I was perfectly capable of rescuing myself? Her example inspired me—and it was one of the reasons why I had refused to call anyone on the telephone to come and rescue me from jail. I had thought of Grandma's words as my cell door slammed shut: *Only women in fairy tales wait to be rescued.*

After Grandma Bebe and I fixed the tire that damp May evening and started down the road toward home again, I was eager for her to continue the story of my great-uncle Franklin and grandpa Horatio.

"So how did you end up marrying Horatio Garner, Grandma? If you went home to the farm and he went back to Roseton again, how—?"

"Patience, Harriet, patience. I'm getting to that part . . ."

Bebe couldn't wait to tell her mother all about the Anti-Slavery meeting as they prepared breakfast the next morning. "You should have come last night, Mama. Lucretia Mott came all the way from Philadelphia, and she told us that—"

"Not now, Beatrice . . . please . . . and mind what you're doing—you're letting the bacon burn."

Bebe slid the cast iron skillet to a cooler place on the stovetop, then turned the crisping pieces with a fork. The fat sizzled, stinging her bare arms like wasps. She knew better than to raise the subject of equality for women after her father and brothers trooped in from the barn, but when the men had eaten their fill and she and Hannah were alone, Bebe brought up the subject again as they washed the breakfast dishes.

"It was such an interesting meeting last night, Mama. Mrs. Mott said that we proved our equality with all the work we did during the war. She said we're entitled to the same rights as men, seeing as we were created equal."

Hannah put away the stack of plates she had dried and closed the cupboard door. "But I don't agree that men and women are equal, Beatrice. God created us to be different, with different skills and qualities that complement one another. Women don't have the muscular strength to be blacksmiths and men don't have the tenderness required to nurture a baby. To say that we are equal is foolishness."

Bebe looked up from her scrubbing, genuinely surprised that her mother disagreed. "But didn't we work just as hard as men while they were away?"

"Those were special circumstances. I don't think

131

you'd want to do men's work for the rest of your life, would you?"

"No . . . but Mrs. Mott said that women are considered inferior to men, and we're not inferior, Mama. So it isn't fair that—"

"It's not a question of who is superior; it's a question of who is the head of the household. Someone has to assume leadership in the home, and God decreed that it should be the husband. This isn't something for you or me or Lucretia Mott to decide. We can't change what's written in the Bible."

Bebe felt confused. Everything had seemed so clear to her at the meeting last night, but she didn't know how to explain it to her mother the way Mrs. Mott had. Bebe finished scrubbing the last pot and handed it to Hannah to dry. "I don't think you understand what I'm saying."

"Listen, Beatrice. The roles God has given us as wives and mothers are of the utmost importance. The standard He set for us is found in the thirty-first chapter of Proverbs. We are to be a helpmeet to our husband so that he can accomplish his God-given work. And we are to raise obedient, moral, God-fearing children."

"Yes, that's exactly what Mrs. Mott said last night. And she said our work is just as important as what men do—maybe even more important."

Hannah smiled and spread her palms. "Then what more could you possibly want?"

Again, Bebe felt confused. "Well . . . Mrs. Mott said that women deserve the same civil rights as men, including the right to vote."

"Why would you want to vote, Beatrice?"

"I-I don't know . . . That's why I need to go to the next meeting, so I can learn more about it. She said that women like us helped win freedom for the slaves, and that equality for everyone should be our next goal. That's what I want to do, Mama. I want to help accomplish something important."

"The most important thing that any of us can do is to serve God and build Christ's kingdom. My religious convictions were what led me to help all those slaves escape. I was simply doing the work that God gave me to do."

Bebe huffed in frustration. She wished she could explain it better. Her mother just didn't understand. "Well . . . well, maybe this is the work God is giving me to do. That's why I want to go to another meeting."

Hannah hung the dish towel near the stove to dry and rested her hands on Bebe's shoulders. "If you would determine in your heart to put that same amount of time and effort into Bible study and prayer, you would find the purpose and contentment that you're seeking."

"Yes, but . . . can I still go to the meeting?"

"That's up to your father, Beatrice."

When Bebe's father learned what the meetings were about, he forbade her to attend any more of them. She voiced her frustration to Hannah, who responded by reciting Bible verses such as "godliness with contentment is great gain." Bebe resigned herself to living a boring life on a boring farm outside a boring town—but she was not very happy about it, let alone content.

She found it especially hard to be content whenever she shopped in the general store and heard the other women discussing the meetings. Mrs. Harrison never failed to invite Bebe to come back. She invited her once again after Bebe drove into town on a beautiful Indian summer day to buy vinegar and salt and the other supplies that she and Hannah needed to make pickles and sauerkraut.

"Thank you, Mrs. Harrison. I would love to come again. Maybe when the harvest is over."

She hurried out of the store to avoid further conversation and noticed an unfamiliar horse and buggy drawing to a halt across the street. No one she knew could afford such a fine rig. Three other women from town had stopped to stare at it, too.

"Who in the world could that be?" one of them asked.

"Someone who is lost, no doubt."

But to Bebe's amazement, the man who stepped down from the high leather seat to tie the horse to the hitching post was none other than Horatio Garner. He looked as rich as the king of England in his waistcoat and bowler hat and shiny black shoes. He would have been right in style on the streets of Philadelphia, but he looked quite over-dressed among the simple, hardworking people of New Canaan. The other women stared at him, as slack-mouthed as a string of dead trout.

Horatio turned when he'd finished securing the reins, and headed across the street toward the women. When he spotted Bebe his grin outshone the moon. He swept off his hat and bowed, his fair hair and reddish beard glinting like gold in the sunlight.

"Good afternoon, Miss Monroe. How fortunate that we should meet this way. You're the very person I came to see."

"Me?" she squeaked.

"Yes, you!" His laughter filled the quiet street. "Why are you so surprised?"

She didn't know what to say. Happiness and dismay began a tug of war inside her heart. She was thrilled to see Horatio again, but he had stumbled upon the real Bebe Monroe, dressed in a patched skirt and a faded shirtwaist, not the idealized version of her that he had met in Philadelphia. Now he would see that her life in the village was as dull as a log of wood, that she lived in a simple frame farmhouse, and that she worked as hard as his servants did.

"Will you excuse us, please?" he asked the gaping women. He grasped Bebe's elbow and gently led her away. "Is there a café where we could find a bite to eat?"

Now it was Bebe's turn to laugh. "This isn't Philadelphia, Mr. Garner. There's no café. In fact, you'll have to drive all the way back to the last town you passed just to find a place to sleep tonight."

"Is your home nearby? Perhaps I could trouble you for a glass of lemonade on the porch?"

"I live two miles down that road," she said, pointing. "But I'm quite sure there are no lemons in the pantry . . . and I wouldn't know how to make lemonade, even if we could afford such luxuries."

"How is Franklin doing?"

"Good . . . good . . . a little better every day."

"I'm very pleased to hear it. And although he is my very good friend, the truth is that it was you I came to see."

Bebe's heart thrummed inside her chest like hummingbirds' wings. She tried to speak but nothing came out.

"I've missed you, Beatrice," he said softly. "Ever since you left Philadelphia, I haven't been able to get you out of my mind."

She had to find her voice, had to say something. "I-I missed you, too. But I'm afraid that you have the wrong impression of me. As you can see, my hometown is—"

"I brought you something. I'm dying to see how you like it." He rooted through his coat pockets while he talked. "I happened to pass a jewelry store one afternoon on the way to my attorney's office, and I saw this in the store window. It was so dainty and beautiful—it reminded me of you."

He pulled out a velvet-lined jeweler's box and opened it to show Bebe a small gold locket inside. She couldn't breathe. How was it possible that a handsome, wealthy man like Horatio had come looking for her, bringing her a present?

"I would be so honored if you would accept it as a gift from me. May I see how it looks on you?" He removed it from the box and reached over her shoulders to fasten it around her neck. They stood inches apart. She smelled the clean, spicy scent of his hands.

"But I . . . this old dress . . ."

"Nothing you wore could ever diminish your loveliness."

"Thank you, I-I . . ." Bebe felt completely over-whelmed. She wanted to let go of all caution and allow herself to be swept away by Horatio, but she was terrified that he would leave when he discovered the truth about her, and she would drown in disappointment.

"I forgot to show you, but look—the locket opens." He took another step closer as he pried it open for her. "See? There's a place inside to put a picture of your beloved or a lock of his hair."

"Oh . . . it's beautiful," she whispered. "Thank you, Horatio. No one has ever given me . . . I mean, I've never . . . I don't know what to say. . . ."

Bebe's heart lost the battle. The grip he had on her was too powerful to escape, even if she had wanted to. Seeing Horatio again thrilled her, and she was so amazed by the gift he'd given her that she wanted to whirl and dance in the street. She could have floated home on a cloud of happiness. She drew a shaky breath and said, "Come home with me, Horatio."

"Thank you. I would be honored."

She untied her own horse and wagon and led the way to her farm. Her mother stopped removing laundry from the line to watch as Horatio's buggy pulled into the yard behind the farm wagon. Bebe took his arm and led him over to meet her mother. Hannah silently eyed the locket.

"Look who I met in town, Mama. This is Franklin's friend, Horatio Garner—"

"I hope that I am your friend, as well, Beatrice."

"Yes, of course. But Franklin knew him first, Mama, from the war. And then they were in the hospital together in Philadelphia . . . and that's where I met him."

Horatio swept off his hat and bowed. "How do you do, Mrs. Monroe?"

Hannah smiled in return. "I'm very pleased to meet you, Mr. Garner. I'm sure Franklin will be glad to see you, too. He's working out in the barn at the moment. If you just walk through that open door across the way, I'm sure you'll find him."

"Thank you." But Horatio gazed at Bebe, not in

the direction where Hannah had pointed. Bebe didn't want to let him out of her sight and would have escorted him to the barn, but Hannah gently pulled her away from Horatio, linking arms with her.

"Come, Beatrice. You can help me finish folding the laundry, and then we'll get started in the kitchen. You'll stay for dinner, won't you, Mr. Garner?"

"Thank you. It's very kind and gracious of you to offer."

Bebe couldn't take her eyes off Horatio as he crossed the barnyard, mindful of where he stepped in his shiny black shoes. She continued to stare at the empty barn doorway after he'd disappeared through it. Hannah finished taking the clothes off the line, then led Bebe into the kitchen.

"I see he brought you a present."

"Yes. Isn't it beautiful?" Bebe fingered the necklace, amazed that he would give her something so lovely.

"It looks very costly."

"I-I guess so . . . Horatio's family is wealthy. His father owns a tannery. They have servants." None of those statements had anything to do with the joy and wonder Bebe felt at that moment.

Mama stopped working and turned to look at her. "Oh, Beatrice," she said with a sigh. "Anyone with a pair of eyes can see that you have feelings for each other."

"Really, Mama? Do you really think he has feelings for me?"

"I don't know where this is going to lead, but before you get swept away, you need to remember that the strongest marriages are between couples who share the same faith and the same values. If money is the most important thing to him—"

"It isn't, Mama! I mean . . . at least it doesn't seem to be important. He has always been very kind and generous to Franklin. They're friends."

"And what about Mr. Garner's faith? Does he trust in God or in his wealth and position?"

Bebe didn't know the answer. She turned away so her expression wouldn't betray her doubts. Horatio had never spoken of his faith.

"It's a wonderful thing to fall in love, Beatrice. But make sure that both you and the man you marry love the Lord even more than each other."

She nodded but her mother's words were sliding off like rain on glass. She felt as though she'd been caught up in a whirlwind as she tried to comprehend the fact that Horatio Garner was here—on her farm. He had come to see *her*. And he had brought her a present.

Horatio looked even more out of place at dinnertime, seated at the table beside her burly father and brothers. But if Horatio felt uncomfortable, he never showed it. He gazed across the table at Bebe as if she were the only person in the room while he filled the normally quiet dinner hour with a never-ending stream of words. Now that he'd entered her world, Bebe would never be content without him. The emptiness he would leave behind would be just like the ache she felt every time she saw her brother Joseph's vacant chair or his unused bed. Was this what falling in love was like?

"What are your plans, Mr. Garner?" Bebe's father asked when dinner ended and Horatio had praised Mama's cooking for several minutes.

"Well, as I explained to Franklin earlier, one of the reasons I've come is to pass along the name of a doctor I've heard about. He has the knowledge and expertise to fix up Franklin with a brand-new leg. And to show my appreciation for the friendship we shared, I also came to offer him a job in my family's business. We're in need of a new clerk, someone to handle the customers' orders and keep the books."

"That's very generous of you, Mr. Garner. I'm sure Franklin is grateful."

"I am," Franklin said. "But I don't think I'd make a very good clerk. I never cared much for schoolwork—and I don't think I'd like to sit at a desk inside a building all day. I'm not exactly sure what I'll do for a job, but thanks for the offer."

"Of course, of course. But be sure to let me know if you change your mind."

"You're welcome to spend the night if you'd like more time to visit," Bebe's mother said. "It's too late to travel anywhere else to spend the night."

"Thank you. It's most kind of you to extend such wonderful hospitality to me. I shan't burden you for very long, I promise. I noticed this afternoon how hard everyone works, and I would hate to get in your way, especially at harvesttime." Horatio glanced at Bebe and smiled before turning back to her father. "But there is one other matter of great importance that I would like to discuss with you, Mr. Monroe. Might I have a moment to speak with you in private?"

Henry nodded in agreement. Horatio started to rise, then quickly sat down again when Henry reached for his Bible to read the evening's Scripture passage. Bebe didn't hear a word of it. Her heart galloped in anticipation of what Horatio was about to ask her father, hoping and praying that he was going to ask for her hand in marriage. She thought her father would never finish reading the passage. His closing prayer seemed endless. At last he said "Amen" and scraped back his chair. As Henry led Horatio into the parlor, Bebe abandoned her mother and the supper dishes and ran upstairs to eavesdrop through the vent in the bedroom floor.

She arrived in time to hear Horatio say, "I want you to know, Mr. Monroe, that I developed very tender feelings for your daughter, Beatrice, during her month-long stay in Philadelphia. I had the opportunity to get to know her as she cared for Franklin, and I discovered what a remarkable woman she is. Those feelings didn't diminish after we parted. In fact, I found myself unable to get her out of my mind. And so what I am trying to say is that I would be very grateful if you would grant me the honor of marrying your daughter—if she will have me."

Tears of joy filled Bebe's eyes. She longed to cover her face and weep at the wonder of Horatio's proposal, but then she wouldn't be able to hear her father's response. She pressed her fist against her mouth. The pressure of holding back her happiness felt like a dam about to burst.

"I want you to know that I am able to provide well for her," Horatio continued. "My family owns a very profitable leather tannery, which I will inherit one day. I'm in a position to build Beatrice the finest house in town and staff it with servants and—"

Henry interrupted with a grunt, as if unimpressed with Horatio's wealth. Bebe held her breath, waiting to hear his reply. "Are you a believer, Mr. Garner?" To Henry, that would be the most important question.

"Oh yes, sir. Most assuredly so. I've been baptized and confirmed in the Christian church, and our family worships together regularly. Your son Franklin can attest to my character, having shared a tent with me while we served together in the army."

Another lengthy silence followed. Bebe peeked

through the grate and saw Horatio perched on the edge of his chair as if anticipating an answer at any moment.

"I'll pray about it," Henry finally said. Bebe closed her eyes in despair, well aware of how long that might take. Why couldn't her father be like other people, who made prayer seem as simple as tossing a ball up in the air and catching it again when it came down?

"Yes . . . of course," Horatio replied. But when her father stood to return to his evening chores, Bebe saw Horatio's shoulders slump. She composed herself and hurried downstairs to rescue him from her father's silence.

"Would you care to go for a walk with me, Horatio?"

"That would be lovely, if . . ." He glanced at Hannah, who was clearing the table, then back at Bebe. "If . . . if you would excuse us, please, Mrs. Monroe."

Bebe led Horatio past the barn and through the pasture and stopped beside the swing overlooking the river. "What a charming swing," Horatio said. "And in such in a charming setting. I can picture you as a rosy-cheeked girl playing here on a summer afternoon."

Bebe nodded, certain that he pictured her in a lacy white dress with her dark hair in ringlets and ribbons. What would he think if he saw her swinging in Franklin's baggy overalls and work boots? "Horatio, I need to tell you about my childhood—"

"I'm certain it was more idyllic than mine. A bout of rheumatic fever as a child left me too weak for outdoor activities. I confess that afterward my mother coddled me in many ways. How I would have loved the rugged outdoor life that Franklin and your other brothers led. But as the only son, I was expected to inherit our family's business."

"That's just the thing . . . you see, while my brothers were away at war . . ."

He turned to Bebe and took her hand. "I've asked your father for your hand in marriage."

"Yes, I know. I was eavesdropping."

"Did I do something wrong that your father didn't answer my question?"

"No, he always takes a long time to pray. That's just Papa's way."

"Then if he agrees, will you marry me? Please say yes, sweet Beatrice."

"Are . . . are you sure you want *me?* Your family is so wealthy and . . . and I don't know anything about your way of life—"

"My life will be empty and pointless without you. Please say yes . . . please!" He dropped to his knee like a prince in a fairy tale, leaving Bebe breathless.

Could she really live the life of a wealthy, genteel woman? She owned only one good dress. The rest were work clothes that were stained and tattered. She needed to confess her ignorance and tell him who she really was. But as Bebe gazed into Horatio's eager, expectant face, she realized that if she could transform herself into a boy during the war and learn to do a man's work, why not transform herself into the woman he thought she was? Anything was better than saying good-bye to him and never seeing him again and living her life without him. If the river of life was going to carry her into marriage and motherhood next, why not choose her own vessel and chart her own course?

"I don't care what my father's answer is, Horatio. My answer is yes! Yes, I will marry you!"

"Oh, Beatrice . . ."

Happiness filled his eyes as he gazed at her. He was speechless for the first time since she'd met him. Then he scrambled to his feet and pulled her into his arms to hold her tightly.

By the time Grandma Bebe and I arrived home from the reunion of the Grand Army of the Republic that Decoration Day, I had a better understanding of what she'd meant when she said that I was here because of my uncle Franklin. But at the same time, I was left with the unsettling feeling that life resembled a game of chance more than a river, and that we were all at the mercy of a heavenly game master. I existed because of the random firing of a minie ball that just happened to strike Great-Uncle Franklin's leg at the same moment that another one struck Grandfather Horatio in the foot.

The minie balls might explain why I was here on earth, but why was I *here*, in this jail cell, some fifty years later?

I rose from the rusty cot to stretch and yawn. My night's sleep had been anything but restful. I paced from one end of the cell to the other for a few minutes, then lay down again. I couldn't help worrying about Grandma Bebe. I loved her so much—and her heart was going to break in two when she found out what I had done.

CHAPTER
10

I heard footsteps in the hallway outside my cell. It was lunchtime, so I figured someone must be bringing me a meal. I sat up, then groaned aloud when I saw Tommy O'Reilly stop outside my cell door. He balanced a tray on one of his brawny hands and fumbled with a ring of keys with the other hand as he tried to unlock the door.

"You can take back the food," I told Tommy. "I'm not hungry." It wasn't true. I was starved. But I thought I should maintain an aggrieved attitude for a while longer.

"Nonsense," Tommy said. That's what he'd said last night, too, when I'd tried to explain what I was doing driving a carful of bootleg hooch.

Tommy finally managed to unlock the cell door. He took a step inside, glancing around for a place to set down the tray before deciding on the floor. It was the only place he could put it other than the bed, and since I was sitting with my legs crossed and my arms folded in a posture of defiance, I didn't blame him for not venturing any closer. Lunch consisted of a cup of coffee, a slice of buttered bread, a bowl of soup—it smelled like vegetable beef—and a dish of pudding. Tapioca. My favorite. It was going to be hard to resist.

"Don't you want to call someone to come down and bail you out, Harriet?"

I heaved a bored sigh. "As I explained to you last night, Tommy, there is no one I can call. Besides, the liquor wasn't mine. I don't understand why you don't believe me."

He looked down, and I had the wild thought that he was staring at his shins, which had received their fair share of kicks from me over the years. The kicks had all been well deserved, I might add, but they had done nothing to endear me to Tommy O'Reilly. He probably thought it would serve me right if I spent the rest of my life in jail.

"Well," he finally replied, "the evidence against you says otherwise, Harriet." His voice was soft and a little sorrowful, I thought. "As an officer of the law, I'm obliged to make assumptions based on the evidence, which in your case was a load of bootleg liquor. It'll be up to a judge to determine your guilt or innocence."

"Oh, I'm quite sure the judge will find me innocent, once the facts are known."

"Maybe so, but why sit here starving in the meantime? In fact, why sit here at all?" he asked with a shrug. "You're entitled to a phone call, you know."

I looked at him in amazement. From all outward appearances, Tommy looked . . . well . . . sympathetic! It must be a trick. He probably thought he could wheedle a confession out of me if he smiled his wide Irish grin and pretended to be nice. Tommy had grown into a fine-looking man, filling out every inch of his policeman's uniform. He'd been blessed with classic Irish good looks: dark, straight hair that fell into his brilliant blue eyes, and shoulders that were broad and strong enough to rescue innumerable damsels in distress. Any other woman might have swooned when he grinned at her the way he was grinning at me, but Tommy O'Reilly and I had a long, checkered history. My heart fluttered only a little.

"I'm sure there must be someone who's getting worried about you by now," he continued. "Someone who's wondering why you didn't come home last night."

I shrugged. My personal life was none of Tommy's business.

"I really hate to see you like this, Harriet."

I sighed again and lay down on the bunk, crossing my ankles and folding my hands behind my head. "Don't you have work to do, Tommy? Aren't there laws in this town that need to be upheld?"

He stared at me for a long moment before walking away, locking the cell door behind him.

My thoughts drifted back to my grandmother. She was going to be so disappointed in me after all her work for the Women's Christian Temperance Union, wielding hatchets and closing down saloons. She had been gloriously triumphant when the Prohibition Amendment had passed a few months ago and might have celebrated with a glass of champagne if she hadn't taken The Pledge years earlier.

I knew full well why she had become involved in the Temperance Union. I groaned and pulled the pillow over my head, wishing I could hide in jail forever.

On her wedding night, Grandma Bebe nearly died of fright. One moment she was sleeping peacefully beside Horatio Garner, nestled in the warm, safe curve of his body, and the next moment a piercing cry startled the life right out of her. She leaped out of bed, terrified, ready to run, and saw that the anguished cries were coming from her new husband. She grabbed his shoulders and shook him.

"Horatio! Horatio, wake up!" His eyes shot

open. He stared at her as if at a stranger. "Horatio, it's me . . . your . . . your wife . . ." When Bebe's heart slowed again and she was able to catch her breath, she sat down beside him on the bed and gathered him into her arms.

"Oh, Horatio . . . what is it? What's wrong?"

"I'm so sorry. I should have warned you . . . but sometimes . . . sometimes I have nightmares. They are always about the war. I dream about all the things I've seen . . . I thought they might go away in time, but . . . but they haven't."

Bebe rocked him in her arms and felt a tremor course through his body, shaking the bed. She wondered if it would help to light a lamp in the unfamiliar hotel room, but he was clinging to her like a drowning man in a flood.

"When my brothers and I used to have bad dreams," she told him, "my mother always made us talk about them. It seemed like the nightmares lost their power once we spoke them out loud. Maybe if you told me—"

"No, Beatrice," he said with a shudder. "You don't want me to describe the things I dream about."

"Yes I do. I think it will help. Please?" He didn't reply. She squirmed out of his embrace and stood to light a lamp, then coaxed Horatio to sit propped against the pillows. She sat cross-legged on the bed facing him, waiting.

"It isn't really a dream," he finally said, "because

I'm remembering things that really happened. It's like . . . like I'm reliving the war all over again. Tonight I was back in Virginia, fighting outside of Richmond." He shivered, hugging himself as if to ward off a chill. Bebe longed to take him in her arms again but was afraid he would stop talking if she did.

"We had fought a hard battle two days earlier . . . and lost nearly two thousand men. Now the Rebels were entrenched behind earthworks at the top of a rise. We all knew there was going to be another slaughter when we tried to take that hill, so the night before the battle, some of the men sewed tags in their clothes with their names and addresses printed on them. That way people would know whose body was whose after the Rebs shot us all to pieces.

"And that's just what happened the next morning. It was a slaughter. The generals kept sending our men up that stupid hill . . . charging forward in nice, neat rows . . . and the Rebels kept mowing us down like a field of wheat. As fast as one row of men would fall, we'd send up the next batch. Our commanding officers were asking us to commit suicide!"

His Adam's apple bobbed as he swallowed a knot of emotion. His voice didn't sound like his own, and Bebe realized that it was the first time she'd ever heard him speak plainly, without all of his flowery words and inflections.

"I was so scared as I waited for my turn," he continued, "that I could hardly stand up for shaking. It seemed like a terrible waste to me, and I didn't want to go. But people were determined to shoot me either way. If I sat down and refused to obey orders or ran off like a coward, the Yanks would put me up before a firing squad. And if I charged up that hill like they were telling me to do, I would face Johnny Reb's firing squad. No matter which course I chose, I was a dead man. So you know what I did? I got out a nickel and flipped it in the air. Heads, I would die by a Yankee bullet, tails by a Rebel one."

"It must have come up tails," Bebe said quietly.

"It did. So I started reciting the Lord's Prayer. Everyone was reciting it. A lot of us were vomiting our guts out, too. I was all set to die, like I'd been ordered to do. But just before my turn came, they stopped the slaughter. Someone finally saw the senselessness of it, I guess. I heard later on that when General Grant ordered another attack, his officers refused. I don't know if that's true.

"But even though the shooting stopped, our wounded men were lying out on that hill, pinned down. You could hear them begging for help, moaning and weeping and dying—all day and all that night. I tell you I cried like a baby for those men. Some of them were my friends. Except for the grace of God, it might have been me."

He swallowed again and drew a ragged breath.

"They say that seven thousand men died that day in less than an hour. *Seven thousand*, Bebe! And I watched it all happen. It's something I'll never forget. And now . . . well, my body may have survived, but my nerves were shot all to pieces that day. Sometimes . . . sometimes I think I would have been better off if I had—"

"Don't say it, Horatio! Please!" Bebe scrambled forward to hold him in her arms again, gripping him tightly as if trying to squeeze her own strength into him. "Don't you ever dare to say such a terrible thing." The tremor that ran through his body was like the rumbling Bebe felt when riding the train.

"You know how much longer we had to keep on killing each other after that battle near Cold Harbor? Ten more months! I felt like a condemned man on death row all that time, following those generals around Virginia as they sacrificed us like so many sheep just to win some little piece of worthless land or a burned-down town. I was one of the walking dead, waiting for my turn to go down into the grave."

Bebe looked into his eyes and brushed his damp hair from his forehead. "But you didn't die, and it wasn't a useless sacrifice. You kept our country united and you won freedom for millions of slaves."

"Well, why couldn't they have settled those issues like gentlemen? Isn't that what governments are for? War is a horrible way to decide an argument, Bebe. You saw the aftermath of it when you visited the army hospital." He released her and fought free of the covers to climb out of bed.

"Where are you going, Horatio? Can I get you something?"

"Stay in bed, dear one. I'll get it myself." He crossed the room to retrieve his small traveling case and set it on top of the dresser to open it. Strapped inside were four glass decanters of golden liquid and two sturdy glasses.

"What is that?" she asked.

"A little something to calm my nerves." His hand shook as he poured a generous amount into one of the glasses and carried it over to her, sitting beside her on the bed. The smell of it made Bebe's eyes water. "Would you like some?" he asked.

"Is it liquor?"

"It's the only thing that helps chase away the ghosts."

She pushed the glass away. "No, thank you. My parents never allowed alcohol in our home. Reverend Webster always preached against strong drink."

Horatio drained half of the liquid in one gulp. "Well . . . I would hate to wake you up again with another nightmare, beloved Beatrice. This was not at all how I envisioned our first night together, and I am so very sorry for frightening you the way I did. You must know that I would never do anything to hurt you." He drained the second half and pulled her into his arms. "Do you think you can ever forgive me for the way this night has turned out?"

"Of course. There's nothing to forgive. You can't help having nightmares."

He stroked her hair. "You're the best thing that has ever happened to me, do you know that? Who would have thought that fighting the war and getting wounded would lead to meeting you?" He kissed her, and she didn't like the taste of the liquor on his lips. When he pulled away again, he looked at her for a long moment, then rose and crossed the room to the dresser. She thought he was going to put the glass away, but instead he poured another drink.

It seemed like a lot.

"Why don't you come back to bed, Horatio?"

"I will in a moment, dearest. I want to make certain that I stay asleep this time." He raised the glass in the air in a toast: "To no more bad dreams." And after he'd refilled his glass a third time and drank it down, there weren't any. In fact, Horatio slept like a dead man. Bebe had to shake him awake in the morning so they wouldn't miss their train to Niagara Falls.

They spent their honeymoon in a lavish hotel near the falls, and the first time Bebe saw the thundering cascade, she clung to Horatio's arm, unable to speak. They stood so close to the rushing water that she could feel the spray on her face when the wind blew their way, and she had to fight against the sensation that she would be swept over the edge.

"Can you feel the river's power, Beatrice?" he asked, raising his voice to be heard above the roar.

"Yes! It's . . . it's overwhelming!"

"That's how I felt when I met you—overwhelmed. Swept away."

Bebe clung to him a little tighter, not caring if it was improper to show affection in public. "The falls are so terrifying . . . and yet so beautiful. I never dreamed I would see anything this magnificent." She drew her gaze away to look up at her husband. "Or that I would ever love anyone as much as I love you."

Bebe would remember those two weeks as the most wonderful days of her life. Horatio didn't have a single nightmare after the first one, and they both believed it was because of the healing power of their love.

Then they returned to Horatio's hometown of Roseton in a mountain valley in central Pennsylvania and Bebe's nightmares began. Her new mother-in-law met them at the front door with crossed arms and an angry glare. "How could you do this to us, Horatio? How could you run off with some . . . some *farm* girl with no thought or consideration at all for our feelings? After everything we've done for you?"

Bebe drew back from the force of her words. Her

instinct was to turn and run, but Horatio remained calm, his smile never wavering.

"I'm sorry you feel that way, Mother, but this is my new bride, Beatrice Aurelia Garner, and—"

"She's a child! Is your marriage even legal?"

"She's not a child; she's merely dainty and petite."

"I-I'm seventeen," Bebe said just above a whisper.

Mrs. Garner ignored her. "It may not be too late to have the marriage annulled, Horatio. Your father can talk to a judge and—"

"He'll do no such thing." Horatio draped his arm around Bebe's shoulders and pulled her close. "I love her, Mother. And if you can't accept my choice, then perhaps Beatrice and I will have to move to her hometown and live with her parents, instead."

Bebe looked up at him, wondering if he'd lost his mind. Then she remembered her manners and turned back to her mother-in-law, offering her hand. "I'm very pleased to meet you—"

Mrs. Garner whirled away with a rustle of taffeta, leaving Bebe on the doorstep with her hand still outstretched. Horatio squeezed her shoulder and led her into the house. "That went better than I expected," he said with a grin.

"Are you joking, Horatio? She hates me!"

"She'll get over it. She's angry because we had a simple marriage ceremony in your church and she didn't have the opportunity to plan a huge, lavish wedding. And also because I chose my own bride instead of marrying someone from her social circle. But don't worry, by this time next week she'll be planning an extravagant ball to introduce you to all her friends."

Bebe didn't know which frightened her more, the idea of meeting more women like Mrs. Garner, or the knowledge that it would be at a fancy ball. She didn't even know how to dance. "Oh, Horatio . . . a ball? I-I—"

"Mother will have so much fun shopping with you, buying your trousseau, outfitting you in a new wardrobe—"

"Outfitting me?"

"Of course." He took her face in his hands. "You're beautiful, Beatrice. You're like a tiny porcelain doll. I can't wait to dress you up and show you off myself."

Show me off? For a second time, Bebe fought the urge to turn and run. She gazed around the mansion's soaring foyer and sweeping staircase—and noticed, for the first time, the row of uniformed servants standing like stiff, unsmiling soldiers. The man whom she guessed to be the butler gave a little bow.

"Welcome home, Master Garner," he said. The row of maids all curtsied.

"Thank you, Robert," Horatio replied. "I trust that you and the rest of the staff will help make my bride feel welcome in every way. You're all dismissed for now." The butler went to see about their luggage. The maids curtsied again and scattered. Horatio smiled as if they'd been greeted with hugs and kisses and a fattened calf instead of harsh words and unfriendly faces. "Would you like a tour of the house, my dear?"

"I-I feel a little dizzy, Horatio." She had made a wrong turn and had wandered onto the pages of a tragic fairy tale. If only she could read the ending and find out what would happen. A week ago she'd been certain that she and Horatio would live happily ever after. Now she wasn't so sure.

"You must be exhausted, my dear," Horatio said as he led Bebe into an enormous parlor. It overflowed with so much overstuffed furniture, gewgaws, and bric-a-brac that she could barely see the walls. He made her sit down on a stiff horsehair sofa. "Shall I have the servants bring you something?"

"I don't want to bother anyone. . . ."

Horatio's laughter filled the high-ceilinged room. "My dear, it's their job to wait on you!" He crossed to a tall cabinet in the corner and took out a glass decanter. It was like the one in his traveling case, only larger. The crystal tumbler that he poured the liquor into was larger, too. Bebe watched him take a long drink. "Would you like some, Beatrice?"

"No thanks. I think . . . I think I need to lie

down." Her nerves felt so fragile that she feared she might throw up or burst into tears—perhaps both—and she wanted to be someplace private when she did. Horatio laughed again and set down the glass. Before Bebe could protest, he scooped her up in his arms and carried her into the foyer and up the stairs. She was in tears before he reached the first landing. "This . . . this is all too much, Horatio!"

He kissed her forehead. "You'll get used to it, my dear Beatrice. I promise you."

But for the first time since she'd met her husband, Bebe had cause to doubt him.

CHAPTER
11

Three days after arriving home with Horatio, Bebe crept down the wide staircase all alone in search of breakfast, leaving her husband asleep in bed. The first two mornings he had convinced her to stay in bed with him and sleep until much later in the day as they rested from their journey. "The maids will serve us our breakfast here," he'd told her.

"You mean we'll eat while lying in bed? Not at a table? I couldn't do that."

"Why not?" He had grinned, as if her efforts to adapt to his lifestyle were very amusing.

"Well . . . I'm just not used to staying in bed past dawn unless I'm sick—and I'm hardly ever sick."

She had yielded to Horatio's wishes and remained in bed for the first two days, but by the third day Bebe couldn't sleep a moment longer. When the hall clock struck seven, she put on her clothes and tiptoed downstairs. She heard laughter and the rattle of dishes coming from the kitchen and would have been content to go through the forbidden doorway and eat with the servants. But Horatio had scolded her for socializing with the help after he'd overheard her chatting with the chambermaid.

"Servants often become lazy and presumptuous if their masters are overly friendly," he told her. In truth, Bebe had much more in common with those simple, hardworking people than with Horatio's family.

Except for the voices in the kitchen, the house was cold and silent. Bebe missed the sound of the rooster crowing in the morning and the cows lowing to be milked, and all of the other clanking, bustling noises of the farm. She crept into the dining room and saw steam rising from a row of silver chafing dishes on the sideboard. She lifted one of the lids and found enough bacon for a dozen people. Should she wait for Horatio's parents? And how in the world would she converse with them without Horatio alongside her?

In the three days that Bebe had lived in the Garner home, her mother-in-law had not once spoken to her or addressed her by name. Mr. Garner had barely spoken to her, either. Horatio had carried the conversation throughout their meals, describing Niagara Falls and the other sights they had seen in such beautiful, poetic language that Bebe could have listened to him for hours.

She replaced the lid on the chafing dish and was about to go back upstairs when Horatio's father strode into the room. He stopped short when he saw her.

"You're up early."

"Yes, I can't seem to sleep past—"

"Where's Horatio?"

"In bed—"

"What did you say? Speak up!"

"I-I said that he is still in bed." She saw no need to mention that the three tumblers of liquor he drank last night had knocked him out cold.

"Well, he needs to get up. I need him at the tannery this morning."

"I'll go wake him." Bebe turned to leave.

"Not you. Sit down. The servants can do it." He sank into his place at the head of the table and rang a little silver bell. Servants poured through the door from the kitchen as if he had opened a spigot. Bebe jumped out of their way.

"Kindly awaken my son," Mr. Garner commanded them. "I would like my coffee and my newspaper right away. Then fix me a plate—but I don't want any of that disgusting orange marmalade on my toast. I'd sooner eat earwax."

The maids scrambled to do Mr. Garner's bidding as if he were King Solomon and they were his many wives. Once he began to read his newspaper, he didn't speak another word to anyone. Someone filled his coffee cup. Another maid prepared a plate for him at the buffet and set it before him. Bebe watched her father-in-law silently turn the pages of his newspaper and tried not to form a harsh opinion of him. Her own father had never been a talkative man, but he wouldn't have ignored another person at the table this way. Nor would he have begun to eat, as Horatio's father had just done, without first offering thanks to God for his food.

Mr. Garner rang the bell once again when he wanted more coffee, pointing mutely to the empty cup. Then, when he'd finished his breakfast, he folded his newspaper, laid it aside, and rang for his carriage.

"I don't have time to wait for Horatio," he told Bebe. "Tell him I left without him." The front door thumped shut behind him.

"Can I get you something, ma'am?" the serving girl asked as she cleared away Mr. Garner's breakfast dishes.

"No, thank you . . . I'm waiting for Horatio."

"If you please, ma'am . . . he told us not to disturb him again for another hour. And then he would like his breakfast upstairs, as usual."

Bebe stood to serve herself from the chafing

dishes, swallowing a knot of tears as she remembered standing at the stove with her brother Franklin, tussling over the scrambled eggs and biscuits.

It didn't take long to eat breakfast alone. She longed to carry her plate into the kitchen, where she would feel more comfortable and where there were other people to talk to, but she didn't dare. She was trying to decide where she should go in this enormous house, and what she should do until Horatio awoke, when Mrs. Garner swished into the room in her ruffled dressing gown, carrying a stack of books.

"Do you know how to read?" she asked.

"Yes, of course, Mrs. Garner. I—"

"Then you'll need to study these." She dropped the pile onto the table in front of Bebe. "They'll teach you proper etiquette and other important social conventions. I don't have time to teach you all of the things you failed to learn on your rustic little farm. And your first social engagement is in a few weeks."

"My first—?"

"When you're finished reading these, I have several back issues of *Godey's Lady's Book* for you to peruse. Have you heard of it?"

"Yes, it's a magazine for women that—"

"You'll need to begin reading it regularly. Otherwise, heaven only knows what you'll find to talk about in polite company. My dressmaker will be coming to measure you at nine o'clock this morning. Kindly be prepared for her."

Bebe wondered what in the world she had to do to prepare to be measured, but before she could ask, her mother-in-law said, "Once you are properly educated and outfitted, you'll be included in the regular round of social duties."

"Social duties?"

Mrs. Garner rolled her eyes toward the ceiling as if beseeching the Almighty for patience. "Your ignorance is astonishing." She turned and swished away, her chin in the air.

Bebe swallowed another knot of tears as she looked at the pile of books in front of her, scanning the titles: *Good Morals and Gentle Manners*; *The Manners That Win*; *Our Deportment*; *The Complete Book of Etiquette*. She opened one of them at random and began to read: *Never loll, fidget, yawn, bite the nails or be guilty of any other like gaucherie in the presence of others.* She had no idea what *gaucherie* meant, but she suspected she would find out after studying all four books. She opened to another place and read, *The proper form of introduction is to present the gentleman to the lady, the younger to the older, the inferior to the superior.*

The inferior to the superior? She thought of the Scripture verse that Lucretia Mott had quoted at the anti-slavery meeting back home: *"There is neither bond nor free, there is neither male nor female: for ye are all one in Christ Jesus."*

Bebe thumped the book shut. Trying to memorize all these trivial things seemed daunting and useless. She recalled, with great regret, the advice her mother had offered: *"If you would determine in your heart to put that same amount of time and effort into Bible study and prayer, you would find the purpose and contentment that you're seeking."*

Bebe was still sitting alone at the table a while later when a maid came in and began preparing a breakfast tray from the food in the chafing dishes. "Is that for my husband? Horatio Garner?"

"Yes, ma'am."

"I'll bring it up to him."

"Oh, no, ma'am. Mrs. Garner would never allow such a thing."

Instead, Bebe waited until the tray was ready, then followed the maid upstairs, lugging the stack of books. Horatio was awake but still in bed. "Why are you dressed already, Beatrice? What time is it, anyway?"

She walked over to his dresser to look at his pocket watch. No one had ever cared about the time of day on the farm, following the rhythm of the animals and the sun and the seasons. But Horatio and his family scheduled everything according to the clock. There were several of them scattered throughout the house, including the tall case clock in the foyer that chimed four times every hour. It made Bebe uneasy to hear regular reminders of the passing of time, especially since so far she had not accomplished anything useful.

"It's ten minutes past eight," she told him. Horatio groaned and closed his eyes. Bebe waited, wondering what to do. "Your father said he needed you at work this morning."

"Too bad. Let him wait. I have a pounding headache, and the last thing I need is all that racket at the tannery. . . . What are all those books for?"

"Your mother loaned them to me. She says I need to read them so I can learn proper etiquette and prepare for my social duties. And a seamstress is coming before long to measure me."

Horatio smiled and stretched out his hand to her. "Come here, my love. Why so glum?" The tears that Bebe had held back all morning spilled over as Horatio pulled her close. "Are you sorry you married me, Beatrice?"

"No! Never! But I wish . . . I wish it could just be the two of us, and that we lived all by ourselves so that I could cook for you and take care of you myself and—"

"It will be that way soon. Didn't I promise to build you your very own house?" He tried to kiss her, but she freed herself from his embrace. "What's wrong, dear one?"

"Your breakfast is getting cold, and your father needs you at work, and I need to get ready for the seamstress. She's coming shortly."

The woman arrived promptly at nine and made Bebe strip to her chemise and drawers while Mrs.

Garner and one of the chambermaids stood right there in the room with her, watching. Then the seamstress measured every inch of Bebe from head to toe, shaking her head and muttering as she bemoaned the fact that Bebe was so small.

"I may have to use children's patterns," she told Mrs. Garner, "and even then they may not fit her properly."

"I'm not a child," Bebe tried to explain. "I'm seventeen."

Mrs. Garner and the seamstress exchanged looks. While Bebe put her clothes back on, the two older women paged through pattern books and examined fabric samples and discussed lace and trim. Neither of them bothered to consult Bebe or ask for her opinions as they planned an entire wardrobe for her. If she had tiptoed out the door, she doubted anyone would have noticed.

"The girl doesn't have a single decent thing to wear," Mrs. Garner told the seamstress. "I'll need to take her shopping for shoes and hats and gloves—and undergarments, too, from the look of hers."

Bebe pressed her lips together and tried not to cry.

Their shopping trip a few days later was an exhausting affair. Back home in New Canaan, Bebe could have purchased everything she needed at Harrison's General Store, but Roseton had so many stores to choose from that she and Mrs.

Garner spent two long days traipsing from one to the next. Mrs. Garner made all of the decisions. When Bebe first arrived in Roseton, all of her belongings had fit inside two modest-sized carpet-bags. But by the time she finished shopping and her new dresses had arrived, she needed a bureau, an armoire, and a vanity table to hold everything. It seemed like a sin to own so much.

"Tomorrow you will receive callers for the first time," Mrs. Garner told her when she and Horatio had lived there for a month. "Be dressed and ready to greet our guests by two o'clock sharp. Wear the blue taffeta gown. My maid will arrange your hair."

"You'll do fine, my darling," Horatio assured her as he kissed her good-bye in the morning. "There's no reason in the world to be ill at ease. You will win over the other women with your charms in no time, just as you captivated me."

Horatio's confidence seemed unfounded to Bebe. But as she gazed at her husband's handsome face, she decided that she would walk through fire and flood for him. Surely a simple tea party wouldn't be so difficult.

That afternoon as Bebe sat in front of her looking glass watching the servant arrange her dark hair in an elaborate knot, all of her confidence suddenly evaporated. What had ever made her think she could transform herself from a simple farm girl into a society woman? Laboring like a man alongside her father had been easy compared to facing a roomful of women like Mrs. Garner. What would she say to them? And how would she ever manage to pour tea with shaking hands?

"All finished, ma'am." The maid had secured the last hairpin in place. "You have lovely hair, ma'am. So full and thick."

Bebe stared at her reflection and saw a stranger. *"Life is always changing,"* her mother had said, *"always flowing forward like a stream."* It was time for Bebe to wade into the current and change, as well. She rose from her seat at the dressing table, gracefully lifting her skirts, and went downstairs to the parlor to face her guests.

Mrs. Garner wore a tense smile as she introduced Bebe to the chattering ladies. Bebe hated being on display, scrutinized by a roomful of strangers. Some of the guests boldly questioned her about her age, others commented rudely on how short and girl-like she was. Bebe wished she could retaliate by pointing out how stout and wrinkled they were or by asking their age in return. But according to the etiquette books, she was supposed to answer their questions politely, no matter how inconsiderate they were, and above all to smile.

As the afternoon wore on, Bebe thought she was doing well until one of the younger women approached and asked her a question she hadn't expected. "Which clubs will you belong to, Beatrice?"

"I-I'm not sure what you mean."

"Which women's organizations do you plan to participate in? Which causes have you supported?"

Bebe stuttered to form a reply. "W-well . . . back home, my mother and I worked with the Anti-Slavery Society."

The woman frowned and waved her hand in dismissal. "That's all in the past. The war is over. The slaves are free."

"Yes, but there is still so much work to do. One of our guest speakers, Lucretia Mott, pointed out that since women proved their equality during the war by running their husbands' farms and businesses, we should be allowed the same civil rights as men, and—"

"Excuse me? You're not talking about woman suffrage, are you?" The room grew unusually still. Bebe felt everyone's attention shift to her. She had no idea what the correct response was, so she told the truth.

"Well . . . Mrs. Mott explained that it was compassionate, educated women like ourselves who have worked hard to abolish slavery. And now all of the former male slaves are being granted civil rights, even though many are illiterate, while literate women are still being denied those rights."

For a long moment, no one seemed to breathe. The room felt as hot as the hayloft on an August afternoon. Bebe had been certain that this gathering of women would agree with Lucretia

Mott's conclusions. Instead, they appeared shocked.

Finally, the woman who had asked Bebe the question mumbled, "I see. Would you excuse me, please?" She scurried away as if Bebe had head lice. Within minutes, everyone seemed to be saying good-bye and leaving. Bebe had no way of knowing if it was because of what she'd said or if afternoon teas always ended this abruptly. She soon found out.

"How could you!" Mrs. Garner roared the moment they were alone. "Didn't you read the books I gave you?"

"Y-yes. All four of them."

"Then why did you decide to ignore all of the warnings about never discussing politics?"

"I . . . I . . . she asked me about the clubs I belonged to, and—"

"And you told her you supported woman suffrage? Of all the outrageous things!"

"I didn't mean . . . I only went to one anti-slavery meeting back home and—"

"You've not only embarrassed me in my own home, you've also ruined your chances of being invited to any of their homes! No one wants to entertain a woman with such radical views."

"But don't women deserve the same rights as—?"

"Certainly not! The public sphere of labor and politics is a man's domain. Ours is the more exalted sphere of home and family. Motherhood is a woman's highest goal. Our success can be seen in the character of our children and in the respite we provide for our husbands at home."

"But—"

"Don't you *ever* mention woman suffrage in my house or in my presence again! Do you understand?"

Bebe wanted to run down the hill and jump into the wide, cold river that flowed through Roseton. She was still in her room, crying, when Horatio returned home from work. He went to her immediately and folded her in his arms. "Oh, my poor Beatrice. Is it safe to assume that the afternoon didn't go very well?"

"It was awful," she whimpered. "I'm so sorry, Horatio. I know how important this event was to your mother, and I embarrassed her, and . . . and I let you down."

"Beatrice, I love you. Nothing will ever change that. I don't care what you said or what happened today. It isn't important to me."

"But your mother—"

"You don't have to be part of Mother's social circle if you don't want to be," he said gently.

"That's good. Because after today, I doubt if she'll ever allow me to be seen with her in public again."

"I'll smooth things over with her. Now, please don't cry anymore. It breaks my heart to see you so upset."

She drew a breath and tried to pull herself

together, but her tears wouldn't stop falling. "But what will I do all day, Horatio? The house is cleaned for us, all of our meals are prepared, our clothes are all sewn and laundered and pressed. The chores that I used to do back home are all done for me, and I have nothing to do. Your mother doesn't like me and never talks to me. You told me I mustn't talk to the servants, and I don't have any friends . . ."

He smoothed her hair off her face. "You'll make new friends soon. The first day of any new venture is always the most difficult one. I'm certain that when you try again, you'll find someone in Mother's crowd or among their daughters who will be a friend to you."

Bebe wanted to believe him but couldn't. She longed to be honest with him, to tell him that she really wasn't graceful and refined, to confess that she had been playacting ever since the day they'd met. But the only certainty in her life right now was that she loved him—more and more each day, if that was possible. And she would do anything in the world for him. She dried her eyes with her new linen handkerchief and smiled up at him.

"Forgive me for complaining, Horatio. I'm so sorry. I'll do better the next time. I promise."

CHAPTER
12

When Tommy O'Reilly arrested me last night, he'd had the audacity to ask if I was married. I stuck out my chin, looked him square in the eye, and said, "No, I am not, Tommy—are you?"

He took a step backward, holding up his hands as if I might take a swing at him. It wouldn't have been the first time. "I meant no offense, Harriet. I just thought that if you were, I could call your husband to—"

"To do what? Come and rescue me? Talk some sense into me? Take control of me?"

"Sorry I asked," he said, shaking his head. He was careful to keep his hands in a defensive position. "And the answer is no, I'm not."

"Not what?" I was too angry to keep track of the conversation.

"Not married. I'm single. Like you." He smiled, and if I hadn't known him as well as I did, I would have thought he was being flirtatious. But I was immune to men's advances in general—and to Tommy's in particular.

Grandma Bebe may not realize it, but she had played a huge part in forming my opinions of men and marriage. To be honest, I couldn't see why I needed either one. She no longer had a husband and she fared just fine without one. She went wherever she pleased and did whatever she pleased, and I planned to do the same. I knew how to start an automobile, how to drive it down the road, and how to take care of it when it rattled to a halt. What did I need a husband for?

My parents' marriage had also contributed to my opinions—but not in a positive way. Mind you, I never heard them arguing, and our house was, for the most part, a peaceful, happy place. But that was largely because my mother treated my father like a maharajah in his palace: *"Yes, dear. No, dear. Whatever you say, dear."* On the odd occasion when my father became unreasonable she resorted to tears, which nearly always worked in her favor. I was much too proud to weep, so how could I have a marriage like theirs? I planned to navigate my own path through life, and I had no intention of handing the rudder over to anyone else.

My low regard for marriage had solidified into rock-solid aversion when my sister Alice became engaged. Where should I begin to describe that turn of events? After breaking hundreds of hearts, Alice finally made up her mind and settled on one beau. If her decision surprised me, imagine the astonishment of her innumerable spurned suitors. The fact that she'd made up her mind at all was shocking. My empty-headed sister had trouble deciding which hat to wear for a stroll down the block, let alone choosing something as momentous as a mate. Alice insisted on seeing the good in everyone, so she had been forced to rely on Mother's skills at dissecting people and analyzing their pedigrees. It was the only way Alice ever could have narrowed her choice down to one.

I was thirteen that spring of 1912 when Alice got engaged. She was twenty. The lucky winner of Alice's heart was a banker's son named Gordon Shaw, grandson of one of Roseton's founding fathers. I had absolutely no idea what Alice saw in him. Gordon was a bore. His favorite topics of conversations were himself and his bank full of money.

But before the marriage could occur I had to endure . . . *The Wedding*. When General Pershing and his troops set off for France in 1917, they didn't go through nearly as much rigmarole as Mother and Alice did as they prepared for *The Wedding*. Digging the Panama Canal was simple in comparison. One afternoon, when they were trying to narrow down the guest list to slightly less than circus-like proportions, the hullabaloo became so unbearable that I fled to Grandma Bebe's house for refuge. I found her seated at her desk, writing a speech for a temperance rally.

"May I move in with you until the wedding is over?" I begged. "Please?"

Grandma smiled and blotted the ink on the last line she'd penned. "Well, as much as I would love your company dear, your mother would never allow it. . . . But as long as you're here, Harriet, maybe you can listen to my speech and tell me what you think of it. I'll make us some tea, first."

I would've rather had a bottle of sarsaparilla, but Grandma didn't have any in her icebox. I sat down at her kitchen table while she put the kettle on to boil, savoring the peace and calm. I liked eating in Grandma's kitchen. Our kitchen was the domain of Bess, our Negro cook, and Maggie our hired girl, and they didn't like anyone venturing into their territory. Grandma didn't have any servants and preferred sitting in her kitchen more than any other room.

"I'm never getting married," I said with an elephant-sized sigh.

"Never is a very long time, Harriet. And marriage is what gives you a purpose in life—not to mention a family. Just think: If I hadn't married Horatio, your mother never would have been born. And if your mother hadn't married your father, you never would have been born." She scooped tea from the canister into the pot while she talked, then set cups and saucers in front of us.

"If having babies is the only reason to get married," I said, "then count me out for sure! The last thing I need is a drooling, squalling baby. And if Alice decides to have one, I'm moving in with you for good."

"Most people get married for love, Harriet. . . . No, don't make a face. I know you don't understand it now, but someday some lucky man will come along, and when you fall in love with him it will be like plunging over Niagara Falls. You won't know how you ever lived without him. That's how I felt about Horatio."

"I don't think Alice 'fell over the falls' with Gordon Shaw. I think Mother steered her straight into him, like beaching a ship on a sandbar. I can't figure out what Alice sees in him. Or what he sees in Alice, for that matter."

"I hope that both of them are looking for the right qualities in each other. And I hope, for Alice's sake, that there is more to Mr. Shaw than a handsome face and a wealthy father."

"Well, there's nothing more to Alice, I know that for sure. Aside from a pretty face and fluffy blond hair, she's completely hopeless. She has trouble remembering how to uncork her smelling salts, and she needs them at least three times a day—that's how often she swoons."

"Now you're exaggerating," Grandma said with a smile.

"What do men see in women like Alice—and my mother? No offense, I know she's your daughter, but Mother doesn't do much of anything except look pretty and fuss over Father and go to club meetings."

"I know. Poor Lucy," Grandma said, shaking her head. The kettle reached a boil and she rose to pour the water over the tea leaves. "Lucy was overly influenced by Horatio's mother, I'm sorry to say. I wasn't home much of the time when she was little, so my mother-in-law made her into the woman she is today. Lucy acquired a taste for expensive things because Mrs. Garner kept buying her extravagant toys—imported dolls, a rocking horse, an enormous dollhouse. She even bought a miniature porcelain tea set so Lucy could learn the tea ritual from a very young age. And the last thing Grandma Garner did before she died was to make sure Lucy married well."

"You mean to my father? He was a prize? I don't believe it. He owns a department store, for goodness' sake. He has a moon face and spectacles. His forehead gets higher and higher every year. What in the world did Mother see in him?"

"He was a very nice looking, up-and-coming gentleman back in the early nineties, when they married. Not as handsome as my Horatio, but not every woman can be as fortunate as I was."

I didn't say so, but I had seen pictures of Horatio and I didn't think he was handsome at all. He looked scrawny and pasty-faced to me.

"Horatio and I went to Niagara Falls on our honeymoon, and it's a perfect metaphor of what love is like: powerful, beautiful, terrifying, overwhelming—and there's no turning back once you fall over the edge."

"But you've told me stories about how hard your marriage was, especially living with Horatio's parents and trying to learn all those society rules. You made it sound horrible."

"Did I? I didn't mean to. Marriage can be difficult at times, I'll grant you that. But being married to Horatio gave me a great deal of joy, as well." She smiled, and even with silver streaks in her dark hair, I could see remnants of the lovely woman Grandma Bebe must have been. She poured tea into my cup and pushed the sugar bowl across the table to me. "Here. I know you like it sweet."

"But you were pretty, Grandma. Mother and Alice are, too. You and my mirror have told me countless times that I'm plain. I look like Father's side of the family. Even if I was interested in marriage, who would want to marry me?"

"Outward beauty can be a distraction for many men. Count it a blessing that you're plain, Harriet. That way, you'll know that a suitor is attracted to the real you, not the fancy wrappings. Believe it or not, I was very plain when Horatio met me. I was dressed in a simple calico gown with my braids coiled up on my head. I was a shy, small-town farm girl with no social graces at all. What he saw in me, I'll never know."

Grandma was getting more nostalgic about marriage by the moment. I needed to bring her back to the present. "I'm going to go to college when I finish school—and not some sissy female seminary, either. I want to go someplace substantial like

Cornell or Oberlin. I want to be like you, Grandma, and do something important with my life. Didn't you say that your work for the Temperance Union gave your life meaning?"

"Yes, but you can be married and still serve a cause. I did. Besides, I probably never would have joined the Union if I had remained single."

"I don't believe it." Her insistence on the joy of marriage was starting to frustrate me. I blew into my cup to cool the tea and my temper, then said, "You need to explain yourself, Grandma."

"It's a long, sad story . . . are you sure you want to hear it?"

"We have plenty of time. I'm not going home until the wedding is over. And if Alice has a baby, I'm never going home."

"Every marriage has its good times and bad, Harriet. Change is the only constant in life. . . ."

By the time Bebe and Horatio had been married for three years, she had perfected her ability to perform in society. She could pay visits to the wealthiest homes in town and make meaningless conversation for hours on end without committing a faux pas or a gaucherie. But even with flawless social skills, Bebe never achieved full acceptance by Mrs. Garner and her friends. That came by birth, not by marriage. She would always be poor little Bebe Monroe, a dairy farmer's daughter. Many of the young women who were Bebe's age held a grudge against her for capturing Roseton's most desirable bachelor. The older women never forgave her for denying them a huge society wedding—a major social event among the well-to-do. They would consider her a gold digger, an upstart, a newcomer in town, even if she resided there for fifty years.

Bebe may not have been allowed to mention woman suffrage, but she did find something more meaningful to do than attend tea parties and social events. Since the Garner men owned one of Roseton's largest industries and employed hundreds of workers, it was the duty of the Garner women to be charitable to the poor workers' families. Once every month, Bebe and Mrs. Garner would travel by carriage to The Flats, as the sorry side of town was called, accompanied by the driver and the family butler for protection, of course.

Before Bebe visited The Flats for the first time, she had never imagined that such poverty existed. Her family had always worked hard on their farm, and life had been primitive in many ways, but at least they'd always had plenty of food to eat. In The Flats, the ramshackle tenements and bungalows were bounded by the river on one side and the railroad tracks on the other. Sewage oozed down open gutters alongside the streets, and freight trains rumbled past day and night, rattling windows and foundations. There was no grass or trees, and the yards behind the buildings were so tiny and barren that the workers couldn't even grow food or raise animals. It seemed like a miserable way to live. Yet in the eight-block area of The Flats, Bebe counted six saloons.

"Those saloons are the reason you must never venture into this part of town alone or at night," Mrs. Garner warned.

On Bebe's first trip to The Flats, they visited a tannery worker's wife, who had recently given birth. "Her sixth or seventh child, I believe," Mrs. Garner said with a sniff. Bebe wondered where everyone slept at night in that tiny, crowded apartment. The new mother barely spoke English, but she did know how to say "Thank you," which she repeated over and over as she expressed gratitude for the meal they'd delivered—as if Bebe and Mrs. Garner had cooked it themselves. Bebe felt like a fraud.

Two of the woman's ragged, barefooted children had coughs and runny noses. The three oldest, who looked as though they should be in school, sat at a table doing piecework with their mother, sewing on buttons. "Can't we do something more for that family?" Bebe asked after they returned to their carriage that first day.

"Of course not. It's important to be charitable, but we mustn't allow the poor to become dependent on us."

"Shouldn't the city officials be doing something about the sewage and all the garbage that's piling up?"

"That's entirely up to our civic government. It isn't our duty to meddle in men's affairs."

Three years after Bebe's first visit to The Flats, the neighborhood looked exactly the same. The garbage and sewage, the fleas and the flies remained unchanged. The only thing that had changed, as far as Bebe could tell, was the population, which had grown considerably larger.

"I don't know how these families can afford to live with so many mouths to feed," Bebe said after delivering yet another meal to yet another new mother. She felt guilty for parading into these families' lives, well dressed and well fed, reminding them of what they lacked. To Bebe, her attempts at charity seemed like a tiny drop of goodwill in an ocean of need. "I counted five children in that apartment, and none of them looked well nourished," she continued. "Surely there must be something more we can do than simply deliver one meal."

"At least these women are willing to have their husbands' babies."

Bebe knew that Mrs. Garner had directed the jibe at her. She had turned twenty in July, she and Horatio had been married for three years, and she had yet to become pregnant. Bebe's insides burned like hot coals as she forced herself to ignore her mother-in-law's barb—just as she ignored count-less other barbs every day. As if it were Bebe's fault for being childless! Mrs. Garner herself had produced only one son. Bebe longed to speak her thoughts out loud but didn't dare, and the coals of her anger burned hotter each day.

Her mother-in-law seemed convinced that Bebe was somehow to blame for her childlessness, when the fault rested entirely with Horatio. A man needed to be at home with his wife at night in order to produce babies, and Horatio rarely was. He arrived home with his father at six every evening, swearing that he'd missed Bebe and professing his undying love. He would eat dinner with her and his parents and then go out again.

"I have business to attend to," he would say if she questioned him. She was often asleep when he returned late at night, the smell of alcohol strong on his breath. "So my nightmares won't bother you, my dear one," he explained. The more Horatio drank, the less he resembled the carefree, talkative man she had fallen in love with. The dis-tance between them seemed to be growing wider and wider.

Bebe arose and got dressed long before he did in the morning, steeling herself to endure another long, lonely day with only his mother and her socialite friends for companionship. During the war years, when her life had been a daily struggle of hard labor, she had feared that the work would never end. Now that she didn't have the usual women's chores to do, her empty, work-free life also seemed as though it would never end. She hated her life. Then one night Horatio stopped coming home for dinner altogether.

"Where's Horatio?" Mrs. Garner demanded when Mr. Garner arrived home alone.

"How should I know?" he replied.

Bebe had been waiting for Horatio in the parlor and didn't intend to eavesdrop on his parents' conversation in the foyer, but there was no other way out of the room without being seen. She shrank away from the parlor door as the Garners began shouting at each other by the front stair-case.

"Well, he was with you all day at work. Why didn't he come home with you?"

"If you must know, your son hasn't been with me all day at work for a very long time. He fails to show up at all, half the time, nor does he do a full day of work when he does show up. He comes in late every morning and leaves whenever he feels like it."

"Where does he go?"

"How should I know? I have more important things to do than follow him around all day. But I'll tell you this much, I'm not going to put up with it any longer. I hired a new general manager last month to replace him. I warned Horatio that I was going to do it, and now I have. As soon as the fellow learns his way around, Horatio can look for work elsewhere, as far as I'm concerned. I'm taking him off my payroll."

"You can't do that! He's your son."

"No, he's *your* son—you spoiled him shamelessly when he was a boy and—"

"Only because Horatio was so ill."

"—and you're still spoiling him to this day. It's your fault that he never grew up."

"How dare you blame me when the fault is yours? I told you not to force him to go to war. I begged you to hire a substitute for him when his draft notice came. He's our only son! Horatio wept and pleaded with you, too, and you turned a deaf ear."

A chill shivered through Bebe at their words. Horatio had told her the opposite story—that his father had offered to hire a substitute, but he had insisted on fighting. She wanted to believe Horatio's version, except his nightmares told her otherwise. She felt stunned. Duped. He wasn't the man she'd thought he was. And what did he do all day if he wasn't working?

"I thought that going away to war would do him some good," Mr. Garner said. "Make a man out of him."

"Well, you forced him to go and look what happened. He not only came back wounded, he brought home that ridiculous wife of his."

"Well, you can't blame me if he doesn't come

home now. He's obviously not very happy with his ridiculous wife or he would be here, wouldn't he?"

Mr. Garner's words hit Bebe with the same shock she'd felt when she'd plunged into the river. Could it be true? Had Horatio stopped loving her? If so, she wanted to sink into the cold, dark water and drown.

Silence settled over the foyer as the Garners stalked off in opposite directions. As soon as the way was clear, Bebe ran upstairs to her room. She refused to come down for dinner and refused the servants' offer of a tray. How could she eat? Horatio didn't love her anymore.

On other nights when Horatio stayed out late, Bebe usually went to sleep before he came home. But tonight she sat up in a chair beside the bed waiting for him, growing angrier and angrier with each passing hour. Horatio was not the man she'd thought she had married. He was an irresponsible liar who seldom went to work, leaving her trapped at home with his hateful mother. He never was going to build a home for her—small or grand. How could he afford one if he never went to work to earn a living?

Anger kept Bebe awake until Horatio stumbled home at two o'clock in the morning. She knew the time by the hall clock, which had chimed every hour, half hour, and quarter hour before he arrived. Horatio blinked when he opened the bedroom door and saw all of the bedroom lamps burning. He shaded his eyes against the brightness. His clothes and hair looked disheveled.

"What are you doing up, my sweet Beatrice? It's very late, you know."

"I know. I've been waiting for you to come home. I need to ask you something."

"What's that, my dear?"

"Do you still love me, Horatio?"

"Of course! Oh, my dearest, how could you even think that I don't love you?" He moved toward her with wavering steps. Drunk.

"You never spend time with me. You didn't even come home for dinner tonight."

"I'm sorry. Something unforeseen came up. But you must believe that I love you, my darling. I adore you."

"I don't know whether to believe you or not, especially when you're like this."

"Like what?"

"You've been drinking. Excessively, it seems." She wanted to confront him with all of the other lies he had told her: how he hadn't really volunteered for the war; how he wasn't going to work every day; how he'd promised to move out of his parents' house and build a house for her. Instead, she continued in a calm voice. "I don't know what to believe. Where do you go all day and all night, Horatio? You're never home. Your father says you haven't been working at the tannery with him."

His smile faded into a troubled frown. "I hate

working there. It's too noisy, for one thing. And Father and I don't get along. He never listens to any of my ideas." Horatio began to undress, kicking off his shoes and dropping his suit coat onto a chair. "He should have given me the foreman's job. It belongs to me. But instead he hired Neal MacLeod, an outsider. So I left."

Horatio turned toward the cupboard where he kept the bottle for his nightly drink, then seemed to change his mind. He wobbled toward Bebe, stopping in front of her chair to face her.

"I wanted to surprise you, Beatrice, but I suppose I'll have to tell you now. I haven't been going to work because I've been looking into another job possibility. I'm tired of being dependent on my father, and I've decided to start a business of my own choosing."

His words offered her a tiny seed of hope, but she was afraid to plant it, afraid that it, too, would shrivel and die. "A job? Doing what?"

"I don't want to say, just yet. I'd rather surprise you. But I'm working on something big."

"Will we be able to move out of your parents' house? They hate me, Horatio, and I'm sick of this boring, shallow life. I want to do something meaningful."

"Yes, my love. We'll move out just as soon as we possibly can." He leaned forward and reached for her hands, gripping them in his. "It will be wonderful with just the two of us. You can do whatever you wish with your time. It will all happen soon, I promise you, my dearest."

"And will you stop drinking, too?"

He released her hands and tugged off his tie, collar, and cuffs, tossing them on the bureau top. He dropped his suspenders and shirt on the floor. "I've tried to stop drinking, Beatrice, you know I have. But the nightmares always begin again."

"But do you have to drink so much? Do you really need to get drunk every night?"

"I don't get drunk—you're exaggerating. Listen, can we talk about this tomorrow? I've had a very long day, and I have a very important appointment tomorrow. Our future is at stake, Beatrice. I need my rest."

She wanted to remind him that he could get all the rest he needed if he hadn't stayed out until two o'clock in the morning, but she held her tongue. He dropped his trousers onto the floor and left them there in a heap, then climbed beneath the covers.

"I've made up my mind, dear Beatrice. I believe I'll accept that business proposition tomorrow. And as soon as the deal is signed, I'll begin looking for a new house for us. Now, please, come to bed, my darling."

Bebe wanted so badly to believe him. She rose from the chair, her muscles stiff with tension, and went around the room picking up his clothes and turning off all the gas lamps. By the time she took off her dressing gown and climbed into bed beside him, he had already passed out.

Horatio slept late the next morning, finally rising at noon. Bebe wondered if he remembered what they had talked about last night—and if he would keep all of his promises. He awoke in such a foul mood that she was afraid to confront him.

"I'll go see about that job now," he said when he'd dressed and had his coffee. He kissed her good-bye and rode off in the family carriage.

Bebe spent the next hour in an agony of waiting. As she paced in their bedroom she tried to think of Horatio's good qualities and the reasons she had married him—but all she could remember were the lies. Maybe he was lying about the important appointment, too, and about the new business venture, and about their new home. When the carriage returned awhile later, she went downstairs to speak with the driver.

"Could you please tell me where you drove my husband?"

His eyes shifted all around. He seemed reluctant to answer. Bebe refused to back down, mustering all of her courage and standing in the man's path as she waited for his reply.

"Same place I take him every day, ma'am—to his gentleman's club on Foster Street."

"I would like you to drive me there. Right now."

Again, the driver hesitated, glancing around as if he wanted to run and hide in the bushes. "Begging your pardon, ma'am . . . but the club is no place for a lady."

"I see. Can you please tell me what Horatio does at this club?"

"It's . . . it's a place where gentlemen go to drink . . . smoke cigars . . . maybe play cards . . ."

"You mean gambling?"

He gave an uneasy shrug. "I can't really say for sure. They don't let me inside, ma'am. And I doubt if they would let you inside, either, even if I did take you there."

"I see."

And she did. There was no important appointment, no new job. There would be no home of their own. Their future was not foremost in Horatio's mind—liquor was. The man she had married was a liar and a fraud. She leaned against the carriage to keep from falling as her world collapsed on its foundations.

"Are you all right, ma'am?"

"Yes. I'll be fine. Wait right here for me, please. I'll be back shortly."

Bebe hurried upstairs to her room, her decision already made. She removed the locket from around her neck for the first time since Horatio had given it to her and laid it on her dressing table. Then she rifled through Horatio's pants pockets and bureau drawers, collecting all of his loose change and dollar bills. After stuffing a few belongings inside two carpetbags, she hurried downstairs to the waiting carriage. The driver tossed aside his ciga-rette when he saw her and crushed it beneath his shoe.

"Where to, ma'am?"

"Please take me to the train station."

CHAPTER
13

Bebe didn't realize how much she had missed home until the crowded city was far behind her and acre after acre of rolling farmland and forests came into view. She had spent the night in the train sta-tion since there wasn't a train home until morning, praying that Horatio wouldn't come looking for her. Thankfully, he hadn't.

The train reached the station in New Canaan by early afternoon. Bebe breathed a sigh of relief that it wasn't market day, when all of the townsfolk would be milling around. Hopefully, no one would recognize her beneath her veiled hat and city clothes, and she would be able to sneak out of the station and walk home unnoticed. She pulled the hat down low over her face, just to be sure, before stepping off the train. But there on the platform, hurrying to put a small stool in place for the con-venience of the passengers, was her brother Franklin. She stared at him in astonishment. His crutches were gone and he was standing on two legs, using Horatio's ebony cane for support. Bebe had to remind herself that her brother was only twenty-three. His trials during the war made him look years older.

"Franklin!"

He looked up at her in surprise. "Bebe? What are you doing here?"

"I could ask you the same question. And why are you wearing that uniform?"

He gave a bashful grin as he helped her down from the train. "I'm the assistant stationmaster now. But . . . why didn't you tell us you were coming? Are you home for a visit?"

Bebe hated to lie, but there were other people on the platform, unloading mail and freight, replenishing the train's supplies of coal and water. If she confessed that she had left her husband and was returning home for good, the news would spread all over New Canaan before she walked through her mother's kitchen door.

"I haven't been home for a visit in three years," she said instead. It was the truth.

"Well, why didn't you tell us you were coming? There's no one here to meet you."

"I wanted to surprise everyone."

"They'll be surprised, all right. I can hardly believe my eyes . . . Say, where's Horatio? Didn't he come?"

Bebe shook her head. She was going to cry, and she didn't want to. She pulled Franklin into her arms, hugging him tightly, avoiding his question.

When she held him at arm's length again, she said, "You look wonderful, Franklin. I'm so happy to see you doing so well."

"I get around pretty good these days on my new leg." He glanced around at the flurry of activity on the platform and said, "Listen, I'm supposed to be working. I don't finish until six but I can drive you home then. Can you wait a few hours?"

She shook her head. "I'm eager to see Mama. I don't mind walking home. I've done it before, you know."

Bebe left her two carpetbags with Franklin and walked all the way home from town. Her fancy city shoes pinched her feet so badly that she took them off and carried them the last mile. Hannah was in the garden, hoeing weeds, but as soon as she spotted Bebe, she put aside the hoe and hurried up the road to meet her. Bebe's tears started the moment she felt Hannah's embrace.

"My goodness, Beatrice. Why didn't you write and tell us you were coming for a visit? I would have driven to the station to meet you. Did you see Franklin?"

"Yes, I saw him. And I'm not visiting, Mama, I'm home to stay. I've left Horatio."

"Oh my." Hannah hugged her again, then said, "Let's go inside. I think there's still some coffee in the pot. And I picked rhubarb yesterday and made pies." Neither of them spoke again until Hannah had poured the coffee and had set a slice of pie and a fork on the table in front of Bebe. "Now, tell me why you left your husband, Beatrice. Does he abuse you?"

"No. Horatio has always been gentle and kind. He would never hurt me."

"Does he fail to provide for you?"

"No. Money isn't a problem . . . even though he skips work most of the time. I suppose it will become a problem if he doesn't start working soon. We live with his parents, and they provide everything for us."

"Is there another woman in his life?"

"I don't think so."

Hannah sighed. "Listen, all married couples have disagreements from time to time, but he is still the head of your household and—"

"This isn't a silly disagreement."

"Then why did you leave him?"

"I don't want to be his wife anymore. He's not the man I thought he was when we married. All this time I thought I was the fraud, and I've been trying so hard to become the woman he thought I was. But now I found out that he's the fraud, Mama. He's been lying to me about everything."

"What aren't you telling me, Beatrice?"

She hesitated. It was a terrible thing to admit that her husband had a weak moral character. And why did she still want to protect him, now that she had left him? She took a breath and finally blurted out the truth. "Horatio is a drunkard. The bottle is his entire life. I thought I could help him. I thought that he would get better—but he's getting worse. And he has been lying to me to cover it up. He has broken every promise he ever made to me. So I left him." She pushed the plate of pie away, uneaten. Her stomach felt as bitter as unsweetened rhubarb.

Mama rose and turned to the stove, poking the coals, checking the stew that was simmering on the back of the stove. Bebe wondered what she was thinking. Mama had tried to warn her before she married Horatio, asking about his faith and questioning her about their shared values. *"Make sure that both you and the man you marry love the Lord even more than each other,"* she had said. Bebe should have listened to her. Horatio had sworn that he was a regular church member, but it had been another lie. He'd only attended services with her half a dozen times in the past three years, sleeping late on Sundays, instead.

When Hannah returned to the table and sat down again, she took Bebe's hands in hers. Her words were unexpected. "You must go back to him, Beatrice."

"Go back! Why? . . . I told you, he's not the man I thought he was."

"Nevertheless, you made a vow before God that you would cleave to him 'for better or for worse, in sickness or in health.' "

"I know, but—"

" 'As long as you both shall live.' "

"But he's a drunkard, Mama. You want me to live with a drunkard?"

"You made those solemn vows to each other before God. If Horatio isn't abusing you, and if he is providing for all of your needs, then you must keep your vows—for better or for worse. I understand that this is one of those 'worse' times, but you made a solemn promise. You have to go home to him."

"Mama, no! Please don't make me go back there."

"It isn't up to me, Beatrice. You promised God. In His eyes, you and Horatio are no longer two separate people. You've become one. And Scripture says, 'What God therefore hath joined together, let not man put asunder.' I would be disobeying Him if I allowed you to stay here."

"But I'm so miserable in Roseton. There's nothing for me to do all day, and his parents hate me, and Horatio doesn't care about me anymore, and I'm so angry with him for lying and for drinking—I don't want to go back to him!"

"You can stay for a visit and take some time to calm down. But you are a married woman now, and the Bible says you must leave your father and mother and cleave to your spouse."

Bebe folded her arms on the table and lowered her head on them. "I can't live that way for the rest of my life!" she wept. "It's like a prison."

"No one says it has to remain that way for the

rest of your life. That choice is up to you. You can always pray for your husband. Ask God to help him overcome his weakness. Fight for him. God is stronger than the enemy who has captured Horatio. Do you believe that?"

"I don't want to fight for him. I don't care what happens to him! I'm tired of holding all my feelings inside, tired of trying to be polite to his hateful mother and trying not to nag my husband. I can't stand living there another day!"

Hannah stroked Bebe's hair. "I hear a lot of anger and bitterness, Beatrice. Even if your circumstances created those feelings, you've been wrong to harbor them and nurture them. Horatio and his family might have helped to sow the seeds, but you're the one who has allowed them to grow in your heart, untended. Bitterness is like a weed. Remember how hard it always was to pull out thistles once they take root? Remember how deep those roots grow, and how if you just snapped off the end of it, the plant would grow right back? You have to dig down deep inside. Let God search your heart. Let Him show you what's there and help you root out all that bitterness. Then you can pray for forgiveness."

"Why should I ask for forgiveness? This is all Horatio's fault."

Mama rose from the table and tied an apron over her dress. She would have to get dinner on the table soon. "You may stay for a few days, Beatrice, and we'll talk some more. I'll pray with you, if you want me to. Once you've asked God to search your heart, you'll be able to go home with a renewed love for your husband. You'll be able to help him. And you'll also be able to show God's grace to his parents."

"They've never liked me, Mama. They're probably glad that I'm gone."

"Nevertheless, it sounds as though they've been showing grace to you if they've been feeding you and clothing you and providing a roof over your head."

Bebe didn't want to hear any more of her mother's advice. And she certainly wasn't going to heed it. The fault in her marriage was Horatio's, not hers. Mama was wrong. And Bebe was never going back to him.

"I'm going for a walk." Bebe knew her mother could use help, but she didn't want to talk about Horatio anymore. She put on her tight-fitting city shoes and went outside. Hannah didn't stop her.

The farm was so beautiful and lush during these early summer months. Bebe had missed the view from the barnyard of rolling hills and fences, the verdant green pastures and trees, the sedate black-and-white cows grazing in the distance. She could see a wide swath of azure sky above the Pocono Mountains, and smell fresh earth-scented air—so different from the city. If Mama wouldn't let her stay, maybe she could find a job in New Canaan like Franklin had, or work as a hired girl for one of the town's more prosperous families. Maybe she could be a schoolteacher. No matter what, she would never go back to Horatio.

Bebe followed the familiar path beside the pasture that led to the river and the rope swing. The riverbank had become overgrown with brush and weeds since she'd left three years ago, and the river had dried up into a stream half its size. She looked around for the swing but it was gone. All that remained was a ragged, rotted end of rope dangling from a branch high above. Bebe felt the loss as if the swing had been an old friend. She sank down in a heap on the dusty ground.

"Let God search your heart," Mama had said. Deep down, Bebe knew that she still loved Horatio—the old Horatio from their days at the hospital in Philadelphia and when they'd visited Niagara Falls. She wanted him back.

Fight for him.

Bebe remembered how she'd nearly drowned after leaping from the swing into the river. That's how she felt now—like she was drowning. She had wanted to die when Mr. Garner said Horatio must be unhappy with his marriage. But should she let despair overwhelm her this way? She had fought to survive her plunge into the river, battling her way back to shore. And if she wanted to save her marriage, she would have to do battle again. Where would she ever find the strength?

A long time later, Bebe returned to the farm-house, still unsure what to do. Franklin had arrived home for supper and her father had come in from the barn. "Hello, Papa," she said as she gave him a brief hug. "It's so good to see you again."

"Where's your husband?"

Bebe glanced at her mother before replying. "Horatio didn't come with me." She hoped her face didn't reveal her emotions as the four of them sat down at the table to eat, along with the hired hand who now worked for her father. Bebe strained for something to say to change the subject. "Mama never mentioned in her letters that you've been working in town," she told Franklin.

"That's because they just hired me about two weeks ago. I can get along pretty good on my new wooden leg, but Pa and I figured out that farming is just too hard for me. Too much mud and manure to slip around on."

"Do you like your new job?" She thought of Horatio and how he hated working at the tannery.

Franklin shrugged. "I'm getting used to it, little by little. Mr. Freeman wants to retire as station-master, so if all goes well, I'll be replacing him in a few years."

"Did Franklin tell you that he has a girlfriend in town?" Mama asked. She wore a pleased smile on her face.

"That's wonderful, Franklin. Who is she?"

Franklin's cheeks colored, and Bebe remembered how ghostly pale he had been in the hospital. "Remember Sadie Wilson?" he asked. "Her pa has a farm west of town. I haven't asked her to marry me or anything. She's only my girlfriend." He paused and his blush deepened. "But I think I might like to marry her, if she'll have me. I'm going to save my money to build a house for us in town, near the station."

Bebe had to hold back her tears when she remembered all of Horatio's promises to build a house for her. She hoped Franklin mistook them for tears of happiness. "I wish you and Sadie a lifetime of happiness," she said.

They finished their meal and the rest of the rhubarb pie, then the men went out to do the evening chores while Bebe and her mother washed and dried the dishes. Late in the evening, after her parents had gone to bed, Bebe decided to confide in her brother. "Can I ask you something, Franklin? . . . Do you ever dream about the war?"

He shrugged. "Not really. Why?"

"Horatio has terrible nightmares about the war. He wakes up screaming and trembling. . . . He says that the only way to make the dreams stop is to drink whiskey."

Franklin sighed and sank onto his chair again, massaging his knee. "We both saw some pretty terrible things, Bebe. Men blown to pieces . . . and some of them were our friends." He shook his head as if to erase the image. "Horatio seemed more bothered by sights like that than the rest of us. I always figured it was because he was a city boy and wasn't used to seeing animals slaughtered— all the blood and guts. . . . Yeah, he had a pretty hard time with it. I was surprised he enlisted in the first place, him being wealthy and all. I always gave him a lot of credit for not buying his way out like a lot of other rich fellows did. But it seems like he got sick more often than anyone else and couldn't always make roll call."

"That's because Horatio was weak and ill as a boy," Bebe said. "His mother told me that they nearly lost him several times from pneumonia, pleurisy, influenza . . ." Bebe didn't know why she had come to his defense. Why make excuses for him if she was furious with him?

Franklin nodded. "I remember one doctor who seemed to have it in for Horatio. He kept sending him back to fight, even if he was coughing or feverish. Accused him of faking. Horatio tried to report in sick on that last day when we were both wounded. Said he had the flux real bad, but the doctor sent him right back to fight with the rest of us. Bad luck that he got shot that day."

Bebe wasn't sure she wanted to know the answer to her next question but she asked it anyway. "How did it happen? Did you see him get wounded?"

"You never see the bullets coming, Bebe. We were fighting side by side. Horatio always stuck pretty close to me. Said I was his good luck charm." Franklin smiled crookedly. "Some charm! Anyway, the Rebels were throwing all the ammunition they had at us. I suddenly felt this jolt in my leg like I'd been kicked by a mule. Then unbelievable pain. Blood everywhere. Horatio put down his rifle and helped me tie a tourniquet around my leg like they showed us how to do. Probably saved my life. He was supposed to keep charging forward with all the others, but he didn't. When I finally got up the nerve to look down again and saw what was left of my leg, I passed out. Horatio dragged me back to an aid station. Next time I woke up, he was still there beside me. He'd been wounded in the foot."

"Was it a minie ball?"

"No, a bullet. Doctor said it was from a revolver—like the one Horatio always carried."

"What are you saying? . . . You think Horatio shot himself?" Along with everything else Bebe was discovering about her husband, she was beginning to fear that she had married a coward.

Franklin held up his hands. "I'm not saying anything. He's a good fellow at heart. And quite a talker. He kept us entertained on those long marches and on the nights before a big battle when we were all too keyed up to sleep."

"I wish you would have told me that he drank a lot. I wouldn't have married him if I had known."

Franklin stared at her in surprise. "I didn't know that he drank, Bebe, I swear. I never saw him drinking—least not any more than the rest of us. If he was drinking on the sly, I think I would have known. Why? Is there a problem?"

She shook her head. Horatio's problem was no longer hers. She had left him for good.

Franklin climbed wearily to his feet, hanging on to the arms of the chair for support. "Well, I'm bushed. We should call it a night.

Can we talk another time?"

"Sure. And I'm sorry for making you think about the war."

"It doesn't bother me."

She watched him hobble toward the downstairs bedroom that used to belong to their parents. It was his now that he had difficulty climbing stairs. "Franklin?" she called. He stopped and turned to her. "Make sure you keep your promise and get that house built for Sadie, even if it's just a cottage. She won't care how fancy it is if she loves you."

"Hey, don't cry," he said when he saw her tears. Franklin was as awkward with his emotions as their father was, but he limped back over to her. "Are you all right? Can I do anything? You helped me out when I was low, Bebe."

And helping Franklin was how she had met Horatio. She quickly wiped the tears away. "I'll be fine. Good night, Franklin."

The rooster awakened Bebe the next morning at dawn. She joined her mother in the kitchen. Bebe hadn't cooked in three years, but she mixed the dough and rolled out the biscuits as if she'd made them only yesterday. She had missed the sticky warmth of the dough beneath her fingers, the velvety softness of the flour. By trying so hard to be the woman Horatio envisioned her to be, she had lost part of herself. Worse, she didn't like the person she had become, a woman who did nothing productive day after day, living a life of gossip and frivolity. But Bebe also realized as the day progressed that she didn't belong here at home, either. She was no longer a child.

After lunch, she joined Hannah in the vegetable garden. The early summer sunshine warmed her back as she attacked a crop of weeds with the hoe. Hannah knelt in the dirt, thinning a row of young carrot plants. "I'm sorry that your life hasn't been what you'd hoped it would be, Beatrice," she said. "I understand how you feel, because the early years of my marriage were very difficult and lonely for me, too."

"At least Papa was never a drunkard."

"True. But like most women, I also came into my marriage with expectations. I imagined that my home here on the farm would be a little paradise, where Henry and I would work together side by side, sharing our lives and our dreams. But you know what a solitary man your father is. He's a good man, and he lives right before God, but he doesn't have any idea how a woman needs to be loved. His first love is for his land. He knows his farm and his animals inside and out, but he doesn't know me at all."

Bebe stopped and leaned on the hoe, looking down at her mother in surprise. She had never imagined that Hannah was discontented.

"The first years after I married your father I was very lonely and unhappy. Henry never knew how to talk to me. Then the boys came along, one right after the other—and they didn't talk to me very much, either," she said with a little laugh. "I don't think I ever told you how grateful I was for your companionship, Beatrice. But by the time you came along I'd learned to turn to God. We can't expect other people to meet all of our needs, all of the time. Only Christ can do that perfectly. That's why I know that if you turn to Him, you'll find contentment."

Bebe didn't reply. She watched as Hannah moved to the next row of carrot sprouts and began to tend them. "I put in many hours of prayer during those years," she continued. "I figured as long as I was going to be down here on my knees anyway, I may as well pray."

"But trusting God comes easy for you, Mama. You've always been devout."

Hannah shook her head. "A life of faith and prayer doesn't come naturally to me or to anyone else. It grows from tiny seeds that we have to plant and nurture ourselves. What I'm trying to tell you is that my marriage hasn't always been easy, either.

211

I felt, at times, like I was Henry's property, not his partner. That instead of appreciating all the work I did for him, he felt that it was his right and my duty. When we don't get our own way, and when our life doesn't turn out the way we think it should, we face a choice. We can let bitterness grow or let the love of God grow. So instead of becoming bitter toward Henry, I asked God to help me change and to use me for His purposes, not my own."

Bebe laid down the hoe and knelt beside her mother to help finish the row. Hannah's words had moved her, and she felt selfish for thinking only of her own unhappiness. "I never knew you were unhappy, Mama. I don't understand why God would allow anyone to struggle. I thought He loved us."

"He does love us. But as the saying goes, 'Smooth seas don't produce skillful sailors.' It's the rough waters that train us to be His disciples. He uses the turbulent times in our lives to prepare us for His purposes—if we'll let Him. God taught me to see the plight of slaves and have compassion for them because I had once felt so unappreciated and used. That's why I became involved with abolition. The rough seas in my life prepared me to reach out to others."

"You were so courageous, Mama, hiding the slaves the way you did and helping them escape."

"I didn't have any courage, Beatrice. I had God.

Over the years, as I drew closer to Him and saw His faithfulness in my life over and over again, I learned to trust Him. But I learned it the hard way—by being tested. That's why I urge you to turn to God. Ask Him to show you how He wants to use your marriage for His glory."

"But I'm miserable there. How can I possibly do any good?"

"There are still many evils in the world, even though slavery has been abolished. And if Horatio can't stop drinking, it sounds like he's as much of a slave as those poor Negroes were. God wants us to fight evil and take part in His redemption. You always said you wanted to do something important with your life, remember? Maybe this is what God is asking you to do."

Bebe wasn't so sure. She was still angry with Horatio, and she still couldn't face the idea of going back to Roseton and living with him and his parents after overhearing their conversation. Yet she couldn't deny what Mama was saying, either. She had long admired Hannah's faith and her willingness to risk going to prison for what she believed.

"How did you know what God wanted you to do, Mama?"

"Have you been reading His Word, Beatrice? It's the best way to get to know God and discover His will. And prayer, of course. I spent a lot of time praying. I did it all day long, while I worked. I still do. And see these weeds we've been attacking?" Hannah yanked out a dandelion and held it up. "They'll take over this garden and choke out all of the good vegetables if we don't get rid of them—every day. We can't see His will clearly until we get rid of our anger and bitterness and all those other weeds that choke out His life. Give up your right to them."

"But Horatio broke my heart. How can I go back to him? I'm not even sure I love him anymore."

"Ask God to heal your broken heart. He can put the pieces back together the right way so you'll be able to love your husband the way God does—forgiving him seventy times seven and wanting only the best for him. Ask God to give you Christ's love for Horatio, not your own imperfect love."

Hannah stood and surveyed the row they had just tended. She offered Bebe a hand and pulled her to her feet. "I won't lie and tell you it will be easy, Beatrice. If you want a fruitful life, it requires a lot of hard work, and daily attention—just like this garden does. But love is the most powerful force there is—Christ's love and our love for one another. It has the power to change us and to save the whole world. It can surely save your husband."

Five days after Bebe arrived at the farm, Horatio drove into the barnyard in a new runabout. Bebe saw him through the kitchen window as she was cleaning strawberries to make jam. For a moment she couldn't breathe. When he drew to a halt, her first impulse was to run upstairs and hide.

"Mama, please! I'm not ready to talk to him yet. Send him away . . . or . . . or tell him I'm not here—"

"He's your husband, Beatrice. You belong with him."

"But I don't want to hear what he has to say. I won't believe a word of his lies anyway."

"You don't have to believe him. But you do have to listen to him with an open heart and with God's love."

"I'm not ready to forgive him. And his parents said such hateful things about me. How can I go back there and live with them? How can I forgive them?"

"Do you deserve forgiveness? None of us do. But we need to forgive each other because God forgave us."

Horatio had walked around to the front of the house. He knocked on the door.

"Go answer it, Beatrice."

"This is too hard! I can't do it!"

"That's what you said during the war when you had to take over your brothers' chores, remember? And do you remember what I told you then? We can do all things through Christ who strengthens us."

Horatio knocked again, louder.

"Go on, Beatrice. I'll be praying for you."

Bebe walked through the house, whispering a prayer for help. She drew a deep breath, then opened the door and looked up at her husband's pale face. He still looked handsome to her with his hair the color of mown hay, and his copper-flecked mustache and beard. His eyes filled with tears.

"I don't blame you for leaving me, Beatrice. I know I lied to you. But I'm telling the truth when I say that I love you. Please forgive me. Please give me another chance."

Bebe couldn't speak through the knot of tears in her throat. Horatio dropped to his knees.

"Please . . . I can't live without you. I don't want to try. I'll change, Beatrice, I can change, I know I can. Can't we please start all over again?"

Bebe longed to believe him. She prayed for the strength to believe him. Then she dropped to her knees, too, and took him in her arms, knowing that she needed forgiveness as much as he did.

Grandma Bebe and I finished the pot of tea at the same time that she finished her story. "So you see, Harriet, I loved Horatio dearly, but liquor had a very tight grip on him at times. We had some wonderful years together when he was sober. But it drove me to my knees—and to the railroad stations to smash whiskey barrels—when he wasn't. Living with him was like soaring on a swing—high in the air one day, feet dragging on the ground the next. But the Lord used the circumstances of my marriage to bring about something good for many, many people."

I stared at Grandma in disbelief. "Was that story supposed to make me eager to get married? I'm sorry, but I still say *no thanks*!"

Grandma Bebe laughed. "You'll have to fall in love in order to understand, Harriet. When you do, I promise you that everything I just told you will make perfect sense."

I was about to ask another question when the telephone rang. Grandma got up from the table and climbed onto a little stool to answer it. I had always admired Grandma for being among the first people in Roseton to purchase a telephone and to have electricity wired into her home. But the man who'd installed the telephone had hung it too high on the wall for Grandma to reach, insisting that all telephones needed to be hung at the standard height.

"Poppycock!" Grandma had told him. He had ignored her protests and mounted it at the standard height, just the same.

"Hello?" she said into the mouthpiece. "Yes, Lucy. Yes, Harriet is here. . . . Yes, I see . . . I'll tell her, dear. . . . Good-bye." She replaced the receiver and smiled at me as she stepped down from the stool. "Your mother is looking for you. You're needed at home."

"Did she say why she wants me? She's not going to make me go shopping with her, is she? Grandpa

Horatio may have had nightmares about the war, but my recurring nightmare is of the time that Mother and Alice made me shop for that horrible dress with all the flounces and frills and furbelows. I don't ever want to—" I stopped short, struck by a newer version of my nightmare. "Mother isn't going to make me dress up in something horrible for The Wedding, is she?"

"Well, you can't go looking like that."

"Why not?" The century was only a few years old, but I'd already discarded my voluminous petticoats in favor of the modern, streamlined look and shorter hemlines. Mother thought I looked scandalous—even though my high-button shoes covered my ankles. "If Mother thinks I'm going to get all done up like a Gibson girl, she's going to be sorely disappointed. I refuse to wear one of those enormous hats with all those ridiculous feathers. And I steadfastly refuse to wear a corset. Ever! Even if I do get a figure someday."

Grandma Bebe rested her hand on my arm. "Calm down, dear. Your mother didn't say anything about shopping for hats or corsets. She would like you to come home and help Alice address her wedding invitations. She said you have lovely penmanship."

I moaned. "Do I have to? You were going to practice your temperance speech on me, remember?"

"Next time, dear."

"And you didn't finish telling your story. What about the right to vote? When did you join the suffragettes?"

"That story can wait for another day."

"Can't I *please* join the suffragettes with you?"

Grandma shook her head. "Your parents said no, and I have to respect their wishes."

I huffed in frustration. "Please don't make me go back to that crazy house."

"Stop being melodramatic, Harriet, and get going." Grandma made sweeping motions as if trying to shoo me out the door with a broom.

I dragged myself to my feet, sighing and making faces, hoping Grandma would feel sorry for me. Instead, she smiled and wiggled her fingers to wave good-bye. I got as far as the back door and turned around.

"Are you sure I can't stay a little longer? You never told me what happened to Horatio. Did he give up the bottle for good that time? You tell all of your stories in bits and pieces, Grandma, and you never finish any of them."

"Another day, Harriet," she called as she walked from the kitchen to her dining room. "Go home."

I realized as I slouched down the street toward home that even though I was thirteen years old, I didn't know what had become of my grandfather. I had never met him, nor had I ever visited his grave.

In fact, I had no idea if Grandfather Horatio was dead or alive.

CHAPTER
14

In the frantic weeks before Alice's wedding, my mother's greatest fear was that Grandma Bebe would get herself arrested again and cause a family scandal. Grandma did have a reputation in town, make no mistake about that. In fact, one of my more memorable fights with the school bully, Tommy O'Reilly, occurred when he started teasing me about her on the way home from school one day.

"Harriet's grandma is a jailbird!" he announced in a singsong voice, loud enough for all of the other kids to hear. His father was the town constable, so he had firsthand knowledge of every arrest in Roseton. I should have ignored him but I didn't.

"I dare you to cross the street and say that to my face!" I yelled in a very unladylike manner. Tommy shouted even louder.

"Jailbird! Jailbird! Harriet's grandma is a jailbird!"

I sprinted across the street and tried to kick him in the shins, but he knew me well enough by then to sidestep my foot. He laughed and said, "You're going to be a criminal just like her!"

I took a swing at him and my fist smacked into his chin. He howled like a baby. "Ow! Ow! You broke my jaw! I'm telling my father to arrest you!"

"Hit her back," one of his friends advised.

"Naw, let's get out of here. Her whole family is crazy! You'll be sorry someday, Harriet Sherwood!"

I was sorry immediately. My hand hurt so badly I was certain I had broken a few bones. At least my parents never found out about the fight because it hadn't taken place on school property, but my hand was sore for a week.

I hated the fact that Tommy O'Reilly had been right: I did grow up to be a jailbird just like Grandma Bebe. This was only my first offense, but Grandma had been arrested several times, following in the footsteps of her heroine, Carrie Nation, who had a reputation for smashing up saloons with a hatchet. Carrie had an alcoholic husband, as well, but other than that she and my tiny grandmother were as different as night and day. Carrie stood nearly six feet tall and weighed at least one hundred eighty pounds, according to the policemen who were required to arrest her. I read one newspaper account where she described herself as "a bulldog, running along at the feet of Jesus, barking at what He doesn't like." She inspired Grandma's temperance group to adopt some of her hatchet wielding tactics—giving my mother good cause to be worried.

"Why not let me live at Grandma Bebe's house until after the wedding is over?" I asked my mother. "She'll stay out of trouble if I'm with her."

"What about school?"

"I can walk to school from her house. It isn't that much farther." My plan had a dual purpose: It would keep me away from the wedding mania that had taken control of my house, and it would provide me with a new route to school that didn't include crossing paths with Tommy O'Reilly—who might be seeking revenge for his aching jaw and injured dignity.

My mother eventually agreed, and I packed a satchel. Deep inside I hoped that I would get to see my grandmother and her axe in action. That's why I was thrilled when she got a phone call from one of her temperance friends on a Saturday night, and the two of them arranged a meeting. I was even more thrilled when Grandma let me come along with her.

The saloon they had chosen was down by the river near the brickyard. Out of the dozen women who showed up, I was the youngest protester by about fifty years and the only one without gray hair. I craned my neck, trying to get a peek inside the "den of iniquity" while Grandma shouted to the saloon owner through the open door, asking for permission to come inside and pray. She didn't seem surprised when he refused.

"Never mind, ladies. Let's all stand out here near the curb," Grandma said. "Remember, we have strict orders from the police not to block the sidewalk or the doorway."

The women arranged themselves in a long row, and after some preliminary throat clearing we began singing hymns. Horses and wagons drove past us on the street, and laborers hurried by on the sidewalk, but nearly every man raised his hat in respect as he passed. After we'd sung two or three hymns and a small crowd had gathered, one of the ladies told the tearful story of how her son had fallen into the clutches of Demon Rum in a saloon just like this one. When she finished her sad tale, the prayer meeting began—and it lasted so long that I began wishing I had a whiskey barrel to sit on. Finally the prayers tapered off, and we ended the meeting with another hymn. I hoped that the hatchets would come out now and I would witness a little excitement, but the ladies simply wished each other a good night and went home. My first temperance meeting was a great disappointment.

"I don't see how praying and singing hymns is going to accomplish anything," I told Grandma when we returned to her house. "I didn't see any drunks suddenly turning sober."

"Progress doesn't happen overnight, Harriet. But if we close down the saloons one by one, the men will finally get out of that terrible atmosphere. A change of scene always worked very well for Horatio—especially when he took a vacation from the city altogether. I noticed the beneficial effects of good country air for the very first time when he came to fetch me from my father's farm after I ran away. We ended up staying there with my parents for a week. . . ."

"This week has flown by," Horatio said as he and Bebe walked along the path from the barn to the river. "It's so peaceful compared to the city. I feel different here."

He looked different to Bebe, too. The sun had bronzed his face during their long walks and burnished his hair. His hands no longer shook the way they had at first. "Why don't we move here, Horatio? Maybe Franklin could help you find work in town."

"That's tempting," he said with a sigh. "Especially when I see how happy Franklin is. But I owe a debt of loyalty to my parents. My father worked hard to build up our family's business, and I'm his only son."

"But you hate working at the tannery."

"I know. But I need to try again, for his sake. We need to go home, Beatrice. I think it will be better for both of us this time. And I'm going to keep my promise to build you a house of your own."

Bebe wanted to trust him, but she was still afraid. They walked until they reached the spot where the swing used to be, and as she looked up at the frayed rope she tried not to think of Horatio's other broken promises. She listened in the afternoon stillness to the sound of the wind in the leaves and the murmur of the river.

"Let's build a small house," she told him. "Just big enough for the two of us. I want to cook for you, and—"

"You shouldn't have to cook. I'll hire servants."

"But I like to cook. I've missed being in the kitchen. Besides, my biscuits are much better than the ones your cook makes." She had hoped to make him smile, but he stood looking into the distance, his face somber. Bebe wondered what he was thinking. "Horatio?"

He turned back to her, and his gaze was tender as he studied her face. He loved her. She had no doubt. "Let me hire just one servant then, my sweet Beatrice. I insist. So you won't become overly tired."

She smiled up at him. "Very well. Just one."

"Things will be different this time," he said as he drew her into his arms. "I promise."

They returned home to a reception that was as frigid as the first one had been. It reminded Bebe of the first winter morning every season when she would awaken to a coating of frost on the hardened ground and tree branches that were barren and brittle. She knew from her mother-in-law's expression that Mrs. Garner hadn't hoped for reconciliation. She didn't speak a word to Bebe for three days.

The first thing Bebe did was to throw out the

whiskey bottle that Horatio kept in their bedroom. He handed over his key to the liquor cabinet in the drawing room and Bebe made sure it always remained locked.

"I've cancelled my membership in the club downtown," he told her. "I promise I'll stay away from there."

Horatio rose early every morning and went to work with his father, even when his nightmares kept him awake much of the night. Father and son arrived home for dinner together in the evening, and Bebe could see their relationship begin to change. Their conversations flowed more easily and the men seemed much more relaxed at the table. Mrs. Garner remained cool and distant, but Bebe consoled herself with the thought that she and Horatio would be moving out soon. Whenever the family carriage wasn't in use, Bebe borrowed it to search for a home of her own to purchase, unwilling to wait for a new one to be built.

On a warm autumn afternoon three months after she and Horatio reconciled, Bebe found the perfect house. She met Horatio in the foyer the moment he returned from work that evening and told him about the house before he even had time to remove his hat.

"I know it's going to seem small compared to this mansion," she said, "but it will be just right for us. It's in a lovely neighborhood on a quiet street, not too far from the tannery or the center of town.

Come with me after dinner and look at it with me. Please, Horatio?"

"If you wish." His voice sounded flat and toneless. She saw none of her own excitement mirrored in his expression. But in spite of his lack interest in the venture, he went to see it with her after dinner. His face fell when he saw it.

"That little cottage? It's much too small, Beatrice. I want something better for you. Why won't you let me build you a proper house? We can hire the same architect that Father used."

"Because it will take too long. I want our own place now. Please? I like this little house."

He was quiet for such a long time that she thought he would refuse. She saw lines around his eyes that she hadn't noticed before, and his face looked strained as he stared at the house. She reached to take his hand, but he held it tightly clenched into a fist. "Is something wrong?" she asked.

He shook his head. "Everything's fine. If you're certain you want this place, I'll go to my lawyer's office tomorrow and ask him to buy it for you." His lack of enthusiasm worried her.

"If . . . if you'd rather not, Horatio—"

"I said I would buy it!" He raised his voice with her for the first time. Tears sprang to her eyes, but he didn't seem to notice. They rode home in silence.

At breakfast the next morning, Horatio still seemed preoccupied. He hadn't said another word to Bebe about the house, and she was afraid to raise the subject again. She watched him poking at his eggs while his father silently read the newspaper and decided not to remind him of his promise. Maybe he would be in a better mood that evening.

Mr. Garner folded the newspaper and rang for his carriage. "You ready?" he asked Horatio. He nodded and pushed away his untouched plate.

Bebe gave his arm a gentle squeeze as he rose to his feet. "I'll see you tonight," she whispered. She remained at the table to finish her tea as the men headed toward the front door. A moment later she heard a loud thud, as if someone had dropped a sack of grain.

"Father!" Horatio shouted. "Help! Somebody, help!"

Bebe ran out to the foyer and saw that Mr. Garner had collapsed to the floor. His face was the color of ashes, his arms and legs splayed lifelessly. Horatio dropped to his knees beside him and lifted his head. "Father? . . . Father!"

Bebe flung open the front door and called to the waiting carriage driver. "Fetch the doctor! Hurry! It's an emergency!"

But moments after he'd collapsed, Mr. Garner died in Horatio's arms.

Bebe stayed close to Horatio's side for the next three days, throughout the wake and the funeral.

His spirits had plummeted into a depression that was as deep and dark as the grave they had dug for his father. Horatio barely spoke. He closed his eyes as the men lowered the casket into the ground. Bebe gripped her husband's hand, trying to will her own strength into him. They rode home in the carriage together after the graveside service, but he wouldn't come into the house.

"I need to go to the tannery," he said. "Father left some unfinished business that I need to take care of."

"Let me go with you, Horatio. I'm sure it will be hard for you to go into your father's office all by yourself and—"

"I would prefer to do it alone. I'll be home shortly." She released his hand reluctantly and climbed down from the carriage. When she looked back to where he still sat, he seemed to have shriveled in size, like bread dough that had been punched down, releasing all the air.

He arrived home after midnight. Drunk.

Bebe's anger kindled when he staggered into their bedroom, bumping into a chest of drawers, knocking over a chair. "How could you, Horatio! You promised me you wouldn't start drinking again and—"

"He was my father!" he shouted. "And he's *gone*!"

The anguish in his voice tingled through her. Bebe laid aside her own anger to offer Horatio comfort instead of condemnation. "Thank goodness you made your peace with him, Horatio. Your father was so glad to have you working with him these past few months, wasn't he? At least you had that time together."

Horatio stood with his fists clenched, just as he had when they'd looked at the little cottage together three days ago. His eyes looked dull and lifeless. "My father fell down dead right beside me . . . I couldn't do anything for him."

"It wasn't your fault that he died. There was nothing you could have done." But Horatio stared straight ahead, not at Bebe, and she saw the gleam of tears in his eyes. He looked as fragile as glass, as though he might shatter if tipped the wrong way, if she said the wrong words. "Horatio, talk to me," she begged.

"Did I ever tell you about my friends? Jacob Miller and Peter Griffin? We met during the war. . . . One day we were all charging forward with our bayonets fixed, one fellow on either side of me. . . ." Horatio held up an imaginary rifle and stumbled forward a few steps to demonstrate. "Then they both fell down dead, just like that . . . and I was left standing. I don't know why God would do that, do you, Beatrice?"

"That's something only He can know."

"So do you know what I did that day? I wasn't wounded, but I dropped down on the ground, same as them. . . ." Horatio sagged to the floor. "And I covered my head, and I . . ." He fell facedown, weeping, his arms folded over his head. Bebe leaped from the bed and sank down beside him to comfort him.

"It's all in the past, Horatio. It happened a long time ago. There was nothing you could have done—"

"Yes there was!" He raised his head to glare at her. "I could have stood up and fought like a man. But I was a coward, Bebe . . . and my father knew it, too. I didn't want to go to war, but he made me go. He refused to pay the money and forced me to go!"

"Shh . . . shh . . ." She pulled him close and sat with his head on her chest, stroking his hair.

"Your brother Franklin wasn't a coward. He wasn't afraid of anything. But when Franklin fell . . . when the Rebels shot him in the leg, I—"

"Hush now!" Bebe put her hand over his mouth to cut off his words, afraid of what else he might confess. He pushed her hand away.

"First thing tomorrow, I'm going to go down and enlist. I'll go out West and fight the Indians and prove to my father that I'm not a coward."

"No, Horatio. Tomorrow you're going to go down and run the tannery in your father's place. You can prove yourself to him that way."

He shook his head. "I don't think I can. Running that place is . . . is too much for me . . . and I . . . I feel like I'm drowning."

Bebe could see how overwhelmed he was. No wonder he had started drinking again. Horatio had never liked working at the tannery in the first place, and now he was in charge of it. She hugged him tightly, rocking him. "You can do it, darling. I believe in you."

He clung to her like a child. "I'm so sorry, Beatrice, but having a drink was the only way that I could cope. You understand, don't you? Just one drink . . . ?"

"We'll start all over again tomorrow." She held him until he relaxed and his breathing eased, then helped him to his feet to undress.

"I never bought that little house you wanted. I promised I would, and now—"

"That doesn't matter right now. Let's get you into bed."

"But don't you see? Now I can't keep my promise. My father is dead, and I own this house."

Bebe froze. "Doesn't it belong to your mother?"

He shook his head. "It's mine . . . yours and mine."

"But what about your mother? Where will she live?"

"She'll live here, too. We have to take care of her from now on."

Bebe fought the urge to moan. She wanted her own house, far away from Mrs. Garner. She wanted Horatio all to herself. She hated this monstrous house and the three years of bad memories that it held. She had hoped to move out soon so she wouldn't have to see her mother-in-law anymore. For the past three days, Mrs. Garner had been insufferable as the grieving widow—more so because Bebe had never seen any sign of affection between the Garners, much less love.

As Bebe's anger and bitterness sprouted and bloomed, she tried to recall the advice her mother had given her. Mama would say that she needed to change her attitude toward her mother-inlaw and learn to love her. She would tell Bebe to let go of her plans and make the best of her situation. Again.

Wasn't that what she had been doing all her life?

Horatio passed out quickly once she helped him into bed. But Bebe lay awake for a long time, unable to sleep.

Bebe wasn't surprised when Horatio was too ill the next morning to get up and go to work. He didn't seem to recall last night's conversation or that he had confessed to being a coward. She left him in bed and went downstairs to eat breakfast alone. The dining room looked the way it always had, with the chafing dishes on the buffet, but now Bebe was the only one at the table. The room was so quiet that she could hear the case clock ticking out in the hallway and the low rumble of the servants' voices in the kitchen. She looked at Mr. Garner's empty chair and marveled at how quickly life could change. Why did he have to die now, just when she and Horatio were going to move out of this place and away from his mother?

Bebe folded her arms on the table and lowered her head onto them. She didn't want her love for Horatio to slowly erode again, but if he continued to drink she feared that it might. The only thing she could think of to do was to pray.

Her prayers, it seemed, went unanswered. Horatio's one night of drinking turned into two, then three. Mrs. Garner was no help to him or anyone else. She remained in her bedroom, consoled by the laudanum pills that the family doctor had prescribed. Bebe felt utterly alone. When she could no longer stand the silence in the cold, echoing house, she decided to follow the maid upstairs when she took Mrs. Garner her breakfast, determined to offer comfort.

Bebe's mother-in-law looked years older, lying in the rumpled bed with her hair loose and disheveled. "Leave the tray on the table," she mumbled to the maid. The girl obeyed, then quickly left the room. Bebe cleared her throat.

"Mrs. Garner? Is there anything I can do for you? I'd like to help."

Mrs. Garner rolled over to face her, frowning. She looked Bebe up and down for a moment, as if wondering who she was and where she'd come from, then pointed to the pile of condolence cards heaped on her nightstand. "You can write thank-you notes on the family's behalf . . . and you can leave me alone." Bebe scooped up the cards and backed from the room.

One week after her father-in-law's death, Bebe was writing notes at the desk in the parlor when someone arrived at the door. "My name is Neal MacLeod," she heard him say to the butler. "I'm the foreman down at the tannery. Might I speak with Horatio Garner, please?"

Horatio was still in bed, of course, passed out cold at eleven o'clock in the morning. Bebe hurried out to the hall, and when she saw a ruddy young man about the same age as Horatio standing in the doorway, she could only stare in surprise.

"Excuse me . . . did I understand correctly that you're the foreman down at the tannery?"

"Yes, ma'am. Neal MacLeod." He swept off his hat and bowed slightly.

No wonder Horatio had viewed MacLeod as a rival. No wonder he had been angry with his father for hiring him. He looked no older or more experienced than Horatio was.

"I'm Beatrice Garner, Horatio's wife." She offered her hand, and it seemed to disappear inside his large, freckled one. "I saw you at the funeral, but we weren't properly introduced."

Neal MacLeod reminded Bebe of one of her father's yearling calves—sturdy and square and large-boned, with all of the latent power of a bull but none of the brashness. His round boyish face and gentle nature made her feel as comfortable with him as with her own brothers.

"My husband isn't feeling well, Mr. MacLeod. May I relay a message to him?"

"I wouldn't want to trouble you, ma'am. I understand that your household is still in mourning. I'll come back another time." He ducked his head shyly and began backing away.

"Wait. Please. It's no trouble at all, Mr. MacLeod, I assure you. Especially if it's important. Won't you please come into the parlor and have a seat?"

He seemed to step carefully as he followed her into the overstuffed parlor,as if picking his way across a stream on uneven stones. He gazed around uncomfortably at the abundant bric-a-brac just as Bebe had the first time, then sat down on the very edge of the sofa, gripping his hat in his hands. Why would her father-in-law, known to be a ruthless businessman, hire such a gentle, unassuming man to run his tannery? Could it be that MacLeod's lumbering physique discouraged arguments among the workers or threats of labor unrest? Judging by his deferential manner and threadbare suit, he probably had grown up in The Flats alongside the other workers.

"Tell me what brings you here, Mr. MacLeod?"

"First of all, please extend my sympathy to your family once again for their loss. Mr. Garner was a very fine man and—" His voice faltered as he choked back his grief. Bebe had no doubt that it was genuine, and it surprised her.

"You were fond of him, weren't you?" She saw his eyes glisten as he nodded.

"He was like a father to me, ma'am. I will miss him. . . . Excuse me . . ." He cleared his throat.

Bebe waited, liking Neal MacLeod more and more every minute.

"I understand that your husband, Horatio Garner, will take over for his father according to the terms of his will. And I know that in the past he didn't always agree with his father's decisions and even argued against some of them. I've been running the tannery the same as usual for the past week, but I've begun to worry that I've been too presumptuous. I came here to ask your husband if I should continue with the plans that his father set in motion before he died, or if he—young Mr. Garner, that is—has different plans."

Bebe's stomach turned over in dread. Horatio wasn't capable of running the business in his present condition—and perhaps not even when he was sober. His father hadn't seemed to trust him and had hired MacLeod precisely for that reason. Nor had Mr. Garner promoted Horatio to the foreman's position even after three months of sobriety. The fact that Horatio hadn't always agreed with his father's more experienced decisions made Bebe feel ill. Might his decisions sink the company, now that he was at the helm?

"I see," Bebe murmured. "I'll certainly convey your message to my husband, Mr. MacLeod. But in the meantime, I don't see how it would be presumptuous of you in the least if you continued to operate the tannery the way you did when Mr. Garner was alive. I'm certain that Horatio would trust your judgment completely until he's feeling better."

And then what would happen? Would Horatio fire Neal MacLeod when he did return to work? Bebe feared that he would. The young foreman's plain, honest face revealed that he had arrived here fearing the same thing. And she had done nothing to relieve those fears.

MacLeod rose to his feet, squaring his broad shoulders. "Thank you, ma'am. I will continue the daily operations as usual, for now. Please tell your husband that I hope he feels better soon. I know that there will be documents that will require his signature, and while I have the authorization to sign in some instances, I don't in all of them."

Bebe remained seated as another wave of fear washed over her. Horatio's oversight would be required soon. If he didn't pull himself together, the business could suffer serious consequences.

"You are welcome to bring the papers here for Horatio's signature whenever necessary, Mr. MacLeod. I'm not certain how long it will be until he's well." Her future rested in his drunken, shaking hands. If only Horatio could go back to her family's farm to dry out again, as he had the last time. If only the farm wasn't so far away. As she finally stood to walk the foreman to the door, Bebe struggled to think of a way to convince Horatio to make the trip.

"We may be leaving the city for a few days so that my husband can rest and recuperate in the countryside. It's so much better for him, you see."

MacLeod nodded. "I know that your father-in-law always enjoyed visiting his fishing cabin up on Iroquois Lake. I can see how spending some time up there might bring consolation. It shocked all of us when he died so suddenly."

Bebe hadn't known about the existence of such a cabin, but she nodded as if she had. "Thank you for coming, Mr. MacLeod. I'm certain that Horatio will be back to work very soon."

As soon as MacLeod left, Bebe hurried upstairs and began packing two satchels with clothing and toiletries for Horatio and herself. The foreman's visit had fueled her rising fears for the future, but he'd also given her hope for a way to help Horatio. He heard her rustling through the bureau drawers and rolled over in bed to face her, squinting in the light.

"What are you doing, Beatrice? Must you make so much noise? What time is it?"

Time for things to change, she wanted to tell him. But she didn't, aware that she needed to console him and coax him, not confront him. "Have you ever been to your father's fishing cabin on Iroquois Lake?" she asked.

"Yes, of course. Why?"

"I think we should go there for a few days."

"What are you talking about?"

"The factory foreman was just here. You're needed at work. He says there are questions for you to answer and papers for you to sign, and you can't do your work when you've been drinking this way."

"I don't think I can—"

"Nothing can bring your father back, Horatio. But if you loved him—and if you love me—then you need to take charge of the business that he worked his entire life to build. You need to stop drinking. And you need to keep all of your promises to me—" Fear and grief choked Bebe's voice. She couldn't finish.

Horatio closed his eyes. "You don't know how hard this is for me. I want to stop . . . and I don't mean to drink so much, but I . . ." He sank back against the pillows and covered his face.

Bebe quickly wiped her own tears. "I know it's hard. But maybe if we went to the lake for a few days, just the two of us . . . Remember how peaceful and rested you felt when you visited our farm?"

"I don't think I can—"

"You have to!" she shouted. She hadn't meant to, but fear drove her to it. "I can't live this way and neither can you!" He stared at her as if she had slapped him. Bebe swallowed, forcing herself to speak calmly. "Please, Horatio."

When he finally agreed, Bebe immediately ordered the driver to prepare the carriage before Horatio could change his mind. "Please pack a hamper of food for us," she told the cook. "Enough for three or four days." All the while, Bebe kept a close eye on Horatio to make sure he didn't bring along any alcohol.

"Do you know the way to Mr. Garner's fishing cabin?" she asked the driver as he loaded their belongings into the carriage.

"Yes, ma'am. It's about an hour's drive outside of town, up the mountain."

Horatio was silent and sullen throughout the trip, slumping forward on the seat with his head in his hands, elbows on his thighs. He seemed oblivious to the beauty all around him, and the flaming colors of the changing leaves. Bebe sat back and enjoyed the view of the countryside, trying to let it soothe her, praying that this cure would work. The road followed the same river that flowed through Roseton, climbing steadily uphill until it reached Iroquois Lake at the top of the mountain. The mirror-like lake was peaceful and serene, surrounded by a forest that was so quiet Bebe could hear her own heartbeat. She wished they had brought enough food for a month.

"It's beautiful up here, isn't it Horatio?"

"I suppose so. The lake is man-made, you know. They dammed up the river about ten years ago to form a reservoir for the city."

The carriage halted in front of a rustic cabin with log walls and a stone fireplace for heat. The driver had to kick the swollen door a few times before it would open. Bebe followed him inside. Judging by the cobwebs on the rafters and the mice nests in the corners, the cabin had been vacant for quite some time. Puffs of dust trailed behind Bebe as she crossed the room to open a window. The curtains crumbled in her fingers when she touched them.

Horatio stood in the doorway, watching her. "This is much too crude for you, my darling. We should let the servants come up here first and clean it before we try to stay here. It's uninhabitable. Let's go back."

"I don't mind doing a little cleaning," she replied. "I can have this place tidy in no time, you'll see. I love it up here." She brushed the dust off her hands as the driver brought in the last of their things. "Please come back for us in four days' time," she told him. She feared it wasn't long enough, but that was as long as Horatio would agree to stay. He stood outside and watched as the carriage drove away as if watching the last ship set sail, leaving them stranded on a deserted island. During the drive up to the cabin the sky had been steadily lowering on them like a gray wool blanket, but the moment the carriage disappeared from sight among the trees, the blanket split open and rain began to pour down. It rained for the entire four days they were there.

Horatio's recovery was much rougher than the last time. His moods rose and plummeted from high to low, from anger to despair, as if he were on a swing and couldn't jump off. Bebe read books to him, prayed for him, talked to him. They took walks together in the dripping woods whenever the rain let up—which wasn't often. Some evenings they stood on the fishing pier in front of the Garners' cabin in the cold drizzle and watched the waves wash over the planks. Little by little Bebe encouraged Horatio to talk about his father.

"I could never please him, Beatrice," he said one stormy afternoon as they sat in front of the fire. "I never heard him say that he was proud of me. Not once. Not even during these past few months when I've been working so hard for him."

Bebe leaned into Horatio's shoulder as she listened, grieving for her husband and not for the man who had hurt him so deeply.

"You know what his lawyer told me after he died? My father put a condition in his will that I have to keep Neal MacLeod on as foreman for at least five years after my father's death. Otherwise, I won't inherit anything. What an outrage! He didn't trust me—his own son! He gave my job to a stranger!"

Bebe squeezed his hand a little tighter and tried

to form her reply. She knew she should be as outraged as her husband was, but instead she felt
relieved to know that Mr. MacLeod would manage
the tannery for a while longer. It would give
Horatio more time to learn the business—and
more time to remain sober. If only Horatio would
see him as a friend instead of a rival.

"Don't be so hard on yourself, Horatio. I'm sure
your father trusted you. It's just that Mr. MacLeod
has had a little more experience than you've had,
hasn't he? Your father loved you. He provided well
for you, didn't he?"

"I suppose so." He stared into the flames for a
long moment before saying, "I never could figure
out the connection between my father and Neal
MacLeod or why he hired him in the first place. He
isn't even from our social class. He grew up in The
Flats. He barely has an education."

"I only met him once," she said, "and it was
obvious to me that he came from the working
class. But please don't hold that against him,
Horatio. I grew up poor, too, you know. Would it
be fair for your mother and her friends to judge me
by where I grew up rather than by the person I am
now?"

"That's different."

Bebe wanted to ask how it was different, but she
held her tongue. "Can't you try to see Mr.
MacLeod as someone who can share the burden
and the responsibilities with you?"

"There was always something between him and my father. I can't explain it. . . ."

"Did you ever ask him about it?"

Horatio didn't seem to hear her. He was sunk too deeply in his own misery. "Father used to brag that MacLeod had earned the Medal of Honor for bravery during the war. He worked with some big general or other. Why does everything always come back to that blasted war?"

Bebe had to change the subject before memories of the war pulled Horatio any lower. "Hey, I think the rain has stopped. Let's go fishing. We can use your father's fishing poles." She jumped up. "Do you think they'll still work?"

"My father taught me how to fish when I was a boy. We had some good times up here—when Mother would allow me to come, that is. I told you how sickly I was when I was young, didn't I?"

"You did. Thank goodness you're strong and healthy now." She dragged over a chair to stand on and managed to lift down one of the poles resting on wooden pegs on the wall, sneezing from the dust. "Look, these rods still have strings and hooks on them. We can dig up a few earthworms and we'll be all set."

Horatio hadn't moved. He wore a frown on his face as he watched her. "How do you know so much about fishing?"

"Franklin used to take me with him once in a while. I was pretty good at it, too. Sundown is supposed to be a great time to catch fish. Come on." She held out her hand to him.

Horatio rose from the sagging sofa like a man twice his age, and they bundled up against the autumn chill. Bebe easily found a few earthworms squirming on the rain-soaked ground, then she and Horatio walked out to the end of the pier together. The wind had stopped blowing, and the lake resembled a wide sheet of smooth gray metal. She watched Horatio untangle one of the poles, attach the bait, and cast his line into the water. The ripple from the hook made an ever-widening circle on the glassy water.

"Look at that," she whispered.

"Look at what?"

"You disturbed the water in only one tiny place, yet the circle is growing wider and wider until it will reach all the way to the shore." She watched as he cast his line, over and over again, and she never grew tired of watching the ripples widen and spread. When a gentle, misting rain began to fall, thousands of tiny raindrops transformed the smooth lake into a mosaic of intersecting ripples. "How could something as tiny as a raindrop create such beauty?" she asked.

Horatio turned to her and caressed her cheek. "I've learned that true beauty sometimes comes in very small packages." He smiled, and for the first time in a very long time, it seemed genuine.

Horatio caught three fish for their dinner. Bebe

cleaned them and cooked them in the fireplace in a cast-iron frying pan. "These are the best fish I've ever tasted," he told her.

Later, as Bebe lay in Horatio's arms, listening to the patter of raindrops on the cabin roof, it seemed as though the rain had finally washed away his grief and nourished his withered spirit. He began to talk to her the way he had in the hospital in Philadelphia, and as he spun stories like silk, hour after hour, the beauty of his words made Bebe remember why she had fallen in love with him.

CHAPTER
15

The rain was still falling steadily when the carriage arrived to take Bebe and Horatio home from the cabin. The driver looked drenched and shivery. "Come inside and warm up by the fire," Bebe told him. "I'll fix you a cup of coffee. Your name is Peter, isn't it?"

"Yes, ma'am."

Horatio looked irritated with her. He probably would scold her later for being too friendly with the help, but she didn't care. She didn't view class differences the way Horatio and his mother did, and besides, the driver's hands were raw from the cold. He wrapped them around the coffee cup she gave him and sat down in front of the fire. Horatio stared out of the window at the horses, huddled beneath the woodshed's sloping roof. Silence settled over the three of them.

"Did you have any trouble making it up the mountain in all this rain?" Bebe asked the driver. "I imagine the roads are very muddy by now."

"Yes, ma'am. I ran into some muddy patches along the way, and a few slippery spots with the wet leaves and all. But I don't think we'll get stuck going home. The horses are plenty strong."

Bebe nodded. Rain drummed against the roof and plinked into the tin pan she'd placed below a leak. "We've certainly had a great deal of rain these past few days, haven't we?" she asked. "Has it rained this much back home?"

"Oh yes, ma'am. Some of the folks down in The Flats are having a really rough time of it."

"What do you mean?"

"The river overflowed its banks down there. You almost need a boat to get around in some places. The floodwaters forced a lot of people out of their homes with no place to go."

"What will happen to them? Where will they live?"

Horatio spun around abruptly to face them. "Fortunately, my father had the foresight to build our home on the ridge, overlooking the river. We'll be high and dry, my dear."

"Yes, I know, but—"

"I think we should get going." He scooped up their satchels himself and carried them outside while the driver gulped the rest of his coffee. Bebe quickly doused the fire. She had the unsettled feeling that Horatio was already thinking about his first drink.

Cold rain and low gray skies greeted them when they arrived in town. The road had disappeared completely beneath the floodwaters in several places, forcing the horses to wade or make a wide detour.

"Do you think the tannery will be flooded?" she asked Horatio. "It's closer to the river, isn't it? Maybe we should go there first."

"Nonsense. I want to get you home, where it's warm and dry. I'll head over there and see for myself after I speak with Mother."

Bebe's loneliness returned the moment she walked through the door into the quiet house. "Where's Mother?" Horatio asked the servant who opened the door for them.

"Mrs. Garner is in bed, sir—where she's been for the past four days."

"Is she ill?" Bebe asked.

The butler shook his head. "It's grief, ma'am."

"I'll go up and talk with her," Horatio said.

Bebe didn't volunteer to go with him. Her conscience whispered that she should, but she had no desire at all to see her mother-in-law. Nor would Mrs. Garner be eager to see her. Horatio returned five minutes later.

"She's fine," he assured her. "But I'll ask Dr.

Hammond to come by and see her today, just the same."

"Why don't you take your coat off and warm up, Horatio. You're all wet."

He shook his head. "I'm going down to the tannery. I'll be home by dinnertime, my dear."

A shiver of mistrust slithered through Bebe as Horatio kissed her good-bye and left the house. Maybe she should go with him. Maybe she should warn the driver not to take him to any saloons. She should have checked with Mr. MacLeod to see if Horatio kept any alcohol hidden at work. As her suspicions rose as steadily as the river, threatening to overwhelm her, Bebe searched for a distraction. She picked up Mr. Garner's newspaper from the table in the foyer, and carried it into the parlor to read. The unused room felt damp and cold, and she knelt by the hearth to light the logs that the servants had laid in the fireplace. The chill she felt didn't come from the cold, rainy weather but from her fear for Horatio.

She pulled a chair close to the fire and opened the newspaper. Bad news covered every page, drawing her in as she began reading about problems larger than her own. The mayor called the flooding the worst the town had seen in fifty years. Workers filled empty sacks with sand to try to protect the downtown area from the swollen river. Store owners scrambled to move their merchandise to the second floor whenever possible. But worst of all, an outbreak of cholera had already taken two lives down in The Flats.

Bebe closed the paper and stared into the flames. After she'd reconciled with Horatio and returned from her parents' farm three months ago, she had vowed to do something purposeful with her life rather than simply attending social events and delivering food that the servants had prepared. Instead, she had wasted the past few months searching for a house to buy—a house she never would live in. The needs she had just read about seemed enormous, and she longed to keep her promise and do something useful to help. But what could she do?

By the time Bebe finished reading four days' worth of newspapers, the family doctor had arrived to see Mrs. Garner. Bebe poked the fire and added more wood as one of the servants led him upstairs. She felt a tremor of fear when she thought about how helpless and self-pitying Mrs. Garner was— and how weak Horatio was, too. Might she end up just like the two of them someday? Bebe brushed sawdust off her hands and went into the foyer to wait for the doctor.

"Do you have a moment, Dr. Hammond?" she asked when he came downstairs from Mrs. Garner's room. "I would like to ask your advice on what I might do to be of help."

"Don't worry, your mother-in-law should be back to normal soon. Grief affects people in different ways—and the gloomy weather and all this rain haven't helped, either. I suggest you spend some time with her, talk with her, read uplifting books to her to help raise her spirits." He reached to remove his coat from the hall tree.

Bebe looked away so he wouldn't see her irritation. "That wasn't quite what I meant. I was talking about the much greater needs here in Roseton because of all the flooding. I've been reading the newspaper reports and wondered what you can tell me about the cholera outbreak down in The Flats."

"You have nothing at all to worry about. It won't spread up here to this part of town."

She nearly stomped her foot in exasperation. "I'm not concerned for myself. Our tannery workers and their families live down in that area."

The doctor stopped buttoning his coat and studied her for a moment. Bebe grew impatient. "I'm not my mother-in-law, Dr. Hammond. I may appear young and delicate to you, but I am determined to help those poor people if at all possible. I need to know what to do."

He exhaled, and she saw the lines in his face soften. "The cholera is being spread through the sewage. Someone must have brought the disease to town unknowingly—perhaps one of the newer immigrants. With all of this heavy rain we've had, the sewage spilled over into the drinking water.

People don't know they're drinking contaminated water and the disease keeps spreading."

"I've visited The Flats on occasion to do charity work. I've seen the open gutters and raw waste. I've also noticed that the sewage is taken care of in this part of town. Why haven't the city officials done something about The Flats long before now? On our farm back home, we kept our barn cleaner than those streets are kept."

"You'll have to ask the mayor and our city councilmen, ma'am."

"Perhaps I will. In the meantime, what can be done for those poor people?"

"The disease could be stopped if they were taught to boil all their drinking water. And once someone becomes ill, people need to avoid contact with contaminated bedding and clothing."

"Is it really that simple?"

"Yes. The problem is, once a mother contracts the disease, her children quickly get sick, as well, because there is no one to care for them or boil their water. The diarrhea can become so severe that if the patient isn't rehydrated, death can occur within several days for an adult, within hours for a child."

"If I gathered together some volunteers, what would we need to do to help?"

"Teach people to boil all of their water. The city is supposed to post signs with the warning—but many of the people in The Flats can't read. Patients that are already ill need to be kept well hydrated with clean drinking water. Get rid of any soiled clothing and bedding—boil it or burn it if you have to—and make sure no one comes in contact with it."

"Would volunteers be in any danger?"

"Not if they're careful. If they scrub their hands in hot soapy water and don't drink any untreated water, they should be fine."

As soon as Dr. Hammond left, Horatio's mother descended the stairs wearing her nightclothes and dressing gown. Her hair hung loose and limp, reaching past her shoulders. She halted on the landing, staring down at Bebe like a hawk watching a mouse.

"Are you feeling better—?"

"I heard what you and Dr. Hammond were discussing just now. I forbid you to get involved, Beatrice."

"But I'm concerned that the cholera outbreak might spread to our workers and their families. Dr. Hammond said it could be stopped with a little effort. Might we ask some of the women we know to help?"

"Absolutely not! I forbid it! You will not embarrass me by making such a request. Women of refinement and delicate sensibilities must be sheltered from such unpleasantness. How can you even think of asking such a thing?"

Bebe felt anger building inside her chest. Mrs.

Garner responded to tragedy by taking a dose of laudanum and going to bed. Worse, she had coddled and sheltered Horatio until he was unable to endure the miseries of life without a glass of scotch. But Bebe carefully suppressed her anger before speaking.

"Helping those poor people is the Christian thing to do, Mrs. Garner. And it needs to be done quickly, before more people die."

Her mother-in-law descended the remaining stairs, standing so close that Bebe could see her jaw trembling with rage. "If you step one foot in that neighborhood in the middle of this epidemic, don't you dare come back to my house!"

Bebe took a deep breath. "This is Horatio's house now, and I'm his wife. I know that I need to ask his permission before I go down there, but I'm certain he won't forbid me to help people who are suffering and dying. Now if you'll excuse me, please, I need to change into my work clothes."

She brushed past her mother-in-law and hurried up the stairs, aware that she probably had sacrificed all hope for a peaceful relationship with her. Bebe slammed her bedroom door a little louder than necessary and tore two buttons off her blouse in her haste to change out of her clothes. Mrs. Garner had purchased these clothes for her, and they were as suffocating and pretentious as she was. The woman was heartless. So were all the other women in her social circle. Mrs. Garner probably had been right about one thing: Those snobs would never lower themselves to help someone else, even if it meant saving a life.

Bebe thought of her own mother as she slipped into the dress that Hannah had sewn for her, the one she had worn when she arrived there three years ago. If only she could be more like Hannah, whose gentle, loving spirit never seemed to waver. But Bebe despaired of ever becoming like her mother.

She sighed and dropped to her hands and knees to search for her sturdy work shoes from the farm, digging through the back of the wardrobe. Horatio had nearly convinced her to throw them away since they were too small for any of the servants to wear, but Bebe's frugality hadn't allowed her to toss out perfectly good shoes.

She tried to think of someone else who might volunteer to help her, and thought of the tannery foreman, Neal MacLeod. If his wife had grown up in The Flats as he had, she might know some of the families in that neighborhood. Since Bebe intended to go to the tannery anyway to ask Horatio for his permission, she could easily ask Mr. MacLeod about his wife at the same time.

Bebe hurried down the servants' staircase and out the rear door to avoid running into her mother-in-law again. In her heart she knew that asking for Horatio's permission was simply an excuse to go to the tannery and check up on him. Was he really at work or had he already left for the saloon?

Bebe had never been inside the tannery before and had viewed it only from a distance—a messy, sprawling collection of buildings situated near the railroad tracks and the river. She asked the driver to take her to Horatio's office, and he halted the carriage in front of a long, low building with a small overhanging roof. The aroma of freshly cut wood scented the air as Bebe climbed down, along with the smell of smoke rising from the tall smoke-stack. But nearly drowning out all the other scents was an animal-like stench she couldn't quite place.

As soon as she walked through the main entrance, Bebe understood what Horatio meant about the terrible noise. The deep rumble of machinery roared in her ears like a dozen locomo-tives, and she had the urge to put her hands over her ears to drown out the deafening sound. Much worse than the noise was the terrible smell that caught in her throat and made her want to gag. She had grown up on a farm and was used to the odor of animals and manure, but this was something altogether new and horrid—a combination of strong chemicals and putrid flesh.

Her eyes adjusted to the dim light, and she saw that the noise came from several huge machines a few yards away. Two workmen stood in front of each one, feeding hides into the machine's mouth while the monster spit piles of discarded animal fat, flesh and hair at their feet. Another row of workers bent over wooden stands, scraping flesh and hair from animal hides with two-handled blades. Farther back in the shadowy building she glimpsed huge wooden vats and bales of hides stacked in tall bundles.

Poor Horatio, forced to spend his days in such a dreary, airless place. No wonder this job had killed his spirit. No wonder he preferred to remain in bed every morning than to come here. The stench of death was everywhere—and Horatio had experienced his fill of that stench on the battlefield.

As she stood looking all around, trying to decide where to go, she saw Neal MacLeod striding toward her. She had forgotten how tall and solidly built the foreman was—like a walking oak tree.

"If you're looking for your husband, Mrs. Garner, he's upstairs in his office. Would you like me to take you there?"

The relief Bebe felt was like shedding a heavy, wet coat. Horatio was at work, just as he said he would be. "Yes, you may take me to him in a moment. But may I have a word with you first?"

"Certainly, Mrs. Garner."

"I've been reading about the cholera outbreak down in The Flats, and I'm worried about our workers and their families. I just spoke with our family doctor, and he believes the epidemic could be stopped if we gathered some volunteers together and educated the people about the need to boil their drinking water. I'm willing to do that, but I'll need help. I wondered if your wife might be willing to assist me."

He looked away, already shaking his head. "I'm sorry, Mrs. Garner, but—"

"We will be perfectly safe," she said angrily, "as long as we take the precautions that the doctor outlined."

He stared at the floor, rubbing his square chin as if she had landed a punch to his jaw. "You've misunderstood me, Mrs. Garner," he said softly. "I was about to say I'm sorry—but I'm not married."

"Oh." Her anger drained away, replaced by embarrassment.

"But my sister Mary may be willing to help you," he continued. "I share a home with her and my mother. I can give you our address, if you'd like. I think that what you're doing is very courageous."

"My fair Beatrice is undoubtedly courageous," Horatio said as he approached Bebe from behind. She hadn't heard him coming because of the factory noise and his voice startled her. He rested his hands on her shoulders as if staking his claim. "How is it that you've discovered my wife's courage?" he asked his foreman.

Bebe saw MacLeod glance from Horatio to her and back again, as if unsure if he should reply or allow her to explain. She quickly told Horatio about the cholera epidemic and what Dr.

Hammond had advised her to do. "You're not going to forbid me to help, are you, Horatio?"

"No, darling. Of course I'm not going to forbid it." But Horatio's cheeks colored as he glanced at MacLeod, and Bebe sensed from the way that he shifted his feet that he might have refused her request if they had been alone. "I'm proud of you for being so brave. You are certain that it is safe, though?"

"Yes, of course. Ask Dr. Hammond."

"Well, then." Horatio smiled. "You had better be on your way while we get back to work."

The carriage driver followed Neal MacLeod's directions, halting in front of a small, plain bungalow on a quiet street. Bebe was surprised to discover that the foreman lived only one block west of the house that she had wanted to buy. She wondered if Horatio had known where MacLeod lived, and if that was the reason he had seemed so tense the day she had taken him to see the house. Bebe suddenly had second thoughts about initiating this friendship. What if it enflamed Horatio's jealousy? She nearly turned away from the door, but Mary MacLeod must have spotted Bebe's carriage through the window because she opened the door before Bebe had a chance to change her mind.

"Please, come inside out of the rain," she said, beckoning to her. Her smile was warm and welcoming. Bebe liked the woman the moment she saw her. Mary was sturdy and large-boned like her brother, with the same ruddy complexion and plain, honest face. Bebe glanced around at the inside of her cottage and wished that she and Horatio lived here instead of in their cold, echoing mansion.

"Thank you so much, Miss MacLeod. I'm Beatrice Garner, Horatio Garner's wife."

"Yes, I know. I saw you at the funeral."

Bebe stared for a moment, too surprised to speak. She could understand why Neal MacLeod would attend Mr. Garner's funeral, but why would his sister? She decided not to pursue it and quickly explained why she had come. "Dr. Hammond assured me that we'll be perfectly safe," she said when she finished, "as long as we're careful to take precautions."

"Of course I'll help you," Mary said without hesitation. She untied her apron, wrapped a warm shawl around her shoulders, and climbed into Bebe's carriage without a second thought. "I'll talk to my minister tonight," Mary promised. "Perhaps we can gather a few more volunteers from my church to help out tomorrow."

"That would be wonderful. I don't think the women from my church would ever volunteer. They're mostly high-society women, and . . . well . . ."

"You don't need to explain," Mary said. "I've lived in Roseton all my life. I understand."

"Back home in New Canaan, the women from

my church would gladly help out. Some of them risked their lives to help slaves escape before the war." Bebe listened to the horses' hooves splashing through the rain-drenched streets, then added, "I wish I could attend a different church, but Horatio's family has belonged to this one for several generations."

"And it isn't our business to judge them, is it? The choices people make are between them and God. And may I say that I admire you very much for going against their opinion and doing this, Mrs. Garner."

"Please, call me Bebe."

By the time they arrived in The Flats, Bebe was certain she had found a new friend. In the few minutes that they had conversed, it seemed as though they had always known each other. But they both fell silent when they reached their destination and saw the devastation. Water flooded the streets in every direction as far as Bebe could see. It surrounded all of the houses and tenement buildings until they appeared to be floating in a vast lake.

"This is as far as I can go," the driver told her. "The water is too deep."

"That's fine. We can walk from here." Bebe's concern for the residents increased as she and Mary climbed out of the carriage and waded into the knee-deep water. Bebe headed for the nearest tenement, snatching down one of the signs the city had posted to warn of the cholera epidemic and carrying it with her.

"How many of these people can even read?" she asked.

"Not many," Mary replied. "Most children are forced to drop out of school so they can work and help support their families."

Bebe pointed to the nearest building and said, "Let's start right here."

Shin-deep water filled all of the main floor apartments. The tenants had salvaged whatever items they could from their meager possessions and carried them to the upper floors. Bebe was astonished to see that many of the families were now living in the hallways or on the landings. She saw small children asleep on the floor beside mounds of soggy bedding, cooking pots, and rickety wooden chairs. Some upstairs tenants had taken pity on their neighbors, jamming dozens more people into the apartments on the upper floors.

For the next few hours Bebe went door to door with Mary throughout that first tenement, then to every other home and apartment building on the block, showing residents the sign and explaining what it meant. "Don't drink that water," she warned, pointing to the public faucets. "It isn't safe. It's making people very sick. Drink only boiled water. You must boil all of the water you use from now on."

In house after house they found the main floors

flooded and the tenants doing their best to live in despicable conditions. "Doesn't the city realize that these people have no place to live?" Bebe asked her new friend. "I wish we could do something."

"I'll ask our minister if we can open a shelter for some of them at our church—if these people will come to it, that is. They don't always like to accept charity."

Bebe nodded. She thought of all the extra rooms in Horatio's spacious home. They could house entire families there. But she knew better than to extend the offer without Horatio's permission. And she knew that his mother would never allow him to grant it.

Bebe and Mary talked to as many people as they could that afternoon, then promised to come back tomorrow with more help. When she returned home, Bebe put her own cook and all of the maids to work preparing extra food to distribute. They filled crocks and pails with clean drinking water for Bebe to take with her tomorrow. She loaded everything into the carriage early the next morning and stopped to pick up her new friend on the way. Mary had recruited six other women from her church. "And a dozen more ladies are working to turn the church into a temporary shelter," Mary told her. "Others are collecting donations of food and blankets and clothing."

"That's wonderful news, Mary." Bebe knew it

was what her own mother would have done—and what all Christians should do—and she made up her mind to live her life differently from then on.

In one of the first tenements Bebe entered, a little girl met her at the door, begging for help. "Please come. My mama is sick. She needs help."

Bebe found the mother and three of her children lying on soiled bedding, sick with cholera. The apartment stank so badly of illness and mildew that Bebe feared she might become sick herself, but she knelt beside the mother's bed with a cup of clean drinking water. "Here, you need to drink this. Your children need water, too."

The woman's lips were parched. She gulped thirstily. She looked both young and old at the same time. "What's your name?" Bebe asked her.

"Millie," she whispered. "Millie White. Please help my babies."

"Don't worry, Mary is taking good care of your children. Let me help you wash and change your clothes and bedding."

"Wait, let me do that job," Mary said, stopping her. "It's not fitting for a woman like you to do it. You shouldn't have to."

"No task is beneath me, Mary. I'll change this bed while you look after the children."

"The baby looks very ill to me," Mary whispered a few minutes later. "He's so weak he can't even swallow."

"I'll run downstairs and have my driver fetch Dr. Hammond."

All day long the women cared for the sick and moved flood victims to the shelter at the church. Bebe and Mary returned the next day and the next. "You are angels, sent from above," an elderly woman told them.

But even with additional volunteers, their efforts weren't always successful. Four days after Bebe first helped Millie White, she watched helplessly as Millie's baby boy died in his mother's arms. Bebe was so furious that she climbed into her carriage and drove straight to the mayor's office.

"Is the mayor expecting you?" his clerk asked.

"I'm Mrs. Horatio Garner," she said with as much dignity as she could, mindful that she was wearing muddy shoes and dripping work clothes. "The mayor's wife and I belong to the same social circle. I need to have a word with him." When the surprised clerk didn't respond, Bebe stormed past him and through the open door into the mayor's office. He appeared surprised and disgruntled, as if she had awakened him from a nap.

"My name is Mrs. Horatio Garner," she began, calmly enough. "My husband owns the tannery, as you well know. I have been helping out down in The Flats for the past several days, and I thought you should know that people are dying. Needlessly! Every single one of the cholera deaths this past week—including Millie White's infant son who died a few minutes ago—could have been prevented if this city had provided proper sanitation down there."

His obstinate expression never changed. With his long narrow face and overly large ears, he reminded Bebe of one her father's mules. "I don't understand how this concerns you, Mrs. Garner. Your family isn't affected in the least."

His attitude fueled her rage. "It concerns me because these are our workers and their families. We owe them a decent place to live. Furthermore, it concerns me as a citizen of this town, because our public works are supposed to be for the good of all, not just for the wealthy. And finally, it concerns me—as it should you—because the Bible commands us to help the poor."

The mayor looked her up and down. "My wife has mentioned making your acquaintance. She told me that you were . . . unusual." He had the audacity to smile as if she were an entertaining child. "You're not originally from Roseton, are you?"

"What does that have to do with anything?"

"You have no idea how we do things here, so allow me to give you some advice. If you value your husband's reputation in this community, I suggest that you run along home now and leave this business to others."

Bebe wanted to leap across the desk and punch

him. "You think this is a joke? How would you like it if I dumped contaminated water into your well or your cistern? How would you like to watch your children die of cholera?"

"Does your husband know you're meddling this way?"

"My husband cares about his workers just as much as I do. And since most of our workers are eligible to vote, perhaps you should care about them, as well. I intend to hold meetings at the tannery and inform our workers of their rights—and of your lack of concern for them during this crisis. The population of The Flats is quite large, you know. We're talking about a sizable group of voters. They may be interested to know how their informed vote can bring about change for their neighborhood. And who knows, perhaps someone from that community might decide to run for councilman—or even mayor."

He pushed papers around on his desk as if Bebe were an annoying fly and he were searching for the swatter. "Are you finished, Mrs. Garner?" he asked without looking up. "I believe I have another appointment."

"I'll see you at the next city council meeting," she said with controlled fury, "along with some citizens from The Flats. We'll see what you have to say then!"

"Women aren't allowed in our council meetings. Only registered voters may attend. Good day."

Bebe had never felt such helpless rage in her life. She stalked out to her waiting carriage, sank down on the seat, and wept with anger and frustration. The driver surely could hear her, but she didn't care. She thought of Millie's heartrending tears as she'd held her lifeless child, and Bebe sobbed harder.

"Shall I take you home, Mrs. Garner?" the driver asked when her tears finally subsided.

"No. Take me back to The Flats, please. I have more work to do."

Horatio stared at Bebe in amazement that evening when she told him about her conversation with the mayor. "You really said all of those things to him, my darling?"

"I would have said a lot more if he had taken me seriously. But he was laughing at me, Horatio!"

"To your face?"

"No . . . but he was laughing inside, I could tell. Lucretia Mott is right, you know. She came to one of our anti-slavery meetings back home and told us that women must win the right to vote. Coldhearted men like the mayor will never have the same compassion for children and poor people that women have. It's going to be up to us to make every neighborhood safe from disease."

By the time the epidemic and the flooding subsided, Bebe and Mary MacLeod had become good friends. "Won't you come inside and share a cup of tea with me?" Mary asked when they finished their last workday together. "Our home isn't fancy, but—"

"I would love a cup of tea," Bebe replied. They sat by a cozy fire in the cottage kitchen, eating Mary's homemade scones.

"I wanted to show you this," Mary said, handing Bebe a photograph. "He's my fiancé, James Lang. He died at the Battle of Shiloh."

He looked like a boy to Bebe. But hadn't they all been mere boys? "He has a very kind face," she said. "I'm so sorry for your loss."

"I loved him," she said simply. "I still love him. No other man can ever take his place."

"I fell in love with Horatio when I visited my brother Franklin in the army hospital in Philadelphia." Bebe remembered how different Horatio had been back then compared to the Horatio who had to get up and work at the tannery all day.

"Do you hear what everyone in The Flats is saying about you?" Mary asked as she poured more tea. "You have won undying gratitude from the workers and their families."

"I'm not finished down there. The cholera epidemic may be over, but the city still needs to do something about the sewage. Are you willing to fight that battle with me, too, Mary?"

"Of course. Tell me what I can do."

Bebe looked up at her new friend and smiled. Mary might have been large-boned and plain, but her kind, gentle nature made her seem pretty. Mrs. Garner's society friends worked so hard at dressing up the outsides of themselves but they could never compete with Mary's inner loveliness and strength.

"I don't know exactly how I'm going to fight that battle, yet," Bebe said. "We need to figure out a way to storm the city council meeting and get someone's attention. We'll talk about it some more tomorrow."

But the next morning when Bebe tried to get out of bed, the room spun so wildly that she had to close her eyes to make it stop. When she opened them again, her stomach seemed to turn inside out and she was struck by such a violent wave of nausea that she barely made it to the chamber pot before vomiting. Nor could she stop vomiting. Horatio leaped out of bed in a panic, ordering the servants to send for Dr. Hammond, immediately.

"Oh, my darling," he moaned. "I was so afraid you would catch that vile disease."

"It's not cholera," she told him. "Vomiting isn't a symptom."

"Please don't die on me! Please! I can't live without you, Beatrice." He looked so pale and shaken that she wondered if he was ill, too.

"I'll be fine," she assured him. But she wasn't fine. She felt so wretched that she had to lie down again.

Dr. Hammond arrived an hour later. By the time he'd finished examining her, he was smiling as he called Horatio into the bedroom. "I expect your wife to make a full recovery in approximately eight months," he said. "That's when your baby will be born. Congratulations, Mr. Garner."

"M-my baby?" Horatio stammered. "She's having a baby? . . . Oh, my darling, how wonderful!" He broke into a wide grin, then hugged Bebe so tightly she feared her ribs might break. When Horatio finished walking Dr. Hammond to the door, he returned to the bedroom. His handsome face was somber as he took Bebe into his arms again.

"Now listen to me, my dearest. No more excitement of any kind for you. No more trips to The Flats, no arguments with the mayor."

She gently freed herself from his arms and started to get out of bed, feeling much better now that the nausea had passed. "But there's more work to be done down there and—"

"No, Beatrice. I withdraw my permission for you to go down to that place ever again. From now on you need to stay at home. In bed. For the baby's sake."

She tried to laugh away his concern. "Don't be silly, Horatio. Women have babies all the time, and they don't stay in bed."

"I don't care what other women do. You're my wife, and I want you to stay home and not exert yourself. I want to make certain our child is delivered safely into this world."

"But I can still do some sort of charity work even though—"

"No. I would never forgive myself if something happened to you down in that terrible place. I want you to follow Mother's example and be a respectable wife from now on. Women from our social station are supposed to have a proper period of confinement when they're in your condition. I'm sure Mother will explain it to you."

"Your mother hates me, Horatio."

"That isn't true. Please give her a chance, Beatrice. My fondest wish is that you and Mother would become friends."

Bebe could only nod. Her own mother had advised her to make peace with Mrs. Garner, too. "I promise to try, Horatio. Now may I please get out of bed? Mary MacLeod is expecting me to call on her this morning."

"We need to talk about her." Horatio looked like a stern schoolmaster about to scold his pupils. "Now that the flooding has subsided, I don't want you to see her anymore."

"But why not?"

"Why not? I hardly know where to start. The MacLeods are not our kind of people, Beatrice. It's bad enough that Father has saddled me with her brother for the next five years, but I don't need you socializing with the rest of his family, as well. Please respect my wishes, darling."

Bebe felt another wave of dizziness, as if the bedroom walls were floating toward her. "But Mary is my friend. Can't I just visit her now and then?"

Horatio looked wounded. "I've given you a life and a home that many women would envy. Isn't that enough for you? Aren't I enough?"

"Of course you are." Bebe pulled him into her arms so he wouldn't see her tears. If she had to choose between losing her new friend and losing Horatio there was no contest. He was working hard and staying sober, and those were the most important things right now, especially with a baby on the way. But she couldn't help feeling the loss of her friend along with her hopes of living a more meaningful life. She would have to lay aside her own wishes once again, and she didn't want to. She felt the seeds of bitterness and resentment begin to sprout in her heart and recalled Hannah's warning about weeding them out before they grew. If only she knew how to do that.

"I'll do whatever you want," she told Horatio.

For now, she said in her heart.

On a warm morning in May of 1869, Bebe went into labor. The delivery proved to be very difficult and painful, lasting nearly two days. Horatio worried and paced and fretted the entire time.

"Your wife is having a hard time," the doctor told him, "because she is so tiny and her baby is so big."

Bebe thought her pain worthwhile, though, when she finally held her daughter in her arms. She was a beautiful baby, ruddy and fair-haired like Horatio. "Are you all right, my darling?" he asked when the doctor finally allowed him into the room.

"I'm fine now. Just very tired." Bebe remembered how disgruntled her own father had been after she'd been born and asked, "Are you disappointed that we didn't have a son, Horatio?"

"Not at all! How could anyone be disappointed in this wonderful child? She is the most beautiful baby in the world!"

"Do you like the name Lucretia? We could call her Lucy." She didn't tell him that she had chosen the name in honor of Lucretia Mott.

"Could we give her my mother's name for her middle name?" he asked.

"Yes, of course."

Horatio lifted Lucretia Frances Garner from Bebe's arms and waltzed slowly around the room with her, talking to her nonstop and telling her what a strong, brave mother she had.

"I'm so tired, Horatio. Can you talk to her later? Lucy and I both need to rest."

"Yes, of course." He gave the baby to the nurse he'd hired and kissed Bebe's forehead. "Go to sleep now, my darling. You deserve a very long nap. The nurse will take good care of both of you."

Bebe sighed and closed her eyes. Moments later, she was asleep.

While she slept, Horatio went downtown to his former club with a fistful of cigars to celebrate his daughter's birth.

He came home roaring drunk.

CHAPTER
16

My sister Alice's wedding was two weeks away, and I was still safely tucked away at Grandma's house, enjoying the peace and quiet. Then Grandma heard about a big temperance rally that was going to be held in the state capital of Harrisburg. "Should we go, Harriet?" she asked. "It would take us about two hours to drive there."

I felt torn. On the one hand, I had promised my mother that I would keep Grandma Bebe out of trouble so there wouldn't be any family scandals before the wedding. But on the other hand, maybe I finally would get to see some axe-wielding at a gathering this big. "What do people do at these rallies?" I asked her.

"Oh, the speeches are very inspirational. Some of our national leaders will be there, and there is usually a call to sign The Pledge and abstain from alcohol. I heard Frances Willard speak at one rally, but she has since passed away, I'm sorry to say."

"Will Carrie Nation be there?"

"She passed away last year."

"Oh. That's too bad." I was beginning to get the feeling that I had missed the boat when it came to the more exciting exploits of the temperance movement. "I would still like to go, Grandma. Can we? Please?"

Grandma agreed. But when we awoke to a downpour on Saturday she began to have misgivings. "I've driven to Harrisburg in the springtime before," she told me. "The dirt roads can be quite muddy this time of year."

"But we *have* to go! Please, Grandma? Please?" She didn't know it, but I planned to surprise her by signing The Pledge, swearing to forsake all alcoholic beverages for the rest of my life. After hearing about my grandfather, I never wanted to take a single sip. Grandma was going to be so pleased.

We left Roseton early in the morning and made it over the first range of hills without any trouble. We saw some pretty huge puddles in the road, and the mud looked deep and squishy in places, but Grandma steered smoothly around all the obstacles. Twenty minutes into our trip, though, we came to a quagmire that had completely swallowed the road. Grandma stepped on the gas to plow straight through it, but the car never made it to the other side. We ground to a halt, stuck in the mud—sunk clear up to our axles, judging by the spinning sound that the wheels made. A shower of muck sprayed out from the rear wheels and splattered down on the rear window. We were going nowhere. Grandma lifted her foot off the accelerator and let the car engine die.

"Oh, dear," she said with a sigh. "I was afraid this would happen."

I started to open the passenger door, certain that if Grandma knew how to fix a tire, she would surely know how to get us out of this mess, too. But she stopped me before I could climb out.

"Where are you going, Harriet? Stay in the car. It's much too wet and muddy out there. You'll ruin your shoes."

"But we're stuck. Shouldn't we do something? Jack up the car, maybe? Or start pushing?"

"No, we'll just wait. Another car is bound to come along soon and help us out."

I stared at her in disbelief. "But . . . but you said that only women in fairy tales wait to be rescued."

"Harriet dear, neither one of us is capable of getting this car out of the mud by ourselves."

"But you said—"

"I know, I know. But there are exceptions to every rule, and this is one of them."

My disappointment was as deep as the mud. How was I supposed to learn anything about life if Grandma was going to contradict herself? I heaved a loud sigh to let her know how frustrated I was. "First you say, 'Don't wait to be rescued.' Now you say, 'Wait for help.' How am I supposed to know what to do when?"

"Well, I suppose time and experience will teach you the difference."

I sighed again and sat back with my arms folded, waiting for an explanation. Grandma stared at the fog-shrouded mountains in the distance for a long moment. Rain pattered softly against the roof and slid down our windshield like thin, glassy fingers.

"Sometimes you can look at circumstances," she finally said, "and you can clearly see what needs to be done. Take my mother's situation, for instance. She didn't wait for someone else to help the runaway slaves; she did what she could to rescue them herself. And in my own situation, I knew that I had to do whatever I could to rescue Horatio so that he wouldn't drink us all into ruin."

I waved my hand impatiently. "I understand that part. Like you said, 'Only women in fairy tales wait to be rescued.'"

"Yes. But there were other times in my life when I took matters into my own hands, and . . . well, things didn't turn out the way I'd hoped. . . ."

Bebe sat in the parlor with her four-year-old daughter on her lap and held up two books for her to choose between. "Which story shall we read today, Lucy?"

"Both! I want to hear both of them!"

"No, we have time for only one of them before your nap."

"But I want both!" Lucy pouted.

Reading stories before Lucy's afternoon nap was one of Bebe's favorite rituals, and one of the few times she had Lucy all to herself. Lucy resembled a little angel, with her halo of curly blond hair and her sweet rosy face—but her temperament didn't always match her appearance. Bebe glanced at Lucy's nanny hovering nearby. The woman always gave in to Lucy in order to avoid a temper tantrum, but Bebe was determined not to spoil her only child. She laid one of the books aside.

"If you can't make up your mind, we'll read this one."

"No! I want two books!"

Bebe ignored her daughter's stubbornness and opened the book, hoping Lucy would settle down once they started reading. Several pages into the story, the front doorbell chimed. Bebe paused, waiting for the servants to answer it, listening to hear who it was. Lucy listened, too, and when it became obvious that a deliveryman had arrived at the front door with a package, she slid off Bebe's lap, squealing with delight and clapping her hands. "For me? Is it for me?"

Bebe laid aside the book and followed her to the front hallway.

"Yes, Miss Lucy. It's for you," the butler said. Lucy snatched the package from his hands without a word of thanks and began tearing off the brown paper wrapping, scattering it all over the floor. Mrs. Garner descended the stairs to watch the destruction, wearing a pleased smile on her face.

"I was wondering when my surprise might arrive for you, Lucy. Open it carefully, dear. You wouldn't want to break it before you've had a chance to play with it, would you?"

Bebe stifled a groan. "Not another toy, Mother Garner. The playroom is overflowing with toys as it is. No child needs that many playthings."

They were expensive toys, too. Last week Mrs. Garner had purchased a wooden rocking horse for Lucy, with a mane and tail made of real horsehair. The week before, she had brought home a stuffed bear with glassy eyes and velvety fur and paws that really moved.

Lucy tore open the box and quickly dug through the straw packing material to retrieve her prize. "Look, Mama! A dolly!"

Bebe crouched beside her daughter. She had to admit that the doll was beautiful—even more so than the five other dolls Lucy already owned. Its hair felt like real human hair and the eyes in its dainty porcelain head opened and closed when Lucy moved her. She even had tiny eyelashes. According to the label, the doll had been imported all the way from Germany.

"She's lovely, Lucy. You must give her a very lovely name to match."

"And you must be careful with her," Mrs. Garner added. "You don't want to get her hair mussed or her clothes wrinkled."

"Aren't toys meant to be played with, Mother Garner?"

The older woman ignored Bebe's question and reached for Lucy's hand. "Come, Lucy dear. Let's go find a place for her in your playroom."

"But it's time for her nap, and—"

"Lucy wants to play with her new doll, don't you, darling?" They walked upstairs together, followed by the nanny.

"Lucy?" Bebe called up the stairs after her. "Did you thank Grandmother Garner for the present?" She didn't reply.

Bebe looked down at the torn paper and straw that Lucy had strewn all over the floor for the servants to clear away. She sighed in frustration and bent to pick up the mess herself. Her daughter was growing into a spoiled, demanding child, who didn't know how to do anything for herself, but whenever Bebe complained to Horatio, he took his mother's side.

"She'll only be a child for a few more years, Beatrice. You want her to grow up happy, don't you?"

"Of course I do." Bebe wanted everyone to be happy—most importantly, Horatio.

His drinking binge following Lucy's birth had lasted nearly a month. Bebe had begged him to stop, appealing to his love for his new daughter and for her. When he finally agreed, she took him up to the fishing cabin for a week. Once again, Horatio sobered up, apologizing and promising that it would never happen again. He had kept his promise for four years now. In return, Bebe had done her best to settle into the Garners' social world at his request, planning dinner parties and open houses and teas, attending social gatherings and balls and fetes. In fact, she was supposed to attend the ribbon cutting ceremony at Roseton's new women's club this afternoon. She wished she didn't have to go.

"I own the tannery now," Horatio had told her. "I have certain duties to perform in this community, and so do you and Mother." Like it or not, those duties included pointless ribbon-cutting cere-monies. Bebe trudged up the stairs to get ready, ignoring the commotion in Lucy's playroom as the nanny tried in vain to coax her into taking a nap.

"Let her stay up and play with her new doll," Bebe heard Mrs. Garner say. "I insist."

Bebe's maid was waiting in her room to help her dress. "Mrs. Garner chose this gown for you to wear today," she said. Bebe nodded, tight-lipped. It seemed as though Horatio's mother made every decision in her life. While the maid tightened her corset laces and slipped the chosen gown over her head, Bebe struggled to stay afloat in a sea of resentment. She hated the control that Mrs. Garner had over her—and now over Lucy. She felt as though she were navigating through rocky waters without a map: praying Horatio would remain sober, trying to please Mother Garner, hoping to maintain a façade of normalcy for her daughter's sake.

As she sat at the dressing table, watching in the mirror as the maid arranged her hair, Bebe thought her life resembled a lavishly written novel without a plot. What good was all of the pageantry and posturing without a purpose? And what good did it do her to look beautiful on the outside when she seethed with frustration and resentment on the inside? She wished she would get pregnant again so she would have something useful to do—and so Lucy wouldn't become so spoiled—but that hadn't happened, either.

Bebe and Mrs. Garner arrived side by side at the ceremony, smiling and greeting the other women as if they were as close as mother and daughter. On lonely afternoons like this one, Bebe longed for a true friend. Her relationships with the other society women were superficial, and none of the women had become what she would call a friend, much less a confidante. She missed Mary MacLeod, even though their friendship had lasted barely a month. After Lucy's birth, she had begged Horatio again and again to allow her to visit Mary, but he always refused.

"Why do you need her?" he had asked. "She's

not like us, Beatrice. Please stay away from her."

Three hours after the ribbon-cutting ceremony began, Bebe returned home, her face stiff from holding a phony smile in place all afternoon. She trudged upstairs feeling exhausted, even though she'd done nothing more strenuous than eat *petit fours* and listen to boring speeches. After changing out of her dress, she sat down in her dressing room to read the newspaper. Mr. Garner's subscription had never lapsed, and Bebe had developed the habit of reading the news every day. Occasionally, she would find an article about the Woman Suffrage movement—the paper always described their activities in negative terms, of course—and sometimes an article would mention Lucretia Mott.

But what interested Bebe even more were the descriptions of a temperance crusade that had swept across upstate New York, Ohio, and Michigan this year, quickly gaining momentum. Like the abolition crusades, it had begun when groups of Christian women joined together in prayer meetings, seeking the abolition of all alcoholic beverages. As the movement spread, the women began holding their prayer vigils on the streets outside of saloons until the embarrassed customers went home and the saloon owners caved in to the pressure and closed their doors. So far, the women had driven dozens of saloons out of business.

Bebe cut out all the articles she could find with news of either movement and kept them in a cigar box in her dresser drawer. If Horatio wouldn't allow her to become involved, she could at least enjoy reading about what other women were doing.

Bebe was disappointed to find nothing about either the Temperance or Suffrage movement in today's paper. Instead, every headline and article described the shocking news that yesterday, September 18, 1873, the nation's best-known banking house, Jay Cooke and Company, had collapsed. Business affairs usually were of little interest to Bebe, but she could tell that this news was momentous. She read every word. Experts predicted that more bank failures would quickly follow; that businesses and industries would be forced to close their doors once they could no longer borrow money; that workers would be laid off, leading to labor unrest, riots, and starvation. The newspaper painted such a grim picture that Bebe whispered a prayer that the experts would prove to be wrong.

Late that night, Horatio startled her awake, moaning and thrashing in bed.

"Horatio! Horatio, wake up!" she said, shaking him. His eyes finally flew open and he sat up, looking frantically around the room as if he didn't know where he was. "You were having a nightmare, Horatio. Everything is fine, it was only a bad dream."

She could feel his body trembling, shaking the bed. Sweat drenched his silk pajamas. He groaned and ran his hands through his hair and then climbed out of bed. Bebe got out of bed, too, and started to light a lamp, but he stopped her.

"Don't! I don't want a light on." She tried to draw Horatio into her arms to soothe him, but he refused her consolation, pushing her away. He began to pace as if trapped in a cage with no way out.

"Tell me about your dream, Horatio. Was it the war again?" He shook his head. She could see that he longed for a drink, and she was glad that she had thrown out every drop of alcohol after his father died. She sat on the edge of the bed, still feeling shaky after being startled awake.

"Please tell me what's wrong." He didn't reply. "Talk to me, Horatio. Are you worried about something? I read in the newspaper about the huge bank that went broke—are you afraid it will affect the tannery?"

He finally turned to her, and she could hear the controlled anger in his voice, even though she couldn't see him clearly in the dark. "This house is my refuge, Beatrice. I don't want to talk about work when I'm at home. Besides, you don't need to concern yourself with financial matters. You shouldn't even be reading the newspaper in the first place. Why can't you read *Godey's Lady's Book,* like other women do?"

His words stung and she knew he had meant them to. She lashed back without thinking. "I don't care about the latest fashions. I care about real life! You think I'm too stupid to understand the news, don't you?"

"I didn't say that. But why concern yourself with the world outside our home? I work hard so that you can be free from worry, like Mother is."

Comparing her to his mother infuriated Bebe. She sprang to her feet. "Well, I'm not stupid! I know that Cooke's was one of our country's largest banks and that business loans are going to be hard to come by in the next few months. I know that if factories like yours can't borrow money to purchase supplies, and if stores can't borrow money to buy stock, then the store shelves are going to be empty by Christmastime and workers are going to be laid off and—"

"Stop it! I never said you were stupid. I said I didn't want to talk about it at home!"

Bebe realized her mistake and softened her tone. "But why can't you share your life with me? We could help each other." She tried to take him into her arms again, but he fended her off.

"You're not the man of the family—I am!" He snatched up his dressing gown and opened the bedroom door. "Go back to sleep. I'm sorry I awakened you." He slammed the bedroom door on his way out.

Bebe sank onto a chair and lowered her face to

her lap. She didn't know what to do. She could hear Horatio wandering around downstairs, unable to sleep, but at least he wouldn't find any alcohol. She sat in the chair for the rest of the night, waiting for him to return to bed, but he never did. In the morning, she saw dark circles beneath his eyes as he dressed for work.

"Horatio, I'm sorry for making you angry." She wanted to hold him, but she was afraid to approach him after he'd pushed her away twice last night.

"I'm sorry, too," he said. "About everything." He reached out to her, and the sorrow she saw in his eyes nearly stopped her short. His grief seemed much deeper than regret over a marital spat. And what had he meant by "everything"? She went into his arms and held him tightly, afraid to risk another argument by questioning him.

"I won't be home for supper tonight," he told her. "We are very busy at work right now, and I'm needed there to handle things."

He still held her tightly in his arms, so she couldn't look into his eyes to see if he was lying to her. "Shall I have the servants save dinner for you?" she asked.

"No. I'll be very late." And he was. But Bebe didn't detect the smell of alcohol on his breath when he did return home, and he didn't appear to be drunk.

The following afternoon, Bebe was sitting in the parlor reading in the newspaper about the growing financial crisis when someone arrived at the front door. Lucy, who was supposed to be napping, barreled down the stairs, shouting, "For me? Is it another present for me?"

Bebe laid down the paper and hurried to the door. When she saw that it was the foreman from the tannery asking for Horatio, her stomach clenched in a knot. "Go back upstairs, Lucy. Right now."

"But I want another present!"

Bebe stood aside and waited while the nanny scooped up the struggling child and carried her upstairs. The dread Bebe felt overwhelmed any embarrassment over her daughter's tantrum.

"Won't you come in, Mr. MacLeod?"

He shook his head, choosing to remain on the front step. "I'm very sorry to bother you, Mrs. Garner, but your husband is needed at work. I'm afraid it can't wait until tomorrow."

The knot of pain in her stomach tightened. "Horatio's not here. . . . Isn't he at the tannery?"

MacLeod's face reddened with embarrassment. "Um . . . well . . . no, ma'am. He isn't." He began backing away, preparing to leave. "I'm sorry I bothered you with this."

"Wait . . ." The foreman halted, but he wouldn't meet Bebe's gaze. "How long ago did Horatio leave?" She was trying to convince herself that he had simply gone for a haircut or a shoeshine.

"About three hours ago. . . . I'm sorry. I never would have disturbed you, but he told me he had another headache, and I thought he said he was going home. I must have misunderstood him. I'm sorry." Once again, he began backing away. Once again, she stopped him as dread and suspicion billowed inside her like smoke.

"Wait! Does he complain of headaches often? Has he left work this early before?" MacLeod hesitated as if he didn't want to reply. "I need to know the truth, Mr. MacLeod. I want to do what's best for the tannery, and I want to help my husband. But I can't do either one if I don't know the truth."

"He has been complaining of headaches for some time now," he said, rubbing his jaw. "Lately, it has become a habit for him to leave work early. Usually around noon. I'm sorry."

"Does he return to work, or is he gone for the remainder of the day?" She dreaded hearing his reply.

"He doesn't return, ma'am. Listen, I'm sorry for disturbing you. I wouldn't have bothered you if I had known . . . I'm sorry . . ."

"Stop apologizing and tell me how long he has been doing this."

He cleared his throat. "For about two weeks."

Two weeks. What had Horatio been doing all that time? Where had he been going? The pain in Bebe's stomach grew so fierce she wanted to double over. Instead, she held her head high.

"Horatio hasn't been coming home with these headaches. And he didn't come home last night until well after dinner. He told me he was working late."

"I'm sor—" He caught himself and stopped. "I worked late last night and . . . and he wasn't there. Listen, I guess this can wait one more day, Mrs. Garner. I'll talk to him about it tomorrow morning. I'm sorry for bothering you."

"No, wait!" He halted again, and this time Bebe paused until he finally looked up at her. "You need to know the truth, Mr. MacLeod. The reason that Horatio isn't here and the reason he's been lying to you about his headaches is probably because he is down in a men's club or a saloon somewhere, getting drunk."

MacLeod didn't reply. Nor did he appear surprised. His emotions were easy to read on his plain, honest face, and Bebe guessed from his expression that many of Horatio's other actions had begun to make sense to him.

"You aren't surprised, are you, Mr. MacLeod?"

"It does explain some things that have happened lately."

"Like what?"

"I would rather not say." He lowered his gaze again to stare at the ground.

Should she go looking for Horatio? Bebe felt so angry and betrayed that she wanted to storm into his club and confront him. She knew that she should wait until she could let go of her anger and could confront him in love, but she felt no love at all for him at the moment. She had given up every-thing for him, had agreed to all of his wishes—and he had deceived her.

"You mentioned that you came here on important business, Mr. MacLeod. I would like you to come with me now and help me find my husband. That way, Horatio will know that he can't lie to us any-more."

"I'm sor—" He stopped and cleared his throat again. "Listen, nearly five years have passed since your father-in-law died. Your husband has already made it very clear that I will be fired as soon as the time is up. He was forced to keep me on as foreman according to the terms of Mr. Garner's will, and . . ." He looked very uneasy. "And when he fires me, I'll need a recommendation from him if I hope to find another job. I don't want to do anything to make him angry."

"Horatio can't run the business by himself," Bebe said. "I think you already know that. Especially if he has begun drinking again. And I believe you know what might happen to the tan-nery during this economic crisis if you're not at the helm."

He didn't reply. His unease grew as he continued to rub his jaw and shuffle his feet, his gaze directed at his shoes. Bebe admired his unwillingness to speak ill of Horatio, even if his motivation was fear of unemployment. But she could no longer disguise her fear from him.

"I know about the banking crisis in this country," she told him. "If Horatio doesn't sober up, we stand to lose everything, don't we? The tannery, all of our income, our savings?"

"Please don't ask me to confront your husband, ma'am. I'm very sorry for disturbing you, but I need to get back to work."

This time he turned around and kept walking without looking back. Bebe closed the front door. It required a great effort on her part to remain calm and not burst into tears of rage and fear and disappointment. Instead, she went out to the carriage house to find the driver. Bebe made up her mind that if Horatio was using the carriage, she would walk downtown alone, searching every men's club in town until she found him and dragged him home. But the driver and all of the horses and vehicles were in the carriage house.

"I need to find my husband," she told him. "He isn't at the tannery. I need you to drive me around to some of the other places he frequents."

The driver didn't reply, but his pained expression told her what she needed to know. He didn't want to be in the middle of this confrontation any more than Mr. MacLeod did.

"I know that you must feel a great deal more loyalty to Horatio than to me," Bebe continued, "but I need your help. If Horatio is drinking during the daytime instead of working, and if we lose the tannery because of it, you could be out of a job."

He lifted a set of reins from a hook on the wall and slowly opened one of the horse stalls to lead the animal out, his reluctance displayed in his every movement. He silently harnessed the horse to the vehicle, then helped Bebe into the carriage. He paused before climbing aboard himself. "I'll take you to a place where he sometimes goes, ma'am."

Bebe closed her eyes. "Thank you," she said softly.

They drove to one of the poorer parts of town and halted in front of a two-story brick building with a striped awning in front. The sign read *Logan's Tavern.* Horatio was frequenting a common saloon. In the middle of the afternoon.

The driver hopped down to help Bebe, but she couldn't seem to move. Lively piano music drifted out of the open door, but the saloon's interior looked very dark, as if the people inside were trying to hide. A deliveryman had propped the door open as he hurried in and out, carrying blocks of ice.

Bebe finally climbed down and went up to the door for a closer look, pausing before entering, waiting for her eyes to adjust to the darkness so she could recognize her husband. Through a haze of cigar smoke, she saw a bartender standing behind a long, wooden counter, wiping glasses. Dozens of liquor bottles filled the shelves behind him, and Bebe fought the urge to pick up the brick that held the door open and hurl it at the shelves, smashing every bottle in the place. She drew a breath to calm herself, inhaling smoke and the yeasty aroma of beer. The row of men who leaned against the counter wore filthy work clothes, their faces smudged with soot and grease, as if they had just finished a day of work and had stopped off for a drink on their way home. Horatio wasn't among them.

Her eyes adjusted a little more and she watched the iceman shove the dripping blocks inside a wooden icebox beside the bar. A rotund man sat on a little round stool, playing an upright piano that sounded as though it needed to be tuned. In between the tinny notes she heard the clink of glasses, the rumble of voices and laughter. The saloon had smoke-stained walls and a wooden floor and a tin ceiling.

In the rear of the long, narrow room, groups of men sat hunched around tables while a woman served drinks to them. One of the men was Horatio. He had a glass in one hand and a fistful of playing cards in the other. He had slung his suit coat over the back of the chair and rolled up his shirtsleeves. He looked happier than Bebe had seen him in months, laughing and tilting his chair back on two legs.

The iceman brushed past her and shoved aside the brick he'd used to prop open the door. Bebe caught the door as it slowly closed, but before she could step inside, the bartender rushed over from behind the counter.

"Whoa, whoa! You can't come in here, lady. Women aren't allowed." He held up his hands to block her path.

"Then kindly send my husband out. His name is Horatio Garner, and he is needed at home."

The man stroked his bushy mustache and shook his head. "I never disturb my customers in the middle of their euchre games. Go home, little lady."

"I said he is needed at home! This is an emergency!" She had raised her voice, hoping Horatio would hear it above the chatter and the music. She hadn't lied about the emergency; Horatio was putting his family's future at risk by neglecting his work at the tannery.

"Sorry, but you'll have to send your driver in to get him. No women allowed." He pushed the door closed in her face.

Bebe returned to the carriage, where the driver stood waiting for her. "I'm sorry," she told him. "I hate to make you take my side over Horatio's, but as I said, you could lose your job if the tannery goes bankrupt. Kindly fetch Mr. Garner for me."

"Yes, ma'am." He shuffled through the door and disappeared inside. Bebe climbed into the carriage to wait. Several minutes passed before he returned with Horatio, and while she waited, Bebe thought of her cigar box full of newspaper articles

describing the new women's temperance movement. She felt much too angry to ever kneel in
front of this saloon and quietly pray the way those
women did. Instead, she envisioned herself
throwing bricks through the windows and
smashing all the tables and chairs to pieces in
anger.

Horatio finally emerged with the driver, wearing
a silly grin on his face, as if he wasn't the least bit
concerned. "What's the emergency, Bebe?"

"Your foreman came to the house. He needs you
at the tannery. You have to come home and sober
up so you can go back to work."

He stood staring at her as if he hadn't understood
a word she'd said.

"Please get in, Horatio. We need to go home."

The driver had to take his arm and help him
climb in. Bebe's tears began to fall as the carriage
jolted up the hill toward home. Horatio had
brought along an unfinished bottle of vodka, but
when Bebe tried to take it from him, he became as
stubborn and petulant as Lucy did during one of
her tantrums.

"No! You can't have it, Bebe. This is mine. I
need it."

She glared at him in disgust and his silly smile
vanished.

"Don't look at me like that, Bebe."

"How should I look at you? You're drunk,
Horatio. You broke your promise to me."

His eyes filled with tears. "Remember the first time we met in the army hospital? You looked at me as though I had just hung the moon in the sky. I saw it on your face . . . in your eyes. . . . You never look at me that way anymore."

That's because you're a drunkard, she wanted to shout. *I gave up all of my own wishes and dreams for you!* But she bit her lip and remained silent.

Horatio finished the vodka at home that evening after locking himself in his father's study. He didn't come upstairs to their bedroom until after midnight. The next morning, when Bebe tried to awaken him for work, he refused to get up.

"Go away and leave me alone," he mumbled.

"Horatio, you have to go to work. Please, for my sake . . . for Lucy's sake . . . for your mother's sake . . ."

He clapped his hands over his ears. "Shut up and leave me alone!"

Bebe got out two satchels and packed clothing for both of them, then shook him awake again. "Everything is ready, Horatio. We can leave for the fishing cabin right away. We'll take Lucy with us this time. She'll like it up there."

"No she won't. She'll hate it."

Bebe knew it was true. Even at four years of age, Lucy was as accustomed to luxury as her grandmother was. Bebe pulled back the covers and tugged on his arm. "Come on, Horatio. You need to go down to the tannery and—"

"I'm never stepping foot in that cursed place ever again!"

She remembered yesterday's visit from the foreman and felt the pain in her stomach return. "Neal MacLeod was here yesterday, and he said there was something important to take care of at work this morning."

Horatio sat up in bed to face her. "Don't ever mention that man's name to me again, do you hear me? And stop telling me what to do, Beatrice. I'm in charge of my life, not you!"

The rage she saw on his face frightened her. She backed up a step. "I know you are in charge, but—"

"All my life, everyone has been telling me what to do. First my mother, then my father, then the army officers . . . Don't you dare start telling me what I have to do, too! This is my life, and I'm never going back to that tannery again! Ever!"

She turned her back on him and walked from the room and then downstairs to the foyer. She needed to get away from him before she said something she would regret. She grabbed her hat and shawl from the hall tree, sick with fear and worry, and hurried outside to the carriage that stood waiting to take Horatio to work. Something was terribly wrong at work, and if Horatio wouldn't go, then she would have to go in his place. She would find out what the crisis was, then return home and beg him to take charge of it. Surely he hadn't meant it when he said he would never go back there again.

She strode through the tannery's main entrance, and the smell of death immediately assaulted her. As she pulled out a handkerchief to cover her nose, she spotted Neal MacLeod examining one of the huge scraping machines as if trying to determine why it had stopped. A workman alerted him to her presence, and he spun around with a look of surprise.

"Mrs. Garner, I hope nothing is wrong."

"May I speak with you for a moment?" She led him further away from the workers so they wouldn't overhear. "Horatio won't get out of bed. He has started on another drinking binge. I know you said yesterday that something important needed his attention, but since it isn't possible for him to attend to it this morning . . ." She paused to swallow her tears. "I-I wondered if you could advise me on the best course of action to take. What exactly is the problem?"

MacLeod hesitated, and she saw his back stiffen. He reminded Bebe of one of her father's mules refusing to follow her order to plow. "Please tell me the truth," she begged. "Is the tannery in financial trouble?"

"Let's go up to the office."

She followed him up a short flight of stairs to a cramped, cluttered office that was not much bigger than her dressing room. Horatio's name was painted in gold lettering on the glass window of the door beneath his father's name. A window on one side of the desk looked down on the tannery floor, offering a view of the workmen and blunting some of the terrible odors and noise. A window on the opposite wall looked out on the tannery yard behind the main building. But that view was far from scenic, marred by untidy storage sheds and a row of railroad cars, a smokestack and water tanks, and piles and piles of tree bark. The river in the distance resembled a sluggish brown smear. Bebe couldn't picture Horatio working in this stifling room all day, nor working down on the factory floor or out in the filthy yard. Yet Neal MacLeod had looked confident and comfortable striding among the men and machines. His work had become part of him. She wondered if Horatio had noticed it, too.

MacLeod closed the door behind them and motioned for Bebe to sit down behind the desk. He pulled up a chair on the other side of it. "Our financial situation is not good, Mrs. Garner. We are nearly out of money. If we can't convince the bank to extend our loan, the tannery will have to close."

Pain gripped Bebe's stomach and twisted it. "Does Horatio know the truth?"

"Yes. I've been begging him to sign these loan forms so we can stay in business, but to be honest, he doesn't seem to care. It's almost as if he wants the tannery to close."

MacLeod paused, and Bebe was surprised to see him struggling to control his emotions. He seemed to care about the tannery's future as much as she did. She wanted to lean on him, and put her trust in his quiet strength and competence. "In that case, you need to take control, Mr. MacLeod. You need to sign the loan forms in his place."

He shook his head. "I can't. I won't be working here much longer. Two weeks ago, your husband went to see his father's attorney to find out exactly when my contract here was finished so he could be rid of me. I don't know what the lawyer told him . . . but that's when he stopped caring about what happened here. That's when he started leaving work early with headaches. I don't have the authority to save this place, even if I wanted to."

Bebe felt her life spinning out of control as if as she were battling a swift current. She remembered the day she had nearly drowned in the river, and once again she was struck by the overwhelming knowledge that no one was going to save her. If she yielded to the current and allowed it to carry her downstream, she would go under. But if she wanted to survive—and if she wanted her family to survive—she would have to fight to stay afloat, fight her way toward the riverbank. She would have to save herself. She gripped the arms of Horatio's chair.

"Then I'll do it. I'll take over for him until he's sober. Give me the loan forms."

The foreman stared at her. "I don't think that's legal—"

"Do you like your job here, Mr. MacLeod?"

"Yes, but—"

"Then we need to make certain that you keep it. Who's going to know that it isn't Horatio's signature, besides you and me?"

He didn't reply. Their staring contest lasted several long moments.

"Are you still unmarried?" she asked him.

"Yes, ma'am."

His answer surprised her. Why would a young, nice-looking man with a good job be unable to find a wife? "Why is that?" she asked him.

"I support my mother and sister."

"What about your father?"

His face colored slightly, but Bebe couldn't tell what had caused it. "He died," MacLeod said. "Why is my personal life so important to you?"

"I'm sorry if it sounds like I'm prying, Mr. MacLeod, but I need to see where things stand. I read the newspaper every day, so I'm well aware of the bank collapse and the financial crisis. I don't want this tannery to shut down. Too many families are depending on us, including yours and mine. Agreed?"

He nodded slightly. "Agreed."

"Good. Then this is the way it is: Horatio has started on another drinking binge. You and I are the only ones in this place who know the truth. Neither of us knows how long it will last this time. Like it or not, you and I will have to run things until he decides to get sober again." She folded her hands on top of the desk, trying to appear calm. "So. Kindly give me the loan papers to sign."

She watched as MacLeod searched through the stacks of documents on Horatio's desk. Bebe didn't want to run her husband's business any more than she had wanted to do her brothers' chores during the war. *This is temporary*, she told herself—just as she had told herself back then. *It's only until this crisis ends—until Horatio pulls himself together.*

The foreman finally produced the documents and spread them in front of Bebe, pointing to the lines that required a signature. She took Horatio's pen out of the holder and dipped it into the inkwell. When she finished signing them, she stacked them in a neat pile and handed them to MacLeod.

"Kindly take these papers to the bank right away. And let's pray that it isn't too late."

CHAPTER
17

Bebe tried in vain to get Horatio out of bed and off to work the next morning. When he wouldn't budge, she knew she would have to get dressed and go in his place. "Please tell the driver to prepare the carriage for me right away," she told the serving girl.

"You mean after breakfast, ma'am?"

"No, immediately. I don't want any breakfast." The food would only seethe and boil in her stomach, along with her anger and fear.

"I'll fetch your shawl and bonnet, ma'am."

Bebe had hoped to leave quickly, before encountering her mother-in-law, but Mrs. Garner swished down the stairs in her dressing gown just as Bebe's carriage arrived. "Where do you think you're going?" she asked.

Bebe hesitated, forming her reply. Horatio needed to stop drinking and take responsibility, but that would never happen if she lied for him and pretended nothing was wrong. She needed to tell her mother-in-law the truth.

"I'm not going to cover up for Horatio anymore. He is on a drinking binge, and he is unable to run the tannery."

"That's a lie!" She rushed toward Bebe as if she wanted to strike her. "Horatio has always had health problems, but to accuse him of drinking—"

"This isn't a health problem, it's a drinking problem. He drank so much last night that he can't get out of bed and go to work this morning. So I'm going to work for him."

"That's absurd! It's unseemly! What will people say?"

"The better question is, what will people say if the business fails and we go bankrupt? How will we continue to live in this house or pay the servants or put food on our table if the tannery closes?"

Mrs. Garner glanced around in horror as if one of the servants might have overheard them talking. She lowered her voice to a harsh whisper. "I don't believe any of this. You're exaggerating. What do you know about such things? You're just an ignorant farm girl."

Bebe held her temper at an enormous cost. The pain in her stomach burned like fire. She knew that arguing wouldn't help any of them, and she refused to stoop to Mrs. Garner's level and hurl insults. "If you don't believe me, then go upstairs and speak with your son. And if you want to be helpful, talk some sense into him. Convince him of the need to sober up so his 'ignorant' wife won't have to run the tannery in his place."

"How dare you speak to me this way!"

Bebe clasped her hands together in frustration. "I don't know how else to convince you that I'm telling the truth. This country is in the middle of an economic crisis. If things go the way the experts are predicting, we'll have to cut back on our household expenses and let some of the help go. At the very least, you'll need to stop buying new clothes for yourself and expensive toys for Lucy every week. And if the tannery closes, not only will your fancy dinner parties have to stop, we may not be able to feed our own family. The morning newspaper is in on the breakfast table. You can read about it for yourself."

"You don't know what you're talking about. If my husband were alive—"

"If he were alive, he would tell you the same thing. It's not just our business that's having trouble, but businesses everywhere. I'm sure that finances are getting tight for your friends, too. They're just not admitting it." She paused and took a calming breath. The maid had returned with Bebe's shawl and hat, holding them out to her. "Thank you. I need to leave now. Kindly explain to Lucy that I've gone out."

Helpless dread overwhelmed Bebe as she rode the carriage to work. What would happen to all of them if the business did go bankrupt? Where would they live, how would they survive? Horatio couldn't get another job in his condition even if he did manage to find one somewhere.

How had she ended up living this useless, lonely existence in the first place? She would like nothing more than to go down to the station and board the next train out of town, leaving everyone and everything behind. She was furious with her husband, sick of her mother-in-law. But where would she go? Her life had deteriorated into a huge mess, and she didn't know what to do about it. What could she do?

Bebe dried her tears as the carriage slowed to a halt at the tannery. She lifted her chin and strode inside, passing the foreman's desk and hurrying upstairs to Horatio's office. She hung her hat and shawl on his coat-tree and sat down behind his desk. A moment later, the foreman knocked on her door. "Come in, Mr. MacLeod."

He stood in the doorway, his head inches from the lintel, his broad shoulders filling the frame. "My husband won't be coming to work today," she told him. "I can't convince him to stop drinking, so I've decided to take his place."

"I see." He rubbed his chin. He seemed incapable of hiding any of his emotions, and she could tell he was not happy with her decision.

"Together, we're going to figure out a way to keep the tannery going, Mr. MacLeod, and to keep our workers employed and pay back the loan I signed for yesterday. I need you to tell me exactly what's going on so I can decide what else I need to do."

He hesitated for a long moment, and she wondered if he was going to become mulish again and refuse to plow under her orders. But he finally pulled a chair over in front of her desk and sat down across from her, accepting the fact that he needed to work with her.

"Business is slowing down in many industries, not just ours," he began. "More and more of our orders are being cancelled. Customers are reluctant to spend money in this economy. The loan you signed for yesterday will tide us over for a while, but if business doesn't improve, we won't be able to make any payments on it. We may have to lay off some of our workers."

"But they'll need money for food and for a roof over their heads. What will those poor people do?"

"I don't know."

Bebe pressed her fist against her stomach to ease the pain. "The newspapers speak about labor unrest and even riots in other cities because of unemployment. I don't want that to happen here."

"Neither do I." He paused for a moment, then said, "I believe we might be able to ward off some of the labor unrest if you and I spoke honestly with our workers. They respect you, Mrs. Garner, because of the way you helped them during the cholera outbreak. And they know that my family was once just as poor as theirs."

"That's a good idea. And maybe I could speak with some of the local charities and churches and women's clubs. If I could convince all these groups to coordinate their efforts during the financial crisis, they would be able to provide for more families. Do you think your sister Mary might help me?"

He looked away. "I can't speak for my sister."

"Listen, I know I treated her very badly. I tried to explain everything to her in my letters—I hope she read them. Horatio didn't approve of our friendship, but he promised he would stay sober if I became more involved with his mother's social circle. . . . As you can see, he hasn't kept his promise."

"I'll talk to Mary."

They spent the morning outlining what they would tell their workers and labor leaders, then gathered them together for a meeting shortly before the whistle blew at the end of the day.

They had agreed that MacLeod would speak first. "We will do our best not to cut jobs or hours," he explained. "But we can't increase wages or pay any overtime until this crisis is over. Please work with us. We're trying to keep the factory doors open and keep all of you employed."

"We'll also try to provide the practical help that your families need," Bebe told them when it was her turn. "Please feel free to come to me whenever you need help. Every one of you should have a decent place to live, and none of you should ever have to go hungry."

Bebe spent the next few days meeting with church leaders and women's clubs in an effort to get them to work together. Mary MacLeod went with her, volunteering to serve as coordinator for the combined charities. The work distracted Bebe from her problems with Horatio and with their finances, but by the end of the week, Bebe was able to leave everything in Mary's hands and return to the tannery. The responsibility frightened her. She felt much more capable running a charity than running a business, and she sat behind Horatio's desk wondering where to begin. She was paging through the ledger books and trying to make sense of them when the foreman knocked on the office door.

"Come in, Mr. MacLeod."

"You're back," he said. She could tell by his somber expression that he was not happy about it.

"Listen, I can see that you're uncomfortable with the idea of having a woman in charge of the tannery, and I want you to know that I'm not happy about this arrangement, either. Horatio should be here, not me. But he isn't, and so we'll simply have to make the best of it. Now, kindly sit down and explain these ledger books to me."

MacLeod picked up a chair and dragged it behind the desk beside hers, drawing out the action as if to display his reluctance. But he spent the rest of the morning going over the books with her and answering her questions. When Bebe finally thought she grasped the bigger picture, she sat back with a sigh.

"If I understand what you're saying, there really is nothing we can do about the orders that have been cancelled. But I believe we would be wise to start searching for new markets. There are more uses for leather than simply for shoes. Couldn't we offer to create new leather products along with sole leather in order to win new customers? And if we shaved off our profits and sold our leather for a cheaper price, wouldn't that win more business for us, too?"

"I suggested that we do all of those things, but your husband disagreed with me."

"Well, I agree with you, Mr. MacLeod. I would like you to explain some of the ideas you have for finding these new markets."

He sat back in his chair and studied her. "May I ask how you know all of this, Mrs. Garner?"

Bebe's temper flared. "What do you mean by that?"

"I'm sorry. I meant it as a compliment, and it came out wrong. It's just that you seem to know how to run a business, and I wondered how you learned."

She shrugged. "It seems like common sense to me . . . and I read the newspaper. Listen, I don't think we need to be so formal. I would like to call you Neal—and please call me Beatrice."

"If you wish."

They worked together all the following week, outlining ideas, forming a plan, delegating duties. When Friday came and the payroll was due, Neal came into her office again. "I hate to mention this, but the five-year anniversary of Mr. Garner's death is next week. I will be working without a contract after that. I know your husband planned to fire me, and—"

"And you know that I can't run this place without you." The thought of losing Neal brought the burning pain to Bebe's stomach again. "I'll speak with Mr. Garner's attorney and have him extend your contract for you."

"Without your husband knowing about it? It won't be valid. The attorney will know very well that Mr. Garner didn't sign it."

"Let me worry about that. Kindly tell me the name of Mr. Garner's attorney."

"William Harris. His office is on Central Avenue."

Bebe went to see him that afternoon and felt even more out of her element than she had when sitting behind Horatio's desk. Legal affairs were a man's domain, not a woman's, and Mr. Harris greeted her with suspicion after his clerk ushered her into his office. He was old enough to be Horatio's father, with a full head of yellowing white hair and a stern expression on his wrinkled face.

"What can I do for you, Mrs. Garner?"

She lifted her chin, reminding herself that the attorney worked for her. She had seen his name in the ledger books for doing legal work for the tannery. "I understand that the contract for Mr. MacLeod's services as foreman is about to expire. I would like you to draw up a new one for him."

His white eyebrows met in the middle as he pierced Bebe with hawkish eyes. "I don't know why you're attending to this business in place of your husband, Mrs. Garner, but I'm quite certain that Horatio did not wish to extend Neal MacLeod's contract."

"He changed his mind."

"And he sent you here? I'm sorry, Mrs. Garner, but I don't believe you. Can you prove to me that you're authorized to act for Horatio?"

Bebe drew a deep breath. She had proven years ago that she could do men's work, and she knew that she could do Horatio's work, too. She kept her head high and her voice level, trying not to be intimidated by Mr. Harris's gaze or his office full of leather-bound books and framed diplomas. She wondered if her mother had felt this way when she faced the gun-wielding bounty hunters on that long-ago day.

"No, sir. I can't prove that I'm authorized. But I'm going to be honest with you in the hope that it will convince you to help me." She paused until the pain in her stomach eased a bit. "The truth is that my husband has been drinking very heavily for the past few weeks. He is in no condition to run the tannery or make wise decisions. If Mr. MacLeod doesn't continue to work as our foreman, we'll lose everything. But in order for him to work, he needs another contract. Once Horatio sobers up, he can hire or fire whomever he chooses, but in the meantime I have a daughter to support and I don't want to lose our home or our livelihood because of my husband's moral failures. Is that clear enough?"

The attorney looked away while Bebe wiped her tears. When he turned to her again, his eyes had

315

lost their hawkish gleam. "I'm very sorry about your situation, Mrs. Garner. I know that you never would have divulged such personal information unless it was absolutely necessary."

She drew a deep breath. "Will you help me?"

Mr. Harris hesitated, propping his elbows on the desk and lacing his fingers. His lips pursed as if he was carefully considering his response. "What I'm about to tell you," he finally said, "is very confidential. Please understand that I will deny I ever told it to you. Is that clear?"

"Yes."

Mr. Harris paused again, staring at the littered desktop as if trying to decide where to begin. Bebe couldn't imagine what he was about to reveal.

"I was your father-in-law's legal counsel before he died. He told me all about Horatio's weaknesses, so what you've just told me isn't news to me. Mr. Garner asked me to put a provision in his will to keep Neal MacLeod on as manager for five years after his death in order to make certain that Horatio had time to remain sober and learn the business. But there was another reason why he made MacLeod his foreman." He paused, looking her in the eye. "Neal MacLeod is Mr. Garner's illegitimate son. Mary MacLeod is his illegitimate daughter."

Bebe heard the words, but it took a moment for her to comprehend them. The lawyer waited, aware that he had shocked her. She suddenly recalled that Mary MacLeod had attended Mr. Garner's funeral with her brother, and it finally made sense to her.

"Mr. Garner supported the MacLeods while he was alive," Mr. Harris continued, "and he wanted to ensure that they were taken care of after his death. However, he didn't want his wife and son to know the truth. If he had made provision for the MacLeods in his will, the truth would have become obvious."

"His wife doesn't know?"

Mr. Harris shook his head. "As far as I know, she does not."

"Does Horatio know?"

"Not until recently," he said with a sigh. "He came to see me for the same reason that you've come—because five years have elapsed since his father's death, and Horatio was determined to be rid of MacLeod. I asked him about the financial situation at the tannery, and he admitted that the business was in trouble. Before he died, Mr. Garner instructed me to tell Horatio the truth if his mismanagement ever threatened the business—or if he continued to drink. I felt I had no choice but to tell Horatio. The news shocked him, to say the least."

Bebe couldn't speak. She couldn't move. Added to the tannery's financial woes, the shock of this revelation would have given Horatio more than enough reasons to start drinking again.

"I'm sorry if I've shocked you," the lawyer said. "It-it's not your fault . . . Thank you for telling me."

Poor Horatio. What a terrible blow he must have suffered. He had harbored jealousy toward Neal MacLeod for a long time, but to discover the truth about his father's indiscretions, along with the reason for his favoritism toward his "other" son— it must have been more than Horatio could bear. How could Bebe let him know she sympathized without telling him how she had learned the truth?

But deciding what to say to Horatio would have to wait until later. Bebe quickly turned her thoughts back to Neal's contract. "In light of what you've told me, Mr. Harris, you certainly must agree that Neal MacLeod should continue as foreman."

He gave a reluctant nod. "Yes, I know it would be what Mr. Garner would want. I'll draw up a contract that will remain in force until your husband is able to take charge again."

When Bebe returned to the tannery, it seemed like a different place to her. She had never felt much affection for her father-in-law, but now that she knew his secret sins and the mess they had created, she felt only hatred toward him. She saw Neal working at his desk on the tannery floor and wondered why she had never noticed before that his hair was the same color as Horatio's—and their father's. He looked up as Bebe approached.

"Is something wrong?"

"Please come upstairs to my office, Neal."

She heard him following her up the steps and closing the door behind them. She hung her hat and wrap on the coat-tree, then drew a deep breath as she turned to him.

"How long have you known the truth?"

It took a moment before Neal seemed to realize what she was asking. He sank down in the chair in front of her desk, and Bebe sat down, as well.

"All my life," he said quietly. "Mr. Garner . . . my father . . . met my mother when she worked here at the tannery. She said that Mr. Garner's wife didn't . . . I-I mean . . . he said he didn't love his wife. He had married her because it was the socially acceptable thing to do. I was born six months after your husband was. My sister arrived a year and a half later."

He paused, staring down at one of the ledger books as if he were the one who needed to be ashamed. "I would like to believe that our father loved us in his own way. He visited us once in a while. He took me to his fishing cabin a few times. When I was old enough to work, he gave me a job at the tannery. When the war started I enlisted right away. Afterward, we often talked about my experiences. My father never said much, but I knew he was proud of me."

Bebe's heart ached for Horatio. He had never felt that assurance from his father. "And did you love him?" she asked.

"Not always. There were times when I resented him. I couldn't understand why he didn't leave his wife and marry my mother, or at least acknowledge her and her children. But he did provide for us. He bought the house where we live and deeded it to me before he died. And he made me his foreman."

"You're his son, Neal," she said softly, still trying to comprehend it. "That's all the more reason why you must continue working here. The tannery can't run without you. The attorney agreed with me and is drawing up a temporary contract."

She saw him smile for the first time.

CHAPTER
18

Grandma Bebe was right in the middle of her story when a farm wagon with a team of horses approached us from the opposite direction. On board were a farmer and his two burly sons. The wagon bed held a dozen crates of wet, squawking chickens.

"Need help, ladies?" the farmer called to us from the other side of the mud bog.

Grandma lowered her window. "Yes! We would be very grateful for your help. Thank you."

The men climbed down and unhitched the horses, then harnessed them to our rear bumper. With the horses pulling from behind and the farmer's two sons pushing from the front, they managed to heave our car backward out of the mud.

"Where are you headed?" the farmer asked after Grandma thanked him profusely.

"We're on our way from Roseton to Harrisburg."

"Well, ma'am, I suggest you turn right around again and go home," he said, shaking his head. "We've just come from that direction and the road gets much worse a little farther along. We were going to deliver these chickens, but we've had to turn around ourselves."

I knew how brave Grandma Bebe was. She would never retreat. "Thanks for the advice," she said with a smile. "As soon as I get this car turned around, I believe we will heed it."

"No, please . . ." I begged. "Don't listen to him." But Grandma started up the engine, and after executing a perfect three-point turn, we headed home to Roseton.

"We could have made it to Harrisburg," I grumbled, slouching in my seat. "What do they know?"

"There is no shame in changing direction, Harriet. In fact, once you've seen the warning signs, it's always wise to turn around."

"You could easily get us there, I know you could. You ran a tannery all by yourself. A little mud is nothing."

Grandma glanced at me in alarm. "I don't know

where you ever got the idea that I'm invincible, Harriet. And as for managing the tannery . . . well, things didn't turn out very well for me, in the end. . . ."

Bebe realized on her way to work one morning that a year had passed since she first went to work at the tannery in her husband's place. She had been reminded of the fact after hearing Mrs. Garner making plans to place flowers on her husband's grave to mark the sixth anniversary of his death. How could so much time have passed so swiftly? And how could Horatio have remained a drunkard for an entire year? Bebe had stopped pleading with him long ago, becoming accustomed to rising early every morning and going to work in his place. She wondered if Neal MacLeod realized how long it had been.

"Come up to my office," she told him as she passed his desk. "There's something I want to tell you."

"I'll be right there."

Bebe enjoyed working with Neal. He had a gentle smile and a quiet strength that enabled him to remain calm in any crisis. Working alongside him reminded her of the war years when she and her brother Franklin had labored together, sharing the chores, becoming friends. Over the past several months, she and Neal had found new customers and gradually improved their sales. None of their workers had been laid off. The fiery pain in her stomach was gone.

Bebe removed her hat and shawl and hung them on the coat-tree, remembering how angry and resentful she had felt a year ago on her first day there. She stood by the window in her office, looking down on the tannery yard and outbuildings, and realized that she knew exactly what each one was for: the drying shed and bark shed, the buildings for the soaking vats and the steam generator, the warehouse to store all the hides that arrived by rail from the slaughterhouses. And as she looked out at the rainy September afternoon, Bebe realized that her anger was gone, too. She no longer cared if Horatio drank all day. Her life had a purpose, just as it had when she'd helped with the cholera outbreak.

She heard someone tap on the door and turned to see Neal filling the doorframe. He was holding a ledger book. "You wanted to see me?"

She smiled up at him. "Do you realize that I've been working here with you for a full year?"

"Has it been that long?"

"Yes. I started in September, five years after Mr. Garner—your father—died. And it will be six years this week."

"The year sure went fast." He rubbed his jaw, smiling slightly. "I hope you take this in the way that it's meant, but when you first came in here and told me that you were going to run the tannery for your husband, I thought we were ruined for certain."

Bebe laughed out loud.

"I was certainly wrong about you," he continued. "You're just a little bit of a thing—no offense—but you have the courage and common sense of someone three times your size. And a real mind for business, too."

"Thank you. No offense taken," she said with a smile. "And I have to say that you surprised me, too. You reminded me of one of my father's mules that first day, and I thought for sure you were going to dig in your heels and refuse to plow for a woman."

"You know, in many ways you're much better at this job than your husband was."

Bebe's smile faded. "I can honestly say that I'm sorry to hear that. I wish Horatio enjoyed working here, but I know that he never did. I don't think he is very well suited to being a businessman. I wish he could find something that he truly enjoyed—besides drinking, that is. I thought he would sober up and return to work here within a few days, and that I would be able to return home to raise my daughter. But that's not what happened."

"I'm sorry about the circumstances, Beatrice, but I'm very glad to have worked with you."

"Please don't say anything more, Neal." She was going to cry, and she didn't want to. She wished she'd had the good sense to marry a man like Neal instead of Horatio.

"Let's change the subject," Neal said. He opened the ledger book he was holding and traced his finger down the page, pointing to the bottom line. "Here, I wanted to show you these figures. Thanks to our new customers, we've made a very nice profit for the third month in a row. That means it might be a trend, not an accident. And if the trend continues, we may be able to pay off our loan ahead of time and save money on the interest. I think the worst is finally over, Beatrice. We're going to stay solvent."

"Oh, Neal, that's wonderful!"

Bebe threw her arms around him and hugged him tightly. She acted spontaneously, responding the same way she would have if she and her brother Franklin had shared good news. But the gesture quickly changed into something more when neither one of them tried to pull away.

Bebe felt the warmth of his body spread through her own as he held her close. She rested her head against his chest and closed her eyes, inhaling his scent. She could feel his heart racing as rapidly as her own. She never wanted to let go of Neal MacLeod.

For months, she had relied on his strength as they'd weathered the financial crisis; now she felt the full force of his physical strength as his arms surrounded her. Horatio hadn't held her this way for a very long time. She wouldn't allow him to if he had been drinking—which was all of the time. Bebe had even moved into a separate bedroom, hoping to bribe him into sobriety. It hadn't worked.

Now the embrace that she and Neal shared lingered much longer than it should have, but she didn't want it to end. He knew the real Bebe, not the false image of her that Horatio had fabricated when they'd met. And she had come to know Neal, as well—his quiet resourcefulness, his integrity and courage.

Neal finally drew back to look into her eyes but their arms still encircled each other. Bebe saw the truth written on his face—he never had been able to disguise his feelings. He was in love with her. She saw it so clearly. And she loved him.

"Neal . . ." she whispered. She lifted her face toward his, longing to kiss him.

Suddenly Neal's expression transformed into one of horror. He released his hold on her and pulled her arms from around his waist.

"What are we doing, Beatrice? We never should have . . . I-I'm sorry . . ." He turned and fled from the office as if the room were on fire.

"Neal, wait!"

He kept going, lumbering down the stairs to the main floor.

Bebe couldn't breathe. Her entire body trembled. She wanted Neal's arms around her again. She wanted him to hold her. Neal MacLeod had become the rock she had clung to in the middle of the rapids, and she didn't know how she would survive without him.

"Please don't leave me . . ." she whispered. But it was much too late for pleas.

She grabbed her hat from the coat-tree and settled it haphazardly on her head. Somehow she kept moving, stumbling out of Horatio's office like a blind woman and hurrying down the stairs. The noise from the tannery floor throbbed in her ears along with her pounding heartbeat, but she kept walking, moving toward the main entrance, then through it. She ran out of the building and onto the street, into the rain.

Bebe had no idea where she was going as she walked and walked. The rain fell steadily, soaking her back and shoulders and thighs, wicking up from the hem of her skirt as it trailed through the puddles. The rain drenched her hat until the ruined straw wilted and dripped. She didn't care. Her tears fell as steadily as the rain, pouring down her face, blurring everything around her.

At last she halted, realizing through her haze of grief that the gray stretch of nothingness ahead of her was the river. She pulled a handkerchief from her sleeve and wiped her tears to look around. She was standing on a deserted stretch of waterfront between the railroad tracks and the wide, rippling water. On her left, fifty yards away, the tall fence that surrounded the sprawling brick factory blocked her path. On her right, beyond piles of gravel and trash, stood the shantytown that bordered the area called The Flats. Walking alone in that direction would be too dangerous. She had no business being in this place—just as she had no business falling in love with Neal MacLeod.

She turned to leave and realized that the deep rumbling sound she heard was a locomotive moving closer and closer. She started running toward the tracks to re-cross them before the train blocked her path, but she was too late. The long line of freight cars created a slow-moving fence, barring her escape. She was trapped by her own mistakes.

What was she doing there? What had become of her life? If only she could figure out how she had ended up at this dead end, maybe she could find her way back. She looked up at the heavens as the rain flowed down her face, but God seemed a long way off.

Bebe knew she had married Horatio for all the wrong reasons—his handsome face and fancy clothes and the way he had wooed her with romantic words like the hero in a novel. But most of all, she had liked the image of herself that she'd seen reflected in his eyes, the beauty and goodness he'd imagined seeing in her—things she knew weren't really there. She had known nothing of his true character, nor had she cared to look beneath the surface. That mistake was hers, not God's. But what should she do about it?

She heard the squeal of steel against steel as the train halted on the tracks, trapping her. She turned around and walked toward the river again, watching the raindrops dimple the surface. The rapidly spreading rings collided and created more rings, roiling the surface. Bebe remembered the day she had stood at the lake with Horatio, watching the spreading ripples, realizing that one raindrop—one person—could make a difference. Multiple raindrops and multiple people, all interacting and colliding and stirring up the placid surface could create a tidal wave of change. Mr. Garner's infidelity had created a son out of wedlock, who had collided with Horatio, leading to his misery, his drunkenness—and because of his drunkenness she had fallen in love with Neal MacLeod. It hadn't happened overnight, but little by little, working with him day after day—the same way tiny raindrops could create a flood.

Freight cars banged and slammed behind Bebe as the locomotive added more cars to the train and released others, coupling and uncoupling. The engine rumbled, hissing steam. She bent to pick up a stick from the ground and snapped it in half.

She had made a terrible mistake. The love she had once felt for Horatio had slowly eroded while her feelings for Neal MacLeod had grown steadily stronger. Had her father-in-law fallen in love with

Neal's mother the same gradual way? Had he over-looked the warning signs, too, until he'd fallen into temptation?

Horatio's drunkenness had happened with one sip of alcohol at a time. He had made the wrong choice day after day until those choices accumulated into something more, just as Bebe's wrong choices had. She knew that she no longer left home every morning to work in the tannery out of necessity. She went every day because she wanted to be with Neal. She loved talking with him, loved the nearness of him when they worked side by side, loved everything about him.

She tossed half of the broken stick into the river and watched the current sweep it away. That's what had happened to her. She had allowed the current to carry her away to a place she had no business going.

God forgive me. God forgive us all.

Bebe glanced behind her. The train hadn't moved. In front of her, the river flowed through town and out of sight. The rain continued to fall. She was soaked to the skin, her dress plastered to her back and arms and thighs. She turned in a circle like a trapped animal with no way out.

Should she go home to the farm? No, that was another dead end. Her mother would never allow her to stay. Hannah would say, *"What God hath joined together, let not man put asunder."* She would tell Bebe that she had to forgive Horatio "seventy times seven." But how could she go back to Horatio when she loved Neal?

Maybe she should go back to the tannery and beg Neal to run away with her.

Bebe's tears flowed faster when she realized that he would never do it. Neal had too much integrity. He had turned away from their embrace before she had, just now, as if fleeing the scene of a crime. And that's exactly what it had been. Bebe was a married woman. And Neal knew firsthand the devastation that adultery always caused.

What was she going to do? She hated living in the mansion on the ridge, hated all the turbulence in her marriage and in her life. Her mother-in-law despised her. Horatio loved liquor more than he loved her. And for the past year, she had spent so much time at work that her daughter barely knew her anymore.

Bebe watched a small ship navigate upriver against the current and remembered her mother's words: *"Smooth seas don't produce skillful sailors."* Mama said that the rough waters in life made people strong, ready for God to use. But what could possibly be God's purpose in all of this mess? She couldn't even remember the last time she had prayed.

Bebe threw the other half of the stick into the water as hard as she could. She longed to shout aloud to the heavens, *"What do you want from me, God?"* Maybe she should leap in after the stick, let the shock of the icy water steal her breath away, let the water fill her lungs and carry her away to the sea.

All of her mistakes were of her own making. She couldn't blame God. Whether she had married Horatio for the right reasons or not, she had vowed to be his wife until death parted them. She knew that her life was never going to get any better than it was right now unless she asked God to change her, first. She had walked into this dead end on her own. Bebe lifted her face to the sky again. *Help me, God. Please show me what to do.*

She heard another crash as more freight cars collided. She turned toward the tracks and saw that the train had begun to move again. She watched it slowly lumber away, and when the track was clear she started walking back the way she had come.

Bebe already knew what God wanted her to do. It wasn't a mystery. She needed to help Horatio get sober so he could return to his job. She needed to pray and ask God to forgive her and restore her love for Horatio. She recalled Horatio's words on the day she had fetched him from the saloon: *"You used to look at me as though I had just hung the moon in the sky. . . . Why don't you look at me that way anymore?"*

Hannah had been right; love was the most powerful force in the world. But Bebe had allowed its strong grip to pull her in the wrong direction, pulling her toward Neal MacLeod and away from

Horatio. Now she had to redirect that force. She had to look at Horatio with love again, to do the loving thing for him whether she felt like it or not. She had to work for his good, encourage him, pray for him.

And if he continued to drink?

Bebe choked back a sob. Regardless of the outcome, she had to turn away from Neal MacLeod and go home to her husband and daughter.

She trudged up the street the way she had come and found herself back at the tannery a few minutes later. Two figures, a woman and a young boy, stood outside the door, huddled beneath the overhanging roof. They looked nearly as drenched as Bebe was. As she drew closer, she saw that the woman held an infant bundled in her arms. Then a third child, a little girl Lucy's age, peeked from behind the woman's skirts.

"Mrs. Garner!" the woman called.

Bebe halted, startled to hear her name.

"You're Mrs. Garner, aren't you?" the woman asked.

"Yes. . . . How do you know my name?"

"I'm Millie White. You helped me once before when I was sick with cholera. Please, Mrs. Garner, I need your help again."

Bebe stared. She was in no position to help Millie or anyone else after making such a mess of her own life. "What . . . what do you want me to do?" she finally asked.

"My husband works at your tannery and today is payday. Please, I'm begging you to give the money to me this week, not him. He'll only drink it away in the saloon. My children need to eat. I need to pay the rent. Can't you please give the money to me?"

Bebe looked at Millie White and saw herself. She easily could have ended up in Millie's situation. Her husband was also a drunkard, and if Bebe hadn't come to the tannery a year ago and taken over for him, she might have lost everything. Her own daughter would be the child who was hungry.

Bebe rested her hand on Millie's shoulder. "I don't know the answer to your question, Millie, but if you'll come inside with me, I'll find out." She would have to talk to Neal MacLeod. She would have to face him again, even if it broke her heart. She opened the door and motioned for Millie and her family to follow her inside.

The children cringed at the noise and huddled around their mother. Bebe led the way to Neal's desk on the main floor. He had all of his drawers open and a wooden crate at his feet, and she realized that he was emptying his desk, packing his things. He glanced up long enough to see her approaching, then looked away. His eyes were red, as if he had been weeping.

Bebe cleared the knot from her throat and quickly explained Millie White's request. "Can we do that, Neal?" she asked. "Can we give Mrs. White her husband's pay?"

He shook his head. "I'm sorry. I would like to help her out, but her husband earned his pay. By law, we have to give it to him."

"Let me work, then," Millie begged. "Give me a job here instead of him."

"But who will take care of your children?" Bebe asked.

Millie pushed her son forward. "Hire my son, then. He can run errands for you or sweep the floor. He's a good boy; he does what he's told."

The boy couldn't have been more than seven or eight years old. Bebe hated the idea of a child laboring in her tannery. It was bad enough that most children did piecework in their tenements at night. But Neal looked at the boy and nodded. "I think I can find something for him."

Bebe imagined her own daughter being forced to work and shuddered. Horatio might be a drunkard, but he owned the tannery and had the means to support his family. Women like Millie had nothing.

Bebe glanced at Neal again and longed to feel his arms around her—just one more time. Tears stung her eyes as she remembered the starchy scent of his shirt and the sound of his heartbeat. She looked down at the little boy instead, and suddenly knew that this family was an answer to her prayer. She swallowed her tears and said, "Listen, Millie. If the only way we can keep our husbands out of the saloons is to close them down, then that's what we'll have to do."

"How can we do that?"

"Can you gather together a group of women who are in the same situation that you're in?"

"Yeah, sure," she said bitterly. "That won't be hard at all."

"Do you know which saloon your husband usually goes to on payday?"

"Ozzie's Tavern down on Sixth Street."

"I want you and the other women to meet me there tonight at six o'clock."

"Meet you . . . ?" She started shaking her head. "You shouldn't go down there, Mrs. Garner, believe me. The tavern is down in The Flats, and—"

"I'm not afraid. I've been to The Flats before. We have to stop the men from getting drunk on their way home, right after they get paid. Will you meet me there?"

Millie nodded and caressed her daughter's damp hair. "Yeah. I'll be there, Mrs. Garner. And I'll gather the other women, too. Thank you."

Bebe waited until Millie left before turning to Neal again. She couldn't meet his gaze. She drew a painful breath as she looked out over the floor of the tannery that had become so familiar to her this past year. "I think my work here is finished, Neal. The tannery is yours to run, alone, until Horatio returns. I don't know when that will be, but I've been reading in the newspaper about a new temperance organization, and I think I'll start a chapter here in town. I'm not going to quit until every saloon is forced to close its doors and my husband—" She paused as her voice broke. She covered her mouth with her hand until she could finish. ". . . and my husband is sober again. Until then, our family would appreciate it if you would kindly manage the business for him."

"Yes . . . of course . . . but listen, Beatrice. I-I'm sorry—"

"So am I, Neal. So am I."

She turned and hurried away from him. She felt as though her heart had been slashed in two. She strode out of the building and back out into the rain, walking all the way home to her mansion on the hill. She went inside through the servants' entrance in the rear of the house and climbed the back stairs to her room, too ashamed to go through the front door, too ashamed to face her mother-in-law. One of the servants met Bebe on the stairs.

"Goodness' sakes, you're soaking wet, Mrs. Garner. Let me draw you a hot bath and take care of your wet clothes."

"That would be wonderful, thank you. Your name is Herta, isn't it?"

"Yes, ma'am."

It shamed Bebe to realize that she had kept all of the servants at a distance, just as Horatio and her mother-in-law did, as if she were better than these simple, hardworking people. That was going to

337

change. From now on Bebe was going to stop trying to fit in with the Garners' socialite friends and be herself—a simple farm girl.

"And, Herta, kindly tell the driver—his name is Peter, isn't it?" The girl nodded. "Please ask Peter to have the carriage ready for me at six o'clock tonight."

Millie White and two dozen other women stood waiting for Bebe outside Ozzie's Tavern when Bebe arrived. They looked desperate but determined, and she felt an instant kinship with them. She should have done this a year ago.

"My husband is a drunkard, too," she told them as they gathered in front of the saloon door. "We're going to pray and ask God to help us close down this place. And we're going to come back here every night if we have to, until it does close."

"It won't help," one of the women said. "Our men will just find another saloon."

"Then we'll do the same thing until that one closes. I've been reading in the newspaper how women in other cities have done this very thing—and it works. Dozens of saloons have been forced to close their doors. The organization is called the Women's Christian Temperance Union. I'll write to them and ask for advice. We'll start a chapter here in town. We'll have more power and influence if we join together with other women."

"What do we have to do?" someone asked.

"Well, besides praying, one of the Union's methods is to write down the names of all the men who are patronizing the saloon and list them in the newspaper. The men should be ashamed of what they're doing, spending your rent money on alcohol and taking food out of your children's mouths. We'll bring their actions out into the open and make people aware of how drunkenness affects families like yours."

"I say let's try it," Millie said. "It can't hurt none."

"Good. Shall we bow our heads?" Bebe closed her eyes as she prepared to pray aloud. She had never done anything like this before, always praying silently in church or in the privacy of her room. "Heavenly Father . . ." she began. Her throat closed with emotion.

Desperation had forced her to turn to God, and she suddenly felt closer to Him than she ever had before. He was here, right beside her. This was the task that He wanted her to accomplish. And although nothing in her life was as it should be, God was still with her and she was going to be fine. She drew a deep breath and started again, pouring all of her passion and sorrow, all of her guilt and grief into her prayer. She didn't stop until the saloon door opened a few minutes later and the owner began to shout.

"Hey! What do you think you're doing out here? You're blocking my door! Get away from here!" He waved his arms as if shooing a flock of chickens.

"This is a public walkway," Bebe told him. "We have every right to stand here."

"You're going to interfere with my business. Go home where you belong!" He looked down the street past the women and scowled. Bebe turned in that direction and saw a group of workmen approaching from the brick factory where their shift must have just ended.

"Let's pray, ladies." Bebe closed her eyes again, ignoring the owner's angry shouts as she beseeched the Almighty to turn the workers' steps away from the saloon and toward their homes. The women joined in with cries of "Yes, Lord!" and "Hear us!"

When Bebe opened her eyes to peek again, the workers had halted at the corner as if afraid to wade through the mob of women. "Come on, come on, gentlemen," the owner called out. "We're open for business. Don't let these crazy women get in your way."

Bebe raised her voice to outshout him. "Ladies! Do you know the hymn 'Give to the Winds Thy Fears'? Come on, sing it with me: 'Give to the winds thy fears, hope and be undismayed; God hears thy sighs, and counts thy tears, God shall lift up thy head.'" Bebe sang with all her might even though only a few of the women joined her and none of them seemed to know all the words.

"'Through waves and clouds and storms, He gently clears the way. Wait thou His time, so shall the night soon end in joyous day.'"

The workmen held a huddled conference on the street corner, then slouched away. The women cheered, drowning out the bar owner's angry rant.

Three months later, Ozzie's Tavern closed its doors for good. Bebe, Millie, and the other women now began gathering in front of Logan's Saloon—Horatio's favorite place—to pray and sing. Bebe had made the rounds to all of the local churches, giving speeches to their ladies' groups about temperance and asking them to join her crusade. Hundreds of women had signed The Pledge, vowing to abstain from alcohol. Her local chapter of the Women's Christian Temperance Union had grown to nearly three hundred members.

On a Friday night well into their crusade, Bebe's women forced Logan's Saloon to close its doors for lack of patronage. Horatio was the last man to stagger out that final night, gripping a half-empty bottle. The bartender cursed at the women as he hung up a *Closed* sign and locked the door. Bebe had the carriage waiting for her husband at the curb, and Peter, the driver, helped him climb in beside her.

"Let's go home, Horatio," she said.

"Are you happy now?" he asked as they rode up the hill in the quiet night.

"Yes. I am." She nestled close beside him and took his hand in hers, lifting it to her lips and kissing it. She didn't feel love for him yet, but God willing it would soon begin to grow.

"Horatio?" She waited until he met her gaze. "I love you."

He looked away as tears filled his eyes. He still gripped the half-empty bottle and she took hold of it, as well. "May I have this, please?" She waited until she felt his grip loosen, then pulled it gently from his hand and dropped it over the side of the carriage. She heard glass shattering on the cobblestone street behind them.

Bebe wondered what Horatio would have done if liquor hadn't been readily available. Might he have found a better way to cope and saved all of them a great deal of grief? She knew in that moment that she wouldn't stop her temperance crusade until every last saloon had closed its doors and alcohol was banned everywhere. With God on her side, how could she lose?

She helped Horatio up the stairs to their bedroom when they reached home, then helped him undress. His clothing stank of cigar smoke.

"You'll be happy to know that the country's financial crisis is much improved, Horatio. The tannery is earning a profit again. You got overwhelmed, I know, but when you go back to work, you'll see the improvement."

He sat on the bed and kicked off one of his shoes.

It fell to the floor with a thud. "Thanks to Neal MacLeod, I suppose?"

Bebe wasn't sure what would anger him more: knowing that Neal had saved the business or that she had helped him. She decided to tell him the truth. "Mr. MacLeod and I worked together until things turned around."

"You worked with *him*?" He kicked his other shoe across the room. "I suppose he found great satisfaction in that. He has stolen everything else from me—my father, my job . . . What's left to steal except my wife?"

Bebe cringed, aware of how close to the truth Horatio's words were. "It isn't like that at all," she told him. "You're my husband, not Mr. MacLeod. You're the man I vowed to spend my life with. And I've kept my vows. But you also made vows to me, Horatio. You vowed to honor and protect and cherish me. You can't do those things when you're drunk."

"I've tried to stop and I can't!"

She helped Horatio put on his pajama top and buttoned it for him. "No one can get through life's trials alone. We all need God's help."

"God wants nothing to do with me, and I want nothing to do with Him!"

His words shocked Bebe, but she tried not to show it. She had to keep coaxing him to talk, to unload all of the reasons he had started drinking in the first place. Maybe then he would be able to stop.

"What makes you think that God doesn't care about you, Horatio?"

"Because God never answers my prayers. He never answers anyone's prayers. Why doesn't He right all the wrongs here on earth? Put a stop to war and killing? All my friends . . . all my friends . . ." He paused, passing his hand over his face. "I prayed for courage, and He didn't give me any. I was scared all the time during that war."

"But Franklin and your other friends will tell you that they were terrified, too. There's no shame in being afraid."

"Neal MacLeod won a Medal of Honor, did you know that? My father made sure that I knew all about it—and he called me a coward. God is supposed to be our Father, isn't He? Well, if He's anything like my father, then I want nothing to do with Him!"

"Oh, Horatio . . . listen—"

"My father turned away from his family, did you know that?"

"Yes, I know, but—"

"He didn't love my mother and me anymore, so he left us and started another family. Then he sent me out to die on a battlefield to be rid of me. How could a loving father do that? How could he force his son go to war? He wanted me to die!"

The anguish in Horatio's voice made Bebe ache for him. She wrapped her arms around him and held him tightly. "I don't know, Horatio . . .

but I know that God isn't like your father at all. God loves you."

"Then why does He stand aside and watch us hurt and betray each other?"

"I don't know the answers to your questions, Horatio. But I promise that we'll try to find them together. . . ."

Grandma and I arrived back in Roseton that rainy afternoon just as she finished telling her story. "So you see, Harriet, there is a time to fix your own flat tires, and a time to recognize that all of your efforts to help yourself are only making matters worse. You'll only end up soaked and muddy and trapped in an even deeper rut. That's when you need to know enough to turn around. That's when you need to call on the Lord for help. Do you understand what I'm saying?"

"I suppose so."

"Listen, I'm sorry that we didn't get to the meeting. I know you're disappointed, but—"

"I was going to take The Pledge today. I made up my mind, and I was going to surprise you."

She looked at me in dismay, not pride. "You're just a child, Harriet. You're much too young to understand what you're promising."

"I'm not too young, I'm twelve! And I know that I'll be promising never to touch a single drop of alcohol all my life and to do my best to stop other people from drinking it, too. I want to get my own pledge book to carry, so I can get other people to sign it, like you do."

"You also would have to promise to banish alcohol from your sideboard and your kitchen, and that's not something you can promise yet. And you would be pledging not to court a man who drinks or to marry one—"

"That's easy. I'm never getting married."

"You see, Harriet? You're much too young to be making such rash decisions. Let's wait a few years to see if you change your mind about drinking alcohol—and about getting married, too."

She parked the car in the garage and went into the house, leaving me sitting there, mystified. Grandma was working so hard to get other people to take The Pledge. Why wouldn't she let me sign it? I didn't understand my grandmother at all. She was turning out to be a woman of great contradictions.

CHAPTER
19

In June of 1912, my sister Alice married banker Gordon P. Shaw. It was the society event of the year in Roseton, and people considered it a social triumph to be invited. I considered it a triumph when I successfully avoided wearing a hat, a corset, and any article of clothing with frills or ruffles. I watched all the other women's heads wobbling beneath the weight of their voluminous hair and enormous hats, and I ran my fingers through my short, bobbed hair and gloated.

The weeks and weeks of fluttering preparations for Alice's wedding, along with several last-minute emergencies, had exhausted everyone in our family. The worst crisis had been the heated argument that had erupted over whether or not liquor would be served. Grandma opposed it, of course, and wanted all types of alcohol completely banned from the event. Mother worried that a "dry" reception might offend the groom and his well-to-do family.

"Poppycock!" Grandma said. "Are they such lushes that they can't celebrate a happy occasion without a drink? If so, perhaps Alice should think twice before marrying into that family. We already know there are lushes on our side."

"Shh! Don't say such things!" My mother always became horrified whenever Grandma implied that drunkenness ran in our family. "Think of the girls! Do you want to tarnish their reputations?" she whispered.

"Our family's 'secret' isn't exactly a secret, Lucy. Everyone in town knows that I'm the president of the local Women's Christian Temperance Union—and most people know why. Besides, how will it look if my granddaughter's wedding reception turns into a drunken brawl, especially after all my hard work preaching temperance?"

"Really, Mother. My friends are respectable people. The reception is hardly going to turn into a brawl. You always exaggerate."

I listened to weeks of such arguments. The truth was, Daddy's relatives also would have been offended if the liquor didn't flow freely. They figured Daddy owed them a lavish party in exchange for the gifts they were giving Alice. My father finally announced his decision, attempting to meet both sides in the middle and avoid a rift between Grandma and Mother.

"Liquor will be served in small amounts," he decreed as he stroked his clean-shaven chin. He looked as wise and decisive as King Solomon had when he'd ordered the baby to be chopped in half. "We will serve enough liquor for a decent toast and a festive celebration, but not enough to encourage drunkenness."

In other words, neither side would be happy.

As I sat at the wedding reception watching the festivities, my father wore the dazed look of a man whose hard-earned money had been stolen by pirates and carted away in fat treasure chests. My mother looked flat-out exhausted. The bright rouge on her cheeks couldn't distract from the dark circles beneath her eyes. Presiding over this lavish wedding had been the pinnacle of all her achievements, the fulfillment of all her dreams. This extravagant party for Roseton's most important citizens had kept seamstresses busy for months, while the local jewelers had made hefty profits polishing everyone's heirloom diamonds. The drama and pageantry of the occasion represented everything Mother loved most in life. In one glorious evening she would exercise all of the etiquette skills she had learned from Grandmother Garner—who would have reveled in the event, too, had she been alive. Best of all, the wedding united Mother to the groom's impeccable family. What would she do for an encore?

I asked to sit beside Grandma Bebe at the wedding reception because I enjoyed her company more than anyone else's in my family. Neither one of us fit in with this crowd. We were two social misfits who didn't care one whit about what people thought of us. By the time I had eaten all of the food I wanted to eat, and Alice and her groom had cut the wedding cake, I was ready to go home. The dancing had begun, and I didn't see a single gentleman in this sorry assembly of social climbers who I cared to dance with—even if I had known how to dance.

Grandma gazed at the waltzing couples in their glittering finery and sighed. "It's on joyous occasions such as this that I miss my Horatio the most." She smiled and yet at the same time she looked sad.

"Whatever happened to him?" I asked, hoping I wasn't opening a Pandora's box of bad memories. "Why doesn't he live with you?"

"Don't be obtuse. You've heard the story a hundred times, I'm sure you have."

"No, I haven't. Mother never talks about him. That's why I'm asking."

"Well," Grandma said with a sigh, "it's really quite a long story."

"Good. The longer the better. This party is boring."

Horatio looked wretched as he sat on the edge of the bed. "Very well, Beatrice, I give up. I'll go up to the fishing cabin with you."

Bebe closed her eyes in joy, wondering if she were dreaming. She had formed the local chapter of the Temperance Union more than a year and a half ago, and had fervently prayed ever since that one day she would hear Horatio say those words. She went to him, hugging him tightly. His embrace felt limp in return. His once ruddy skin had turned dull and gray, his sunken eyes looked lifeless. But Bebe believed that the man she once loved still lived inside this sad, tired body. He would be his old self again once he quit drinking.

"Thank you, Horatio. It will be wonderful to get away from here for a while, you'll see." She got out their satchels and began to pack. "I'll tell Peter to get the carriage ready and—"

"No, don't. I want to drive up there myself. Tell him we'll take the runabout."

Bebe hesitated, wondering if she should try to

talk him out of it. It would be easier for Horatio to change his mind and return home if he didn't have to wait for Peter to come back for them. On the other hand, he might decide not to go to the cabin at all if she argued with him. She decided to say nothing and let him drive the runabout. She had waited much too long for Horatio to get sober.

After Bebe and her temperance women had closed down Horatio's favorite saloon, he had found another—and another. Then he'd begun drinking at home. Neal MacLeod continued to operate the tannery for them in Horatio's absence, but Bebe was careful never to mention his name.

Forgetting Neal proved much harder than she ever imagined. She kept busy with her temperance activities: holding prayer vigils in front of saloons, attending rallies and conventions, writing articles and speeches that told about the high cost of alcoholism. Now, as she prepared to climb into the runabout with Horatio to drive to Iroquois Lake, she was almost afraid to hope that her prayers were finally being answered.

Rain began to patter against the roof of the runabout before they even left the city limits. Thunder grumbled in the distance. Bebe nestled closer to Horatio. "Good thing we bundled up in our warmest clothes."

"It always rains when we go up to the cabin. Did you ever notice that?"

"No, I can't say that I have. But it's nearly April,

351

after all—and you know what they say about April showers. Besides, I don't care if it does rain. We can just sit by the fire together in the cabin."

Fifteen minutes later, the sky opened up and rain poured down on them. The canopy could barely keep them dry. "Maybe we should turn back," Horatio said. "We're getting wet, and besides, I've never seen the river this far over its banks before."

Neither had Bebe. The rain-swollen river they had been following up the mountain had seeped into the woods, leaving trees stranded and the forest flooded with several feet of water. It surged across their path in some places as if trying to swallow the road. She urged him on. "The weather won't matter once we're up there. And I'm sure everything will be dried out by the time we go home."

The higher they climbed, the more rapidly the river seemed to flow. Once again, Horatio talked about turning back. "I don't like the look of that current, Beatrice. I've never seen it flowing so swiftly."

"We're almost there now, aren't we?"

Thankfully, he kept going. But as they neared the lake, Bebe heard a roaring noise in the distance like the rumble of a locomotive. "What's that sound, Horatio? Stop the carriage for a minute." He pulled to a halt and listened with her. It wasn't the wind. And it sounded much louder than the rush of rapids in the nearby river.

"I don't know what that is," Horatio said. "A train, maybe?"

"It sounds like a waterfall, doesn't it? Remember our wedding trip to Niagara Falls? Remember how loud the water was?"

"I remember." He flicked the reins and the horse started moving again. "I'll be glad when we're inside, out of this rain."

The roaring sound grew louder the farther up the mountain they climbed, and when they neared the dam that had created Iroquois Lake, the mystery was finally solved. "Look, Horatio. It *is* a water-fall! I don't remember seeing it before—or hearing it, either. Do you?"

"That's because it isn't supposed to be here. There isn't supposed to be that much water going over the dam. It was just a trickle the other times we came up here, remember?"

Horatio drove the wagon a little farther up the road and stopped when they reached a clearing. "Look at that!" he breathed. Bebe gaped in awe at the power of the water thundering over the earthen dam. Behind it, the lake looked twice as vast as she remembered. It seemed to strain against the flimsy barrier that held it back.

"I've never seen the lake so high . . . or the water flowing over the dam so fast," Horatio said. "They must have had a lot of snow higher up in the mountains last winter, and now it's all melting."

Bebe rested her hand on his knee, worried that he

would decide to turn back. "The waterfall brings back memories, doesn't it? It's hard to believe we've been married for more than ten years already, isn't it?"

"Mmm . . ." He didn't seem to be listening. He stared at the falls and shook his head before moving forward again. "I don't like the look of that dam, Beatrice. It was built right after the war, you know. It was never designed to hold back so much water."

They barely recognized the cabin when they finally reached it, either. The beach along the lake-front was under water, the fishing pier submerged. The lake engulfed all the trees that had once stood near the shoreline, and Bebe had to remove her shoes and lift her skirts to wade from the road to the doorstep.

"The flooding up here seems even worse than the last time," she said. "That was when we had the cholera epidemic in town, remember?"

"Maybe we should go back."

Bebe shook her head, aware of the temptations he faced in town. "We'll be fine. I'm just remembering."

Two days later it was still raining. Horatio couldn't stop worrying about the earthen dam. He walked outside so often to check on it that Bebe wondered if he had a flask of alcohol hidden somewhere. She watched him from the cabin window as he waded down the beach for the third time that day and disappeared among the trees.

"The dam doesn't look sound to me," he told her when he returned. "The structure has aged over the years, and it has developed a nasty bulge on one side. I wonder if anyone from town has bothered to inspect it lately."

"Who is in charge of the dam?"

Horatio shrugged. "This land is all privately owned up here. I suppose all of the landowners are."

Each day the lake continued to swell before their eyes. Horatio worried and paced, walking out in the rain every few hours to check on the dam. By the end of the week the waves lapped at their doorstep. "I think we should go home," he said. "I want to send someone up here to inspect the dam and see if it's sound."

Bebe resisted his pleas, convinced that Horatio wanted an excuse to go home and get drunk. His latest binge had lasted more than two and a half years—much longer than any of his others had—and she knew it would probably take more than a week for him to dry out. She had been afraid this would happen when he had decided to drive up here himself. Having transportation handy made it too easy for him to leave before he was ready.

That afternoon, when he returned from his walk, he begged Bebe to come outside with him. "Please, I want you to look at it for yourself, Beatrice. You'll see why I'm so concerned."

She pulled on a pair of his trousers and waded

out to the dam with him, slogging through water up to her thighs in places. She heard the roar of the falls long before she saw them. Horatio stopped in a clearing overlooking the dam, and what Bebe saw frightened her so badly that she clung to his side. Water rushed over the dam with unstoppable power. The river below the falls had become a raging rapids.

"Can you see how the dam is bulging over there?" Horatio shouted above the noise. "It's only made of earth. I'm afraid it's going to burst."

"What will happen if it does?"

"If that dam gives way, all of the water in Iroquois Lake will go surging down the river at once. The houses in The Flats would be demolished by the tidal wave. Remember the flood eight years ago when we had the cholera epidemic? If this dam lets go, that entire neighborhood could be washed right off its foundations."

Bebe knew he wasn't exaggerating. Even as they stood watching, a small, boulder-sized section crumbled away before their eyes. Horatio gripped her arm. "Look, Beatrice. It's starting to go! We have to go home and warn people!"

He grabbed her hand as they hurried back to the cabin, struggling as if in a dream to move through the deep water. Bebe packed as quickly as she could while Horatio harnessed the horse to the runabout. For the first time she was grateful that they had driven up to the lake and wouldn't have to wait for the driver to return for them. But when the vehicle was ready, Horatio stopped her from climbing on board.

"I want you to stay here, Beatrice. The road follows the river most of the way and if the dam bursts while we're on our way home . . ." He drew a breath as if his chest ached. "If it bursts, we'll never make it. We'll be washed downstream with the surge, carriage and all."

Bebe's heart hurt from pounding so hard. "Well, if it's too dangerous for me, then it's too dangerous for you, too."

"I can drive faster if I'm alone. I'll come back for you when it's safe. I want you to stay here on higher ground."

"Never! I'm going with you, and don't you dare try to stop me!" She clutched his jacket in her fists as if she never intended to let go. "I love you, Horatio Garner, and if you get washed away, then I want to be right beside you."

"What about Lucy? She needs a mother—"

"And she needs a father, too. Now, come on. You're wasting time. Let's go."

He lifted her onto the wagon and they took off down the mountain as fast as they dared on the flooded road. "I hope you're praying," Horatio murmured.

"Yes—with all my might." Bebe pleaded with God to help them make it back to town before the dam burst. He had protected her and her mother from the bounty hunters years ago, and she prayed that He would send His angels to protect her and Horatio now. *"When you obey the Lord,"* Hannah had said, *"He will always be with you, no matter what happens."* Bebe prayed that her mother was right.

Horatio sat on the edge of the seat, concentrating on the path ahead as they traveled down the steep, muddy road as fast as the horse would go. Bebe helped point out some of the deeper ruts and holes, while glancing anxiously at the swollen river on their left. The current had uprooted trees, carrying them along in the brown, swirling water. The river rushed madly alongside them as if they were in a race against it. Perhaps they were.

Please help us, God, she silently pleaded. *Please spare the town and our home. Please help us make it in time to warn people. . . .*

She suddenly remembered how much Lucy and Mrs. Garner loved to go shopping downtown. She tugged on Horatio's sleeve in panic. "What about the downtown area? Do you think the tidal wave will hit there, too?" She tried not to picture her daughter and mother-in-law strolling innocently down Central Avenue when the flood hit.

"I don't know," he mumbled. "I don't know. . . . The stores aren't far from the river."

Horatio had to stop three times and climb down from the runabout to lead the horse through the deep water that flooded the road. The sound of the rushing river spooked the animal, and Bebe saw its eyes rolling in fear. Horatio was getting soaked but he spoke calmly as he coaxed the horse along. He looked strong and determined. She had never loved him more.

Whenever she thought about the crumbling dam and the water that was powerful enough to sweep them away, Bebe could barely breathe. *Please, God . . . please . . .* she prayed. And when the town finally came into sight below them, she wept with relief. "We made it! Thank God!"

"Yes, we're almost there," Horatio breathed. "Hang on, darling."

The lathered horse was panting with exertion when Horatio stopped at the tannery. They came to it first along their way, and he rushed inside, shouting, "Shut the place down, MacLeod! Send everyone home! The dam on Iroquois Lake is going to burst. Everyone who lives near the river needs to evacuate. Now!"

They stopped next at the mayor's office, where Horatio delivered the same warning. "Sound all the town's fire alarms! Get the police and firemen to spread the word! Everyone needs to get up to higher ground!"

Bebe chewed her fingernails while she waited for him. Fear gnawed her insides. Finally, Horatio turned the exhausted horse up the hill toward home. Bebe didn't even wait for the vehicle to halt out front before she leaped off and ran up the steps into the house.

"Lucy!" she cried. "Lucy, where are you?" If her daughter were downtown, how would Bebe ever find her in time? She would have to go from store to store, searching for her. "Lucy!"

It felt like an eternity before the playroom door opened at the top of the steps and Lucy's golden head appeared. "I'm up here, Mama."

"Thank God! Thank God!" Bebe bounded up the stairs toward her daughter, tripping over the last step, struggling to her feet again, hugging Lucy tightly. "Thank God, you're safe!"

"Ow . . . not so hard, Mama. You're wrinkling my dress!"

Mrs. Garner emerged from her bedroom down the hall. "What's going on? Why all this shouting?"

"The dam up on Iroquois Lake is going to burst," Bebe said breathlessly. "All that water is going to flood the town. People have to get out. Horatio says the tidal wave could wipe out The Flats."

Horatio had followed Bebe inside after tethering the horse. He stood downstairs in the foyer, calling up to them. "Are all of the servants at home, Mother?"

"Yes, I believe so."

Horatio ran into the parlor, dripping muddy water on the floor, and rang the service bell to summon them. One after another, they hurried to the front hallway in response. Bebe saw him counting heads to see if they were all there.

"Make sure everyone stays inside," Horatio told the butler. "Don't let anyone go downtown. It's not safe. The dam up on Iroquois Lake is about to give way and all of that water . . . ."

"Don't stand there with the door open," Mrs. Garner told him as she descended the stairs. "Come upstairs, Horatio, and let the servants fix you a hot bath. You need to change out of those wet clothes before you catch your death of pneumonia."

He shook his head. "I'm going back out to finish sounding the warning."

"I'll go with you." Bebe released her hold on Lucy and started down the stairs.

"Oh no, you won't," Horatio said. "You're staying right here with Mother and Lucy."

"And you're staying, as well," Mrs. Garner said. "There's no reason in the world why you should risk your life. You can very well send someone else."

Horatio took another step toward the open door. "People are going to need a place to go for shelter. I'm going to bring as many people as I can up here to the ridge where it's safe." He turned to the servants, who were whispering fearfully among themselves. "Get some coffee and food ready for them. I'll be back shortly."

"No, Horatio. I forbid it!" Mrs. Garner said. Lucy began to wail as if the panic had become contagious.

"Daddy, Daddy!" She started down the steps toward her father, stretching out her arms to him. Bebe caught her and tried to comfort her, but she squirmed in protest, trying to reach Horatio. He was almost through the door when Peter, the family's carriage driver, stepped forward.

"I'll go with you, Mr. Garner. We can rescue more people if we take two vehicles."

"Very good. Thank you, Peter." They left hurriedly, making plans.

"Daddy! I want Daddy," Lucy cried. Bebe finally released her after the door closed behind Horatio, and Lucy fled into her grandmother's arms.

Mrs. Garner glared at Bebe as if the commotion were all her fault, then turned her attention to Lucy. "There, there. Come with me, dear. The cook will fix us some tea and cookies." She led her away by the hand.

For the next hour, Bebe tried to distract herself from her fears by helping the servants turn the house into a shelter for the refugees. Church bells clanged incessantly all over Roseton and fire bells sounded a warning in the distance. When Bebe went into the parlor to build a fire to warm the room, she found Lucy and Mrs. Garner sitting side by side on the horsehair sofa, sipping tea. Bebe wasn't sure if she should be irritated with Mrs.

Garner for not helping or grateful that she was distracting Lucy.

"What are you doing?" Mrs. Garner asked as Bebe knelt to pile the wood in the fireplace. "Let the servants do that."

"I don't mind. I'd rather work than pace the floor and worry. And I'm sure everyone will be wet and cold when they arrive, so I thought I would warm the room for them."

Mrs. Garner surveyed the overstuffed room with a worried look. "You're not going to allow strangers to come into my parlor, are you? What about all of my things?"

"That's all they are, Mother Garner—things. People's lives are at stake."

But Mrs. Garner rose from her chair like a queen rising from her throne and strode from the room with Lucy close behind her. Bebe crumpled up a piece of newspaper and lit a match to it. By the time she got the fire kindled, her mother-in-law had returned with two chambermaids.

"I don't care what you were doing," Mrs. Garner told them, "I want you to help me protect my things." She paraded around the room, pointing to all her bric-a-brac and silver pieces. "Take this . . . and this . . . and this . . . upstairs to my bedroom suite for safekeeping." Lucy followed her grandmother around, whining for attention as Mrs. Garner pointed to each item. The maids ran up and down the stairs, hauling everything away.

Two hours after he left, Horatio returned. Bebe felt weak with relief as she hugged him, not caring if she got wet. He led a bedraggled group of people into the house, half of them small children. "I'm so proud of you," Bebe whispered as she brushed his wet hair off his forehead. A moment later, Lucy raced into the foyer to see her father.

"Daddy! Lift me up, Daddy," she said, reaching up to him. "Carry me."

He patted her head. "Not now, sweetheart. I'm all wet. Your nice dress will get all wet."

Bebe looked at the frightened, shivering children that Horatio had herded into the foyer and saw them gaping at the enormous rooms and sweeping staircase. She remembered how overwhelmed she had felt the first time she'd entered Horatio's home—and these poor souls were fleeing for their lives.

"Come, Lucy. Let's take these children upstairs and show them where your playroom is. They must be terribly frightened."

Mrs. Garner moved to bar their way. "You can't be serious! These people can't be trusted. They'll break all her nice things."

Bebe winced at her mother-in-law's insulting words, spoken loudly enough for the children and their mothers to hear. "We can always buy more, Mother Garner," she whispered. "Please, I don't want Lucy to grow up to be selfish." She motioned to the refugees again. "Come, children. This way.

Mothers, too, if you wish. Lucy, you go first and show them where your playroom is."

Mrs. Garner glared at Bebe, then turned to Horatio. "Aren't you going to stop her?"

He shook his head. "They need a place to stay. It isn't safe downtown. The warning is going out, and we're evacuating all the people—"

"Good. Then you can change out of those wet clothes right now, and warm up. You look drenched, Horatio."

"We're not finished, Mother. It's a big town, you know. I won't rest until I've made sure everyone has heard the warning."

Bebe halted halfway up the steps when she heard Horatio's words. The refugees continued on as she hurried back downstairs to him. "You can't go out there again! What if something happens? The dam could break any minute. You said yourself how dangerous it was."

He glanced around at the flurry of activity all around them and reached for Bebe's hand. "Will you excuse us please, Mother?" He led Bebe into the dining room, where no one could hear them, then took her other hand as he faced her. "I have to do this, Beatrice. I'm tired of being a coward. Why should you be the only brave one in the family?"

"No! I won't let you go!" Bebe clung to him, weeping, not caring how wet he was. "Please don't go back out there, Horatio! Please! It's too dangerous. Stay here with me. I need you! You're not a coward, I know you aren't."

He pried her arms from around his waist and looked down at her, holding her hands in his again. Tears filled his eyes. "I know the truth, and I'm tired of running scared. I want you and Lucy to be proud of me for once. Most of all, I want to be able to face myself in the mirror every morning. I have to do this, Bebe." He kissed her forehead and turned toward the foyer.

"No!" Bebe clung to his clothing, desperate to hold him back.

"Don't, my darling," he said quietly. "Let me go. Let me do this."

Bebe saw his courage and determination and released her hold. "I love you, Horatio." For the first time in months, she meant it. He nodded and hurried through the door, closing it behind him. Bebe sank down on the bottom step, covering her face.

"I hope you're happy now!" Mrs. Garner said before swishing past her up the stairs.

Several minutes passed as Bebe sat on the stairs. She knew she had to pull herself together, but fear for Horatio threatened to overwhelm her. She felt a hand on her shoulder and looked up. It was one of the refugees.

"My husband is helping, too," she said.

Bebe wiped her eyes and let the woman pull her to her feet.

Peter returned to the house three more times that afternoon, bringing more refugees to safety. Nearly one hundred people crowded into the downstairs hallways and rooms, and Bebe did her best to help them get dried off and settled and fed. During a lull in the activity, she went up to her own bedroom and fell on her knees to pray. Suddenly, above the rumble of voices in the rooms below her, she heard a loud roar outside in the distance.

The dam had burst.

She fell on her face, pleading with God for Horatio.

Bebe had no idea how long she had prayed when she heard hoofbeats and the sound of a carriage rolling to a stop outside. She raced downstairs and threw open the front door, expecting Horatio. Instead, Peter sat on the driver's seat, badly shaken. His carriage full of refugees appeared dazed; many were weeping. Bebe wanted to weep with them, but she opened the carriage door and offered her hand to help them down.

"Please, come inside where it's warm. We have coffee and food waiting." When the last one climbed out, she looked up at the driver. He hadn't moved. "Where's Horatio?"

Peter stared into the distance as if he hadn't heard her. "I've never seen anything like it," he mumbled. "The dam burst. The water was like a wall—"

"Is Horatio with you?"

He slowly shook his head. "The water carried trees and debris, and everything crashed into the railroad bridge north of town . . . a-a huge pile! It got hung up on the railroad trestle, but then that gave way and the bridge collapsed and all the debris thundered into town. I-I saw freight cars carried away like toys!" He paused when his voice broke. Tears overflowed and ran down his face. "The water crushed every building in The Flats into matchsticks. Houses were lifted right off their foundations by the force of the water and carried away downriver. I saw . . . I saw people hanging from their windows, screaming for help. . . . There was nothing we could do. . . ."

Bebe climbed up to his seat and grabbed the front of his jacket, shaking him. "Peter! Where's Horatio!"

"I-I don't know. We split up hours ago. He was driving the other carriage."

"Driving it where? Did you see where he went?"

"No, ma'am. We went in different directions. I'm sorry. . . ."

Bebe knew better than to direct her anger and fear at Peter. She released her grip on his jacket. It was drenched. She dried her hands on her skirt. "Come inside and get dried off and warmed up," she told him. "We'll fix you some food and hot coffee. It was very courageous of you to help Horatio this way. I'm glad you're safe."

She kept busy for the rest of the evening, soothing people, making them comfortable, feeding them. Herta, one of the maids, tried to offer Bebe a plate. "Here, Mrs. Garner, sit down and have something to eat. You must be hungry, too."

"No, thank you. I can't eat."

At last she went upstairs to the playroom searching for Lucy, longing to hold her and fill her empty arms. A dozen children were playing quietly with Lucy's toys, carefully watched by their mothers. "Have you seen my daughter, Lucy?" she asked.

"Her grandmother came for her a few hours ago," one of the mothers said.

Bebe went down the hall to Mrs. Garner's bedroom suite and knocked on the door. "Come in," Mrs. Garner said. Lucy lay asleep on her grandmother's lap.

"Have you eaten anything, Mother Garner?" Bebe asked. "Would you like me to bring you something?"

"Where's Horatio? It's getting dark outside."

"He's still out there, helping people."

"The fool!"

"He's not a fool. He's a very courageous man." She lifted Lucy from her mother-in-law's arms, holding her closely for several minutes before laying her on the bed. "I'll be downstairs if you need anything." Bebe left, closing the door behind her.

Later that night, the servants brought out every blanket and pillow in the house for the refugees to use, and they bedded down wherever they could find space, sleeping on the parlor floor and in the dining room and even in the front hallway. Everywhere Bebe looked she saw bedraggled people, some sleeping, some talking quietly, others holding children in their arms, soothing them to sleep.

She finally went upstairs to her bedroom—Horatio's bedroom—but she didn't undress. She would never be able to sleep. She found her Bible and opened it to her mother's favorite psalm: *"God is our refuge and strength, a very present help in trouble. Therefore we will not fear, though the earth be removed, and though the mountains be carried into the midst of the sea; though the waters thereof roar and be troubled . . ."*

At dawn Bebe went downstairs. Peter was gathering all of the able-bodied men to go downtown to help. "I want to go with you and look for Horatio," she told him. "Show me where you last saw him, please."

He shook his head. "You'll only be in the way, ma'am. There's work to do, and they'll need the carriage and horses."

"I can help—"

"No, ma'am. People are buried under all that mud and debris. It's not something a woman should see. Mr. Garner would never forgive me if I let you go down there."

Three days passed before it was safe enough for the women and children to leave Bebe's house. When the ordeal ended and the last refugee had moved out of the mansion, Bebe finally walked down the hill alone. Some areas of town were still under water. Others had mud and wreckage piled as high as the windowsills. Most of the downtown area had flooded, and many buildings had sustained damage. Debris floated everywhere in the hip-deep water, pieces of people's lives and possessions—a chair, pots and pans, an oil lantern. Bebe saw the bloated bodies of rats and dogs and horses. Trees that had avalanched down the mountain in the flood lay piled everywhere, along with ragged planks of wood from houses, shards of window glass, bricks, and shingles.

There was nothing left of The Flats. Not a single house remained standing along either side of the river. Bebe never could have imagined that the once-placid river could cause so much destruction. It had destroyed her town, her life.

Fifty-six people perished in the flood along with her husband. According to the newspapers, the death toll would have been much, much worse if not for the heroism of Horatio T. Garner.

CHAPTER
20

Bebe barely coped with her sorrow. Horatio's funeral was one of many, many others in town, yet she felt utterly alone in her grief. She walked through the motions of laying her husband to rest as if walking in her sleep. The nanny took little Lucy home after she threw a tantrum during the church service, and Bebe longed to throw herself on the floor, too, and weep like a child. If she could just get through the burial, she told herself, then she could break down.

The ground at the cemetery felt wet and spongy beneath her feet as she climbed from the carriage. The air smelled of damp earth and rotting wood. The graveyard sat high on the ridge above the city, but Bebe couldn't bring herself to look down at the flooding and destruction in the town below. The river had become her enemy, snatching Horatio from her arms and turning her world upside down. The future seemed hidden from her sight, as completely as Roseton's once-familiar streets lay hidden from view. God seemed very far away.

"Whatever will I do?" she asked herself again and again. "Whatever will I do?"

She didn't hear a word the minister said as they prepared to bury Horatio. She was aware of Mother Garner sitting stiffly by her side, but a vast ocean could have filled the space between them. Neither of them could offer comfort to the other. Horatio's mother never shed a tear throughout the ordeal, while Bebe's tears never stopped flowing.

At last the burial service came to an end and a line of mourners walked past, offering Bebe their condolences. Among the strangers was a familiar face: Neal MacLeod's. He removed his hat to bow slightly, and his golden hair—so like Horatio's—shone in the pale spring sunlight.

"Mrs. Garner . . . Beatrice . . ." he began. "I'm so sorry for your loss—"

"You!" They had been sitting in chairs beside the grave, but Mrs. Garner stood suddenly, toppling hers. "How dare you come here?" Her face shook with fury beneath her black net veil.

Bebe sprang to her feet, too. "Mr. MacLeod manages our tannery, Mother Garner—"

"I know exactly who he is!" she said in a harsh whisper. "And who his sister is!"

Neal ducked his head, his face bright with shame. "I'm very sorry for upsetting you. Please excuse me." He turned and hurried away, just as he had run from Bebe on her last day at the tannery. Her tears started again as she remembered how Horatio also had turned away from her on their last day. *Let me go, Bebe. Let me do this.* He had received what he'd wanted most in life—a chance to redeem his past. But he was never coming home to her.

Home. Bebe returned to the huge, gaudy house that had never been a home to her, hating it more than ever before. The servants tiptoed from room to room, staring at their shoes. Lucy was inconsolable, crying for her father, unable to understand his death, and blaming Bebe for it, for some unfathomable reason. Mrs. Garner never left her room or her bed, numbing her grief with laudanum. And as badly as Bebe longed to lie down in a fog of sleep, as well, she knew it was up to her to keep the household moving forward. Each day felt longer and darker than the previous one.

"A Mr. William Harris is here to see you, ma'am," the maid told Bebe one afternoon. She had been dozing in a chair in the bedroom she had once shared with Horatio when the knock on her door awakened her. It took her a moment to recall that Mr. Harris was the family's attorney.

"Show him into the parlor, please. Tell him I'll be right down." Bebe stood to straighten the wrinkles from her black crepe mourning dress and tidy her hair. When she gazed at her reflection in the mirror she hardly recognized herself.

"I've come to talk about your husband's will," Mr. Harris began after offering his condolences once again. "I know that you and your family are still grieving, but I believe that your husband would want his estate to be settled quickly, and for you to know how things stand financially."

"Yes," she murmured. "Thank you." She heard

the lawyer speaking, but she was still groggy with sleep and grief and had trouble comprehending him. The word *will* reminded her of a verse of Scripture—*"Not my will, but thine, be done."* Jesus' words echoed through her mind as Mr. Harris continued.

"Horatio made provisions in his will for his mother and daughter, of course, but you have inherited the bulk of your husband's estate: this home, the tannery, his real estate holdings, bank accounts, and shares of stocks and bonds. I will be happy to provide the details, if you wish—perhaps at a better time. But for now, I want to assure you that the business is doing very well, thanks to Neal MacLeod, and to let you know that your life can continue as before. Nothing will need to change."

She looked up at him, certain he had missed something very important. "But everything will change, Mr. Harris. Horatio is gone."

"I know, I know. And again, I'm very sorry for your loss. But I want you to know that you have been very well provided for, Mrs. Garner—and for many of my clients that isn't always the case. Too often, I'm afraid, widows are forced to change their entire way of life after such a loss. Their lives are never the same."

After Mr. Harris left, Bebe sat in the parlor, unmoving. The attorney had done his best to reassure her that her life wouldn't change, but she knew that it wasn't true. Once again, she would have to start all over again. How many times had she been in this place? Three weeks ago she had been ready for a new start as she'd packed Horatio's bags to go to the fishing cabin. Would it have worked this time? Would he have remained sober? And if so, for how long?

"Nothing will need to change," Mr. Harris had said, but the truth was, nothing would ever be the same. *"Remember how life changed when the war started and the boys left home?"* Mama had once told her. *"And how it changed again when Franklin had to leave? Life is like that, Beatrice—always changing, always flowing forward like a stream. Things never stay the same. And we have to move on and change, too."*

"What if I don't want things to change?" Bebe had asked her mother.

"You can't fight against the current. You need to trust God and be prepared for wherever the river of life will take you next."

Trust God. Was she angry with God? How could Bebe be angry when He had answered her prayers? She had prayed that Horatio would return to the cabin and sober up, and he had. God had answered Horatio's prayers, too, finally granting him the courage and redemption he had long sought. *"Not my will, but thine, be done."* Bebe repeated the verse over and over, praying that she could mean it.

For the next few weeks, Bebe watched from her bedroom window as the floodwaters receded and the townspeople prepared to rebuild Roseton. In most ways her life hadn't changed, just as Mr. Harris had promised. She had lived without Horatio's companionship for a very long time, even though they'd shared the same house, the same bedroom. But as she thought about the provisions of Horatio's will—and about God's will—she became increasingly aware that a great injustice had been done. When she finally made up her mind what should be done about it, Bebe made an appointment with Mr. Harris, then sent Neal MacLeod a note, asking him to meet her at the lawyer's office.

Bebe hadn't been to the downtown area in weeks, and as her carriage drove through the streets she saw the last remnants of the floodwaters and piles of debris still waiting to be burned. A muddy watermark stained many of the surviving buildings, showing how high the water level had reached. Mr. Harris's office on Central Avenue stood high enough above the river to be spared, for the most part.

Neal was already waiting in the outer office when Bebe arrived. He looked unchanged to her, as sturdy and strong and capable as ever. He stood up the moment she entered. "Listen, Beatrice, I want to apologize again for upsetting Mrs. Garner at the funeral. I didn't know that she would recognize me. I wasn't aware that she knew about . . . about Mary and me."

"It's not your fault, Neal. I didn't know, either. She never said a word to me about you and Mary in all the years I've lived with her." She was about to ask Neal how he was doing when Mr. Harris emerged from his office.

"Please come in, Mrs. Garner, and have a seat." He waited until Bebe and Neal were seated in front of his desk and then said, "Once again, I want to say how sorry I am for your loss. Your husband will be remembered as a very great man in this town."

"Thank you, Mr. Harris. You know our foreman, Neal MacLeod, don't you?"

"Yes, of course." The two men shook hands. "What can I do for you, Mrs. Garner?"

Bebe lifted her chin. "You told me that according to Horatio's will, I have inherited all of his property, including the tannery. But now that I've had time to think about it, I don't believe this arrangement is entirely fair. Mr. Garner had two sons— Horatio and Neal. I believe that, by rights, half of the tannery belongs to Neal."

Neal shifted in his chair, suddenly uncomfortable. "What? Wait a minute. . . . You can't be serious."

"Yes, I'm quite serious."

"But . . . I mean . . . that's obviously not what my father wanted or he would have—"

"I disagree. Your father thought very highly of you and wanted *you* to run the tannery, not Horatio. The reason he didn't acknowledge you publicly was to spare his wife's feelings. But since Mrs. Garner is aware of the truth, I believe that his two sons should each inherit half of his business." She turned to face the lawyer. "I would like you to transfer half ownership to Neal, Mr. Harris."

"Wait!" Neal interrupted again. "I don't think you should do this, Beatrice. I . . . I *can't* let you do this."

"Why not? You've been operating the tannery all these years, so it's not as though I'm giving it to you for free—you've earned it. You're the one who has made it profitable. Besides, if part ownership is in your hands, then my daughter and I will be even better off than we are now. I'm sure you'll be motivated to work even harder if half of the tannery belongs to you."

Neal slumped back in his seat, shaking his head in disbelief, but Bebe remained determined. "Can you arrange for the transfer, Mr. Harris?"

The lawyer had been watching and listening without commenting, but he finally spoke up. "Are you certain you wish to do this, Mrs. Garner?"

"Yes. I'm absolutely certain."

"Very well. I'll respect your wishes. I'll prepare all of the necessary documents and deeds."

Neal followed Bebe outside afterward, stopping her as they reached the curb. "I still can't believe you would do this, Beatrice. It's a very kind, generous thing to do. I don't know how I can ever thank you."

"It was the right thing to do, Neal. You're Mr. Garner's son—I'm only his daughter-in-law. Besides, I watched you work at the tannery for more than a year, remember? I saw how much you love that place, how it has become part of you."

"Yes . . . well . . . in any case, thank you. I'll make certain you won't regret it."

Bebe's carriage was parked nearby and the driver had opened the door for her. She had accomplished her task and had no reason to linger, yet neither she nor Neal seemed in a hurry to leave.

He cleared his throat. "Maybe . . . maybe this isn't the best time to discuss this, for I know that you loved your husband and that you're still in mourning. But I think you also know that I . . . I have feelings for you."

"Yes. I know," she said softly.

"During the time we worked together, it would have been wrong to tell you how I felt because you were a married woman. But now it's no longer a sin. . . . I fell in love with you, Beatrice. Whenever I've thought about you for the past year and a half, I've wished that I had told you."

"I knew. And you must have known that I fell in love with you, too. I realized too late that it was wrong. I should have guarded my heart better."

Neal had been staring at his feet as they talked

but he finally looked up at her. "Someday . . . in a year or two . . . do you think there could ever be a future for us?" She saw love and hope and fear in his unguarded expression.

"Oh, Neal . . ." She closed her eyes, longing to share his hope, longing to fall into his arms. "I would love to believe that we might have a future together after enough time has passed, after I finish grieving for Horatio. But Mrs. Garner knows who you are. And if I left her to be with you . . ." Bebe shook her head. "I could never hurt her that way."

Neal exhaled. "Yes, of course. I understand." The muscles in his face worked as he battled his emotions. "I'm a reminder of her husband's infidelity."

"She has lost so much more than we have. Her husband betrayed her, her only son is dead, and the only thing she has left, besides Lucy and me, is her social position. I can't take that away from her. Believe me, I don't want to stay in that horrible house and live an empty life. I would much rather be with you. But I have to stay, for her sake."

Do the right thing, Bebe's mother would have told her, *and trust God to bring good out of it.* But she wondered as she watched Neal wipe away a tear that had escaped, if she ever would find the contentment and peace that Hannah had found.

"I might have chosen differently before I started working for the Temperance Union," Bebe continued. "I used to think only of myself and what I wanted. But if there's one thing I've learned from that amazing group of women, it's that God puts other people in our life so that we won't have to suffer through it alone. I can't leave Mrs. Garner all alone. God loves her, even if I find it hard to. And I'm responsible before God for how I treat her."

"You're a good woman, Beatrice," he said, swallowing. "I never dreamed you would give me a share in the tannery. In fact, whenever I've thought about you and the possibility of a future together, I was afraid that it would seem as though I was pursuing you so that I could inherit it. It never would have been my intention to marry you for the business."

"I know, Neal. I know you would never do that."

"Well . . . maybe we should leave things the way they are—strictly business." He looked up at her again, and she saw both love and pain in his eyes. She still could change her mind; she had only to speak the word and they could be together.

"Strictly business," she whispered. She could barely see him through her tears. Bebe loved Horatio. He had just died, and she still couldn't accept his loss. But she loved Neal MacLeod, too. Was such a thing possible?

"Are you going to be all right?" he asked. She nodded. "You could always come back to work with me at the tannery, you know."

"The tannery is your life's work, not mine. I have to move forward, not backward. And change is a part of life. I learned that growing up on the farm—sowing, growing, harvesting—life always goes on."

"What will you do, then?"

It was becoming clear to Bebe that she would continue her work with the Temperance Union even though her family was no longer affected. As the wife of Roseton's new hero, her voice would carry a great deal of clout. "With so much reconstruction taking place around here," she said, "I need to make sure that all the saloons aren't rebuilt, as well."

"I know how smart and capable you are. I have no doubt at all that you'll succeed in whatever you try to accomplish."

"Thank you."

The street had been free of traffic as they'd talked, but when a wagon and team of horses approached, Neal took Bebe's arm and gently guided her away from the curb so the approaching vehicle wouldn't splash them. "Why does life have to be so hard?" she asked after it passed.

"I don't know. I guess that's just the way it is." He released her arm and began backing away from her, as he always did. She wanted to embrace him one last time but knew that she didn't dare.

"Thank you again, for what you did with the tannery," he said. "I'll run it well, for both our sakes.

I'll make sure that you're always well provided for."

"I know I'm in good hands. Good-bye, Neal."

"Good-bye."

Bebe took one long, last look at him as he continued to back away from her. Then he finally turned and hurried off. "God go with you," she whispered.

Bebe went upstairs to her mother-in-law's room and knocked on her door as soon as she returned home. Trading a future with Neal MacLeod for a future with Mrs. Garner had been one of the hardest things she had ever done, but she knew she had made the right decision. Again, she thought of the words *Not my will, but thine, be done.*

"Mother Garner?" she said after knocking a second time. "It's me, Beatrice." When she still didn't hear a reply, she went inside. The shades were drawn in the unkempt room, and Mrs. Garner lay buried beneath a mound of blankets and pillows. Bebe scooped up the tin of laudanum pills from her nightstand and slipped it into her pocket, then opened all the curtains and window shades.

"What do you think you're doing?" Mrs. Garner asked. The pillows muffled her voice.

"You have to get up, Mother Garner. You need to answer all of these condolence cards."

"You do it."

"I already answered the ones that were addressed

to me. But good manners require you to respond to the ones addressed to you."

"Who are you to lecture me about good manners?"

Bebe drew a deep breath and slowly let it out. "I share your grief, Mother Garner. I loved Horatio, too. But he wouldn't want us to stop living. He would want us to carry on with our lives and learn to be happy again."

The covers rustled as Mrs. Garner sat up, leaning on her elbows. "What reason do I have to be happy? I have no one left."

"That's not true. You have Lucy . . . and me."

Mrs. Garner stared at Bebe as if questioning her sincerity. "I suppose you'll sell my home out from under me now, and everything will change. You never wanted anything to do with this house or our way of life."

"I'm not selling the house, and nothing is going to change. You're Horatio's mother, and he loved you. I'll always take care of you, for his sake. And for Lucy's sake. She loves you, too."

Mrs. Garner's eyes were cold as she stared at Bebe. "If you hadn't made him go up to that cabin with you, he would have been here at home where it was safe when the dam burst."

Her mother-in-law's words couldn't hurt Bebe. She had punished herself with them a hundred times since Horatio died. "Maybe so," she said quietly. "But thousands of innocent people would be dead." She walked toward the door, then turned back. "I'm going to send Herta up with a tray of food. You need to eat something, Mother Garner, and regain your strength. I'm planning to invite a small group of your friends to come for tea next week. They are concerned about you. Besides, according to all the etiquette books, holding a small reception is the proper thing to do."

Bebe felt a double measure of sorrow as she descended the stairs to speak with the cook—sorrow over Horatio and over Neal. Yet God seemed very close to her at that moment, as close as He had been the first time she'd prayed in front of a saloon. Loving her mother-in-law was the task that He had given to Bebe for now. And though nearly everything else in her life had been taken away, God was still with her.

And she was going to be fine.

By the time Grandma Bebe finished telling her story, I was crying. Tears flowed down her cheeks, too. I felt terrible for putting them there. I never should have made her relive that terrible day— much less relive it during Alice's wedding reception. The musicians played a stately waltz, people laughed and danced—while we cried our eyes out.

"I'm sorry," I said, hugging her. "I heard about the Great Flood of 1876 in school but no one ever told me what my grandfather did. Why didn't you tell me this story before?"

"Don't be silly. You've heard the story."

I shook my head. "No, I haven't. . . . I don't even know where he's buried."

"I'll take you there some time. . . . Well, I'm ready to leave, are you? There is entirely too much drinking at this shindig for me to want to stay."

I told Daddy we were going home, and I climbed into Grandma's car with her. I expected her to go straight home, but instead she drove to Garner Park and stopped at a spot overlooking the river.

"I know you've been to this park before, Harriet. You must have seen the monument stone."

"I guess I have," I said with a shrug. "I know your name is Garner and that this is Garner Park, but my name is Sherwood . . . and I guess I never gave it much thought."

"Well, come on, then."

Dew dampened my shoes as we walked across the grass. A half-moon lit the way for us, and stars shone above our heads. Grandma halted beside a granite marker that was taller than she was. It looked like a giant tombstone. I had never bothered to read the engraving before, but this time I did: *In memory of Horatio T. Garner, whose courage and heroism saved thousands of lives in the Great Flood, March 25, 1876.* The names of the fifty-six other people who had perished along with him were inscribed beneath his name in smaller letters.

"The city proclaimed your grandfather a hero,"

Grandma told me. "They named this park after him. They said he saved thousands of lives, but my poor Horatio was washed away with the floodwaters. They found his body nearly a mile downstream." She sighed and gestured to the trees and pathways and flower beds all around us. "This park is where The Flats used to be. After the disaster, the city decided to move the workers' neighborhood to higher ground. They built those levies along the riverbanks for protection."

"No one ever told me," I said softly.

"Well." She sighed again. "I can't imagine why not. My Horatio was quite famous, dear." She gazed off at the distant river. "It was always very hard for me to talk about losing Horatio. I imagine it must have been even harder for your mother. How do you explain heroism to a child, especially when she misses her daddy?" Grandma Bebe pulled a handkerchief out of her sleeve and wiped her eyes.

"I'm sorry, Grandma. I didn't mean to spoil this happy day."

"You didn't spoil it, dear," she said with a smile. "Joy and sorrow are two sides of the same coin. They both come in seasons, just like floods and droughts. I loved my Horatio. I think about him nearly every day."

She reached to take my hand and we walked side by side, back to her car.

"He was a good man underneath it all," she said

as she slid behind the steering wheel. "But in a way, he really died years earlier on a battlefield in Virginia. I guess it just takes some men longer than others to fall down dead. My brother Joseph was one of the lucky ones who died quickly."

I was afraid to ask any more questions, but as we drove away, I wondered when Grandma had moved out of Horatio's big mansion on the ridge. She had lived in her modest house overlooking the river for as long as I'd known her. The view from her bedroom window was of the river. I wondered if it reminded her of Horatio.

She halted the car in front of her garage, but we didn't get out right away. The gaslights up and down the street gave off a warm glow as we sat in the dark, talking.

"I loved him, Harriet. There was goodness and joy in him in spite of all the sorrow he brought into our lives. If only he could have believed in himself and overcome his drinking. But alcohol had a grip on him, and he couldn't shake free. That's why it should be outlawed. It ruined the life of a good man.

"Some people call our temperance crusade the Women's Whiskey War," Grandma continued. "And it is a war, make no mistake about that. We've had to fight hard to make this community aware of all the hardship that comes from alcohol, aware of the children who live in appalling conditions and die from poor health because their fathers drink away all of their earnings. We'll do whatever it takes to win this war, whether it means praying in front of saloons or smashing whiskey barrels at the train depot."

"But after Horatio died, you had no reason to keep fighting, did you? Why not just live peacefully?"

"I couldn't do that. I knew about the evil of alcohol firsthand. What better work could I ever do than to help others fight it? The other women and I do what we need to do—and lives are saved. I would like to think that in his short, tragic life, Horatio saved this town from more than the flood."

"But you did all the work, Grandma, not Horatio."

She shook her head. "Marriage is always a partnership, dear. I loved Horatio."

"How could you still love him after everything he put you through?"

"Love isn't always a feeling. Sometimes it's a decision. I can only pray that you and Alice will find love and meaning in your marriages, too."

"I'm never getting married," I mumbled, crossing my arms. I meant it now more than ever before. Why suffer all that pain and sorrow?

Grandma smiled at me through her tears. "We shall see, Harriet, my dear. We shall see."

CHAPTER
21

Who knew that life in jail could be so boring? Grandma Bebe had been arrested several times, so you'd think she would have at least mentioned it. If only someone would bring me a book to read—I would have even settled for some needlework to help while away the hours, and heaven knows I never have been one to sit and stitch. I seemed to be the only person in jail that day, which meant I had no one to talk to. Time passed as slowly and as annoyingly as a dripping faucet.

I finally sat up and ate my lunch. The glistening tapioca pudding wore down my resistance. I never could turn down a good bowl of tapioca. When that was gone and I had licked every slick, lumpy morsel off the bowl and spoon, I decided I might as well eat the vegetable soup and the bread, too. There is no point in attempting a hunger strike if you're going to make an exception and gobble down your dessert.

"The soup was watery and the bread was dry," I told the man who came to retrieve my lunch tray.

"Ain't that a pity now?" I could tell by his smirk that he didn't care. He slammed the cell door closed as if to remind me that I was incarcerated.

The afternoon dragged even more slowly than the morning had. Worrying about my fate didn't help my mood, either. Prohibition had become the law of the land only a few months ago, and I was one of the very first people in Roseton to get caught breaking it. I had no idea how long my jail term might last. Spending one day in this place was bad enough; I couldn't imagine spending several years this way. If prison was meant to be a deterrent to a life of crime, then I was ready to repent of my misdeeds and forswear all criminal behavior forever.

I slumped against the cold brick wall and sighed. I had been asking myself the same questions over and over ever since Tommy had locked me in here last night. How in the world had I ended up here, so far from where I imagined life would take me? And how would I ever find my way back to where I should be? I had hoped to stumble upon the answers by reminiscing about my grandmother's life. So far, it hadn't worked.

When my supper tray arrived hours later, I was very surprised to see that once again, Tommy O'Reilly delivered it. "Is our town so short of policemen that you not only have to arrest all the criminals but feed them, as well?" I asked.

"I was worried about you, Harriet. I wanted to see how you were doing."

I tried to think of a witty retort but couldn't. Boredom had dulled my mind. "I'm fine," I said, "considering my circumstances."

What really confused me was the fact that I was

happy to see him. Both times that Tommy had made an appearance I had felt a jolt of adrenaline go through me, just as it had when we were kids. Back then, the spurt would come as I readied myself for a fight. But he was behaving so nicely today. Why was my heart speeding up? Could it be a learned reaction that I'd developed over the years? I didn't want to believe that it was because Tommy had grown into a good-looking man with a grin like ivory piano keys.

"Here you go," Tommy said as the cell door creaked open. "Dinner is served."

This time he came all the way inside and set the tray on my lap. The aroma of roast beef drifted up to my nostrils. A mound of mashed potatoes with gravy and a pile of green beans lay alongside the slab of meat. There was a hefty slice of chocolate cake for dessert. My traitorous mouth began to water.

"Thanks," I told him.

Tommy started to leave but made it only as far as the cell door before turning back. "Are you sure I can't do anything else for you, Harriet?"

I studied him with suspicion. Why was he being so nice? Why couldn't he have been this nice during our school years instead of tormenting me day after day? He had been nice last night, too, when he'd stopped my car and seemed to genuinely regret the need to arrest me.

"As a matter of fact, there is something you can

do," I told him as I speared a forkful of mashed potatoes. "You can notify the Sunday school superintendent at my church that I won't be available to teach my class tomorrow—unless the girls want to come down here for their lesson."

"Harriet . . ." he said with a sigh.

"Tommy . . ." I said, imitating him.

"I don't understand you," he said, leaning against the bars. "I never did. You were never like any of the other girls in school."

"Oh? How was I different? Aside from the fact that I stood up to you and the other girls all ran away in fear?" I continued to eat my dinner. Mother would call it unladylike to talk with my mouth full or to eat in front of someone who wasn't eating, but I was hungry.

Tommy smiled. "You were always just like this—sassy and bold. And you were also a lot brighter than the other kids, even the boys." He hesitated, and he appeared to be considering something. "I've been thinking about your arrest all day, Harriet. I want you to tell me your story again. How did you end up with all that bootleg liquor in your car?"

"I knew you weren't listening to me last night."

"You weren't exactly reasonable last night."

After a moment's reflection I knew it was true.

"The thing I don't understand," he continued, "is that your grandmother is notorious here in Rosetor for busting up saloons and smashing whiskey barrels. We have quite a collection of hatchets that once belonged to her."

"I used to buy her a new one for Christmas every year."

"So why are you carting liquor around for a bunch of bootleggers?"

I didn't reply. My reasons no longer made sense to me in the light of day. I sawed into my roast beef with the dull knife.

"I was thinking that maybe I could get you out of jail myself," Tommy continued. "I'm off duty until Monday. I could keep you under house arrest until your hearing before a judge—and in the meantime, maybe you can explain everything to me in a calm, reasonable fashion."

"You coming to Sunday school with me, too?" I asked with my mouth full.

He shrugged. "I suppose I'll have to."

I studied him with narrowed eyes. "Is this some sort of policeman's trick?"

"What would I gain from it?"

"I don't know—fame, a big promotion for capturing such a notorious criminal. Maybe you dream of becoming police superintendent like your father."

"You have quite an imagination, Harriet."

"I've studied police procedure, you know," I said with a half grin. "I'm a big fan of 'The Keystone Cops' and Fatty Arbuckle."

"Hey, me too! There's a new episode playing at

the movie theatre this week—have you seen it yet?"

I gestured to my surroundings and shook my head before gulping the last bite of my chocolate cake.

"So what do you say, Harriet—have you had your fill of this place? Are you ready to be set free?"

I knew I should keep my mouth shut and let Tommy spring me from jail rather than spend another night here, but I couldn't let my suspicions rest. "I need to know why you would do this," I told him.

"Look, I live in this town, too, so I'd like it to be a safe, law-abiding place. My job is to keep the peace and arrest people who break the law. Our hands have been full of lawbreakers ever since Prohibition started. The moment the government made liquor against the law—which I think is a good thing, by the way—there was suddenly a lot of money to be made by breaking that law. It's supposed to be up to the federal agents to enforce Prohibition, but there aren't enough of them to go around."

"I think it's ironic that we're both on the same side for once, Tommy."

"Yeah, me too." He smiled his magnificent smile, erasing all traces of the bully I once knew. "Listen, why are we still talking in here? Let me see about getting you out of jail, all right?"

I remembered how the farmer and his sons had pulled Grandma and me out of the mud. Maybe this was one of those times when it was better to be rescued than to be stubbornly self-sufficient. *"There is no shame in changing direction,"* Grandma had said.

"All right. If you insist, Tommy. But I really have no place to go."

"Where are your parents? And your famous grandmother? . . . Although, under the circumstances, I think I understand why you may not want to call her. Don't you have a married sister who lives here in town?"

"You seem to know quite a lot about me."

"Roseton isn't that big. Listen, do you really want to spend another night in this place?"

"Not if I can help it."

"Sit tight, then," he said as he took my supper tray. "I'll be back."

"I'm not going anywhere," I assured him. I lay down on the cot and folded my hands behind my head as he hurried out, locking the door behind him.

Funny he should ask about my parents. My mother's life was another complicated story. I decided to consider the part that she played in this drama while I waited for Tommy to return.

My mother's childhood was worlds apart from the simple farm life that Grandma Bebe had known.

Lucretia "Lucy" Garner was born with the prover
bial silver spoon in her mouth, and she knew it
She quickly acquired a taste for the finer things in
life, and by the time she learned to walk, any lesser
type of spoon left a very bad flavor on her palate.

Her earliest memory, so she has told me, was o
the day she peeked over the upstairs railing when
she was supposed to be napping and sav
Grandmother Garner's elegant friends arriving fo
afternoon tea. Lucy looked down at their flower
strewn hats and swirling satin gowns and though
they looked like the brilliantly colored birds in on
of her picture books. When the ladies all disap
peared into the parlor, Lucy tiptoed down the stair
to follow them, their voices and laughter drawing
her like the sound of gurgling water.

Inside the echoing room, Grandmother's fines
china teacups clinked and tinkled along with th
laughter. Silver serving pieces that usually rested
on the dining room sideboard shone in all their
glory on marble-topped side tables. Parlor maids in
black uniforms and starched white aprons flitted
around like chickadees, serving the guests. Lucy
stared in openmouthed awe at the beautiful spec
tacle.

Then the nanny, who should have been watching
Lucy, caught up with her and snatched her away
from the doorway. "You're supposed to be taking a
nap," she whispered as she carried her toward the
stairs. Lucy howled in protest.

Grandmother Garner set down her teacup and strode into the foyer to see what all the fuss was about. "Whatever is the matter, Lucy darling?"

"I don't want to take a nap, Grandmama. I want to come to your party."

Mrs. Garner smiled regally, careful not to disturb her calm composure. She reminded Lucy of a queen in a fairy tale, royally elegant with her swishing dresses and straight-backed posture, commanding obeisance from all the household servants and respect from all the society matrons. "You certainly shall attend one day, my dear. But first, we must make certain you are properly attired and instructed. These social gatherings require a great deal of training, you know. Now, toddle along upstairs and I will talk to your father about it tonight—there's no sense trying to discuss anything important with your mother."

Lucy wasn't happy about being left out of the festivities, but she did what she was told. And Grandmother Garner kept her promise. The very next day she gave Lucy a miniature porcelain tea set decorated with red roses and gold trim so she could begin to learn the rituals. The porcelain felt cool and smooth beneath Lucy's fingers.

"You must be very careful when you play with it, Lucy. You wouldn't want to break any of the pieces."

"I would never break it, Grandmama!" She carried the tea set up to her playroom so she could recreate her grandmother's party, planning to invite her stuffed bear and all of her dolls. She invited Mama the next morning at breakfast. "I'm having a tea party today like Grandmama's. Will you come?"

"I'm sorry, darling, but I have to go down to the tannery to work." Mama was always going to the tannery and was seldom home during the day. Every morning after breakfast she would pin on her hat and kiss Lucy good-bye, and she wouldn't return until suppertime.

Lucy decided to invite Daddy, instead. He slept very late every day, and she wasn't allowed to see him until he woke up. But when the maid brought him his tray of coffee and toast, Lucy tiptoed into his bedroom along with her as she did nearly every morning.

"I'm having a tea party today, Daddy. Would you like to come?" He squinted at her as if the room were very bright, even though all the curtains were still drawn. Then he smiled.

"Are men allowed to come? Your grandmother never invites men to her tea parties, you know." He pulled himself upright in bed so the servant could set the tray on his lap, then patted a place beside him, inviting Lucy to sit. She climbed up next to him and held out her hand for a lump of sugar. He gave her two. They both laughed at their familiar ritual as she savored the sugar's crunchy sweetness.

"It's *my* party, Daddy, and I can invite whoever I want, and I want you." He tousled her hair, then leaned over to kiss her forehead. Lucy loved her daddy's scent, like the rum cakes their cook made at Christmastime. The smell of bay rum aftershave always reminded Lucy of him.

Later that afternoon, when Lucy had everything ready, her father came to her tea party, sitting cross-legged on the playroom floor beside her, wearing his blue silk bathrobe. He held a tiny teacup in his hand and made slurping noises as he pretended to drink. Cook had baked tea cakes with pink frosting for Lucy to serve along with the pretend tea. They laughed and laughed. Lucy loved her carefree, golden-haired daddy—the most handsome daddy in the whole world. When she looked at herself in the mirror on her dressing table, she could see that she had fair hair and blue eyes just like his. She didn't look at all like Mama, who had dark hair and dark eyes and a dark frown.

Once Lucy began to learn proper social skills, Grandmother Garner planned a glorious party for her fifth birthday in May of 1874. Grandmother's friends filled the parlor, wearing their colorful afternoon gowns and bringing their little daughters and granddaughters along with them. It was a real grown-up tea party—Lucy's first. Her dress was the prettiest one, hand-sewn by Grandmother's seamstress and decorated with imported lace and embroidered smocking. Lucy stood in the front foyer to properly greet her guests, saying "Welcome" and "So glad you could come" just as Grandmama had taught her. She loved the envious looks the other girls gave her when they saw her dress and the satin bows that Nanny had tied in her shining golden ringlets.

Everyone brought Lucy a beautifully wrapped present, and she gave each child a little present to take home. The dining room table overflowed with food and candy and other treats, and Lucy ate and ate until her stomach ached. Then Cook brought in a towering cake with birthday candles. "Make a wish and blow them out, dear," Grandmama said.

Lucy closed her eyes and silently wished that Mother and Daddy could be there for her party. She must have closed her eyes too tightly, because when she opened them again, the candles seemed to waver behind a curtain of tears. It took her two tries to blow out all five candles.

A few minutes later, part of Lucy's wish came true when her mother rushed home from the tannery in time to eat a piece of birthday cake. She wasn't dressed as elegantly as the other women were, and she looked small and plain and out of place among the guests with their glittering necklaces and earrings. Lucy was sorry she had wasted her birthday wish.

"Where's Daddy? Why didn't he come?" she asked.

"I wish he could be here, Lucy. He loves you so

402

much." Mother quickly finished her cake and swallowed her tea, then took Lucy aside. "I need to go back to work now," she whispered. "I love you, sweetheart."

Daddy didn't return home until very late that night after Lucy was already asleep. He tiptoed into her room carrying a candle and sat down on the edge of her bed, softly calling her name and stroking her fair hair until she woke up. She recognized his sweet scent. "Hi, Daddy."

"Hey, my darling girl. I'm so sorry I had to miss your birthday party. Something important came up, and I couldn't get away." Even in the middle of the night Daddy seemed happy, his face glowing with pleasure—unlike Mama, who always looked vexed and worried.

"That's okay, Daddy," she said sleepily. "Grandma didn't invite any men. You would have been the only one there."

"But I didn't forget your birthday, sweetheart. Here. I brought you a present." He held out a small box, and Lucy scrambled to sit up so she could unwrap it. Inside was a fine golden chain with a dark green gemstone dangling from it, shaped like a teardrop. "It's an emerald, sweetheart. Your birthstone. Here, let me put it on you." He fumbled to fasten the clasp around her neck. When he finished, Lucy hugged him tightly.

"I'll never, ever take it off! I love you, Daddy, more than anyone in the whole world."

"And I love you, too. Now, make a wish and blow out the candle, sweetheart. I'll see you in the morning."

Lucy didn't know what to wish for. She had everything she could ever want, except . . . maybe . . . a pony of her very own. She closed her eyes and wished for one, then blew out her father's candle.

Most of Lucy's days were spent with her nanny, but sometimes Grandmama would invite Lucy into her bedroom suite to read to her from etiquette books or look at fashion magazines. "I'm going to teach you how to be a proper young woman so you can attend society events someday," she told her. "You should be very proud of your high standing in this town. Our family owns one of the largest businesses. You can marry anyone you choose." At age five, Lucy imagined that getting married would be like kissing the handsome prince in the fairy tales Mother used to read to her—the end of the story, not the beginning.

Lucy admired her austere grandmother but was a little in awe of her. She especially loved the stately way her grandmother walked and the swishing sound her skirts made. "You can learn how to walk the same way, Lucy, by balancing a book on top of your head for practice." Grandmama showed her how, and Lucy practiced and practiced with Nanny, but no matter how hard she tried, Lucy couldn't get her dresses to make the swishing sound.

"I want more petticoats so my dresses sound like Grandmama's," she told her mother one morning at breakfast.

Mother laid down her newspaper and frowned. "You have enough petticoats. You're a little girl, Lucy. How can you run around and play in such stiff clothing?"

"I don't want to run, I want petticoats! Buy me some right now!" She stamped her foot for emphasis. Mother's frown deepened.

"Lucy, you may not talk to me that way."

Lucy had learned how to throw a temper tantrum to make Nanny do her bidding, and she decided to throw one now for her mother, kicking her feet and making as much racket as she could. Nanny ran into the dining room in alarm, but Mother calmly returned to her newspaper. "Carry Lucy to her room until she can control herself," she ordered. But as soon as Mother left for the tannery, Grandmother Garner came to Lucy's rescue.

"There, there, don't cry, darling. If you want more petticoats, we'll go shopping today and buy you some."

Lucy loved to shop. The carriage driver took them down to Central Avenue and Lucy held Grandmother's hand as they went from store to store, buying three of the prettiest, noisiest petticoats they could find. When Mother came home at suppertime, Lucy twirled in happy circles to show them to her—and to let her know that she had won the contest. Mama sighed and frowned and looked unhappy. Mother always gazed at Lucy as if she were aboard a ship that was slowly sailing away. She wondered why Mother didn't jump on board with her.

Then one day her mother didn't leave to go to the tannery after breakfast. Lucy found her sitting at the little writing desk in the morning room, instead. "What are you doing, Mama?"

"I'm writing letters to some very important people, dear." She didn't look up.

"Why?"

"Because I need to convince them to make some changes in our community, and—" She paused, finally looking up from her work. "It's hard to explain, Lucy."

"Are you going to the tannery after you finish writing the letters?"

When Mother's eyes filled with tears, Lucy feared she had said something wrong. "I won't be working there anymore," she said softly.

Lucy thought it was going to be wonderful to have her mother home again, but nothing changed very much in the months that followed. Mother's new work always occupied her: writing letters, reading pamphlets, organizing meetings. She never attended Grandmama's tea parties even though she was at home, nor she did she go calling in the afternoon like all of the other women did. But nearly every evening after dinner, Mother gathered up her picket signs and banners and left the house, staying out until long after Lucy fell asleep. Daddy seemed very angry with her and Lucy overheard him shouting at her one morning after the maid brought him his coffee. Lucy stood outside his bedroom door, listening.

"Where are my friends and I supposed to go now that you've closed down the place?"

"That's the point," Mother said. "You're not supposed to go anywhere. You're supposed to stop drinking every night and stay home with us." Her voice sounded very calm even though Daddy was angry. "I'm doing this for Lucy's sake. She loves you so much, you know. But how will she feel in a few years when she learns the truth about where you spend all your time?"

"You wouldn't tell her!"

"No, of course not. But other people here in town know the truth, and someday she'll find out, too, and it will destroy her love for you. Please, Horatio. I'm begging you to stop."

"Go away and leave me alone."

Lucy had no idea what they were fighting about, but everyone she loved seemed angry and sad all the time, even Grandmama. The tension made Lucy feel sad, too. And frightened. Her nanny tried to keep her occupied during the day and always closed the door to Lucy's playroom or bedroom or took her for a walk when her parents began to argue. But one morning on Nanny's day off, Lucy

407

overheard her mother and grandmother fighting as she tiptoed downstairs for breakfast.

"I insist that you stop these crazy campaigns of yours," Grandmama said. "They are an embarrassment to me, to our family, and to yourself. You should be ashamed of such behavior." Lucy could tell by the sound of Grandmama's voice that her face was turning very red.

Mother's voice sounded as hard and tight as a fist when she replied. "Your son is the one who should be ashamed and embarrassed, not me. Why don't you ask him how he spends his evenings?"

"Because it's none of my business. Besides, his actions aren't described in vivid detail on the front pages of the newspaper every morning the way yours are."

"I spend my evenings praying and singing hymns—how is that disgraceful?"

"Because you do it on street corners in the most disreputable parts of town and in the company of the most disreputable sort of people. Don't you care at all about Lucy's future?"

Lucy's cheeks started growing warm when she heard her name. She worried that she had caused the argument somehow, but she didn't know what she had done. She wanted to run into the dining room and tell them to stop fighting, but every time in the past that she had come between the two women, she always felt like the rope in a game of tug-of-war, pulled in opposite directions.

"I care very much about my daughter's future," Mother continued. "And in that future she deserves to have a father she can respect."

"What about a mother she can respect? You're earning a terrible reputation in this town with your shenanigans."

"I'm trying to improve this town by closing down the multitude of saloons that have sprouted like weeds, and if some people don't like that, it's just too bad. Are you aware of the social problems caused by alcohol? You can read all about them in the Temperance Union's newsletter. Or you can open your eyes and see what's happening in your very own home."

"I can't talk to you anymore. You not only have no common sense, you've become some sort of religious fanatic."

"You're calling me a fanatic because I trust God and ask for His help? Or is it because I've chosen not to attend your church anymore?"

"That so-called church you attend is filled with religious fanatics just like yourself. There isn't a respectable citizen among them."

"Thank God for that! Thank God they're not too respectable to offer help during a cholera epidemic or to give aid to families with drunken husbands and fathers. I won't spend one more Sabbath in a church that ignores Christ's command to help the poor. Maybe you're comfortable in such a place, but I'm not."

As soon as the topic switched to churches, Lucy began backing away from the door to run upstairs. When Mother had decided to join a different church than the one Grandmama always went to, Lucy had felt like a piece of taffy, stretched and pulled in two directions at once. The tug-of-war continued until the two women finally asked Lucy to choose which church she liked the best. She hadn't known what to say. Of course, she wanted to please her mother, but she didn't know any of the other girls at Mother's church, and besides, they dressed so differently than she did. In the end, Lucy chose her grandmother's elegant church because that was the one that Daddy used to go to when he was a little boy. The distance between Lucy and her mother seemed to grow wider each day.

In the spring of 1876, Grandmother began planning a lavish party for Lucy's seventh birthday. Lucy decided to ask for a pony that year, along with her very own pony cart to ride around in. But when she followed the maid into her father's bedroom one morning with his coffee and toast, she sensed right away that something had changed. For one thing, Mother was in his bedroom, too, and she was stuffing Daddy's clothes and toiletries into a suitcase. Daddy sat on the edge of the bed with his shoulders slumped. He looked very sad. His blue eyes weren't sparkling anymore, and he had dark circles beneath them.

"Are you going away on a trip, Daddy?" she asked.

Mother answered before he did. "We're going to stay at Grandfather Garner's fishing cabin for a few days."

Lucy skirted around her mother and ran to him. "I want to come on the trip, too, Daddy."

He tucked a strand of her hair behind her ear. "You wouldn't like it up at the cabin, sweetheart."

"Yes I would. I want to go. Why can't I go?" She stomped her foot and started to cry, certain that Daddy would give in, but her mother gripped her firmly by the shoulders and turned her around.

"Stop it, Lucy, and listen to me. Remember when Nanny took you upstairs to the attic and showed you where the servants sleep? Well, the cabin that we're going to is even more rustic than the attic is. It has spiders living there. And mice."

"You're just saying that. It's not true. I want to go!" Her tantrum didn't do any good. Her mother finished packing and prepared to leave.

"I'm sorry, Lucy," Daddy said as he kissed her good-bye. "I promise to buy you a very special present for your birthday when I get home."

"A pony. I want my own pony."

Daddy smiled faintly, but he didn't promise. Lucy tried one last time to throw a tantrum to get her own way, but Nanny held her back until her parents' runabout disappeared from sight.

She was playing with her dolls in the playroom a

week later when Mother burst into the house shouting, "Lucy! Lucy, where are you?"

Lucy stood and went to the playroom door. "I'm up here, Mama." Her mother bounded up the stairs in a very unladylike way, then hugged Lucy so tightly it made her ribs hurt.

"Thank God! Thank God!" Mother murmured. She wasn't wearing a hat and the rain had soaked her clothing and hair. Her body shivered so badly it might have been snowing outside instead of raining. Daddy came inside, too, shouting something about the dam on Iroquois Lake. He rang the service bell to summon all the servants. Grandmama came out of her room and tried to get Daddy to close the front door and change out of his wet clothes, but he wouldn't listen.

Lucy had no idea what was going on, but everyone was shouting, and the household had never been in such an uproar. It made her feel very frightened. She started down the stairs toward her father, calling, "Daddy, Daddy!" but her mother caught her instead, and wouldn't let go of her until after her father left with the carriage driver. "Daddy! I want my daddy!" she wept, but it was too late. He was gone. Lucy fled into her grandmother's arms, instead.

"There, there," she soothed. "Come, my dearest. I'll tell Cook to fix us some tea and cookies."

Before Lucy had time to finish her cookies, Mother and Grandmama began to quarrel. The servants started moving all of Grandmama's pretty things out of the parlor and upstairs to her bedroom. Then Daddy came back with a carriage load of strangers—horrible, dirty people who crowded into Lucy's house, dripping water on the carpets and hardwood floors. Most of them were children, foul-smelling and dressed in rags, and elderly people with wrinkled faces, who spoke in languages she couldn't understand.

"Lift me up, Daddy. Carry me." She reached up to him but he only patted her head.

"Not now, sweetheart. I'm all wet. Your nice dress will get all wet."

"I don't care." She wanted his arms around her and everything changed back to the way it used to be, so she could go into his bedroom and talk to him every day.

She blamed her mother for all of this chaos. Mother was giving everyone directions and inviting them into the house, saying, "Please, come inside and get warm. We have food and hot coffee prepared." But when Mother suddenly said, "Come, Lucy. Let's take these children upstairs and show them where your playroom is," Lucy was too horrified to reply. She was desperate to stop the horrible children from going into her special room and was about to shout "No!" and throw a tantrum, but Grandmother Garner spoke up first.

"You can't be serious, Beatrice. These people

can't be trusted. They'll break all of Lucy's nice things."

Mother waved her away. "I don't want Lucy to grow up to be selfish," she said. Lucy couldn't think what to do! Mother plunged ahead, saying, "Come, children. This way. Lucy, you go first and show them where your playroom is." The raggedy children started moving up the stairs.

"Aren't you going to stop her?" Grandmother asked Daddy. He shook his head. Lucy scrambled up the stairs as fast as she could go, racing toward the playroom to protect her toys. She would get the servants to help her move everything into Grandmama's room the way they had moved all of the valuables out of the parlor and dining room.

Lucy reached the playroom first, ready to scream or cry or throw a tantrum, if need be, in order to keep the dirty children out. But a strange thing happened when the first few children reached the playroom behind her: Instead of running and grabbing and breaking her things, they stood huddled near the door, as unmoving as store mannequins, gazing around the huge room. The pause gave Lucy a few moments to calm down.

Then one little boy, the bravest one, took two halting steps inside. He had hair the color of wet sand and ragged clothing that hung from his slender body like a scarecrow's. She couldn't tell if all of the spots on his dirt-smudged his face were freckles or filth. He made a sweeping gesture with his scrawny arm, pointing to her shelves and toy boxes and to the pile of dolls in the middle of the floor that she had been playing with a few hours ago. "What are all these things?" he asked.

"They're called toys. Haven't you ever seen toys before?"

He lifted one bony shoulder in what might have been a shrug. "What do you do with them?"

Lucy had never met such a stupid boy. "What do you think you do? You play with them!" She watched as his gaze roamed the room, taking it all in. Then he spotted her wooden rocking horse and he took a few more steps inside, halting alongside it.

"What's this for?" He reached out his hand to stroke the horsehair mane.

"You ride on it. Like this." She pulled the horse out of his reach and climbed on, gripping the handles to rock back and forth. The horse was a baby's toy, and Lucy had been bored with it for the past year, but when she saw the boy and all of the other children watching in amazement and admiration she decided that she liked the rocking horse again.

"Can I try it?" the boy asked.

"You mean, '*may* I?'" He looked at her as if she had spoken a foreign language. "You're supposed to say '*may*' I try it, not '*can*' I."

"I want to ride it," he said matter-of-factly, and Lucy recognized something in his gray eyes, a deep sadness that seemed very much like her own.

"Well . . . I suppose you may," she told him. "But you'd better be careful and not break it."

A huge smile spread across his face as he climbed on. She guessed that he was a little older than she was because his two front teeth were growing in and her baby teeth were just falling out. He had holes in his shirt and one button missing. The other three buttons didn't match each other. His pants were too short, his shoes too large. He wasn't wearing socks. But he laughed out loud as he rocked back and forth, and it was such a joyous sound that Lucy couldn't help smiling.

The other children watched him from the doorway, and since the stampede she'd feared hadn't happened, Lucy began walking around the room taking toys off the shelves, showing everyone how to play with them. She didn't show them her newest doll or her very special things like the porcelain tea set, but she decided that the strangers could play with her older toys and the things she had outgrown. Slowly, tentatively, the children inched forward to watch. Their mothers stayed close beside them and seemed as awestruck as they were.

"This is my rubber ball," Lucy said, showing two children how to roll it across the floor to each other. "And this is called a top." Three other children took turns spinning it. One little girl seemed content to rock Lucy's empty wooden doll cradle. Another hugged her old, worn-out rag doll in her arms. "Watch this," Lucy said as she taught two youngsters how to build a tower with her wooden blocks. They took turns building and toppling the blocks. She gave two small girls her chalkboard and some chalk to use. When everyone was occupied, she walked back to the first boy, who was still rocking on her horse, grinning as if it was the most fun he'd ever had.

"What's your name?" she asked him.

"Danny Carver. What's yours?"

"Lucretia Frances Garner. You may call me Lucy."

"I like your horse."

"It's all right, I suppose. Daddy is going to buy me a real pony for my birthday."

"I like this one."

"Well, when is your birthday? Why don't you ask your daddy to buy one for you?"

His smile faded. He lifted his shoulder in another shrug. "We got no room for one. Our house is too small. . . . Hey, can my brother have a turn?"

"I suppose so. If he's careful."

Danny helped a smaller boy climb on, and while he rocked, Lucy decided to show Danny her wooden train. He seemed more fascinated with the train than she had ever been, coupling and uncoupling each of the cars and imitating a train whistle as he pushed it across the floor.

A little while later, more children arrived. As the afternoon grew late, some of the youngest children fell asleep on their mothers' laps. Everyone was behaving nicely until the servants came into the playroom with a tray of sandwiches and set it on Lucy's table. Danny and the other children dropped their playthings and raced toward the food. They had no manners at all, snatching up the sandwiches in their filthy fingers and gobbling them down as if they hadn't eaten in a very long time. They created such an uproar that Grandmother came into the playroom to see what the racket was all about.

"What's going on in here, Lucy? Are you all right?" Her queenly face was no longer serene, and she looked angry and fearful. Lucy could tell that she didn't like all the upheaval in their household. "Come, Lucy. Let's take your nice things to another room." She helped Lucy gather up her favorite dolls and her tea set and carry them into Grandmama's bedroom suite. Lucy stayed there, eating from the tray of food the servants brought them, and later fell asleep in her grandmother's arms.

Lucy lost track of how many days the ragged, dirty strangers lived in her house, but it seemed like a very long time. They occupied every room downstairs, sleeping on the floor and eating her food and playing with her toys. She made friends with Danny, but the other children were too shy to talk to her or even tell her their names. Danny took turns playing with each of her toys, but what fascinated him the most were her picture books. She sat on the floor beside him one afternoon and told him the stories from memory. He studied each page with such concentration that she often grew impatient and pulled the book from his hands to turn to the next page. She had never met anyone quite like him before.

Years later, Lucy saw photographs of the disaster and learned what the Great Flood of 1876 had done to her town while Danny and the other children had stayed at her house. The photos showed mountains of mud as high as the door lintels; piles of debris and downed trees; vast lakes of water that surrounded all of the buildings and flooded the city's main street where she used to go shopping. The neighborhood where Danny and the other children had lived resembled a garbage heap.

Lucy waited and waited for her Daddy to return home, but he never did. When all of the dirty people were gone and the house was quiet once again, she asked, "When is Daddy coming home?"

Mother pulled her into her arms and held her tightly. "He isn't coming home, Lucy." Mother shivered, even though the room felt warm. Lucy didn't understand what her mother meant.

"Well, where is Daddy going to live from now on if he isn't coming home? I want to go live with him."

"I'm sorry, but you can't, Lucy. He died in the flood and now he's in heaven. He'll be laid to rest in the cemetery beside Grandfather Garner."

Everyone called Lucy's daddy a hero and said how courageous and brave he was, but Lucy didn't care what he had done for everyone else in town. She wanted her daddy back, dressed in his blue satin bathrobe, smiling and giving her lumps of sugar while he drank his morning coffee. Her last glimpse of him had been when he had walked out of the front door and into the rain.

The memorial service was like a bad dream, with everyone dressed in black and walking as if they were asleep. Mother couldn't stop crying, but Grandmama held her head high and tried not to show her feelings in public, just as she had taught Lucy to do. Hundreds of people filled the church along with huge bouquets of flowers, but Lucy's father wasn't there. When she'd had enough of all the sorrow and the meaningless words, Lucy sank down in the aisle of the church and threw a tantrum.

"I want my Daddy!"

For the first time in her life, she didn't get what she wanted.

CHAPTER
22

I will always remember Alice's wedding because of what I learned about Grandfather Horatio that night. And just as the Great Flood of 1876 proved to be a turning point in Grandma Bebe's life, the wedding opened a floodgate of changes in my mother's life. That's when she woke up one morning and discovered that she had nothing to do. She turned to me, sizing me up as her next project like a bear circling a bee tree, wondering how she could get at all that honey.

"Nothing doing, Mama!" I held up my hands, backing away like Neal MacLeod used to do. I had to stop when I backed into a wall. "I don't want you to turn me into another Alice. And there won't be another wedding, because I'm never getting married!"

She poked at my short hair, wrinkling her nose. "You're like a wild thing, Harriet, and it's all my fault. I should have kept a closer eye on you. As it is, I fear I've let you go for much too long."

I grabbed the telephone and called Grandma Bebe, pleading with her to come over and rescue me. "Please hurry!" I begged. "You should see the way Mother looks at me—like she wants to cinch my waist in a corset and pin a gigantic hat on my head. I won't let her do it, I tell you! I'll run away from home, first!"

"Calm down, Harriet. I'll be over as soon as I can."

By the time Grandma arrived, Mother had all of my bureau drawers open and the doors to my wardrobe thrown wide. She was shaking her head and clicking her tongue as she examined my clothing. "This won't do . . . and this *certainly* won't do. . . ."

"See?" I whispered to Grandma. "I told you she's lost her mind."

Grandma nodded and approached Mother as if soothing a spooked stallion. "Lucy, listen to me. You need to leave Harriet alone. She is already her own person. Alice was very much like you, but Harriet isn't like you at all."

Mother turned to us, smoothing back her golden hair, wild from her rummaging. Her eyes had a wild look to them, too. "But whatever will Harriet do in life? She has no aptitude for proper manners and absolutely no social contacts."

"I don't have any manners or social contacts, either," Grandma said, "and I'm perfectly happy. You know very well that when you were growing up, I wanted nothing to do with Grandmother Garner's women's clubs and teas. But I let you get involved with her social set, even though I thought you were wasting your time, because that was what you wanted. Alice wanted that type of life, too, but Harriet doesn't. Besides, times are changing. Women are moving beyond the home and developing interests other than marriage and motherhood."

Mother's expression showed her horror. "But what else is there? I will not have Harriet getting caught up in all your protests and things. I don't want her singing hymns outside those disreputable saloons and marching in parades."

"Neither do I, dear. And I don't think she wants

to be involved in my work, either. But think about it, Lucy—would you have wanted me to force you to take up all of my causes? You can't expect Harriet to become like you any more than you would have wanted to become like me."

"But she's turning into a wild thing," Mother insisted. "Just last week I received another note from school about her unladylike behavior."

Grandma gave me a glance that was more conspiratorial than condemnatory. "What did she do this time?"

"She kicked the police superintendent's son in the shins!"

"He deserved it, Grandma. Tommy O'Reilly is a big, mean bully!"

Grandma paused before responding, biting her lip as if laughter might bubble out any moment. "All I'm saying is, we have to let our children lead their own lives. Let Harriet be herself, Lucy. Let her find her own way in life. She's a smart young woman. She'll do all right."

Mother sighed and pushed the wardrobe doors closed. I sank down on my bed with relief. But Grandma Bebe turned to me, her forefinger raised as she gently scolded me. "I want you to promise your mother that you'll behave in school from now on. No more shin-kicking, do you hear?"

"I'll try." It would be a small price to pay for my freedom. I thought the episode was over, but when

I glanced at my mother I could see that she was still upset.

"I was always a disappointment to you, wasn't I?" Mother murmured. She was talking to Grandma Bebe.

"I was wrong to feel that way, dear," Grandma replied. "I had to learn what you're learning now—that our daughters aren't the same people we are, nor are they extensions of ourselves. They are unique individuals in God's eyes, responsible to Him for the choices they make, not to their mothers."

"I know you've always thought my life was shallow because I didn't share your values or your passion for all of your causes—"

"It isn't up to me to judge anyone's life."

"But I always knew you felt that way. That's probably why we were never close."

Grandma Bebe's expression turned sad. "I'm afraid it goes back a few more generations before us," she said. "My mother was dismayed by the choices I made, too—marrying Horatio, not being a woman of prayer like she was. The letters she wrote to me were very carefully worded, but I avoided visiting her because I could see that we valued different things and that she was disappointed in my choices. By the time I became involved with the Temperance Union and learned what it meant to really lean on God, my mother was already in heaven."

Mother closed the drawers to my bureau, then leaned against it. "Grandmother Garner understood me, even if you didn't. I knew exactly how to win her approval. But I always felt as though pleasing her meant displeasing you."

I listened to their conversation, aware that I was repeating their pattern. My mother was disappointed in me, too. We would probably never be close because I refused to join her social world. But the things that were important to Mother just didn't matter to me. I wanted to please her and make her proud of me, but it seemed impossible unless I turned myself into another Alice. I also wanted to make Grandma Bebe proud of me, but pleasing her meant disappointing my mother. I felt hopelessly confused.

"I was not the wife that Mrs. Garner would have chosen for her son," Grandma Bebe continued. "I was an embarrassment to her and to you. Admit it, Lucy. I still embarrass you, sometimes."

"Yes, I admit it. And I still don't want a life like yours. But lately, when I look at my life, it seems like such a waste. . . ."

I sat up in concern when I saw that Mother was close to tears. I was afraid that I had caused them. It wouldn't hurt to *try* to be more ladylike in the future. But my behavior wasn't what had upset her.

"I keep thinking of all that time I wasted making

sure that Alice's wedding was perfect . . . all the money I spent . . . I just wanted her to be happy, and now . . . now . . ."

"When one era in our life comes to an end," Grandma said, "and we have to start all over again, it can be a good thing. It gives us a chance to decide what's really important. Nobody likes change, Lucy. But even if everything else is taken away, God is still with us."

Mother didn't seem to hear her. "I just want you to be happy, too, Harriet," she said, turning to me. "Why won't you let me do that?"

I'll be happy if you leave me alone, I wanted to say, but Grandma said it for me.

"Harriet has to find her own happiness in life, and living to please another person is never going to accomplish that. Living to please God is what matters. Meanwhile, we have to trust that He'll arrange the events in Harriet's life in order to lead her to the purpose He has for her."

I looked to see what my mother's response would be, but it seemed as though she had suddenly popped open an umbrella to fend off Grandma's words and keep them from soaking in. Her spine stiffened and she assumed the faint smile and detached pose she always adopted for her society friends.

"Would you like some coffee, Mother? I'll go and ask Bess if there is any left." She floated from the room as if we had just arrived to pay a social call and she'd been neglecting her duties. Grandma looked at me and shrugged.

Grandma Bebe may have won me a reprieve from a life of foolish fashion, but my mother still drifted aimlessly without a project. I watched her wander around like a child who had lost her way, turning in circles on an unfamiliar street, searching for the way home. I felt torn. I hated seeing her so sad, but I wasn't willing to sacrifice my liberty for her happiness.

Then at breakfast one Saturday morning, Father slid his newspaper across the table to her before leaving for work. "There's an article on the front page you might like to read. It's about your father."

Mother read the social pages every day but seldom looked at the rest of the news, insisting that it only distressed her. *"I would rather not know what's going on in the world,"* I'd once heard her tell Alice. *"I have enough to concern me in my own household. I'll leave it up to the politicians to fix the messes they create. That's their job."*

The United States had managed to fight a war with Spain right under Mother's dainty nose without her ever knowing about it. I don't think she was aware that the *Titanic* had sunk two months before Alice's wedding, either, killing thousands of people. After all, Mother had flowers to choose and invitations to address.

But as I spread a thick layer of orange marmalade on my toast, I saw her reach for the paper and pull it toward her as if it were a sack of snakes. She opened it to the front page. When I looked up again, her face had turned so white I thought I might have to run and get the smelling salts. She had tears in her eyes as she laid the paper on the table again.

"Mother? Are you all right?"

She nodded, but I could see that she wasn't. When she stood and tried to walk, her legs didn't seem to work right, as if she were wearing someone else's shoes. Somehow, she managed to wobble from the room and climb the stairs.

I grabbed the newspaper, of course, and quickly scanned the front page. The feature story wasn't even about Horatio, but about a local man who had leaped into the Iroquois River to rescue some children after their homemade raft had capsized. He managed to drag three of the boys to safety, but he and a fourth boy drowned after the current swept them away. The mayor called him a hero. A brief sidebar article reminded readers of Horatio Garner's heroism thirty-six years ago during the Great Flood of 1876.

Mother never returned to finish her breakfast. I reread the two paragraphs about her father, failing to see how the matter-of-fact prose could have evoked such a dramatic response. After the strange way she had reacted the other day in my bedroom, I feared that my mother would need a sanatorium soon. Father had left for work, and since our hired girl wanted to clear the breakfast table, I tiptoed upstairs and knocked on Mother's bedroom door. I heard weeping.

"Mother? Are you all right?"

"Go away, Harriet."

I decided to walk to Grandma Bebe's house and see if the story had affected her the same way. I found Grandma seated at her cluttered table, counting names on a batch of petitions. She held up a finger to keep me from interrupting.

"Did you see the story in the newspaper about Horatio?" I asked when she finished.

"I saw it."

"Are you all right?"

"Why wouldn't I be, dear? The flood happened nearly forty years ago."

"Mother read the story and she got so upset she started crying. For a minute there, I thought she was going to faint."

Grandma removed her spectacles and laid them on the table. "Oh, dear. Lucy never reads the paper. I was hoping she wouldn't see the front page."

"Daddy gave it to her. I read the article, too, and there were only two paragraphs about Grandpa Horatio. I don't know why her face turned so white. I nearly ran for the smelling salts."

Grandma slowly shook her head. "I don't think it was the story about Horatio that upset her. Lucy was—" She halted, covering her mouth with her fingers as if she had already said too much. That made me curious to hear more, of course. I stepped into the kitchen and got out Grandma's teapot and two cups. While the kettle heated on the stove, I flopped down on a dining room chair with my legs outstretched to let Grandma know I wasn't going anywhere until she explained herself. Mother would have told me to sit up straight and cross my ankles, but I could be myself at Grandma's house.

"Well?" I prompted.

Grandma had been staring out of the window while I'd put the kettle on to boil, and she turned to me as if she'd forgotten I was there. "Hmm?"

"Mother has been acting very strange and melancholy ever since Alice's wedding," I said to get her started. "But today, when she read the newspaper, it was like the Iroquois Dam had burst all over again."

"Your mother has been working too hard. She's overwrought." Grandma played with a corner of the paper in front of her. She was looking through the window, not at me. I knew she was hiding something.

"You should have seen her reaction, Grandma. She went upstairs to her room, and I could hear her crying, even though the door was closed. Is she going to be all right?"

"It depends on whether or not she turns to God for help. It can be a very difficult time for a woman when her children don't need her anymore. You'll see, one day."

"No I won't because I'm never getting married, remember?" I waited, but Grandma still said nothing. I huffed in frustration. "Are you going to tell me why the newspaper made her cry or not?"

She closed her eyes. "Your mother knew the man who drowned."

"What?" I grabbed Grandma's copy of the newspaper, lying open on the table, and sucked in my breath when I reread his name: Daniel Carver. "Was he the same Danny who played on her rocking horse during the flood?"

Grandma's brows lifted in surprise. "Why, yes . . . how did you know about that?"

"Mother told me the story, once." I could tell there was a lot more to this mystery, so I waited, jiggling my foot impatiently. "Was that the only time Mother met this Danny fellow?"

She glanced at me, then quickly looked away. "I think your mother should decide whether or not to tell you about Daniel Carver."

Now I was thoroughly intrigued. And frustrated. "But she won't tell me! Mother never talks about anything interesting or important—just the news on the social page."

The kettle whistled, and Grandma got up to turn it off. She didn't pour the water into a teapot, though. "I think you should go home and talk to her, Harriet. If she's as upset as you say she is, maybe talking about it will help."

"You come, too, Grandma. We'll both talk to her."

She shook her head. "Your mother misses Alice very much. You don't have to take Alice's place, but you should try to spend a little more time with your mother. Get to know each other."

I winced at the idea of spending time with my mother, especially if she was going to weep, but it seemed to be the only way I would ever hear the whole story. I hemmed and hawed until I realized that Grandma wasn't going to change her mind, then I trudged home again.

I found Mother in her little sitting room upstairs. A pile of correspondence sat in front of her but the pen was still in the inkwell, the stationery untouched. She sat with her hands folded in her lap as she stared out of the window above her desk. The wadded handkerchief on her desktop looked very damp.

"I'm so sorry about your friend Danny Carver, Mother."

Her eyes looked red and swollen as she turned to me. "I haven't thought about Danny in years, and now I see his name on the front page . . . and such a tragedy."

Her tears started again. A childhood friendship of two or three days didn't explain so much grief. I made myself comfortable on the floor at her feet and waited to hear the story.

A brass band played a dirge in the distance as Lucy stood on a grassy rise, gazing at the river that had swept her father away when she was a child. The shimmering water appeared deceptively placid, and she had trouble imagining that it could have done so much damage eleven years ago or caused so much sorrow.

She hadn't wanted to come to this commemorative event today, but her mother had insisted. "It wouldn't be right if you didn't come, Lucy. After all, they are honoring your father. Besides, Grandmother Garner might need you."

Lucy had watched in detached silence as city officials dedicated Garner Park to her father's memory and unveiled the newly erected monument stone. The town's brass band played mournful music and a group of soldiers who had served in the army with Horatio saluted in tribute. Grandmother Garner, the honored guest for the ceremony, had presented a wreath in her son's memory. Now Lucy had drifted away from all the fuss while the city's elite soothed Grandmother Garner and Mother talked with Uncle Franklin, who had arrived by train for the event.

For the moment Lucy stood alone, trying to find the daddy she remembered in all the glowing tributes she had just heard. No one had mentioned how his eyes had sparkled when he looked at her, or how he would laugh as they sipped pretend tea together. She worried that she would forget what he looked like. She had a photograph of him in his army uniform and another of him with his arm around her mother's shoulder, taken shortly after they were married, but neither photograph had captured the father Lucy remembered.

The brass band finished their dirge and began playing a lively march. Lucy didn't hear the man approach until he spoke to her. "You're Horatio Garner's daughter, aren't you?"

She turned to see a tall young man who was about her age. She backed up a step when she saw that he was a common laborer. "How do you know me? Who are you?"

"My name is Danny Carver. I met you once before, but you probably don't remember."

Lucy couldn't imagine ever meeting him. His overalls and work shirt were stained with red clay from the brick factory. He ran his hand through his hair, which was the color of wet sand, and she saw red stains beneath his fingernails and in the creases of his knuckles.

"I came to your mansion during the flood. You let me play in your playroom and ride on your rocking horse."

He smiled—a wry grin that laughed at the world—and Lucy did remember him suddenly. But she was too proud to admit it. "Dozens of children stayed with us during the flood," she said primly.

"I know. And I always respected your family for that."

Lucy didn't respond. She had been taught to act

very coolly toward young men who were attracted to her beauty, especially unsuitable strangers.

"I just wanted to tell you how sorry I was about your father—even though it happened eleven years ago. He saved my life, you know."

"He saved many lives."

"Yeah, but he saved me in person. He came up to my family's apartment and warned all of us to get out. Said the dam was about to break. My grandmother was old and couldn't walk too good, so your father carried her out to his carriage in his arms."

Lucy watched Danny's face as he spoke and saw that his emotion was genuine, his sneer a shield of defense. "Then your father came back for me and my brother. He put Jake on his shoulders because the water was so deep, but he said I looked like a big brave fellow, and he was sure I could get through it on my own. My mother had to carry the baby. I remember how cold the water was as I waded into it, and how your father whistled 'Yankee Doodle' as if we had nothing at all to worry about. He let me hang on to the back of his coat, and he lifted me up into his fancy carriage when I finally made it there. I had never ridden in a carriage before. "

Tears came to Lucy's eyes as Danny brought her father to life again. She had forgotten how he had loved to whistle.

"We lost everything in the flood," Danny continued. "Not even a blanket or a tin pot was left. Our tenement and everything in it simply vanished. All that remained of our neighborhood were piles of junk and tons of mud. But at least we got out alive. Your father was a brave man."

"Thank you. It was very kind of you to tell me your story. I miss my father. You might have been one of the last persons to see him alive."

"I was on my way over there," he said, pointing to the levy. "I wanted to see where our apartment used to stand. Want to walk there with me?" He had a kind face, a respectful voice, and Lucy thought that he might be nice looking if he were properly dressed. She glanced back at the crowd and saw that her mother and grandmother were still occupied.

"I would like that," she replied. They started walking together, with Lucy carefully picking her way in her dainty shoes. He slowed his stride to match hers.

"Do you remember what The Flats used to look like before the flood?" he asked.

"No. I'm sorry, but I was only six years old at the time."

"Yeah, and you probably weren't allowed down in this part of town, were you? . . . No, don't apologize," he said as she started to. "I don't blame your family for keeping you away from that place. You probably shouldn't go near the new workers' neighborhood they built to replace it, either."

He halted a few minutes later in the middle of a bare, grassy area and pointed to the place where they stood. "Here. This is where I used to live."

Lucy glanced around and saw nothing that made this spot of land distinguishable from the rest of the park. "How do you know that this is the place?"

"See that church steeple on the hill across the river?" he asked, pointing to it. "I used to see it from my apartment window. It was straight across the river." He paused, closing his eyes for a moment. "My tenement was three stories tall with four apartments on each floor—packed with people of all ages, shapes, and colors. You could hear three or four languages at a time, and people yelling, laughing, cursing . . . babies crying . . . It seemed like there was always laundry hanging out, day and night, and I remember that our drinking water tasted terrible. But all the families watched out for each other, you know?" He smiled his crooked grin again. Lucy nodded, but she had no idea what he meant.

"Most of the fathers worked at the brickyard or in your tannery. None of us had very much, but it was home. We lived on the top floor, and I loved to watch the boats go by on the river. We'd go for a swim in the summer when our apartment got too hot, and my father used to take me fishing sometimes on Sunday afternoons. That was his only day off. . . . He died in the flood, too."

Lucy stared at him in surprise. "Why didn't he get out when you did?"

"He was at work when the alarm sounded. They shut down the brick factory and told everyone to get to higher ground, but he decided to help with the evacuation. They said he was trying to convince two elderly sisters to leave their house. It was further downstream and right on the riverbank. When the logjam at the railroad trestle broke, the river swept the house and all three of them away."

"I'm so sorry!" Lucy rested her hand on his arm. "It seems we have something in common then, don't we?" She had never met anyone who truly understood her loss, and she felt a kinship with him.

He raked his fingers through his sandy hair and nodded. "The word *hero* never meant much to me when I was a kid. It didn't change the fact that my father was never coming back. I couldn't understand why he left us. I was furious."

"I've always felt the same way. I would much rather have my father back than have him applauded as a hero. To tell you the truth, I didn't care about all the people he saved. I didn't know any of them. I felt like they stole my daddy from me. My eighteenth birthday is coming soon, and he won't be here to celebrate it with me. The other girls will all get roses from their fathers when we graduate from the female academy in a few months, but my father won't be there." She stopped, surprised by the strength of the emotions Danny had stirred. Then she realized what she had just said. "I'm sorry. You were one of those people he saved. I didn't mean—"

"That's okay. I know exactly how you feel. For a long time I used to hate those two stubborn old sisters who wouldn't leave their house. I figured they'd killed my father just as surely as if they'd stabbed a knife through his heart. It probably wasn't right to hate them, but he was dead and their stubbornness was to blame."

"I blamed the entire town. I hated the mayor and the police and the firemen—it was their job to save and protect people, not my father's." Lucy didn't say it aloud, but she also blamed her mother. It had been her fault that Daddy went up to the cabin in the first place. If he had stayed home, he never would have known about the dam. He would have been drinking his coffee in bed when the dam burst. But Lucy didn't tell Danny that part, because if her father had lived, he and his family would have died.

The band played a lively tune in the background as they stood side by side remembering the disaster, and it seemed inappropriate. She suddenly thought of something else. "Your father's name must be on the new memorial, too."

"It is. That's why I came today. I wanted to see it."

"Well, I would like to see it, too. Will you show it to me?"

"Sure." They walked back across the grass together, but when Lucy looked closely at the granite marker, she regretted her request. Her father's name stood above all the others, chiseled in huge letters. She found Henry Carver's name listed below it in much smaller letters.

"That's not fair," she murmured. "They died doing the very same thing."

"Life is seldom fair, Miss Garner. And you know what else? They put the names of the two spinster sisters my father was trying to save on there, too. See?"

Lucy looked where he pointed and read their names: *Elizabeth Dawes, Esther Dawes.* It seemed so unfair. As Lucy's memories returned, she recalled how angry and cheated she had felt in the weeks following the flood.

"Our home was a terribly sad place after my father died," she said. "I was planning a huge party for my seventh birthday, but I never had it. I was going to ask Daddy for a pony—a real one this time, not a wooden one like the one you rode. That probably sounds selfish and petty considering all that you lost, but I was very young and I couldn't understand all the changes in my life."

There must have been changes in Danny's life, too, she realized. How had his family survived?

Lucy's family had income from the tannery, and she hadn't lost her home. She had never given much thought to all of the people whose homes had been destroyed while hers had been spared. The differences seemed unfair to her now—like the big and little letters on the monument.

"How did you get by after your father died?" she asked. "Where did you live?"

"We managed." He lifted one shoulder in a casual shrug, and she recalled the gesture from eleven years ago. "They set up a tent city for a while, and it developed into a sort of shantytown."

"Who supported your family?"

When Danny didn't answer right away, Lucy was sorry she had asked. He looked away but not before she saw his cheeks flush. "My mother found work. And I did odd jobs and things—delivering ice and newspapers, running errands. I took a job at the brickyard when I was fourteen. They thought I was much older."

"Lucy!" She whirled at the sound of her grandmother's voice. "It's time to leave."

"Good-bye, Daniel. Thank you—" But before Lucy could finish, Grandmother Garner gripped her arm and yanked her away.

"Why in the world were you talking to that person?" Her voice sounded as cold and hard as the monument stone. "Don't you know it's unseemly to talk to such people?"

"He was telling me about Daddy. He said that

Daddy rescued him from the flood and saved his life."

"You can't believe a word those people say. They'll tell you anything to win your trust."

"But it's true, Grandmama. Danny's father died in the flood, too. He was helping Daddy save people. I saw his name on the marker."

Grandmother didn't seem to be listening. "It's bad enough that your mother fraternizes with those people, which is why she isn't invited to all of the places that you and I are. But you mustn't ruin it for yourself the way she did. Come along now."

Lucy glanced over her shoulder as her grandmother led her away, but Daniel Carver had disappeared in the milling crowd. As Lucy rode home in the carriage, her heart felt lighter in spite of the somber occasion and the memories it had evoked. For the first time in her life, she had met someone who understood the loss she had lived with for so many years—someone who understood that a father couldn't be remembered in a granite marker and flowered wreaths.

CHAPTER
23

Lucy was reading a book in her room a few evenings later when one of the servants interrupted her. "I'm sorry to disturb you, Miss Lucy, but there is someone at the back door asking to speak with you. He is not a respectable gentleman and I refused to let him in the house, but he insisted that I—"

"Did he tell you his name?"

"Yes, Miss Lucy. Daniel Carver." Lucy's skin prickled and warmed as if she had stepped into a tub of steaming water. "Shall I send him away, Miss Lucy?"

"No! I'll speak with him." Lucy found it hard not to run. She used the servants' stairs to get to the back door, aware that her grandmother would never allow Danny into her house, nor would she want Lucy speaking with him. She couldn't say exactly what drew her, but her heart raced as if she had run up all those steps instead of down them.

Danny Carver smiled when he saw her, his admiration as clear as his gaze, then he snatched off his hat and lowered his head. "Excuse me for bothering you again, Miss Garner, but after we talked the other day I remembered something that's been eating at me all these years." He dug in his pocket and pulled out a small lump of wood, handing it to her. It took Lucy a moment to recognize it as a toy boxcar just like the one that had belonged to her little wooden train.

"It's yours," he said. "I stole it from your playroom eleven years ago. I've felt sorry about it ever since and more than a little guilty, but I was too ashamed to walk all the way up here and return it to you. Besides, my life was . . . Well, things were pretty hard after the flood. But anyway, I wanted to give it back to you. I knew it was wrong to steal."

"Then why did you take it?"

He lifted his shoulder in a shrug. She followed him as he turned and walked a few paces into the garden, then hoisted himself onto the low stone wall. She remained standing.

"I don't really know why I took it. But this house, all your toys and things, all the food . . . it felt like a dream. I guess I wanted something that would help me remember that it was real. Then when I found out we'd lost everything in the flood . . . I don't know, but for a long time that little boxcar was the only thing I owned. My father was dead, and it reminded me of him for some reason. And I didn't want to forget him."

"To tell you the truth, I never even noticed it was missing. I had so much more." She spun one of the little wooden wheels with her finger, aware that she took for granted her way of life and all her possessions. It occurred to her that she was the one who should feel guilty, not Daniel.

Lucy was silent for so long that Daniel finally slid off the wall, brushing dirt from the seat of his pants, and said, "I guess I should go."

"No, wait! I-I enjoyed talking with you the other day."

He smiled his crooked grin. "Yeah, me too."

"Tell me more about yourself. Where do you live now? What's your life like?"

"There isn't much to tell. I've worked in the brickyard for the past six years—"

"Six years? How old are you? And what about school?"

His only reply was a shake of his head as he hoisted his lanky body onto the wall again. "I live in a boardinghouse in New Town—that's the workingman's part of town that they built to replace The Flats. And I'm twenty."

"Do you live all alone? What about your family?"

"I don't have one, really. My baby sister died the first winter after the flood, and my brother, Jake, has been on his own almost as long as I have. We don't see our mother much."

The tragedy he had faced made Lucy feel ashamed of her pampered life. She was glad that the darkness hid her flushed cheeks. "Why did you let me go on and on about not having a seventh birthday party or a new pony?"

"Because I don't think grief and loss are something you can measure, Miss Garner. We both have a hole in our childhood where our fathers used to be, and that makes us alike, no matter how different we are."

"Please, call me Lucy."

"If you want." Except for his first glance, Danny had averted his eyes the entire time he'd talked to her, as if he'd been taught that laborers didn't look wealthy young ladies in the eye. But he looked at her now in a way that made her heart pound.

"Do you have a girlfriend?" she asked. He shook his head, his gaze still fastened on her. Lucy knew how to make polite conversation, but she struggled for something to say. "Do you enjoy your work?"

"Not really. It's boring and backbreaking. But I consider myself lucky to have a job at all. Especially with all the new immigrants coming to town who would gladly do my job for less money."

"Is there some other job you'd rather have in the future?"

He scratched his head. "I guess I just don't think that way, Lucy. I know what you're really trying to ask—what am I looking forward to in the future, what do I hope for and all that. You mentioned yesterday that you were graduating from school soon, so I assume you're looking forward to starting something new. But things don't work that way for people like me. If we have a decent job, we hang on to it. Maybe we'll wind up as foreman someday and make a little extra money, maybe not. But from where I stand, the future looks pretty much like the present, so why waste time trying to see into it?"

His words appalled Lucy. "How can you live without hope?"

He gave his now-familiar shrug. "I guess you don't miss what you never had."

"You've lived your entire life without hope?"

"Pretty much. I used to hope that my father would come back, but that didn't get me anywhere. And for a while I hoped that my mother would change, but . . ." He looked away.

"Let me help you, Danny. I can talk to our foreman at the tannery and see if he can get you a better job, and—"

He held up his hands to stop her. "Don't start down that road, Lucy. It isn't going to take me anywhere. Believe me, I know."

"I . . . I don't know what to say. I've never met anyone like you before."

"Listen, why don't you tell me more about your life?"

"Because it seems shallow and selfish beside yours."

"I would still like to hear about it. If you want to be friends, that is."

"Yes, I really would like to be friends. You're the only person I've ever met who understands how I've felt all these years about losing my father."

"Good. Then tell me what it's like to be Miss Lucy Garner."

"Well . . . I live here with my mother and grandmother. I don't have any sisters or brothers." She could hear the apologetic tone of her voice and was certain that Danny could hear it, too. "I attend a small, private female academy here in town—I'll graduate in a few months."

"What do they teach you in school?"

She was ashamed to tell him she was taking classes in French and watercolor painting and piano. "I like geography," she said, instead. "It's interesting to learn about other countries. Grandmama said that I might—" Lucy stopped, embarrassed to say that they had talked about traveling to Europe someday. "My grandmother has been to Paris," she amended, "and she says it is very beautiful."

"Do you have any boyfriends?"

"No." She was glad he couldn't see her blushing. "We see boys at social events, but it's all very stiff and artificial. I've never talked with any of them the way I'm talking with you. And not even my best friend understands how I feel about losing my father. But then how could she, since her father is still alive? It's so nice to know that you understand."

"Miss Lucy?" She recognized the butler's voice and turned to see him standing near the back door. "It's chilly out here. I think you'd better come inside."

"I'll be right there, Robert."

Danny slid off the wall again. "I'll come back another time if you want, and we can talk some more. Which room is yours?" He tilted his head toward the rear of her mansion. "I'll throw some pebbles at your window to get your attention, next time. I don't think your servants like me very much."

"It's that window," she said, pointing. "The second one from the left."

"Well, I'd better get going. My day starts pretty early."

"Please keep this," Lucy said, pushing the little boxcar back into his hands. His skin felt as rough as an emery board. "I think it means much more to you than to me."

He looked surprised. "Thanks. Have a good evening, Miss Garner—I mean, Lucy. Until next time . . . ?"

"Yes. Good night, Daniel."

Four months later, Lucy sat near her bedroom window on a warm July night, waiting for Daniel's now-familiar signal. As soon as she heard the tap of a pebble against the glass, she hurried down the back staircase, then carefully closed the outside door behind her, hoping that none of the servants had heard her leaving the house. She stood on the back step for a moment as her eyes adjusted to the darkness, then saw Daniel standing in the shadows near the carriage house. She ran to him and let him pull her into his arms. Lucy felt at home there, comfortable with his embrace, his touch.

"I've told myself a dozen times to stop coming to see you," he murmured, "but I can't make myself stop."

"I don't want you to stop."

"Come on, let's find a better place to talk," he

said, taking her hand. "There's a full moon tonight, and I don't wantyour servants to see us." He led her further into the garden, stopping when he found a bench beneath the rose trellis, where they could hide from view. The summer night was warm, the moon very bright, and she could see his beloved face clearly by the light of the moon. Something was bothering him.

"Why would you want to stop coming?" she asked. "We always have so much to talk about, don't we?"

"Yes. But I've been wondering where this can possibly lead."

"I-I don't know what you mean." She traced her fingers along his jaw, feeling the rough stubble of his whiskers. She had grown to love the roughness of his skin, the coarseness of his work clothes, the hardness of his muscles. Everything in her world was soft and refined, and she loved the novelty of him.

"Come on, Lucy. I think you know that we've become much more than friends. I think you know that I'm falling in love with you."

They had never talked about love before, and it made Lucy's heart speed up. She had wondered during the past few weeks if this was what love felt like: wanting to be with Daniel all the time; counting the minutes and seconds until night fell and she would hear the pebble strike her window; wishing the time they spent together could last twice as long as the time they spent apart. She had read about love in romance novels, of course, but books couldn't begin to describe the happy, breathless way she felt whenever she was with him.

I'm falling in love with you. No one had ever said those words to Lucy before, and she felt like whirling in giddy circles the way she had as a child with her brand-new petticoats. Danny Carver loved her! And she loved him, too, she was certain of it. So why had he turned so serious? Why was he talking about not coming anymore? She couldn't bear the thought of never seeing him again.

"Is that such a bad thing?" she asked. "That we've become more than friends?"

Danny released her hand and stood up. "No, of course it isn't a bad thing. But . . . but that river down there isn't a bad thing, either, when it's flowing along nicely. But when it goes beyond its banks, when it goes into places it shouldn't . . . that's when trouble happens."

"I don't understand." She watched him pace in front of her, a frown on his face, and she was afraid that he was angry with her.

"I don't belong up here on the ridge, in your world. And I know for sure that you don't belong down in mine. I've overstepped my bounds, Lucy, and it can't end well. For either of us."

"But I don't want it to end."

"I know." His frown melted into a look of sadness. "Me, either. But I don't see how . . ." He paused, clearing his throat as if to rid it of the emotion that thickened his voice. "The first time I came here, I told you that I didn't dare to gaze into my future and start hoping for things to change, because my future was always going to look like my present. That's the way things are in my world. And I was fine with that—until I met you. Now when I look into the future, I want you there beside me. But I don't see any way that we can possibly be together—and I'm not fine with that."

"But there has to be a way, Daniel. What if I asked my family to give you a job at the tannery? I know how hard you work, how honest and good-hearted you are."

"They will never allow it," he said, continuing to pace in front of her. "They would say I'm only after your money."

"But that isn't true. I know it isn't."

"They would point out that I never finished school. That I can barely read and write."

"But you're not stupid, Daniel. You could easily get an education if someone gave you a chance. You could be anything you wanted to be."

He stopped and looked at her. "But that's just it. I wouldn't even know what to wish for." He sank down beside her on the bench again. "Everything I own fits into a room in a boarding-house that I share with three other men. You're used to . . . to all of this." He made a sweeping gesture with his arm.

"That doesn't matter. My mother came from a very poor family, too, but my father loved her and married her anyway, and she came here to live. I would gladly share everything I have with you."

"I don't know if I could ever get used to a place like this. Besides, I saw the way your grandmother looked at me the first day we talked in Garner Park. You saw it, too, I know you did. She would never accept me."

"She looks only at the outside of people." Lucy swallowed the bitter taste of guilt, knowing she had done the same thing before she met Daniel. "If people only knew you the way I do—"

"Don't give me hope, Lucy. You'll only break both of our hearts in the end."

"But it can't end! Please don't stop coming to see me. Give me a chance to figure out how to make this work. There has to be a way that we can be together."

He took her face in his hands and kissed her. Afterward, they clung to each other.

"I'll keep coming as long as you want me to, Lucy. When the night comes that you don't answer my signal"—he nodded toward her bedroom window—"then I'll know that it's over."

Lucy stayed awake for most of the night, trying to figure out a way that she and Daniel could be together. She considered eloping, coming home a married woman and forcing her family to accept him, but she was too afraid to leave home on her own. She had never ventured anywhere without a chaperone or with friends or family.

Her thoughts kept returning to her mother and how she had come from humble beginnings to live in this house, eventually adjusting to this life. Bebe still wasn't afraid to "fraternize with the riffraff," as Grandmother Garner called it. Lucy realized that the only solution was to get her mother on her side. She had to talk Bebe into helping her and Danny so they could be together. After a short, restless night of sleep, Lucy began a conversation with her mother at the breakfast table the following morning.

"I wish there weren't barriers between rich people and poor people," she said as she pushed scrambled eggs around on her plate.

"Education is the key," Bebe said. "If we can help poor children get an education, we'll give them a better chance in life. That's one of our Temperance Union's goals."

Lucy resisted rolling her eyes. For her mother, the Union was always foremost in her mind. She tried a different approach. "Did you marry Daddy for his money?"

Bebe finished stirring milk into her tea and laid down her spoon. "Maybe I did, in a way. I worked so hard during the war, doing my brothers' chores on the farm, that I think I liked the idea of having servants. It overwhelmed me to think that such a wealthy, sophisticated man as your father wanted to marry me. But I truly loved him, Lucy. Most of all, I married for love."

Lucy twisted her napkin nervously. "And what advice would you give someone who wanted to do the same thing—marry for love, I mean—in spite of other differences?"

"I would say . . . that they should think twice. It took me years and years to adjust to our differences, and in many ways I still haven't adjusted, as you well know. I embarrass you at times. I'm not like all of your friends' mothers, am I?"

Lucy didn't know what to say. She remembered how small and plain and out of place her mother looked at the graduation reception a few months ago. As Lucy fumbled for what to say next, her mother suddenly reached for her hand and took it in both of hers. "I know about him, Lucy. I know all about Daniel Carver. That's who you're really talking about, isn't it?"

"How . . . how do you know?" she asked in a whisper.

"The servants told me. They've known for some time that you've been sneaking out at night to see him."

Lucy pulled her hand free. "How dare they spy on us!"

"They did it because they love you, Lucy. Robert and Herta and Peter have known you since the day you were born. They would never let you come to harm or allow a stranger to take advantage of you."

Lucy imagined them peeking at her and Daniel through the curtains, seeing all their private moments together, and her anger threatened to boil over. "If you knew all about Danny, I'm surprised you didn't lock me in my room and forbid me to see him!"

"I considered it," Bebe said calmly. "But then I recalled the night that Horatio asked my father for permission to marry me. And I remembered that it wouldn't have mattered if my father had refused— I would have defied him. I didn't want you to make a mistake out of anger or defiance, Lucy. Marriage is one of the biggest decisions you'll ever make. . . . And you're so young."

"I'm older than you were."

"Not by much. And that's why I'm glad you're asking me for advice."

"But I'm not asking for advice—I'm asking you to help us. You can give Danny a decent-paying job in the tannery. You can let him move in here, like you did."

"What about your friends? What advice do they have for you?"

"They're so shallow and superficial. I can't talk to any of them the way I talk to Danny. And never about important things."

"So you haven't told your friends about Danny?"

"They wouldn't understand. But Danny lost his

father, too. He shares the grief I've felt all these years."

"I share it, too, Lucy. I lost your father, too. And I found comfort in God, not in another person. He knows what it's like to lose someone dear to Him."

"Why do you keep changing the subject? Are you going to help me or not?"

"I am trying to help you. You need to think everything through so you can make a mature, informed decision."

Lucy exhaled, forcing herself to be calm so her mother would take her side. "I'm sorry. Go on."

"Can you picture Danny at all your social events? Or are you going to give up your social life?"

"He could learn to fit in. He's very smart, Mother. And the rules of etiquette aren't that hard to learn."

"Danny Carver could hire the finest tailor," Bebe said quietly, "and get every detail of your social world letter-perfect, and he still wouldn't be accepted. Believe me, I know. Besides, have you asked him if he wants to be part of all that? I know I never did. I hated it. What if Danny hates it, too?"

Lucy saw him in her mind, seated at her grand-mother's elegant dinner table, hiding behind his careless half shrug and his laugh-at-the world grin, and knew that he would hate every minute of it—especially Grandmother Garner's cold, undisguised disdain. Lucy let her mother's question go unanswered.

"So the real question is," Bebe continued, "are you willing to change for him? That's what you must decide. Don't expect him to change. You're the one who must change. Do you love him that much? Could you give up your way of life and live in his world for his sake? Or are you expecting him to fit into yours?"

"It doesn't matter where we live. I love him, Mother. I know you're going to say that I'm too young and that I don't know what love really is, but it's true—I love Daniel Carver!"

"I believe you. But even when people love each other, it doesn't always mean that they should get married."

"Are you talking about Daddy? Are you sorry that you married him?"

"No. I'm talking about someone else." Her mother looked away, sighing softly. "After your father died, someone else asked me to marry him."

Lucy's jaw dropped in shock. "Who?"

"It doesn't matter, dear. I loved him but I didn't marry him because . . . because I knew it would hurt you and Grandmother Garner. You would have felt that I was betraying your father. I can tell that I've shocked you now, even though your father has been gone for more than a decade."

Lucy struggled to digest this news as her mother continued. "Grandmother Garner will feel even more shocked and angry and betrayed than you do right now if you marry Danny. It will break her heart. You're all she has. That's why you need to carefully consider if you really want to do this to her."

Lucy recalled how her grandmother had yanked her away from Danny on the day the memorial stone was dedicated. But she also knew that her grandmother had never denied her anything she'd wanted. "Grandmother always lets me have what I want. She won't stand in the way of my happiness."

"You might be surprised, Lucy. She would have gladly had my marriage annulled even though she knew I made Horatio happy. . . . Listen, there is one more question you need to consider, and it's an important one. What about Danny's faith? My mother tried to advise me to make sure your father and I had a common faith in God. No marriage can get along without Him at the center."

Lucy had no idea what Danny believed. They had never talked about God or religion. "What difference does it make what church he goes to?" she asked.

"I didn't ask about his church—I asked about his faith. There is a huge difference."

Bebe's questions frustrated Lucy. She wanted answers, not questions. "So, will you help Danny and me or not?"

Bebe wrapped her hands around her teacup,

staring down at it as if deep in thought. "I want you to make a well-informed decision, not one you'll long regret," she finally replied. "If you promise to agree to my conditions first, then I'll agree to help you."

Hope and suspicion battled inside Lucy. "What do you want me to do?"

"Tell Danny you can't see him for two weeks."

"Mother, no!"

"True love can certainly endure a separation of two weeks. You both could use some time apart to get some perspective on your relationship. That's my first condition—and the servants will be sure to let me know if you try to cheat. During that time, I want you to come with me to get a firsthand look at the world that Daniel comes from. It's important that you understand him and why he thinks the way he does. You've never been to New Town, have you?"

"Danny and I aren't going to be living there, so I don't see the point. But I'll go, if you insist. Is that all?"

"No. I know that you've been invited to the Midsummer Ball at the Opera House later this month. Grandmother Garner is looking forward to showing you off to the town's royalty. I want you to go with her and enter into the festivities with the same enthusiasm you would have shown if Daniel Carver wasn't in the picture. Those three things are all I'm asking you to do."

Lucy knew that her mother was trying to shock her by taking her to New Town, but she made up her mind not to be shocked. As for Grandmother Garnerand the ball, Lucy didn't see how it would hurt to go. She could get on her grandmother's good side by being cooperative, and maybe then she could talk to Grandmama about Daniel. The hardest condition would be spending two weeks away from him, but that was a small price to pay for a lifetime together.

"I'll agree to all three conditions," she told her mother, "so start counting off the two weeks. I'll tell Danny tonight."

Two days later, Lucy accompanied her mother to New Town. "A woman who attends my church just had a baby," Bebe told her. "Our ladies' group always brings a meal to new mothers, along with some clothes and things. I told the other ladies that we would deliver everything."

The working-class neighborhood was just as Lucy had expected it to be: overcrowded, smelly, and disgusting, but she worked hard to hide her shock from her mother. She thought of her beloved Daniel growing up in such a sad environment, and she was all the more determined to lift him out of this way of life.

So many ragged children played in the street that Lucy feared the horses would trample one of them as the carriage waded through the melee. The driver halted in front of a dilapidated two-story building with several of its windows boarded up. It looked as though it already was falling apart, even though the neighborhood had been built only eleven years ago, after the flood. Lucy hooked the basket of food over her arm, steeling herself to go inside and get this "lesson" over with. But before she could take a single step, dozens of children mobbed her, thrusting their filthy hands in her face and shouting, "Please, miss! Please! You have a penny for me?"

She wanted to turn and flee to the safety of the carriage, but her mother simply smiled and shouted to them above the noise. "All right, children. Let us through, please. We have to bring these things to Anna Walsh and her new baby. We'll have something for all of you when we come out."

The clamoring mob parted, and Lucy and Bebe made their way up the steps and into the building. The smell of urine assaulted Lucy in the vestibule. "Oh! That's revolting!" she said before she could stop herself. Bebe said nothing as she led the way upstairs to the second floor. The apartment door was open, and she knocked on the doorframe and peered inside.

"Anna? It's me, Bebe Garner."

"Come in, Mrs. Garner, come in."

The room was tiny and smelled of kerosene and perspiration. It was so hot that Lucy couldn't breathe. Not even a hint of a breeze blew though the windows, which stood dangerously open to the two-story drop below. Two toddlers sat bare-naked on the wooden floor. A line of laundry was strung across one end of the room, dripping into a sink and onto the floor. Anna Walsh sat on a sagging bed on the other end of the room, nursing her baby. She couldn't have been much older than Lucy was, but she looked as timeworn as Grandmother Garner. She thanked Bebe over and over for the food and clothing and other supplies.

"Is there something more we can do for you while we're here?" Bebe asked. "Do you have some work that my daughter, Lucy, and I can help you with?"

Mrs. Walsh wouldn't hear of letting them work for her, and after Bebe rocked the new baby for a few minutes and the two women chatted, she and Lucy left again.

"An apartment like this is all that Daniel can afford on his salary," Bebe told her on the way down the stairs. "This is how you would have to live, unless he relies on you to support him." Lucy nodded, refusing to reply. "My experience tells me that most men take a great deal of pride in being the breadwinner. How do you think Daniel will feel, knowing he has to rely on his wealthy wife for charity for the rest of his life?"

"He's willing to work if you give him a chance. He could work for us at the tannery."

"That decision isn't entirely up to me. I would have to talk it over with Mr. MacLeod."

Before they emerged from the building, Bebe pulled a bag of penny candy from her basket and held it out to Lucy. "Here. You can pass these out to the children."

Lucy shrank back. "I don't want to. You do it." She would need to take a bath after touching all those filthy fingers. But her mother pushed the bag into her hands.

"I have a pocketful of pennies to pass out."

Lucy did as she was told, gritting her teeth and bearing her penance. She would be home soon. And once the two weeks were over, she could be with Daniel.

"How much do you know about Daniel's parents?" Bebe asked on the ride home.

"His father died while helping people escape from the flood, just like Daddy did."

"And his mother?"

"He doesn't talk much about her."

"I think I know why," Bebe said quietly. "I met Mrs. Carver a few years ago in one of the saloons we were trying to close down. Do you understand what it means if I tell you that Daniel's mother survived after her husband died by selling her body?"

"You're lying! You're just trying to shock me!"

"No, it's the truth, Lucy. I'm trying to help you understand the man you love. Women aren't paid the same wages as men, even if they do the same job in the same factory. They can never earn enough to pay the rent and feed their children. Besides, who would watch her children while she worked a twelve-hour shift? After Mrs. Carver's husband died, she must have faced all those dilemmas. The only way she could make a living and keep a roof over her head was to solicit business in a saloon every night."

Lucy didn't reply. She couldn't stop the tears that rolled down her face. It explained why Danny had quit school and gone to work at such a young age. And why he wouldn't talk about his mother.

"Mrs. Carver's situation is one of the things that our Temperance League is working so hard to change. If we could get equal wages for women and affordable housing and childcare for widows like her, they wouldn't be forced into such a tragic position. I'm certain that Daniel feels shame because of what his mother does, and I'm sorry that you were forced to see his shame. But you know your grandmother and her friends very well, Lucy. Will they ever accept Daniel, knowing what his mother does for a living?"

"That's not fair! It's none of their business!"

"Life isn't fair. That's what I'm trying to show you. And you need to remember that it will be just as difficult for Daniel to change and enter your world as it would be for you to enter his."

Lucy longed to talk to Daniel about what she'd seen today. She wanted to tell him that she loved him and that the differences between them didn't matter. And she wanted to hear him say the same thing. But she also knew that she could never shame him by admitting that she knew the truth about his mother. Unless he chose to tell her, it would be one secret that would always stand between them.

At dinner that evening Grandmother Garner began making plans for the Midsummer Ball. "Lucy, darling, we need to go shopping as soon as possible. If we don't order our new gowns soon, all of the finest seamstresses will be spoken for."

"Why don't we go first thing tomorrow morning, Grandmama?"

Lucy loved to shop. She and her grandmother drove downtown as soon as the stores opened the next day. But as they made their rounds, it distressed Lucy to realize that her grandmother had a hard time keeping up. When had Grandmother Garner become so frail and out of breath, her steps so slow and halting?

"Sit down, Grandmama," Lucy said over and over. "You should rest a bit. We don't have to keep going."

"Nonsense. I'll be fine." But Lucy listened to her painful wheezing and worried, just the same.

As they paged through pattern books and selected fabric and lace and ribbon, Lucy couldn't help remembering all of the happy hours she had spent shopping with her grandmother as a child.

She tried to imagine the two of them sitting side by side this way, choosing the wedding gown she would wear when she married Daniel, and found that she couldn't do it. Her mother had been right about that much. If Lucy married Daniel Carver, she would break her beloved grandmother's heart.

Lucy forced all these disturbing thoughts from her mind over the next few days as she prepared for the ball. She made luncheon dates with some of her school friends to compare notes about their dresses and giggle about all the young gentlemen they would meet at the upcoming event. She had forgotten how much she enjoyed their girl talk, even though she found herself avoiding their questions about what she'd been doing all summer. As the day of the ball neared, Lucy grew more and more excited. She no longer thought about Daniel a dozen times a day as she had when the separation first began. She was much too busy deciding how to arrange her hair and which shoes would be more comfortable for dancing. When the night finally arrived, Lucy felt like a princess in a fairy tale.

"You look beautiful, my darling girl," Grandmother said as Lucy descended the stairs. "The young men will be fighting to fill your dance program." And they did. The moment Lucy entered the ballroom, dozens of young men in tuxedos clamored for a chance to dance with her, the way the street urchins had clamored for pennies. She was swept away into the glory of it all, surrounded by colorful ball gowns and flowers, glittering candles and elegant music. And she loved every elegant minute of it. Lucy never wanted the evening to end.

Halfway though the ball, Grandmother Garner parted the sea of Lucy's admirers and linked arms with her. "Come, my dear. There is someone I'd very much like you to meet. I hope you saved a dance or two for him."

Lucy could tell that she dazzled John Sherwood the moment they met, and she savored the power she held over him. She was discovering how much fun it was to flirt and tease and make a man laugh at all her charms. And John instantly held her interest, as well. His hands were soft and clean, his scent spicy and intoxicating. His tuxedo was the finest one she'd seen all evening, exquisitely tailored to fit his tall, sturdy body.

"I had it custom made," he explained. "Our family owns several men's haberdasheries, here and in various neighboring towns. But now that I've graduated college and have entered the family business, I have plans to expand our stores and turn them into fine department stores like the one I've visited in Chicago recently. Imagine, floor after floor with everything a woman could ever want to shop for, all under one roof."

"I would be your most devoted customer, Mr. Sherwood," she said with a smile. She tossed her dance card aside to waltz with him for the remainder of the evening, listening in awe as he described his recent trip to Paris.

"I would like to ask your family for permission to court you," he said as the night drew to a close. "May I?"

For the first time all evening, Lucy thought of Daniel. She tried to picture him there at the ball, but he wasn't wearing a tuxedo or whirling with her around the ballroom floor. Instead, she could only imagine him standing near the door, looking ashamed and uncomfortable in his coarse, work-stained clothes. Once again, Lucy knew that her mother had been right—Daniel would hate all of this. And he would never fit in.

"In fact, Miss Garner," John Sherwood continued, "our family is planning a dinner party for next Thursday evening. If you are free, would you be kind enough to join us?"

"I would love to," she replied. She began planning what she would wear, forgetting that her two-week separation from Daniel ended that night.

On Thursday evening, when Danny Carver tossed a pebble against her bedroom window, Lucy wasn't home to hear it.

"I was so shallow, Harriet!" Mother said when she finished telling me her story. "I liked my pampered life too much, and in the end that's what I chose. I wanted to wear beautiful gowns and attend lovely parties and travel to Paris. I loved wealth and ease more than I loved Danny."

"Didn't you love Father at all?" I asked in horror.

"Of course I did," she said, blowing her nose. "But I thought I loved Danny, too, and I decided not to marry him for very selfish reasons. I didn't want to be poor and live in New Town and have a mother-in-law like his mother. And I knew he would never fit into the life I wanted, either."

I exhaled, alarmed to learn how close my mother had come to throwing everything away for Daniel Carver. I admired Grandma Bebe even more for her wisdom and ingenuity.

"Don't get me wrong," Mother said, "I care very deeply for your father. We've had a good life and two beautiful children together. It's just that . . . I confess to feeling guilty at times for the pain I must have caused Danny. I've often wondered what became of him and what our life together might have been like. Who would I be today if I had chosen differently? And now he's dead." She blew her nose again and dropped the handkerchief onto her desk.

"Lately, I can barely look at myself in the mirror," she said tearfully. "I look around at my elegant home and my wardrobe filled with clothes . . . I think about how much money I just spent on Alice's wedding, and I'm horrified with myself. My father was a hero who died saving people! My mother has dedicated her life to helping others and improving our community. And me? All I ever think about is myself, Harriet . . . only myself. . . ."

I didn't know what to say to my mother. I reached for her hand and patted it uselessly, saying nothing.

CHAPTER
24

The day after Mother told me about Daniel Carver, we went to church as usual. She seemed to be holding herself together during the service, but that afternoon, while my father dozed on our sun porch, my mother dressed in black from head to toe and pinned a huge black hat on her head. "Where are you going?" I asked her.

"I've decided to attend Danny's funeral." She lowered the black mesh veil over her face, which still looked red and puffy to me. I was worried about her. She certainly hadn't been herself lately. I would have called Grandma Bebe again for help, but I remembered the advice she had given me about spending more time with my mother.

"I'll go with you, if you want," I said. I thought she would refuse, but she didn't. I quickly changed back into my church clothes while she called a taxi—Mother didn't drive. And she would have fainted dead away on the floor if she ever found out that I did.

We arrived at the cemetery near New Town at the

same time as the funeral procession. We remained at a discreet distance, standing in the shade of a huge oak tree that had obviously survived the Great Flood. "It said in the newspaper that Danny had a wife and four daughters," Mother whispered to me. "I wonder what will become of them."

We saw them a few minutes later, dressed in black and seated in chairs beside the open grave. But I counted six women, not five. Maybe the blowsy gray-haired one was his disreputable mother.

"Danny once told me how difficult it is for widows and orphans to survive without a father," my mother said. "His mother was a widow, and she—" A sob caught in her throat. She slid her handkerchief beneath her veil to wipe her tears.

A dozen raggedy young boys suddenly surged forward to gather around Danny's grave. I wondered if the three boys he had rescued were among them. They parted as the pallbearers moved Danny's casket into place, then a man in a ministerial collar stepped forward to speak. I nudged my mother closer to the gravesite so I could hear what he was saying.

"Danny Carver died the same way he lived— helping others. He was a true hero. Some of you may remember Danny from his earlier years, and if so, you know how the Lord transformed his life when he came to know Jesus. By his own confession, Danny found hope, for the first time in his life, in Christ. Afterward, he spread that hope to everyone he met, not caring that his own circumstances hadn't changed, but working to provide a better future for others. That was how his ministry to these young boys began. Danny fed them from his own table, bought shoes for those who needed them, took youngsters fishing on Sunday afternoons, and encouraged them to stay in school and get a good education. Above all, he shared his faith with these boys." The minister's voice choked with emotion, and he paused to clear his throat. "I'm sure the Lord must have a good reason why He needed Danny Carver in heaven, but frankly, I don't know how we'll get along without him here on earth."

Mother sobbed beneath her veil as the six pallbearers lowered the simple wooden coffin into the ground. We could hear the hollow thumps as his family dropped clods of earth on top of it. As the other mourners filed past to pay their respects, Mother moved forward, as well. I stayed close beside her as she halted in front of the minister.

"I would like to do something for his family," she told him. "If . . . if they need money . . ."

Up close, I could see that the minister's face had been ravaged by his grief. His voice was hoarse with it, too. "Money is important, of course. But it's really a matter of vision. Danny Carver could look into a young person's future and see hope when everyone else in New Town saw it as hopeless. I don't know where we'll ever find another man like him."

"Please, tell me what I can to do for his family. Shall I bring them a meal? That seems so paltry. I want to help, but I'm not sure what to do."

He shook his head like a man trying to awaken from a bad dream. "Come and see me next week," he said. "I-I can't think straight at the moment. I still have the funeral for the young boy who drowned. I'm sorry . . ." Another woman got his attention, and he turned to speak with her.

While my mother had been talking to the minister, I noticed that the gray-haired woman, whom I had assumed to be Danny's mother, had been listening to their conversation. She rose abruptly from her chair and strode toward us, and I could tell by her stiff posture and glaring eyes that she wasn't coming over to thank us for attending. I wanted to grab my mother and run, but I was too slow.

"You rich women from up on the ridge are all alike!" Her voice was low and filled with rage. I could smell alcohol on her breath as she leaned close to us. "You leave your pretty little world, do a few acts of charity, and go home again. You think you're better than everybody else, and you look down on women like me from on high. But we're the ones your husbands turn to for love and excitement. There would be no need for us if rich men like your husband weren't willing to pay for our services." She turned and strode away again before I could draw a shocked breath.

Mother was quiet all the way home. I was sure she would collapse in another fit of weeping as soon as she reached her bedroom, and I figured I should call Grandma Bebe right away. But as we stepped from the cab, Mother turned to me and said, "I'm going to do something meaningful with my life from now on, Harriet. Just wait and see if I don't!" She marched upstairs and changed out of her mourning garb without shedding another tear.

The way the women in Mother's club tell the story, she barreled into their next meeting like Annie Oakley riding into the Wild West Show with guns blazing. "Ladies, I have a project for our club to undertake. If you would like to join me, I would be happy for your help. If not, I plan to tackle it with or without your help."

The president inched toward Mother as if she may not have fired all of her ammunition yet and might still pose a danger. "Are you feeling all right, Lucy?"

"I have never felt better. But I've been thinking about how shallow we have become in our elegant little women's club. All we ever focus on in our meetings is ourselves—improving ourselves and entertaining ourselves and pampering ourselves. What about service to our community? Isn't it time that we, who have been so richly blessed, did something to help the women and children in

Roseton who aren't as fortunate as we are? I, for one, have vowed to commit myself to bettering the lives of the downtrodden here in our town."

The president patted Mother's shoulder as if soothing a barking dog. "There, there . . . Why don't you sit down, Lucy. You don't need to shout. You're among friends."

"No, thank you. I can think much better standing up."

"Tell us your plan, Lucy," a matron in the front row said. "We're listening."

"I would like to start by doing something for the family of our New Town hero, Daniel Carver. As you know, my father, Horatio Garner, died as a hero in the Great Flood of 1876. My family was well provided for by his estate, but unfortunately that isn't true for Mr. Carver's family. He labored in the brickyard all of his life. His wife and daughters have no way to support themselves now."

"What do you suggest?"

"I suggest that we provide some sort of short-term relief for them, certainly. We can at least help his wife and daughters find employment—perhaps as domestics in our homes. But the Carvers aren't the first family to lose their sole breadwinner, and they certainly won't be the last one. Why not invest the money that we usually spend entertaining ourselves every month to start a charitable foundation to help the women and children of New Town who have nowhere else to turn?"

"Good idea," someone called out. "Write up a motion, and we'll vote on it at our next meeting."

Mother smiled. "I'll do that—but there's more." The club's president had been about to lift her gavel, but she settled back in her seat.

"I spoke with the pastor of Daniel Carver's church," Mother continued, "and I learned that before he died, Mr. Carver dedicated all of his spare time to helping the young boys who lived in New Town. You see, unlike our sons, those poor boys have little hope for a better life. If their fathers worked in the brickyard, that's where they're destined to work, too. Daniel's vision was to start a boy's club for them—a place where they could be encouraged to dream of a better life. I would like to help him make that vision a reality."

It is a credit to my mother's charming personality and newly awakened leadership skills that the women in her club embraced her proposals. Not every woman shared her enthusiasm, certainly, but enough of the important ones did to quickly endow Roseton's new charitable fund. They also sent a delegation to other towns to research how they had sponsored boys' clubs. Mother stopped her weepy-eyed moping and launched into her new tasks with the same energy that she'd poured into planning Alice's wedding. The change in Mother seemed instantaneous and complete. I didn't understand it. And I certainly didn't like it. Neither did my father.

He threw down his napkin at the dinner table one night, interrupting Mother's rant about the town council's resistance to change, and shouted, "What has gotten into you? I thought you wanted nothing to do with your eccentric mother and her crazy causes."

"Perhaps I finally see the point of them," she said quietly.

"Why now, Lucy? Why all of a sudden?"

"Why not now?"

Father exhaled. He sounded like one of our overheated radiators when the repairman vented the steam. "I think you should go up to Saratoga Springs for a few weeks and take a cure. I'm worried that you're heading for a nervous breakdown. You overtaxed yourself with Alice's wedding."

The calm, placid expression never left Mother's face. She had worn it ever since we returned from Daniel Carver's funeral, and it worried me. It was so unlike her usual worried, hand-wringing appearance. "Going to Saratoga won't change a thing, John. I'm tired of all my vain, empty pursuits. I'm starting a new life."

Father and I exchanged looks. "You're still a wife and mother, Lucy. Aren't they the most important roles there are for a woman?"

"Of course they are. And the work I'm doing in our community is a natural extension of those roles. Why not share my motherly skills with families in real need?"

"What about Harriet? She needs a mother, too, you know."

"Harriet doesn't need me," Mother said with a wave of her hand. "She never did need me. No, my life is going to change now that Alice has left home, and it may as well be for the better."

"For the *better*? What more could you possibly want, Lucy?" Father slapped the table in exasperation. "I provide for all your needs, you don't have to lift a finger here at home, you have your women's club and dozens of friends—why isn't that enough, all of a sudden?"

"I don't know, John . . . but it just isn't."

I started going to Grandma Bebe's house after school every day since Mother was never at home anymore. I was helping Grandma design a newspaper advertisement for the Temperance Union one afternoon when Mother burst into our cozy little world, uninvited.

"I can't even begin to tell you how frustrated I am," she said as she unwound the fur boa from around her neck. "I was certain that our mayor and city council would welcome our plans. After all, we're simply trying to improve Roseton and the lives of its women and children. Imagine my surprise when they turned down our request to convert the old Columbia Building into a boys' club! They wouldn't even let us explain our proposal at the town council meeting. It seems there's a long-standing bylaw that doesn't allow women to attend the meetings unless they're invited, and they refused to invite us! Can you imagine? I would love to see every last one of those hardhearted scoundrels voted out of office at the next election, but—"

"But women aren't allowed to vote," Grandma finished. "It's a vicious circle, Lucy. That's why the Women's Christian Temperance Union joined forces with the suffrage movement. The male politicians have continued to ignore our demands, which means we can't accomplish anything worthwhile until we have a voice."

"I know! Our women's club was so frustrated today that we passed a unanimous resolution to enroll our club in the National American Woman Suffrage Association."

"Well, glory be!" Grandma Bebe leaped up and threw her arms around Mother. "I never thought I'd see the day when you would finally live up to your namesake! I named you after Lucretia Mott, you know. Grandmother Garner must be rolling over in her grave."

I sat slumped in the chair with my arms folded and my legs outstretched, pouting. My mother didn't even try to correct my posture. I was angry about the change in my mother and didn't know why.

The changes continued, building in momentum and menace like a great storm. The only things I had ever seen my mother reading were the society pages and party invitations, but now that she was receiving information about the women's movement, she read religiously. Her reading also included the daily newspaper. My father was not at all happy about sharing it with her every morning.

"Must you drip orange marmalade on the stock market report?" he grumbled. "My fingers are sticking to the page."

"But, John, how will I be able to vote intelligently once I do win the right to vote, if I don't know what's going on in the world?"

"Can't you read my newspaper while I'm at work?"

Of course not. She would be busy with meetings all day. Father left for work muttering darkly beneath his breath.

Instead of lecturing me about poise and manners, my mother now delivered sermons on woman suffrage at every meal as if she expected me to memorize the details of the movement the way I'd once memorized which fork to use for my shrimp.

"Are you aware, Harriet, that Elizabeth Cady Stanton, Lucretia Mott, and the other women signed the Declaration of Sentiments and Resolutions in Seneca Falls, New York, on the same day that Grandma Bebe was born?"

"Yes, Mother," I said dully. "Grandma told me all about it."

"July 19, 1848, was a very important day for all women. But I must say, we don't seem to have made much progress in the past sixty-four years. . . ."

I deliberately slurped my orange juice and said, "That's because the suffrage movement didn't have you helping them." My sarcasm was wasted on her.

"I was a mere child, Harriet, when Susan B. Anthony delivered ten thousand signatures to the U.S. Senate, asking for a suffrage amendment. That was in 1877, the year after the Great Flood, and those men laughed right in her face. The following year she persuaded a senator to propose the amendment again, and it has been introduced every year since—and defeated every year since, I'm sorry to say."

"Am I supposed to be memorizing all of this for a quiz or something?" I asked, licking jam from my fingers.

"I wish I had done more to help, all those years," she said with a sigh, "instead of shopping and sipping tea all day."

I rolled my eyes and reached across the table for more toast, instead of politely asking her to pass it to me. She never even noticed.

"Of course, I shouldn't say that we've made no progress at all, Harriet. There are five states that have already granted women the right to vote. Wyoming was the first one, then Colorado, Utah, Idaho . . . and what was the other one again . . . ?"

She stared at the ceiling above the china cabinet, scratching her chin.

"Washington," I told her.

"What did you say, Harriet?"

"I said, Washington State granted voting rights to women, too. Grandma Bebe told me all about it."

"Yes, I believe you're right about Washington. Very good, Harriet."

I was afraid she might pat me on the head. I grabbed my toast, scraped back my chair, and fled without waiting to be excused. My mother was taking all of the fun out of swimming against the stream.

I wondered where in the world all of these changes were taking my mother, and I soon found out—to Pennsylvania Avenue in Washington, D.C. Nearly one year after Alice's wedding and Daniel Carver's funeral had begun the transformation process, Mother decided to travel to Washington on the eve of President Woodrow Wilson's inauguration to take part in a huge suffrage parade. I had heard her and Grandma Bebe discussing it and wondered when she would muster up the nerve to ask my father for permission to attend. I wanted to be there to watch the fireworks.

I knew she was up to something one morning when she came to the breakfast table dressed in blue—Father's favorite color—and wearing his favorite perfume. I also noticed that the orange marmalade was missing, replaced by cherry jam, another of his favorites. As he began unfolding the morning newspaper, she began her appeal. "I would very much like to go to Washington, John, and take part in the suffrage parade next week."

"Don't be ridiculous."

"Let me explain why I want to go. Women need to be able to vote in order to be good mothers and protect children's interests. We deserve the right to participate in decisions that will affect our homes and families—issues like better education, free public libraries, and playgrounds for poor children. We're not only caretakers in our own homes; we're caretakers of our communities. But we have no voice, John."

"Do I really have to listen to all of this? Can't I eat my breakfast in peace?" He made the mistake of looking up at Mother. She smiled at him. My mother was still a very beautiful woman, able to blindside my father with her charms.

"If you give me your blessing, dear," she said, "I'll spare you the speech and the sermon. Otherwise, if I have to convince you of the rightness of our cause and the reason for our methods, it might take some time, and you won't get to work until well after lunchtime."

"It isn't necessary to preach to me." He finally managed to tear his eyes away from her. He started scanning the headlines.

"I can show you the materials that the organization sent us describing the march, if you're interested."

"I'm not."

"It's a very well-organized event. Prominent women from all across the country will be there, including Miss Helen Keller."

"I'm not married to Helen Keller, nor is she responsible for running my home and raising my daughter."

"So, may I go, dear?"

He looked up again. "What happens if I say no?"

I wondered if she would turn on the tears. Perhaps Father was wondering the same thing. But Mother didn't even reach for her handkerchief.

"Why, I suppose . . . I suppose I will go to Washington just the same."

For a moment he looked stunned. "Then why bother asking me?" He raised his newspaper like a shield and disappeared behind it.

"Well, I . . . I would like to know that I have your blessing, John."

He was silent for a long moment before lowering the paper again. "Promise me that you won't turn into your mother."

"Good heavens, John!" She had no trouble at all looking appalled. "This is going to be a nice, peaceful march down a very respectable street, not a prayer meeting in front of a saloon. We simply want to get our point across to the new president, and all the other politicians who are ignoring us, that we deserve to be heard. I would never take up any cause that requires me to raise an axe or lower my dignity. Mother and I are two entirely different people."

When it looked as though my father was about to give in, I decided to speak up. "May I go, too?"

They answered simultaneously. "No!"

"Don't be ridiculous," my father added.

"You're only thirteen," my mother said. "You can't miss school, Harriet."

I begged and pleaded to be allowed to come, but to no avail. I even threatened to leave home and travel down to Washington on my own, but Mother knew it was an empty threat. I didn't have money for a train ticket, and it was a very long walk from central Pennsylvania to Pennsylvania Avenue. I burned with envy when my mother and Grandma Bebe left without me.

The train they took to Washington was very crowded, with barely an empty seat. Lucy hated being crushed together with a carful of rude, smelly strangers, even if it was for a worthy cause. It turned out that the overflowing train was just the beginning of Lucy's ordeal. Once she and Bebe reached Washington, they could barely move through the train station, much less find a cab to drive them to where the parade started. Grandma Bebe linked arms with her to prevent them from becoming separated and said, "Let's walk, Lucy. I'm sure it isn't that far."

They started toward Pennsylvania Avenue, following groups of excited, sign-toting women. The closer they got to the starting place, the more crowded the streets became.

"Isn't this intoxicating?" Bebe asked. "There's something about being part of a group, united for one cause, that's so energizing! It's like we're tiny drops of water in a powerful stream, all flowing in the same direction toward the same goal. I feel like shouting!"

Lucy had never shouted in her life and couldn't have shouted now even if she had wanted to. She couldn't seem to draw a breath as strangers pressed in on her from all sides. The march seemed like a disorganized mess to her, with chattering women milling around, drums rattling, and uniformed musicians warming up on their instruments. The parade floats sat mired in the muddy grass, looking as though they weren't going anywhere.

"Who's in charge?" Lucy asked. "When are we going to get started? Where are we supposed to go?" She had been too excited to sleep well the last few nights and had risen early to catch the train. Now she felt close to tears. She could no longer see how being part of this swarming, chaotic throng was going to help her win the right to vote.

"According to the instructions I received," Bebe told her, "we're supposed to march with our state delegation. Let's walk this way and look for their banner, shall we? I see New York State's sign . . . and there's Virginia's over there . . ."

"Oh, look, Mother . . ." Lucy pulled Bebe to a halt to watch a cluster of professional women lining up, grouped by their occupations. She saw nurses in white uniforms and stiff caps, women doctors with white coats, and college women in their academic gowns. "I feel so inadequate compared to them," she murmured. "I'm only a housewife." She felt close to tears again, but Bebe pulled her forward.

"You mustn't think that way, dear. You know what an important job motherhood is. Come on, I think I see our Pennsylvania banner over there."

They found a place to stand among their state delegation, and someone handed Lucy a picket sign to carry. Her legs were already weary from so much walking and standing, and she hadn't even begun marching yet. The streets were so crowded! Lucy was about to lay down her picket sign and pull a folding fan from her bag to cool her flushed face when she saw that the first few groups were starting to line up in an orderly fashion. She caught a glimpse of a woman wearing a white cape and riding on a white horse, preparing to lead the march down Pennsylvania Avenue. The parade finally began to move. The colorful floats eased off the grass and onto the pavement. The marching bands fell into their ranks and began to play. The music cheered her.

"I would have loved to meet some of the pioneers of the women's movement," Bebe said.

"According to the printed program, they are among the first ones marching today. It seems fitting, doesn't it? They led the way for women, and now they are leading the way in the parade."

"There are so many people here!" Lucy said, feeling faint again. "How many do you suppose are marching?"

"I think they expected around five thousand women from all across the country. The politicians will have to take notice of us from now on. They can no longer justify excluding us."

The crowd moved and swarmed around Lucy like a living thing as more and more groups started marching down the parade route. She couldn't breathe. She needed to sit down somewhere. She was searching around frantically for a place to sit when the signal came that her state delegation was next. Lucy and her mother lined up like soldiers and marched out onto Pennsylvania Avenue.

"Isn't this marvelous?" Bebe asked.

To Lucy, it was anything but marvelous. The gawking spectators who lined the parade route were mostly men, in town for the next day's presidential inauguration. They stared at her as she marched past, making her feel naked and exposed. It was one thing to dress up for a ball or to be on display for her husband's important clients. It was quite another thing to parade down a public street with a picket sign, deliberately drawing attention to herself. It went against everything that

Grandmother Garner had taught her. Proper young ladies did not allow themselves to be publicly conspicuous.

In spite of Lucy's self-consciousness, everything went well for the first few blocks. Then she sensed a change in the mood when one of the spectators shouted, "Go back to your kitchens, where you belong!" The other men rewarded him with cheers and laughter, and soon more men began to jeer and shout. The farther the women walked, the worse the taunting became. Lucy was shocked to hear cursing and foul language and filthy jokes. She forced herself not to cry.

"Ignore them, Lucy," Bebe told her. "It's to their shame, not ours."

Lucy knew that her mother had sometimes endured public humiliation while holding vigils in front of saloons, but Lucy had never been treated this way in her life. Women were supposed to be revered and respected, not made to be the butt of jokes.

Soon the men were no longer content to stand alongside the curb and shout rude comments. Hundreds of them surged into the street to try to halt the parade. When the men had managed to squeeze the procession down to a single file, Lucy dropped her sign on the ground and gripped her mother's arm, terrified that they would become separated.

"Keep moving forward, ladies," Bebe shouted to

encourage everyone. "We can't let these brutes stop us." Lucy held on tightly. She saw several policemen up ahead and breathed a sigh of relief, certain they would restore order. Instead, the policemen joined in the mockery, laughing at the crudest, most ribald jokes Lucy had ever heard. Bebe shouted above the noise, "Pay no attention to them, ladies. Keep marching."

The women's perseverance seemed to anger the men. Lucy saw rough hands reaching out toward her, grabbing and shoving and groping. Someone stuck his foot in her path and she stumbled forward, nearly tripping. She lost her grip on her mother's arm, and when she turned to find her, Lucy saw another woman trip and fall flat on the pavement. A second woman tripped over the first one, then others tumbled down on top of them. She heard Bebe shouting, "Stop! Help them up! They're being trampled!"

In spite of her tiny stature, Bebe managed to steer the parade around the fallen women, then she quickly took charge, helping the uninjured ones to their feet. But the women on the very bottom of the pile hadn't fared so well. Several of them sat on the pavement moaning, bruised and bleeding. One woman cradled a broken arm, another a rapidly swelling ankle. The first woman to fall wasn't moving at all.

"Somebody call an ambulance," Bebe shouted. "People are injured over here." Lucy stood above her mother, wringing her hands. "Go on without me, dear," Bebe told her. "I'm going to stay here until the ambulance comes."

"No. I don't want to get separated." Lucy backed away a few steps and watched as Bebe and a few other women tried to administer first aid. She felt faint and wished she had brought her smelling salts. The parade that continued to stream past them seemed absurd to her now. What good were decorated floats and marching bands when women sat huddled on the street, mocked and weeping and bleeding?

"Where is the ambulance?" Bebe asked again and again. When it finally arrived, the driver was as enraged as the women were.

"I would have been here sooner, but they wouldn't let me through! I had to fight my way through all the spectators just to get here. I'm sorry, but I had to park about a block away."

"Come on," Bebe said, "I'll help you get these people to the ambulance." Lucy followed her mother and the others, feeling nauseous. The taunting continued, even though it was obvious that the women were injured. Lucy battled tears. Women were supposed to be placed on a pedestal, admired as gentle creatures, the weaker sex. She wanted nothing more to do with this march. All she wanted to do was to go home and crawl into her bed and weep.

Lucy never did reach the end of the parade route

at the Treasury Building. She read about the inspiring pageant that she had missed in the newspaper the next day. One hundred women and children had presented an allegorical tableau on the steps of the building, dressed in flowing robes and colorful scarves to portray Justice, Charity, Liberty, Peace, and Hope. Trumpets had sounded and a dove of peace had been released. The *New York Times* called it "One of the most impressively beautiful spectacles ever staged in this country." Meanwhile, Woodrow Wilson, the newly elected president, had arrived at the railway station expecting to see a huge crowd and had found only a handful of people. Everyone else was watching the suffrage parade.

Lucy also learned that more than one hundred women had to be shuttled to the hospital by ambulance before the day ended. The chief of police had finally called the secretary of war, requesting that the cavalry be sent from Fort Myer to help control the crowd. They arrived too late to do Lucy's dignity any good. After the last patient had been helped to a hospital, Bebe finally noticed Lucy sitting forlornly on the curb.

"My poor dear," she said, stroking her windblown hair from her face. "Where would you like to go? Shall we find the other marchers and see the end of the parade?"

"I want to go home."

They walked the eight blocks to the train station.

Lucy paid for two extra fares so they could have a compartment all to themselves. The tears she had bravely held back all day could finally flow.

"I feel dirty and tattered and heckled and scorned. I've worked so hard for the suffrage movement, but it hasn't done one bit of good. Those men will never accept us as equals."

"Why are you doing all of this, Lucy? Why did you want to go to the march today?"

"Because I vowed to change and to become a better person. Alice is married now, and Harriet doesn't need me, and . . . and I just felt so empty and worthless. I could barely get out of bed in the morning."

"Oh, Lucy, only God can fill the emptiness you feel. Why didn't you turn to Him?"

"Because I couldn't! I needed to make it up to Him first, for the way I've lived all these years and for all of the shallow choices I've made. I felt so guilty for the way I treated Daniel. He died a hero, just like Daddy and his own father had, while I've done nothing worthwhile all of these years."

"Listen," Bebe said as she pushed her own hand-kerchief into Lucy's hand. "Harriet told me what Daniel's pastor said at the funeral, and it sounds to me that Daniel's faith was what motivated him. He didn't just pull up his socks one morning and resolve to be a better person. God changed him from the inside out."

"I tried to change and do something meaningful for God, but I'm just so tired of it all. I didn't feel like I was part of the parade today—I hated it!"

"I think you may have gotten everything turned around, dear. You're supposed to work *with* God, not *for* Him. Let Him change you first, and then He'll give you the strength and motivation you need for each task."

"Well, what am I supposed to do now?"

"You need to stop all this work and go away by yourself for a while. Start talking to God. Let Him fill the emptiness in your life. Then, once you get to know Him, He'll tell you what He wants you to accomplish next."

Lucy couldn't seem to stop crying. "I'm so sorry for disappointing you. I'm sorry I can't do all of the things you do."

"Oh, Lucy," Bebe said, pulling her into her arms. "I don't expect you to fight the same battles that I do. We're two different people, just as my mother and I were two different people. God arranged the events in my life to give me a different task than the one He gave to Hannah, and He has a different plan for you, too. Once you put God in the center of your life, I know He's going to use you. And He's going to use you just the way you are right now."

"But how can He? I'm so shallow and empty-headed and . . . and all I've ever cared about is socializing."

"Do you honestly believe that women should have the right to vote?"

"Yes, but I hated marching and picketing and being heckled today. I would rather die than make a public spectacle of myself again. If God tells me that I have to do that all over again—"

"God has never told anyone to grab a picket sign and march for woman suffrage. What He does tell us to do is to feed the hungry and help the oppressed and share His love with others. Women of faith could change the world if we were given half a chance. But what we've discovered is that we won't get that chance until we're treated as equals. The fight for suffrage is simply a means to a greater end."

Lucy blew her nose, then leaned her head against Bebe's shoulder. She wondered how her mother had grown so wise.

"God never asks you to be someone you're not, Lucy. He asks you to use the talents you already have. You are in a perfect position to use your club friendships and the social connections you have to butter up our legislators and convince them to support suffrage. Have tea with politicians' wives, get them to support our cause, too, so they'll pressure their husbands. Hold dinners and other events to raise funds for candidates who do endorse suffrage. Your natural charm and social skills will get you through doors that are closed to me. And these are things that you love to do and are skilled at doing."

They were almost home. Lucy finally dried her tears and pulled herself together. "Will you promise me something, Mother?"

"What's that, dear?"

"Promise me you won't tell John what happened today. Or how useless I was."

Bebe hugged her tightly. "Your secret is safe with me, Lucy."

CHAPTER
25

Much to my surprise, Tommy O'Reilly returned to my cell with the necessary paper work to spring me from jail. I had been rescued. I stood outside on the front steps of the police station a few minutes later and inhaled deeply. Fresh air and freedom had never smelled so good.

Tommy took my elbow and guided me forward. "Now that I've sprung you from jail, where would you like me to take you?"

"I know the secret password to a little speakeasy down the block."

"Very funny, Harriet. How about if I take you home?"

"Well, I suppose I should go home and prepare my Sunday school lesson for tomorrow. . . ."

"Seriously? You mean you weren't making that up about teaching Sunday school?"

"I knew you didn't believe a word I said."

"That's not what I meant, Harriet."

"No? What exactly did you mean?" I stopped walking and stood with my arms crossed, feeling belligerent for some reason. Tommy halted, as well.

"I meant that you're so smart and modern. . . . Sunday school seems so . . . old-fashioned. Aren't Sunday school teachers usually elderly women with snowy hair and whalebone corsets and high-button shoes?"

I had to laugh, in spite of myself. "You're describing the teachers I had when I was a girl. Look, I may be modern in some ways, but I'm old-fashioned in others. If you're really going to keep me on a leash all weekend, then you'll have to come to Sunday school with me tomorrow."

"Fine. So, should I take you home now? So you can prepare your lesson?"

I remembered that I would have to face my father if I went home, and I shook my head. "No. I don't want to go home. Take me to that café over there and buy me a cup of coffee."

I thought he would argue with me, but he didn't. We walked across the street, and since Tommy was wearing his police uniform he was greeted with smiles and nods of respect as we entered the café. We took a seat in a booth. Tommy's coffee was free. Our waitress batted her eyes at him and offered him a piece of blueberry pie to go with it. "It's free, too, Officer O'Reilly. Just for you." I don't know why, but I had the urge to kick her in the shins.

He gave her his finest smile. "No thanks, Sue. Just coffee tonight."

Once we had our coffee in front of us, Tommy picked up where he had left off. "Listen, Harriet, I'm sure your family must be very worried about you. It's been nearly twenty-four hours since I arrested you. Why don't you at least call them and let them know you're all right?"

"Has anyone telephoned the police station looking for me?"

"Not that I'm aware of."

"Well, there you are." He continued to stare at me, waiting, and I knew I owed him an explanation. "Look, I can't call my grandmother. She joined the Women's Christian Temperance Union and took the pledge not to drink alcohol before I was even born. After all the hard work she has done to get Prohibition passed . . . well, she'll murder me. And then you'll have to arrest her, too."

"I understand that. But what about your parents?"

"My mother isn't worried about me because she isn't even home."

"Where is she?" He poured about a table-spoonful of sugar into his coffee and stirred it patiently.

"Don't you ever read the newspaper, Tommy? The U.S. House of Representatives passed a suf-frage bill in January of 1918, and—"

"I was over in France in 1918. I think I missed that piece of news."

"You fought in the war?" I asked in awe. He nodded. "Was it as bad as everyone said it was, with mustard gas and trenches and everything?" He nodded again. Who knew that Tommy O'Reilly's life could be so interesting? I wanted to pursue this topic of conversation further, but Tommy was a relentless interrogator.

"Let's get back to your mother."

"I haven't seen much of her since the bill passed and the momentum started building toward a suffrage amendment. And by the way, did you hear about the women who protested outside the White House all during the war? Wasn't it ironic that President Wilson had you fighting for freedom and democracy halfway around the world while denying those same democratic freedoms to half of the population of America—its women? Did you hear how the suffragettes were eventually thrown into jail and force-fed with tubes shoved down their throats when they went on a hunger strike?"

He held up his hand to stop me. "So is that where your mother is? In jail?"

"Are you kidding? She wouldn't be caught dead in jail. She prefers to work behind the scenes, throwing parties for political candidates—she's great at throwing parties. Anyway, last year the suffrage bill passed in the Senate, too, but then it had to be ratified by two-thirds of the states. She has been hard at work, and now all we need is one more vote. My mother is in Tennessee right now, probably on her knees, praying for their legislature to ratify the amendment. If they vote to pass it, we'll win. Women will finally have the right to vote."

"That's a fascinating story, Harriet. So tell me, is your father in Tennessee, too?"

His question caught me by surprise. "Huh? . . . No. No, he's here in town. But I don't want to involve him."

"You're his daughter. I'm sure if you had called him last night, he would have come down and bailed you out of jail, wouldn't he?"

"Not unless I cried a gallon of tears. That's what Alice and my mother used to do whenever Grandma Bebe got arrested, but I'm not the type to weep and beg. Why do you think women want the right to vote, Tommy? It's so we can stand on our own two feet and be taken seriously. We're tired of depending on a man to run to our rescue and bail us out whenever we're in trouble."

Tommy bit his lip, staring at his coffee and frowning fiercely in what I guessed was a desperate struggle not to laugh. "What's so funny?" I asked.

"Nothing."

I suddenly figured out the joke, and it was on me. My indignation vanished. "Oh. You're a man. And you just bailed me out of jail, didn't you?"

"It seemed like the gentlemanly thing to do." His smile broke free, and I almost smiled in return. "But I didn't think of it as rescuing you," he quickly assured me. "If I've learned anything about you over the years, Harriet Sherwood, it's that you can take care of yourself. I'm sure you would have managed just fine if you had to spend another night or two locked up. Even the trustee was a little frightened by you. But I know there has to be more to your story than what I can see on the surface."

"And so you're going to follow me around like this until you crack the case? Our city is going to need a pretty big police force if they have to assign one cop for every person out on bail."

He looked down at his coffee. He was still stirring it relentlessly, causing a tiny typhoon in the cup. "I have a confession to make, Harriet. I don't have to follow you all around. I trust you not to flee. I'm following you because I want to."

"Because you want to—what? Torment me? That's what you always did best, you know. All through school, you were always pulling my pigtails or taunting me or bullying me."

"You know why I did all those things?" he asked. He looked up at me with a shy grin on his face. "Because I liked you."

"You're joking. If you liked me, then tormenting me was a pretty stupid way to show it."

"I know. But I was a kid," he said with a shrug.

502

"What did I know about women? I liked you because you weren't like all the other girls. You had guts. You were just a little bit of a thing—you still are. Yet you stood up to me like someone three times your size. I admired you for that. I still do. I just wish that you hadn't . . . you know. . ."

"Broken the law?"

"That's what we need to talk about. Tell me what's going on. Convince me that you're innocent."

"I'm not innocent. You caught me red-handed. . . . But there are innocent people involved. And as I told you last night, they're the ones I'm trying to help. The really bad criminals are the ones who belong in jail. But if the people I'm protecting are arrested, then innocent children are going to go hungry."

"Then help me catch the real criminals."

"If I do that, if we catch the bigger crooks, will you let me and the others go free?"

"I'll do my best, Harriet."

"How do I know I can trust you to keep your word?"

He looked hurt. "People can change, you know. I'm not the same bully I was when we were in school. Besides, I think you can trust me more than some federal agent you've never met before, can't you?"

"I guess so . . . I'm in a whole pile of trouble, aren't I?"

"I'm afraid so."

He had become so solemn that I began wringing my hands like the heroine in a melodrama. "Oh no! Please save me, Tommy! I'll go insane if I have to remain behind bars! The meat was so rubbery that I bent the knife, and the tapioca pudding came out of the bowl in one huge, gummy lump and—"

"I wish you would be serious."

"I'm sorry." And I was. "I'm sorry I became involved in this mess in the first place. If I could do it all over again, I would do everything differently."

"Why did you do it?"

"I'm still not exactly sure. . . ."

But after thinking about it for the past twenty-four hours, I was beginning to figure it out. The waitress brought us more coffee, and Tommy sat back and listened patiently while I told him.

In April of 1917, two months before I graduated from high school, America went to war. I thought I had drawn a nice, neat map for my life, but the war turned out to be one of those unexpected changes Grandma Bebe had warned me about. I had every intention of steering a course straight toward college in the fall, but the rudder slipped from my grasp and I drifted, instead, into a job at my father's department store.

My change of course started where so many other events in my life have started—at the breakfast table. It was a beautiful morning in May and my father had just read an article in the newspaper about the new Selective Service Act that required all men between the ages of twenty-one and thirty-one to register for the draft. His newspaper rustled like a forest fire as he refolded it angrily and voiced his frustration.

"I don't know how I'm expected to run a business without employees. According to this article, nearly all of my department managers, buyers, and bookkeepers are about to be drafted. I've had several good men enlist already, and it's impossible to find anyone to replace them."

"I could do it," I said. "I could work for you." The prospect of a long, boring summer loomed ahead of me now that both my mother and grandmother were occupied with their causes. Neither one of them would allow me to come with them and get involved—licking stamps didn't count, in my opinion. "Why don't you hire me to work in your store, Father?"

"Don't be ridiculous." He waved me away without even considering the idea.

"I'm serious!" I banged my fist on the table to get his attention, rattling his coffee cup. He looked up, startled. "I'm graduating from school in two weeks and I have nothing else to do. I'm very smart, according to all my teachers. Twice as smart as any boy. Why won't you hire me?"

"Because these aren't jobs for women."

"Why not? What difference does my gender make? Your male employees just sit behind desks all day anyway, don't they?"

"The only women I hire are all salesclerks. My department managers, buyers, and bookkeepers are men."

"Why?"

"Because that's the way it's done."

"Well, you might have to change the way it's done now that we're at war. Grandma Bebe had to take over for her brothers when they went to war, and she ended up doing all their farm chores—plowing and baling hay and everything. And then she helped run her husband's factory when he was . . . unwell."

"Your grandmother's example is hardly one that I want my daughters to follow," he said, shaking his head. "Women have no business running a factory or a department store. And besides, aren't you supposed to be going to college soon?"

"Not until the fall. I have all summer free. And if you give me a job, it might help me decide what I want to study in college. Won't you at least think about it?"

"Women work fine as salesclerks, but I don't need any more clerks at the moment. I need managers—men."

I huffed in frustration. "The United States government is hiring women in Washington to fill men's positions because of the shortage. I just read

about it in the paper the other day. If the government thinks women are capable of doing men's
work, why not hire them for your store? All I'm
asking for is a tiny little department to manage."

"My department managers are all men. You're a
woman." My father was repeating himself. Either
he had run out of arguments or he wasn't listening
to me.

"Your managers *were* all men," I told him. "You
just said yourself that they were all leaving to
enlist or were about to be drafted—and that there
aren't any men to replace them. I would say you're
out of options." When Father didn't reply, I added,
"I could dress up in a man's suit and tie, if you
think it would help."

"Don't be ridiculous."

"Look, you need employees, right? What's so
hard about a manager's job that a woman couldn't
do it?"

"It's a question of respect. The salesclerks are
mostly young women your age. Managers need to
be mature. They need to be men."

"But I'm the store owner's daughter. That should
win me some respect. And believe me, I can be
very bossy—the boys at school tell me I'm bossy
all the time. "

The more I thought about it, the more I liked the
idea of working in the department store, but my
father looked as though he wasn't even going to
consider it. I was wondering how I could convince

him when, much to my surprise, my mother rose to my defense—and she did so without resorting to tears.

"Why don't you let her try it, John? What could it hurt? If you need help as badly as you say you do, it seems you should give Harriet a chance. She is very quick to learn things, you know."

"Yes, Father. Why not let me try it? Let's say . . . for two weeks? If you're not completely happy with the work I'm doing by then, I'll agree to come home again."

I don't think anyone was as surprised as I was when my father finally agreed. It showed how truly desperate he was for help. I would have gone to the store with him that very morning, but he made me wait until after graduation. "I need to shuffle people around and find a suitable department for you to manage," he explained.

He didn't want me to run Ladies' Fashions or the Millinery Department, because I wasn't the least bit fashionable. I couldn't tell a Gainesboro hat from a Shepherdess style. Likewise, I was the wrong person to run the Jewelry, Perfume, and Shoe departments. All of the men's departments were off the list because the middle-aged male clerks—not to mention the customers—would never take me seriously. "The Children's Department is much too important," Father said, "to be managed by a woman with a strong aversion to marriage and children"—and I had been outspoken about both. In the end, Father ranked all of the departments in order of importance and gave me the most unimportant one he could find: China, Glassware, and Silver Goods.

"What an excellent choice for me, Father," I said, pretending to be overjoyed. "As you know, I'll bring a great deal of experience to my work. Mother has trained me quite well in understanding the differences between a salad plate and a dessert plate, between a tablespoon and a dessert spoon, between a—"

"That's quite enough, Harriet."

"But I was just explaining about the differences—"

"The most important difference you need to know is that male managers don't aggravate me with their excessive talking."

"Yes, sir."

I had never even seen the China, Glassware, and Silver Goods Department in my father's store until my first day of work. It was in such an out-of-the-way location in the basement of his vast emporium that I was going to need a map to find it again tomorrow. Mine was a small department with only three salesclerks, Bertha, Claudia, and Maude. They weren't much older than I was. Their shifts were staggered so that no more than two of them were on duty at one time, and only Bertha and Claudia were there to greet me on my first day. They stood at attention in my father's presence, gracing me with a small curtsy after he introduced me as Miss Sherwood, their new department manager. Next, Father showed me my desk—piled high with sample catalogs, invoices, and order forms—behind a curtain in the back room. I shared the space with three other department managers and shelves full of inventory.

"You can ask Mr. Foster from Linens, Pillows, and Bedding to show you how we do things," Father said. He nodded toward an elderly gentleman at the neighboring desk, who looked as though he had been selling pillows and bedding since the War Between the States.

The first thing I did after my father returned to his office was to peruse my new domain on the showroom floor. It consisted of a tall shelf of glassware on the back wall and four long display counters—one for ridiculously elaborate silver serving pieces, another for silver tableware in silk-lined boxes, and two for porcelain dishware. My two salesclerks were busy trying to look industrious. Bertha twirled a feather duster over the glassware while Claudia rubbed tarnish off a silver pickle castor as if she expected a genie to pop out and grant her three wishes.

"Tell me how my predecessor used to run this department," I said after gathering them into a huddle. They looked at each other, then at me.

"Mr. Osgood had his rules," Claudia said, "and as long as we remembered them, he left us alone."

"What kind of rules? Can you give me some examples?"

Claudia gazed at the ceiling as if she had pinned a crib sheet up there. "Um . . . we had to say, 'May I help you, ma'am?' right away whenever a customer came. And when there weren't any customers we had to keep busy. No sitting allowed."

"And we can't chew gum," Bertha added—although I thought I spotted a wad of it tucked in her cheek. "Our clothes have to be pressed and neat, our hair clean and tidy, and our shoes shined. And if we get married, we lose our jobs."

The last rule seemed arbitrary and unfair to me, but I kept my thoughts to myself. "Do you like working here?" I asked.

Not surprisingly, they both replied, "Yes, ma'am."

I spent the entire day familiarizing myself with all of the paper work I would be required to do and listening as Mr. Linens, Pillows, and Bedding droned on and on about ledger books and accounting practices. My eyes started to glaze over, and if I hadn't pleaded so fervently for this job in the first place, I might have decided to enlist in the army myself. When I emerged from my underground kingdom at the end of the day, I was glad to see sunlight again.

"How was your first day?" Mother asked.

"Wonderful! I learned so much! I never knew they made sterling silver mustard pots." I didn't mention that we hadn't had a single customer. At least reordering new stock would be simple.

By the end of my first week as manager of China, Glassware, and Silver Goods, I knew I had to do something differently in my department or die of boredom. I decided to go on a spying mission to our competitors' stores, comparing their selection and services to ours. I returned to give Bertha, Claudia, and Maude my report.

"The clerks in the other stores acted so haughty and superior, they made me feel like I was trespassing. I was afraid to peruse the shelves or ask them any questions. I don't want you to be that stuffy. Smile and be friendly to our customers. Ask about the occasion for the gift and whom they are buying it for. Show some interest in our customers."

I got the standard reply of "Yes, ma'am." But as I turned to leave, I thought I heard Bertha whisper, "What customers?"

Yes, something would have to be done about the customer problem.

During my second week of work, I marched into Father's office on the top floor and asked, "What's my budget for newspaper advertisements?" He stared at me as if he'd forgotten my name. "I'm great at writing ads," I told him. "I used to help Grandma Bebe write them all the time."

"Budget?" he finally replied. "You don't have a budget. Our advertising department handles everything. That's their job. Your job is to sell china, glassware, and silver goods."

"How am I supposed to do that if nobody can even find my department?"

"Well, it's your job as manager to figure that out. Now go away and stop bothering me, Harriet. I'm busy."

I spent a week pacing the floor of my department, desperately searching for an idea. "How would you describe our typical customer?" I asked my salesclerks one day. Claudia began to giggle as if the notion of having actual customers was hilarious.

Bertha pushed her gum aside with her tongue and said, "They're mostly girls who are about to get married. They come in to pick out their wedding presents."

I sat at my desk in the back room beside Mr. Linens—whom I suspected was asleep most of the time—and thought about it some more.

I came up with a brilliant idea.

I ran up the stairs from the basement two at a time—the elevator was much too slow—and hurried outside to the nearest newsstand, where I bought all three of our town's daily papers. When I got back to my department, breathless, I gave one to Bertha, one to Maude, and kept the third. "Open it to the social pages," I told them, "and find the engagement announcements for me." They did as they were told, but they were eyeing me warily.

"Now, add up the engagements. How many are there?" Bertha counted four, Maude had three, and I struck gold with seven.

"Here's my idea: Sherwood's Department Store is going to offer the happy bride-to-be a free sterling silver serving spoon in her choice of four different patterns as our way of congratulating her."

"Free?" Bertha echoed, nearly swallowing her gum.

"Yes, free. Once she has that first spoon, you see, it will be your job to convince her that she needs the rest of the set, as well. That means service for at least twelve with all of the accessories to go with it—gravy ladles, carving knives, pickle forks, jelly knives, salad sets. And why not add a beautiful set of berry spoons and shrimp forks?"

My staff appeared dubious, but they set to work cutting out the engagement announcements for me while I got out order forms for Rogers Brothers Silver and boldly ordered six sets of serving spoons in four of our most popular patterns. Then I went upstairs—taking the elevator this time—and borrowed several sheets of Sherwood's Department Store stationery from my father's office. That evening I typed up letters of congratulations on Grandma Bebe's typewriter to all fourteen prospective brides. I mailed them on my way to work the next day.

"Now, this is the most important part," I told my clerks. "The free spoons are going to be in a box on my desk, but don't run into the back room and bring it out to the customer right away. Make her wait a few minutes so she has time to wander past our display counters and examine the dishes and the sterling silver tea sets while she's waiting. Suggest that she sign up for our wedding registry. The free spoon will draw new customers in, and before you know it, every bride in town will have registered their silverware selections at our store."

My gamble worked. All fourteen brides-to-be hurried into the store for their free spoon. I sent out more letters. Business boomed. Then my father heard about my scheme.

"What's this I hear about you giving away my stock for free?" he asked at the dinner table one evening.

I quickly explained my idea to him and finished by saying, "It's just a serving spoon. And dozens of new customers have come in already to get theirs."

"Can't you give away teaspoons? They're cheaper."

"I know, but a teaspoon is too small. The bride will toss it into her hope chest and forget about it. But a serving spoon carries a lot more weight. It's big and shiny and elegant, and she'll put it on her bureau top and dream about serving mashed potatoes to her new husband every evening."

"Don't be ridiculous."

"You won't think I'm ridiculous when you see our sales figures in a couple of months. I've sent out thirty-five letters so far. And do you know how many brides came in for their free spoon? Every single one of them. We counted them. And every single one of them signed up for our gift registry. You can bet they'll be back for the rest of their silverware in the pattern of their choice."

"Well . . . I suppose you can continue."

"You won't be sorry. But listen, Father. I'm going to need some help typing letters. I can't keep doing them all myself. Grandma's typewriter ribbon is about worn out and my salesclerks need me on the floor."

"I suppose my secretary can do them."

By the time summer ended, China, Glassware, and Silver Goods was thriving down in the basement of Sherwood's Department Store.

And I loved my job.

CHAPTER
26

I was supposed to start college in the fall of 1917, but I no longer wanted to go. "You need me at the store," I told my father. "The war is far from over, and besides, the college campus is like a ghost town with all the young men overseas." From my desk in the back room I could hear Bertha, Claudia, and Maude bemoaning the shortage of men, too, as they kept our stock shiny in between customers. But they complained about the shortage for an entirely different reason than my father did. All three of my clerks desperately wanted to get married and live happily ever after, but only Bertha had a steady boyfriend. His name was Lyle, and she worried about him constantly.

"He's going to get called up, I just know it!"

He did.

"He's going away for training, and I'm going to miss him so much!"

She did.

"I'm going to worry myself sick if he gets sent overseas."

She did after he did.

One weekend in November, Claudia and Maude asked if they could work extra hours to cover Bertha's shift and give her the weekend off. "Lyle is home on leave," Claudia explained. "This will be the last time Bertha will get to see him before he sails for France." I gave her the time off. She cried for days after he left. Once Lyle landed in France, Bertha kept track of his steps and all the battles he fought more diligently than General Pershing did. Her daily news reports brought the war right into China, Glassware, and Silver Goods. It didn't look like the war would be over anytime soon, which was bad news for Bertha and Lyle, but it was great news for me. I loved my job.

I did miss spending time with Grandma Bebe, however, now that I worked such long hours. In December, she called one day to ask if I would drive her to the train station and water her violets while she was away. "Where are you going, Grandma?" I asked.

"To Washington, dear. I don't know if you've been following the news, but the prohibition amendment is coming up for a vote before both houses of Congress this month. I can't sit quietly at home and wonder about the results. I've waited much too long to see this day and worked much too hard for it."

I was happy for her, but a little sad that I had become so wrapped up in my job that I had lost track of her progress. America had been fighting in Europe for only nine months, but Grandma Bebe had been waging war against alcohol since she was my age. I eagerly awaited news from her in Washington. On December 17, the House of Representatives voted to pass the amendment. The next day the Senate did the same. I thought Grandma Bebe would be triumphant when I picked her up at the train station again, but she seemed surprisingly subdued. Considering how hard she had worked to get the amendment passed, it seemed to me that she should be jubilant—even if she couldn't toast her success with champagne.

"What's wrong, Grandma?"

"We can't sit back and rest just yet. The amendment still needs to be ratified—which means getting thirty-six out of the forty-eight states to approve it. Many state legislatures won't even get around to voting until after the Christmas recess."

"How many years have you been fighting this battle, Grandma?"

"Oh, I don't know . . . let me think. We started our local chapter of the WCTU before the Great Flood of 1876 . . . so it has to be more than forty years by now."

"So it shouldn't be too hard to wait a few more weeks until after Christmas, should it?"

"We'll still have our work cut out for us, though," she said with a sigh. "The temperance chapters in each state will have to work to get the amendment before the state governments, which means talking to legislators, signing petitions, gathering support . . . Yes, we still have a lot of work to do. But I keep thinking of all the families and the children whose lives are ruined by this evil every day. They are the reason I'm doing this, Harriet."

I carried her suitcase into her house for her and saw the mountains of paper on her dining room table, and I wondered what Grandma would do with herself once the amendment passed. I knew what she would do if it didn't pass—continue working, of course.

Christmas approached, and as I was strolling past Woolworth's on my lunch hour one day and saw rolls of brightly colored wrapping paper in their store window, I came up with a great idea for the holidays: free gift-wrapping. I went inside and bought a dozen rolls of paper and fifty yards of ribbon with my own money. When I told my staff my idea, Bertha claimed to be an expert at wrapping packages. She offered to teach my other salesclerks how to do it.

"First you fold the ends in like this . . . then you crease it real good. . . ." I watched Bertha work, admiring her graceful hands—and suddenly noticed a plain gold band on the ring finger of her left hand. "And then you tie it like this. See, Miss Sherwood? Doesn't it look pretty?"

She looked up, expecting praise, and must have seen my puzzled frown. She looked down again, following my gaze, and gasped. She snatched the ring off her hand and stuffed it into her pocket, but of course it was too late.

"You're married." It came out as a statement, not a question.

"Please don't fire me, Miss Sherwood! Please! I need this job and—"

"You and Lyle got married."

Tears filled her eyes at the mention of Lyle's name. "We eloped the weekend before he was shipped overseas. I wanted to be with him and be his wife so badly . . . just in case he . . . you know . . ."

I was too surprised to reply, even though I shouldn't have been surprised at all. Bertha had talked about Lyle constantly since I began working at the store seven months ago. She was in love and love led to marriage. I had seen the same starry-eyed look in my customers' eyes when they came in for their free spoon, a symbol of their brand-new life. And even though I had forsworn love and marriage and all the rest, there were times when I looked at all those brides-to-be and I felt something very close to jealousy. I felt it now after learning the truth about Bertha and her beloved Lyle.

"I know there's a rule that says I can't work in this department store and be married," Bertha said between sobs, "but Lyle and I need the money, Miss Sherwood, and I don't want a factory job. And I can't just sit at home all day, either, because I'll go crazy worrying about Lyle and—"

"I'm not going to fire you, Bertha."

"Y-you're not?"

"I always thought it was unfair to fire a perfectly good salesclerk just because she got married. When men get married, the store gives them a raise."

"But . . . but your father is the one who made that rule in the first place, and you might get into trouble if—"

"My father's rule is unfair, and I'm not afraid to tell him so—if he asks."

Justice was on my side. I thought of my great-grandmother Hannah, who had defied the unfair Fugitive Slave Law. Nevertheless, I didn't plan to confront my father unless I got caught. "I'll look the other way, Bertha. But make sure you don't wear the ring to work again." She hugged me in gratitude.

Free gift-wrapping turned out to be another successful idea, and other departments throughout the store soon copied it. My father, however, never breathed a word of praise or acknowledgment to me.

January of 1918 turned out to be brutally cold, and business slumped when a deadly flu epidemic swept across the nation. I begged Grandma Bebe to cancel all her meetings and stay home so she wouldn't risk getting sick. For once, she listened to my advice. My mother traveled to Washington with a group of her friends after President Wilson spoke up publicly in support of the suffrage amendment. She was in the audience chamber in the House of Representatives on January 20 when they narrowly passed the amendment. But she arrived home discouraged after the Senate decided to postpone the debate on the amendment until the fall.

Meanwhile, state legislatures across the country began to ratify Grandma Bebe's prohibition amendment, bringing the total to eleven states by the time spring arrived and the wedding season was about to begin. Of course, the war meant fewer weddings, since a sizable percentage of prospective grooms were overseas, but that didn't stop me from coming up with more new ideas for

China, Glassware, and Silver Goods. In fact, when Mr. Linens, Pillows, and Bedding announced that he was retiring, I begged Father to combine the two departments and allow me to run both of them. The Linens Department couldn't be that hard to manage, since I suspected that Mr. Linens had actually been asleep at his desk for the past few years.

"We could call it the Home Goods Department," I told Father. "Our slogan could be 'Everything a woman needs for a comfortable home.'" I hatched plans to pair damask tablecloths and napkins with my dishes and glassware to create beautiful table settings for our customers to covet. "There may not be too many weddings this year," I told Father, "but once the soldiers return . . ."

My father eventually agreed. He had no choice. He couldn't find a replacement for Mr. Linens, Pillows, and Bedding no matter how hard he tried. My kingdom expanded to twice its size, and I was on my way to becoming the queen of the basement of Sherwood's Department Store. In April I decided to have a Hope Chest Sale in my combined departments. Young ladies could prepare for the day when their sweethearts returned from France to pop the question by making sure their hope chests were well stocked with china and bed linens.

One morning as we were setting up for the sale, I took a good look at Bertha and realized that she was pregnant. "Please don't fire me, please!" she begged when I pulled her into the back room for a talk. "I'll go crazy at home all day, and we really, really need the money, Miss Sherwood, especially with a baby on the way. Please!"

I had grown very fond of all my clerks by now, but I would especially hate to lose Bertha. She was my best salesgirl and could probably talk the Rogers Brothers silversmiths into buying one of their own pickle castors from us. I was counting on her to teach my new clerks from Linens, Pillows, and Bedding how to sweet-talk our customers into buying more than they intended during the Hope Chest Sale.

I gave the matter a great deal of thought and decided that I could disguise Bertha's condition for a while longer if I gave blue cotton smocks to all of my salesclerks to wear over their clothing. I told my father that not only would the baggy smocks protect the girls' blouses from tarnish stains, but our customers would be able to distinguish our staff members much more easily in their smocks.

The Hope Chest Sale was such a success that I decided it should become an annual event. Bertha continued to work for a few more months. When she began to waddle, the girls and I gave her a baby shower in the back room after the store closed on her last day. I sent her a sterling silver teething ring and a twenty-five dollar war bond after she gave birth to Lyle Jr. in August.

Life couldn't have been better for me. I was enjoying my work and accomplishing great things for our store—maybe not of the caliber of Mother's and Grandmother's accomplishments, but I couldn't help noticing that we were all working hard for our community, each in our own way. And in the past, women in our nation hadn't been allowed to accomplish very much at all.

By fall, almost half of the required states had ratified Grandma's Prohibition Amendment. I held a sale in my new Home Goods Department on warm bedding and china teapots in preparation for winter. And my mother and her suffragette friends were waiting anxiously for the promised debate in the Senate on the woman suffrage amendment. When the amendment lost by only three votes, Mother was heartbroken. And furious. But she refused to give up.

"We'll show those hardheaded old men," she told me. "There's an election coming in November, and we're going to target all of the senators who voted against the bill to make sure they lose their Senate seats. The amendment is going to pass the next time, you'll see."

On November 11, everyone rejoiced when the armistice was signed. The war in Europe was over. I visited Bertha and her baby and learned that her husband, Lyle, had managed to survive the war unharmed. He was coming home. I hired three more salesclerks and ordered a case of silver serving spoons in anticipation of the flood of engagements that would soon follow.

During the first two weeks of January 1919, there was a flurry of voting all across the country as more and more states ratified Grandma Bebe's prohibition amendment. Then, on January 16, Wyoming became the thirty-sixth state to ratify it. She now had the necessary votes to officially amend the United States Constitution to prohibit alcohol. The saloons she had fought so hard to close would have to shutter their doors for good. Grandma Bebe invited me to the celebration at her house, along with Millie White and all of the other longtime members of the Women's Christian Temperance Union. No one at the party needed champagne in order to celebrate. It was a good thing the amendment passed when it did, too, because Grandma was seventy years old, and I couldn't help noticing that she was starting to slow down. Her days of smashing whiskey barrels at the train depot were all behind her.

She was jubilant, though, her cheeks glowing like a schoolgirl's. "The last time I felt this ecstatic," she told me, "was the day I learned that the slaves had been set free. . . . Or maybe it was when I learned how to soar on my brothers' swing with the sky above me and the wind in my hair. . . . Or it might have been when I first saw Niagara Falls with my dear, sweet Horatio by my side. . . ."

Meanwhile, Mother's goals were also within

sight. She had worked hard to help pro-suffrage candidates get elected to the Senate, and on June 4, 1919, when a vote was taken once again, the woman suffrage amendment passed. Once thirty-six states ratified the amendment, women would achieve equality at last. I couldn't help feeling proud of the women in my family. Great-Grandma Hannah had helped bring about the abolition of slavery. Grandma Bebe had saved America from Demon Rum. And now Mother was close to victory, as well. All three women had worked hard and had accomplished their goals—and my mind spun with all the plans I had for our family's flourishing department store.

Two days after my mother's latest victory for woman suffrage, my father called me upstairs to his office at work. I assumed it was to congratulate me on three straight months of record sales figures in the Home Goods Department. With the surge of engagements and June weddings, I was mailing out letters and handing out free spoons at a record rate. I strode confidently into Father's office and found him conversing with a tall young man with an army haircut.

"Harriet, I would like you to meet Robert Morton. He was discharged recently from the army, and I've just hired him to manage my Home Goods Department."

I think I stopped breathing for a moment. I tried not to panic. I managed to swallow my fear and say, "How nice for you. And which department will I be managing from now on?"

Father looked confused. "You're going off to college."

"What? No I'm not! I like working here."

Father had the good sense to ask Mr. Morton to kindly wait outside. Then he cleared his throat and said, "Now, Harriet, I admit that you've done a good job here. But you always knew that your position was only temporary."

"No I didn't—"

"This is men's work."

"What!"

"And now that the war is over and the men have returned home, it's time to give them their jobs back."

"But it's *my* job, not theirs! I'm the one who created the Home Goods Department in the first place. I'm the one who boosted sales to record numbers by giving away spoons. I don't want to go to college anymore. I want to keep managing my department, just like I've been doing for the past two years."

"Mr. Morton has a family to support."

"I don't care! There must be another job in the store you can give him. Or at least give me a different job to do. You hire lots of people, don't you?"

"The women who work for me are all salesclerks and typists. I'm sure you don't want one of those jobs."

"Why do you keep insisting that there's such a thing as men's work and women's work? Don't you know that women have done all sorts of 'men's jobs' during the war? There were women car mechanics and telegraph operators and streetcar drivers. Women worked on factory assembly lines and plowed fields and served as traffic cops."

"But they aren't doing those things anymore, Harriet. The soldiers have come home and they need their jobs back."

"But those aren't *their* jobs anymore!"

"You can go to college in the fall like you planned. Isn't that what you wanted to do?"

"I don't want to go to college anymore, I want my job back! I want to work in this store—our family's store. Your father let you join the business years ago, didn't he? Suppose I was your son instead of your daughter."

"That would be different."

My pulse rate soared along with my anger. "Why? Why would it be any different?"

"Men have to work to support their families. Women get married and have children."

"Not me! I'm never getting married!"

"It doesn't matter if you get married or not, Harriet. My mind is made up."

I hated myself for it, but I began to cry. I couldn't help it. "Please, Father. Please let me stay here and work for you. I want to come into the business with you."

My tears made him uncomfortable, but they didn't change his mind. He started leading me toward the door. "I'm sorry, but it just isn't done. Now, if you were to settle down with a husband someday and he wanted to work for me, I would consider bringing him into the business."

There aren't enough words to describe my outrage.

I don't know how long I stood outside his office door and wept. His secretary came over with a handkerchief to console me but wisely refrained from asking me what was wrong. When I finally dried my tears, I went downstairs to say good-bye to the girls in my department. I didn't see any reason to delay my departure, nor would I stick around and help Mr. Morton learn how to manage the department he had just stolen from me. I gave free spoons to Maude and Claudia, who had both become engaged to returning servicemen. Then I left Sherwood's Department Store for good.

It was pouring rain outside, but I was so furious that I didn't care how wet I got. I walked all the way to Grandma Bebe's house, remembering how she had walked through a downpour, too, after leaving her job at the tannery—and leaving Neal MacLeod. I knew that she would understand the terrible loss I felt at that moment, if not my rage.

"Why, you poor thing," she said when I appeared at her door, shivering. "Where's your umbrella? Why aren't you at work?"

The second question brought more tears. "Father fired me!"

"Fired you? Why? What happened?"

"He said that since the servicemen have all returned, he doesn't need me anymore. It's so unfair!"

Grandma Bebe pulled me into her arms and let me cry. Even in my anger and grief I was aware of how frail she had become—and how dear she was to me. When I finished crying, she took me into her kitchen and made tea.

"You're right, Harriet. That was completely unfair of him. But I don't suppose anyone is going to convince him to change his mind, are they?"

I shook my head, rainwater dripping from my hair. "Even Mother's and Alice's tears wouldn't do me any good this time."

Grandma fetched a towel and gave it to me to dry off. "I know that right now you want sympathy more than advice, Harriet, but I'm going to give you some advice anyway. Just two words: Trust God."

I looked away. She was right—I didn't want to hear it.

"You have to trust that He is arranging the events in your life in order to lead you to the purpose He has for you," she continued. "Sometimes those events are tragic and painful. But He uses them to shape us into the people He wants us to become."

"But I loved my job. And I was good at it!"

"Did you ever stop to think that maybe God has an even better job for you? You're so young, Harriet, and working at the store was the first challenge you ever faced on your own. But what if God has planned something even better for your future? Would you want to end up stuck at the store all your life and missing something great? Remember poor Horatio and how much he disliked working in his father's business? I always thought he was destined for better, greater things, but he was stuck there. He had no choice. He was expected to continue his father's work. And poor Neal MacLeod, who was so well suited for the job, was written right out of his father's will."

I tossed the wet towel down on the floor. "Life is so unfair."

"Yes, it is. But in spite of that fact, we can trust God to always do what is best for us—best for *His* purposes. If working at the store is His choice for you, then He'll arrange circumstances to lead you back there. Maybe your father's attitude will change. But in the meantime, go to college. Find out more about yourself and your gifts. Women will be able to vote soon, and then watch out. There will be no limit to what we can accomplish."

"My life was going along so nicely," I said. "And now I have nothing."

"Remember what my mother once told me, Harriet? She said, 'Life is always changing, always flowing forward like a stream. Things never stay the same. And we have to move on and change, too.' She was right, you know."

I heard what Grandma was saying, but disappointment and rage kept her words from sinking in. "I want to move in with you," I told her. "I hate my father and I'm never going home again!"

She stood to pour water from the boiling kettle, then said, "You may stay for a day or two. . . . After all, I would hate to see you commit patricide. But eventually you will have to forgive him."

"Never! What he did was unforgivable!"

Grandma smiled sadly. "Your father grew up in an era when a man's role was that of provider and protector. Whether men went to war or to work, they did it so that the women they loved could stay home where they were safe and cherished. That's the way your father was raised, and in his mind he is doing what's best for you—saving you from being forced to earn a living. He thinks he's your knight in shining armor, doing battle in the business world so that he can give you and your mother everything you need, without you having to lift a finger. That's the only way he knows to show his love for you. He can't change his role overnight. Imagine how threatened men like your father must feel now that women are coming into their own, working in professional fields, voting to change things. Look how much your mother has changed in the past few years. In many ways, your father's entire way of life is coming apart."

"Don't ask me to feel sorry for him, Grandma. I can't do it."

"I know, dear. But you are going to have to forgive him."

I closed my eyes, picturing my beloved Home Goods Department, knowing I would never work there again. I shook my head. "Forgiving him is impossible."

CHAPTER
27

I decided to start college in the fall of 1919 and faced a new injustice. When I reapplied to the school that had accepted me two years ago, I discovered that the admissions office was now giving preference to the men who had served their country during the war. And because so many men enrolled that fall, there was no room for me. Grandma Bebe would have told me that it was another instance of God ordering the circumstances in my life for His purposes, but if that was the case, I was starting to feel pretty angry with God, too.

I ended up attending a small female college in Roseton and living at home. My classes weren't nearly as challenging as my job had been. I signed up for a liberal arts degree with no clear goals in mind.

On January 29, 1920, Grandma Bebe's prohibition amendment went into effect. It was now officially against the law to manufacture, transport, or sell alcoholic beverages in the United States. "You have a right to be proud," I told Grandma. "You've accomplished all your goals."

She must have detected a note of jealousy or maybe bitterness in my voice, because she caressed my cheek and said, "Your day will come, Harriet. Just be patient."

That August I was on summer break and sitting around feeling sorry for myself when Maude called to tell me that Bertha and Lyle had just had a second child. I decided to pay Bertha a visit and surprise her with a gift. I found her in tears.

"Bertha, what's wrong?" It was probably a stupid question. She had a runny-nosed two-year-old hanging on to her apron and a fussy newborn in her arms. The apartment looked much too cramped for a family of four, and the temperature inside felt ten degrees hotter than outside. I would weep, too, if I were Bertha.

"Oh, Miss Sherwood. Lyle and I are in a terrible pickle. He . . . oh, maybe I shouldn't tell you. He said not to tell anybody, but I . . . I just don't know what we're going to do!"

I guided her to a chair so she could finish feeding the baby, then gave her two-year-old the stuffed bear I had brought him. Both children were content momentarily, so I encouraged Bertha to confide in me. "You know that I would never share your secrets with anyone—and maybe there's something I can do to help."

Bertha wiped her eyes on the burping cloth that was slung over her shoulder. "You see this crummy apartment? It was all we could afford, and now we can't even afford to live here. If we don't pay the rent by next week, they're going to throw us out."

"I thought Lyle had a good job."

"He did! But they went on strike a month ago and now we're all out of money."

"Maybe I could loan—"

"I'm not even to the worse part, Miss Sherwood."

I could see that this might take a while, so I sat down on one of Bertha's splintery kitchen chairs to listen.

"Please don't get me wrong. My Lyle is a very good man, and he knows that he never should have done such a stupid thing, but with two children to take care of and no money for the rent, he was desperate. So when a friend told him how he could make a little extra money . . . well . . ." Bertha's voice dropped to a whisper. "He got mixed up with the wrong kind of people, and . . . and he agreed to smuggle liquor across the border from Canada."

"Oh my."

"Transporting liquor is against the law, Miss Sherwood, and if Lyle gets thrown into jail, we'll starve. I didn't know he was planning to do it until it was too late. He had already gone up to Canada and he never said a word about it until I saw him bringing all the crates of liquor and beer into the apartment, and I—"

"Wait a minute, slow down. He brought the liquor in here?"

"Yes, here! Lyle hid it here in our apartment."

I took a quick glance around the two rooms and knew it wouldn't be too hard for me or anyone else to find it. The baby had fallen asleep in Bertha's arms, so she laid him in a laundry basket that she was using for his cradle. Now that her hands were empty, she began wringing them. "I don't know what to do!"

"Why didn't Lyle just deliver his cargo right away?" I asked. "Why bring it here?"

"They told him to wait a couple of days and to use a different car in case the police were watching him and were planning to follow him to the delivery place. When he told me all this . . . honestly, Miss Sherwood, I had a fit! We have two children to think about. Lyle told the people that they would have to come here and get the liquor themselves, but they explained that transporting it is the part that's against the law. They said that Lyle has to deliver it, but now he's afraid to. And I'm afraid to let him. Oh, I just don't know what to do!"

"If I were you, I think I would dump it all down the sink."

"We can't. The people loaned him the money to drive up to Canada and buy it. Beer costs five dollars a case up there and sells for twenty-five dollars a case down here, and after Lyle pays the people back, plus a little bit for interest, we were supposed to keep the rest. Now we're in even more debt."

It sounded like a very well-planned operation where the bad guys made desperate people like Lyle and Bertha take all of the risks. "Have you considered going to the police?" I asked.

"We can't. Lyle broke the law. We'll starve while he's in jail, and once he has a prison record, he'll never be able to get another job. I know you're very smart, Miss Sherwood, and you're always thinking up new ideas and things—please tell me what we should do."

"Wow." I couldn't think of anything else to say. I ran my hands through my short hair as I pondered Bertha's dilemma.

She was an excellent salesclerk, but she would never be able to find a job now that she was married. Besides, who would take care of her children? The women like Millie White who had come to Grandma Bebe for help had faced the same dead end, and Grandma had begun her temperance crusade to help them. My mother's involvement with the suffrage movement had started after Daniel Carver's wife and children were also left destitute. Mother had enlisted the help of her women's club the very next day. Now it was my turn to come up with a solution to rescue someone in need. I rose from the chair and started to pace.

I could borrow Grandma Bebe's car and deliver the liquor myself, but I would be taking a huge risk. Then again, Great-Grandma Hannah had taken a risk when she hid escaped slaves in the back of her wagon. And Grandma Bebe had not only risked contracting cholera in order to help out, but she had been willing to go to jail to close down saloons. My mother had risked losing her reputation and all of her society friends when she stood up in front of her club members and declared her intention to help families in need. And I wanted to help this family.

"I'll deliver the liquor," I told Bertha. "And collect your money."

"Y-you will?"

"Yes. But I need you to swear to me that you and Lyle will never do anything this stupid again."

"I do swear! On my very life! And I'll make sure that Lyle swears, too."

I borrowed Grandma's car that evening. As I drove back to Bertha's apartment I felt like Joan of Arc or Queen Esther, or some other noble heroine racing to the rescue. I admit that the thought of breaking the law—for a worthy cause—was very exciting. And heaven knows I hadn't had much excitement in my life lately.

My apprehension began as I watched Lyle loading all the liquor into the car. "I never imagined that there would be so much of it," I told him.

"Yeah," he said, wiping sweat from his forehead.

"And I don't think it's all going to fit in your trunk."

"How did you get all of this across the border?"

"They gave me a special car to drive, with compartments to hide it all in."

"Well, I'm not making two trips," I said. "You'll have to pile the rest of it in the back seat and cover it with a blanket. I want to get this over with."

Lyle gave me the address where I was supposed to deliver the liquor, along with his profuse thanks. "Good luck, Miss Sherwood."

I started the car and took a moment to wipe my sweating palms on my thighs before shifting into gear. The excitement I had felt on the way over began to drain away once I started driving through town. Fear replaced it. What in the world was I doing? I pushed down on the accelerator, driving a little faster, eager to get my good deed over with. That's when I heard the siren behind me.

My first impulse was to press the accelerator all the way to the floor and make a run for it, but then I recalled how Hannah had stopped and waited for her pursuers. I pulled the car over to the side of the road, hoping the police car would drive past, hoping the blaring siren wasn't meant for me, after all. But the police car came to a stop behind me. I thought I knew how Grandma Bebe felt when the bounty hunters had halted their horses beside her wagon and the dogs started sniffing around. I tried to act calm, but my entire body was trembling.

Imagine my surprise when I looked in the mirror and recognized the officer who was walking up to my car window.

"Would you step out of the car, please?" Tommy asked.

I could barely stand and found I had to lean against the fender for support. Too late, I noticed that the blanket had slipped off, exposing my cargo in the back seat. I watched in a daze as Tommy uncorked one of the bottles and sniffed. How could this be happening to me?

"I'm going to have to arrest you, Harriet," Tommy said. He seemed truly surprised. I was even more surprised. Unlike my great-grandmother Hannah, I had been caught with the goods!

"So you see?" I told Tommy, "I did it to help a friend in need. Bertha and Lyle have two small children, and I don't have anyone to worry about but myself. I don't intend to make a career of rum running, and neither do they. I just wanted to do a good deed."

I didn't tell Tommy, but after thinking about it for the past twenty-four hours, I also think that I did it because I was angry with all of the maddeningly heroic people in my family: Great-Grandma Hannah, who helped free millions of slaves; Grandpa Horatio, who saved an entire town; and Grandma Bebe, who not only conquered Demon Rum in our family and our town but also helped the entire nation go dry. And even my lovely, shallow, socialite mother was about to succeed in a way that would change the life of every woman in America. And what had I ever done?

"I come from a long line of heroes and heroines, Tommy, and I wanted my chance to be brave. But there aren't any more causes to fight for. I've been left out and left behind. I'm plain-faced and ordinary. And now, apparently, I'm also a criminal."

"I don't know where you got that idea," Tommy said, looking up at me. "You're not plain-faced. And you're certainly not ordinary."

"Thanks." I wasn't sure if I believed him. I wondered if he believed me.

"The funny thing is," Tommy said, leaning back in the booth, "I believe your story."

"You do?"

"No one could make up something as wild as that," he said with a grin.

I felt only a small measure of relief. "So I guess Lyle was right. I guess the police were watching his house, after all."

Tommy's brow furrowed. "I wasn't watching his house. I stopped you because you were driving too fast."

"You're joking!"

"No. When I saw that it was you, I was going to let you go with a warning—but then I spotted all those bottles in the back seat and I had no choice."

"The blanket must have slipped off."

542

"Apparently. The liquor was in plain sight."

"Poor Lyle," I said with a sigh. "I don't know how he'll ever pay back all the money he owes. Some very big people are going to be awfully mad at him."

The furrow in Tommy's brow deepened, but I didn't think he was worried about Lyle and Bertha. "So that means . . . Lyle's customers must still be waiting for their delivery," he murmured.

"I suppose they are. . . . Why? What are you thinking?"

"I was thinking that if I called in some federal agents to help me, we could go raid the place. You had an awful lot of alcohol in your car, Harriet, so I'm guessing it must be a very large operation. Do you still have the address?"

"I do."

Tommy leaned forward, his gaze intense. "Listen, if you give it to me and we're able to catch the big guys, maybe the judge will be more lenient toward you and your friends for cooperating."

I did some quick thinking, and I didn't like Tommy's idea. "Your plan would get my friends into trouble, and right now you don't have any evidence against them. The liquor was in my car. But if you go crashing in to catch the bad guys, they will think Lyle tipped you off. And if Lyle doesn't pay back the money he borrowed, he and Bertha will be even worse off than when they started."

"Maybe so, but—"

543

"I have a better idea. Let me make the delivery and collect Lyle's money first. Then you can move in and make your arrests."

"I can't involve you in this. It's much too dangerous."

"Well, I'm not giving you the address unless we do it my way." I crossed my arms and lifted my chin. Tommy would recognize the pose.

"Now, Harriet—"

"Look, I was going to drive there last night and make the delivery, so how is this any more dangerous? Please, let me try to undo some of the harm I've already done."

We argued about it until we had each drunk enough coffee to keep us awake for a week. In the end, Tommy reluctantly agreed with my plan, since it was the only way he would ever make the arrest and close down a secret gin joint. We walked back across the street to the police station. Night had fallen by now, and it was dark outside.

I sat in a wooden chair in the back room and listened while Tommy made some phone calls and enlisted two federal agents to help him. "Okay, it's all set up," he finally told me. "Your car is still behind the police station, where my partner parked it last night. The alcohol is in the evidence room, but we'll put it all back in the car. . . . Listen, are you sure you won't change your mind and just give me the address?"

"Quite sure."

I watched the police load all of the liquor into my car. I felt exhausted. I hadn't slept very well last night on that squeaky iron bunk, and I just wanted to get this over with and go home.

"I still have reservations about this," Tommy said as I slid behind the steering wheel. "I don't like putting you in danger."

"You didn't put me in danger. I did it to myself with my misguided notion of becoming a heroine. Besides, you'll be watching out for me tonight, right?"

"Every step of the way."

"And listen, Tommy. Please wait until I drive away so the bad guys won't think Lyle tipped you off. And please let him and Bertha keep the money. They really need it."

"I'll do my best."

"Thanks. Okay, then," I said with a sigh, "let's get going. I have a Sunday school lesson to prepare, remember?"

I put the car in gear and drove away, careful not to speed this time. My nerves felt jitterier than they had last night—but that might have been from all the coffee. The address Lyle had given me was on the other side of town and belonged to a run-down warehouse next to the brickyard. I could see the dark void of the river behind it and Garner Park in the distance. Tommy and his agent friends would be disappointed if this turned out to be just a storage facility and not a gin joint, after all.

Presumably he had followed me, even though I hadn't seen his car's headlights.

I pulled around to the back of the building as Lyle had instructed me to do. The windows were all boarded up, but I did see a door. I parked as close to it as I could and got out of the car. I knew that I should have been nervous or excited or something, but I wasn't. I felt wide awake from all the coffee, but otherwise numb. I took a deep breath and knocked on the door. A middle-aged woman wearing a lot of lipstick and rouge opened it a moment later. I was relieved to hear lively music and laughter coming from inside. It was a gin joint. Tommy would be pleased.

"I have a delivery from Lyle," I told her.

"Just a moment."

She closed the door, and as I stood waiting in the shadowy alley, I suddenly realized why Tommy had been worried about my safety. These people could tie me up and toss me into the river and keep both the liquor and the money. Who would ever know? I hoped he was watching out for me.

The door opened again, and three burly men came out. I backed up a few steps, but they were interested in my cargo, not me. The woman held the door open for them, counting the bottles as they carried the crates inside. When they finished, she pulled a fat wad of bills from her pocket and paid me.

That was it. The end of my adventure. The police

didn't swoop in with guns blazing, as I half expected them to do. The alley was quiet except for a train whistle in the distance. Tommy and I hadn't discussed what I should do afterward, so I got back into Grandma's car and drove to her house. She was in her nightgown and robe.

"Where in the world have you been?" she asked when she saw me. "You look like someone dragged you through a mud puddle."

"You would never believe it."

"You joined the circus and they shot you out of a cannon?"

"No . . . I spent last night and all day today in jail."

"Oh, dear. Well, you'd better sit down and tell me all about it." I followed her into her dining room, then halted in shock when I saw her table. It was bare! I was looking at a shiny wooden tabletop for the first time in my life. There wasn't a paper or leaflet in sight—only my grandmother's Bible lying open on top of it.

"Grandma! What happened?"

"I cleaned my table off," she said with a flip of her hand. "And it was about time, too, don't you think? But sit down, dear, and tell me why you were in jail."

I drew a breath as if I were about to leap off Grandma's swing into the river. My words all came out at once. "I'm only out on bail and I'm still in a whole lot of trouble, but Tommy said he would testify in court that my story was true and he

547

thinks the judge might be lenient with me because I cooperated with the police and helped them arrest the really bad guys."

I had just thrown a great deal of information at her, but when I paused to take another breath, she had only one question for me. She smiled when she asked it. "Who's Tommy?"

"Huh? . . . Oh, you wouldn't believe that, either."

"Try me."

"He's Tommy O'Reilly, the police superinten-dent's son. Remember the bully whose shins I used to kick all the time? Well, he grew up to be a policeman, and he's the one who arrested me last night."

"For kicking him in the shins?"

I shook my head. I felt close to tears because I was afraid to tell her the truth. "I was only trying to help a friend, Grandma. I wanted to do some-thing brave and noble and heroic like you and Mother and Great-Grandma Hannah did. I even prayed for help the way Hannah did, and asked God to blind Tommy's eyes, but it didn't do any good. He saw what I had in my car, and he arrested me."

"I'm guessing you weren't hiding slaves."

"No," I mumbled. "Alcohol."

"I see."

"I don't understand why God didn't answer my prayer like He did for Hannah. She broke the law, too, by helping slaves escape."

"Prayer isn't a magic trick, Harriet. When my mother prayed, it was to a Savior she knew and loved and talked to all the time."

I propped my elbows on the table and rested my head in my hands. "I'm so sorry, Grandma. I know you must be so disappointed in me. I know how hard you fought for this law and how much you hate alcohol, and the only reason I did it was because a friend was in trouble and she has two small children who were going to suffer, and besides, I wasn't going to drink any of it or make any money for myself, but even so, I wouldn't blame you if you were furious with me and—"

"Harriet, Harriet . . . I'm not angry with you." She stood next to my chair and wrapped her arms around me, resting her cheek on my hair. I hugged her tightly in return and sobbed. When I finally stopped crying, she sat down on a chair beside me.

"You're right, I have worked hard to make certain that alcohol was banned. I've devoted my entire life to temperance because I saw how much pain and suffering alcohol caused. But you know what? Every day now I read in the paper about the crime spree that Prohibition has caused, and I wonder if I've been fighting the wrong battle all these years."

"What do you mean?"

"Jesus' harshest words were for the moral guardians of His day—the Pharisees. They wanted to dictate morality, too, but Jesus called them hypocrites and whitewashed tombs. It isn't our calling as Christians to write laws that force people to live moral lives. As much as our communities might need it, and as bad as things are, imposing our morality on others isn't the answer. It doesn't work. People may be forced to give up alcohol, but they are still going to hell. That's our calling—to bring people to Christ—not to force them to behave the way we want them to or to solve all their external problems."

She reached for my hand and held it in her own. Her skin felt as soft and fragile as tissue paper. "We can make stricter laws, Harriet, but people will just figure out a way around them if their hearts are hardened. The Emancipation Proclamation freed the slaves, but it couldn't make people accept the Negroes. They're still hated and treated unfairly and given only the poorest paying jobs. When the suffrage amendment passes and women are allowed to vote, there will still be many more battles to win. Men who are biased against women aren't going to treat us equally overnight. No, there aren't enough laws in the world to change human nature. We've had the Ten Commandments since Moses' time, and people still murder and steal every day. Only God can change people."

"But your work wasn't in vain, Grandma, just because people are breaking the Prohibition laws."

"That's true. But I've come to realize that our

short time here on earth isn't about what we accomplish, but about what sort of people we become. I'm at the end of my life now, but when I look back on the work I've done, I see that God was using it to teach me to care about someone besides myself. He's been working compassion in your mother, too. And also in you, judging by the risk you just took for your friends. And God also uses our circumstances to teach us to rely on Him. That was the first lesson I ever learned when I helped deliver those slaves in our wagon. That's why my mother brought me with her in the first place. She told me that we grow stronger every time our faith is tested. That's how we learn to trust God."

"Am I ever going to get a real task to do?" I asked. I gestured to her barren dining room table. "Look—your work is all done. Even the table is finally cleared off. And Mother's suffrage amendment only needs one more state to approve it and it will become a law, too. What's left for me to accomplish?"

"Harriet, God has already given you a task to do for Him."

"He has? What is it?"

"Jesus told us to go into all the world and preach the gospel to every creature."

I sighed. "Where in the world do I begin doing that job?"

Grandma smiled. "Why, you start by teaching your Sunday school class tomorrow."

It seemed like a very paltry beginning.

I thanked Grandma for forgiving me and went home so she could go to bed. I tried to sneak into the house and go upstairs to work on my lesson, but my father must have heard me because he came out to the hallway.

"Where have you been?" he asked.

I was about to give a sarcastic reply, asking the reason for his sudden concern for my welfare, but he broke into a smile.

"I've been waiting all evening to tell you the good news. Look, your mother sent us a telegram." He waved a yellow paper in the air. "It says, 'Tennessee voted to ratify. Suffrage amendment passed!'"

I could see that Father was proud of my mother, happy for her. He loved her. And maybe the fact that he could celebrate Mother's victory meant that his attitude toward women was slowly beginning to change. Grandma was right; he was a good man at heart.

"That is good news," I said.

"Yes . . . and perhaps Lucy will stay home from now on." He didn't add *where she belongs,* but I could tell that he was thinking it. I thought about all the changes he had endured since my mother became a suffragette, and I felt sorry for him. Sympathy was a tiny step toward forgiving him.

"Thanks for waiting up to tell me the news," I said.

I went upstairs to my room and opened my Sunday school book to tomorrow's lesson—and I laughed out loud at God's timing. The lesson was on one of Jesus' most famous parables. Two men decided to build houses, one on a rock, the other on sand. The storms came and the floodwaters rose—just like the great flood that had taken Grandpa Horatio's life. The foolish man's house, which must have been built in a place like The Flats, was demolished by the floodwaters. But the wise man's house, built high on a ridge like the Garners' home, was able to withstand the deluge.

This was the lesson that Grandma Bebe had been trying to teach me all along. It wasn't enough to build my life on doing good deeds and heroic things such as helping Bertha and Lyle. I needed to get to know Jesus first, and obey His commands.

And I knew very well that one of those commands was to forgive my father the way God had forgiven me. I closed my eyes and prayed—a real prayer this time.

I had just finished dressing for Sunday school the next morning when I heard a knock on our front door. I sprinted down the stairs and opened it to find Tommy O'Reilly on my doorstep. I was surprisingly happy to see him. And judging by the grin on his face, he was happy to see me, too.

"What are you doing here?" I asked. "Don't tell me you've come with leg irons to haul me back to jail?"

"Not at all. I'm supposed to be watching you so you don't flee to Canada, remember?"

"Well, you're just in time to help me repair my still. I'm turning grain alcohol into gin down in the basement."

"Very funny."

"How did it go last night?" I asked, leaning against the door-frame.

"The federal agents were quite impressed. The warehouse you led us to was a speakeasy, and we found a lot of valuable evidence inside. We uncovered a large rum-running operation, involving people in several communities. Yes, I would say it went very well."

"Congratulations."

"Thanks." Tommy had an incredible smile.

"Now, if you're really intent on watching my every move," I told him, "I'm on my way to church to teach my Sunday school class."

Tommy hesitated, ducking his head as a shy grin spread across his face. "Listen, Harriet. May I come with you as a friend and not as your jailer? I would really like to be . . . um . . . friends."

Now it was my turn to hesitate. I knew I had foresworn love and marriage and all the rest, but Tommy O'Reilly had changed a lot in the past few years. And my attitude toward him had changed, as well.

"I would like to be friends, too," I finally said.

I could almost hear the roar of a waterfall in the distance and Grandma Bebe laughing as she said, *"We shall see, Harriet, my dear. We shall see."*

DISCUSSION QUESTIONS

1. Throughout the novel, Harriet is trying to answer the question, "How did I end up here in jail?" What insights does she gain from recalling Great-Grandma Hannah's story? Grandma Bebe's story? Her mother Lucy's story? How does she ultimately answer the question?

2. What strengths did each of the four women—Hannah, Bebe, Lucy, and Harriet—possess? What were each woman's weaknesses?

3. Which woman did you identify with the most? Why?

4. Hannah tells Bebe, "'Smooth seas don't produce skillful sailors.' . . . God uses the turbulent times in our lives to prepare us for His purposes—if we'll let Him." What were some of the rough waters in each woman's life that led them closer to God?

5. After the episode with the bounty hunters, Hannah tells Bebe, "Someday . . . God is going to give you a task to do in your own time and place. Then you'll have to put

your faith in Him as you follow your conscience." What tasks did each woman feel God was giving her to do? How did the circumstances in her life lead her to this task?

6. Near the end of the book, Grandma Bebe tells Harriet, "Our short time here on earth isn't about what we accomplish, but about what sort of people we become." What are your thoughts regarding her comments? What other insights did Bebe share with Harriet regarding each Christian's task?

7. Grandma Bebe is born on the same day, month, and year that the first Women's Rights Convention was held. The story ends with the news that the suffrage amendment has passed. How did each woman's "cause" contribute to its passage: Hannah and the Anti-Slavery Society? Bebe and the Women's Christian Temperance Union? Lucy and her women's club? Harriet's job and the need for workers during World War I?

8. What was your reaction when Harriet's father "fired" her from her job in the department store? How would you have reacted in that situation? As a young

woman living in 1919, what recourse did she have to fight his decision? What other instances of discrimination against women did you see in the story?

9. What was the prevailing attitude toward women and their roles in each generation throughout the book? Did you see a change in any of these attitudes? If so, what caused it?

10. What qualities did each woman see in the man she married: Hannah and Henry? Bebe and Horatio? Lucy and John? What qualities do you think Harriet and Tommy are beginning to see in each other? Do you think Bebe should have married Neal MacLeod? Should Lucy have married Daniel Carver? Why or why not?

11. What do you think the next chapter in Harriet's life will be?

Center Point Publishing
600 Brooks Road ● PO Box 1
Thorndike ME 04986-0001 USA

(207) 568-3717

US & Canada:
1 800 929-9108
www.centerpointlargeprint.com